ENCYCLOPEDIA OF ARCHAEOLOGICAL EXCAVATIONS IN THE HOLY LAND

VOLUME I

EDITOR, ENGLISH EDITION:
Michael Avi-Yonah

ASSOCIATE EDITOR:
Ephraim Stern

EDITORIAL DIRECTOR:
Joseph Aviram

ASSISTANT EDITOR:
Essa Cindorf

ILLUSTRATIONS EDITOR:
Joseph S. Schweig

Published in cooperation with the Israel Exploration Society, Jerusalem

CONTRIBUTORS TO THIS VOLUME

PROF. YOHANAN AHARONI, Tel Aviv University — *Arad, Tel Beersheba*

PROF. WILLIAM F. ALBRIGHT (deceased), Johns Hopkins University — *Tell Beit Mirsim*

PROF. RUTH AMIRAN, Israel Museum, Jerusalem — *Arad*

PROF. EMMANUEL ANATI, Tel Aviv University — *Tell Abu Hawam*

PROF. NAHMAN AVIGAD, Hebrew University, Jerusalem — *Beth Alpha, Beth She'arim, Capernaum, Chorozain*

PROF. MICHAEL AVI-YONAH, Hebrew University, Jerusalem — *Abu Ghosh, Ashkelon, Beth Govrin, Bethlehem, Caesarea*

MR. DAN BAHAT, Dept. of Antiquities and Museums — *Beth-Shean*

PROF. OFER BAR-YOSEF, Hebrew University, Jerusalem — *Abu Uṣba Cave*

MR. MEIR BEN-DOV, Israel Exploration Society, Jerusalem — *Belvoir*

DR. AMNON BEN-TOR, Hebrew University, Jerusalem — *Azor, Bab edh-Dhra'*

DR. ABRAHAM BIRAN, Director, Dept. of Antiquities and Museums, Jerusalem — *Tel Dan*

PROF. JOSEPH A. CALLAWAY, Southern Baptist Theological Seminary, Louisville — *Ai*

MR. RUDOLF COHEN, Dept. of Antiquities and Museums, Jerusalem — *Churches*

PROF. FRANK M. CROSS, JR., Harvard University, Cambridge, Mass. — *el-Buqei'a*

PROF. MOSHE DOTHAN, Haifa University — *'Afula, Tell el-Asawir, Ashdod, Azor*

PROF. TRUDE DOTHAN, Hebrew University, Jerusalem — *Deir el-Balaḥ*

MR. ABRAHAM EITAN, Israel Museum, Jerusalem — *Aphek (Sharon)*

DR. ISRAEL EPH'AL, Tel Aviv University — *Ashkelon*

DR. GIDEON FOERSTER, Dept. of Antiquities and Museums — *Dor*

PROF. H.J. FRANKEN, University of Leiden — *Tell Deir 'Alla*

PROF. ANTONIO FROVA, University of Milan — *Caesarea*

DR. ROBERT W. FUNK, Drew University, Madison — *Beth-Zur*

DR. DAVID GILEAD (deceased), Tel Aviv University — *Wadi Beidha*

DR. ZEEV GOLDMANN, Tel Aviv University — *Accho*

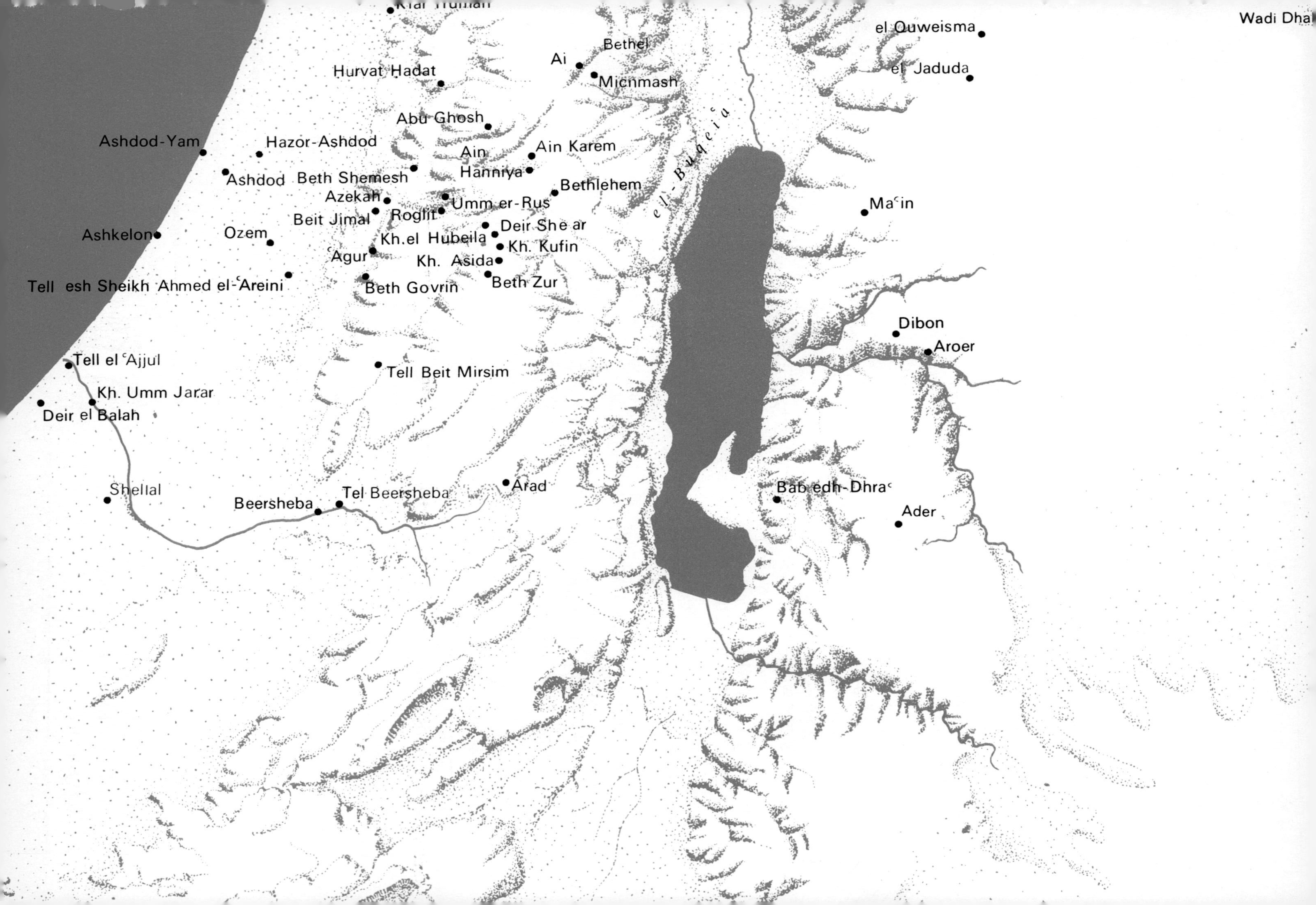

Wadi Dha
el Quweisma
el Jaduda
Bethel
Ai
Michmash
Hurvat Hadat
Abu Ghosh
Ashdod-Yam
Hazor-Ashdod
Ain
Ain Karem
Hanniya
Ashdod
Beth Shemesh
Bethlehem
el-Buqei'a
Azekah
Umm er-Rus
Ma'in
Beit Jimal
Roglit
Deir She ar
Ashkelon
Ozem
Kh.el Hubeila
Kh. Kufin
'Agur
Kh. Asida
Tell esh Sheikh Ahmed el-'Areini
Beth Govrin
Beth Zur
Dibon
Aroer
Tell el 'Ajjul
Tell Beit Mirsim
Kh. Umm Jarar
Deir el Balah
Shellal
Arad
Bab edh-Dhra'
Beersheba
Tel Beersheba
Ader

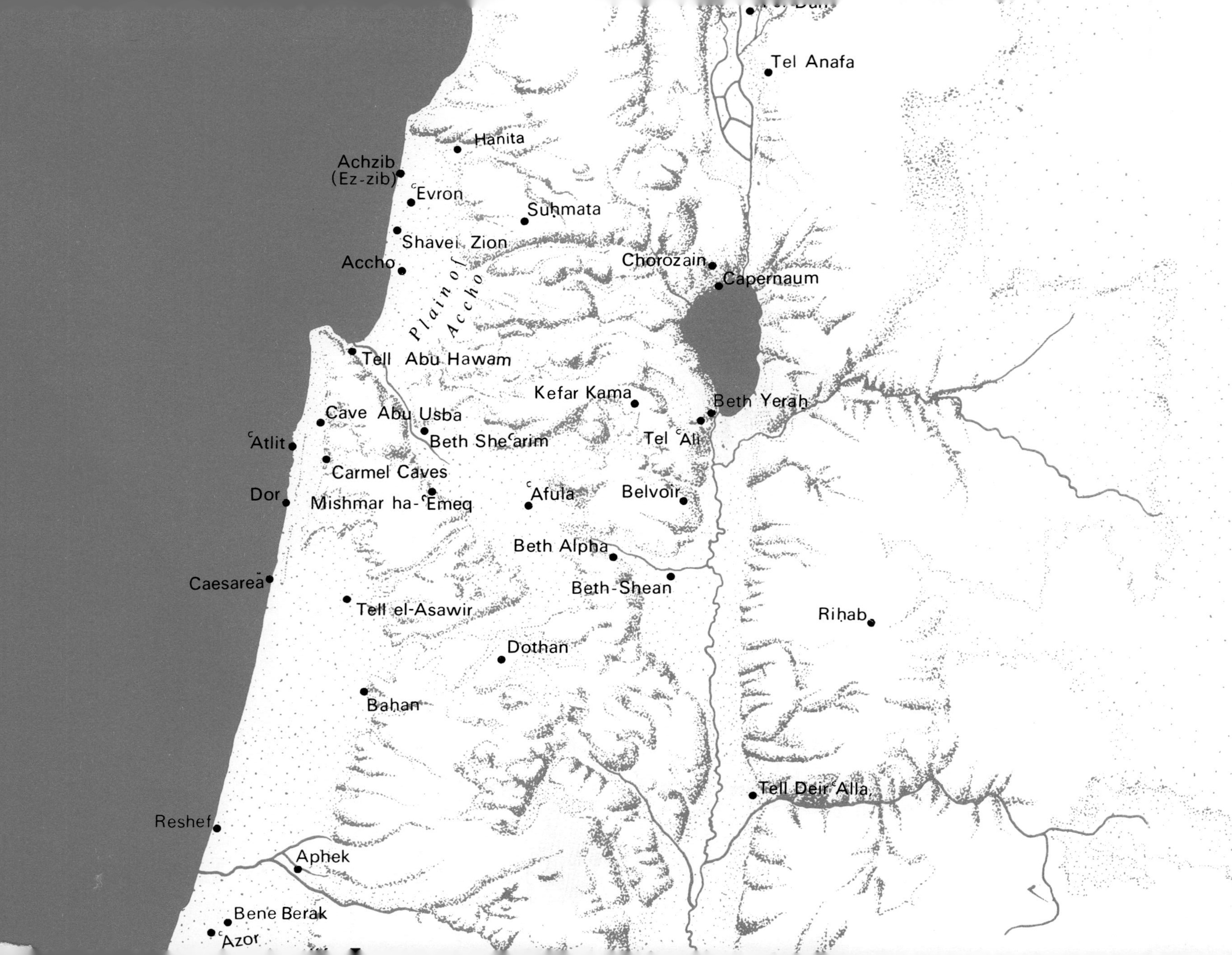

Tel Anafa
Hanita
Achzib
(Ez-zib)
ᶜEvron
Suḥmata
Shavei Zion
Accho
Plain of Accho
Chorozain
Capernaum
Tell Abu Hawam
Kefar Kama
Beth Yeraḥ
Cave Abu Usba
Beth Sheᶜarim
Tel ᶜAli
ᶜAtlit
Carmel Caves
Dor
Mishmar ha-ᶜEmeq
ᶜAfula
Belvoir
Beth Alpha
Caesarea
Beth-Shean
Tell el-Asawir
Riḥab
Dothan
Bahan
Tell Deir ᶜAlla
Reshef
Aphek
Bene Berak
ᶜAzor

MR. RAM GOPHNA, Dept. of Antiquities and Museums, Tel Aviv — *Beersheba*

MRS. RUTH HESTRIN, Israel Museum, Jerusalem — *Beth Yeraḥ*

DR. FRANCES JAMES, University Museum, Philadelphia — *Beth-Shean*

MR. CEDRIC N. JOHNS, Aberystwyth, Wales — *'Atlit*

DR. JACOB KAPLAN, Museum of Antiquities, Tel Aviv–Jaffa — *Ashdod-Yam, Bene-Berak and Vicinity*

PROF. JAMES L. KELSO, Pittsburgh Theological Seminary — *Bethel*

MR. AHARON KEMPINSKI, Tel Aviv University — *Beth-Shean*

DR. MOSHE KOCHAVI, Tel Aviv University — *Ader*

PROF. BENJAMIN MAZAR, Hebrew University, Jerusalem — *Beth She'arim*

PROF. ABRAHAM NEGEV, Hebrew University, Jerusalem — *Caesarea*

DR. TAMAR NOY, Israel Museum, Jerusalem — *Carmel Caves*

R.P. EMILIO OLÁVARRI, Jerusalem — *Aroer*

M. JEAN PERROT, French Archaeological Mission, Jerusalem — *Abu Ghosh, Beersheba*

DR. MOSHE W. PRAUSNITZ, Dept. of Antiquities and Museums, Jerusalem — *Plain of Accho, Achzib, Tel 'Ali*

PROF. MOSHE STEKELIS (deceased), Hebrew University, Jerusalem — *Bethlehem*

DR. EPHRAIM STERN, Hebrew University, Jerusalem — *Azekah*

DR. OLGA TUFNELL, Archaeological Institute, University of London — *Tell el-'Ajjul*

DR. A.D. TUSHINGHAM, Royal Ontario Museum, Toronto — *Dibon*

MR. NEHEMIAH TZORI, Dept. of Antiquities and Museums — *Beth-Shean*

DR. DAVID USSISHKIN, Tel Aviv University — *Dothan*

PROF. SAUL S. WEINBERG, University of Missouri — *Tel Anafa*

MR. ELIEZER WRESCHNER, Haifa — *Carmel Caves*

PROF. G. ERNEST WRIGHT (deceased), Harvard University — *Beth-Shemesh*

MISS EFRAT YEIVIN, Tel Aviv University — *Wadi Dhobai*

PROF. SHMUEL YEIVIN, Tel Aviv University — *Tell el-'Areini*

DR. ZEEV YEIVIN, Dept. of Antiquities and Museums, Jerusalem — *Chorozain*

ENCYCLOPEDIA OF ARCHAEOLOGICAL EXCAVATIONS IN THE HOLY LAND

ENCYCLOPEDIA OF ARCHAEOLOGICAL EXCAVATIONS IN THE HOLY LAND

VOLUME I

Editor, English Edition
Michael Avi-Yonah

Prentice-Hall, Inc., Englewood Cliffs, N.J.

LIBRARY OF CONGRESS CATALOGING IN PUBLICATION DATA
MAIN ENTRY UNDER TITLE:
THE ENCYCLOPEDIA OF ARCHAEOLOGICAL EXCAVATIONS IN THE HOLY LAND.
1. Palestine — Antiquities — Dictionaries.
2. Bible — Antiquities — Dictionaries. I. Avi-Yonah,
Michael, 1904– ed.
DS111.A2E5 220.9'3 73–14997
ISBN 0–13–275115–1 (v. 1)

Simultaneously published in Great Britain by
Oxford University Press, London

Printed in Israel by Peli Printing Works Ltd.

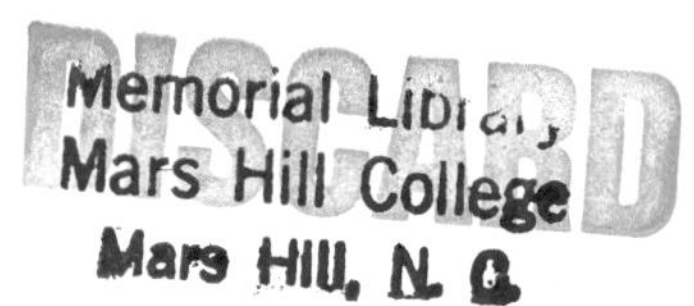

ABOUT THIS EDITION

The publication in Israel of the ENCYCLOPEDIA OF ARCHAEOLOGICAL EXCAVATIONS IN THE HOLY LAND marked a milestone in the history of archaeological research. For the first time the information dispersed in hundreds of books and articles, in addition to material previously unpublished, was collected and condensed into two convenient volumes. At the outset of the planning of the encyclopedia, it was felt that the use of the work should not be restricted to readers of modern Hebrew and that an English-language edition should be prepared and published.

When the present editor was entrusted with the task of preparing the English text, careful consideration had to be given to the special requirements of the new edition. As a result the encyclopedia was divided into four volumes instead of the original two, since the English text is, by virtue of the language, longer than the Hebrew. Moreover, with a few exceptions, the original text included only those sites where work had begun before 1967. The present edition was brought up-to-date through the end of 1971, and a score of new sites was added to the original 160. Where work had continued on sites begun before 1967, the excavators were asked to add the latest information and to supply new illustrative material. It is gratifying to note that all of them responded to our request, in spite of the inconvenience and additional work imposed on them.

Those articles originally written in English have been reproduced as written after revision by the authors. Several of our most eminent contributors, to our deep regret, have died since the publication of the Hebrew edition: W. F. Albright, R. de Vaux, I. Dunayevsky, N. Glueck, P. Lapp, M. Stekelis, and E. Wright. Their contributions had to be updated by others.

Use of the present edition is facilitated by the adoption of the names by which many of the sites are commonly known in scholarly circles, rather than adherence only to official usage. Thus "Beth 'Eglayim" appears under *A* as *el-'Ajjul, Tell* (disregarding, of course, Petrie's inappropriate "Ancient Gaza"). New sites, however, are listed under the names by which they became known, *e.g., Poleg, Tel*. Some exceptions to this rule have been made for the sake of convenience: southern Tell el Far'a (Petrie's "Beth Peleth") appears as *Sharuḥen, Tel* to avoid its being confused with Tell el Far'a (North). Ample cross-references and the index to be added at the end of Volume IV will help, it is hoped, in all doubtful cases. The biblical names are in the forms used in the Revised Standard Version; the Greco-Roman names are given in their Latin form. The various periods are given their archaeological or historical appellation as circumstances warrant.

A list of abbreviations is provided in every volume. A glossary of Hebrew terms will be added to Volume IV.

The bibliographies have been brought up-to-date as far as possible; the less important Hebrew books and papers have been omitted and those remaining are followed by "Hebrew" in parentheses.

The Executive Board and this editor wish to thank Mrs. Essa Cindorf, who revised the English text and copyedited the manuscript, and Mmes. Eshel and Philips who retyped it.

Mr. Joseph Aviram has been the *spiritus moveus* of this undertaking, as he has been for so many others for several decades. He was assisted by his staffs at the Israel Exploration Society and the Institute of Archaeology of the Hebrew University.

In expressing his expectation of a successful conclusion of the whole, the editor hopes that this English encyclopedia will serve abroad the cause of archaeology of the Holy Land as well as the Hebrew edition has served it at home.

Jerusalem, 1973 — M. AVI-YONAH

The Editorial Board regrets to announce the untimely death of Professor Michael Avi-Yonah, who died after a long illness on March 25, 1974, at the age of 69.

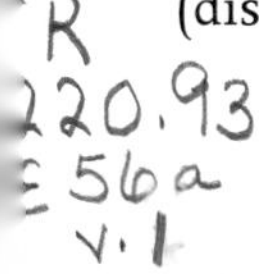

FROM THE INTRODUCTION TO THE HEBREW EDITION

Since 1890, when Sir Flinders Petrie laid the foundations for scientific study of the stratigraphy of mounds in the Holy Land through his excavations at Tell el-Ḥesi, the country has witnessed a steady increase in archaeological expeditions. Under the British Mandate, and even more during the past two decades, this activity advanced greatly both in scope and in quality. Numerous sites on both sides of the Jordan have now been unearthed by scholars from Israel and from abroad. At the same time rapid progress has been made in the methods of archaeological research. As a result, there has been collected a very rich and varied body of archaeological material bearing on all aspects of man from prehistoric as well as historic periods. These discoveries have also cast new light on the cultural history of Palestine, including that of the biblical period, within the framework of the cultures of its neighboring lands. In addition, the past few years have seen an increase in publications dealing directly or indirectly with Palestinian archaeology: excavation reports, general works, documents, articles, monographs, etc. Despite the wealth of publications, however, there has been a paucity of reference works designed to aid the student of Palestinian archaeology, in all its ramifications, toward a fuller understanding of the recent discoveries by incorporating evaluations of the archaeological results and achievements and discussing the dilemmas and difficulties they pose. Consequently the need was felt for a comprehensive work that would present a summary of excavation work in Israel. Thus the Executive Board of the Israel Exploration Society approved the timely suggestion of Professor Y. Yadin to mark the fiftieth anniversary of the Society with the publication of an encyclopedia of archaeological excavations in the Holy Land.

The encyclopedia is arranged in the alphabetical

order of the excavated sites. An individual entry is devoted to each site. In addition, there are composite articles, *e.g., Churches; Megaliths; Monasteries; Synagogues;* as well as articles on specific areas, *e.g., Accho, Plain of; Jordan Valley.* Chronologically the encyclopedia ranges from prehistoric times through the Crusader period. The geographic limits are the historic borders of the Holy Land on both sides of the Jordan, from the Ladder of Tyre and Dan in the north to the Gulf of Elath in the south.

Most of the contributors to the encyclopedia are Israelis, but a number of archaeologists from America and Europe — primarily those who have headed archaeological expeditions to Israel — have also participated. Although the editors have made every effort to maintain a measure of consistency, the fact of the large number of contributors is reflected in the articles: some writers have stressed the stratigraphy and chronology of given sites; others have emphasized the finds or the historical and cultural aspects of sites; still others have expressed views that are in opposition to those of the majority of scholars.

Each entry is followed by a selected bibliography. Since visual material forms an integral part of archaeology, many illustrations and plans have been included (most of them prepared specially for this work) and in large part provided by the contributors themselves. These have been carefully selected to supplement and elucidate the written text.

The Executive Board wishes to express its gratitude to all the writers for their contributions and to the editorial staff for their dedicated work. Special thanks are due to the coordinator, Mr. Joseph Aviram, without whose great efforts and initiative in all phases of the work, this project could not have been accomplished. The scientific secretary, Mr. M. Broshi, assembled and processed all the material and coordinated the work of the staff. Dr. D. Rokah checked the references from the Talmud and the spellings of Greek and Latin words. Mr. S. J. Schweig selected the photographs, many of them his own work, and Carta, Jerusalem, reshaped the plans and maps for publication.

In addition we wish to thank the institutions and persons who so generously assisted in this project: The Department of Antiquities and Museums and its director, Dr. A. Biran, scientific secretary, Mrs. Inna Pomerantz, director of archives, Mr. J. Landau; and the librarians, Dr. Milka Cassuto-Salzmann and Miss Wanda Aftergut; as well as the Institute of Archaeology of the Hebrew University and its staff, in particular Mrs. Nehamah Litani.

Our thanks are also due to the following institutions and persons: Encyclopedia Biblica, Jerusalem; W. F. Albright Institute, Jerusalem; British School of Archaeology, Jerusalem; Ecole Biblique et Archéologique, Jerusalem; the late I. Dunayevsky; Hebrew Union College, Cincinnati and Jerusalem; Government Press Office; Stadium Biblicum Franciscanum, Jerusalem; University Museum, Philadelphia; British Museum, London; Israel Museum, Jerusalem; Danish National Museum, Copenhagen; Collection of Egyptian art, Bavarian State Museum; Royal Ontario Museum, Toronto; Museum of Antiquities of Tel-Aviv–Jaffa; Sha'ar ha-Golan Museum; Oriental Institute, University of Chicago; Pontifical Biblical Institute, Jerusalem; Expedition of the Centre National de la Recherche Scientifique, Jerusalem; Colt Expedition; Penguin Books, Harmondsworth; Prof. Y. Perry; Palestine Exploration Fund; Wellcome-Marston Fund; Dr. B. Rothenberg; Mrs. Esther Reifenberg; National Parks Authority.

Jerusalem, 1970 THE EDITORIAL BOARD

LIST OF ABBREVIATIONS

Abel, GP. F. M. Abel, Géographie de la Palestine 1–2, Paris 1933–1938

Aharoni, LB. Aharoni, Y: The Land of the Bible, London, 1966

Alt, KSch. A. Alt, Kleine Schriften zur Geschichte des Volkes Israel 1–3, München 1953–1959

Avi-Yonah, HL. Avi-Yonah, M.: The Holy Land, Grand Rapids, 1966

Benoit et alii, Discoveries 2. P. Benoit — J. T. Milik — R. de Vaux, Discoveries in the Judaean Desert 2 (Les Grottes de Murabba'at), Oxford 1961

Bliss — Macalister, Excavations. F. J. Bliss — R. A. S. Macalister, Excavations in Palestine during the Years 1898–1900, London 1902

Brünnow — Domaszewski, Die Provincia Arabia. R.E. Brünnow — A. V. Domaszewski, Die Provincia Arabia 1–3, Strassburg 1904–1909

Clermont-Ganneau, ARP. Ch. Clermont-Ganneau, Archaeological Researches in Palestine 1–2, London 1896–1899

Clermont-Ganneau, RAO. Ch. Clermont-Ganneau, Recueil d'archéologie orientale 1–8, Paris 1888 ss.

Conder-Kitchener, SWP. C. R. Conder–H. H. Kitchener, Survey of Western Palestine, Memoirs 1–3, London 1881–1883

Crowfoot, Early Churches J. W. Crowfoot, Early Churches in Palestine, London 1941

EI. Eretz-Israel, Jerusalem 1950 ff.

Enc. Miqr. Encyclopaedia Biblica, 6 vols, Jerusalem 1955 ff.

Frey, Corpus. J. B. Frey, Corpus Inscriptionum Iudaicarum 2, Roma 1952

Goodenough, Jewish Symbols. E. R. Goodenough, Jewish Symbols in the Greco-Roman Period 1–12, New York 1953–1965

Guerin, Galilée. V. Guerin, Description géographique, historique et archéologique de la Palestine, Galilée, Paris 1868–1880

Guerin, Judée. V. Guerin, Description géographique, historique et archéologique de la Palestine, Judée, Paris 1868–1869

Hill, BMC. G. F. Hill, Catalogue of the Greek Coins in the British Museum, Palestine, London 1914

Klein, Corpus. S. Klein, Jüdisch-palästinisches Corpus Inscriptionum, Wien-Berlin 1920

Kohl-Watzinger, Synagogen. H. Kohl — C. Watzinger, Antike Synagogen in Galilea, Leipzig 1916

Lidzbarski, Ephemeris. M. Lidzbarski, Ephemeris für semitische Epigraphik 1–3, Giessen 1902–1915

Musil, Arabia Petraea. A. Musil, Arabia Petraea 1–3, Wien 1907–1908

Pritchard, ANET. J. B. Pritchard (ed.) Ancient Near Eastern Texts Relating to the Old Testament, Princeton 1950

Robinson, Biblical Researches. E. Robinson, Biblical Researches in Palestine, London 1841

Saller-Bagatti, Town of Nebo. S. J. Saller — B. Bagatti, The Town of Nebo, Jerusalem 1949

Schürer, GJV2. E. Schürer, Geschichte des jüdischen Volkes im Zeitalter Jesu Christi, Leipzig 1907

Sukenik, Ancient Synagogues. E. L. Sukenik, Ancient Synagogues in Palestine and Greece, London 1934

Vincent-Abel, Jérusalem Nouvelle. L. H. Vincent—F. M. Abel, Jérusalem nouvelle 1–2, Paris 1912–1926

Vincent-Steve, Jérusalem. L. H. Vincent — M. A. Steve, Jérusalem de l'Ancien Testament 1–4, Paris 1954–1956

Watzinger, DP. K. Watzinger, Denkmäler Palästinas 1–2, Leipzig 1933–1935

Wilson-Kitchener, Special Papers. Ch. Wilson — H. H. Kitchener, The Survey of Western Palestine, Special Papers, London 1881

AAA	Annals of Archaeology and Anthropology
AASOR	Annual of the American School of Oriental Research
ADAJ	Annual of the Department of Antiquities of Jordan
AJA	American Journal of Archaeology
AJSLL	American Journal of Semitic Languagues and Literatures
'Alon	Bulletin of the Israel Department of Antiquities
APEF	Annual of the Palestine Exploration Fund
'Atiqot	'Atiqot, Journal of the Israel Department of Antiquities
BA	Biblical Archaeologist
BASOR	Bulletin of the American Schools of Oriental Research
BBSAJ	Bulletin, British School of Archaeology in Jerusalem
BIAL	Bulletin, Institute of Archaeology, London
BIES	Bulletin of the Israel Exploration Society (1951–1962), continuing
BJPES	Bulletin of the Jewish Palestine Exploration Society
BMB	Bulletin du musée de Beyrouth
BPM	Bulletin of the Palestine Museum
BS	Bibliotheca Sacra
BZ	Biblische Zeitschrift
CRAIBL	Comptes-rendus Academie des inscriptions et belles-lettres
HUCA	Hebrew Union College Annual
IEJ	Israel Exploration Journal
ILN	The Illustrated London News
JAOS	Journal of the American Oriental Society
JBL	Journal of Biblical Literature
JCS	Journal of Cuneiform Studies
JEA	Journal of Egyptian Archaeology
JNES	Journal of Near Eastern Studies
JPOS	Journal of the Palestine Oriental Society
JRAI	Journal of the Royal Anthropological Institute
JRAS	Journal of the Royal Asiatic Society
JRS	Journal of Roman Studies
MDOG	Mitteilungen der deutschen orientalischen Gesellschaft
MUSJ	Mélanges de l'Université Saint Joseph de Beyrouth
OLZ	Orientalistische Literaturzeitung
PEFA	Palestine Exploration Fund, Annual
PEFQSt	Palestine Exploration Fund, Quarterly Statement
PEQ	Palestine Exploration Quarterly
PJB	Palästina-Jahrbuch
QDAP	Quarterly of the Department of Antiquities in Palestine
RAr	Revue Archéologique
RB	Revue biblique
RHR	Revue de l'histoire des religions
TLZ	Theologische Literaturzeitung
VT	Vetus Testamentum
Yediot	Continuation of BIES (1962–1968)
ZAW	Zeitschrift für die alttestamentliche Wissenchaft
ZDPV	Zeitschrift des deutschen Palästina-Vereins

ABU GHOSH

IDENTIFICATION. The present-day village of Abu Ghosh lies some 15 kilometers (9 miles) southwest of Jerusalem on the road to Tel Aviv and Jaffa.

PREHISTORIC REMAINS

The prehistoric settlement is located in an olive grove on the slope of the valley, northwest of the village, on either side of the old road near a well (Bir Ankush).

As early as 1928, the Benedictine Fathers who cultivated the land drew the attention of R. Neuville to flint implements and stone vessels collected in their fields. A few exploratory trenches, however, yielded meager results.

In 1950 a grant from the Commission des Fouilles in Paris enabled J. Perrot to resume exploration. In one of the trenches (70 square meters), he found material in situ and established the stratigraphy. New excavations took place in 1967 with the support of the Centre National de la Recherche Scientifique. During four seasons of work an area of 600 square meters was excavated, and the following stratigraphy of the site was determined:

a. Surface layer, with terra rossa and coarse gravel, containing mixed material (flints and Byzantine-Arab pottery) circa .3 meters thick.

b. Gray organic soil with angled flints — archaeological layer — .5–1.1 meters thick.

c. Sterile red clay on bedrock.

The architectural remains are close to the surface, and hence badly damaged. Three building levels have been distinguished, but structures could be identified only in the middle level. The walls, .6 to 1.1 meters wide, are built of two faces of rough stones. The buildings are rectangular, and each consists of one living unit. One house (6.5 by 6 meters) contained a polished white plastered floor with a band of red paint at the edge. Another house, also with a plastered floor, had a row of three small cubicles (.8–1 meters wide) along one of its walls. A kind of enclosure, with a wall 18 meters long, was also uncovered, as were stone-lined pits, hearths, and the remains of pavements. Twelve human skeletons (some incomplete) have been found. Two of them, which had been buried below the plaster floors of one house, were without

Ashdod. Cult stand with musicians.

skulls and only the lower jaws were found. All the skeletons were in a flexed position.

The flint industry was characterized by the frequent use of very fine brown, cream-white, or violet flints. The two-stroke method of working was followed. The tools found include finely denticulated sickle blades (circa 40 percent); arrowheads of varied types with tang, wings, and notches, or tanged or foliated, made by abrupt retouch or pressure flaking (circa 20 percent); retouched blades (17 percent); burins (8 percent); borers (4 percent); and scrapers (3 percent); a few large almond-shaped axes, small partially polished axes, and small picks (4 percent). Obsidian finds are few: one small arrowhead and several bladelets.

The limestone grinding tools include equipment such as querns, pestles, finely polished bowls, and larger vessels. A few bone tools were also found: awls, needles, and spatulas. Some animal figurines of unbaked clay were recovered, but no pottery was found.

The fauna remains, which are being studied by G. Haas, consist of ox, goat, gazelle, fox, pig or wild boar, tortoise, and wild cat.

According to a survey, data acquired from test trenches, and electric resistivity data (two series of measurements have been made by A. Hesse), the site apparently extended little beyond the area excavated. In view of the remains of architecture, the settlement seems to have been of a sedentary type, with large and solidly built houses and perhaps facilities for storage. No data concerning the economy of the inhabitants have been collected so far. No seeds were recovered. And until the study of the fauna is completed, it is impossible to say whether or not the animals were domesticated.

No charcoal for radiocarbon dating could be collected at Abu Ghosh, but the assemblages and the types of houses and of burials can be paralleled with those of the pre-pottery Neolithic B levels of Jericho, the pre-ceramic levels at Munhata (6–3), and the Neolithic levels of Beidha (VI–I) in Jordan. This stage is dated at Jericho and Beidha to the seventh millennium B.C.

Polished handaxes; pre-pottery Neolithic B.

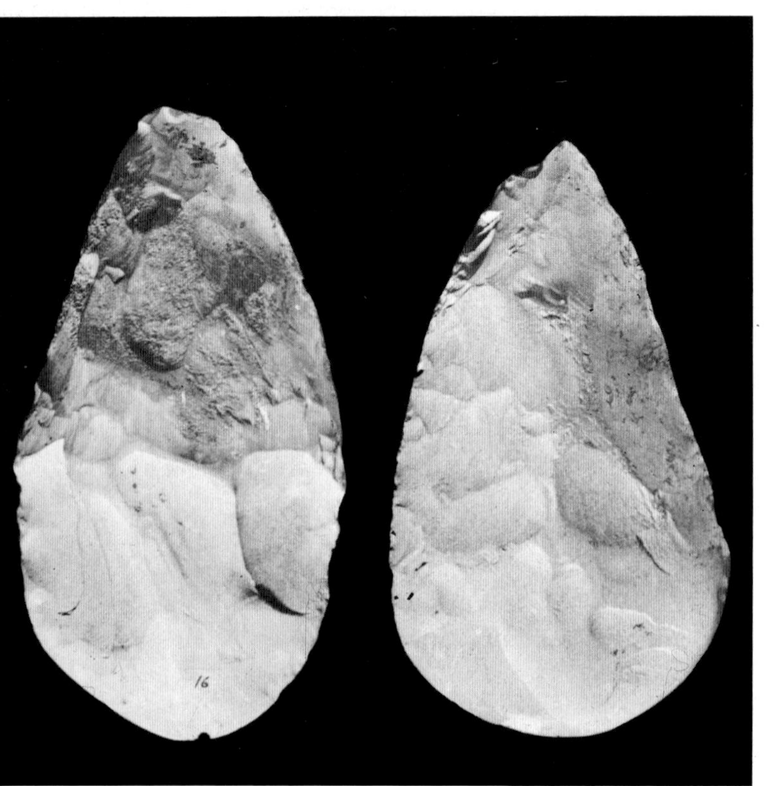

Mameluke caravanserai. Crusader church center top.
existing conjectured Crusader.

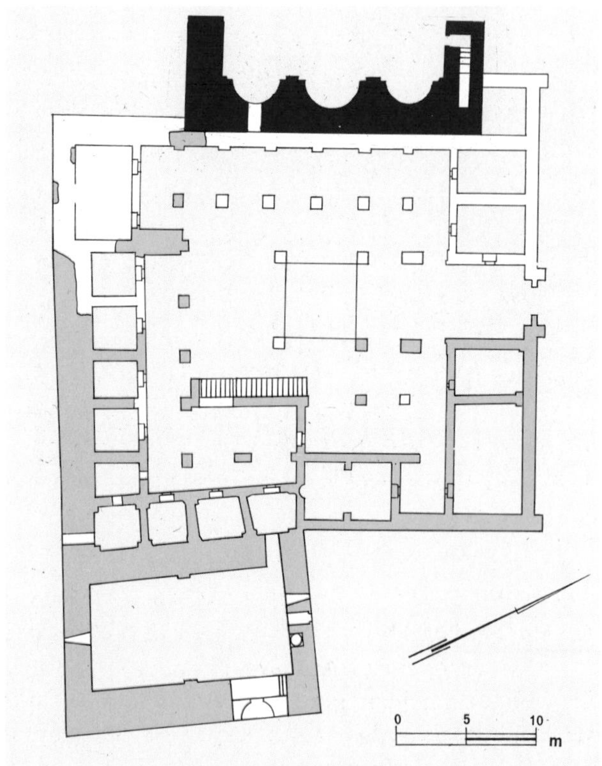

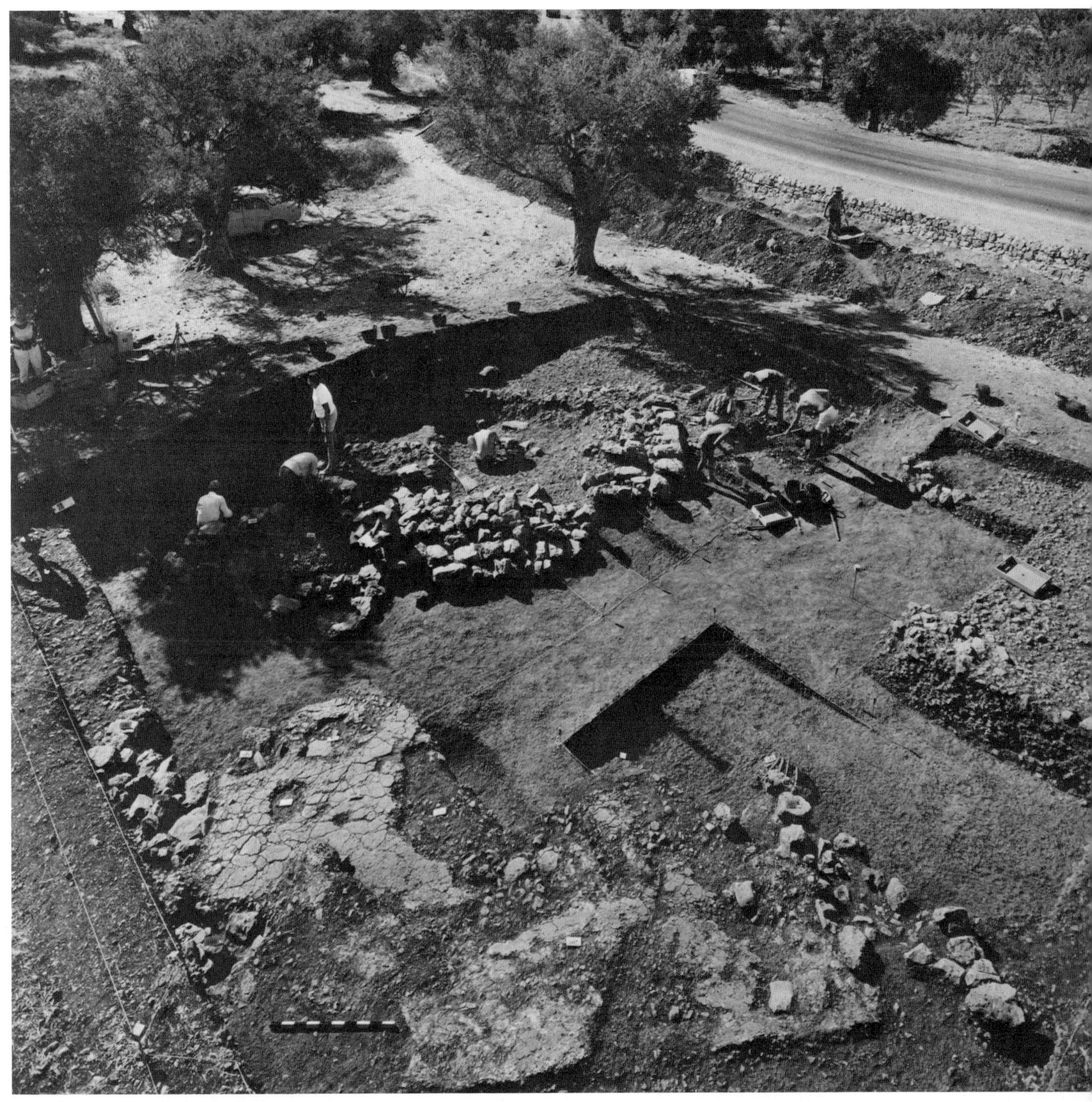

General view of the excavations.

The material of Abu Ghosh is kept in the collections of the Department of Antiquities in Jerusalem and the Mission Archéologique Française. Surface finds are exhibited at the Monastère Saint Sauveur at Abu Ghosh. J. Perrot

BIBLIOGRAPHY

J. Perrot, *Syria* 29 (1952), 119–45 • R.J. Braidwood and G.R. Willey, *Courses Toward Urban Life,* Chicago, 1962, 147–64 • G. Dollfus and M. Lechevallier, *Syria* 46 (1969), 277–87 • M. Lechevallier, *IEJ* 20 (1970), 222–23; 21 (1971), 226–27.

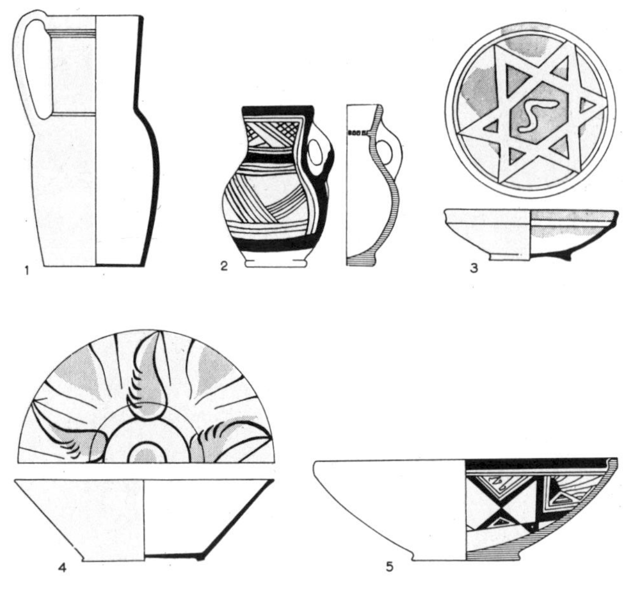

Selection of pottery. 1, 4: tenth – eleventh centuries. 2, 3, 5: Crusader and Mameluke periods (above). The crypt (below).

LATER REMAINS: AREA EAST AND SOUTH OF THE BENEDICTINE MONASTERY

In 1941, and more extensively in 1944, the Ecole Biblique Française, under the direction of R. de Vaux and A. M. Steve, excavated this area, situated west of the village near the Crusader church above the spring. They also investigated remains of Roman installations around the spring. The following structures were found in this area:

The Roman Reservoir. Circa 20.7 by 16.25 meters. Two stepped passages hewn in the rock led to the reservoir. The steps are still in use in the crypt of the Crusader church. The reservoir was used by the detachment *(vexillatio)* of the Tenth Roman Legion *(Legio X Fretensis)*, which was stationed on the Roman road ascending to Aelia Capitolina by way of Colonia (Moza; Arabic Qalunya).

The Caravanserai. The main buildings of the caravanserai date to the time of the Abbasid

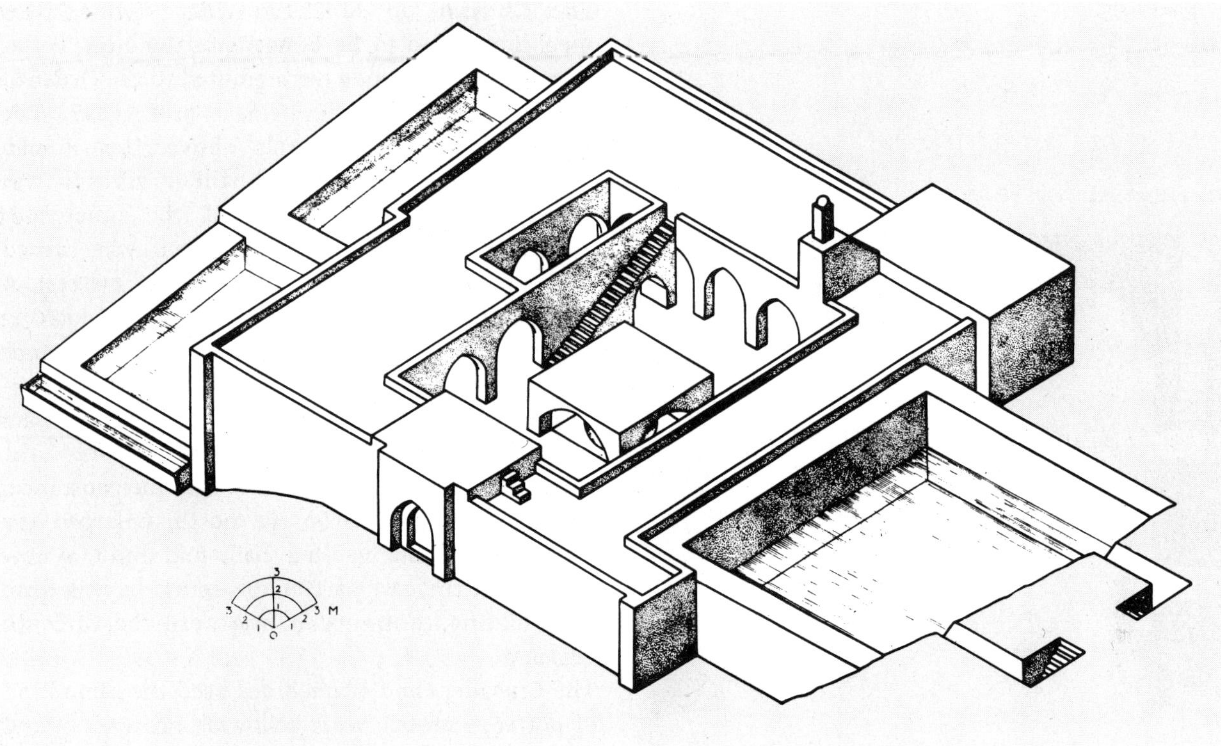

Early Arab caravanserai; isometric reconstruction.

dynasty. It was built east of and tangent to the Roman reservoir. The plan is that of an open court surrounded by vaulted arcades with pointed arches. The court has a wide entrance on the north, near which was the main road to Jerusalem. In the center of the court a small pool was built beneath a pavilion roof whose corners were supported by pillars. Water was conveyed to the pool from the Roman reservoir, and water flowed from the pool through a channel to a thick-walled reservoir. According to the excavators, there was yet another reservoir on the north side of this one. A trough was connected with it on its north side near the road passing by the caravanserai.

On the south and east sides of the court, vaulted rooms were built behind the arcades. A flight of steps led to the flat roof above the arcades and apparently also to rooms on the second story. A small mosque, with the mihrab pointing to Mecca, was built in the southwestern corner of the arcades of the court. On the northeastern side of the mosque were thick foundations (3 by 1.78 meters) cutting through the adjacent arcade, which were probably the base of the minaret of the mosque. In the southeastern corner of the arcade a cistern was dug under the courtyard. Beyond the staircase was another, smaller paved court (7.5 by 3.25 meters) that served the adjoining rooms.

The excavators concluded that the caravanserai was built in about the mid-ninth century. This estimate was based on the following: (a) a comparison with other buildings from the time of the Abbasids, (b) the use of the measurement 1 foot equals 54 centimeters in planning the building, and (c) a date in a fragmentary Kufic inscription found at the site in 1902. The caravanserai continued in use up to the time of the Crusaders.

Two main groups of pottery found at the site are attributed to the Abbasid period: (a) glazed ware decorated with floral and geometric patterns in green, brown, purple, and jasper, and also monochrome glazed pottery with leaf decoration; (b) plain pottery with band burnishing and white or white-slipped vessels (mostly jugs with flat bases and cylindrical bodies); the decoration is incised in various geometric patterns. Also found were shards of large bowls and jars with incised decoration, lightly fired, which continue the Byzantine tradition. The white ware is very similar to pottery found at Khirbet el-Mefjer.

The church; plan and view.

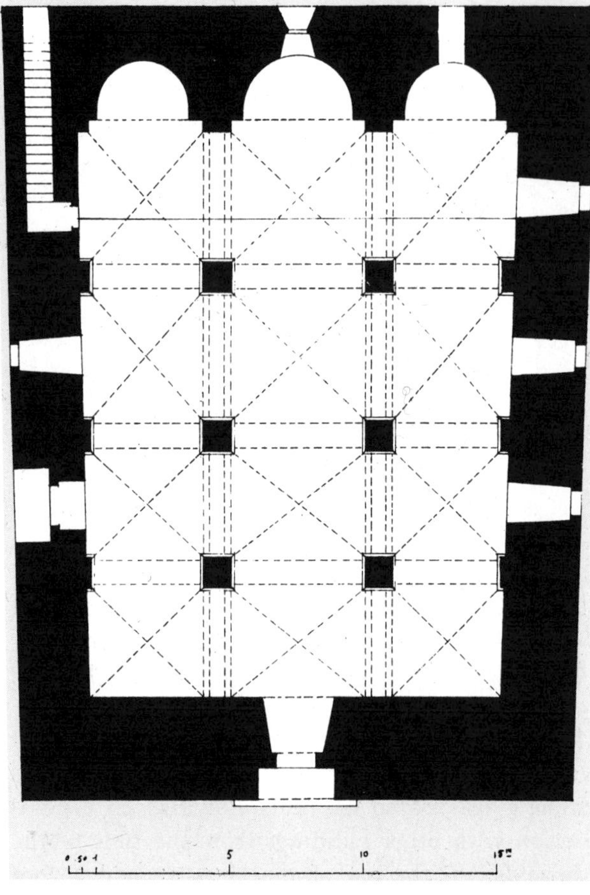

The Church. In 1142 the village (which was then considered to be Emmaus of the New Testament) and all its lands were granted to the Order of the Hospitalers, which held it until 1187. The Crusaders built a church above the Roman reservoir. Most of the church still survives (it was partly restored at the end of the nineteenth century). The Roman reservoir itself was turned into a great vaulted hall (14.25 by 7.5 meters). A window was cut in its south wall and a cooking stove installed in the northeast corner. The cistern in the corner of the arcade served as a toilet.

The Restored Caravanserai. Between the years 1350 and 1400, the Mamelukes restored the caravanserai. They vaulted over the entrance, added rooms near it on the north, enlarged the west wall of the vaulted hall, and built a new mosque in the east part of the court. In this form the building continued in use until the fifteenth century.

The Crusaders and Mamelukes used the same kind of pottery: vessels with yellowish-brown slip and brown-purple geometric decorations in such designs as parallel lines, broken lines, triangles, lozenges, squares, checkered patterns, etc. A common vessel is the jug with a long, wide neck and strainer and a globular body on a flat or ring base. The vessels are richly decorated over most of their area. Also typical are glazed shards with geometric motifs, sometimes decorated under the glaze. The lamps and other finds are of the usual type for the period. The excavations at Abu Ghosh are of special importance because of the detailed classification of its pottery, which served to verify the results of the excavations at Khirbet el-Mefjer and at 'Atlit and forms a bridge between them.

Tombs in Vicinity. In 1923 the Benedictine Fathers excavated two tombs from the Herodian period. In tomb A the entrance had three steps, with the burial chamber slightly sunken in the center. In tomb B a rolling stone was found at the end of a short corridor; the tomb itself consisted of a shaft with elliptically shaped trough graves behind partitions on three of its sides.

M. Avi-Yonah

BIBLIOGRAPHY

The Herodian tombs: F.M. Abel, *RB* 34 (1925), 275–79 • **The Arab Caravanserai:** R. de Vaux, A.M. Steve, *Fouilles à Qaryet el-'Anab (Abu Gôsh)*, Paris, 1950.

ABU HAWAM, TELL

IDENTIFICATION. Tell Abu Hawam, the site of an ancient harbor city, is situated near the spot where the Kishon River empties into the Mediterranean Sea. Before modern building activities, the flat tel extended over an area of about 1.5 hectares on the banks of the Kishon River, approximately 800 meters from the coast. P. L. O. Guy had conjectured that the settlement was originally located directly on the seashore but that in the course of time the coastline had changed due to the silt carried by the Kishon. This supposition was confirmed in the excavations of 1963. About 20 meters west of the Late Bronze Age city wall, on the side facing the sea, a thick wall built of large rough stones was discovered. In the layer of sand at the foot of this wall, shards were found covered with a concretion of seashells. From these finds it can be concluded that in the second half of the second millennium B.C., the settlement was located directly on the coast, and the mouth of the Kishon was apparently the site of an ancient harbor at the foot of Mount Carmel. M. Avnimelech has summarized the evidence of the geological changes that took place in the vicinity of the tel during the Holocene.

B. Mazar has suggested that the site be identified with the Roman Mutatio Calamon, which is the Talmudic Ṣalmona. This name probably derives from Wadi Ṣalman, which joins the Kishon near Tell Abu Hawam.

EXCAVATIONS

The archaeological investigation of Tell Abu Hawam and its environs began in 1923 when a road was being paved on the slopes of Mount Carmel and a group of graves was discovered about one kilometer south of the mound. Guy excavated the graves and assigned them to an Israelite settlement. He also conducted a preliminary survey on the mound and found that it had been settled from the Late Bronze Age until Byzantine times. In 1932, R. W. Hamilton, then deputy director of the Department of Antiquities of the British Mandatory Government in Palestine, carried out the first of two seasons of excavations on the site. He distinguished five strata of settlement: V — the lowest — Late Bronze Age; IV and III — Iron

From top to bottom: Imported Mycenaean pottery (Late Mycenaean III-B); stratum V; LBA II. Cypriot tauromorphic rhyton, related to base-ring ware; stratum V. Faience rhyton in the shape of a ram's head; LBA II.

Age I–II; II — Persian period; and I — the top stratum — a mixture of Hellenistic to Arab finds.
During development projects in the Kishon port in the early 1950's an ancient cemetery was discovered about 500 meters east of the mound. It was excavated in 1952 by E. Anati on behalf of the Department of Antiquities. The entire area was strewn with shards, but most of the graves had been destroyed by river floods and by changes in the level of the sand. Thirteen soundings were made; ten Late Bronze Age burials were discovered, but only one was in an undisturbed condition. Nearby, M. Prausnitz discovered the burial of a child in a jar.
In 1963 another excavation was undertaken on the mound itself, under the direction of E. Anati, and sponsored by the Department of Antiquities. In the Late Bronze Age stratum, three phases were distinguished.

RESULTS OF THE EXCAVATION AND HISTORY OF THE SETTLEMENT

Up to the last excavation (1963) opinion was divided as to the date of the founding of the

Foundation of building; stratum IV.

settlement. Hamilton had assumed that it was first settled in the fourteenth century B.C. Most of the material he discovered, however, was of a later date, which led Mazar and others to conclude that the settlement was founded circa 1300 B.C. In the 1952 excavations in the Late Bronze Age cemetery, Mycenaean and Cypriot pottery was uncovered dating to the fourteenth century (Mycenaean III-A, and base-ring ware). In the 1963 excavations on the mound, finds from the fourteenth century B.C. were also discovered.

Stratum V. In the Late Bronze Age there were three occupation phases distinguished from one another by their buildings and destruction layers. During this relatively short period the city was evidently destroyed twice and rebuilt twice. The numerous shards of imported vessels are evidence of the commercial ties between this port and the centers of Mycenaean and Cypriot culture in the fourteenth and thirteenth centuries B.C.

PHASE A. The earliest level on the site belongs to a temporary settlement, of which only hearths and a flooring of pebbles or pisé de terre remain. Tents were apparently pitched on this flooring. Sea and crab shells found among the remains indicate that this was a fishing village. This phase was overlaid with sand, probably because the place had been abandoned for some time.

PHASE B. The site was resettled and a fortification wall and buildings were erected. A large building, probably the governor's residence, was discovered in the southwestern corner of the settlement, between the sea and the mouth of the river. Another structure was somewhat similar to the Canaanite temples discovered on several sites in Palestine. It may have been a public building, but it is difficult to establish its exact nature from the finds there. Since traces of large-scale planning were found in this second phase, the settlement might be dated to the reign of Pharaoh Seti I. Mazar has suggested that the city was a base for the Egyptian navy — a suggestion that seems likely.

PHASE C. The governor's residence was destroyed, and other buildings were erected on top of it. The fortifications were also repaired extensively in this phase. The city was destroyed and abandoned at the beginning of the twelfth century B.C., apparently when the Sea Peoples roved in this district during the reign of Ramses III.

Stratum IV. After an interval of about a century a new settlement was founded, smaller than the previous one and different in the quality of its buildings. Several small residential units have been discovered, each consisting of two rooms and a closed court. Judging by the material culture, this settlement existed in the second half of the eleventh century and the beginning of the tenth century B.C. It was probably destroyed in the course of David's campaign.

Faience rhyton; LBA II.

Stratum III. New fortifications were built, but sections of the previous wall were reused. A large structure, probably a public building, has been found near the assumed site of the city gate. This stratum contains Samaria ware and imported Thessalian ware, which date it to the tenth and ninth centuries B.C. The city was destroyed at the end of the ninth century, probably during the Aramaean invasion. It was abandoned and not resettled until the Persian period.

Stratum II. Buildings and a wall were constructed in the sixth century B.C., and the settlement continued to exist until the Hellenistic period, about the end of the fourth century B.C.

Stratum I. The uppermost stratum is mainly in ruins. The finds were Late Hellenistic, Roman, and Byzantine. It was evidently a small, unwalled village, and the remnants of the fortifications were no longer used. The last precise information about this settlement comes from the Bordeaux Pilgrim (A.D. 333), who mentions a station called Mutatio Calamon — a name close to its ancient one, Ṣalamon or Ṣalmona.

SUMMARY

The history of this ancient harbor city is summarized in the table below.

E. ANATI

BIBLIOGRAPHY

Excavation reports: P.L.O. Guy, *PMB* 1 (1924), 47–55 • R.W. Hamilton, *QDAP* 3 (1933), 74–80; 4 (1934), 1–69 • E. Anati, *'Atiqot* 2 (1959), 89–102; *RB* 71 (1964), 400–01 • W.A. Heurtley, *QDAP* 4 (1935), 181 • H.L. Vincent, *RB* 44 (1935), 416–37 • W.F. Albright, *AASOR* 21–22 (1934), 6, n. 2 • B. Maisler (Mazar), *BASOR* 124 (1951), 21–25 • G.W. Van Beek, *ibid.* 28; *ibid.* 138 (1955), 34–38 • M. Avnimelech, *'Atiqot* 2 (1959), 103–05.

STRATUM	PHASE	SETTLEMENT AND MAIN FEATURES	CONJECTURED DATES B.C.
V	A	Fishing village.	14th century
	B	Fortified port city; governor's residence, apparently built during the reign of Seti I.	13th century
		Destruction of the city.	13th century
	C	The city rebuilt without the governor's residence.	End of 13th century
		The city destroyed and abandoned during the reign of Ramses III when the Sea Peoples were active in the area.	12th century
IV	A	A settlement smaller than the previous one; part of its wall reused.	Mid-11th century
	B	Improvements in the buildings.	End of 11th century
		Destruction of the city by David.	First half of 10th century
III	A	A fortified village with a large central building.	Mid-10th century
	B	Additions and improvements in the buildings.	End of 10th, beginning of 9th century
		The settlement destroyed and abandoned.	End of 9th century
II	A	Small fortified settlement erected; reused part of the walls of the previous phase.	6th century
	B	Additions and repairs.	Probably 5th century
		The settlement destroyed at the beginning of the Hellenistic period.	End of 4th century
I		An open settlement founded in the Late Hellenistic period.	End of 4th century
		The settlement abandoned in the Byzantine period.	4th or 5th century A.D.

ABU UṢBA, CAVE

IDENTIFICATION. The Abu Uṣba Cave is situated high above the riverbed in a bluff on the left bank of Naḥal Oren (Wadi Falah), near the point where it emerges from the mountains (map reference 14802385). The cave consists of three chambers: the first (10 by 15 meters) is accessible through a corridor (about 6 meters long) and is lighted by daylight. The second is smaller, and the third, the largest, is pitch dark. At the entrance of the cave is a small terrace with a radius of 18 meters.

EXCAVATIONS

In 1941 M. Stekelis explored the cave and discovered that its prehistoric occupants had settled mainly in the first chamber, which receives daylight; the third chamber contained only insignificant remains. A sounding made on the terrace yielded mixed finds: a collection of Roman-Byzantine shards, Upper Natufian and Mousterian flint implements, and pottery similar to layer C material (see below).

Since deposits in chamber I were undisturbed, Stekelis was able to establish their stratigraphic sequence:

A 0–0.9 meters: black earth with modern remains

B–1 0.9–1.15 meters: soft reddish-brown cave earth; flint implements, potsherds, and fauna

B-2 1.15–1.65 meters: compact reddish-brown cave earth; flint implements, potsherds, and fauna

C 1.65–2.35 meters: stalactite crust, breccia with bones and Levalloiso-Mousterian flint implements

D 2.35 meters: bedrock.

Both phases of layer B (B–1 and B–2) yielded an industry that was named Usbian because of its unique characteristics. Although this layer was found only in chamber I, the abundance of its material caused it to become the essential part of the excavation.

In layer C about 350 objects were collected, including twenty-one retouched points and eighteen side scrapers. This industry was correlated with the Upper Levalloiso-Mousterian stratum B at Tabun and with stratum G at el-Wad.

In layer B the flint implements could be divided into two groups: one related to the Upper Natufian and the other hardly distinguishable from the Natufian itself. To the first group belong microburins, lunates with Heluan-type retouch, blades with inverse retouch, Natufian sickle blades, truncated burins, retouched microliths, scalene triangles, and various scrapers. To this group Stekelis added three adzes, similar to those found at el-Wad in Natufian layer B–1. The second group included primitive arrowheads with points but without tangs, as well as denticulated (saw-like) sickle blades made by the pressure retouch technique.

The pottery found in this layer was of poor quality, handmade and fired on an open hearth. Some shards had been petrified by the infiltration of calcium carbonate. A few showed traces of red-brown, yellow-brown, and gray-brown paint. Others bore incised decorations. The few fragments that were found belonged to various parts of vessels: rims, walls, bases, and handles, the latter including lug and knob handles.

In Stekelis' opinion, layer B represents a homogeneous culture belonging to a small and poor community that may have occupied the site only for a short time. The inhabitants were primarily hunters and fishermen, but the sickle blades, axes, and pottery indicate incipient agriculture.

The fauna of layer B was studied by G. Haas. Attention was focused on the microfauna, for it represented many biotopes. Since the cave is situated in a mountainous ridge, next to a spring and not far from the coast, the fauna represents a cross section of different regions. The amphibian species point to the existence of a spring near the site and of swamps on the shore. The reptilian remains belong to a species living exclusively in Mediterranean evergreen scrubwood. The birds include rockbreeders, forest dwellers, and winter residents. The existence of a forest is proved by the presence of mammals as well as the absence of arid-region rodents. Alongside the forest dwellers, land animals living in open spaces, *e.g., Gazella, Hyaena, Equus,* are also found. Haas does not consider the preponderance of *Gazella* over *Dama* to be proof of climatic variation, for biotopes suitable for both animals existed side by side. Possibly, too, hunters preferred one animal to the other.

The biotope of layer B at Abu Uṣba is not different from that found on the site today, except that it had a much denser forest than at present. The faunal study shows the coexistence of forest dwellers with arid-land animals.

After the results of the excavation had been published, Albright and others contended that layer B was a mixture of Natufian flint implements with Neolithic or Chalcolithic pottery. They did not accept Stekelis' assertion that it was an undisturbed layer with very early pottery which could not be dated by its decoration but could be compared with a coarse, equally undatable pottery found by Dorothy Garrod at el-Wad. In Albright's view, a pre-pottery Neolithic period existed between the Upper Natufian and the pottery-Neolithic as it appeared in Garstang's excavation in Jericho. He considered layer B at Abu Uṣba a mixed layer with both Natufian and pottery-Neolithic. The former included mainly the lunates with Heluan-type retouch and the sickle blades, and the latter the denticulated sickle blades, the arrowheads with pressure retouch, the adzes, and the pottery. In Stekelis' opinion, layer B was undisturbed and belongs to the pottery-Neolithic culture in which earlier elements were preserved, particularly tools of Natufian tradition.

O. BAR-YOSEF

BIBLIOGRAPHY

M. Stekelis, *BASOR* 86 (1942), 2–10 • W.F. Albright, *ibid.*, 10–14 • M. Stekelis, *ibid.* 89 (1943), 22–24 • W.F. Albright, *ibid.* 24–25 • M. Stekelis, *QDAP* 11 (1944), 115–18; *idem,* with G. Haas, *IEJ* 2 (1952), 15–47 • M. Almagro, *Ampurias* 14 (1952), 184–86.

ACCHO

IDENTIFICATION. Accho (Arabic 'Akka), harbor city at the north end of Haifa Bay. The unchanged name and the remains make the identification certain.

HISTORY

Accho is first mentioned in the later group of the Egyptian Execration Texts (generally attributed to the end of the nineteenth century B.C.). In inscriptions of the Pharaohs Thutmose III, Seti I, and Ramses II, and in the el-Amarna letters and Ugaritic texts, Accho appears as a royal Canaanite city and a flourishing harbor town from the fifteenth to the thirteenth centuries B.C. At that time it was situated on a large mound — Tell el-Fukhar ("Napoleon's Hill") — circa 1.5 kilometers (1 mile) from the present Old City.

The potsherds scattered on the surface of the mound show that the site was inhabited throughout the Bronze and Iron ages, and also later down to early Byzantine times (fifth to sixth century A.D.). In the Persian period (from the sixth century B.C.), the city had already begun to spread westward to the sea, with people settling in the plain at the foot of the mound, as well as on the peninsula

which forms the northern end of Haifa Bay. There, at the northern end of the peninsula, the port of the city was located from the Persian period onward, and the commercial center of the town grew up around it.

Information about Accho in early Israelite times is scanty. In the Bible it is mentioned only in Judges 1:31: "Neither did Asher drive out the inhabitants of Accho, nor the inhabitants of Zidon," and in the corrupted form עמה — *Umma* in Joshua 19:30 (Septuagint — 'Ακχω) where Accho is listed as one of the coastal cities of the tribe of Asher.

The city occurs more frequently in Assyrian texts, which describe it as an important Phoenician city both politically and economically during the eighth and ninth centuries B.C. It was even one of the centers of rebellion against Assyria during the reign of Ashurbanipal. In Persian times it was a royal fortress and a military base for actions against Egypt ('Ακή — Ps. Scylax 104). Its heyday began after it had been taken without resistance by Alexander the Great in 333 B.C. Alexander set up a mint in Accho that was in continuous use for more than six hundred years.

On the coins of Ptolemy II the monogram of the city (πτ) appears for the first time — indicating a change of name to Ptolemais, the Greek name for the city, in honor of Ptolemy II Philadelphus. This name remained in official use until the Arab conquest.

Accho; general view from the southeast (opposite). Third-century coin of Ptolemais (below).

In 200 B.C. Ptolemais was annexed by the Seleucids after the victory of Antiochus III over the Ptolemaic army at Paneas. It remained under Seleucid suzerainty until the campaign of Pompey in Syria and Palestine in 64/63 B.C.

During the Maccabean revolt the town was hostile to the Jews of the Galilee. In 164/63 B.C. Simon the Maccabee had to come to the rescue of his Galilean brothers. Simon defeated his enemies and drove them "to the gate of Ptolemais" (I Maccabees 5:14–15, 20–23).

Jonathan the Hasmonaean was treacherously invited by Tryphon to Ptolemais and was taken prisoner there (143 B.C.) while his soldiers were slain (I Maccabees 12:48). Ptolemais was besieged by Alexander Janneus in 104 B.C., but the siege was raised at the approach of Ptolemy IX Lathyrus. Julius Caesar visited Ptolemais in 47 B.C. From that date till the time of Alexander Severus (A.D. 229–30) the city counted its years by an era beginning in 47 B.C.

In 39 B.C. Herod landed at Ptolemais, and from there he began his campaign of conquest of the territories that the Romans had bestowed on him. In the time of Nero, Ptolemais became a Roman colony (Colonia Claudia Ptolemais). Soldiers discharged from the Third, Fifth, Tenth, and Twelfth Legions were settled there, as can be seen from coins struck in honor of the event.

During the First Jewish Revolt (A.D. 66–70) the inhabitants of Ptolemais were again hostile to the Jews. Josephus Flavius reports that about two thousand Jews were killed by them. In the second year of the Revolt, Vespasian made Ptolemais his military base for the repression of the rebellion in Galilee.

Christianity spread early among the inhabitants of Ptolemais. Paul the Apostle spent a day there during his third voyage (Acts 21:7). Its first known bishop was Clarus (A.D. 190).

The town surrendered to the Arabs in 636 and resumed its ancient Semitic name, which had remained in use in the Talmudic sources throughout. In the reconstructed shipyards, which had survived from Byzantine times, the first Umayyad Caliph, Mu'awiyah, built a fleet in order to invade Cyprus and attack North Africa.

In the ninth century Ibn Ṭulun ruled 'Akka from

Egypt. He rebuilt the port, which later became the main harbor of the Crusaders; extensive remains survive to this day.

The city was captured by Baldwin I in 1104 with the help of the Genoese fleet. In 1187 the city fell to Saladin, but in 1191 it was retaken by Richard the Lion Hearted and Philip Augustus during the Third Crusade. From this date (1191) to 1291 the city was known as St. Jean d'Acre and was the capital of the Latin Kingdom under the direct rule of the king. A high official, a viscount, governed it in his name.

The military orders had their headquarters and monasteries there, each in its own quarter: the Order of St. John (the Hospitalers) in the center of the city, the Templars at the southern end (near the present lighthouse), the Teutonic Knights in the east, and the Order of St. Lazarus at the northern end in the suburb of Montmusart.

The Italian colonies (Venetian, Genoese, Pisan, etc.) were settled around the harbor. Much merchandise passed through the port of Acre on its way to and from the Near and Far East. The city prospered, and its population grew to some fifty thousand inhabitants.

In 1291 the Mameluke sultan el-Malik el-Ashraf captured the city after a siege of two months and razed it to the ground. The fall of Acre marked the end of the Crusader Kingdom in Palestine.

The Druze Emir Fakhr e-Din rebuilt part of the city at the beginning of the seventeenth century. The full reconstruction of the town began in the mid-eighteenth century, under the rule of Dhaher el-'Amr (1750–75) and Ahmed el-Jazzar (1775–1804). Dhaher el-'Amr rebuilt the city wall (today the inner wall). Jazzar Pasha built the outer wall, the Great Mosque (1781), the Khan el-'Umdan, and the Turkish bath (Hammam el-Basha), in which the municipal museum is located today. Both these rulers and Jazzar's successor, Suleiman Pasha, worked on the citadel in the center of the city on the large ruins of the Hospitalers' convent. In 1799 Jazzar successfully resisted a siege by Napoleon and the French Expeditionary Army. The siege

The refectory and its vicinity. 1. Underground passage. 2. Turkish bazaar. 3. El-Bosta. 4. Municipal museum (Hamma el Basha). 5. Unexcavated hall. 6. Refectory.

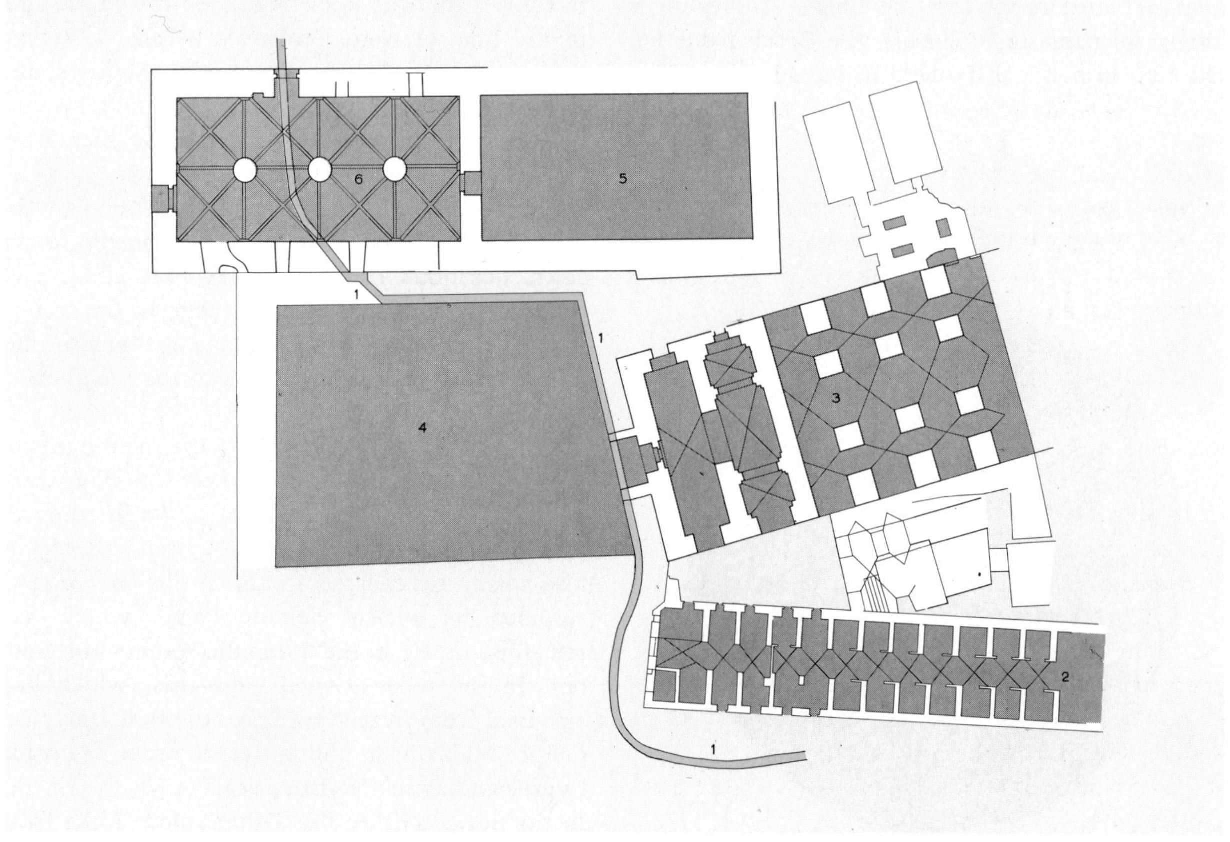

lasted two months and had important historical repercussions.

EXCAVATIONS

Large-scale systematic excavations have not yet been undertaken in or near Accho. The following is a chronological list of the work done so far:

Hellenistic-Roman Graves in Housing Project C. This first excavation was directed by Ruth Amiran in 1950 on behalf of the Department of Antiquities. Several types of burials were discovered: graves without receptacles; burials in pottery coffins, sometimes placed in a plastered tomb; burials in a built tomb with floors of dressed flagstones, occasionally containing a wooden coffin.

Two Graves in Amidar Housing Project. These were excavated by Z. Goldmann in 1953 on behalf of the Department of Antiquities. The two graves were built of large flagstones and were oriented east–west. They date from the third/second centuries B.C. Among the finds were bronze cosmetic vessels. These graves belong to a large cemetery situated north of Tell el-Fukhar.

Graves from Late Bronze, Hellenistic, and Later Periods in Accho-Manshiyeh. These graves were excavated in 1955–56 by S. Levi on behalf of the Department of Antiquities. Five graves were discovered: one belonged to the Late Bronze Age; two were Hellenistic-Roman; one was Roman-Byzantine; and one dated to the Middle Arab period (twelfth century). The Late Bronze Age grave was a simple infant burial. The Hellenistic-Roman graves were built of large dressed flagstones. In the Roman-Byzantine grave, fragments of a large pottery coffin were found.

In another Hellenistic-Roman grave built of large flagstones, which was excavated by Z. Goldmann (1956) at the same site, about 110 fragments of a gilt bronze sheet were found.

The Cemetery on the Seashore. In 1961–62 excavations were carried out by an Italian expedition under the direction of Maria Theresa Fortuna. About two hundred graves were cleared, most of which had been dug in the sand. Burials in wooden coffins were found in several graves. Only a few were built of dressed *kurkar* stone.

In this cemetery three periods could be identified. About one third of the graves are from the end of the Persian or the beginning of the Hellenistic period (second half of the fourth century B.C.);

The refectory (above). Fleur-de-lys ornament on corbel in refectory (below).

most of them were dug deep in the sand or the *kurkar*. The body was placed on its back with the face turned to the east. The few finds from the graves include juglets and lamps of Early Hellenistic type. A few graves of the Hellenistic period — third/first centuries B.C. — were also found. Two fragments of plastered *kurkar* tombstones belong to this period.

Graves of the Hellenistic and Roman periods make up about 60 percent of the total, the majority being very poor. Nails were found, which suggest burials in wooden coffins. Many of the graves contained offerings of glass vessels, including unguentaria. Two graves contained some thirty-seven glass bottles.

The Hellenistic Wall. Sections of the wall of Hellenistic Ptolemais were discovered in different places by Z. Goldmann. One section of the wall was exposed at a depth of 1.8 meters while drainage ditches were being dug in Trumpeldor Street. The wall is 3 to 5 meters thick and runs north-south. At the southwest corner of Ben-Ami and Jabotinsky streets, the Hellenistic wall was discovered at a depth of 1 meter. It was also found in the antitank ditch east of the Accho-Nahariya highway. Remains of two parallel walls were discovered south of Ben-Ami Street, between Weizmann and Jabotinsky streets.

In 1956 Z. Goldmann cleared remains of a bath, an abattoir, and a glass furnace in Trumpeldor Street.

The Bath. Plastered walls and floors were found very close to the surface. The pink color of the plaster resulted from the addition of crushed pottery. On the north side a pool was found, 15 meters in length, its walls built of rough boulders arranged in alternate courses of large and small stones. Only a few centimeters beneath this were the remains of an earlier bath with grayish-white plaster. The earlier bath is certainly Roman, the later one Byzantine (or Early Arab).

Nearby, to the west, there were four or five walls of a large building that was also built in alternate courses of large and small boulders. The floor of the building was covered by a great quantity of animal bones. Undoubtedly this is one of the buildings called "boverie" (abattoir) on the Marino Sanuto map (from the end of the thirteenth century).

The Glass Furnace. The glass furnace was discovered near the east side of the abattoir. It consisted of a container for the molten glass built on the rock out of dressed *kurkar* stones that were coated on the inside with crude glass, and a fireplace hewn in the rock below, at a depth of 3 meters. In this area it was possible to distinguish two strata: a Crusader stratum down to a depth of 1.3 meters and a Hellenistic-Roman stratum to a depth of 3 meters. In and around the furnace was found a thick layer of ashes, which contained a large quantity of Hellenistic-Roman shards. The opening on the eastern side of the rock was apparently the firing chamber. Only a few shards were found there.

The Hellenistic Temple. A small Hellenistic temple came to light in 1959, when S. Applebaum, on behalf of the Department of Antiquities, excavated at the building site of the new post office. Before the excavation a complete Greek inscription had been found, dedicated to "Zeus Soter" on behalf of King Antiochus VII Sidetes, by the chief secretary of the Seleucid Army and district governor, in the year 130/29 B.C. The inscription undoubtedly belonged to the temple.

Opposite the temple on the south side, foundations of a long narrow building were discovered (2.5 meters wide) — perhaps a barracks, workshop, or stable. An elephant bone was found there. The building seems to have been part of the military installations of the late Seleucid kings.

The temple was destroyed in the Roman period (not before the first century B.C.). To the north of it a water-supply system was erected. When the water channels were no longer utilized, workshops were built in their place and remained in use until the third century. The orientation of all these buildings is east-west. In the Byzantine period another building with a plastered floor was erected over the remains of the workshops, with a southeast–northwest orientation.

In the Arab period pits were dug in the Byzantine stratum, thus disturbing its stratigraphy.

Among the noteworthy finds of this excavation are forty stamped Rhodian jar handles dating between 220 and 100 B.C.; seventy-three bronze coins, four of them Hellenistic and the rest later; many shards of Attic, Megarian, and terra-sigillata wares; and the hand of a marble figure.

Plain of Accho; LBA bronze mirror of Egyptian origin, from a tomb.

Crusader tombstone: the deceased is seen praying to a saint in the garments of a bishop, perhaps St. Nicholas.

The Refectory of the Order of St. John (The "Crypt of St. John"). Excavated between 1955 and 1964, this "crypt" is one of the many large subterranean halls under the present government hospital. It was full of an earth and stone fill, which extended above the capitals of the thick round columns. This fill was brought into the halls in the eighteenth century in order to prevent them from collapsing under the weight of the new stories that the pashas of Acre were then building on top of the halls for their citadel.

Originally this hall was situated above ground level, and its popular designation "crypt," is a misnomer. From the shape of the two-aisled hall and from the existence of three chimneys on the eastern wall (two added outside the wall and one within), it was concluded that this building served as a refectory. The hall is built in the transitional style, from Romanesque to Gothic. In the middle of the hall heavy cross-rib vaults spring from a row of three huge columns, each almost 3 meters in diameter.

Two fleurs-de-lys were carved on consoles in the refectory, one in its northeast corner and one in the southeast corner. They may prove that the building was erected about 1148, the year in which Louis VII, leader of the Second Crusade,

Cemetery north of town: Tomb B-3 with trident, sword, pottery, and skull of a young man (top). Clay bathtub (bottom); LBA.

resided in Acre and most probably established the lily as the arms of the French kingdom.

The floor level of the hall is about 2 meters above bedrock. It was built on top of earlier remains and formed a kind of cellar. On the west side a quarry was discovered, indicating that the Crusaders had cut their building stone on the spot. On the south side appeared a wall built much deeper than the level of the Crusader columns. It seems to belong to the Hellenistic-Roman period. On the east side — beyond the western column — 350 meters of an underground passage were cleared. It led north to the city walls and south to the port. Partly cut through the rock and partly built, the passage was at a level lower than the columns of the hall.

The earliest finds on the floor of the passage are Hellenistic-Roman. Because the passage was reused by the Crusaders, the two periods could be clearly distinguished. At the point where the tunnel passes beneath the outer (southern) wall of the hall, its level was raised considerably by the Crusaders. That is, its ceiling "climbed up" to 30 centimeters above the floor level of the hall. At the place where the hall and the corridor joined, the Crusaders installed a kind of communicating window into the tunnel by placing in the wall a large stone with a semicircular niche along its whole length.

The Crusaders' entrance to the tunnel was situated just outside the southern wall of the hall below street level. The entrance was a square shaft built of well-dressed stones. All the other Crusaders' additions were similarly built, in contrast to the rubble stones of the Hellenistic-Roman period.

The el-Bosta Halls. The six parallel underground halls beneath the present Arab School east of the museum are called *el-Bosta* by the local inhabitants. They open through large gates southward into a courtyard and northward toward the street through windows. In the fifth hall a gate was built into the street instead of a window. This plan of parallel halls opening onto a courtyard is similar to the typical design of a khan (caravanserai), and the six halls seem to be the northern wing of a large khan, dating to the Fatimid period (eleventh to twelfth century).

A large horseshoe arch, springing from the southern edge of the eastern wall of the khan, forms the beginning of a portico around the courtyard, which is poorly preserved.

Above the northern side of the el-Bosta building in its second story (today the ground floor), an ornate gate has been preserved; it now forms the entrance to the Arab School, but it certainly belongs to the original structure. The gate was constructed with alternate courses of dark and light stone. Its pointed arch is formed by parallel radiating teeth. Strips of carved decoration run on either side of the gate and are reminiscent of typical Fatimid wood carvings of the eleventh and twelfth centuries. Beyond the six halls of el-Bosta there is another single hall in the courtyard, perhaps a small mosque.

City plan.

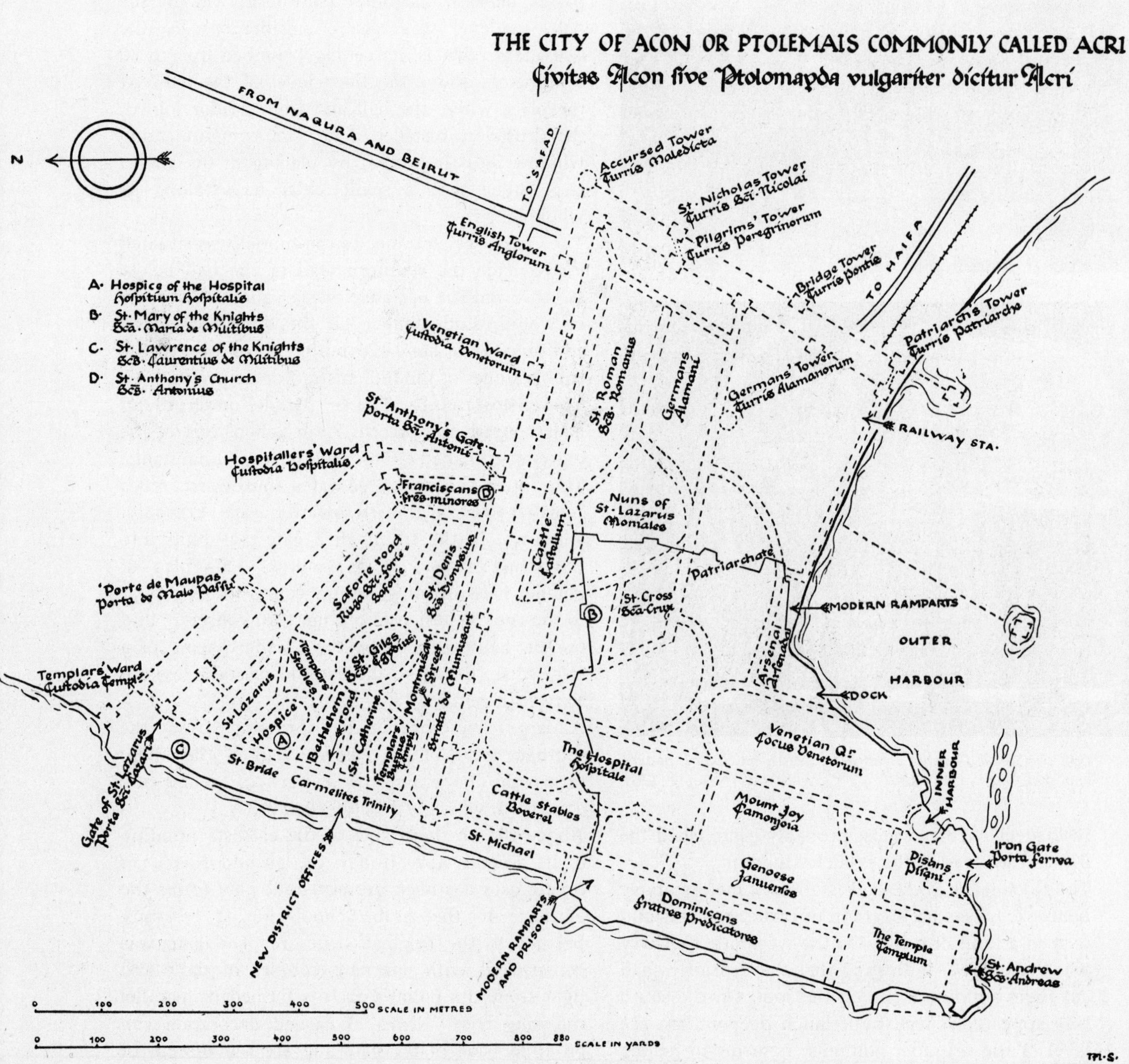
THE CITY OF ACON OR PTOLEMAIS COMMONLY CALLED ACRI
Civitas Acon sive Ptolomayda vulgariter dicitur Acri
FROM NAQURA AND BEIRUT
TO SAFAD
N
Accursed Tower
Turris Maledicta
St. Nicholas Tower
Turris Sci. Nicolai
Pilgrims' Tower
Turris Peregrinorum
English Tower
Turris Anglorum
Bridge Tower
Turris Pontis
TO HAIFA
Patriarch's Tower
Turris Patriarche
A. Hospice of the Hospital
Hospitium Hospitalis
B. St. Mary of the Knights
Sca. Maria de Militibus
C. St. Lawrence of the Knights
Scs. Laurentius de Militibus
D. St. Anthony's Church
Scs. Antonius
Venetian Ward
Custodia Venetorum
St. Roman
Scs. Romanus
Germans
Alamani
Germans' Tower
Turris Alamanorum
RAILWAY STA.
St. Anthony's Gate
Porta Sci. Antonii
Hospitallers' Ward
Custodia Hospitalis
Franciscans
Fres. minores
Castle
Castellum
Nuns of St. Lazarus
Monales
Patriarchate
St. Cross
Sca. Crux
MODERN RAMPARTS
OUTER HARBOUR
'Porte de Maupas'
Porta de Malo Passu
Saforie road
Ruga Sci. Sforie
Saforie
St. Denis
Scs. Dionysius
St. Giles
Scs. Egidius
Templars Stables
Mommusart Street
Strata de Mumusart
Arsenal
Arsenale
DOCK
Templars' Ward
Custodia Templi
St. Lazarus
Hospice
Bethlehem road
St. Catherine
Venetian Qr
Locus Venetorum
The Hospital
Hospitale
INNER HARBOUR
St. Bride
Carmelites
Trinity
Cattle Stables
Boverel
Mount Joy
Gate of St. Lazarus
Porta Sci. Lazari
St. Michael
Iron Gate
Porta ferrea
Pisans
Pisani
Genoese
Januenses
NEW DISTRICT OFFICES
Dominicans
Fratres Predicatores
MODERN RAMPARTS AND PRISON
The Temple
Templum
St. Andrew
Scs. Andreas
0 100 200 300 400 500 SCALE IN METRES
0 100 200 300 400 500 600 700 800 880 SCALE IN YARDS
M. S.

The halls of el-Bosta were used in Crusader times as an infirmary and appear as such on the map of Marino Sanuto. Traces of Crusader and Turkish repairs and rebuildings are noticeable in many places. The ceiling — beginning from the third hall — was reconstructed by the Crusaders in the shape of cross vaults made of brick-sized stones, whereas the original ceiling was built of large dressed stones in the lower part of the vault and progressively smaller ones toward the top. The original ceiling was preserved only in the tunnel vaults of the two façades of the building, toward the street to the north and toward the courtyard to the south.

Of the two remaining halls, the original vault is almost entirely preserved in the first hall. In the second many repairs are evident. In the single hall of the courtyard, the original (double) tunnel vault has been preserved in large part. During excavations a complete Latin inscription was discovered in the single hall. It is a memorial inscription for the eighth master of the Order of St. John, Pierre de Vieille Brioude. The date of his death is mentioned — October 17, 1242 — along with several historical facts of the time: the release of the count of Montfort together with many other barons from "Babylonian" captivity in Egypt and the rebuilding of the walls of Ashkelon by Richard of Cornwall.

Remains of a large Byzantine building were discovered under the existing walls in all the halls except the first. The most substantial find made under the eastern wall of the fourth hall is a cross-shaped fragment of a Byzantine pillar. These remains apparently belong to a monastery that once stood at the same site. Z. GOLDMANN

BIBLIOGRAPHY

J. Prawer, *EI* 2 (1963), 175–84 (Hebrew) • *'Akko, Survey and Planning,* Department for Landscape Improvement, Prime Minister's Office (Hebrew) • N. Makbouly and C.N. Johns, *Guide to Acre,* Jerusalem, 1946 • M.T. Fortuna, *Istituto Lombardo — Accademia di Scienze e Lettere, Rendiconti Classe Lettere* 98 (1964), 171–82, 203–12.

Coinage of Accho: L. Kadman, *The Coins of Akko-Ptolemais,* Jerusalem, 1961 • H. Seyrig, *Syria* 39 (1962), 193–207.

Excavations: Z. Goldmann, *Christian News from Israel* 13 (1962), 1–2 • M.T. Fortuna, *Journal of Glass Studies* 7 (1965), 17–25 • M.T. Fortuna, N. Haas, H. Nathan, *Memorie dell' Istituto Lombardo di Scienze e Lettere, Classe Lettere* 29 (1966), 441–577 • Z. Goldmann, *Archaeology* 13 (1966), 182–89 • G. Edelstein, *Qadmoniot* 5 (1972), 19–21.

Epigraphy: M. Avi-Yonah, *IEJ* 9 (1959), 1–12 • Y.H. Landau, *ibid.* 11 (1961), 118–26.

ACCHO, PLAIN OF

IDENTIFICATION. The fertile Accho Plain, crossed by important roads throughout history, contained numerous settlements in antiquity. This article deals with three partly excavated mounds in the plain: Tel Ma'amer, Tel Regev, and Tel Bira (see separate articles for Tell Abu Hawam and Tell Keisan).

TEL MA'AMER (Tel Geba'-Shemen, Tell el'Amr) Tel Ma'amer is situated on a natural ridge about 250 meters in length, lying in the narrow passage between the Jezreel Valley and the Accho Plain (map reference 159237). At the north end of the ridge stood a fortress; the fortifications are visible on the surface. The fortified area of the mound is about one acre. The Kishon River passes at the foot of the eastern and northern slopes and turns westward from this point.

In 1922 excavations were conducted on the mound under the direction of J. Garstang on behalf of the British School of Archaeology in Jerusalem. The excavators cut five sections in the attempt to discover the gateway of the stronghold and to investigate the fortifications. The thickness of the archaeological strata did not exceed 2.5 meters. In several places Iron Age remains were discovered on the surface of the rock. The pottery that was found dates to the Middle Bronze Age II, the Late Bronze Age I, the Iron Age (ninth and eighth centuries B.C.), and the Hellenistic period.

In 1959 A. Druks, on behalf of the Israel Department of Antiquities, excavated shaft tombs on the southern slope of the ridge, where he discovered abundant pottery from Middle Bronze Age II (corresponding to Megiddo XIII–XIV).

On the identification of the site with Geba'-Shemen, see Y. Aharoni, *The Land of the Bible,* London, 1967, 148, 156; J. Garstang, *Joshua–Judges,* London, 1931, 296–97; Abel, *GP* 2, 343–44. On the excavations: B. Mazar, *HUCA* 24 (1952–53), 80; *BBSAJ* 2 (1922), 14–15.

TEL REGEV (Tell el-Harbaj)

Tel Regev, situated north of Kefar Hassidim, about 400 meters west of the foothills of the Galilee Mountains, rises 12 meters above the plain (map reference 158240). Its area is about 8 acres. At the foot of its southern slope, passes the Zippori Valley, its catchment area the Beth Netopha'h Valley. The Kishon flows north of the mound. J. Garstang, on behalf of the British School of Archaeology in Jerusalem, conducted trial excavations both on the mound and in the cemetery east of it. On the strength of the pottery finds, the fortifications, and other remains, the settlement can be ascribed to Early Bronze Age III, Middle Bronze Age I, Late Bronze Age I–II, and Iron Age I. In a later survey Hellenistic pottery was also found on the surface of the mound.

On the identification of the site with Achshaph, see B. Mazar, *Enc. Miqr.* 1, 282–83 (Hebrew) (with bibliography), Y. Aharoni, *The Land of the Bible,* London, 1967, 148.

On the excavations: *BBSAJ* 2 (1922), 12–14; 4 (1924), 45–46.

TEL BIRA (Tell el-Bir el-Gharbi)

Tel Bira is situated about 9 kilometers (5.5 miles) southeast of Accho on the westernmost foothills of the Galilee Mountains bordering the Accho Plain in the lands of Kibbutz Yasur (map reference 166256). Important routes running from east to west (from the interior of the country to the coast) and north to south pass at the foot of this mound. W. F. Albright suggested identifying it with the Canaanite city of Rehob within the territory of Asher (Joshua 19:30, Judges 1:31).

In 1959 and 1962 an expedition of the Department of Antiquities under the direction of M. Prausnitz conducted salvage excavations of the Tel Bira cemeteries; tombs of Middle Bronze Age I–II, Late Bronze Age II, Iron Age I, Iron Age II (ninth/eighth centuries B.C.), and the Hellenistic period were uncovered. In the "lower town," situated at the foot of and around the mound, remains of walls and floors as well as sections of the city wall, the revetment, and a glacis were examined. The ramp rising toward the city gate presumably began on the northeastern side, at a distance of about 50 to 100 meters from the gate. At the foot of the upper city, remains of an exterior wall consisting only of a glacis and revetment have been uncovered. The wall encircled an area of about 40 acres, including the "upper town," — that is, the mound itself, whose area is about 12 acres.

In one section, which was apparently part of the approach ramp leading toward the city gate, the outer city wall was found to join the inner defenses of the ancient city proper. In the limited area of

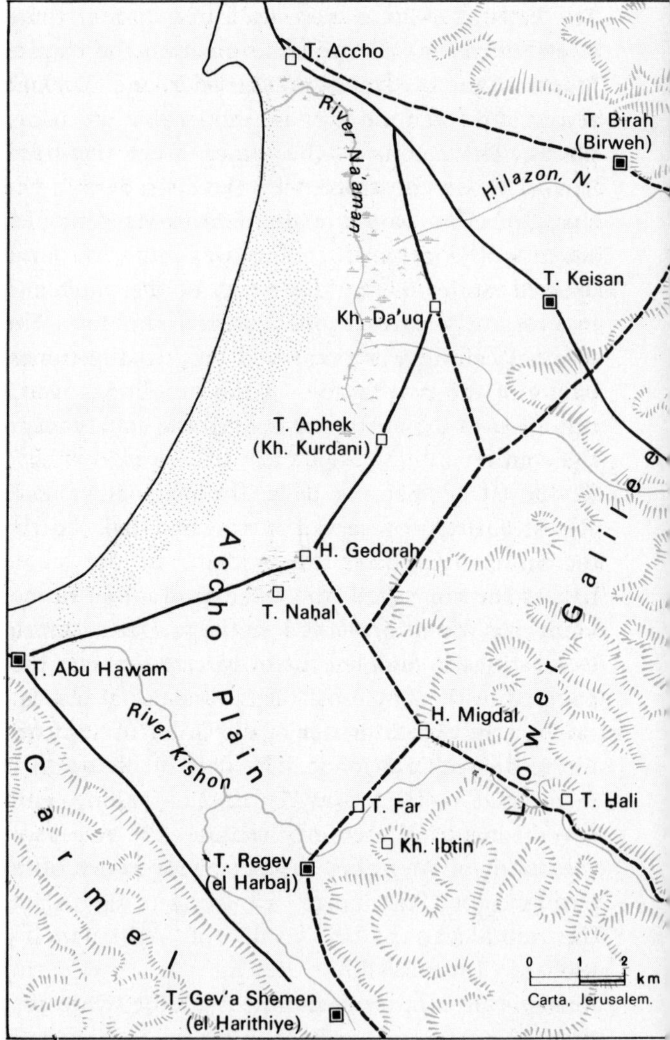

T. = Tel, Tell; H. = Horvat; Kh. = Khirbet; Swamps Dunes; --- Ancient road; —— Roman road ▣ *Excavated mound;* □ *Mound (Tell)*

the excavations, three layers of foundations, floors, and walls were discovered. On the floors of the lowest layer were found several juglets, the black "teapots" decorated with white lines, which are characteristic of Middle Bronze Age I. The two upper layers belong to Middle Bronze Age II. The remaining walls and floors of storehouses adjoin the outer wall, as evidenced by the jugs and large storage jars as well as the limestone and flint tools found there.

The burial forms of the region were explored in the cemetery. Middle Bronze Age burials were accompanied by numerous funerary offerings, such as pottery, tableware, juglets, bowls, and plates similar to finds in contemporary tombs at other sites. The burials in this period consist of pits cut into the rock.

A different type of burial was found dating to the transition from the Middle Bronze to the Late Bronze Age. In these burials the body was laid in a grave measuring 2 by .5 meters, and weapons, lamps, juglets, and other utensils were placed around it. A structure was erected around the burial place, and a carefully built wall separated the tomb from a long passage cut into the rock. Around the passage, burials from Iron Age I (eleventh/tenth century B.C.) were found. Here the bodies were laid on their backs on a stone bench with stones arranged around them. On them were heaped earth and stones. Accompanying the bodies were juglets, flasks, pins, and other personal belongings. At the foot of the "stone bench," cult objects and offerings such as incense burners, lamps, jugs, and similar vessels were deposited.

The tombs of the Iron Age II (ninth/eighth century B.C.) were intended for single and sometimes double burials. Some of the tombs are cut into the rock, their size corresponding to a normal burial (1.8 by .5 meters). Near the tomb a niche was cut, into which offerings were placed.

The hewn tombs of the Hellenistic period (more than 2 meters long) were also divided into two by partition walls. The smaller compartments were used for offerings.

The surface survey of the mound and its surroundings, carried out before and during the excavations, uncovered remains dating from the Early Bronze Age I–III, Late Bronze Age I, the seventh and sixth centuries B.C. (the time of Assyrian and Babylonian rule), and the Persian and Hellenistic periods.

After the Hellenistic period the site was probably abandoned; a new settlement was founded nearby on the site of the village of Birwa.

On the excavations see M. Prausnitz, *IEJ* 12 (1962), 143; *RB* 70 (1963), 566–67.

SUMMARY

The results of the excavations suggested several patterns common to the settlements in the Accho Plain. At the beginning of the Middle Bronze Age, the settlements were characterized by growth and expansion; in Tel Bira a lower town was even discovered that dates from this period. From the beginning of Middle Bronze Age II-A, fortifications and a glacis began to be built (Tel Ma'amer, Tel Regev). During the whole of Middle Bronze Age II, occupation was apparently continuous. From several layers and from the abundant finds, it may be concluded that the settlements enjoyed a period of prosperity and flourished without any break from the Late Bronze Age to the beginning of the Iron Age. In the Hellenistic period the settlements on the summit of the mound ceased to exist, and villages and towns were founded in the lower open plain, where there was more room for expansion. M. Prausnitz

BIBLIOGRAPHY

See under the items above.

Cylinder seal in Syro-Mitanni style, from Tel Bira.

ACHZIB (EZ-ZIB)

IDENTIFICATION. Ancient Achzib, located on the coast 14 kilometers (9 miles) north of Accho, was settled from the Middle Bronze Age until the Crusader period. The ancient name of the site has been preserved until modern times by the fishing village ez-Zib. The ancient city was well protected by the Mediterranean Sea on the west, a creek on the south, and the Chezib River on the north. To the east the Middle Bronze Age builders of the port and city cut a ditch to connect the estuaries of the Chezib and the creek and thus to isolate the settlement. Achzib is mentioned in the Bible as one of the Canaanite cities that the tribe of Asher failed to inherit (Joshua 19:29, Judges 1:31). Assyrian sources relate that Sennacherib conquered the city, as well as Sidon and Accho in the year 701 B.C. during his third campaign. Greek and Roman sources and Josephus (*Antiquities* V, 85; XIV, 343; *War* I, 257) record the name of Ἔκδιππα. According to the Tosephta, Achzib had a Jewish community and a synagogue (Tosephta *Terumoth* 2:13, etc.). The Crusaders called the city Casal Lamberti.

EXCAVATIONS

In the years 1941–44 the Department of Antiquities of the Mandatory Government conducted excavations, under the direction of I. Ben-Dor, in two cemeteries situated east and south of Achzib. In the eastern cemetery, called er-Ras, burials were found from the end of the Bronze Age, as were numerous rock-cut tombs from the Iron Age. Similar rock-cut tombs were discovered in the southern cemetery, called Buqbaq. These Phoenician tombs consisted mainly of burial chambers in which the dead were laid on benches hewn out of the rock.

In 1958, 1960, and 1963 M. Prausnitz excavated in the two cemeteries on behalf of the Israel Department of Antiquities and the University of Rome. The burial chambers of the southern cemetery were found to differ from the shaft graves uncovered in the eastern cemetery, the main difference being that the ceiling of the burial chambers in the southern cemetery had been cut open, only to be closed by a superstructure and a *massebah,* or altar, placed above the tomb. This was a confirmed Canaanite tradition practiced by the Sidonians.

Hearths and potsherds in the southern cemetery

Southern cemetery. Red-burnished jug — "Achzib ware"; end of the eighth century B.C. *(left). Selection of Phoenician pottery; eighth century* B.C. *(below).*

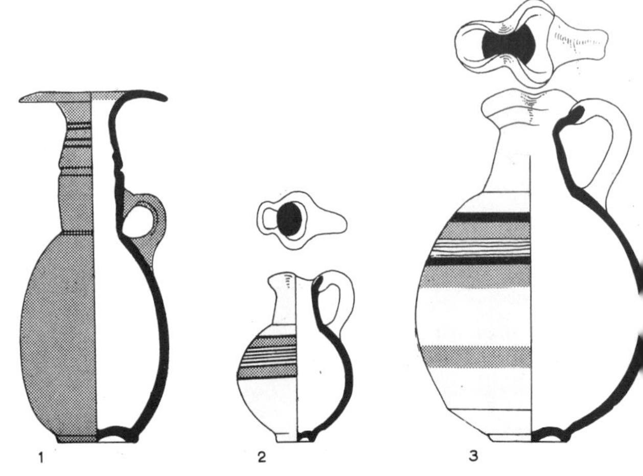

were found either above the entrance shaft or in the burial chamber. Single inhumation and cremation graves, with offerings in pits adjacent to the burial, were also uncovered. Some of the stelae erected above the burials were recovered.

Most of these graves were dated to the eighth century B.C.; others were later ones, dating to the seventh and the first quarter of the sixth centuries B.C. A number of inhumation graves that had no offering pits but were grouped around a central quadrangle belonged to the ninth century B.C. Above the quadrangle were found offerings and remains of meals. These types of burial were absent in the eastern cemetery, where the prevailing grave was the simple shaft tomb used by several generations of one family as is common in Israelite burials. In both cemeteries the rock-cut family tombs each contained about four hundred bodies that had been interred in the course of two hundred fifty to three hundred years, from the tenth to the end of the eighth century B.C.

Among the objects excavated were ritual vessels, incense burners, petaled stands and figurines, masks, and clay models. The cremated remains were usually buried in urns covered with a lid. A pitcher and a jug of the well-known Phoenician red-slipped ware were deposited nearby. The same red-slipped, or painted, pitchers and jugs also accompanied the dead in the eastern (Israelite type) cemetery of Achzib.

In 1963–64 the twin mounds of Achzib were excavated. Outside the city walls cist tombs constructed of large, well-hewn slabs were found. A double ax, lance heads, iron blades of bronze daggers, and characteristic fibulae date these cist tombs to the end of the eleventh century B.C.

One area was excavated on the southern of the twin mounds, which have existed on the tel of Achzib since Roman times. In the southern area, foundations of the Crusader period rested on structures dating to the Roman and Hellenistic periods. Beneath the latest Hellenistic stratum a series of occupation layers, substantial walls, and pavements indicate the prosperity that Achzib enjoyed during the second and third centuries B.C. In the fill of the Hellenistic house, a late Phoenician stele depicting the bottle-image, well known from North Africa and the Punic colonies, is evidence of the persistence of the close relations of the latter with the homeland across the Mediterranean.

The northern part of the mound was examined

Eastern cemetery. Pit tombs; Persian period.

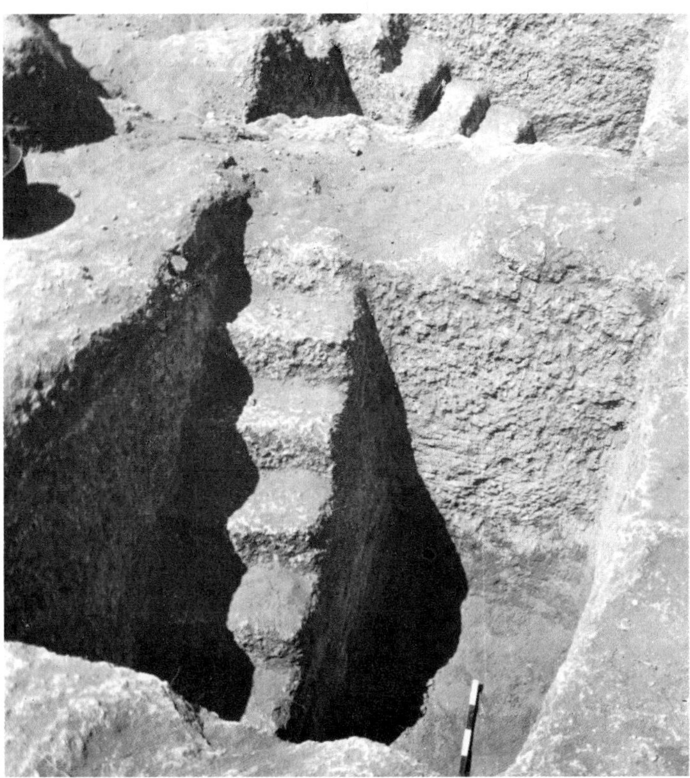

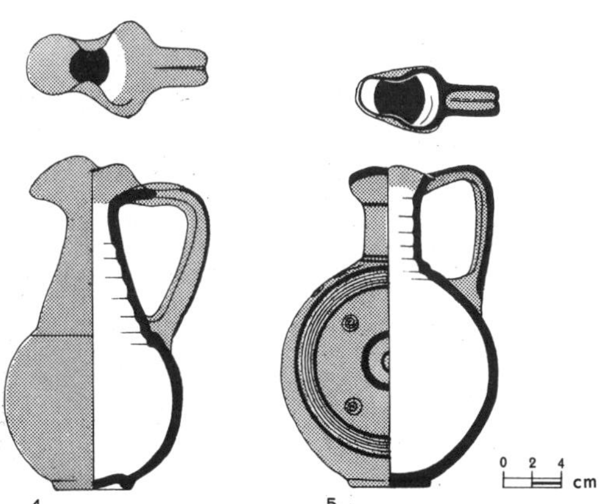

mainly in a forty-meter-long, east–west, trench, which revealed the Middle Bronze Age rampart fortifications. Pottery found in the fill of the brick core, the rampart, and the pisé de terre coating of the revetment indicate that Achzib was first fortified sometime in the mid-eighteenth century B.C., *i.e.,* at the very beginning of Middle Bronze Age II-B. The rampart fortifications as revealed consisted of a fosse in the east and a stone revetment about 5 meters high. A thin coating of clay was still visible on top of the stones. The rampart was heaped up against an earth core that was formed mainly of decomposed bricks. Nothing was found to indicate whether walls, towers, or other types of defense works had crowned the steeply inclined rampart. These Middle Bronze Age fortifications were violently destroyed in the beginning of the Late Bronze Age. Shards of Late Bronze Age II suggest a renewal of building activities. By the end of the Late Bronze Age the defenses again collapsed and were leveled inside the city. From the tenth to the sixth centuries B.C., Achzib reached its greatest expansion, having an area of 20 acres (8,000 square meters) within the fortified city.

Tombstone of "Eved Shemesh ben Ashi" (top left).
Stele of "Zakarmilk," from the cemetery (bottom left).
Shard with Phoenician inscription Adnmlkh ("Adonmelekh"); fifth century B.C. *(below).*

Opposite, counterclockwise: Tomb 14; cat figurine. Clay figure kneading dough; IA II. Pottery figurine of seated pregnant woman, from the cemetery. Horse figurine from Phoenician cemetery; sixth/fifth cent. B.C.

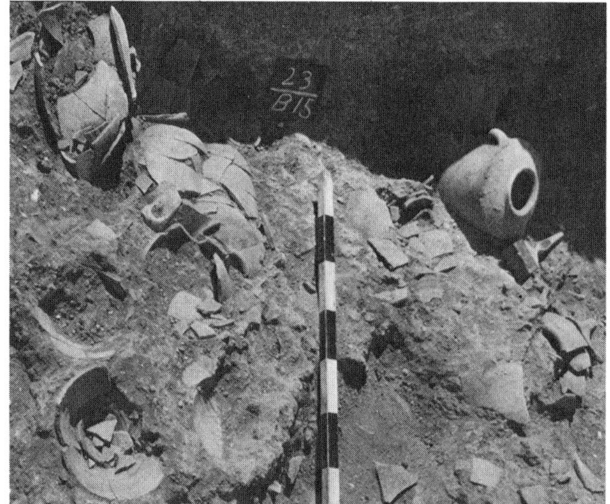

Inside the city, in the northern part of the mound, the Hellenistic, Persian, and Iron Age strata disclosed a number of public buildings adjacent to the eastern defenses of the city. The buildings served as storerooms, as is shown by the numerous jars found standing side by side. Some bore such Aramaic inscriptions as "To my Lord the King." A number of the now-famous Achzib figurines were found on the floors of the public rooms and could be dated within their context. The well-known red-slipped pottery found in the tombs at Achzib and throughout the Mediterranean was found to continue at Achzib into the seventh-century strata. Inside the city in the north, excavations were continued down to the final Late Bronze Age destruction layers. M. PRAUSNITZ

BIBLIOGRAPHY

I. Ben-Dor, *Enc. Miqr.* s.v. "Achzib" (Hebrew) • M. Prausnitz, *IEJ* 13 (1963), 337–38; 15 (1965), 256–58; *idem, RB* 69 (1962), 404–05; 72 (1965), 544–47; *idem, Iron Age Tombs at Achzib* (in press); *idem, Oriens Antiquus* 5 (1966), 177–88; *idem, Proq. 1st Int. Congr. of Cypriote Studies,* Nicosia, 1972, 151–56 • F. Michelini-Tocci, *Oriens Antiquus* 3 (1964), 133–34.

From top to bottom: Stacked jars in situ in storeroom, from the mound; 8th–7th cent. B.C. *Excavated grave with one jar left on the body; from the cemetery; 9th–8th cent.* B.C. *The same grave before excavation with seven storage jars placed above it and cremation crater in foreground; 9th–8th cent.* B.C. *Cremation crater covered with lid and sealed with mud clay; 9th–8th cent.* B.C. *(opposite).*

ADER

THE SITE AND ITS IDENTIFICATION. Ader, an extensive ruined site, is situated on a hill 7 kilometers (4.5 miles) northeast of Kerak. The site, divided by a depression into a "small tel" and a main tel, is occupied at present by the Arab town of Ader.

The earliest reference to the locality is found in Stephanus of Byzantium: "Adara, a large village between Characmoba [Kerak-Moab] and Areopolis [Rabbah]." The edict of Beersheba, which contains a list of taxes levied on the settlements of the Limes Palaestinae, also mentions Ader. In Abu Sama's biography of Saladin, Ader is referred to in the account of Lejjun's expedition against Reginald of Chatillon (1184).

EXPLORATION

U. J. Seetzen discovered Ader, followed by J. L. Burckhardt. Both were impressed by the menhirs (stone pillars) that were then still in situ. A. Musil (1907) gave the first detailed description of the site. In 1924 a survey expedition, under the direction of W. F. Albright and M. G. Kyle, inspected the site. The Byzantine inscriptions they recorded were later published by A. Alt.

Early in 1933 the site was surveyed by N. Glueck. Late in that same year the American Schools of Oriental Research, in cooperation with the British School of Archaeology in Jerusalem and the Transjordan Department of Antiquities, initiated excavations. The Ader expedition, under the direction of W. F. Albright and R. G. Head, found that the remains of the ancient temple discovered in the survey in 1924 had been destroyed during a building boom in the village. The excavators therefore confined their activity to exploratory excavations in various parts of the site. The results were published in a preliminary report; in 1960 the material was revised and published by R. L. Cleveland, who was not a member of the original expedition.

EXCAVATIONS

An exploratory excavation was undertaken in the lower part of the mound, north of the wall that encompasses the main tel. The excavated area was 10 by 4 meters and extended down to virgin soil. Three occupational levels were distinguished. The earliest, level III, contained potsherds dating back to the end of the Early Bronze Age. These were embedded in a thin layer of yellow clay. The excavators also assigned to this period a shaft grave cleared on the small tel, in which they found similar potsherds and a number of flint artifacts. In the intermediate stage, level II, the same type of potsherds were found, as were other potsherds assigned by the excavators to the beginning of the Middle Bronze Age I. All these potsherds were scattered among collapsed clay bricks, which bore traces of a conflagration. In the uppermost stage, level I, which contained many potsherds of the Middle Bronze Age I, there were uncovered two brick walls on stone foundations representing the corner of a structure destroyed by a great conflagration.

In the northwest corner of the wall surrounding the main tel some masonry and fragments of walls were found; these the excavators ascribed to the Iron Age II, the period to which Glueck also dated the shards found there. The city wall itself was built in the second/third century A.D. One of its excavated corners contained a room with a tomb beneath its floor. In this Roman level, in which Nabatean potsherds were also found, the excavators distinguished two stages of construction. Among the debris of stones covering the room in the wall, they found a carved stone bearing what they believe to be a Hebrew inscription of the

Byzantine period. A tower protruding from the general line of the city wall was uncovered near the eastern corner. This tower, built in the Late Roman period, had a fine front wall of ashlar. Its upper courses, which receded somewhat from the lower ones, are a part of the tower that had been repaired in the Byzantine period.

The excavations failed to clarify the character or to determine the date of the most interesting structures in Ader, the temple and the menhirs. According to the statements of various investigators, the menhirs seem to have been on an average of 4 meters high, 1 meter wide, and .4 meters thick. One menhir, still in situ not far from the temple, is called *sarbut Ader* by the Arabs of the vicinity. Three others were found lying on the ground near the sanctuary.

In the course of the excavation at the assumed site of the destroyed temple, an excellently built wall was uncovered, but the excavators were unable to establish with certainty whether it had belonged to that edifice. According to the sketch made during the survey of 1924, which is for the most part an unreliable reconstruction based on conjecture, the temple (25 by 22 meters) consisted of three halls built on an approximately east–west axis.

The entranceway (10 meters wide) was in the middle of the western wall and contained two steps on which one of the menhirs stood. The halls narrowed in the direction of the cella, and the walls of the central hall seemed to protrude somewhat on the south and north sides. Near the temple the investigators noticed an altar of offerings — a smoothed stone slab with two round depressions.

The temple of Ader, insofar as the above sketch can be relied on, consisted of a succession of broad halls on a longitudinal axis, similar to the temples of the Bronze Age found at Ugarit, Hazor, and Alalakh. Menhirs were also found at Lajjun, in the vicinity of Ader, near the temples at Byblos, at Gezer, and Tell Huweirah in northeastern Syria.

M. Kochavi

BIBLIOGRAPHY

Musil, *Arabia Petraea* 1, 29 f. • W.F. Albright, *BASOR* 14 (1924), 10 • A. Mallon, *Biblica* 5 (1924), 453 ff. • A. Alt, *ZDPV* 51 (1928), 218–33 • W.F. Albright, *BASOR* 53 (1934), 14 • R.L. Cleveland, *AASOR* 34–35 (1960), 79–97, figs. 8–15, pls. 19–24.

ʻAFULA

THE SITE AND ITS IDENTIFICATION. The site is situated within the modern town of ʻAfula. Only a small part of it has been preserved, most having been destroyed in the course of the development works. Its original area was approximately 6 acres, but remains of the settlement, especially graves, are scattered over a wider area. The mound stands some 11 meters above the surrounding area. E. L. Sukenik explored the northern and central sections of the site, and I. Ben-Dor and M. Dothan excavated its southern part. The excavations indicated that the settlement was not continuous, but that is possibly due to the previous destruction of considerable portions of the mound. Some periods are represented only by graves, found mainly at the edges of the mound.

The origin of the name ʻAfula is evidently Semitic — *ʻOphel*, "citadel." The name was possibly mentioned in the Egyptian Execration Texts of the nineteenth century B.C. (number E-42), and it might be identical with ʻApr (Apl) in the list of Thutmose III (number 53), which cannot be identified with any other known city of the Late Bronze or Iron ages. The city developed mainly during the Early and Middle Bronze II ages; later it was evidently a small settlement in the territory of Manasseh, one of the "daughters" of Megiddo (Joshua 17:11). It is apparently identical with the Arbela of Eusebius (*Onomasticon* 14:20) and the "Afel" of the Middle ages.

THE EXCAVATION IN THE NORTH AND CENTER OF THE MOUND

In 1926 and 1931 E. L. Sukenik supervised the work carried out at the northern edge and in other parts of the site. In 1937, during the construction of a water tower about 300 meters north of the center of the mound, Sukenik, assisted by N. Avigad, carried out a trial excavation under the auspices of the Hebrew University. Among the pits dug (named A–K) for examination of the deep layers, the important ones were A, B, D, E, F, and H. Numerous graves were found from older strata of the settlement. Among the nineteen graves uncovered, two were from Early Bronze Age III, six from Middle Bronze Age II, nine from Late Bronze Age II, while the other two were from the Hellenistic and Roman periods.

The first settlement on the site belonged to the Ghassulian culture. The remains of the settlement were discovered at a depth of about 3 meters. Fragments of "churns," cornets, fenestrated pedestals, and fan scrapers were found. The remains of the next settlement were dated to the end of the Chalcolithic period or the beginning of Early Bronze Age I (depending on the definition of these periods). The preserved building remains included a wall made of plano-convex bricks and an oven. Vessels characteristic of the period were found on the floors of the houses—gray-burnished carinated bowls with knobs and jugs with everted rims.

The next period of settlement dates to Early Bronze Age I. Among the pottery found are hole-mouth jars with ledge handles. The most common decoration is the band slip. From the Early Bronze Age II an important group of pottery is decorated with pattern combing. The next period, Early Bronze Age III, is represented by Khirbet Kerak ware: burnished jars, stands, and lids, found mainly in graves. Among the few finds from the relatively short phase at the end of the Early Bronze Age IV and the Middle Bronze Age I, pottery with folded ledge handles is particularly noteworthy. The cooking pots with perforations below the rims evidently date from the beginning of Middle Bronze Age II–A. The graves from Middle Bronze Age II, especially Middle Bronze Age II–B, were rich in finds and included juglets of the Tell el-Yahudiyeh type. In the graves of Late Bronze Age II, the vessels imported from Cyprus are especially important. From Late Bronze Age II down to the Hellenistic period, there is a gap in this area of the settlement and in graves.

During exploration in the area of the mound, an oil press from the Byzantine period (J) and a square fort (K, 19 meters long with walls preserved in places to a height of 5.5. meters) were found. In some places stone coffins were reused in the citadel walls of dressed stone. The excavators dated the building to the Mameluke period, but according to the finds of stratum I in the excavations of the mound, which correspond to the period of the fort, it probably should be dated to the eleventh/thirteenth centuries A.D. (see below).

Although the most important finds were discovered in the graves, it is also possible to trace the history of the settlement through the less numerous finds discovered in the strata situated outside the citadel of 'Afula. The settlement outside the walls developed mainly in the Chalcolithic and Early Bronze ages. It is important to note that the Chalcolithic stratum with Ghassulian finds lay beneath the stratum that held the gray-burnished pottery. This is the first evidence for the correct stratigraphical sequence of these finds. After the Middle Bronze Age I, the area outside the citadel was turned into a cemetery, and until the Roman period settlement was limited to the mound itself.

EXCAVATIONS IN THE SOUTHERN SECTION OF THE MOUND

I. Ben-Dor excavated the site, June to September, 1950, and March to April, 1951, and M. Dothan excavated from May to December, 1951. Both were assisted by Y. Shapira. The excavations were carried out on behalf of the Israel Department of Antiquities. Only partial results have been published. However, from the excavation, which established the stratigraphy in the southern part of the tel, from exploratory soundings, and from finds in the graves, the history of the settlement at Tel 'Afula can be reconstructed from the end of Chalcolithic (or the beginning of Early Bronze Age) down to the Late Middle Ages.

Stratum X, Late Chalcolithic Period (or the beginning of Early Bronze Age I). The period is represented mainly on the northern and southern flanks of the excavated area. Two pits dug in virgin soil were discovered; apparently they had served as granaries. The southern pit (1.75 meters in diameter, .4 meters deep) is lined with stones. Nearby was found a hearth with many shards among the ashes. The northern pit (1.45 meters in diameter and depth), also lined with stones, contained a layer of ash in which animal bones and many potsherds were found. Characteristic of the pottery finds were carinated bowls with knobs of the gray-burnished type.

Stratum IX, Early Bronze Age I. The finds in this stratum were meager and occurred mainly in the center of the excavated area. Stone wall foundations were discovered, preserved to a height of .3 meters. Many shards typical of the period were found scattered over the entire surface of the central section of the excavations. The most noteworthy ceramic finds were jars decorated with a band slip.

Stratum VIII, Early Bronze Age III. No building

remains attributable to this period were found. However, pottery vessels typical of the Early Bronze Age III, especially of the Khirbet Kerak type, occurred among other Early Bronze Age IV finds. Thus, the buildings discovered in stratum VII probably stand on foundations belonging to stratum VIII.

Stratum VII, Early Bronze Age IV. Here, remains of buildings with a clear plan were discovered for the first time. The foundations of eight buildings were found, probably parts of one large complex. The rooms are almost square; the largest is about 5 meters long. The foundations, built of large, rough stones, are very narrow (circa .3 meters). Two ovens were also discovered. The pottery included many jars with folded ledge handles.

Stratum VI, Middle Bronze Age I. This settlement was erected on the ruins of stratum VII. Its remains consisted chiefly of three pottery kilns. The transition from stratum VII to stratum VI could be established clearly, since one of the kilns was built on the foundations of walls of the previous stratum. Moreover, a pit dug in the ground had damaged one of the earlier buildings. The largest of the three kilns had an oval shape (2.1 by 3.45 meters) and was preserved to a height of 1.5 meters. Its upper part was vaulted. One of its sides, with two brick piers projecting from the wall, was well preserved. A pier segment from the opposite side also survived. It can therefore be surmised that four piers supported the vault and the ceiling and perhaps the ledges upon which was placed the pottery to be fired.

In the pit (1.8 meters in diameter, .5 meters deep), which damaged one of the walls of stratum VII, several skeletons of boars were found. The pit may have been an oven, for it contained a large quantity of ashes. Since the skeletons were complete, it is likely that they represent a burnt offering.

Stratum V, Middle Bronze Age II-B (Hyksos Period). The main buildings of this stratum were found in the northern sector. Some of these

Remains of a house and pottery kilns; transition period from EBA to MBA.

remains indicate that they belonged to a carefully planned settlement. Segments of two streets were found, one of which was preserved to a length of 15 meters, with an average width of 1.5 meters. Buildings and courtyards stood on both sides of the streets. North of these streets a building complex was discovered. One of the rooms measured 5 by 7 meters. In the southwestern section of the excavations was a pit (circa 1 meter in diameter, 1.5 meter deep) that contained many shards of unfired pottery, mainly Tell el-Yahudiyeh ware. The vessels had broken before they were to be fired in the kiln of the nearby potter's workshop, and they were probably thrown into the pit as refuse. Fired pottery of the same type was found not far from the edge of the pit. These vessels are of the Hyksos type, and this is the first evidence that such pottery was also produced in Palestine.

In the central and northern parts of the excavated area, thirty-eight graves were found most of which are assigned to the Hyksos period. Several belong, however, to a later phase, as they were dug into the buildings of the stratum. The bodies were placed in a flexed position, and their orientation differs from grave to grave. A row of identifying stones was found on several graves. Among the funeral offerings were bowls and juglets typical of the Hyksos culture. Jars were also found in some graves, as well as scarabs, weapons, and toggle pins. Some of the bowls placed next to the bodies contained traces of food.

Stratum IV, Late Bronze Age II. On the eastern flank of the mound, a few burials of this period were discovered. Many shards were scattered over the surface, including imported Mycenaean and Cypriot ware. Many of the graves were dug in virgin soil. Ceramic finds in these graves included large amphorae with button bases and carinated shoulders. Some of the vessels were covered with small bowls, and inside them, or nearby, dipper-juglets were found.

Stratum III, Iron Age IA-B. This stratum was uncovered in a strip almost 25 meters long in the southwestern part of the mound, about .5 meters below the surface. In some places it was possible to distinguish two phases (B and A) according to changes in the building, new flooring, and various other evidence. The main building was built of brick walls on stone foundations and included at least four broad rooms surrounding three sides of a large courtyard. One of the rooms was bisected by a row of four columns. Similar buildings were found at Tel Qasile (stratum X) and Tel Sharuhen (building VE), and in both places they date from the Philistine period. Granaries, a kiln, and a board game made of a stone tablet with perforations were also discovered in this stratum. One of the cemeteries on the eastern edge of the mound is also attributed to this period.

The pottery of phase III-B continued the local pottery tradition of the end of the Late Bronze Age. Thus, some Cypriot shards were found alongside pottery characteristic of the beginning of the Iron Age. This pottery has been dated accordingly to circa 1200–1150 B.C. Phase III-A can be dated by the appearance of Philistine pottery (including a unique jug). At the same time, vessels of the previous phase continued to be made, including store jars with ridged necks and shallow cooking pots with collar rims.

The settlement of stratum III was destroyed in the second half of the eleventh century B.C., perhaps in the time of Saul. It apparently lay in ruins between strata III and II, *i.e.,* approximately from the last quarter of the eleventh century to the middle of the ninth century B.C. Above stratum III no remains of buildings were found, except for a pottery kiln. However, some pottery and many shards were found, including Samaria ware, thus indicating the existence of a relatively modest Iron Age II settlement. In the excavated area very few remains were found dating from the Persian to the Early Roman period.

Pot (Khirbet Kerak ware); EBA III.

Stratum II. Few remains of buildings were discovered in this stratum, for it was leveled at the time the buildings of stratum I were erected. Roman coffins were reused in building the walls of the Crusader (?) fortress east of the excavation; they belong to stratum II. On the basis of the finds, this stratum should be attributed mainly to the second/third centuries A.D. There are few remains from the Byzantine period, but a settlement of sorts undoubtedly existed on the mound at that time.

Stratum I. Two phases of this stratum were discovered, mainly in the central and northern sections of the excavations. The buildings of the main phase, I-B, include one with dressed-stone foundations. On one side of the central wall there were at least three rooms, and on the other side, a portico. Two cisterns were found south of the building. Characteristic of both phases of stratum I are painted or glazed vessels decorated with geometric designs and graffiti. This stratum is to be assigned to the Crusader and Ayyubid periods — from the eleventh to the thirteenth century.

SUMMARY

The settlement of Tel 'Afula, from its beginning at the close of the Chalcolithic period until its end in the Middle Ages, was not a continuous one, at least not in the southern part of the mound, the excavated area. Additional soundings, however, have revealed finds from periods not represented on the mound and have thus reduced the gap in the history of the settlement. The following sequence of the strata can now be established:

STRATUM	PERIOD
I	11th–13th century A.D.
II	2nd–4th centuries A.D.
III-A	IA I-B
III-B	IA I-A (circa 1200–1150 B.C.)
IV	LBA II
V	MBA II-B
VI	MBA I
VII	EBA IV
VIII	EBA III
IX	EBA I
X	Late Chalcolithic

M. DOTHAN

BIBLIOGRAPHY

E.L. Sukenik, *PEQ* (1936), 150–54; *idem, JPOS* 21 (1948), 1–79 • I. Ben-Dor, *'Alon* 3 (1951), 33–34 (Hebrew) • M. Dothan, *'Atiqot* 1 (1956), 18–63 (Hebrew).

AI

IDENTIFICATION. Ai (Heb. העי, "the ruin") was a city of 27.5 acres in Ephraim, settled in Early Bronze Age I-B (circa 3100 B.C.) and occupied until Early Bronze Age III-B (circa 2400 B.C.), at which time it was destroyed and abandoned. At the beginning of Iron Age I (circa 1220 B.C.), a 2.5-acre unwalled village was established in the acropolis area of the ancient ruin. It was occupied until about 1050 B.C., when the village was abandoned and never resettled.

LOCATION

Biblical tradition places Ai east of Bethel (Genesis 12:8, Joshua 7:2). Two sites in the vicinity of modern Deir Dibwan, 3 kilometers (2 miles) east of Beitin (Bethel), were suggested by E. Robinson in 1838 as possible locations of biblical Ai. Et-Tell, the imposing mound shown on p. 51 was the obvious choice, but because of its name Robinson preferred Khirbet Ḥaiyân at the south edge of Deir Dibwan. The Palestine Exploration Fund Survey located Ḥaiyân a generation later. A third ruin, Khirbet Khudriya, located 2 kilometers (1 mile) east of Deir Dibwan, was proposed by V. Guérin in 1881.

W. F. Albright published a paper in 1924 advocating et-Tell as the site of Ai. His surface survey of the region east of Bethel convinced him that no other proposed site could possibly date to the time of the Israelite conquest. The etiological tradition that Joshua "burnt Ai and made it a heap [tel] for ever" (Joshua 8:28) seemed to support his position. Albright's identification has not been seriously challenged. Et-Tell, in the view of the writer, is the site of Ai.

EXCAVATIONS

The Garstang Soundings. The first brief excavation at Ai was conducted by J. Garstang in the fall of 1928. Eight trenches were located along the south and west parts of the Early Bronze Age city, five against the outer face of the city fortifications and three inside, near the sanctuary and acropolis sites. The only report from this excavation was a three-page summary and sketch plan filed with the Department of Antiquities at the conclusion of the work.

Aerial view of temple (extreme right), citadel (right center), postern gate and tower (upper right), and IA village (left center).

Garstang's later assertion that Late Bronze Age pottery — specifically, the wishbone handle of a Cypriot bowl — was found in this excavation is not mentioned in his summary report, and the relevant finds cannot be located.

The Rothschild Expedition. The second excavation project at Ai was the Rothschild Expedition, led by Judith Marquet-Krause in three campaigns from 1933 to 1935. Her untimely death in July, 1936, abruptly terminated the work before the fourth campaign was scheduled to begin. She wrote two preliminary reports before her death, one of which was published in *Syria* (1936). Her husband, Y. Marquet, compiled a register of pottery and objects from the expedition records and in 1949 published the register along with the two preliminary reports and an atlas of photographs, plans, and drawings of artifacts.

The Rothschild excavations were confined to the upper part of et-Tell, between contours 835 and 850 on plan on p. 50. Most of the initial expedition in 1933 was concentrated in the acropolis area at contour 850, the highest part of the mound. Some clearing of the sanctuary site west of the acropolis was carried on, and the Early Bronze Age tombs east of the mound were excavated. But 1933 was mainly "the year of the palace," as Marquet-Krause designated the acropolis building.

An unusually long and productive six-month campaign in 1934 allowed considerable expansion of the excavations. The Iron Age village on the east terraces near the acropolis and the lower city fortifications near contour 835 on plan on p. 50 were discovered and explored. The main discovery of 1934, however, was the sanctuary. A rich find of alabaster and pottery cult objects made this campaign "the year of the sanctuary" in public interest.

The 1935 campaign was one of consolidation and extension of the lower city and Iron Age village areas. Fortifications were exposed in the lower city as indicated on plan on p. 50, but the postern gate with its elliptical tower was the most significant discovery. A large area of the Iron Age village was cleared inside contour 850, confirming beyond doubt that the Iron Age I houses were built upon the ruins of the Early Bronze Age III city with no intervening occupation strata. For biblical scholars, this campaign was "the year of the Iron Age village." For persons interested mainly in the Canaanite city, however, it was "the year of the postern gate," because this was the first entrance to an Early Bronze Age city found in Canaan.

The Joint Archaeological Expedition to Ai. The third archaeological project at Ai was directed by the writer from 1964 to 1970. This expedition was sponsored by the American Schools of Oriental Research in cooperation with the Southern Baptist Theological Seminary, the Perkins School of Theology, the Harvard Semitic Museum, and a consortium of eighteen other institutions. Five major expeditions were fielded by 1970, followed by two small problem-solving operations in areas already open in 1971–72.

Eight sites were opened at et-Tell in areas adjacent to the Marquet-Krause excavations and in new areas along the lower east fortifications of the city: site A, the sanctuary and citadel; site B, the Iron Age village; site C, the lower city fortifications; site D, the acropolis, and site G, the lower city residential area, all above contour 835. Sites H, J, and K were new areas against the lower east walls of the city.

Four other sites at a distance from et-Tell were opened to seek evidence bearing upon the biblical city of Ai. Khirbet Ḥaiyân, located on plan on p. 48 at the south edge of Deir Dibwan, was excavated in 1964 and 1969 as site E. It was found to be a Byzantine settlement, the earliest datable evidence being coins of A.D. 68 on bedrock. Khirbet Khudriya, east of et-Tell, was excavated in 1966 and 1968 as site F and was also a Byzantine settlement, possibly a monastery. Tombs adjacent to the settlement yielded pottery and objects from as early as the first century B.C.

Salvage excavations were conducted in 1969, 1970, and 1972 at Khirbet Raddana, in the north edge of modern Bireh, with sites designated R and S. This small project was begun because hewn pillars of two Iron Age I houses, contemporary with those of site B at et-Tell, had been exposed during the construction of a road a new subdivision in Bireh. The evidence of these houses, it was thought, would supplement and perhaps illuminate the Iron Age village at et-Tell. Preliminary study indicates that the sites were indeed contemporary and culturally related.

ARCHAEOLOGICAL RESULTS.

Summary Introduction. In summary chart form, the results are as follows:

STRATUM	PHASE	SIGNIFICANCE	PERIOD	CHRONOLOGY
Preurban	I	Founding of unwalled village	EBA I-B	3100–3000 B.C.
	II	Village occupation and destruction	Same	
Urban A	III	First major walled city of 27.5 acres	EBA I-C	3000–2860 B.C.
Urban B	IV	Remodeling phase of city buildings and fortifications	EBA II-A	2860–2720 B.C.
	V	Destruction phase of same (by earthquake, apparently)	EBA II-B	
Urban C	VI	Reconstruction of entire city and fortifications	EBA III-A	2720–2400 B.C.
	VII	Remodeling phase of city buildings and fortifications	EBA III-B	
	VIII	Destruction of entire city and abandonment of site	EBA III-B	
Iron Age	IX	Settlement of unwalled village above contour 845	Iron Age I-A	1220–1050 B.C.
	X	Remodeling; abandonment of site	Iron Age I-B	

Early Bronze Age I-B. An unfortified village was established at Ai circa 3100 B.C. on the upper terraces, above contour 835. Remains of simple village houses have been found underneath the first city walls at sites A and C, as well as inside the walls at sites A and D. The village was 200 meters long, making it larger than the Iron Age village built circa 1220 B.C., and as large as many of the cities of Iron Age II, a period of prosperity and expansion.

There were no inhabitants at Ai prior to the settlement in Early Bronze Age I-B, so the village seems to have been settled by the overflow population from other sites, together with an increment of newcomers.

The artifacts at Ai reflect a mingling of foreign and indigenous elements that must have occurred in the region before the village was established, because the village was settled after the decline of Chalcolithic culture by a people already amalgamated. Chalcolithic influences are evident in angular jar neck and rim forms, as well as in angular bowl forms. Foreign, or new, influences appear in carinate platters, hole-mouth jars with inward-rolled rims, and painted decorations of line-group designs. In one instance the new line-group decoration characterizing Early Bronze Age I-B appears on a thin, tapered jar rim, a form carried over from Chalcolithic by the indigenous population.

The people at Ai buried their dead in caves on the northeast slopes of the hill on which they lived, and the tomb deposits reflect the mingling of cultures noted above. The earliest pottery from tombs B, C, F, and G is closely related to that from Jericho tombs A–94, level II-A, A–13 II-I, and K–2 phase II, characterized as Protourban B by Kathleen Kenyon. This may indicate that the settlement at Ai grew out of movements into the hill country by way of Jericho.

The new elements in the village culture at Ai eventually dominated in later periods as the Chalcolithic influences faded away. This was brought about by successive migrations of people from the same general region during later times, which reinforced the new cultural influences and added new features. Their ultimate place of origin is to the north of Canaan. J. B. Hennessy suggests

EBA city walls.

a local origin of the Early Bronze Age I-B tradition, but P. Lapp points out a closeness to the Ciradere tradition in Anatolia, assigned to Early Bronze Age I-B on the basis of stratigraphy at Alishar Hüyük. This Anatolian origin places the Early Bronze Age I-B migration in the succession of an earlier Early Bronze Age I-A movement from eastern Anatolia and Syria, recognized by Hennessy, and possibly as far north as southern Russia, as suggested by Lapp.

Early Bronze Age I-C. A planned, walled city enclosing 27.5 acres (see p. 50) was constructed at the beginning of Early Bronze Age I-C (circa 3000 B.C.). Components of the city that are now known are the impressive acropolis building at site D, an industrial area at site C, a residential area at site G, and four city-gate complexes located at sites A, K, J, and the lower city of Marquet-Krause.

The acropolis complex at site D, in the center of the photograph on page 37, dominated the Early Bronze Age I-C city. Central in the complex was a large rectangular building about 25 meters long, built of large, uncut stones and with walls 2 meters wide. An entrance, now lost by erosion, apparently opened toward the east in the broad wall of the structure, possibly into a large courtyard. Five flat-top columns inside the building supported the roof of the large hall in the interior.

G. E. Wright has argued that this building was a temple, against the theory of Judith Marquet-Krause that it was a palace. The former view is supported by recent discoveries.

It now seems certain that the same structure, rebuilt in Early Bronze Age III-A, was a temple. Two alabaster bowls like those found in the Early Bronze Age III-B sanctuary at site A were discovered in the Early Bronze Age III-A rooms of the acropolis building. Secondly, a large complex of rooms, almost equal in overall size to the central building, has been defined on the west side. This adjoining structure was built on a smaller scale, but two parallel rows of small columns allowed the roof to span about as wide an area as that in the temple. A bench, characteristic of houses in the Early Bronze Age, was constructed against the temple's west wall, which supported the roof of the second building on the east side. This undoubtedly was the residence of the ruler at Ai in Early Bronze Age I-C.

Thirdly, a 2-meter-wide enclosure wall, constructed in distinct sections around the west side of the acropolis complex, fortified the residence of the ruler. This wall is visible on the right of the main buildings on photo on p. 37. On the south, the upper side of the photo, the enclosure seems to join a fortified tower. The enclosure continued in use in Early Bronze Age II, but the royal residence inside was constricted in size, making the complex larger in Early Bronze Age I-C than at any later period.

Four gates have been discovered in the Early Bronze Age I-C city. Three of these — *i.e.*, the citadel, postern, and corner gates — were 1 meter wide, constructed straight through the wall. The walls on each side of the postern gate passage were 3 meters high when excavated, so it is probable that the passage was roofed to stabilize the sides and to add to the security of the gate. The fourth gate at Ai—*i.e.*, the valley gate at site J—was only partially excavated in its Early Bronze Age I-C phase, the north half being in the balk, but the exposed part is more than 1 meter wide, indicating that it is larger than the others.

The first three gates mentioned above were fortified either by elliptical or semi-elliptical towers in Early Bronze Age I-C. The citadel gate was secured by a tower on its south side, with one straight face along the approach road leading to the gate and an elliptical face on the opposite side. The elliptical tower at the postern gate is well known. A large circular tower at the south-east corner of the city, site K, fortified the corner gate. All of the towers were external, built against the outer face of the city walls.

Comparative analysis of the Early Bronze Age I-C pottery forms and the decoration places this phase in the same cultural context as Jericho phases L–K in areas E-III–IV, tomb A–108, and some elements of Garstang's level V and tomb 24; tomb 14 and *périodes* 1 and 2 at Tell el-Far'a (N); Lapp's first urban phase at Bab edh-Dhra'; and Arad stratum III. In a wider context, the artifacts in this phase relate to the Late Gerzean and early First Dynasty in Eypt, Late Amuq F in Syria, and the Jemdet Nasr period in the upper Euphrates Valley.

The Early Bronze Age I-C city was inhabited by a substantial element of indigenous people whose

Plan of the site, and a conjecture of its area. 1. Temple. 2. Acropolis and citadel ("palace"). 3. IA village. 4. Lower city. 5. City fortifications. 6. Cemetery.

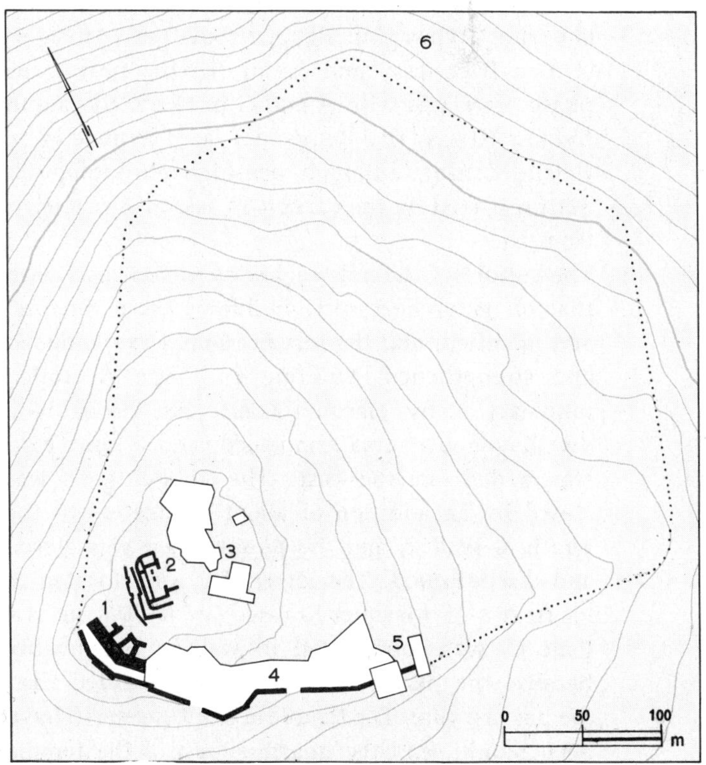

pottery culture is rooted in the Chalcolithic period, indicating that the village population in Early Bronze Age I-B probably was absorbed by the newcomers in Early Bronze Age I-C. However, the radical change evident in the new city and in the imaginative planning behind its construction indicates that new leadership was imposed from the outside. Antecedents of this culture are traced to coastal and northern Syria as well as southern Anatolia.

Early Bronze Age II. About 2860 B.C. the first great period of Ai was abruptly terminated by violent destruction. The citadel at site A was stormed and burned by an unknown enemy, and the acropolis buildings were burned to the ground. Scorched stones on top of the citadel and a blanket of ashes in the acropolis area underlying the Early Bronze Age II buildings attest to the fury of the destruction.

New leadership seems to have been imposed upon the population at Ai, and the city was rebuilt in the third major phase of its history. The construction evidence of this phase is assigned to Early Bronze Age II-A on the basis of stratified parallels with phases K-ii–H in areas E-III–IV at Jericho, some elements of Arad strata III–II and *périodes* 2–3 at Tell el-Far'a (N). In the context of the Near Eastern culture area, this relates to the late First Dynasty in Egypt, from Djer (Albright) or Den (Hennessy and Lapp). To the north, the phase correlates with Amuq G in North Syria and Byblos III as the sequences are arranged by Helene Kantor, although her high chronology is not supported by the Carbon 14 assays of materials from Ai.

The culture of the new regime at Ai contrasts with that of its predecessors. Buildings were repaired and modified, and the fortifications were widened and strengthened. Building C at site A, called sanctuary C by Marquet-Krause but probably a dwelling house, was remodeled, and a courtyard was added on the east. The citadel gate was closed by an addition of about .75 meters to the width of wall C, and the postern gate was closed and discontinued. The lower city gate, located at locus 242 of Marquet-Krause, *Les fouilles de Ay,* Plate C, was constructed in wall B, presumably because the place was more easily fortified than the postern gate. The temple at site D seems to have been rebuilt, and the quarters west of the temple were reconstructed about half the size of the previous building. A wall with curved corners, laid between the two rows of columns in the center of the Early Bronze Age I-C structure, enclosed residential quarters of the acropolis complex on the west side. All these modifications may be described as functional ad hoc structures with a tendency to retrenchment.

Two distinctive new pottery forms suggest the origins of the new people. The first is a carinate bowl with outward curving rim; the second is a jug with a tall, cylindrical neck and high loop handle. These vessels appear to be common at Tell el-Far'a (N) in late Early Bronze Age I-C, but appear at Ai at the beginning of Early Bronze Age II-A. The authentic bowl form is not found at Arad, although local imitations occur in stratum II. Most significant, however, is the appearance of the carinate bowl in phase K-ii of the tel at Jericho, which is the destruction layer of the Early Bronze Age I-C city. This suggests that people associated with the carinate form had something to do with the termination of the Early Bronze Age I-C Jericho, and the presence of the form in the construction layers of Early Bronze Age II-A at Ai indicates that the same people may have participated in its violent overthrow.

A movement from north to south in Canaan is indicated by the pottery, supporting the conclusion that the transition from Early Bronze Age I-C to Early Bronze Age II-A at Ai was brought about by local conflict rather than by an intrusion from the outside. Ultimately, outside influences can be traced to North Syria and the coastal cities, but those elements seem to have settled in northern Canaan first.

A disaster of massive proportions brought the Early Bronze Age II city to an end. At every excavated site the buildings and walls were in ruins, and there was generally evidence of fire. Building B at site A collapsed, depositing a half meter of roof-fall and brick debris on its floors. Fire, trapped under the heavy fall, smoldered with enough intensity to break down wall stones into calcined masses. Up to 1 meter of bricky ruins covered houses at site C, and thick layers of ash lay upon the floors of the acropolis complex. The total destruction of everything standing seems to have been caused by an earthquake. Evidence of this is strongest at site D, where a rift in bedrock through the temple room extends through the north wall, and the stones tilt into the break. The curved wall on the west side of the temple was shifted, and when it was rebuilt in Early Bronze Age III-A, the angle of tilt westward was preserved in the reconstruction.

Since the general destruction terminated the Early Bronze Age city, pottery and artifacts from this phase are assigned to Early Bronze Age II-B. The pottery horizon compares with phases J–G of areas E-III–IV and tomb A-127 at Jericho, and *périodes* 3–5 at Tell el-Far'a (N), although *période* 5 probably terminated after the destruction at Ai.

A conspicuous new kind of pottery appears in Early Bronze Age II-B. The prevailing form is a small juglet of pinkish-orange and light greenish ware, decorated with alternating horizontal and wavy lines and suspended triangles. This is the Abydos ware, known from discoveries at Saqqara in Egypt. Other examples occur at Jericho in tomb A–127, and in the Kinnereth tomb. A similar decoration appears on large jars at Arad in stratum II. North of Canaan, a crude form of the same decoration is found at Judeidah in Syria, in Amuq G (and H).

The Early Bronze Age II-B city at Ai was probably destroyed before the end of the Second Dynasty. A group of four Carbon 14 assays yields a date of circa 2720 B.C. for the termination of the city, or about twenty years before the beginning of the Third Dynasty.

Early Bronze Age III-A. The Early Bronze III spans some three hundred years and includes two major phases of city fortifications and buildings.

Early Bronze Age III-A at Ai is a distinct period of construction, occupation, and destruction, dating circa 2700–2550 B.C. After the paralyzing destruction of the Early Bronze Age II-B city, both houses and fortifications required rebuilding. The construction seems to have moved slowly: The city wall at site A was rebuilt first, then the houses inside the walls were built against it. Erosion in the doorway of an Early Bronze Age II-B house suggests that twenty years may have elapsed between the rebuilding of the walls and of the houses inside. A minimum period of rebuilding would therefore be about twenty years, or from 2720 to 2700 B.C., and a maximum could be as much as forty years.

There is positive evidence of Egyptian involvement in rebuilding the city. The evidence is twofold. First, there are construction features in the Early Bronze Age III-A temple at site D that are best understood if attributed to Egyptian craftsmen. Foremost among these are the raised-top column bases of temple A, which superseded the flat-top bases of temples C/B. The sharply defined rectangular top of the former, shown on page 45, was shaped by sawing four thin grooves 3 centimeters deep into the top of large, flat stones. All the stone outside the grooves was then chipped away to the bottom of the cut, leaving the center

The citadel on the acropolis (area D); called "palace" by Marquet-Krause, "temple" by others (plan and view).

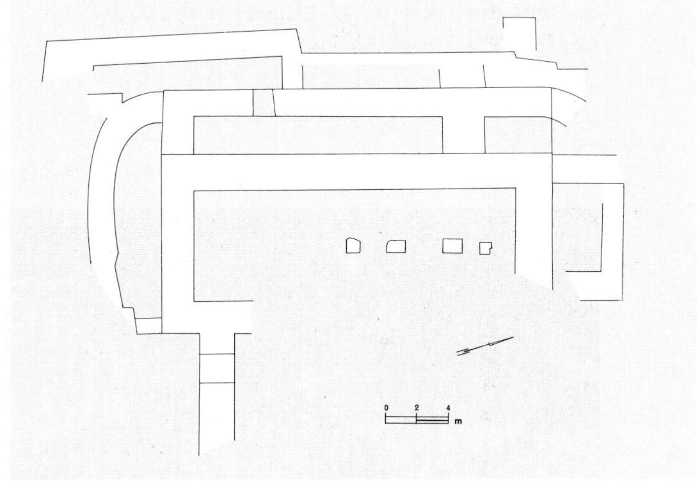

rectangle 3 centimeters above the base. Copper saws capable of shaping the raised-top bases are known in Egypt from the reign of Zer in the First Dynasty and are not known outside Egypt.

Another Egyptian feature is the manner of construction of the 2-meter wall of hammer-dressed stones in temple A. The stones are shaped roughly to the size of bricks and laid in mud mortar throughout the thickness of the wall. This unique way of building a wall of stones without a rubble core is Egyptian, dating to the beginning of the Third Dynasty.

The bricklike stone wall of temple A at site D was only the core, and a sophisticated plastered surface finished the structure on the inside. Mud mortar like that between the stones formed the first layer over the wall. This was covered by a thick layer of *khamra,* or red clay, mixed with straw for a binder. The finishing layer was fine white plaster over the *khamra,* extending to a floor made of the same material. Piers of stones set on the raised-top bases probably were plastered in the same manner, giving the temple interior an elegance which points to Egyptian influences.

Additional evidence of Egyptian involvement is the imported alabaster and stone vessels found in the ruins of sanctuary A at site A. These vessels have been associated with First and Second Dynasty parallels in Egypt, and many have thought they were brought to Ai before the time of sanctuary A, or Early Bronze Age III-B. A careful study of the Early Bronze Age III-A building at site A, preceding sanctuary A, reveals no evidence of cultic vessels or installations. In fact, the building seems to be a dwelling house with a courtyard. On the other hand, two alabaster bowls made of materials like those in sanctuary A were recovered by Marquet-Krause from the Early Bronze Age III-A phase of

Pillar building of the IA village with hewn roof-support pillars on the right and stacked stone piers on the left.

the temple at site D. Ruth Amiran has recently restored the bowls, and she has shown that both indeed are from the temple. Thus, there are cult vessels from temple A in Early Bronze Age III-A, suggesting that the alabasters in sanctuary A, dating to Early Bronze Age III-B, were moved from temple A to the sanctuary in the transition from Early Bronze Age III-A to III-B.

There may also be evidence of Egyptian involvement in constructing the water reservoir at site K in Early Bronze Age III-A, but this cannot be demonstrated yet. The reservoir was built inside the southeast bend of the city wall, closing off the corner gate and creating the earliest known city water system in Canaan. Deceptively simple, the system consisted of an open, kidney-shaped reservoir, built above ground level but designed to capture rainwater channeled from the upper city.

Careful engineering is evident in the structural features of the reservoir. The stone-paved floor, shown opposite, was closely laid on a backing of *khamra,* which becomes practically impermeable when moist. Also, large stones were set into a thick dam of *khamra* to prevent erosion of the dam's face. There was one meter of clay behind the upper part of the dam, and a thick bed of clay supported the lower part of the dam. To provide runoff for any leakage of the dam, a fill of loose stones was placed between the *khamra* on the left and the city wall on the right.

The reservoir has a calculated capacity of more than 1,800 cubic meters, being 25 meters wide and $2\frac{1}{2}$ meters deep. The depth changes with the rise in bedrock to the west, and the east–west size varies because the installation is fitted into the corner of the city wall. A study of water consumption made in an arid region of the Lebanon some twenty years ago has revealed that people there got along very well on 1 cubic meter of stored water yearly per capita. With the added supply of the small spring in the Wadi el-Jaya at Ai, this implies a minimum population of about two thousand inhabitants in Early Bronze Age III-A.

Two gates of the Early Bronze Age III-A city are known. The Early Bronze Age II valley gate was blocked by an erosion control dam similar to that at the reservoir, and a new and smaller gate, fortified by two towers, was constructed on top of the blockage. A second gate was located at

EBA III-A water reservoir in area K IX, with stone-paved dam in the lower right (top). Raised-top column base, shaped by copper saws, in the EBA III-A temple at site D (bottom).

site C in the south wall of the city. Only the east side of this south gate remains; the west side was apparently broken down, along with more than ten meters of the city wall, in the assault on the city that terminated the Early Bronze Age III-A phase.

Early Bronze Age III-B. Some revolutionary changes seem to have occurred at Ai in the transition from Early Bronze Age III-A to Early Bronze Age III-B (circa 2550 B.C.). The changes must be attributed to external influences — specifically, to influences in the north of Canaan, associated with the Khirbet Kerak culture.

That the city was captured is evident in the broken-down wall west of the south gate at site C and in evidences of intensive burning at the citadel fortifications of site A. A new city wall was constructed against the outer face of the Early Bronze Age III-A rampart, making the combined Early Bronze Age III-A–B fortification eight meters wide at site H, where the excavated structure still stands 7 meters high. The south gate was closed and discontinued, but the valley gate at site J was rebuilt and continued in use as a minor entrance. No other Early Bronze Age III-B gate has been discovered.

The most remarkable changes occurred at sites A

Incense burners; EBA III (left); IA I (right).

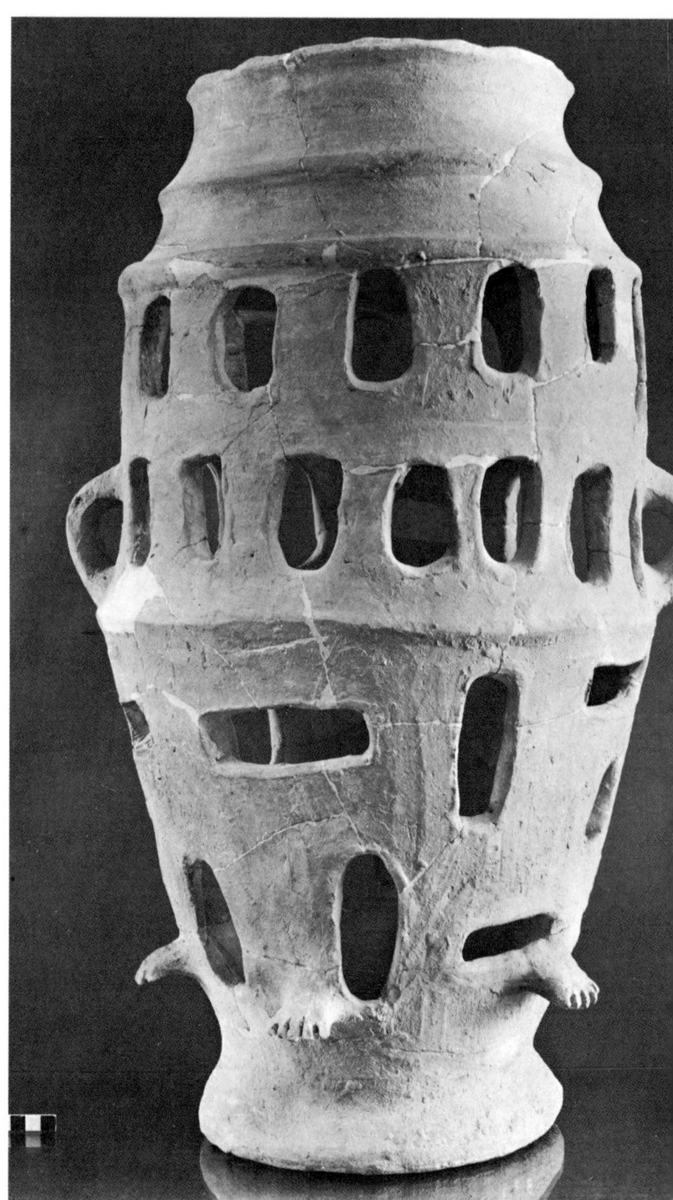

and D. As noted previously, an Egyptian-inspired temple was constructed at site D in Early Bronze Age III-A. At the beginning of Early Bronze Age III-B, the alabaster and pottery cultic vessels were moved from the temple and installed in the building known as sanctuary A at site A (see p. 45). The temple building at site D was apparently remodeled into a residence for the new ruler of Ai. The temple complex served as a fortified temple and royal residence from its beginning in Early Bronze Age I-C. In each successive phase of rebuilding the complex was constricted, with only the temple maintaining a constant size. In Early Bronze Age III-A the earlier enclosure wall around the site was abandoned, and the outer walls of the royal quarters of the Early Bronze Age II phase became the fortified enclosure.

In Early Bronze Age III-B the rooms around the central temple building seem to have been filled with debris, making the temple hall the last remaining habitable space on the acropolis. In this situation either the cult or the ruler had to move. Since the cultic apparatus was discovered at site A in newly prepared surroundings, it is apparent that the cult was moved.

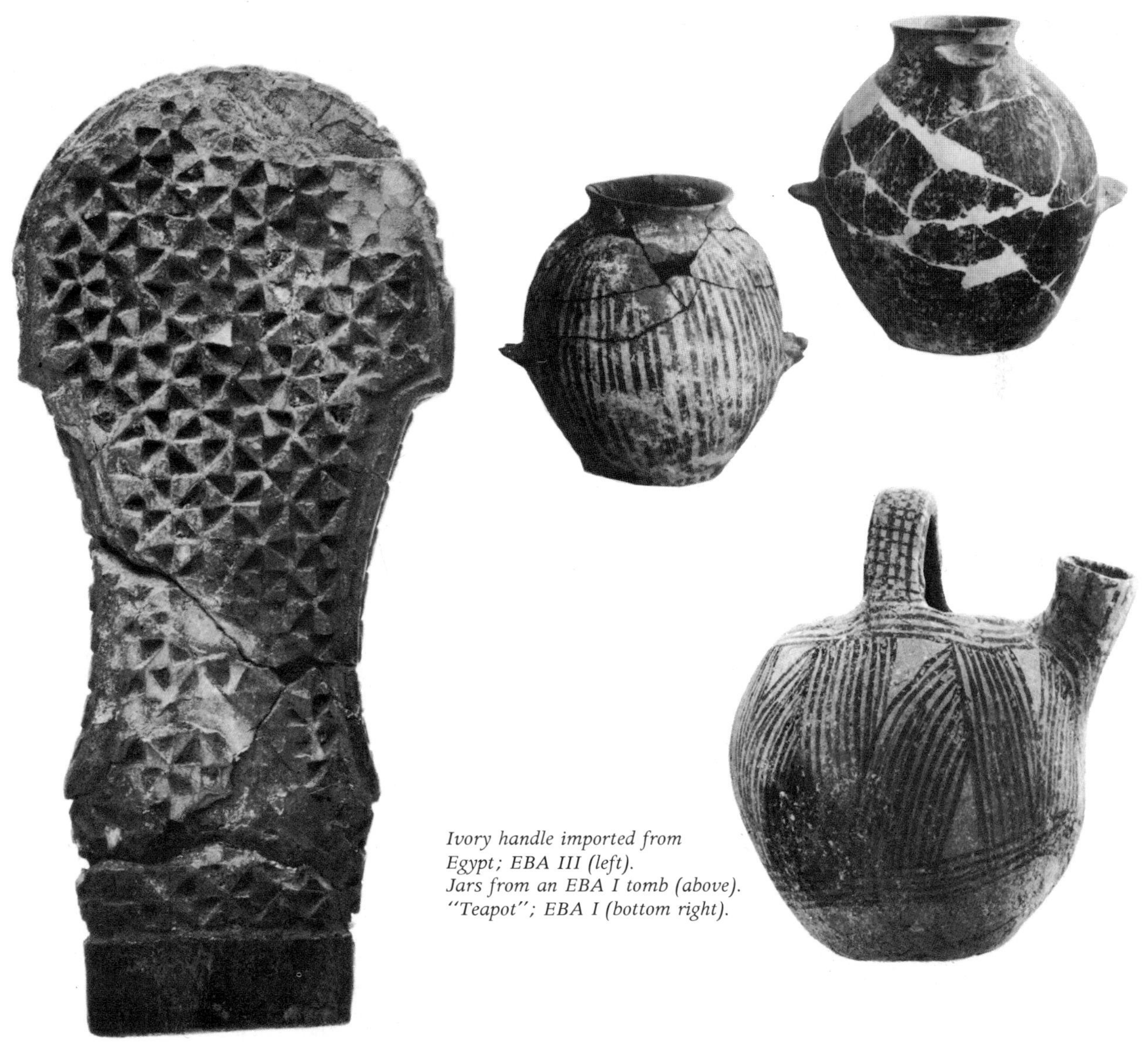

Ivory handle imported from Egypt; EBA III (left).
Jars from an EBA I tomb (above).
"Teapot"; EBA I (bottom right).

There are further reasons for reaching this conclusion. First, the building known as sanctuary A seems to be a remodeled domestic house, a kind of ad hoc sanctuary. The altar in our area III (Marquet-Krause room 133) was actually built in the courtyard of the house located in area II (Marquet-Krause room 116). This court area was probably not roofed in the sanctuary phase but area II on its south, where most of the cultic vessels were found, was covered. Area II was the "holy of holies," if there was one, and entrance was gained via the court.

Second, the transfer of imported Egyptian cultic vessels from the temple to a remodeled house reflects a downgrading of Egyptian influence. A study of the sanctuary artifacts reveals a large number of Khirbet Kerak and northern-oriented objects, especially in association with the altar and "holy of holies," implying a reorientation of the cult in Early Bronze Age III-B. These objects include the pottery votive cups found on the altar and in various rooms by Marquet-Krause, which are paralleled by cups from Beth-Shean XII–XI in the context of predominantly Khirbet Kerak ware. The decorated bone tubes and cups, whose closest parallels are found in Syria in Early Bronze Age III (Prausnitz) where the Khirbet Kerak culture was dominant, are more examples of the same trend. In fact, the carved tube from Ai resembles a find from tomb F-4 at Jericho, which occurs in a context of authentic Khirbet Kerak ware. Both Ruth Amiran and Hennessy have shown conclusively that the small stand, or plaque, found in the sanctuary assemblage is also northern-oriented, with parallels at Beth-Shean and Khirbet Kerak in Canaan and at Judeideh and Ta'yinat in Syria.

Therefore, sanctuary A represents a most curious

The immediate region of et-Tell, with sites excavated 1964–70.

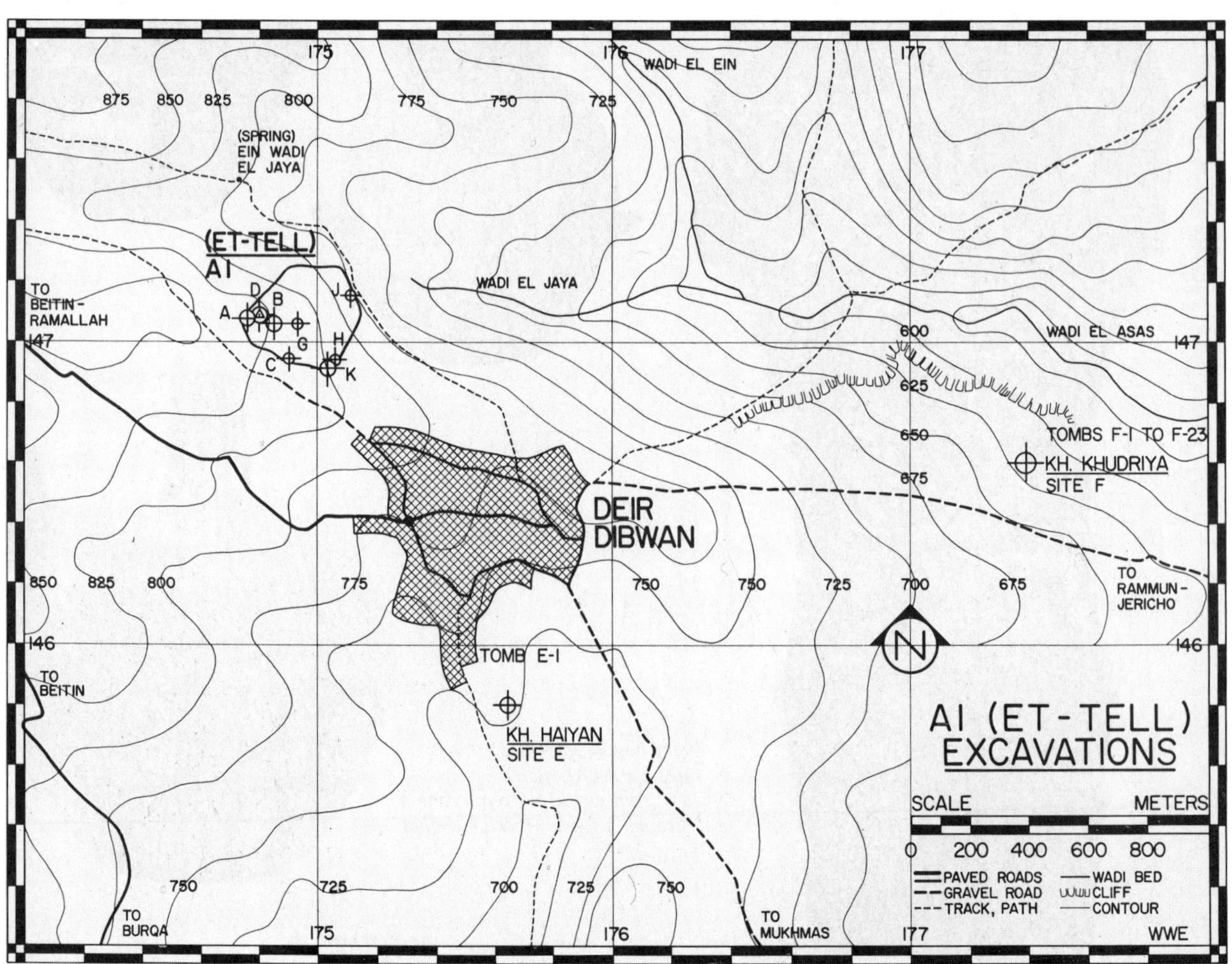

amalgam of Egyptian and Khirbet Kerak cultic objects, housed in ad hoc structures at site A. The primary fact is that Egypt lost whatever influence she had at Ai in Early Bronze Age III-B. The incumbent ruler, at Ai, meanwhile, seems to have accepted halfheartedly the cultic influence of the new, northern-oriented powers in Canaan, and at the same time sought to secure his city and personal residence. The 8-meter-wide city walls and excessively buttressed royal residence on the acropolis reinforce the observation of a local peasant worker, who helped uncover the 7-meter-high fortification at site H. "The people who lived here," he observed, "were afraid."

Violent destruction overtook the city about 2400 B.C., during the Fifth Dynasty. No definite identity of the aggressor is known, but a scene in the tomb of Inti at Dishashi depicts the capture of a Canaanite city, and a mutilated inscription names two cities, neither of which can be identified. If the city at Ai was taken from the control of Egypt in Early Bronze Age III-A, during the Fourth Dynasty, it would be among the first cities targeted for recapture in any Egyptian campaign to regain control of Canaan. Possibly the Egyptians did take the city, but it was never rebuilt, because the "dark age," which is what Wright calls Early Bronze Age IV, descended upon the land with the appearance of nomadic invaders from the desert.

Iron Age I. The site of Ai was abandoned and left in ruins after its destruction circa 2400 B.C. Albright suggested that Bethel was settled by people displaced from Ai. In any case, the site of Ai lay in ruins until circa 1220 B.C., at the beginning of Iron Age I, when people from the north or east established a settlement on the terraces below the acropolis, down to contour 845 on plan on p. 50. By that time the name of the original city must have been lost, for the name "Ai," which undoubtedly dates from the Iron Age I village, seems to be a popular designation of the mound as a regional landmark.

The settlement at Ai was one of many established in the region about the same time, apparently by people who moved in and occupied sites that had been abandoned or strategic places where no previous settlements existed. Among the former were Ai, Tell en-Naṣbe, and Gibeon (el-Jib). New sites that became villages were Mukhmas (Michmash), Rammun (Rimmon), eṭ-Ṭaiyiba (Ophrah?), Raddana (Bireh), el Ful (Gibeah), and many small campsites on hilltops in the region. The Iron Age village at Ai, therefore, was settled as part of a large influx of newcomers, who apparently met with little or no resistance.

Several distinct characteristics of the new culture are evident at Ai. First, the village was not fortified, a characteristic found at the other sites, with the possible exception of Bethel and Gibeon (and about them there is some question). The walls of the Early Bronze Age stood at Ai, but they were not secure. The new village occupied about 2½ acres of the acropolis area, while the ancient walls surrounded the 27½-acre site. There is no evidence that any attempt was made to repair the Early Bronze Age walls, probably because the small number of people in the village could not possibly defend so large a site.

Second, the houses were characterized by a pillar, or pier, a technique of construction first pointed out by Albright at Bethel. One of the better houses, shown on page 44, illustrates the technique. Outer walls, such as the one on the right in the photograph, were constructed of parallel courses of fieldstone masonry, with a core of rubble and earth stabilizing the center. However, the inner walls, supporting long transverse wooden beams, had hewn pillars or piers of stacked stones supporting the beams at intervals of about 1.25 meters, and the interstices between the pillars were closed with rubble walls. These beams were about 25 centimeters thick, evident in the preserved aperture in a house wall, and the lower side was about 1.6 meters above the floor surface. Apparently, wooden slats were laid across the beams, and *huwar* was placed on the slats to seal the roof.

Third, four arch constructions were found in house walls. The arches ranged from .8 to 1 meter high, and usually joined a small room to a larger one. In one case the arch may have joined a small enclosure for animals with the main house, but this does not satisfactorily explain all the occurrences. The arch, however, is a distinctive feature of the houses, without parallel, at least to the writer's knowledge, in this period.

Fourth, the houses at Ai depended largely upon cisterns for a water supply. The meager spring in the Wadi el-Jaya, half a kilometer away, was an added source, but every house had its own

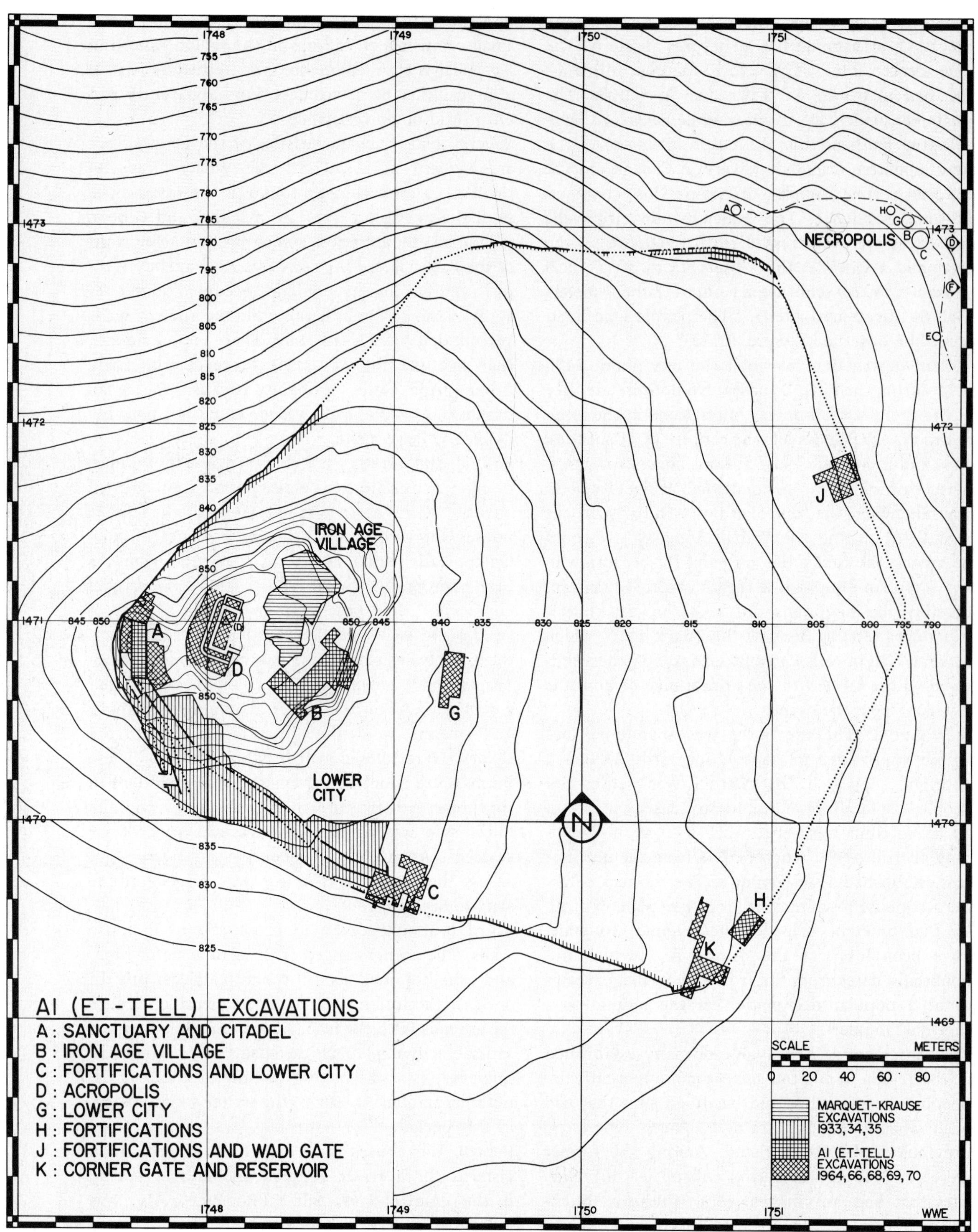
AI (ET-TELL) EXCAVATIONS
A: SANCTUARY AND CITADEL
B: IRON AGE VILLAGE
C: FORTIFICATIONS AND LOWER CITY
D: ACROPOLIS
G: LOWER CITY
H: FORTIFICATIONS
J: FORTIFICATIONS AND WADI GATE
K: CORNER GATE AND RESERVOIR
NECROPOLIS
IRON AGE VILLAGE
LOWER CITY
SCALE
METERS
0 20 40 60 80
MARQUET-KRAUSE EXCAVATIONS 1933, 34, 35
AI (ET-TELL) EXCAVATIONS 1964, 66, 68, 69, 70
WWE

cistern in the village, hewn in the soft Senonian chalk of the acropolis area.

An appreciable sophistication is evident in the construction of the cisterns. The houses were located only where the Senonian layers are found at Ai and at the other Iron Age I sites mentioned above, indicating that the settlers arrived with experience in cistern building. This chalk becomes practically impermeable when wet. No evidence of plaster was found in a cistern that was not reused in the Byzantine period, so the newcomers may not have plastered their cisterns. Water was captured by surface channels and from roofs. It appears that the cistern openings were equipped with traps that would catch the larger impurities in surface water. Two cisterns are visible in the large room of the house shown on p. 44. The larger one apparently collected water drained from the roof. However, the small one in the center of the room was connected to the larger one by a small aperture near the top of the cavity. Water, therefore, filled the large cistern, with impurities settling to the bottom, before the small one was filled by the overflow. This arrangement provided cleaner drinking water in the small cistern.

Fifth and last, the people at Ai were farmers and shepherds. An Iron Age I agricultural terrace was excavated at site G, on plan on page 50, suggesting

Plan of et-Tell, with sites excavated by Judith Marquet-Krause (1933–35) and the Joint Expedition (1964–70) (opposite).
Aerial view of et-Tell and Wadi el-Jaya on north side of mound leading from left to upper right toward the Jordan Valley (below).

that the terraces below contour 845 were probably cultivated. Stone saddles, querns, mortars, pestles, and one iron point attest to the agricultural dimension of village life, and numerous bones of goats and sheep in every house indicate the possession of flocks. One cistern containing Iron Age I pottery was found in the bottom of the valley leading to the Jordan Valley. No settlement was nearer than Ai, so the cistern must have been cut for shepherds to use in watering their flocks.

Two phases of the Iron Age village have been defined in both the houses and pottery. These are actually two subphases of one major building period, because the same houses continued with minor modifications, such as blockage and relocation of doors, repair of walls, and resurfacing of floors.

The characteristic pottery of the first phase of the construction of the houses is the long, collared-rim store jar with high flaring rim. This form is common at all the earliest Iron Age I sites in the region. A low-profile, collared-rim jar, and one with beveled rim and no collar, characterize the last phase. No burnished pottery has been found, so the village must have terminated sometime in the eleventh century, circa 1050 B.C. It is possible that the abandonment occurred after a minor battle, as slingstones were found on the floors of houses. There is no evidence, however, that the village was burned; on the contrary, the houses seem to have been left standing, as the back wall of the house shown on p. 44 is still preserved to more than 2 meters high. J. A. CALLAWAY

BIBLIOGRAPHY

W.F. Albright, *AASOR* 4 (1924), 141–49 • S. Yeivin, *PEF QSt* (1934), 189–91 • J. Marquet-Krause, *Syria* 16 (1935), 325–45; *idem, Les fouilles de 'Ay (et-Tell), 1932–35,* Paris, 1949 • M. Noth, *PJB* 31 (1935), 7–29 • L.H. Vincent, *RB* 16 (1937), 231–66 • J.M. Grintz, *Biblica* 42 (1961), 201–16 • J.A. Callaway, *Pottery from the Tombs at Ai (et-Tell),* London: Colt Archaeological Institute, Monograph Series, No. 2 (1964); *idem, BASOR* 178 (1965), 13–40; *idem,* (with M.B. Nicol), *BASOR* 183 (1966), 12–19; *idem, JBL* 87 (1968), 312–20; *idem, BASOR* 196 (1969), 2–16; *idem, BASOR* 198 (1970), 7–31; *idem* (with R.E. Cooley), *BASOR* 201 (1971), 9–19; *idem* (with K. Schoonover), *BASOR* (in press); *idem* (with N.E. Wagner), *PEQ* (in press) • *The Early Bronze Age Sanctuary at Ai (et-Tell),* London, 1972 • M. Prausnitz, *Annual Report,* Institute of Archaeology, University of London, 1955 • R. Amiran, *IEJ* 17 (1967), 185–86; 20 (1970), 170–79 • G.E. Wright, *AOT,* Festschrift für Kurt Galling, A. Kuschke, and E. Kutach, eds., (1970), 299–319 • F.M. Cross and D.N. Freedman, *BASOR* 201 (1971), 19–22 • Y. Aharoni, *IEJ* 21 (1971), 130–35.

EL-'AJJUL, TELL
(Beth 'Eglayim)

IDENTIFICATION. The site of Tell el-'Ajjul, one of the major cities in Canaan in the Bronze Age, lies some 6 kilometers (4 miles) southwest of Gaza on the north bank of the silted estuary of the Besor Valley (Wadi Ghazzeh). Although partly obliterated on its western flanks by encroaching dunes, and denuded as far as the south corner by seasonal floods, the mound of 28 to 33 acres has retained a roughly rectangular plan.

Petrie concluded that Tell el-'Ajjul was the site of Gaza during the Middle Bronze and part of the Late Bronze ages. It is more probable, however, that ancient Gaza was located within the confines of the modern city, where a sounding uncovered remains from the Late Bronze and Early Iron ages. Thus, Tell el-'Ajjul should probably be identified with Beth 'Eglayim, which Eusebius described as a village on the coast, eight miles from Gaza (*Onomasticon* 48:19).

EXCAVATIONS

Tell el-'Ajjul was the third site excavated by the British School of Egyptian Archaeology after Tell Jemma and Tel Sharuhen (el-Far'a). Work continued there under the direction of Petrie from 1930 to 1934, with a further short season under field directors E. H. Mackay and Margaret A. Murray in 1938. Reports were published in a series of five volumes called *Ancient Gaza.*

EARLY SETTLEMENTS

Although a Chalcolithic and Early Bronze Age settlement was found by J. L. Starkey on the south bank of Wadi Ghazzeh, nothing of these periods was reached at Tell el-'Ajjul. Nor was anything found on the mound from the subsequent period, called Copper Age by Petrie, which is represented by large cemeteries east and west of the mound. Petrie and Starkey were the first to recognize that the contents of cemeteries 1500 and 100–200 represented a culture new to archaeology at that time, and Petrie named it the Copper Age because of the number of copper weapons found in the tombs. Since then, however, other names for this period have been substituted — Middle Bronze Age I or Intermediate (Early-Middle) Bronze Age (following the terminology of Kathleen Kenyon).

In the same years, 1930 to 1934, Albright uncovered stratified deposits at Tel Beit Mirsim containing pottery of the same type, which was later found at other sites in Syria and Palestine as well.

TOMB TYPES AND POTTERY

The burial customs of this period were extremely varied. In the western cemetery 1500 (not to be confused with cemetery 1500 on the mound, published in *Ancient Gaza* III), the predominant tomb plan was rectangular, containing — as a rule — single, intact, crouched burials. Jars found with them were exclusively flat-based vessels, often with vestigial ledge handles and with or without a spout. In cemetery 100–200 east of the mound, most of the tombs had rounded shafts and chambers, although some retained rectangular cutting for the shaft alone. Some burials were intact, but in most cases the bones had been disturbed or scattered. Few of the jars had ledge handles. The burials were accompanied by shallow bowls and deep cups.

METAL

A striking difference between the two cemeteries is the presence of daggers — often the only offering — in cemetery 1500, whereas in the larger cemetery 100–200, only two examples were found. In a study of these weapons, Kathleen Kenyon noted that the tombs lined with stone, rubble, or brick, which formed a concentrated block in the center of the group, each contained a dagger, which may suggest that they are among the earliest tombs in the cemetery. The so-called poker-butt spears found in the eastern cemetery derive from a type known in Mesopotamia in the Early Dynastic III period. They also occur in Western Asia toward the end of the third millennium B.C. Ornaments were confined to a few beads for which Petrie noted Egyptian Old Kingdom parallels.

Mound and excavated areas. 1. Palace. 2. LBA (18th Dynasty). 3, 4. MBA II-B (Hyksos) and MBA II-A cemeteries. 5. The big fosse.

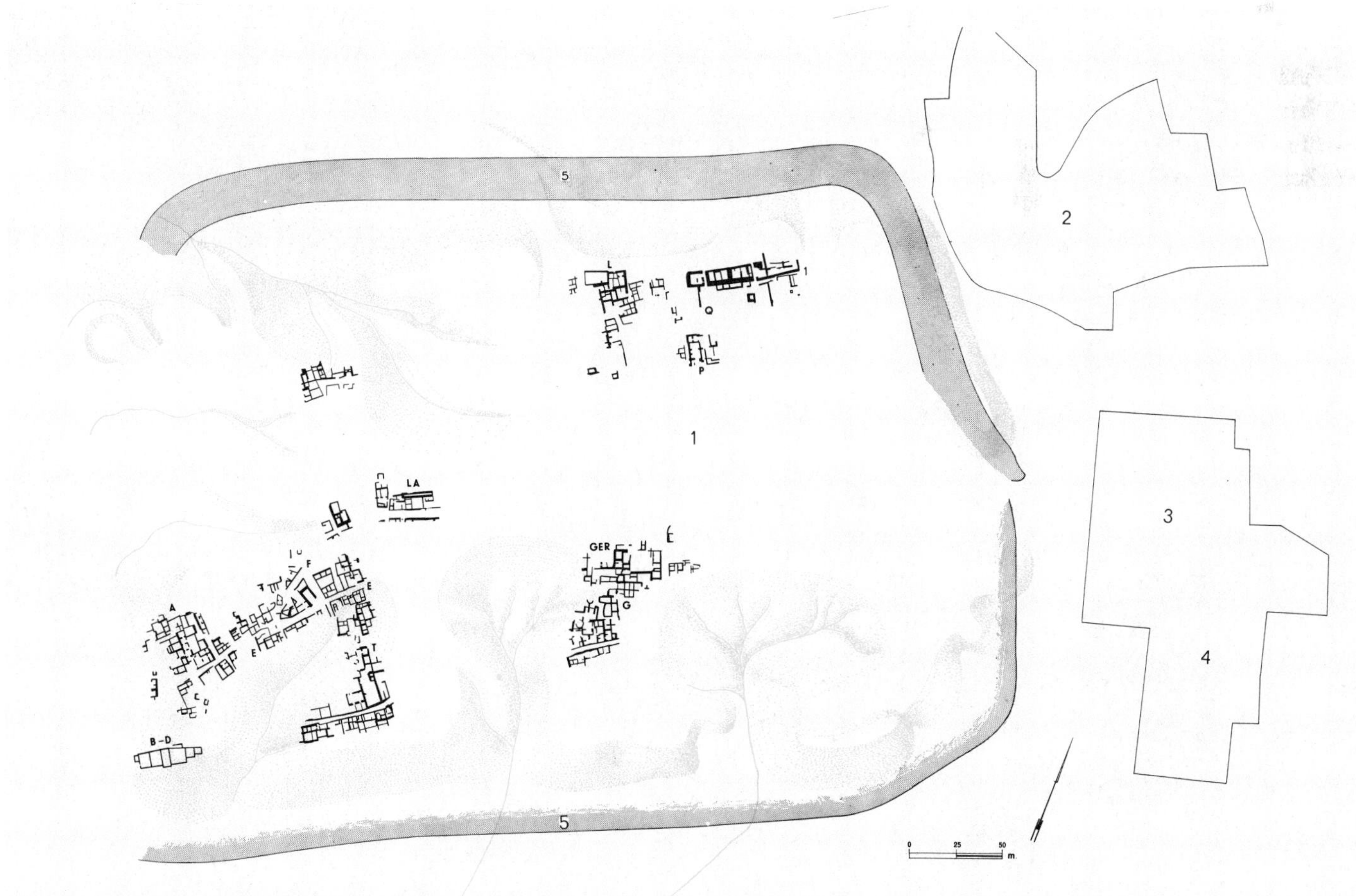

Plain of Accho; tomb finds.

DATE. In general, the date of these cemeteries falls within the range of the First Intermediate Period in Egypt, from circa 2300 to before 2000 B.C.

MIDDLE BRONZE AGE I TO LATE BRONZE AGE

Courtyard Cemetery. The earliest deposits so far discovered on the mound were burials cut in marl or sandstone on either side of a gulley near the north corner. It is possible that erosion destroyed some intervening burials and the builders of the first palace therefore constructed a revetment to arrest the damage at this place.

Detailed study of the burial customs and grave goods has revealed that the single burials can be divided into six phases within the Middle Bronze Age, developing from a crouched to an extended position. The earliest tombs were rectangular in plan. Groups 1 and 2 have affinities with Schaeffer's cultural group *porteurs de torques*. Group 3 was remarkable for the concentration of angular carinated bowls also found at Tel Beit Mirsim G–F, Rosh ha-'Ayin, and Hazor.

There was a break in continuity between Groups 3 and 4, when the first small flared carinated bowls and the first pyriform juglets appear with two scarabs of non-Egyptian design. The pottery of Group 5 shows links with the earliest layers of the contemporary tombs excavated at Jericho in 1952–54. The characteristic vessels at Jericho, such as the pedestal vases, are hardly represented at 'Ajjul.

Included in Group 6 is the burial of a child wearing gold ornaments, which was found under a corner of palace II. This burial may represent a foundation deposit heralding the most prosperous period at 'Ajjul in the seventeenth/sixteenth centuries B.C.

BURIAL CUSTOMS. Single burial continued to be practiced in the courtyard cemetery, as in the preceding Middle Bronze Age I. However, a variation in orientation of the graves and the position of the bodies was found between the groups. Outstanding is the two-chamber tomb of a warrior and a similar one in the eastern cemetery, both containing metal weapons. With some exceptions, the trend of single burial continued throughout later phases of the Middle Bronze Age and Late Bronze Age cemeteries at 'Ajjul.

In addition, a rare class of tombs forming a compact group was found north of the upper tunnel in the eastern cemetery, and other tombs were disposed around the eroded fringes of the mound itself. A few tombs were rectangular in shape, but the majority were circular pits from $2\frac{1}{2}$ to 4 meters in diameter. The bodies of three to eight occupants were laid in alcoves scooped in the sides of the pit, but the main space in several cases was filled by the partially dismembered skeleton of an equid.

Near the mouth of the upper tunnel was a curious deposit of limbs in articulation, including ass, gazelle, horse, ox, and man. Other bones were scattered on top of a pit dug into the walls of forts III–IV, and these may have been remains of a feast following the sacrifice of a horse. This custom is also found in the warrior tomb mentioned above, but only rare occurrences are recorded elsewhere on the Syro-Palestinian littoral, although it appears more common in Asia Minor. Deliberate dismemberment of human bodies is obvious in pit TCH, burial 1702, where two heaps of bones were found with the skulls placed separately in a row; some of them lacked the lower jaw.

South Town. A settlement may have existed on the south end of the mound during the Twelfth to Thirteenth Dynasties. The carnelian bead bearing the name of Amenemhet and scarabs of Egyptian officials, as well as the statuette of Khentiu-ka, all point to this period, although it seems that none of the buildings in the area can be dated so early. A layer of burning sealed off Petrie's "XIIth Dynasty" town (level III, block B-D) from his "XVth Dynasty" buildings (level II, block A).

DEFENSE SYSTEMS. The expansion of the city began with the digging of the fosse, its soil banked to a height of 3 meters around the top of the slope. Traces of early buildings on stone foundations were found in the southeast quarter. From a small town, the site was soon transformed into a vast enclosure, nearly twice as large as Megiddo. It was defended on at least three sides by a fosse 6 meters deep, best preserved on the west. The fourth side may have been sufficiently protected by the estuary at the foot of the slopes. These defenses differ from numerous other camp enclosures, for they were merely cut out of the marl or sandstone, and no constructional packing and consequently no plaster or stone facing was required. A wall of black brick was found on top of the slope on the northwest side, presumably contemporary with palace III and partly built of the same material.

Almost midway along this side, a road cut the

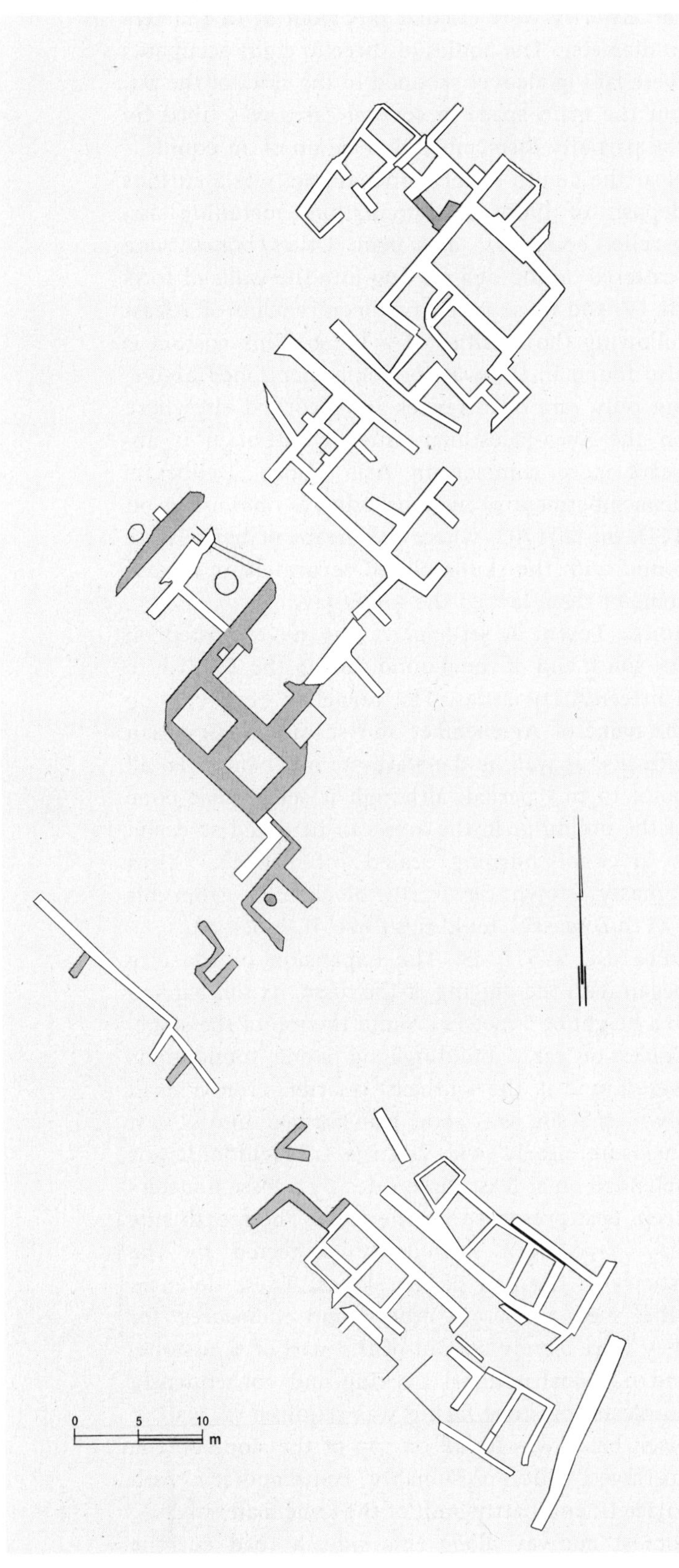

line of the fosse and led up to the mound from the direction of the sea. It was in this vicinity that most of the small stone weights, averaging half an ounce (14 grams) were found — in no less than eight standards of unit, which Petrie interpreted as pointing to an international trade in spices or precious metal. The main and original entry was apparently in the center of the northeast side facing modern Gaza, where a strip of marl some 7.62 meters wide was not removed for the fosse. It formed a convenient causeway entrance, edged with a balustrade of round-topped stones.

TUNNELS. Emerging from the causeway and extending some 152 meters into the plain were curious tunnels, less than 2 meters in depth, with openings at intervals in the roofs. As Petrie has stated, the plan of the tunnels was obscured by denudation and their purpose is unknown. In the writer's view, they could have been connected with an irrigation system similar to the *qanats* of the Iranian plains. The tunnels must predate the cutting of the fosse, and they remained partially open, although not necessarily in use, until the Eighteenth Dynasty, as shown by the Egyptian drop-shaped vases in the fill.

CITY LEVELS III–II. Once the defenses were complete, a city plan was laid out on orderly lines. A ring road encircled the city within the line of the fosse, flanked by buildings. Another thoroughfare ran diagonally from the southeast to the northwest corners. A branch road took a circuitous route toward the same point.

After a fire destroyed buildings on the south end, the population seems to have moved toward the northeast, where a great building program was carried out. The main structure, GER, was planned around a large pit. The purpose of the pit is unknown, for there were already several wells nearby. East of the pit was a small court containing a round tomb with alcove burials, similar to those

Area G, upper level; beginning of the LBA.
early phase *late phase.*

Equid burial; on the right and left, human burials and funerary offerings; MBA II-B (opposite, left).

Sanctuary in southern part of mound seen from the east; contemporary with palace II (opposite, right).

containing skeletons of equids. It is difficult to decide which came first, the tomb or the building. The street plan of level II followed the line of its predecessor, although the ring road was narrower and access to the great pit was not retained. Two parallel lanes, which ran from east to west and led to the palaces are best seen on the upper plan. Preoccupation with ablutions, both domestic and ceremonial, is particularly marked in block A, built about this time to the west of the south town. Besides the "shrine" AF, there were several plastered areas sloping to a sump, as well as decorative pavements laid in seashells.

PALACES. Massive orthostatic slabs of sandstone with rougher blocks between them formed the foundation of palace I. The stone was no doubt excavated from the fosse, and both constructions were probably successive stages in one coordinated plan. The first building measured 165 by 127 feet (or 2,000 square meters by Albright's calculation), but it may be incomplete on the west, and the south side may have undergone two phases of construction or repair. A small room at the northeast corner had a sloping plastered floor and a jar to catch water sunk in the ground.

In its present incomplete state the plan of palace II was small compared with palace I, although it may once have extended to the edge of the mound. The yellow brick walls without stone foundations were half as thick as in the preceding building. Palaces III–V seem like fotresses, as Albright observed. The thickness of the walls suggests that they may have been massive fragments of the defense system at the highest point of the mound, from which the garrison could command a view of the coast road from the north. Associated with III was an isolated brick tower or cenotaph. The first hoard of gold jewelry was found on the floor of the square-paved chamber, including a set of bracelets and two toggle pins. Palace or fort IV was a restoration of III, and was chiefly remarkable for the nearby pit containing equine bones.

POTTERY. Plain pottery, both above and below the burned layer in the south town, has much in common, although it lacks the characteristic features of earlier Middle Bronze Age deposits elsewhere. Gray-burnished and other decorated juglets appear, but the most striking innovation is the so-called bichrome pottery, boldly painted in black and red with bands and metopes, containing bulls, birds, and fish. The subject has been competently treated in recent studies, and the remaining point at issue is the relationship between this splendid ware and the equally remarkable jewelry, which may be contemporary, although there is little to prove it.

JEWELRY. J. R. Stewart noted that "the art of the jeweler is better represented at Tell el-'Ajjul than at any other Palestinian site, and with Enkomi in Cyprus, Ras Shamra in Syria, and Troy in Asia Minor it ranks amongst the places which have produced the most gold work in the coast

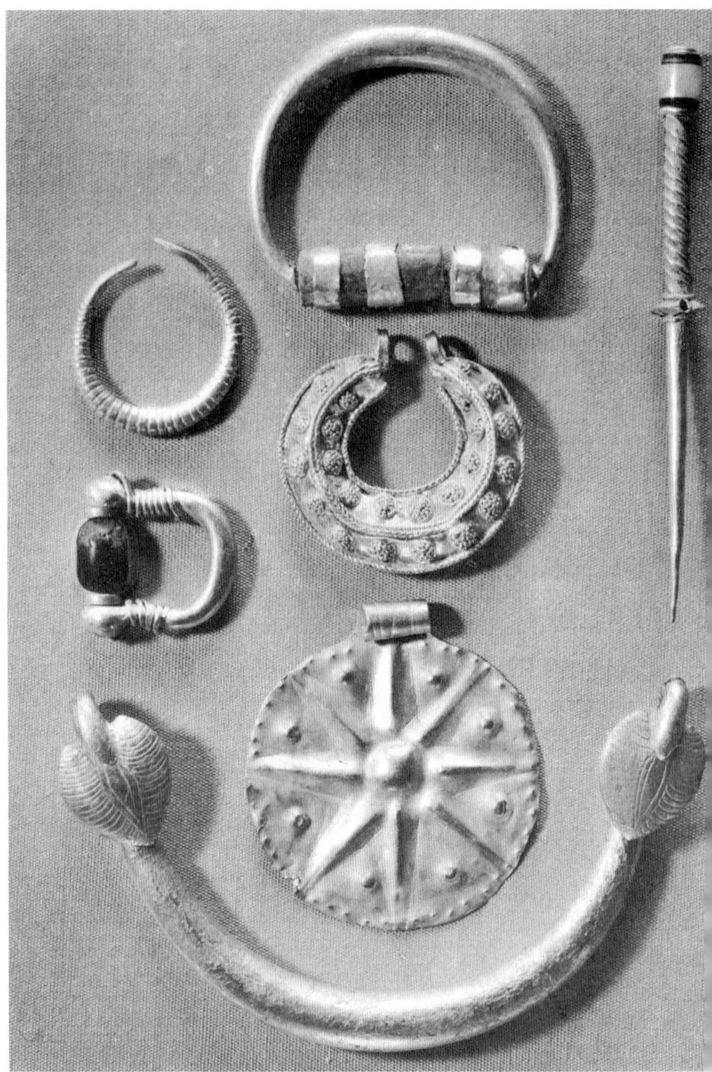

lands of Western Asia." Electrum and silver were also employed, and even lead was occasionally used to make ornaments and amulets.

Such sudden signs of wealth followed a period of exceptional poverty in personal adornment, and for the first time the mixed population of 'Ajjul wore pendants, earrings, and bracelets, elaborately made in sophisticated techniques. Solid gold toggle pins were richly fashioned, and one of the finest pieces was found in a single grave containing several scarabs, including one naming Aa-user-Re (Apophis), last of the great kings of the Fifteenth Dynasty. He reigned over thirty years and was still alive at the beginning of Kamose's reign, who triumphed over him soon after 1570 B.C. It is clear, therefore, that at least some of the gold work was made before the fall of Avaris, and another scarab of the same king confirms that the buildings of level II block A were abandoned about the same time.

SEALS AND CYLINDERS. No other site in Palestine has produced so many inscribed seals, mostly scarab shaped. About 62 percent of the scarabs came from city levels including graves; 28 percent were found in the northern cemeteries and 10 percent are cylinders fairly evenly divided between city and cemeteries. All but about 15 percent bear designs current in the Middle Bronze Age, and the remainder are datable to the Eighteenth Dynasty. The sequence of royal names begins with a cylinder seal, naming Amenemhet III (1842–1797 B.C.). Neferhotep I is represented by two scarabs (circa 1740–30 B.C.), but Ma-ib-Re Sheshi of the Fifteenth Dynasty, who reigned for about a decade shortly after 1674 B.C., left nine scarabs on the site. Lesser monarchs of the Sixteenth Dynasty fill in the gap between him and Aa-user-Re, who contributes the best evidence available for the floruit of gold work at 'Ajjul. This would seem to precede the desertion of building block A, which probably took place at the end of the same reign. Grave 1165 also produced a scarab that, for the first time, represented an animal resembling a horse.

From the beginning of the Eighteenth Dynasty, there are no royal scarabs from the mound, and

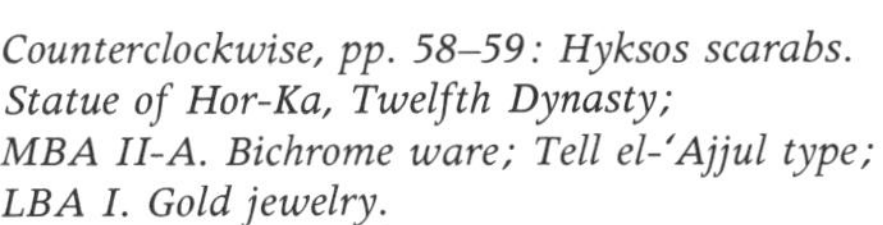

Counterclockwise, pp. 58–59: Hyksos scarabs.
Statue of Hor-Ka, Twelfth Dynasty;
MBA II-A. Bichrome ware; Tell el-'Ajjul type;
LBA I. Gold jewelry.

only a single piece naming Amenhotep I (1546–26 B.C.) from the cemeteries. However, part of a jar impressed with the cartouches of Hatshepsut and Thutmose III during their coregency, which ended in 1483 B.C., testifies to an Egyptian presence on the site. The jar fragments probably came from the debris of palace III. Thutmose III and his immediate successors are well represented in the northern cemeteries, and for Tutankhamen there is a splendid gold signet ring. The last royal name is that of Ramses II, showing that the cemeteries were still in use until at least 1200 B.C.

IRON AGE AND LATER SETTLEMENT

Albright suggested that palace V might belong to the tenth century B.C. If so, it would be the only Iron Age building on the mound. Apart from a few iron arrowheads, there are no recognizable objects of the period on the mound, although some graves in the cemetery contained Cypro-Phoenician black-on-red III juglets and pottery of Philistine derivation.

Hellenistic and Roman pots and part of a funerary inscription dated in year 666 of Gaza = A.D. 603 are among the few remains of later ages. Arab painted pottery and glass bangles found near the mound and along the coastal dunes testify to a flourishing community in the neighborhood between the thirteenth and fifteenth centuries A.D.

SUMMARY

The site of the great city of Tell el-'Ajjul was chosen not for reasons of defense but because it was situated at the junction between important trade routes, with access to the sea. Burials in two large cemeteries indicate that the north bank of Wadi Ghazzeh was already settled before 2000 B.C., but no trace has yet been found of contemporary dwellings. Most of the mound is still unexcavated, and the earliest remains so far recovered date from an early phase of the Middle Bronze Age. The last graves in the same region, which was later occupied by the courtyard of palace I, date from the end of the Twelfth Dynasty. About this time a settlement was established on the southeast corner of the mound. The inhabitants left clear traces of their contacts with Egypt. But the great period of the site began with the construction of the earthworks, planned on a large scale and completed with dispatch. Stones dug from the fosse were used for the foundations of the first palace and for a temenos wall, and houses were built in orderly array flanking a ring road and lining diagonal streets leading toward the palace. At much the same time, a monumental building, GER, was erected on the landward side.

The domestic buildings were constructed in two phases, both within the Thirteenth to Fifteenth Dynasties — the first came to a sudden end in a conflagration, which left a thick layer of ash. Graves, dug shortly afterward in this debris, were particularly numerous in block G, and the phase is well dated by scarabs naming Neferhotep Sheshi and lesser kings of the Sixteenth Dynasty. Before long the former buildings in block G were repaired and rebuilt, and a further complex of rooms was constructed over the ashes of the old town near the southeast corner, which continued in use until the reign of Aa-user-Re (circa 1570 B.C.).

Some walls were standing to a height of 3 meters, so it can be assumed that the rooms were deserted but not destroyed. The relationship between the southeast buildings and the so-called palaces near the northwest corner cannot be clarified on stratigraphic or architectural grounds, due to denudation and insufficient excavation. However, it seems that during the occupation of the first and second palaces, bichrome ware and the presumably contemporary gold work were in use. That distinctive pottery hardly penetrated into Egypt, and the application of granules onto gold plate was a technique that flourished in the later Twelfth Dynasty but was missing in the jewelry of Queen Ah-hotep, mother of Ahmose. It is not surprising that both these skills, so foreign to Egypt, did not reappear there till the later years of the Eighteenth Dynasty.

The first four kings, circa 1570–04 B.C., were not represented by scarabs from the mound at 'Ajjul, and no buildings can be dated with certainty to that time. One reliable fact that can suggest the date of the jewelry is a massive gold toggle pin discovered in a grave containing a scarab naming Aa-user-Re, in whose reign the buildings of block A were deserted. Whatever menace was at hand, the inhabitants had time to hide their valuables in expectation of an attack, and the region was left unoccupied thereafter.

The next signs of occupation were concentrated near the northwest corner. Joint cartouches of Hatshepsut and Thutmose III prove an Egyptian presence during their coregency, which ended in 1483 B.C. The quantities of leaf-shaped bronze or copper arrowheads from the upper levels are clear signs of later enemy action, perhaps during Thutmose III's first Syrian campaign. Apart from the fragments of a Mycenaean III-A-2 krater, scattered in area LA, few traces remain of Eighteenth to Nineteenth Dynasty pottery or structures on the mound. It must be assumed that either they were swept away by wind and rain, or the main population had by then moved to the site of modern Gaza but continued to bury their dead in the long-established cemeteries.

OLGA TUFNELL

BIBLIOGRAPHY

B. Maisler (Mazar), *ZDPV* 56 (1933), 186–88 • Abel, *GP* 2, 265 • F. Petrie, *Ancient Gaza* 1–4, London, 1931–34; *idem* (with E. J. H. Mackay and M. A. Murray), *City of Shepherd Kings* and *Ancient Gaza* 5, London, 1952 • W.F. Albright, *AJSIL* 55 (1938), 337–59 • J.R. Stewart, Tell el-'Ajjul, Sydney n.d. (Privately circulated) • K.M. Kenyon, *ADAJ* 3 (1956), 41–55 • C. Epstein, *PEQ* (1961), 137–42 • O. Tufnell, *BIAL* 3 (1962), 1–37 • W.A. Heurtley, *QDAP* 8 (1939) • C. Epstein, *Palestinian Bichrome Ware,* Leiden, 1966 • O. Negbi, *Studies in Mediterranean Archaeology* 25, Göteborg, 1970 • M. Negbi, *IEJ* 21 (1971), 219.

Tel 'Ali, pottery figurine; pre-pottery Neolithic B.

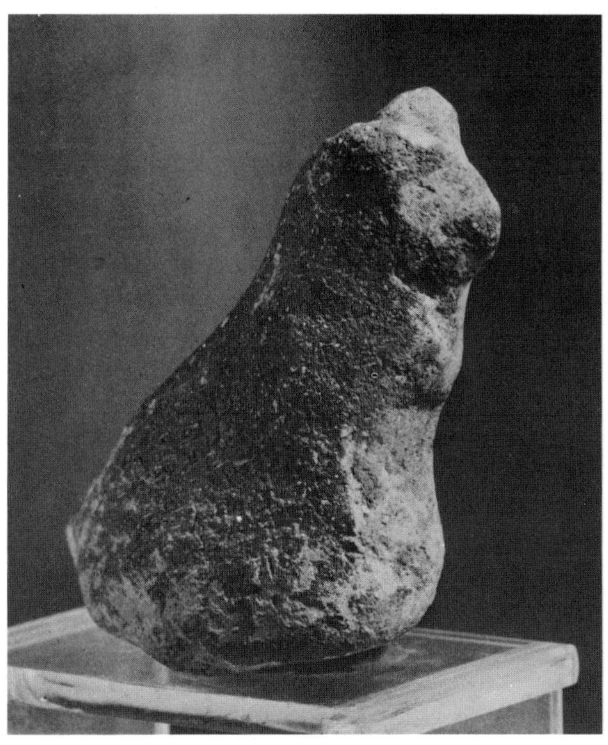

'ALI, TEL

IDENTIFICATION. Tel 'Ali ('Eli, Khirbet esh Sheikh 'Ali), a Neolithic and Chalcolithic site, is situated on a terrace on the slopes of Lower Galilee descending to the Jordan Valley. It stands about 1.5 kilometers (1 mile) southwest of the exit of the Jordan from the Sea of Galilee (map reference 202234), 200 meters below sea level. Due to its position near one of the fords of the Jordan, on the road leading through the Yabneel Valley toward the Yarmuk, it was of considerable importance in the prehistoric and protohistoric periods.

From 1955 to 1959 four seasons of excavations were conducted on the site under the direction of M. Prausnitz on behalf of the Israel Department of Antiquities. An area of 300 square meters was explored, and three trenches were cut. The remains of pre-pottery Neolithic settlements were found to extend over a large area along the terrace, although there was no connection between them. The pottery Neolithic settlements, however — which certainly practiced agriculture on irrigated soil — were situated among the lots cultivated by their inhabitants. The structures of the uppermost layer, dating from Early Chalcolithic, form a large and densely built village. No important remains from the end of the Chalcolithic or the beginning of the Early Bronze Age were found at Tel 'Ali.

EXCAVATIONS

In the lowest level of the mound (stratum 4–B) remains of foundations of round houses and stone implements were uncovered. These were ascribed to pre-pottery Neolithic, also known as Tahunian. Near the mound and on the same terrace, a village settlement was surveyed. It consisted of a group of round houses, contemporaneous with the early remains found on the mound proper.

The basalt objects found in this stratum included long pestles pointed at both ends; carved slabs with sockets that were used as table tops; anvils; and weights of fishing nets, as well as loaf-shaped grinding stones. Among the flint implements were axes, whose working edges were sharpened by transversal blows (tranchet), and especially pointed picks, made of basalt or flint, which were probably used for tilling the soil.

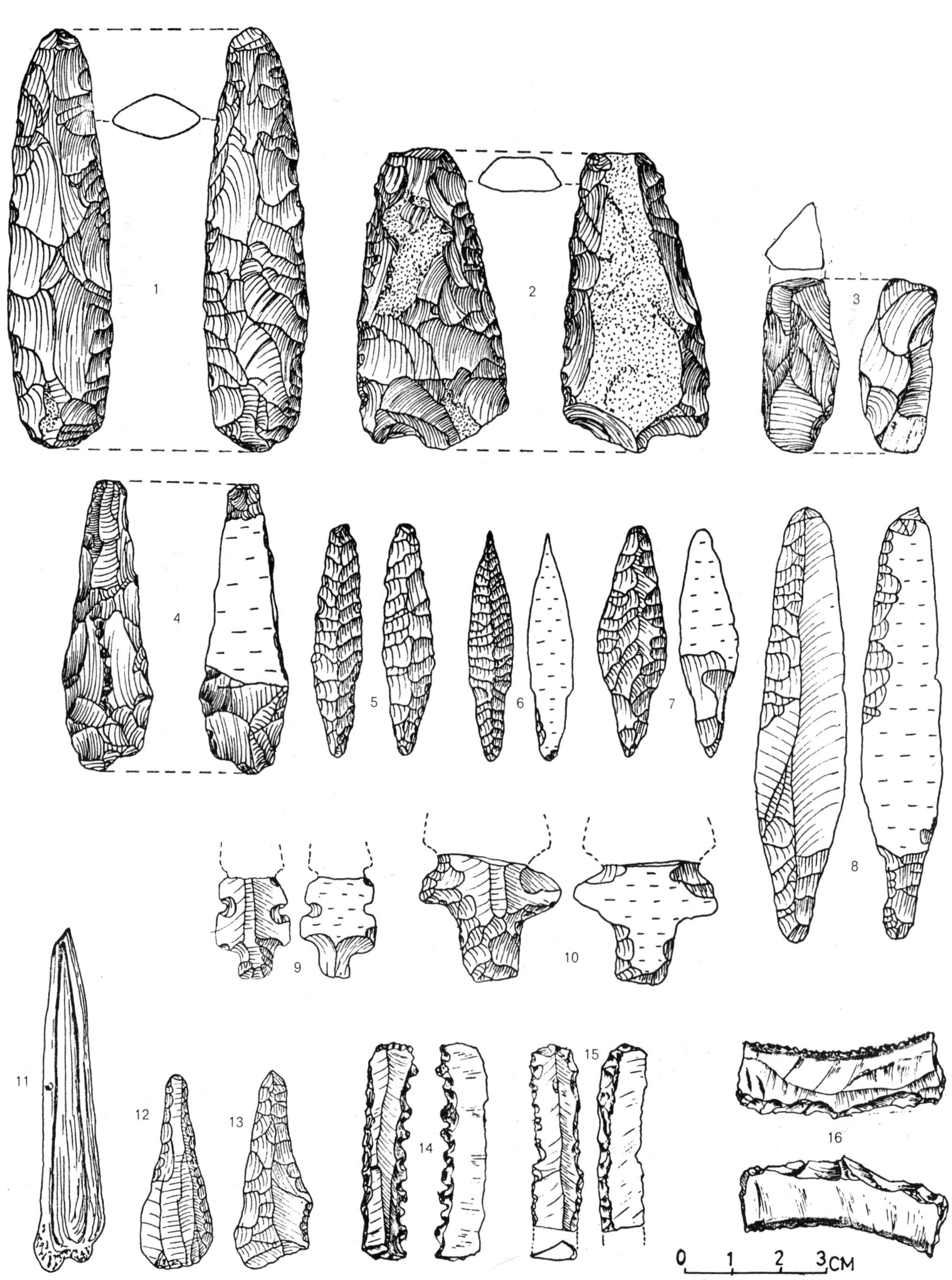
1
2
3
4
5
6
7
8
9
10
11
12
13
14
15
16
0 1 2 3 CM

Pickaxes and net weights show that the main economic activities in the pre-pottery Neolithic village were agriculture in its early stages (cultivation of wild-growing edible grass) and fishing.

On the virgin soil of clay, foundations of buildings were found which were attributed to stratum 4–A, situated between strata 4–B and 3. Clay figurines are ascribed to stratum 4. In stratum 3 no pottery was in evidence. In the same stratum burials were cleared on clay floors, placed along straight walls. The skeletons found there had been decapitated.

In stratum 2, inter alia, a large rectangular building was excavated. Its long walls were built of large, rough stones. Alongside the walls, small cells or rooms were built around an inner courtyard. Stratum 2 contained the earliest pottery found on the site.

In the uppermost level (stratum 1) three stages could be distinguished. The two upper stages (1–A and 1–B) are pre-Ghassulian, and stage 1–B was called, at Jericho, Pottery Neolithic B.

Continuity could be established between strata 3 and 2, but a gap existed between strata 4 and 3 — and perhaps also between strata 2 and 1.

FLINT IMPLEMENTS

Comparison between the flint implements from strata 4–A and 3 and those of strata 2 and 1 reveals several facts:

(a) In the lowest level, stratum 4, the industry of long blades, made of selected pyramidal and bipolar cores, attains its peak.

(b) In strata 4–A and 3 pressure flaking appears as well as a splendid collection of projectile points, for both war and hunting, such as spearheads, javelin points, and arrowheads.

(c) After stratum 4, microliths disappear.

(d) In stratum 3 the ax with its working edge retouched by transversal blows (tranchet) goes out of use and the polished ax appears in its place.

(e) In strata 3–2 the number of sickle and saw blades shows a continuous increase.

(f) From stratum 1–B onward, projectile points disappear, and numerous large flint implements made from flakes and from core waste, cutting tools, scrapers, borers, burins, chisels, and other rough working tools make their appearance.

POTTERY

A figurine of fired clay was found in stratum 4, but pottery vessels appear only in strata 2 and 1. In stratum 2 three kinds of pottery, all handmade, were found. They include the following:

(a) Shallow bowls with round or flat bases, decorated with red-burnished bands alternating with incisions and impressions made in the soft clay before firing. The interior of open bowls also display incised or stabbed decorations. Both sides of the rims are decorated with a red-burnished stripe. While these vessels are fashioned to perfection, the firing is poor.

(b) Large vessels, mostly hole-mouth jars with large lug handles, similar to oval ledge handles.

Selection of flint implements. 1. Adze. 2. Ax with edge broken from use. 3–4. Chisels. 5–7. Leaf-shaped and tanged arrowheads. 8. Tanged spearhead. 9–10. Tanged and notched arrowheads. 11. Bone borer. 12–13. Borers, pressure flaked. 14–15. Neolithic sickle-saw blades. 16. Chalcolithic sickle-saw blade (opposite). Skeleton without head buried beneath floor of stratum III (right).

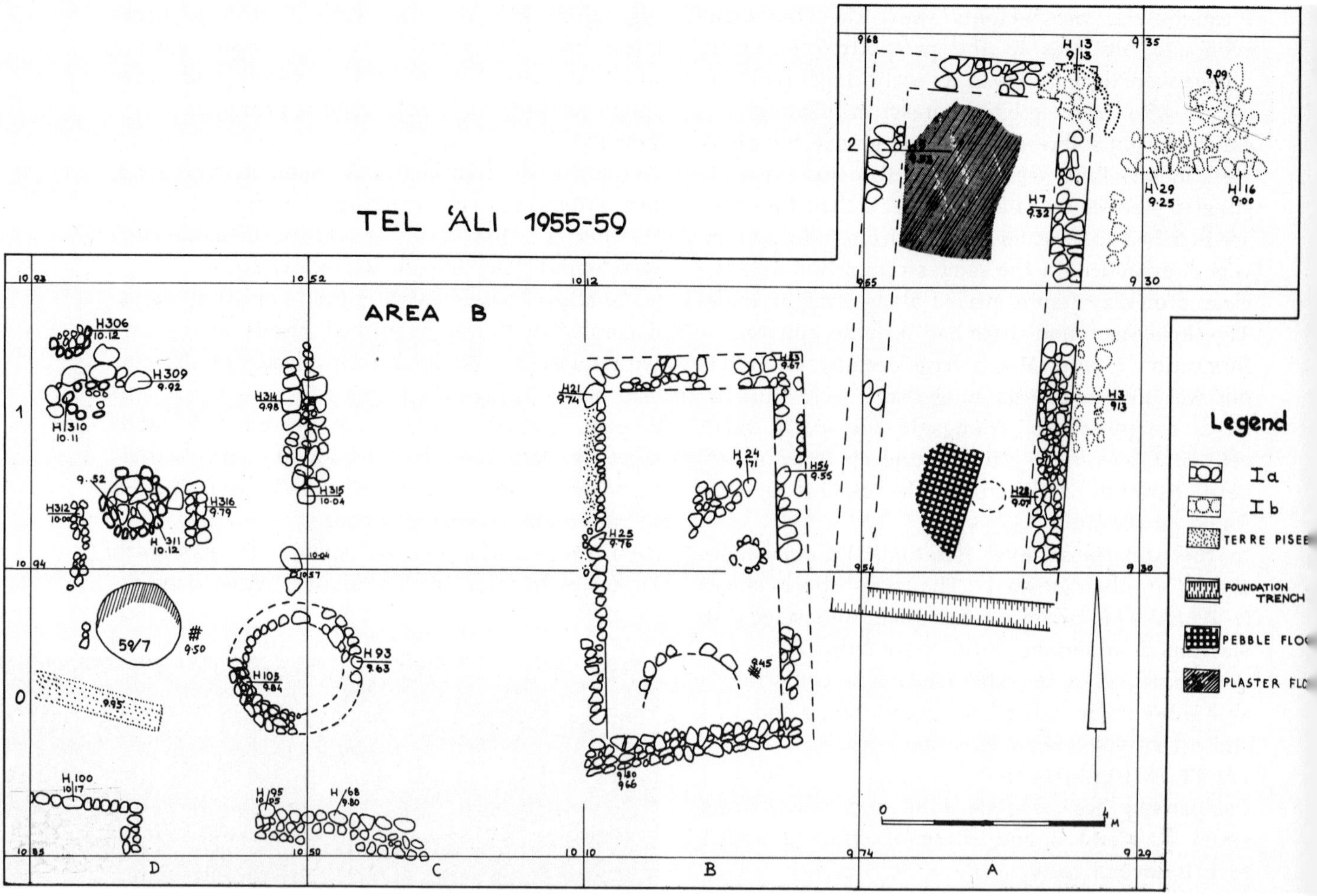

TEL 'ALI 1955-59
AREA B
Legend
Ia
Ib
TERRE PISEE
FOUNDATION TRENCH
PEBBLE FLO
PLASTER FLO
D
C
B
A

This pottery was simple, thick, and coarse, and very poorly fired. The early Neolithic potter used straw as binding material.

(c) A rare type of pottery, similar in quality to that of the first type mentioned but decorated with splashes of paint applied at the top of the vessel and allowed to trickle down over the whole surface to the base. Parallel lines in red, dark red, and even brown are thus formed. Gritrock was used as binding material.

Among other vessels in strata 1–C and 1–B, were two types of pottery. Monochrome pottery with a very fine burnish in various shades of red (black) appears in stratum 1. This differs completely from the so-called gray burnished ware and is akin to the dark-faced burnished ware. The most frequent shapes are cups, shallow and deep bowls, and small vases.

In stratum 1–C pottery with painted decoration is common. These vessels are not incised but have parallel painted stripes and geometric designs. The most characteristic types are bow rims decorated with monochrome burnish or wash or parallel painted bands.

In stratum 1–A fragments of churns and of large vases, decorated with bands of thumb impressions, were discovered.

COMPARATIVE TABLE

STRATUM	PERIOD	PARALLEL SITES
1–A	Ghassul	—
1–B	Early Chalcolithic	Byblos neorecent
1–C	Pottery Neolithic	Byblos neomoyen
2	Pottery Neolithic	Ugarit V-a
3	Pre-pottery Neolithic B	Ugarit V-b–c
4	Pre-pottery Neolithic	

M. Prausnitz

BIBLIOGRAPHY

M.W. Prausnitz, in: *Proceedings, Sixth Pre- and Protohistoric Congress,* II, Rome 1962–65, 216–18; *idem,* in: "From Hunter to Farmer and Trader," Jerusalem/Bonn, 1970, 84–144.

Opposite, counterclockwise: Long rectangular houses with pits and silos, strata I-A and I-B. Stone storage bin; stratum I-B. Stratum III wall in center of picture. (Scale rests on foundation of round hut of stratum IV).

ANAFA, TEL

IDENTIFICATION. Tel Anafa in Upper Galilee is situated at the base of the Golan Heights, between Kibbutz Shamir and Kefar Szold. The mound, about 160 meters long and 110 meters wide, rises 10 meters above the plain (page 66). Judging from the level of the Hellenistic houses that surround the tel, the full depth of habitational debris may reach 12 to 13 meters, an accumulation representing a period of some three millennia. In Hellenistic times the mound served as the acropolis for a much larger lower town. This has not yet been investigated, and chance finds give no evidence for pre-Hellenistic occupation in the plain. After three eight-week seasons of excavations (1968–70), there is still no indication of the ancient name of the town in Hellenistic times, the only period which has thus far been investigated on the mound.

EXCAVATIONS

The excavations of Tel Anafa have been undertaken by the Museum of Art and Archaeology of the University of Missouri, financed by a foreign currency grant from the Smithsonian Institution. In twenty-four weeks some 344 square meters of the tel were dug to depths of as much as 3.5 meters, and the work has only barely penetrated into remains of the Persian period. When it was found that there was more than 3 meters of Hellenistic accumulation, well stratified into three major architectural phases with many subphases, it was obvious that the first investigation should be devoted entirely to the Hellenistic remains. Large areas were therefore opened to permit deeper digging. Work has been carried on thus far in four main areas, which were selected on the basis of topographical considerations and surface indications, aided by aerial photographs and finds obtained from nonarchaeological digging, such as military slit trenches and drainage ditches. Aerial photographs show an enclosure wall around the top of the mound and several large building complexes within it. Many of the walls can be traced on the surface without difficulty. In the northeast corner there are great rocky outcrops.

The Buildings. The northeast sector of the excavations was placed just to the south of the outcropping of rocks and has shown that the peribolos wall was built immediately south of the rocks and, in fact, partially over smaller rocks. No Hellenistic debris was found north of the wall. The peribolos wall, almost 2 meters wide, has been cleared for 14 meters and can be traced farther both to the east and west. It belongs to the middle architectural phase, from the second half of the second century B.C. By the end of that century it had been taken down to the lowest foundation courses. At that time a large structure, probably residential, was built over it, as well as over the flagstone-paved road that ran along the south side of the peribolos wall, sloping down to the east.

This large building provided the best evidence for the last Hellenistic architectural phase, which cannot have lasted much more than thirty years, until the end of the settlement — not later than 75 B.C. Within this short time the building has five subphases. Substantial stone walls, often covered with stucco, are features of this building complex, as are good clay floors (those of the court are partially paved with flagstones), and a colonnade with a single-course stylobate laid on the earliest court floor.

The second architectural phase is best illustrated by a very large building complex in the east–central sector. Here stone walls are preserved to as much as 2.75 meters in height, with the bottom not yet reached. Ashlar blocks used as headers are interspersed with the large fieldstones of which the exterior walls are built. The interior walls were made of mud brick on substantial stone foundations. One section of mud-brick wall is preserved to a height of almost 1.5 meters. The building apparently had a second story. The debris from the collapse of these great stone and brick walls accounts for the 2–2.5 meters of Hellenistic deposit that everywhere marks the end of the second architectural phase. While not yet certain, it appears that the mass of fragmentary stucco decoration, elaborately painted and gilded and

General view from the west.

found largely in the eastern part of this sector, comes from the upper story of this building.

A third sector of excavation is in the northwestern part of the mound, at almost its highest point. Here an Arab cemetery has disturbed the uppermost layers, but the deep deposits of the second architectural phase are largely intact. A courtyard area in the eastern half of this sector has produced a most interesting sequence of double ovens (see below), the latest pair faced with large cobblestones rather than the usual covering of large potsherds set into a heavy coating of mud. Each of the ovens was provided with a flue formed by the neck of a Rhodian wine jar, which lay on the court floor outside the oven and connected with a hole in the oven wall. A deep probe in the western part of this sector revealed very heavy foundations, built of large fieldstones, which constitute the first Hellenistic building phase, provisionally dated to the first half of the second century B.C. A similar foundation is in the east-central sector.

The fourth sector, on the south, is a step trench down the slope of the tel. Since it is outside the acropolis enclosure wall, the architecture is on a smaller scale and comprises houses on either side of a street. The profusion of court floors, often flagged and amply provided with ovens, emphasizes the domestic nature of the area. Remains of the latest architectural phase are scant; those of the second phase are much more substantial. Some earlier walls have also been found. A large area of burned debris, evidence of a violent conflagration, can tentatively be assigned to the end of the Persian period.

Dating. The dating of the architectural phases suggested above is based on the large number of coins and stamped amphora handles that were found. Of the one hundred and eleven coins, only three have beginning dates later than 85–84 B.C., and all three were found in topsoil. Most of the coins are either of Seleucid kings or are city coins, chiefly of Tyre and Sidon, dating between 150

Second cent. B.C.: Stone statuette of deity, probably Demeter (left). Rhodian stampled amphora handle (top). Stone-faced double ovens, with flues made of amphora necks (bottom).

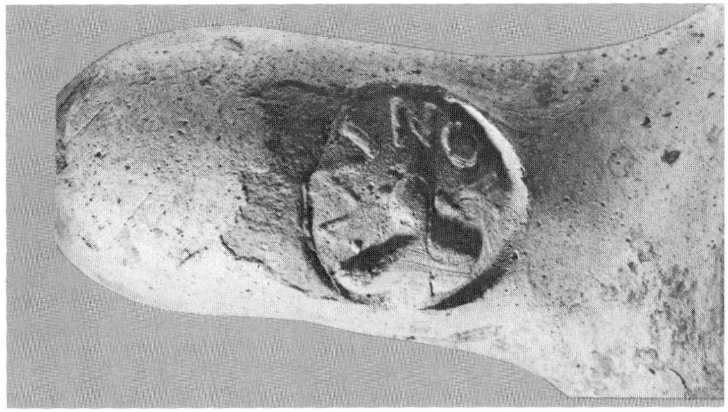

and 85–84 B.C. Only five date earlier than 150 B.C. From the coins it is clear that the earliest Hellenistic architectural phase falls in the first half of the second century B.C., the second phase in the second half of the century, and the third phase in the first quarter of the first century B.C. The abandonment of the settlement certainly came before 75 B.C. All but one of the forty-four stamped amphora handles are Rhodian, and with one exception, they belong to the period between 146 B.C. and a little after 80 B.C. The one exception dates about 220 B.C.

Finds. The finds from Tel Anafa all contribute to an impression of exceptional wealth in the town, especially the very elaborately decorated stucco (page 69), the moldings covered with gold leaf and the richly painted and paneled walls, adorned with columns and pilasters, as well as niches and windows. Floors were covered with mosaics made of exceptionally small stone and glass tesserae. No second-century B.C. parallels for such rich appointments have yet been found in Israel.

Equally unparalleled is the abundance and variety of molded glass vessels found everywhere on the site in levels beginning about 150 B.C. Fragments of about seven hundred and fifty glass bowls and cups, conical or hemispherical, with cut lines on the interior and/or exterior, or ribbed, have been found thus far. Thus, the number in use during the seventy-five years of the settlement's history, both on the acropolis and in the lower town, must have run to many tens of thousands. Yet glass was still a scarce material and glass vessels of this kind have been likened to precious metals in cost and rarity. The only explanation for their abundance at Tel Anafa must be that they were made nearby. This must also be true for the fine red-slipped pottery, which also appeared at Tel Anafa about 150 B.C., and which occurs in great quantities (page 69). No other Hellenistic site has produced the quantity and variety of these red wares known from Tel Anafa, and it seems, therefore, that it should be considered a local ware.

The repertory of semifine, undecorated, and

Left to right, top to bottom: Bronze ladle; second century B.C. *Bowl of bronze ladle; second century* B.C. *(bottom and full view). East Greek relief bowl; second century* B.C. *Red-ware plate with graffito; second century* B.C. *Ashlar block decorated with painted and gilded stucco.*

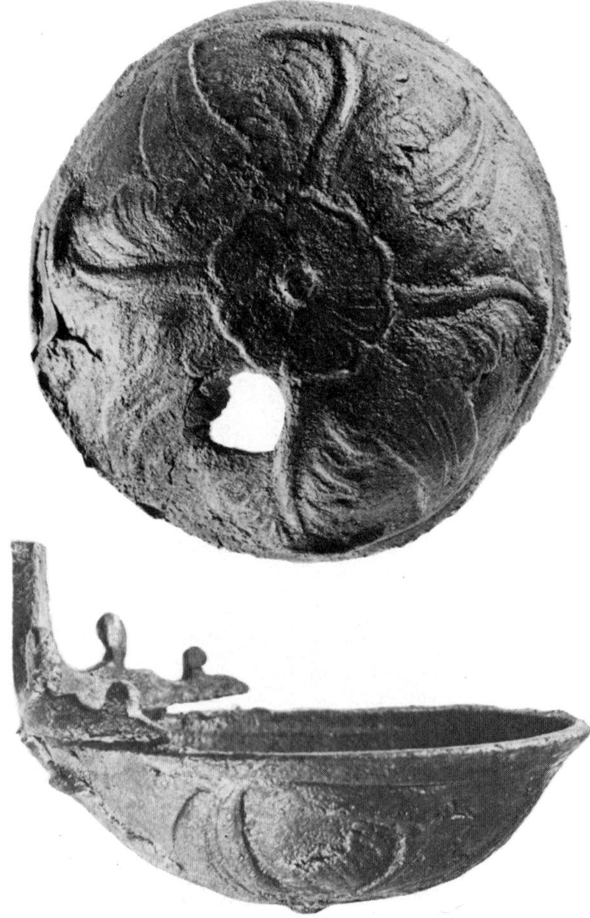

kitchen pottery is equally large. Imported fine pottery, like the many Rhodian wine jars, is largely of East Greek origin, indicating a flourishing trade with this region. A great variety of Hellenistic lamps has been found, but Tel Anafa is particularly rich in the type decorated with two figures of erotes flanking the fill hole, so much so that these too may be considered as having been made locally.

The rich and varied metal finds from Tel Anafa are are equally indicative of the town's wealth. While very few objects of silver and gold were found, fine bronze vessels occur, as well as a multiplicity of iron utensils and weapons. A small cache of semiprecious jewels, beautifully cut, found together with four glass "gems," are of types known in elaborate Hellenistic jewelry.

The striking Greek nature of the town is clearly attested in the written documents found. Besides the coins and stamped amphora handles, the many graffiti on the red ware are all in Greek. Only on one clay sealing is there a single line in a West Semitic alphabet, not yet identified; the other three lines are Greek. Unfortunately, none of the written documents gives any clue as to the name of the site.

SUMMARY

The history of the site in Hellenistic times is already known in general outline. Founded at least by the early second century B.C. under the Seleucids, the town flourished until the end of the first quarter of the first century B.C., when it probably fell to the forces of Alexander Janneus, who incorporated the province of Gaulanitis into the Hasmonaean Kingdom before his death in 76 B.C.

S. WEINBERG

BIBLIOGRAPHY

S. Weinberg, *MUSE,* Annual of the Museum of Art and Archaeology, University of Missouri, 3 (1969), 16–23 • Gladys D. Weinberg, *Journal of Glass Studies* 12 (1970), 17–27 • S. Weinberg, *MUSE* 4 (1970), 15–24; *idem, Qadmoniot* 3 (1970), 135–38 (Hebrew); *idem,* The Israel Museum, Excavation Exhibit at the Rockefeller Museum, No. 1, 1970; *idem, MUSE* 5 (1971), 8–16; *idem, IEJ* 21 (1971), 86–109.

APHEK (SHARON)

IDENTIFICATION. Tel Rosh ha'Ayin (Arabic, Tell Ras el'Ain) lies very near the source of the Yarkon River. It is generally identified with biblical Aphek (Joshua 12:18, etc.). This identification is based on the reference to the tower of Aphek by Josephus (*War* II, 513). The site is probably that of the Aphek mentioned in the Egyptian Execration Texts of the nineteenth century B.C., in Egyptian documents of the Eighteenth Dynasty, in the Bible, in Assyrian sources dating to the time of Esarhaddon, and in an Aramaic letter from the sixth century B.C. This was also the site of Pegae (Πηγαί, the "sources") also called Arethusa in the Hellenistic period, and of the town Antipatris, built by Herod. In the Crusader period it was called the Tower of the Silent Fountains (*Le Toron aux Fontaines Sourdes*). In the seventeenth century the Turks built on the mound a stronghold or a fortified khan, called Qal'at Ras el'Ain, the remains of which still survive.

EXPLORATION

In 1923 Albright conducted a survey on the mound and collected Middle and Late Bronze Age pottery as well as Israelite Age I shards. In his opinion these confirmed the identification of the site with Aphek. Hellenistic and Roman pottery was also found.

EXCAVATIONS

In 1935–36 two areas and two test pits were excavated under the supervision of J. Ory on the north side of the mound in connection with installations for the projected Jerusalem water supply. In the first area (42 by 18 meters), dug on the upper part of the north slope, Early Bronze Age I and Middle Bronze Age II pottery was uncovered as well as sections of two city walls ascribed to these periods. It should be noted, however, that the information obtained regarding the exact stratigraphic relation of the pottery contexts to the walls was inadequate. The wall ascribed to Early Bronze Age I is 2.5 meters wide; it is built of uniformly hewn rubble on virgin soil, and it appears to have been subsequently repaired with brickwork. The city wall ascribed to the Middle Bronze Age II (traced for 13 meters) is about 4 meters wide and built of brick. It runs along the line of the earlier wall but at a generally higher level.

The second area (about 42 by 12 meters) was excavated at the northern limit of the mound, about 40 meters west of the former area. The lowest stratum reached in this area contained four built graves and two open graves dating to the Middle Bronze Age II-A. The built graves are rectangular in shape, 2.2 meters to 2.6 meters long, .75 to 1. meter wide, and .6 to .9 deep (one, evidently the burial of a child, is smaller). All are oriented east-west, the dead being buried with their heads to the east and their knees bent. Only the long sides of the rectangular grave pits were lined with masonry (three to five courses of partly dressed stones). The short sides were left without facing. Large stone blocks laid transversely formed the roofing. The graves had a recess in one of the long walls in the bottom course. In one grave two such recesses were found containing bones and pottery. According to the excavator there was evidence of secondary burial in these graves. Among the vessels found in the built graves is a group of jugs with painted geometric designs of triangles filled with a net pattern (on the shoulder). This style of ornamentation is often considered evidence of the possible connection of the Middle Bronze Age II-A pottery with the Khabur ware.

In the stratum above the graves a brick wall on rubble foundation was uncovered. Its width is uncertain since it was cut at an angle. The wall, which overlay one of the built graves, is dated by the pottery found above its foundation to the Middle Bronze Age II-B. It may be assumed that this wall and the brick wall uncovered in the first area form parts of the same city wall. Late remains, including a massive Byzantine wall (traced for 19 meters) and a lime pit (or kiln) of undetermined (perhaps medieval) date, have disturbed the upper Middle Bronze Age II stratum.

The only information given by the excavators regarding the two test pits was that an Egyptian scarab ascribed to the Thirteenth Dynasty was found in one of them (at a level corresponding generally to that of the built graves) and that the Late Bronze and Iron ages were entirely unrepresented. Further excavations were carried out in 1961 by A. Eitan on behalf of the Department

Plain of Accho; Aegean kylix, from a tomb.

of Antiquities and Museums. These were in three areas (I, II, III) along the foot of the southeast slope of the mound.

Area I. In this section near the southeastern corner of the mound, a thick ash layer containing flints, bones, and Early Bronze Age I pottery was uncovered .3 to 1.5 meters below the surface, probably on virgin soil. No building remains were found. A grave pit containing a single burial and a few pottery vessels dating to the Middle Bronze Age II, as well as a pit (penetrating into the Early Bronze Age I ash layer) with several Late Bronze Age II *bilbils,* were also uncovered in this area. Early Bronze Age I and Late Bronze Age II finds were discovered only in area I.

Area II. When this 60 by 6 meters section along the foot of the slope, about 150 meters north of area I, was excavated, two strata were distinguished. In the lower one a paved strip 5 meters wide, built of rubble stones laid closely together and bordered on both sides with large stones, is in all probability a section of a paved road that led toward the mound (possibly to a gate). A bronze bowl and other objects were found together, somewhat lower, at the edge of the road. They had probably been deposited in a pit.

The upper stratum consists of a surface of rubble stones, forming what seems to be some kind of rough pavement, which extends all over the excavated area. The pottery found on the pavement is predominantly Middle Bronze Age II, but it is mixed with some Iron Age pottery.

Pottery, coins, and other objects belonging to the Hellenistic, Roman, and Byzantine periods were also found in area II, but not in a clear stratigraphic context. A built cist tomb, uncovered at the southeast edge of the area, contained a single burial with remains of a wooden coffin and a few objects dating to the first half of the second century A.D.

The Late Bronze Age II and Iron Age pottery from areas I and II, although not found on the mound proper, indicate some occupation at the site during these periods. The conclusion reached from the previous excavation — that there was a gap from the sixteenth century B.C. to the Hellenistic period — should be corrected accordingly.

Area III. In this area, situated on the lower part of the slope between areas I and II, the remains of a mausoleum from the Roman period were dis-

Coin of Antipatris; first half of the third century A.D. (above). Bottle; MBA II-A (below).

covered. Built and paved with ashlar masonry, it consists of a burial chamber (measuring 3.5 by 3.5 meters, its walls 1.2 meters thick), an anteroom (4.7 by 3 meters), and an open courtyard (10 by 8.5 meters). A stairway descending to the courtyard gave access to the mausoleum from the west. A large stone sarcophagus was found standing on the floor of the burial chamber, which was surrounded along three walls by a built bench, or shelf, one course high. A wide recess in the southern wall, together with the shelf along this wall, formed a raised platform on this side of the chamber. Its doorway, in the opposite wall, leading from the anteroom, was provided with a sliding door, as indicated by the channel cut in the threshold stones, extending into the hollow wall to the west.

The eastern façade of the anteroom, entirely open to the courtyard, served as an entrance to the complex. Several ornamented stones, belonging to an arch that stood above the entrance, were found lying on the threshold. A built cist tomb containing a stone sarcophagus was discovered underneath the courtyard pavement, in front of the anteroom façade.

A layer of ashes .5 meters thick and the broken objects found scattered everywhere show that the mausoleum came to a violent end. Only the cist tomb containing the stone sarcophagus escaped destruction. The objects found in it, mainly glass vessels, date to the late first century or first half of the second century A.D. Fragments of four other sarcophagi of the same type, found mostly in the burial chamber, probably stood on the shelves and in the recess before being smashed.

The finds in the mausoleum are divided chronologically into two groups. Apart from the sarcophagi and the finds in the cist tomb, the earlier group, dating from the end of the first century or the first half of the second century A.D. consists mainly of glass vessels, possibly from the broken coffins. In the later group, dating from the second half of the third century to the first half of the fourth century A.D., amphorae and store jars (found mostly in the anteroom) are more common. According to the finds, the mausoleum was built in the late first century or early second century A.D. and existed for 150 to 200 years until its violent destruction, which occurred in the late third or fourth century A.D. A. EITAN

BIBLIOGRAPHY

History of the site and its identification: W.F. Albright, *JPOS* 3 (1923), 50ff; *idem, BASOR* 11 (1923), 6ff; *idem, BASOR* 81 (1941), 18–19 • S.E. Loewenstamm, *Enc. Miqr.* 1, 501–03 (with bibliography) (Hebrew) • B. Mazar, *EI* 3 (1954), 24 (Hebrew) • S. Yeivin, *ibid.,* 35 (Hebrew) • M. Noth, *Das Buch Josua,* Tuebingen, 1953, 72 • M. Avi-Yonah, *The Holy Land,* Grand Rapids, Mich., 1966, 145–47.

Excavations: J. Ory–J.B. Illife, *QDAP* 5 (1936), 111–26 • J. Ory, *ibid.* 6 (1937), 99–120 • A. Eitan, *IEJ* 12 (1962), 151–52; *idem, RB* 69 (1962), 407–08; *idem, EI* 8 (1967), 114–18 (Hebrew); *idem, 'Atiqot* 5 (1969), 49–68 (Hebrew — with English summary) • M. Kochavi, *IEJ* 22 (1972), 238–39.

Jugs; MBA II-A.

ARAD

HISTORY AND IDENTIFICATION OF THE SITE. Arad, an important city in the Negev in the Canaanite and Israelite periods, has been identified by most scholars with Tel 'Arad, situated about 30 kilometers (18½ miles) east-northeast of Beer-sheba (map reference 162075). It is mentioned in the Bible as a fortified Canaanite city in the eastern Negev. "King of Arad, which dwelt in the South" prevented the Israelites from penetrating directly from the Negev into the Judean mountains (Numbers 21:1, 33:40). Arad appears in the list of conquered Canaanite cities (Joshua 12:14) but nothing is said about its conquest, except that "the children of Hobab [the Kenite]," Moses' father-in-law (Judges 4:11), went up out of the city of palmtrees with the children of Judah into the wilderness of Judah, which is in the south of Arad. They dwelt with the people [Amalekites] (Judges 1:16).

Since an Israelite sanctuary was found in the excavated site, it can be assumed that the Kenite clan related to Moses is mentioned in connection with some focal acropolis that became a royal Israelite sanctuary in the days of Solomon. Arad also appears in the list of the cities of southern Judah (Joshua 15:21 — reading Arad for Eder) and in Pharaoh Shishak's list of cities drawn up after his campaign in the fifth year of Rehoboam's reign: "Hgrm 'rd rbt 'rd n-bt Yrḥm" (numbers 107–12), that is, "The *ḥagrim* ["the citadels"] of greater Arad and of the house of Jeruḥam (Jerahmeel)."

There is no further information on the site except for the testimony of Eusebius (*Onomasticon* 3, 14), who mentions a village by the name of Arad, situated four miles from Molestha (identified with Khirbet Kseifeh) and twenty miles from Hebron, distances that agree with the location of Tel 'Arad.

The mound, which has retained its ancient name to this day (Tell 'Arad in Arabic), dominates the plains of the eastern Negev. The small mound (the upper citadel) with its deep stratification rises prominently above an extensive area of low hills (the lower city). The bedrock crops up in many places. Because the site lacks a spring or well, the

water supply depends entirely upon the storage of rainwater in cisterns. The site stands on a hill of Eocenic rock that contrasts strongly with the white Senonian rock characteristic of the area. Since the Eocenic rock is impervious to water, it was possible to dig cisterns capable of retaining water. The site was therefore well suited for a settlement in antiquity.

EXPLORATIONS

The excavations at Arad were sponsored by the Israel Exploration Society; the Hebrew University, Jerusalem; and the Department of Antiquities and Museums. The first season (1962) was directed jointly by Y. Aharoni and Ruth Amiran and concentrated mainly on the high mound, with only exploratory excavations undertaken in the lower, Canaanite city. The second season (1963) was directed by Y. Aharoni, assisted by M. Kochavi. Excavations were conducted both on the mound proper and in the lower city. From the third season (1964) onward, Y. Aharoni directed the excavations on the mound, and Ruth Amiran directed those of the Early Bronze Age city. The excavations on the mound continued yearly until 1967; excavations of the lower city were conducted from 1962 to 1966, and were resumed in 1971.

Y. Aharoni

EXCAVATIONS

The Lower City. Six seasons of excavations were carried out in the Early Bronze Age city. The designation "city" is used here with good cause: The size of the settlement, selection of the location, water-supply system, well-planned and well-built fortifications, functional division of the city area into private dwelling quarters and a public-buildings center, all clearly indicate a developed conception of urbanization and planning.

TOPOGRAPHY. The city, circa 90 dunams (22 acres) in area within its fortifications, lies on the moderate slopes of a horseshoe-shaped depression eroded into the sides of a chalky hill. The city wall, 2.3 to 2.4 meters thick and circa 1,200 meters in circumference, was built on the crest line of this configuration — the most suitable line for defense. The site appears to have been chosen for

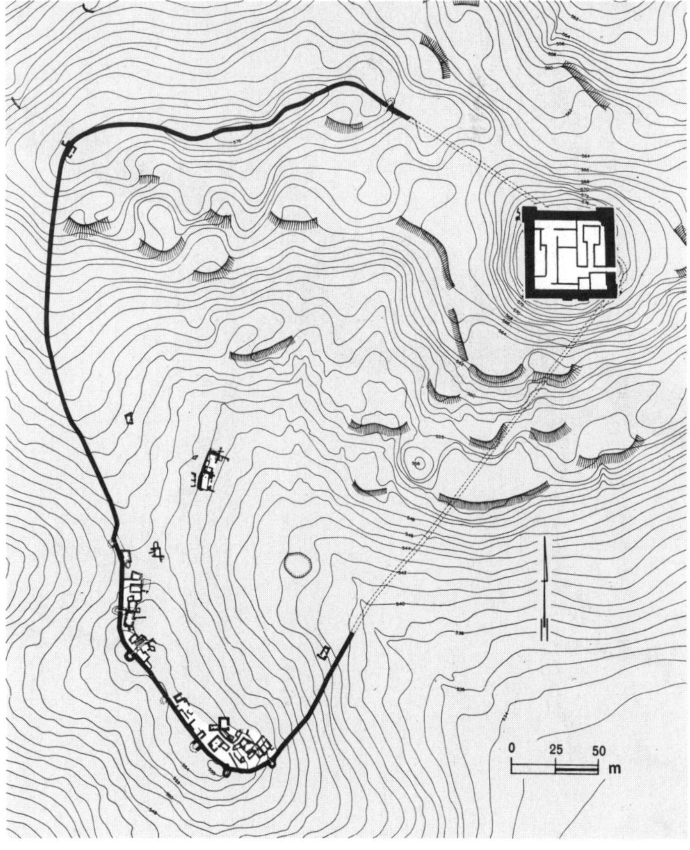

Houses and streets in the EBA II lower city (opposite). Part of wall and bastion of lower EBA city; stratum II (top right). General plan of site (bottom right).

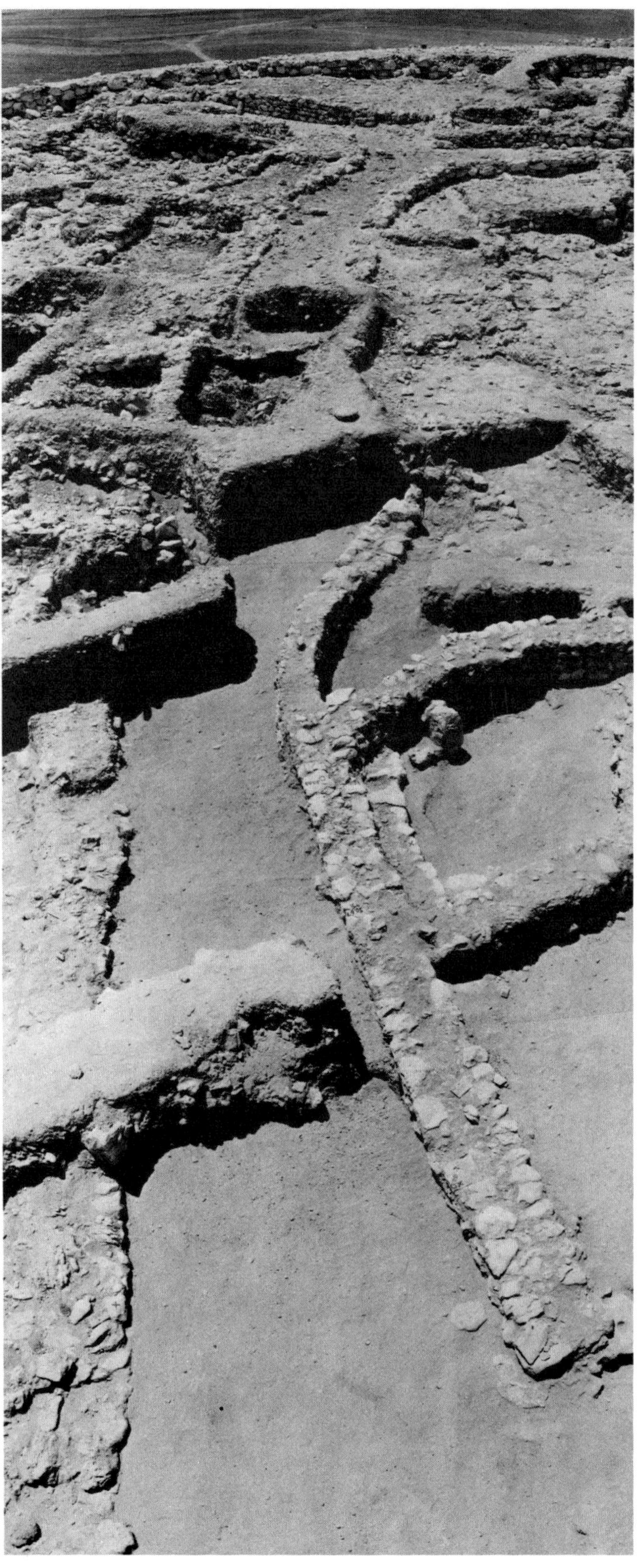

settlement because of its topography, which facilitates the maximum drainage of runoff rainwater into the center of the city. Evidence for this assumption is provided by the artificial depression in the lowest part of the bowl-shaped configuration, most probably the reservoir for storing the rainwater thus collected.

EXCAVATED AREAS. During the first seasons the areas of excavation were distributed throughout the site so as to probe into its various parts. Areas H, N, and K were located adjacent to the city wall on its western flank; M on its southern flank; R in the northeastern corner; and S in the northwestern corner. Area L is in the middle of the slope near the center, while area T lies in the center of the city at the bottom of the bowl-shaped configuration. All the areas except T proved to be parts of dwelling quarters. Area T produced a twin temple, part of a public building, and part of another public-building complex. Sections of the city wall were partly excavated, and partly only traced, to a total length of circa 970 meters. Since 1965, work has concentrated on the enlargement of areas K and T. The aim has been to study as extensive a dwelling area as possible in K, with its houses, streets, open spaces, and stratification. The aim in T is to obtain more and better evidence for the assumption that all the public buildings of the city were purposefully located in its center.

STRATIGRAPHY. The city had four successive strata of settlement: The lowest, stratum IV, predates the erection of the city wall — the people settled in natural caves and caverns. Strata III and II represent the flourishing period of the city, while stratum I follows upon the final destruction of the city at the end of stratum II. The end of stratum III may possibly have come about by enemy attack, and the same seems to be true for the final destruction of II. The stratigraphic relationship between the city strata is relatively easy to distinguish, because they appear immediately beneath the surface. The site has not been disturbed. Materially, the four strata follow each other with no apparent gap and, to judge by the material culture, with no changes in the ethnic composition of the population.

FORTIFICATIONS. The city's fortifications show a knowledge of planning of an organized community and a distinctive military-architectural style. The

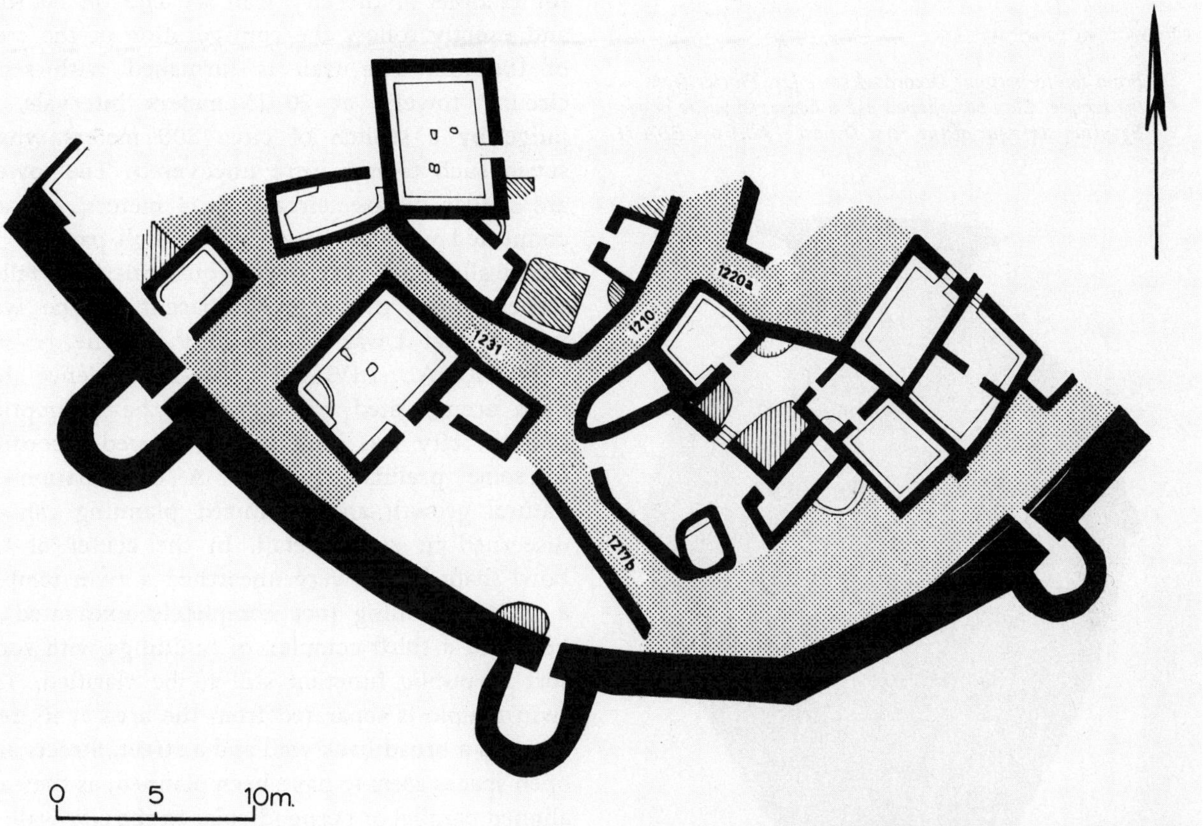

Area K: View of houses and streets descending the slope toward the main water reservoir, looking west (opposite).
Plan of area K: city wall with semicircular towers, houses, and streets (above). Area T: the twin temple; bamah and laver in the courtyard (right). EBA temple in lower city.
existing restored (below).

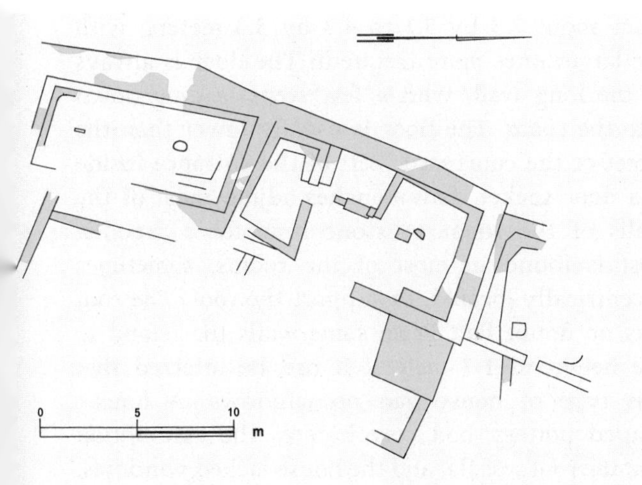

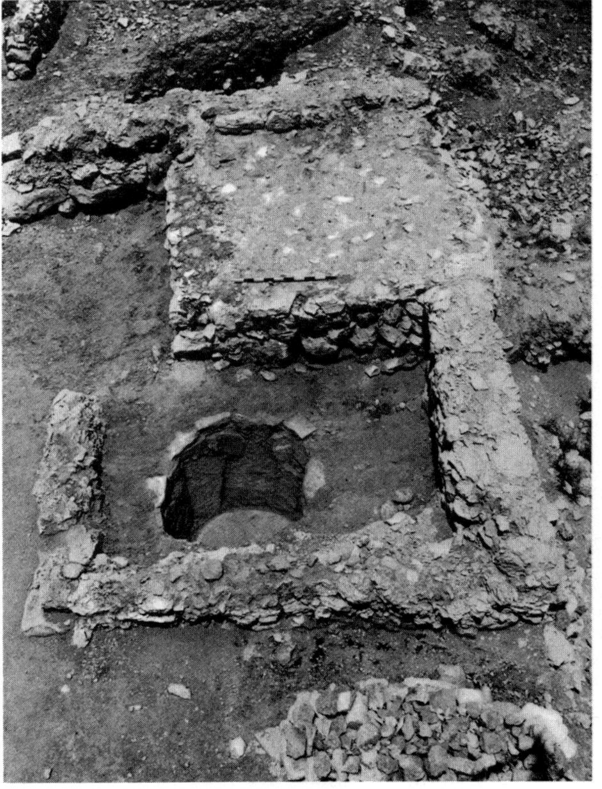

From top to bottom: Decorated store jar. Platter from the temple. Clay box shaped like a house. Opposite page: Egyptian store jar of the First Dynasty. All from EBA II.

foundations of the city wall are laid on bedrock and exactly follow the configuration of the crest of the hill. The wall is furnished with semicircular towers, at 20–25 meters intervals, to judge by a stretch of circa 200 meters where seven such towers were uncovered. The towers are similar in size, circa 3 by 4 meters, and are connected with the city area through passages in the wall. The very large quantities of fallen stones filling the houses adjacent to the wall indicate that it was built entirely of stone.

FUNCTIONAL DIVISION. Much evidence has been accumulated corroborating the assumption that the city was built and developed according to some preliminary plan. A combination of natural growth and organized planning can be discerned in every detail. In the center of the bowl-shaped city were unearthed a twin temple, a public building (not completely excavated as yet), and a third complex of buildings with some sort of public function still to be clarified. The twin temple is separated from the area at its rear by both a broad back wall and a street. Streets and open spaces seem to have been planned, as they are aligned parallel or perpendicular to the city wall.

THE DWELLING HOUSES. This is perhaps the most conspicuous feature of the architecture of Arad, and of the Early Bronze Age II in general. One type of house is typical of the three strata of the city (III, II, I). The Arad House is of the broad-room type, containing in its basic unit one main room, an additional room (kitchen or storeroom), and a courtyard. Variations and developments of this are found, especially in stratum II, the apex of the city. The size of the rooms ranges from about 7.3 by 5.1 to 4.3 by 3.3 meters, with the larger ones more frequent. The door is always in the long wall, with a few steps leading down into the room. The floor is usually lower than the street or the courtyard. Left of the entrance inside is a door socket. Low benches adjoin most of the walls of the room. A stone base for a wooden post is found in most of the rooms, sometimes eccentrically located, to support the roof. The roof was no doubt flat. From some walls that stand to the height of 1.7 meters, it can be inferred that this type of house had no windows. A house-shaped pottery box corroborates the assumption that the roof was flat and the house lacked windows. The houses contain great quantities of broken pottery vessels. Mortars and grinding querns were found in almost every room. There was also charred grain in large quantities, some of it still adhering to the bottoms of containers (such as hole-mouth pithoi or mortars). Fragments of poorly baked clay receptacles found in some houses may have served as storage bins for grain. There were also copper tools, flint implements of various kinds, bone needles, bone spatulae (for weaving?), beads of various materials, and mother-of-pearl pendants.

THE TWIN TEMPLE AND OTHER PUBLIC BUILDINGS. The broad-room type also dominates the larger architecture, *i.e.,* the public buildings. The twin temple is composed of two large halls with a short wall in common. Both halls open onto courtyards, and both face east (have their entrances in the eastern façade). The northern of the two temples was built in stratum III and underwent changes in stratum II. The southern hall was added in the latter stratum. The northern temple has a bamah in the courtyard, built into its eastern façade, and a laver in the corner of the courtyard immediately next to the bamah. Four bases for posts stood in this hall in its early phase.

In stratum II the hall was divided into a closed room, a small cella, and a covered (?) smaller hall. The southern hall has two bases for posts, one of a large stelelike character. This hall was full of pottery and other objects. Contrary to the assemblage normally found in private dwellings, here not one vessel of the hole-mouth, cooking-pot type was found.

This twin temple is similar to the Early Bronze Age I twin temple of Megiddo (4050 +4047), the Chalcolithic temple of En-Gedi, and the Early Bronze Age II temple on the acropolis of Ai (in its original shape). North of the twin temple, again having in common with it the short northern wall, part of another public building was excavated.

South of the twin temple, at a distance of some 5 to 7 meters, excavation of a complex building was started, probably also of a public nature. One room, as yet only half excavated, shows benches and bases for posts and large quantities of pottery vessels. A small stone stele was also found, made of the local chalk. On its face is an incised scene: two identical human figures, one upright and one lying within a frame. Both have their arms raised

and fingers outstretched, and both have an ear of grain instead of a human head. It is possible that they represent one and the same being, and the ear of grain may help to interpret them as representing Dumuzi of the Grain, one of the aspects of the god Tammuz.

In addition to the pottery and other utensils, mention should be made of a cylinder seal and two stamp seals, all made of the local chalk, found together with the stele just mentioned. They are evidence of a local artistic style in seal carving and sculpture. Clay figurines of animals and one statuette of a bull corroborate this conclusion.

THE POTTERY. Much of the crushed and broken pottery in the houses and the public buildings

Counterclockwise: Pillar-handled jar and another specimen showing details of upper part. Small jar, red-slipped and highly burnished, with four degenerated long handles. Pithos with unusual rope decoration at the base of the neck. Hole-mouthed jar. Globular hole-mouthed cooking pots.

(temples) could be restored. The corpus includes various kinds of vessels: bowls, platters, bowl lamps, juglets and jugs, small bowl cups, and a series of different-size jars — small, medium-size, and pithoi. In addition, there are hole-mouth jars, hole-mouth cooking pots, kraters, and hole-mouth pithoi. Of special interest is the quantity of painted vessels in the style known until now only in small juglets from Beth-Shean, Jericho, Beth Yeraḥ, and Ai, and from Egypt in First Dynasty tombs. The vessels from Arad are big, medium, or small jars. As yet no specimens of the jug types were found. This style appears at Arad already in stratum III, but its flourishing period is stratum II.

FOREIGN RELATIONS. The Egyptian pottery found in each of the four strata (together with small Egyptian objects) shows clearly that the economy of the city included distant trade, alongside its basic field cultivation and flocks. Imports from afar are also attested by the temper noted in the clay of the hole-mouth cooking pots. Petrographical analysis by J. Glass has proved with certainty its nonlocal origin — namely, weathered sand produced by granite rock. To find such sand the potters of Arad had to travel to the Araba or the valleys of southern Sinai. In addition, on the basis of the Egyptian pottery at Arad together with the Canaanite painted and plain pottery from the tombs of the kings of the First Dynasty in Egypt, a close synchronism

between Canaan and Egypt during this period can be established. The following table shows the synchronism resulting from the study of the Arad and the Egyptian material.

Stratum IV	Second half of the EBA I	First kings — Narmer and Hor-aha
Stratum III	EBA II	Djer, Uwadji, and part of Den
Stratum II	EBA II	Den, perhaps to Semrekhet
Stratum I (squatters)	End of EBA II	Some time at the end of the First Dynasty

Stratum IV is thus understood to be a prologue of the city, before the city wall was built by the same people who subsequently populated strata III–I of the city.

The excavations at Arad also revealed the existence of an earlier settlement or settlements in that area, namely the Chalcolithic remains of pits dug in the loess soil. These pits are probably bases for reed huts, containing pottery and other objects typical of the Beersheba-Ghassul culture. The Arad Basin seems to have been part of the Beersheba culture during the Chalcolithic period, and this is gradually coming to light under the Arad city strata.

RUTH AMIRAN

Aerial view of the Israelite city at the end of the fourth season of excavations (1965) (above). Fragment of a bowl on which the name Arad is scratched seven times (in mirror image) (left).

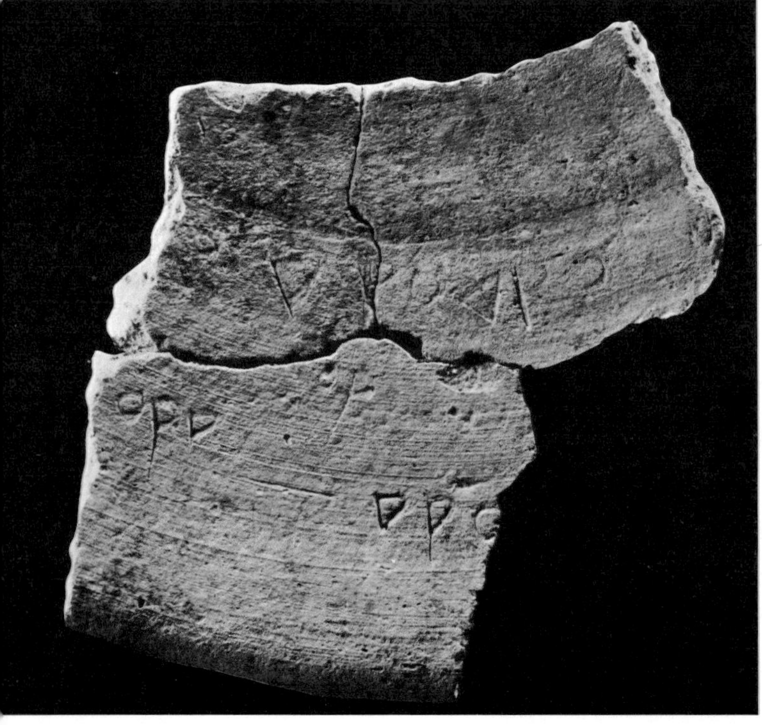

The Upper Mound.

THE ISRAELITE CITADELS. A new settlement on the site arose after an interval of about 1,500 years. Its center was on the high mound that extended along the southeastern ridge surrounding the ancient city. The first settlement here apparently goes back to the twelfth to eleventh centuries B.C. From the days of Solomon to the Roman period, strong fortresses were built here with settlements around them.

On the high mound some remains of the Early Bronze Age were reached. Above them twelve strata appear in the following order:

STRATUM	PERIOD	APPROXIMATE DATES	BUILDINGS
I	Arab	10th–16th centuries A.D.	Graves
II	Early Arab	7th–8th centuries A.D.	Inn
III	Early Roman	70–106 A.D.	Citadel
IV	Hellenistic	3rd–2nd centuries B.C.	Tower and settlement
V	Persian	5th–4th centuries B.C.	Settlement
VI	Iron Age II-C	Late 7th century — beginning of the 6th century (Josiah–Zedekiah)	Citadel
VII	Iron Age II-C	7th century B.C. (Manasseh)	Citadel
VIII	Iron Age II-C	Late 8th century B.C. (Hezekiah)	Citadel
IX	Iron Age II-C	8th century B.C. (Uzziah)	Citadel
X	Iron Age II-B	9th century B.C.	Citadel
XI	Iron Age II-A	The second half of the 10th century B.C. (Solomon)	Citadel
XII	Iron Age I	12th–11th centuries B.C.	Settlement

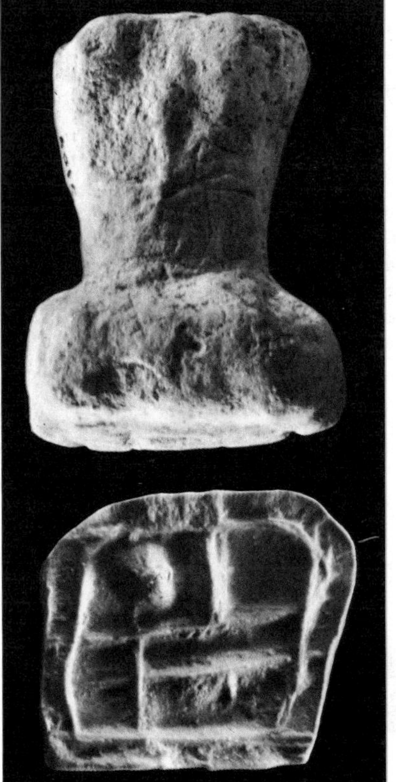

Seal and its impression, possibly plan of citadel (left). The IA citadel (end of 8th cent. B.C.). 1. Temple. 2. Water system. 3. Wall. 4. Retaining walls. 5. Citadel gate used in the 9th cent. 6. New citadel gate. ▬ *existing* ▭ *conjectured.*

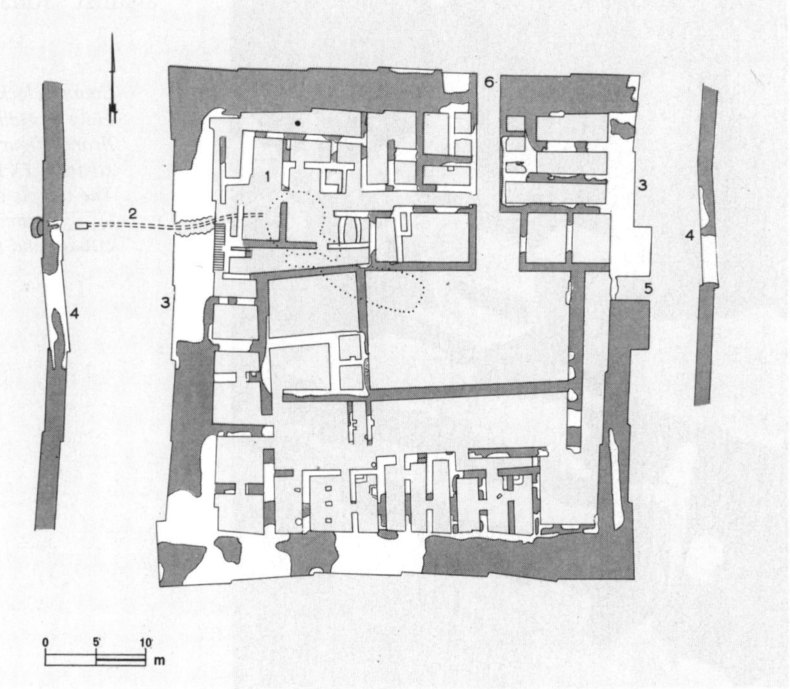

The six Israelite citadels are the largest and strongest structures on the site. The earlier citadels measured circa 50 by 55 meters; the later ones were somewhat smaller. The earliest fortress (stratum XI) was surrounded by a casemate wall with protruding towers. It was erected on an artificial fill, .5 to 1. meter thick, which was heaped up to level the area and to increase its height. In stratum X, which dates to the ninth century, the fortress was surrounded by a solid wall 3 to 4 meters thick, with small indentations at intervals of 9 to 10 meters. This wall continued in use also in strata IX–VII, with further parallel inner walls added later.

The last Israelite fortress (stratum VI) was encircled by a casemate wall with projecting towers, similar to the citadels of Kadesh-Barnea, Ḥorvat Uzza, and elsewhere. In a number of walls of stratum VI, dressed stones were found with margins that had first been trimmed with a broad chisel and later with a toothed adze, while the center was left rough and unworked. All these stones were reused in walls of stratum VI, and they therefore appear to have come from one of the central buildings of strata VIII–VII.

The many finds on the floors of stratum IX indicate that it was a prosperous and flourishing city. It was probably destroyed by the Edomite raid during the campaign of Rezin and Pekah against Judah (734 B.C. — II Kings 16:6, II

Counterclockwise: Altar for burnt offerings in the temple. Holy of Holies in the sanctuary; end of 9th cent. B.C. *Bronze figurine of a crouching lion. The temple of stratum IX (Uzziah)* ▬ *existing* ▭ *conjectured. The temple of stratum X (9th cent.* B.C.*)* ▬ *existing* ▭ *conjectured* ░ *benches. A wall of the IA citadel and the water conduit; 9th cent.* B.C.

Chronicles 28:6). Stratum VIII was evidently destroyed in the campaign of Sennacharib (701 B.C.). Stratum VI existed almost to the end of the First Temple period (598 or 586 B.C.).

Traces of conflagration and the abundant vessels found on the various floors suggest that all six citadels were destroyed by sudden attacks. The site obviously was strategically important as a frontier fortress. The numerous strata of the relatively short period between the middle of the tenth and the beginning of the sixth century allow us to assign with strong probability a definite date in a specific historical context to every stratum. Arad has now the most detailed Iron Age II stratigraphy in Judah. The many typical vessels found in the various strata may provide a more accurate basis for dating other Judean sites.

Besides the rooms in the wall and the storerooms, the citadel area also contained dwellings as well as various industrial installations evidently connected with metal casting and perfume making. The many shekel weights also testify that the inhabitants engaged in commerce. A sanctuary was discovered in the northwest corner of the earlier citadels. Its plan is a broad room with a central adyton, the Holy of Holies. The entrance is from the west, and the Holy of Holies is oriented to the west, similar to the Solomonic Temple in Jerusalem. The walls of the sanctuary and of the Holy of Holies are covered with a strong, thick

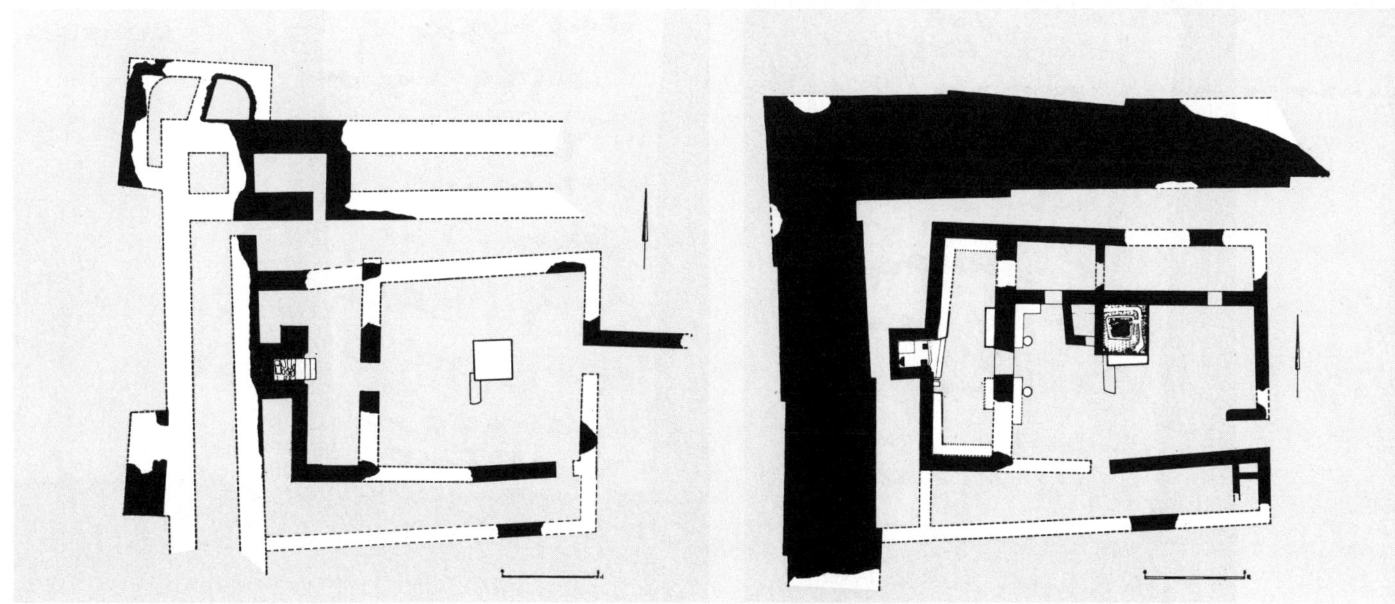

plaster, which has been well preserved.
Three steps lead to the Holy of Holies. On one of them were found two incense altars of stone, .4 and .51 meters high. The tops of the altars are concave, in the form of a flat bowl. Upon them was found a layer of burned organic matter, probably the remains of animal fat. Inside the Holy of Holies was a paved platform (bamah) and a stone stele (a massebah) about one meter high, smoothed and painted red.
Two apparently earlier stelae were built into the wall and covered by plaster. An altar for burnt offerings stood in the courtyard. Built of brick and rubble in accordance with biblical law (Exodus 20:25, etc.), it is circa 2.5 meters (*i.e.,* five cubits) square, exactly like the altar of the Tabernacle (Exodus 27:1) and perhaps also the original altar in Jerusalem (II Chronicles 6:13).
Among the finds several ostraca with Hebrew names deserve special mention, among them a reference to the priestly families of Pashhur and Meremoth. The temple was built on an ancient acropolis, which was in the center of the early unfortified settlement (stratum XII).
From the location of the sanctuary inside the royal Israelite citadel, and from its contents, there can be no doubt that this is a Yahwistic-Israelite sanctuary — the first one uncovered in archaeological excavations. It was built in the tenth century (stratum XI) and continued in use with slight alterations throughout strata X–VII. After its destruction at the end of stratum VII, it was never reconstructed. The casemate wall of stratum VI, which was apparently built by Josiah, cuts through its center. This is a striking confirmation of the biblical account of the great religious reform carried out by that king.
Special significance attaches to the extensive epigraphic material of the various strata. Part of it is incised on potsherds, but most consists of ostraca written in ink. In stratum IX were found fragments of a bowl on which the letters ערד = Arad were incised seven times from left to right (in mirror writing). The most important documents found date to about 600 B.C. Most are letters and dockets addressed to one Eliashib, son of Eshiahu.

Below left, right: Two ostraca from Eliashib's archives ca. 600 B.C.; the second mentions the "House of Yhwh."

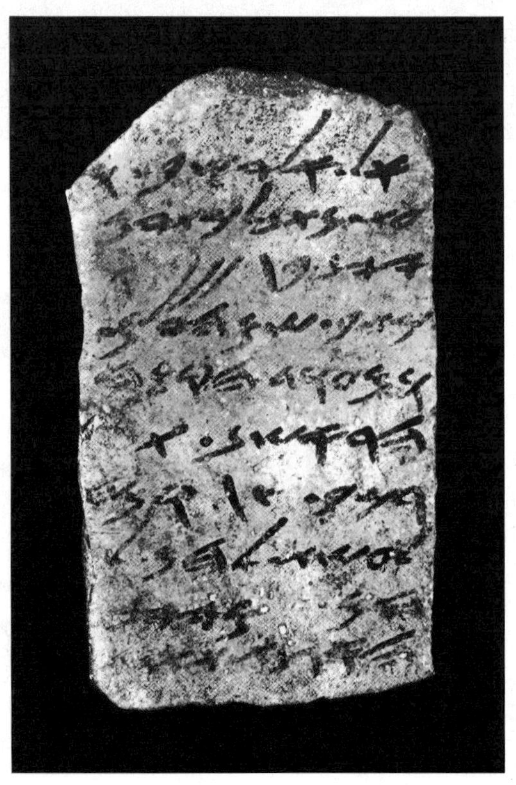

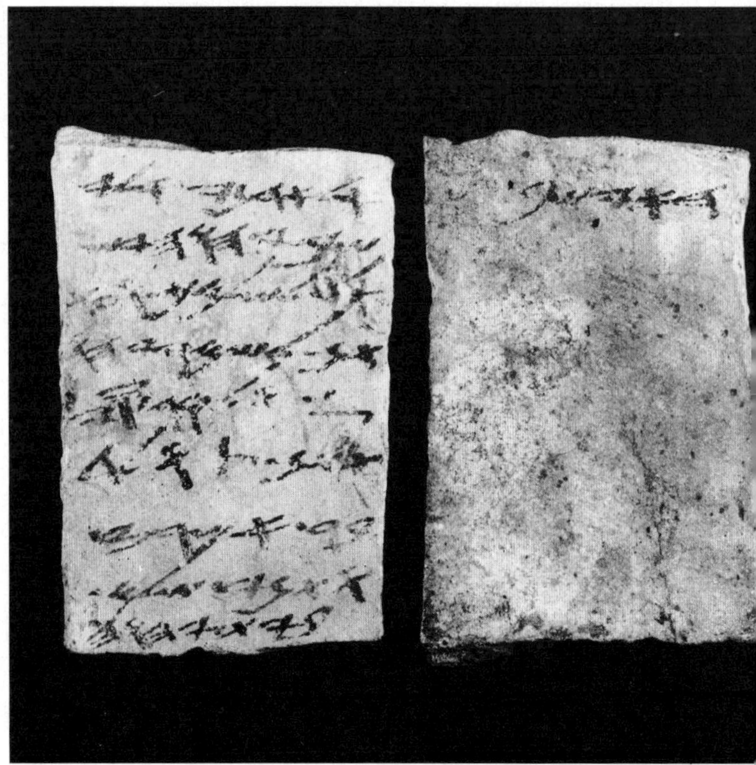

They deal with the distribution of bread, wine, and oil to various persons. One letter mentions "The House of Yhwh" (בית יהוה, the Temple?) and another contains an urgent order to send men to Ramat-Negev against an Edomite attack. The main value of the earlier ostraca, found in strata XI–VII, is paleographic-chronological, since on the greater part of them only isolated characters have been preserved.

THE LATER STRATA. After the last Israelite citadel had been destroyed, the site was abandoned for some time. Settlement on the high mound seems to have been renewed in the fifth century B.C. It was probably again a fortress, but a smaller one than before. The principal find in this stratum (V) are numerous well-preserved ostraca containing the names of men and lists of merchandise. The writing is very similar to that of the Aramaic ostraca of Ezion-Geber and can probably be dated to the beginning of the fourth century B.C.

At the top of the mound, in the center of the courtyard of the Israelite citadels, a strong tower was built about the third century B.C. (stratum IV).

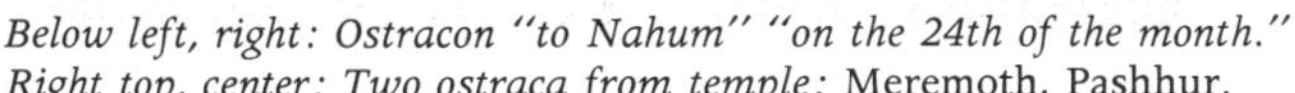

Below left, right: Ostracon "to Nahum" "on the 24th of the month."
Right top, center: Two ostraca from temple: Meremoth, Pashhur.

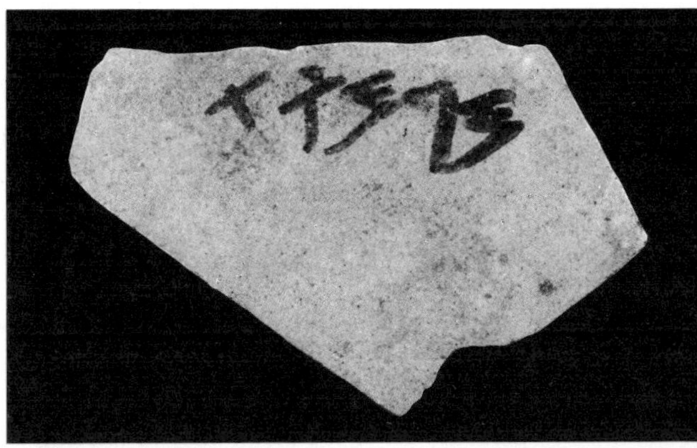

It was surrounded by several rooms. The tower itself is square (12 by 12 meters) and stands on a platform (19 by 19 meters) whose foundations are laid on rock. In this area the earlier remains were all destroyed in the course of its construction. To all appearances this is one of the Hellenistic towers built along the highways and the frontiers, such as the πύργος at Malathah (Tel Malḥatah) mentioned by Josephus (*Antiquities* XVIII, 147). This tower was evidently destroyed in the second century B.C.

Stratum III is a Roman fort consisting of a central courtyard surrounded by rooms on at least three sides. On the basis of the scanty material found on its floors, including a Greek ostracon, it has been dated to approximately the first century A.D. It thus appears to have belonged to a network of fortifications of the *Limes Palaestinae* and to have gone out of use completely with the annexation by Trajan of the Nabataean Kingdom in A.D. 106.

It is surprising that no remains of the Byzantine period were found on the site. Apparently the fort was not resettled, and its buildings gradually deteriorated. The Byzantine village mentioned by Eusebius seems to have been situated on one of the hills in the vicinity. Only at the beginning of the Arab period in the seventh century was building on the mound resumed, this for the last time (stratum II). The new buildings, which include three courtyards surrounded by rooms that cover an area of approximately 40 by 45 meters, were probably used as an inn for wayfarers. Besides the stoves and the usual utensils, a number of ostraca were found with Kufic characters. A hoard of glass vessels was concealed in a chamber in the wall in a corner of one of the rooms.

SUMMARY

The findings unearthed by the excavations again raise the question of whether this site is to be identified with ancient Arad. Since no remains of the city were found dating from the Middle and Late Bronze ages, it is impossible to identify the site with Canaanite Arad. Two theories have been proposed to solve this problem, one by B. Mazar and one by Y. Aharoni.

It has been suggested by Mazar that Canaanite Arad was not a city but rather the name of the entire district, which would account for the designation "in the south of Arad" in Judges 1:16. We are also told that the king of Arad smote the

Three seals: "To Eliashib son of Eshiahu" (top). Decorated shell; end of the seventh century B.C. (bottom).

children of Israel in Hormah. According to Mazar, Hormah was the city where the "king of Arad" resided. It should probably be identified with Tel Malḥatah (Tell el-Milḥ) 12 kilometers (7½ miles) southwest of Tel 'Arad. This is also the place where the principal wells of the district are situated and where remains of the Canaanite period were uncovered. It is perhaps also the place mentioned in the Egyptian Execration Texts (ḥ- r/l – m) and in an inscription from the Sinai mines of that same period. In the Iron Age the clan of Hobab the Kenite, Moses' father-in-law, settled in the Negev of Arad. The clan erected an acropolis in Tel 'Arad, around which the settlement developed in the course of time.

Aharoni assumes, however, that Canaanite Arad was situated on Tel Malḥatah. Hormah is to be identified with Tel Masos (Khirbet el Meshash), 6 kilometers (3½ miles) west of Tel Malḥatah. The two mounds are situated along the same riverbed, and there are no wells in the district except in these two sites. The story concerning the war in Hormah is based chiefly on the interpretation of the name of this city. As a proof one might cite the opposite tradition, according to which the children of Israel defeated the Canaanites in this place (Numbers 21:3). The account of the conquest of Hormah (Judges 1:17) revolves around Zephath and not Hormah. In the Iron Age the Jerahmeelites settled south of Arad, which is the Jerahmeelite Negev. The Kenite clans settled in the north of the city, and this is the Kenite Negev and the cities of the Kenites (I Samuel 27:10, 30:29).

The clan of Hobab erected the acropolis on the high hill commanding the entire district. In building the network of forts in the Negev, Solomon did not content himself with fortifying old Arad. He also built the main citadel in Tel 'Arad. This place was chosen because of its strategic importance, for it commands the main road to Edom and Elath, and also because of the traditional sanctuary. It was converted into a royal temple, to which an important place was allotted in the citadel. Proof for this is to be found in Shishak's list, which mentions two citadels *(ḥagarim)* named Arad: Arad Rabbat, the chief citadel (Tel 'Arad); and Arad of the house of Yrḥm, which is Arad of the Jerahmeelites (Tel Malḥatah).

Tel 'Arad is generally identified with Israelite Arad, and this identification now finds epigraphic support in the inscribed bowl and the ostraca found in the excavations. The Israelite citadels that were built here from the time of Solomon, and the sanctuary that was constructed within them, served also as a center of administration in the south of the country.

Y. AHARONI

BIBLIOGRAPHY

Y. Aharoni and Ruth Amiran, *Yediot* 27 (1963), 217–34 (Hebrew); *IEJ* 12 (1962), 144–45; *RB* 70 (1963), 565–66; *IEJ* 14 (1964), 131–47; *Archaeology* 17 (1964), 43–53 • Ruth Amiran, *BASOR* 179 (1965), 30–33 • Y. Yadin, *IEJ* 15 (1965), 180 • B. Mazar, *JNES* 24 (1965), 297–303 • Y. Aharoni, *IEJ* 16 (1966), 1–7; 17 (1967), 233–49 • Ruth Amiran, *IEJ* 16 (1966), 273–74 • S. Yeivin, *ibid.*, 153–59 • Ruth Amiran and Y. Aharoni, *Ancient Arad,* Catalogue of the Israel Museum, 1967 • C. Nylander, *IEJ* 17 (1967), 56–59 • Y. Aharoni, *BA* 31 (1968), 1–32 • Ruth Amiran and Elise J. Baumgartel, *BASOR* 195 (1969), 50–53 • Ruth Amiran, in *Essays in Honor of Nelson Glueck, Near Eastern Archaeology in the Twentieth Century,* ed. J.A. Sanders, New York, 1970, 83–100 • Y. Aharoni, *BASOR* 197 (1970), 16–42 • Ruth Amiran, *IEJ* (1972), 86–88.

EL-'AREINI, TELL ESH SHEIKH AHMED

(Tel 'Erani)

IDENTIFICATION. Tel 'Erani, one of the most important ancient sites in the eastern part of the coastal plain, lies at kilometer 19 on the highway connecting the Coastal Road (near Ashkelon) with Beth-Govrin, opposite the remains of the abandoned village of 'Iraq el-Manshiyyeh. Naḥal No'am runs south of the site, and Naḥal Lachish north of it (map reference 129113). It is also known as Tell esh Sheikh Aḥmed el-'Areini. The total area of the site exceeds 25 hectares, but its exact limits have not yet been defined (see below).

HISTORY

V. Guérin was apparently the first scholar to visit the site, in May, 1867. C. Conder, who was there in the 1870's, proposed to identify it with Libnah (Joshua 15:42; "The White One"), on the assumption that the settlement had been named after "the hills near it [which] are of very white chalk." H. Guthe was the first to suggest its identification with Gath of the Philistines. W. F. Albright, who visited the site twice in the early 1920's, independently proposed (in 1923) the same identification, and this was accepted by numerous scholars (Beyer, Alt, and others). The Israel Geographic Names Committee named the site "Tel Gath." However, later evidence (see below) invalidated that identification, and the site was renamed Tel 'Erani. Possible identifications of the site, suggested by the excavator, are 'Eglōn and Mamshat (if H. L. Ginsberg's explanation of this name proves incorrect), while B. Mazar (in an oral communication) proposed a possible identification with Libnah (as previously suggested by Conder).

DESCRIPTION

The site consists of three parts:

a. **The acropolis** (the high mound), which has a nearly flat top of about 1.6 hectares and rises 32 meters above the level of the surrounding plain (152 meters above sea level). The slopes of the acropolis hill are quite steep, especially on the east and north. At the highest point of the mound stands a small *weli*, the tomb of Sheikh 'Aḥmed el-'Areini, after whom the mound was called by the local Arabs. The *weli* is surrounded by modern burials.

b. **The high terrace,** stretching around the acropolis hill on three sides (west, south, and east) over an area of about 24 hectares (including the area under the acropolis). This terrace rises 15 to 18 meters above the surrounding plain, and at its highest point it reaches 138 meters above sea level. The acropolis is nearly 17 meters higher than this terrace.

c. **The lower terrace** around both the acropolis and the higher terrace, gradually sloping down toward and merging into the surrounding plain. To establish its exact extent, further trenching along its edges will be necessary (see below).

HISTORY OF THE EXCAVATIONS

During six successive seasons (1956–61) the site was excavated by the Israel Department of Antiquities, and from the fourth season jointly with the Italian *Centro per le antichita e la storia dell'arte del vicino oriento* of the *Istituto per l'Oriente* of Rome. S. Yeivin directed the work during all the seasons, assisted by S. Levy until 1960.

In May, 1956, the Department of Antiquities made a detailed surface survey of the site, discovering ancient remains on the two terraces surrounding the acropolis. In the course of the survey, eight areas were chosen for excavation: three on the acropolis (areas A, E, G), three along its foot (areas B, C, F), one on the southern edge of the high terrace (area D), and one in the abandoned village (area H, to examine the possible site of the ancient cemetery). The expedition has not investigated B and E. In the course of the work a further area was excavated in the abandoned village (area J, a monumental Byzantine burial structure) and four additional areas on the high terrace (K-N). A trial trench was opened down the northwestern slope of the acropolis (almost to the level of the high terrace) south of area G.

THE COURSE OF THE EXCAVATIONS AND THE FINDS

Areas A and G. The whole summit of the acropolis was used as a cemetery in post-Byzantine times. During 1956–57 about two hundred burials were uncovered in area A, dating from the Early Arab period to the seventeenth century. These interments disturbed the upper strata on the acropolis down to an average depth of 2.5 meters

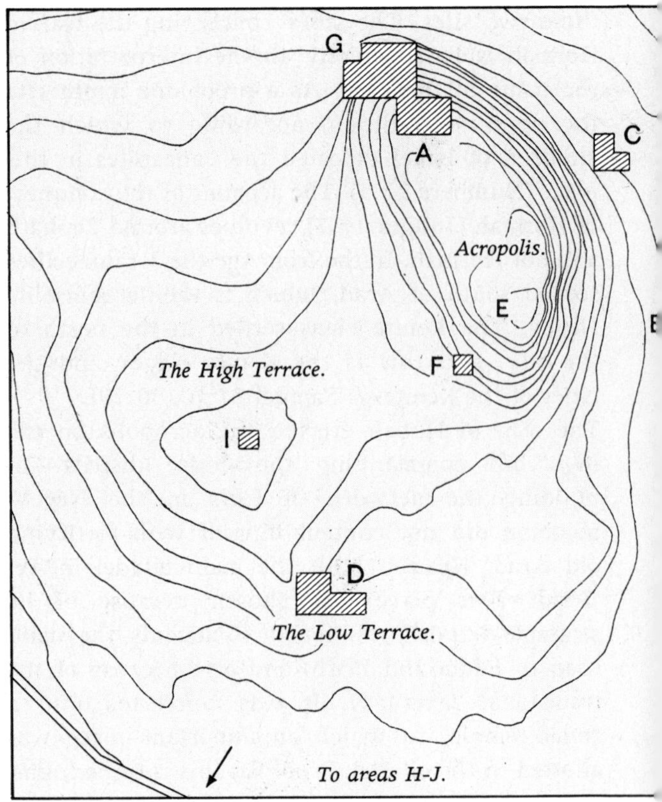

The mound and areas of excavation.

below the present-day surface. Potsherds and small sections of surviving foundations in this disturbed debris indicate that it initially included remains of at least three occupation levels, dating to the Late Israelite (Persian) and Hellenistic periods. Only at a depth of 2.25–2.5 meters below the surface of area A did more extensive architectural remains begin to appear. These represented a lower occupation layer (stratum IV), which were not disturbed by the tombs of later periods. However, this stratum, as well as the underlying one, were also badly disturbed by round silos dug by the inhabitants of the Persian strata (II–III).

Pottery found in stratum IV dates it to the end of the seventh or beginning of the sixth centuries B.C., but no plausible plan of its architectural remains could be established. Although the underlying layer (stratum V) was also heavily damaged by the Persian silos, certain features could be observed. At different spots, remains of two oblong ovens were uncovered full of ashes. Both were lined inside with coarse pottery, and near each were found small heaps of slightly flattened spherical pottery "sinkers" covered with ashes.

Also in this stratum, outlines of a narrow lane of stratum XX (about 1.5 meters wide) could be observed for the first time. It apparently led from the square in front of the gateway (see below) into the interior of the settlement.

On the slope of the acropolis, some 20 meters west of area A, a small area was investigated in the attempt to find the gateway to the acropolis. Here were revealed remains of four superimposed fortification systems. Of the upper three, only stone foundations of what appeared to be casemate walls have survived. But below the level of these systems, and a short distance west of them, were the remains of a fourth defense wall built entirely of baked bricks. In it was a gateway (2.7 meters wide). In front of it, outside the walled-in city, was a pavement of baked bricks, continued southward by a stone-paved approach road, completely destroyed at a short distance to the south. This defense system showed marked signs of a conflagration, which must have destroyed this walled settlement.

Potsherds were very scarce, and it was thus difficult in the first season to assign dates to the different systems of fortifications. Southwest of these fortifications, the slope of the acropolis was covered by a continuous stretch of a glacis, built up of large rectangular mud bricks smoothed over with a thin facing of mud plaster. The glacis was laid over a layer of beaten earth containing some shards of the Early Israelite period.

In the following season (1958), the connection between areas A and G was investigated (see above). At the western edge of area A, ruins of a square structure were uncovered immediately below the surface of the slope. They comprised a square room (about 3.2 by 3.2 meters) with remains of a stone pavement in the southwestern part, and a Γ-shaped corridor in its southeastern and southwestern parts. The latter structure had been erected over an artificial fill, rising (at the foundations of its walls) to a height of about 1.5 meters above the level of the pavement of the square just inside the highest of the four fortification systems in area G. This must have been the town square in front of the gateway to the acropolis (inside the city), similar to squares uncovered in Israelite strata at all other excavated sites.

The aforementioned lane leading into the city, traces of which had been previously unearthed in strata IV–V, probably started from the southeastern corner of the town square. It also continued to be observed deeper down, in strata VI–VIII.

On the strength of the results obtained during the first five seasons and from the trial trench dug in the sixth season, the stratification in this area may be summarized as follows:

STRATA I–III. A thick conglomeration of disturbed debris originally containing Hellenistic remains (fourth–second centuries B.C) — stratum I. Some corners of rooms with beaten-earth pavements containing pottery of the Late Israelite (Persian) period — stratum II. Numerous remains of silos were dug in the same period in both this level and the underlying one (stratum III). These two strata belong to the end of the sixth or beginning of the fifth/third centuries B.C. A gap of some seventy to eighty years apparently existed between the occupation of stratum III and the underlying stratum IV.

STRATUM IV, dating to the Iron Age III (beginning of the sixth century B.C.), had been heavily dis-

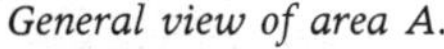
General view of area A.

turbed by silos dug into it from the Persian levels, but parts of rooms and remains of ovens were distinguished, as well as traces of a lane leading from the gate into the city.

STRATUM V also dates to the Iron Age III (probably the end of the seventh century B.C.). It had also been disturbed by silos. However, remains of three rather large buildings as well as wide, pebble-paved courtyards, one with an industrial installation, can be partially traced. The finds include carinated, burnished bowls and fragments of jar handles stamped *lamelekh*.

STRATUM VI belongs to the Iron Age III (beginning of the seventh century B.C.). This was the latest layer in which it was possible to trace complete plans of houses: two adjacent four-room buildings (houses shaped like π in plan) connected by a communicating doorway, both situated northeast of the previously mentioned lane. The walls were built of mud brick on foundations of one or two courses of pebbles. The outer walls were thicker than the inner ones. The longitudinal, lateral rooms were each separated from the inner courtyard (the room between them) by a row of columns (?) erected on stone bases. Near the eastern building on the pavement of the lane were found fragments of a four-handled amphora, each handle stamped with the impression *lamelekh/Hebron* above and a four-winged scarab below. The number of shards of carinated, burnished bowls diminishes considerably in this stratum.

STRATUM VII also belongs to the Iron Age III (end of the eighth–beginning of the seventh century B.C.). Under the π-shaped buildings of stratum VI lay remains of two inner-courtyard structures, with adjacent inner courtyards. Each was surrounded on its other three sides by a row of rooms, one deep on the southwestern side and two deep both on the northwestern and northeastern sides. The houses were entered from the

Graffito on shard; possibly name of Pharaoh Narmer (left). Cylindrical jar, coarsely made; Late Chalcolithic period (right).

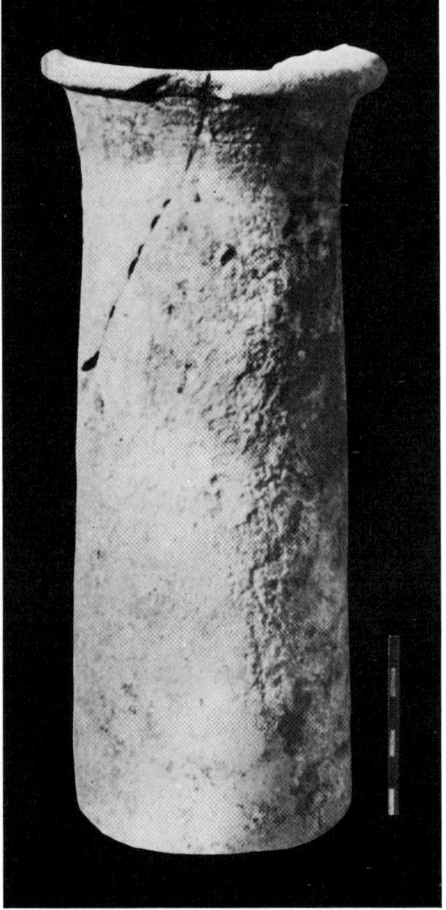

lane through doorways in the southern corner of the western building and near the western corner of the eastern building. Each doorway led into a long corridor communicating with its inner courtyard by means of a second doorway at its opposite end, thus forming an indirect type of access to the house. In the courtyards there seem to have been sheds with roofs supported on wooden (?) poles, which left clearly visible holes in the ground. The lane near the entrances to the buildings was paved with pebbles, and its western part was covered with a thick and hardened lime plaster. A group of pottery vessels found smashed on the floor in one of the rooms of the northwestern building fully established the date of this stratum, which was further confirmed by the paleographic evidence of a graffito incised on the shoulder of a broken pot, which read *lyḥz*.

STRATUM VIII apparently also belongs to the Iron Age III (late eighth century B.C.). Under the northwestern building of the inner-courtyard type in stratum VII, were uncovered remains of a similar type structure, the courtyard of which showed signs of two phases of building. Remains of another similar building were found under the adjacent house, to the southeast.

Stratum IX. At a depth of some 10 to 15 centimeters below the foundations of the building of stratum VIII an extensive area of whitewashed mud plaster was uncovered on which no signs of buildings were visible. Near the northern end of the lane, where it opened onto the square in front of the town gate, a rectangular pit was found almost full of slaked lime, which was undoubtedly the source of the whitewash covering the whole of the area east of the lane. The purpose of this area is not clear, but it seems that it covered a deep fill of earth. This is the only way to account for the sagging of the northwestern corner of the western building in stratum VII, which broke up (diagonally) the paving across a room into two levels, and also lowered the central part of the western building in stratum VI, tearing away its southern wall from its western one.

It seems probable that the uppermost of the casemate systems of fortifications in area G (see above) and the paved open square in front of its gateway belong to stratum X — *i.e.,* the one beneath the aforementioned whitewashed mud plaster-covered fill.

Pottery from stratum IV; Late Chalcolithic period.

INDUSTRIAL INSTALLATIONS. In the courtyards of all the superimposed buildings of strata VIII–V in area A were discovered remains of industrial installations which, for the most part, were similar to one another. The installations in stratum V were destroyed beyond any possibility of examination. All the installations of strata VII–VI, however, were similar. Each consisted of an oblong rectangular structure with rounded corners, plastered and whitewashed on the outside, about 1 meter high. The upper surface of each structure showed an oval depression, equally plastered and whitewashed. In the center was a slightly raised clay collar surrounding a deeper oval hollow, both again mud plastered and whitewashed. Professor

Heiman, of Haifa Technion, suggested that these may have been used in the manufacture of cheese. CONCLUSIONS. The presence of ovens, near which were found small heaps of baked clay sinkers (to retain heat), probably for Sabbath observance, and numerous finds of handles stamped with *lamelekh* impressions, seem to negate the identification of this site with Gath of the Philistines. The two opposing lines of fortifications, at some distance northwest and southwest of the plain surrounding this site, also militate against such an identification.

Areas C and F. Area C (at the foot of the acropolis, on the north) and area F (on the south) were examined for traces of a possible fosse round the defenses of the acropolis, but none was found. In area F there was uncovered, at some depth, a small area paved with pebbles, upon which was pottery of Iron Age I. This may indicate temporary squatting by a seminomadic population.

No traces of ancient burials were found in area H. But to the northwest, in area J, there were fairly well preserved remains of a large stone tomb of the Byzantine period, which contained numerous disturbed burials (including skulls).

Area D. To probe the date and extent of the settlement on the high terrace, a square trench (20 by 20 meters) was opened along the southern edge of the terraces. Mud-brick walls began to appear immediately below the present surface of the ground. Associated with these was pottery of the Early Bronze Age II and some Early Bronze Age III shards found on fragmentary pebble pavements at the highest levels of the excavated area. These almost entirely defaced remains of dwelling houses seem to represent the last level of occupation in area D **(stratum I)** below which were the fragmentary remains of mud-brick walls, standing on both sides of a narrow lane running east–west. These were associated with the Early Bronze Age II pottery.

The walls were mostly built in two header courses put end to end to form the thickness of the wall, bedded on one or two courses of rather small pebbles as foundation. Some areas inside each complex were paved with pebbles or stamped earth. These seem to represent open courts, whereas the smaller unpaved spaces were rooms. Two round storage areas were similarly paved with pebbles. No evidence of violent destruction was visible in this stratum, and the settlement was probably gradually abandoned.

At a depth of about one meter below the surface there began to appear remains of **stratum II.** Here, too, the building remains were badly disturbed, and it was extremely difficult to trace plans of building units. The lane uncovered in the overlying stratum was discernible, however. This stratum apparently contained five phases of occupation.

In these two uppermost strata an unusual structure was found south of the lane. It is a broad-house type oriented east–west, with a large courtyard on the east. It had undergone several reconstructions, but its main feature, a circular mud-brick structure in the center of the room, persisted. Scanty remains of flooring were found in the room, some near the northern wall (pebble pavement), others near the southern one (mud plaster over stamped earth). West of the room was a rather large, fenced-in area, remains of a mud-brick pavement, and another room. The circular structure in the center of the first-mentioned room seems to have been a ritual offering table. This building may possibly be compared with the Chalcolithic temples of Megiddo and En-Gedi. In one of the earlier phases of occupation of the building, a large shallow bowl containing the femur of a hippopotamus was found on the floor of the room, near the north wall. Thus, this structure may perhaps be considered a sanctuary dating from the first half of the third millennium B.C.

In room 2050 of stratum II, phase C, seven skeletons of the proto-Mediterranean type were found. Two were quite tall women with slender bones, and one was a man shorter than the women and with heavier bones. This discovery does not seem to be a normal burial inside a house. Rather it is likely the result of some accident, perhaps a collapse of the building that buried the inhabitants under the ruins. In phase C, too, the aforementioned lane is cut off at its eastern extremity, turns north at a right angle, and becomes a dead end leading to a complex of rooms and courtyards on the north and east.

At an average depth of 70 centimeters below the level of phase C (stratum II) there begin to appear remains of **stratum III**, the buildings and lanes of which (as far as was discernible) completely differ in outline and layout from those of the overlying strata. They are oriented almost exactly northeast–

southwest. Although only a small part of this stratum was cleared, it seems to follow the orientation and planning of stratum IV.

Stratum IV was uncovered at an average depth of 50 centimeters below the level of stratum III. It is especially important for dating the settlement in area D, for in a burned deposit in one of the rooms on the edge of the high terrace was found a hoard of crushed large jars containing seeds of various crops — wheat, barley, and flax (on first examination). Some of these burned seeds were submitted to Carbon-14 tests, which dated the destruction of the occupation in this stratum to 2550 ($\pm$250) B.C. The maximum limit in this case (circa 2800) corresponds to approximately the end of the Early Bronze Age I.

Stratum IV also contained the remains of a building with a large enclosed courtyard paved with stamped earth. Northwest and southeast of the court are groups of rooms, parts of which have the same paving. In the northern end of the court a thin semicircular partition fences off a silo. In the southern part there is an installation suggesting an olive press: a large pithos almost completely sunk into the ground and surrounded by a pebble pavement. Olive pits were found in the pithos.

This stratum shows, for the first time, that the area of the settlement sloped considerably from west to east, with the architectural remains on the east about 2.1 meters lower than those on the west. Here, too, remains of a large building begin to appear. Its outer wall on the southeast is 18 meters long. At its northern corner it joins the northeastern wall at a right angle, while at its southeastern end it curves to the northwest.

The remains of **stratum V** lay at an average depth of 60 centimeters below those of stratum IV. This stratum, too, is important for dating the settlement in area D, for here — and almost only here — there was found a comparatively large quantity of Egyptian-type pottery of the late predynastic and early proto-dynastic periods (but not later than the middle of the First Dynasty). The most characteristic vessels are covered with a white slip, with or without burnish. They consist mainly of long cylindrical jars of various sizes. Some shards have an incised decoration derived from Late Chalcolithic designs but of more artistic workmanship. Among others, there were also fragments of large storage jars, equally characteristic of the same period in Egypt. Three of them bore incised graffiti, two with the name of Meri-Nar (Narmer), who in the opinion of several scholars is to be identified with Menes, the traditional founder of the First Dynasty (according to Manetho).

A fragment of a cooking vessel was found by Dr. Klimovsky on the surface of the terrace, slightly east of area D. This shard bears several lines, incised before firing, which most probably formed part of a typical design of the same period (a head of a horned bull, a bucranium). Some of these vessels may have been imported from Egypt, but many were undoubtedly local imitations of Egyptian work and technique.

In this stratum it was possible to definitely trace the southwestern limit of the large edifice first noted in the overlying layer. Although originating in lower strata, it had been partly repaired and used in this stratum (and to a lesser extent also in stratum IV). It represents a large public building, the main feature of which is an inner pebble-paved courtyard, surrounded by storerooms on three sides and opening onto an outer court on its fourth side. The latter was also pebble paved and exhibits ruins

Figurine of horseman; Persian period.

of storerooms on at least one side. Discoveries in trench N (see below) prove that this settlement was surrounded by a massive mud-brick wall.

North of this building ran a street (average width 2.4 meters). Beyond it, at the northern edge of the excavated area, a group of rooms with stamped-earth floors was uncovered. On one floor was the impression of an oval reed mat, similar to those seen at Jericho.

Stratum VI, the remains of which begin to appear at an average depth of 70 centimeters below the level of stratum V, shows signs of a violent destruction (more pronounced in the corresponding layer in trench N, see below). This stratum is characterized by a combination of three ceramic features: 1.) the presence of some typical Early Bronze Age I ware; 2.) the appearance of some clear Late Chalcolithic pottery; 3.) the first appearance of a peculiar ware. (Since no complete assessment of the ceramic finds from area D has yet been made, it is possible that a few isolated examples of this ware are to be attributed to stratum V.) Outstanding among these vessels are quite wide and deep goblets, with either pointed, rounded, or button bases. Also typical of this ceramic culture is the relatively large proportion of miniature juglets, with or without a high handle, possibly used as containers for rare perfume oils. There are also jugs with round bases and the so-called flower pots, some of them with straight sides, others with flaring. All of them have flat bottoms, some perforated in the center. Typical also of this stratum is the relative abundance of fragmentary animal figurines of baked clay.

The large building already partly traced in strata IV–V takes on a definite plan in this stratum. The large inner courtyard in the southeastern part of the edifice was roofed over in this stratum, its ceiling resting on three rows of wooden (?) columns. Each column stood on a large, round, flat, thick stone placed in the center of a square pediment built up of mud bricks to an average of 70 centimeters. One of these pedestal stones was found in situ; another (of the nearest column to the west) was found overturned at the foot of the mud-brick pediment. The easternmost pediment had been razed by a deep pit dug later in stratum IV. A carcass of an equid had been thrown (or buried) in this pit.

Some 30 to 60 centimeters below the threshold of the entrance to this public building (in stratum VI) appeared the remains of the same building in **stratum VII.** The clearly visible threshold of this stratum was uncovered 30 centimeters below the threshold of stratum VI. Storerooms were ranged on three sides of the inner courtyard. On the fourth (southeastern) there was only the enclosing wall, with more storerooms along it (on the outside, *i.e.,* in the outer courtyard). The outer courtyard was paved with a deep fill of pebbles, and its average level was 50 centimeters below that of stratum VI.

Remains of **Strata VIII-XI** were uncovered only in the deep trial pit dug outside the southwestern wall of the large public building. The northeastern section of this pit shows clearly that the public building had originally been erected in stratum VIII. Virgin soil was reached in the pit about 3 meters below the foundations of level VII. In it were found round dwelling pits **(stratum XII).**

The trial pit was deepened in parts up to 2 meters into virgin soil (124 meters above sea level), where M. Avnimelech found indications of marshy soil.

A group of objects found in area D, in a sand-filled hollow in the northeastern corner of the area, include a number of terra-cotta figurines and two fragments of crude limestone statuettes, all of the Persian period. Below this group was found a late green-glazed scarab of the Saitic period. The hollow seems to have been a burial hole *(genizah)* for disused ritual offerings from a sanctuary of the Persian period — which probably existed on the acropolis at the time and may still be buried under the unexplored part of its surface. Similar finds under identical circumstances were made at short distances from the perimeter of Tel Makhmish and Tel Ẓippor.

Areas K–M. To ascertain the density of occupation on the high terrace, three spot areas were explored on its surface. In area K, at the highest point of the terrace (139 meters above sea level), remains of some pavements were uncovered to a depth of about 1 meter below the surface soil, swept down from the acropolis by winter rains; more especially at 138.4–138.5 meters above sea level, where remains of a potter's kiln, a cooking oven (?), and small sections of stamped-earth pavements were uncovered, all of them dating to the Middle Iron Age II period. At a depth of some 2.5 meters below the surface (almost at the level of the latest remains in area D) appeared sections of mud-brick walls of Early Bronze Age II.

In area L, on the northwestern part of the high terrace, the surface of which was lower than that of area K, remains of mud-brick walls were uncovered just below surface level. These also dated to Early Bronze Age II.

In area M, southwest of area L, on the western edge of the high terrace, were similar mud-brick remains belonging to Early Bronze Age II, including a broad stretch of a mud-brick belt that could later (in the light of discoveries made in area N) be identified as ruins of the thick wall that encompassed the city (see below).

Area N. An aerial photograph taken before the start of the excavations showed a sharp and clearly marked boundary line between areas of differing colors along the northern edge of the high terrace. It was therefore decided in 1960 to examine this region. A trench was opened, running a long distance south of the edge of the terrace at this spot, up to the aforementioned boundary line. It was later extended far to the northwest, into the surrounding plain, by means of small, square pits.

At a depth of a few centimeters below the surface of the high terrace, mud-brick structures appeared in the trench (area N) along its entire length. Ceramic evidence pointed to the Early Bronze Age II. In the small pits sunk in the lower area outside the border line, scattered shards of the same period were found, mixed with alluvial soil, down to a depth of about 1 meter below the surface level.

The most interesting finds, however, were uncovered on the border line seen in the aerial photograph, which coincided with the edge of the high terrace. Immediately below the surface an extensive belt of mud bricks came to light. It soon became apparent that this represented a massive circumvallation protected on the outside (north) by a thick, mud-plastered glacis. Over the latter there were uncovered (near the edge of the wall) remains of a small, square tower. And west of it, at a distance of 5 meters, were scanty remains of the eastern part of a similar tower.

This trial trench was widened in 1961. It was then ascertained that here the thickness of the wall was at least 8 meters. On top of the glacis a miniature juglet was found with a rounded base and a disproportionately large loop handle, characteristic of the ware associated with stratum VI in area D. It seems probable, therefore, that the wall existed already at the time of the occupation of stratum VI. Trial sections cut in the inner and outer faces of the wall showed that originally — apparently at the occupational level corresponding to stratum VII in area D — a mud-brick wall some 2 meters thick (at the rear of the later massive circumvallation) was erected around the settlement. It seems that this original fortification had been intentionally set on fire (by a besieging force?), as indicated by a thin, vertical line of burned material along its outer face, and was then rebuilt by the settlers of stratum VI in its massive form.

Although the city of stratum VI had been stormed (there were traces of burning at this stage), the same system of fortifications seems also to have protected the settlement of stratum V. The remains of stratum IV (in area D), on the other hand, seem to lie over the line of the wall (seen in the aerial photograph), indicating that the settlement was an open one like that of stratum III.

A new aerial photograph taken by the Israel Air Force shows that the northern end of the eastern fortification wall crossed Naḥal Shiqma, turned at a sharp angle southwestward, recrossed Naḥal Shiqma, and continued in the same direction toward the line uncovered in area N. Thus, the wall enclosed a built-up area of about 25 hectares.

Among the finds unearthed in area N is an almost complete horn of a mouflon (unfortunately so badly burned that it powdered to dust immediately after having been photographed in situ) that was found on the burned floor of the lower occupational level inside the wall (stratum VII?). Another find was a group of copper scales fixed together, as proved by the later discovery of similar scales in the treasure trove of Kefar Monash (see Sharon). These were found in the upper level of occupation inside the wall (stratum VI). In a burned layer outside the wall, probably corresponding to stratum VIII (in area D), was found a copper ax of Late Gerzean Egyptian type.

S. Yeivin

BIBLIOGRAPHY

S. Yeivin, Encyclopaedia Biblica (Language Academy Publications), VII–VIII, Jerusalem, 1960, 224; *idem, IEJ* 10 (1960), 193–203, Pls. 23–24; 11 (1961), 191; *idem, RB* 67 (1960), 391–94; 69 (1962), 395–97; *idem, First Preliminary Report on the Excavations at Tel "Gat" (1956–58),* Jerusalem, 1961 • D. Ferembach, *ibid.,* 19–20, Pls. XI–XII • A. Ciasca, *Oriens Antiquus* 1 (1962), 25–29; 2 (1963), 45–63 • S. Yeivin, *ibid.,* 205–13; *idem, Fourth World Congress of Jewish Studies* I, Jerusalem, 1967, 45–48; *idem, JNES* 23 (1968), 37–49.

AROER

IDENTIFICATION. The site of biblical Aroer, which the deuteronomist (Joshua 12:2; 13:9, 16; Deuteronomy 2:36; 3:12, 4:48; II Kings 10:33; Jeremiah 48:19) and the Mesha Stone (line 26) cite as being situated on the bank of the Arnon, is actually located at Khirbet 'Arâ'ir, 4 kilometers ($2\frac{1}{2}$ miles) east of the Madeba-Karak highway on the northern slope of Wadi Mojib (the biblical Arnon).

HISTORY

Archaeological excavations clearly show that Aroer was never a town or settlement. It was a strategically positioned fortress guarding the King's Highway, which crossed the Arnon (Jeremiah 48:19). Little is known of Aroer's history. According to the Bible it was first occupied after the Israelite conquest by the tribe of Reuben, who settled on the plain north of the Arnon (I Chronicles 5:8). Aroer remained in the possession of the Israelites throughout the period of the Judges (Septuagint version, Judges 11:26) and the United Monarchy. It marked the southern boundary of the Israelite territories in Transjordan. In the wake of the successful campaigns of King Mesha (circa 850 B.C.), Aroer, which was then in existence, was annexed to the Kingdom of Moab. As related in the Mesha Stone (line 26), the king made the highway in the Arnon and "built Aroer."

A short time afterward, in the second half of the ninth century B.C., the kings of Damascus conquered the Israelite territories in Transjordan, which extended between the rivers Arnon and Yarmuk (II Kings 10:33). Aroer remained in Syrian possession until the fall of Damascus during the

The northwest trench at the end of the third excavation campaign (August, 1966).

Outer northeastern wall of the fortress of Mesha before the excavations.

Assyrian expansion (732 B.C.). According to Josephus (*Antiquities* X, 181), the destruction of the Aroer fortress took place in the course of Nebuchadnezzar's campaign against Moab (582 B.C.). From that time Aroer was rebuilt only partially and transitorily.

EXCAVATIONS

Members of the Spanish Center, Casa de Santiago, in Jerusalem, under the direction of E. Olávarri, carried out excavations on the site of Aroer during three seasons (1964, 1965, 1966). They uncovered six archaeological levels corresponding to as many periods of occupation. Level VI, the earliest, is composed of two superimposed phases: VI-B (Intermediate Bronze Age I, circa 2250–2050 B.C.) and VI-A (Intermediate Bronze Age II, circa 2050–1900 B.C.). Level VI-B shows evidence of a seminomadic occupation in which agriculture was practiced. The domestic utensils (pottery, flint implements, etc.) represent an evolutionary continuation of Early Bronze Age III. In level VI-A are the remains of very rudimentary domestic constructions in stone, and the pottery includes clear examples of the so-called Palestinian caliciform ware, from the time of the Amorite invasions.

After a gap in settlement, which lasted throughout the Middle Bronze Age, Aroer was again inhabited toward the end of the Late Bronze Age and the beginning of the Iron Age (level V). To this phase belong the houses discovered in trench D, loci 206 and 208, and the passage flanked by the strong walls of locus 204 that formed part of the complex of the Israelite fortress conquered by King Mesha of Moab. The new fortress (level IV), which was built by this king over the earlier one, occupies an area of 50 square meters. It is constructed of very solid masonry and includes three parallel circumvallating walls: an exterior one, 2 meters in width; an interior one, which served as a buttress to the central area of the fortress; and an intermediate wall, 1.5 meters thick. The two inner passages running between these three walls were filled with debris of former buildings, thus forming a defensive structure of great strength. The southeast and southwest sides of the fortress were built upon the steep cliffs of the Arnon, which served as a natural glacis. An additional double defense wall was put up on the northwest side, which faces the plain and is consequently more vulnerable. As in Dibon, King Mesha built a reservoir in Aroer to store rainwater in an artificial basin in front of the northwest wall of the fortress.

From the seventh to the third centuries B.C., Aroer experienced a further period of abandonment. This period coincided with the domination of the Qadarites and Lyhianite nomads over this region. The abundance of Hellenistic pottery (level III) testifies to a new occupation during the third and second centuries B.C. Only a few houses, plus the rough reconstruction of two farms within the fortress, remain of this period indicating the seminomadic character of the Hellenistic settlement.

During the Nabataean period (level II, first century B.C. and first century A.D.), the population increased.

To this period belong four excavated houses and the greater number of the cisterns that surround the ruins of the fortress, some of them still in use. The absence of monumental buildings in this place, however, underlines the fact that during the Nabataean period Aroer had already lost its former strategic importance. After the Roman conquest of the Nabatean territories by Cornelius Palma (A.D. 106), Aroer was again partially inhabited during the second and third centuries A.D. Although the houses of this period (level I, loci 111, 112, 113, and 300) present a greater architectural unity, they no longer form the nucleus of a stable, permanent settlement.

E. OLÁVARRI

BIBLIOGRAPHY

E. Olávarri, *RB* 72 (1965), 77–94; 76 (1969), 250–59.

EL-ASAWIR, TELL

THE SITE AND ITS IDENTIFICATION. Tell el-Asawir, called Tel Arubboth today, is situated at the southern entrance of Naḥal 'Iron (Megiddo Pass) near the so-called "Via Maris," about 10 kilometers (7 miles) north of Ḥederah (map reference 152209). The site, which covers an area of about 3 hectares and rises 7 to 11 meters above the surrounding country, lies in the midst of an area of rich soil and abundant springs. In the course of a survey conducted on the surface and at the foot of the mound, and in exploratory excavations on the summit, potsherds were found indicating that a settlement existed on the site from the Late Chalcolithic period until the end of the fifteenth century B.C. and again from the ninth century B.C. up to and including the Byzantine period.

A. Alt's identification of the mound with Yaham, which is mentioned as the starting point of the march against Megiddo by Thutmose III, is not shared by most scholars, who are inclined to identify Yaham with Khirbet Yamah, 13 kilometers (8 miles) south of Tell el-Asawir. Alt later identified the site with Arubboth, a place included in Solomon's third district (I Kings 4:10), but this identification is unconvincing since no potsherds of the tenth century B.C. have been found on the mound.

EXCAVATIONS. BURIAL CAVE

Several burial caves were found near the mound, especially to the east of it. One of the caves, found in the bed of Naḥal 'Iron, about 500 meters east

Selection of pottery (below). Gray-burnished bowls (opposite, bottom); red-burnished jugs (opposite, upper two); EBA I.

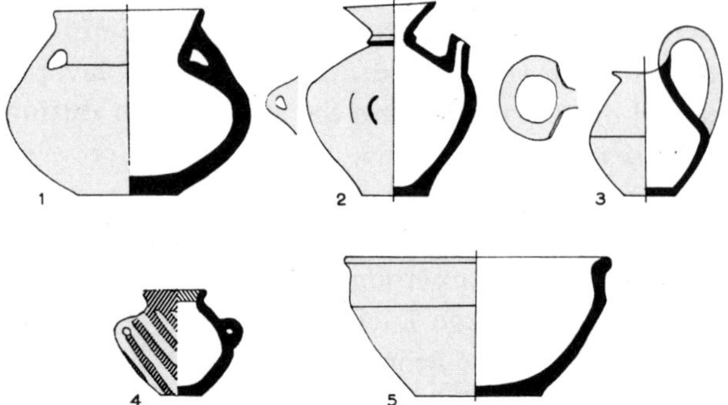

of the mound, was excavated by M. Dothan at the end of 1953 on behalf of the Department of Antiquities. The mouth of the cave was covered with a layer of debris. Underneath were five steps leading to an irregularly shaped room (maximal length and width about 6 meters, height about 1.8 meters). The upper graves, found at a depth of about 50 centimeters, contained skeletons and pottery. From the position of the skeletons and the distribution of the vessels, it is evident that the grave had been looted.

On the basis of the potsherds, especially those of the jugs and bowls, these burials appear to date back to the second half of Middle Bronze Age II-B, approximately the seventeenth century B.C. At a slightly lower level were found four clay vessels but no remains of a grave. The vessels date from Middle Bronze Age I-A and are evidently the remains of an extensive burial area inside the cave, which was cleared for burials in the Middle Bronze Age.

The Late Chalcolithic Period. Two layers of graves were uncovered in the loose, moist soil at the bottom of the cave. It was impossible to distinguish clearly between them since the graves and the funerary offerings of both layers were mixed together. Hundreds of vessels, many intact, were found, and in several places the bones of skeletons and a number of skulls were uncovered. The skulls were severed from the bodies and only a few bones were scattered around them. Most of the bones were found inside vessels that covered almost the entire floor of the cave.

The condition of the bones indicates that this was a grave in which limbs were reburied (fractional burial). The burial offerings included beads,

pendants, flint and stone artifacts, and brass rings. This burial layer, which was rich in finds, dates to the last stage of the Late Chalcolithic period.

The Finds. Most of the pottery is similar to that found at other sites of the Late Chalcolithic period. The vessels were handmade for the most part, but some were made on a tournette. A few were burnished. The main forms include a jug with a high loop handle; a red-burnished jug with a spout and a ribbed neck; a red-burnished pitcher in the form of a gourd; a gray-burnished bowl, which is the distinctive hallmark of the period; also found were a red-burnished bowl and pots with painted decoration, which were well known in this period, especially in the southern part of the country.

Many of the pottery types are derived from the Ghassulian culture, but they were also prevalent in the Late Chalcolithic and beginning of the Early Bronze ages. Parallels are also found in the pre-dynastic cultures in Egypt (Gerzeh, Ma'adi) and Mesopotamia (Uruk). Among the other finds was a pendant shaped like a bull's head, which had its origin in the pre-dynastic period in Egypt, and three rings made of almost pure brass.

Human bones were found in at least sixty-five clay vessels, but there must have been many more: Many vessels were found overturned and the bones scattered beside them. A minimum estimate (based on a count of complete sets of human teeth) of the number of people buried in the clay vessels would be thirty-eight; the maximum estimate is 105. Of the four complete skulls, two are of the dolichocephalic type and two of the brachycephalic (Alpine), the earliest skulls of this type found in the country (except for the find of the Mesolithic period in the Carmel caves).

Tomb Cave.

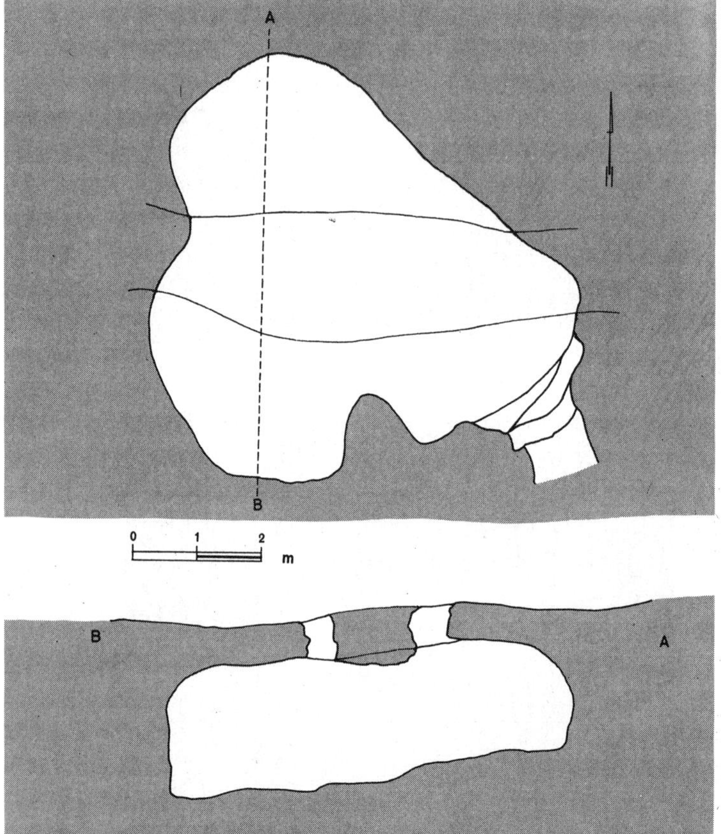

SUMMARY: THE RELATIVE AND ABSOLUTE CHRONOLOGY

The finds in the earliest layer of the grave indicate that the culture of the early stage of the Late Chalcolithic period had been perpetuated, but they also contain elements belonging to the Early Bronze Age. The pottery of this phase found at Tell el-Asawir shows characteristics of both the southern and northern parts of the country. Several objects clearly exhibit their Egyptian origin. A communal burial of limbs and severed heads, known from Mesopotamia and Egypt, was here uncovered for the first time in Palestine. Its closest parallels in the country have been discovered in a number of cemeteries in Jericho and Gezer.

The date of the grave, phase II of the Late Chalcolithic, was determined according to relative chronology, by a comparative study of finds from parallel sites, such as Tell el-Far'a (N), Beth-Shean (stratum XVI), Megiddo (part of stratum XIX and stages 6–7), Jericho (part of stratum VII), various graves in Wadi Ghazzeh, site H and others. On the basis of Egyptian chronology, the absolute date of the grave can be fixed in the thirty-second century B.C., a date that tallies with the results obtained from a Carbon-14 examination of a grave (A–94 at Jericho) of the thirty-second century, where the finds were similar to those of Tell el-Asawir.

M. Dothan

BIBLIOGRAPHY

A. Alt, *Kleine Schriften* 1, München, 1959, 102 • M. Dothan, *IEJ* 3 (1953), 263 • D. Ferembach, *IEJ* 9 (1959), 221–28.

ASHDOD

IDENTIFICATION. Tel Ashdod lies about 4 kilometers (2½ miles) inland, east of the sand dunes. It is difficult to determine the exact extent of the mound since the remains of the ancient settlement were partly destroyed by the cultivation of its fields over many generations and by building activity on the site. The two main parts of the mound can be clearly distinguished: the acropolis, with an area of appoximately 20 acres, and the lower city of at least 70 acres. The mound is about 50 meters above sea level and rises about 15 meters above the surrounding area.

Ashdod was a major city mainly in the Late Bronze and the Iron ages. Its name has been preserved in the name of the Arab village of Isdud, situated 14.5 kilometers (9 miles) northeast of ancient Ashkelon and 6 kilometers (3½ miles) southeast of modern Ashdod. The mound of ancient Ashdod rises in the center of the village.

HISTORY

The city and its inhabitants are first mentioned in several written sources of the Late Bronze Age II discovered at Ugarit. An Akkadian text relates that a merchant, Šukuna, received six garments and other merchandise, including two thousand shekels (weight) of purple wool from Ashdod. This indicates that Ashdod served as a textile center from which dyed garments were traded during the Late Bronze Age II. An alphabetic text from Ugarit names an Ashdodite, Aryn, who belonged to a group of merchants *(bdl)*.

Among the long list of Ashdodites *(add[y])* mentioned in Ugaritic texts, most seem to be West Semitic, while a few may be Hurrian. The Ashdodites never appear as a separate legal entity in the documents, perhaps indicating that they were merely maritime traders who happened to operate in Ugarit.

Another Akkadian document from Ugarit provides evidence that three Palestinian cities were involved in trade with Ugarit: Accho, Ashkelon, and Ashdod. Up to the present time, however, only the Ashdodites are known not only to have traded with Ugarit but also to have lived there or in its port town (Minet el-Beidah or Ugarit).

Ashdod is further mentioned in the list of place-names, composed by the Egyptian Amenopete in the eleventh century B.C. (number 263). In the Bible Ashdod appears many times: "Ashdod, its towns and its villages" is included in the list of the cities of Judah (Joshua 15:47), but the date of this source is controversial. Nothing is said in the Masoretic text of Judges 1:18 about its conquest, but according to the Septuagint version of this passage, it can be argued that Ashdod was conquered by the tribe of Judah.

Ashdod was almost always a non-Israelite town, being one of the five cities of the "lords of the Philistines" (Joshua 11:22; 13:3). The Ark of the Covenant was brought to the Temple of Dagon at Ashdod (I Samuel 5). Uzziah, King of Judah, "broke down... the wall of Ashdod, and built cities about Ashdod and among the Philistines"

The mound and the areas of excavation.

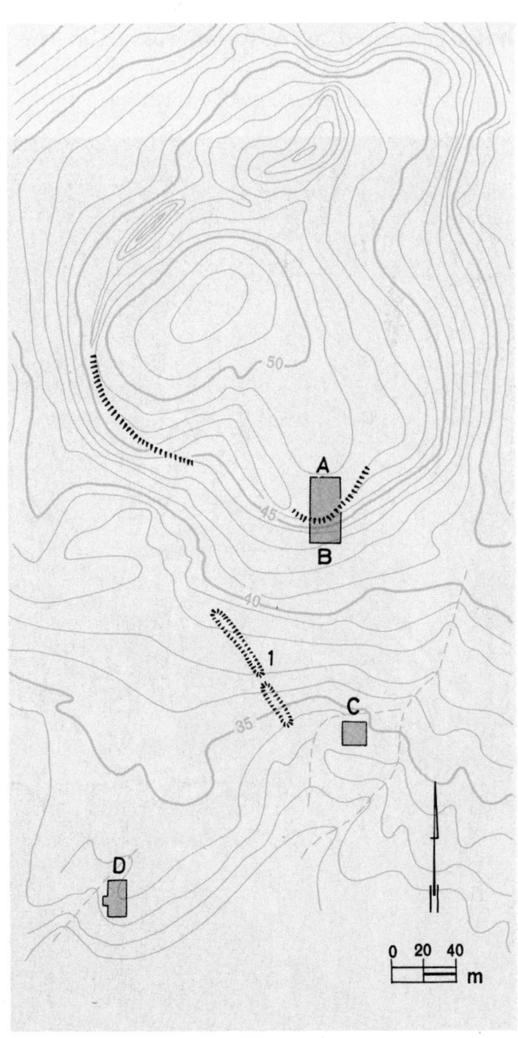

(II Chronicles 26:6). The judgment of Amos on Ashdod (Amos 1:8) probably relates to the same period. Isaiah (20:1) states that Sargon, the Assyrian king, sent Tartan (the commander in chief) against Ashdod and conquered the city. This episode and the relations between Assyria and Ashdod are described in detail in the Assyrian Prism Inscription of the Annals and in the Display Inscription of Sargon II.

According to Assyrian sources, Ashdod revolted against the king of Assyria. During the Assyrian military reprisal, Azuri, king of Ashdod, was dethroned and replaced by his brother in 712 B.C. One year later Ashdod again revolted, under the leadership of Iamani (a Greek, probably from Cyprus), and Sargon once again put down the revolt. The rebel fled to Egypt, the town was conquered and sacked, and the territory of Ashdod was annexed by the Assyrians.

The kings Mitinti and Ahimelekh are known to have governed as Assyrian vassals at the time of Sennacherib and Esarhaddon. Herodotus relates that the city was besieged after the downfall of Assyria by the Egyptian king Psamtik I for twenty-nine years (II, 157). When the Babylonians conquered the country, the king of Ashdod was taken prisoner and the region became a Babylonian province.

The destruction of Ashdod in this period is referred to by the prophets Jeremiah (25:20), Zephaniah (2:4), and Zechariah (9:6). After the return from the Babylonian exile, the Persian province of Ashdod became an enemy of Judah, as reported in the book of Nehemiah (13:23–24). The history of the city in the Hellenistic and Roman periods, when it was known as Azotus, is well documented, especially in the books of the Maccabees and the works of Josephus. Jonathan the Hasmonaean demolished the temple of Dagon in Ashdod (I Maccabees 10:84). The town was held by Alexander Jannaeus at the beginning of his reign (*Antiquities* XIII, 395), and it is thus assumed that

Aerial view of the mound; 1962 excavations.

the city was conquered by John Hyrcanus. Pompey separated the city from Judea (*War* I, 156), and Gabinius reconstructed it (*ibid.,* 165–66). Herod was granted Ashdod by Augustus. He willed it to his sister Salome, who left it to Livia. It thus became part of an imperial estate. During the First Revolt Ashdod surrendered to Titus (*ibid.,* IV, 130). Eusebius speaks of "Azotus" as being only "a townlet of a certain importance" (*Onomasticon* 18, 20:11, 22). By that time "Ashdod Yam," the harbor city (Azotus Paralius), had begun to replace the inland city (Azotus Mesogaeus) as a local center.

EXCAVATIONS

Seven seasons of excavations have been carried out so far (1962, 1963, 1965, a small-scale sounding in 1967, 1968–72), first as a joint project of the Pittsburgh Theological Seminary, the Pittsburgh Carnegie Museum, and the Israel Department of Antiquities, and from 1965 on, as a joint project of the last two institutions. D. N. Freedman, J. Swauger, and M. Dothan headed the project, and M. Dothan served as Director of Excavations. During the first season, excavations were conducted in four areas: A, B, C, D (area B is a continuation of area A, but at the beginning of the excavations the level of area A was 6 meters higher, since the section of the mound containing area B had been previously removed by settlers). In the second season, excavations were carried out in areas A, B, D, G, and during the third season (1965) in areas D, G, H, and K. Trial soundings were also made in areas E and F, to determine the extent of the mound. Small-scale soundings in area D were conducted in 1967.

Areas G, H, and K were the main areas of work during the fourth and fifth seasons. In 1969 area M was also opened. Areas M and G were further excavated during 1970. Work on area M continued in 1971 and 1972. Areas A, B, G, H, and K are situated on the acropolis; areas D, C, and M in the lower city; and area E on a hill northeast of the

General view of area G; MBA II-C/LBA II.

acropolis. Area F forms a part of a cemetery located approximately 1.5 kilometers east of the mound. Altogether more than $1\frac{1}{2}$ acres (6,500 square meters) were excavated.

On the basis of the correlation between the strata of the various areas, and on the stratigraphy of the mound as a whole, a tentative chronology has been established as follows: stratum I, Byzantine; stratum II, Roman; stratum III, Herodian; stratum IV, Hellenistic; stratum V, Persian; strata VI–IX, Iron Age II; stratum X, Iron Age I–II; strata XI–XIII, Iron Age I; strata XIV–XVII, Late Bronze Age II; stratum XVIII, Late Bronze Age I. The soundings in area G in the northern part of the mound show that Middle Bronze Age remains are partly concealed within the mound well below stratum XVIII, and that the establishment of the city dates from Middle Bronze Age II–C (circa 1650–1600 B.C.).

Middle Bronze Age II. Although scattered shards dating to the Chalcolithic and Early Bronze Age were found on the mound, the first fortified city, built on bedrock, dates to Middle Bronze Age II-C. A fragment of a massive brick gate from this period was found in area G. The gate was built on the straight entry plan and has a pair of piers on both ends of its parallel walls, narrowing the passage to 3.5 meters. Short walls supporting the gate on both sides were anchored in a glacis that was preserved to a height of circa 40 centimeters. This layout is similar to that of the east gate at Shechem. The finds point to the second half of the seventeenth century B.C. for the establishment of these defenses, probably in the days of Apophis I.

The acropolis was apparently surrounded by a strong brick wall, of which only the foundation trench was preserved in area B on the edge of the occupied area of the lowest stratum (XVIII). During this period the lower city was not occupied, and outside the wall there was probably a fosse. In area G a building was found above the site of the Middle Bronze Age II–C gate. It therefore seems that from the Late Bronze Age I on, the gates must have been farther north and had eroded. The scant finds from the Late Bronze Age I strata include bichrome pottery and imported Cypriot ware.

Beth Yeraḥ; assorted beads and gold plaque from tomb; EBA II.

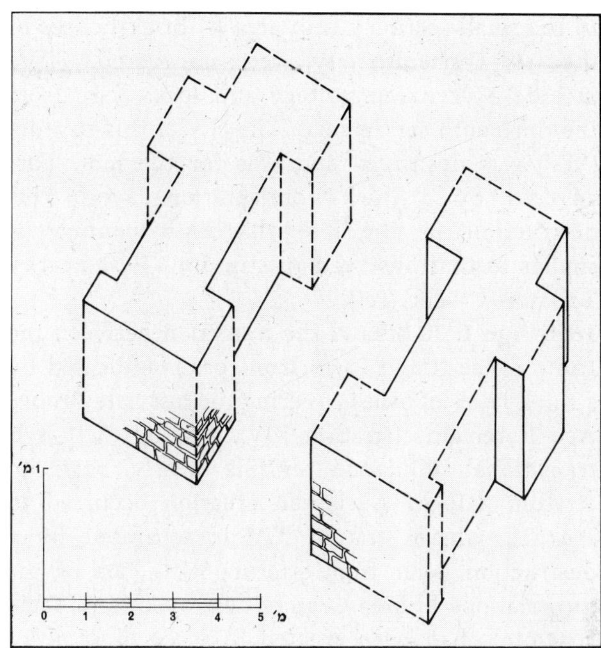

Isometric plan of gate, area G; MBA II-C.

Late Bronze Age II. The next four strata (XVII–XIV) belong to Late Bronze Age II (circa 1450–1230 B.C.). In stratum XVII sections of some brick buildings and stone pavements, perhaps of courtyards or streets, were uncovered in area B. On the strength of the pottery finds, including local painted ware and Cypriot imports, this stratum can be dated to the end of the fifteenth century B.C. The buildings and pottery of strata XVI and XV are similar. A large public (?) brick building was discovered (thickness of the walls 60 to 70 centimeters), consisting of rooms built on two sides of a central courtyard. Finds, characteristic of the fourteenth century B.C., include pottery, scarabs, and figurines. The last phase of the Late Bronze Age (stratum XIV) is scarcely represented here. Since this stratum is situated on the surface level of area B, it was heavily disturbed in modern times. Only some floors and grain silos were preserved.

In area G strong brick fortifications or buildings that may have been fortified continued through strata XVII to XIV, with only minor changes in plan. They consisted of three parallel lines of rooms and courts. The brick walls, 1.2 meters wide, stood on high stone foundations. In one of the courts a plastered cistern was found which collected rainwater from the roofs and conveyed it through a channel to another deep cistern.

In the small section cut in area H, brick houses of the last Canaanite city were uncovered. Finds include Mycenaean pottery and local ware from the thirteenth century B.C. The city of this stratum (XIV) was destroyed and was for the most part covered by a thick conflagration layer. This destruction in the late thirteenth century is similar to that observed in stratum VII at nearby Tel Mor (v. Mor, Tel).

Iron Age I. In area A the transition between the Late Bronze II and Early Iron ages is indicated by a thick layer of ashes covering the last Late Bronze Age II remains (stratum XIV). Stratum XIII–B is transitional. Philistine remains clearly begin in stratum XIII–A. A similar situation occurred in area H, where stratum XIV is separated by a destruction layer from stratum XIII. Part of the fortifications in area G were destroyed, and some structures had been erected in place of some of the walls. This does not necessarily imply that the entire city of Ashdod was destroyed at the end of the Late Bronze Age. However, the discovery at Ashdod of a number of stratified Mycenaean III-C–1 shards (starting in stratum XIII-B), usually dated to circa 1200 B.C., may indicate that a wave of Sea Peoples preceded their great invasion and subsequent settlement associated with the eighth year of Ramses III. Such movements may perhaps be indicated by the stratigraphy at Ashdod. The first wave destroyed part of the Canaanite city (stratum XIV) during the last quarter of the thirteenth century. The second wave brought about Philistine rule in the first quarter of the twelfth century. The Philistine city seems to have flourished mainly in strata XII and XI.

In the limited area of strata XI and X of the Early Iron Age excavated in area A, sections of a fortress were discovered. Only the northern part of this rectangular structure is preserved, because the southern part stood on the level that has disappeared in area B. The brick walls of the fortress are about 1.25 meters wide and are preserved in some places to a height of 2 meters. A part of the wall probably belonged to the western gate tower of the fortress. The main floor of the fortress dates from the eleventh century B.C. and contained pottery characteristic of that period, including Philistine ware. This fortress, which probably stood inside the city and was surrounded by a wall, was built by the Philistines in the twelfth century B.C. and continued to exist — with some changes — through the eleventh century B.C. It was destroyed at the beginning of the tenth century B.C.

In area G the main Philistine stratum (XII) was found. It was built after a short period (stratum

View of Area B; LBA II.

Area B: plan of LBA II dwelling.

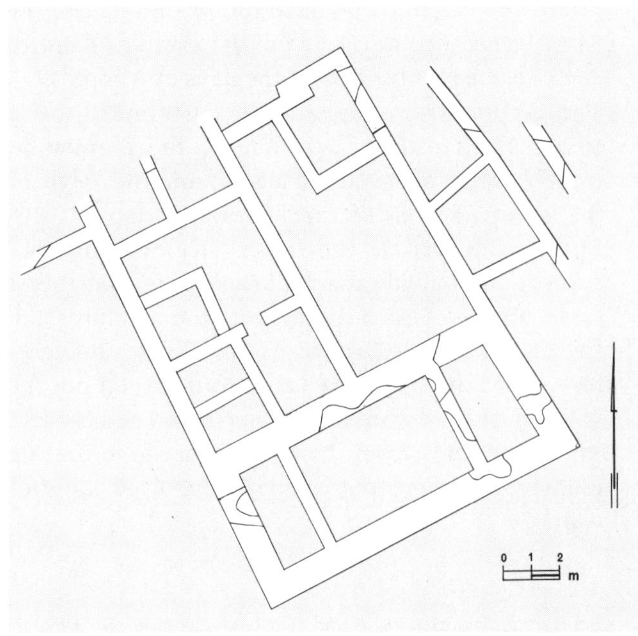

XIII) during which houses and cult installations were erected in the area that had previously been an open space partly covering the fortified walls. The inhabitants reused the remains of the Canaanite fortified building and adapted it to their defense line, creating a casemate wall with a group of rooms and courts beyond it, which served mainly as workshops.

Area H contained three Philistine strata. A section of the well-planned Philistine city containing two building complexes divided by a street was uncovered in this area. The northern complex consisted of a small apsidal structure. To the north of it were a row of rooms and a large hall with two stone bases, which probably originally supported columns. In addition to the Philistine pottery, many small objects, including jewelry, were found in these rooms. The single most significant object of the Philistine strata in area H was a figurine of a seated woman, which forms part of a throne. This figurine probably represents a Philistine goddess whose prototype seems to be the figurines of the Mycenaean "Great Mother."

Two seals were found engraved with signs similar to the Cypro-Minoan script that was used in Cyprus and the eastern Mediterranean during the thirteenth and early twelfth centuries B.C. On one of the seals were representations of men and

Gates in Area M: [light hatching] *11th century* B.C. [dark hatching] *end of 10th century* B.C.

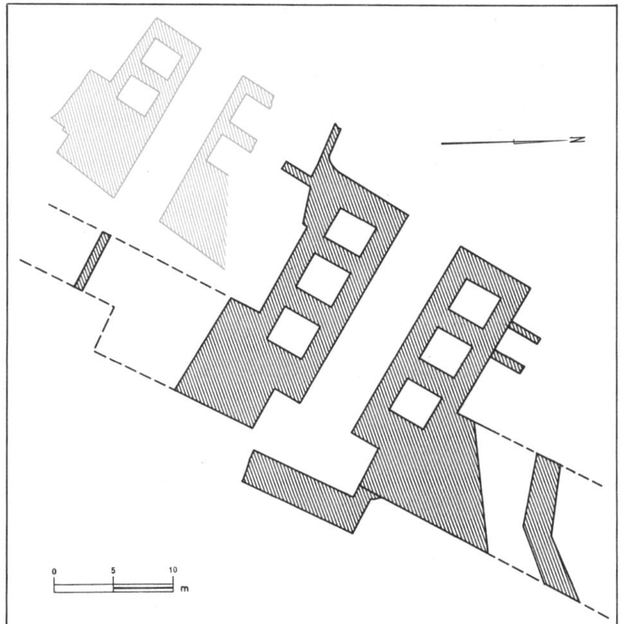

Stratum XII: apsidal building, area H; 12th cent. B.C. *(top). Area M: corner of northern gate tower. Note ashlar stones with bosses and destruction level above; end of 10th cent.* B.C. *(bottom).*

Anthropomorphic votive jar; IA II. Stratum XII: gold cover of pommel; twelfth century B.C. *(opposite page, top). Figurine of seated woman; Philistine stratum. Lead plaque of female deity (opposite page, bottom). Fragment of kernos; IA II. Fragment of chalice with image of goddess; IA II (below left and right). Cylinder seal, early Babylonian period; sixteenth century* B.C. *Seal impression of lyre player; end of eleventh century* B.C. *(bottom left and right).*

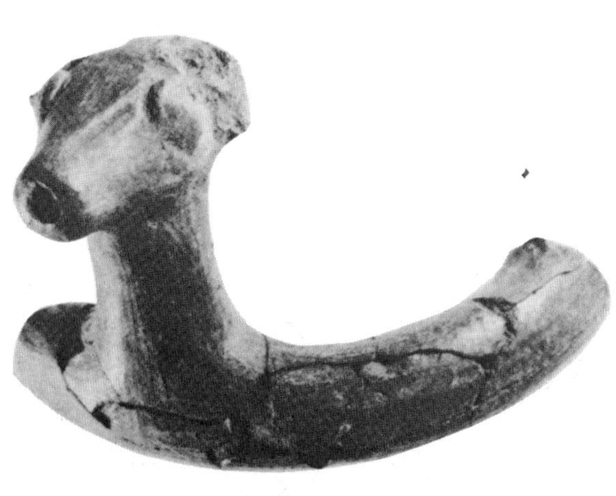

animals in the Aegean style. The seals may be regarded as the earliest written evidence found in a Philistine context.

In the middle of the eleventh century B.C., the city of Ashdod spread outside the acropolis, first as a small settlement in the lower city (area M, stratum X–B) where it is evidenced mainly by the presence of several kilns. Area M was later (stratum X–A) enclosed in a fortified area. Two solid towers stand at the entrance to the gate in the east, while two compartments are joined to each tower in the west. Most of the walls were built of sun-dried bricks, but in several places the walls were strengthened with stone. The gate is 13.7 meters long, 16.2 meters wide, and the passageway 4.2 meters wide. A wall 5 meters wide was attached to the southern tower of the gate. Pottery finds indicate that the gate was destroyed in the first half of the tenth century, perhaps at the end of the reign of David or during the expedition of Pharaoh Siamon, about 960 B.C.

Three superimposed ovens found opposite the passageway of the gate inside the city were in use during a transitional stage between the gate of

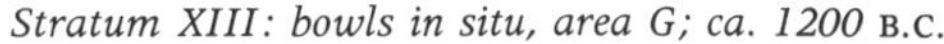

Stratum XIII: bowls in situ, area G; ca. 1200 B.C.

Mycenaean III-C I shards (opposite page, top). Fragment of Mycenaean charioteer vase; Mycenaean III-B (top left). Philistine craters; twelfth century B.C. *(above and opposite). Stratum XII: bathtub in secondary use, area G; twelfth century* B.C. *(below).*

stratum X and a later gate built in stratum IX. No building remains related to the transitional stage have yet been found. The fortifications in area M probably lay in ruins, and the area was an unfortified settlement for some time during the tenth century B.C. The next fortified lower city belongs to the Iron Age II.

Iron Age II. Relatively few significant remains of the Iron Age II were found on the acropolis. In area A some of the walls of the Philistine fortress were reused at this time. In area G a fragment of a brick wall was found which probably encircled the acropolis. A section of a well-planned city from the tenth century was uncovered in area K. The consecutive strata (X–VI) had a central street and drainage channel. The houses facing onto the street were built on stone foundations.

The most significant areas of this period, however, were uncovered in the lower city. A large gate in area M (stratum IX) is located south of the earlier (stratum X) gate. Built of unbaked brick on a stone foundation, this gate consists of two towers with three rooms each. Hewn as well as some dressed stones were used in the corners of the gate, and a gateway 5 meters wide passes between the two towers of the gate and continues into the city. The gate measures 20.5 by 18.25 meters.

It seems that the rooms of the first storey of the towers were sealed off from the passageway, at least in its earliest stage, and the entrance to them was from within the city. A wall 8.7 meters wide north of the gate continues for at least 40 meters and becomes narrower (5 meters) in its continuation to the south of the gate. The gate is similar in plan and measurements to those found at Gezer, Megiddo, and Hazor, which are linked with the building activities of Solomon. Those gates, however, have an additional compartment in front of the three divisions of the gate which is lacking in the Ashdod gate.

The additional width of the Ashdod walls may be due to their being solid brick walls rather than casemate walls on stone foundations, as in the other three cities. The first phase of the Ashdod gate probably dates to the last third of the tenth century. It may have been destroyed by King Uzziah of Judah.

The Iron Age II city was also well represented in area D (in strata IX–VI). The three uppermost strata were surrounded by a brick wall circa 3 meters thick, which probably served as an inner wall of the lower city in this area. The remains of stratum IX included brick foundations of a large building and some additional floors on which pottery, now called Ashdod ware, was found. This distinctive ware — red-burnished vessels decorated with black bands — began in other areas in stratum X immediately after the extinction of the

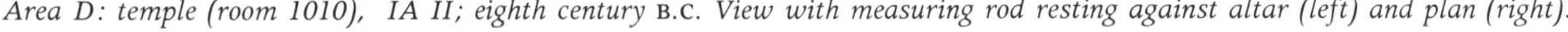

Area D: temple (room 1010), IA II; eighth century B.C. *View with measuring rod resting against altar (left) and plan (right).*

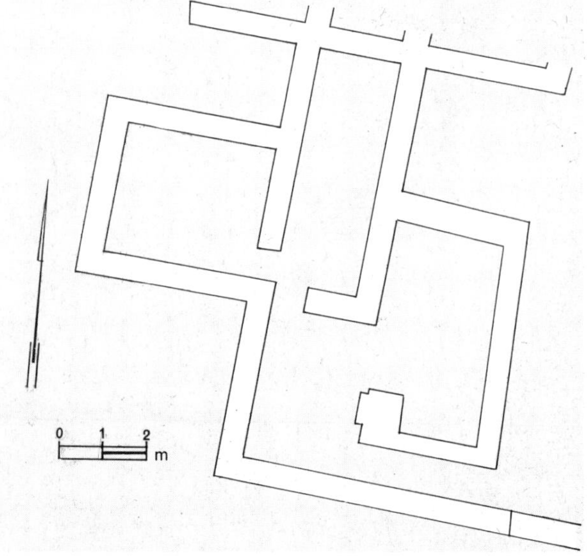

typical Philistine pottery. The richest strata in this area were VIII–VII.

In stratum VIII a small temple, consisting of several rooms, was discovered. Attached to one of the long sides of the main room was a rectangular brick structure that may have served as an altar. Near it, and in the adjacent rooms, a large quantity of cult objects, such as pottery figurines of domestic animals, were found, most of them used for libations in the temple *(kernoi)*. The many male and female figurines that were uncovered probably belonged to miniature clay offering tables. Figurines of the plaque type, especially female ones, were also found. Part of the finds of stratum VIII was discovered in pits containing refuse and ashes in stratum VII, as well as on the surface near the temple, mainly because deep plowing had turned up part of stratum VIII. There is no doubt, however, that the finds belong to stratum VIII, dating to the eighth century B.C., which was destroyed at the end of that century. Groups of skeletons and bones in secondary burials with some funeral offerings were found in several places. The remains belong to some three thousand individuals who probably died during the conquest of the city by Sargon II.

Besides the evidence from biblical and Assyrian sources, three fragments of a basalt stele found in the area of the acropolis bear witness to this

Eighth century B.C.*: Pottery kiln with hole-mouth jars (top); shard with inscription* [h]pḫr *(bottom left); figurines (bottom right).*

destruction. The inscription on the stele in Assyrian cuneiform shows it to be a duplicate of the type of victory stele at the Assyrian capital, Dur Sharrukin (Khorsabad). Although the names of Ashdod and its ruler were not found on these fragments, it may be assumed that they were indeed mentioned on the stele found at Ashdod, as it was the practice of the Assyrian kings to inscribe the names of conquered towns and their rulers on their victory stelae.

In area D, stratum VII (first half of the seventh century), the potters' quarter was preserved, with its street, houses, and courtyards used as workshops. Its main feature was pottery kilns, mostly of the elongated type, some preserved with their air vents. Hole-mouth jars were found in one of these. Stratum VII was probably destroyed by Psamtik I of Egypt.

On the acropolis an inscription in Hebrew characters — which reads *[h]pḥr,* "[the] potter" — was found incised on a fragment of an eighth-century B.C. jar. The discovery at Ashdod of additional inscriptions in the Hebrew script of the Iron Age II on such objects as a *nṣf* weight, a possible *beqa'* weight, a *pym* weight, and a jar handle stamped with a *lamelekh* inscription and the royal symbol (the first such stamp found outside the kingdom of Judah) seems to indicate trade and possibly even a closer relationship between Ashdod and Judah, mainly during the seventh century B.C. (Ashdod strata VII–VI). Perhaps Ashdod was even conquered by Judah in the days of Josiah and remained in the kingdom until his death in 609 B.C.

The Persian Period (Stratum V). Remains of this period were uncovered in the second season of excavation, mainly in area A and, during the third and fourth seasons, in area K. Most of the remains in area A were destroyed when the Hellenistic buildings were erected, and only a few walls of buildings and a deep fosse near the edge of the Philistine fortress were discovered. The fosse was perhaps dug during the Philistine period. However, it was cleaned at a later time, for the earliest objects discovered in it belong to the Persian period. Uncovered in area K were the stone foundations of a large public building, which

Stratum VIII: destruction level of Sargon II, area D (left). Fragment of stele of Sargon II of Assyria, set up after 712 B.C. (right).

possibly served as the administrative center during this period. So far, only four large halls have been excavated.

Besides typical local pottery of the period, this stratum also contained Attic ware, especially of the black-figured type, as well as jewelry in the Persian style and an ostracon with an Aramaic inscription. The ostracon describes the quantity of wine delivered in the name of Zebadiah. On the basis of the paleography, this inscription, which may be written in the Ashdodite dialect known to Nehemiah (Nehemiah 13:24), can be dated to the beginning of the fourth century B.C.

The Hellenistic Period. The Hellenistic buildings in area A — which penetrated deeply into the strata of the Persian period and of Iron Age II, destroying them in the process — belong to a city showing careful town planning. Streets in the excavated section were laid out between groups of buildings. The main building probably belonged to the agora of the city. A special technique employing brick foundations and stone walls was used in building its walls. In the main room large pottery jars, similar to Rhodian wine jars, were discovered. One of the corners of the room served as a place of worship, as may be inferred from an altar found there, formed of two flat stones that served as feet and a third stone laid across them forming the top. Nearby two miniature stone altars were found, as well as weapons and a lead plaque probably representing a deity with a fish tail. These finds, dated mainly to the end of the second century B.C., were discovered in a deposit of ashes that may be related to the destruction of the town by the Hasmonaeans. Among the coins in the deposit, the latest was a coin of Antiochus VIII dated to 114 B.C., thereby establishing a terminus post quem date for John Hyrcanus' conquest of the city.

The Roman and Byzantine Periods. In area A the general layout of the Hellenistic city was maintained also in stratum III, which dates mainly from the time of the Herodian dynasty. The pottery included an abundance of terra sigillata and Megarian wares. With the destruction of this stratum, probably during the First Revolt (A.D. 67), Ashdod's period of greatness came to an end. The city of stratum II dates from the Late Roman and Byzantine periods. Since it was situated close to the surface, few remains were found. Most of the

Potsherd with "Ashdodite" inscription; fifth century B.C. (top). Gold earring in the shape of a goat's head; circa fourth century B.C. (bottom).

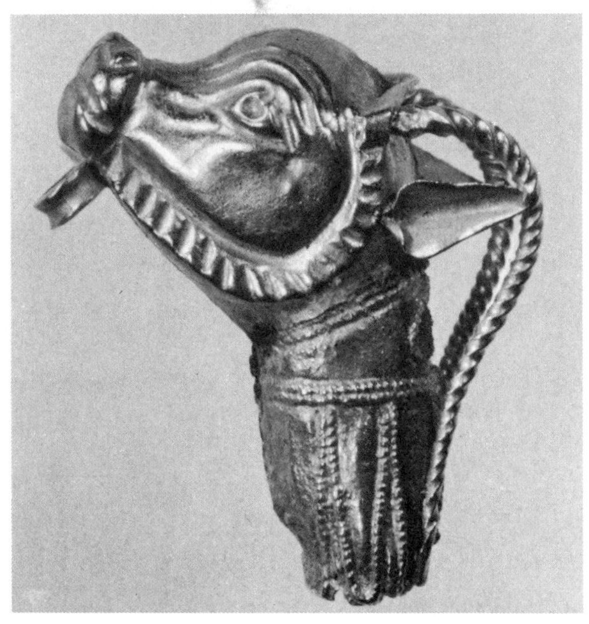

Area A: general view of Hellenistic structure.

buildings are small. A pit full of ashes and of debris from workshops was cleared.

In the topmost stratum (I) the remains of some houses were found. These were also heavily damaged due to their proximity to the surface. The remains of houses, grain silos, and various agricultural installations (such as wine presses) show that Ashdod had declined into a large village by the end of the Byzantine period and the beginning of the Umayyad dynasty. The semi-agricultural settlement spread to the hill opposite the acropolis (area E). A marble slab with Jewish symbols may have belonged to this settlement. Another marble fragment with the beginning of a Samaritan inscription and a Samaritan talisman serve as evidence for a Samaritan population at Ashdod at this time. Ashdod, which for two thousand years had been the capital of a kingdom, a province, and an independent city, lost its importance in the Byzantine period and never regained its previous splendor. M. DOTHAN

BIBLIOGRAPHY

B. Mazar, *Enc. Miqr.* 1, 750–52 (includes bibliography) (Hebrew) • H. Tadmor, *BIES* 18 (1954), 140–46 (Hebrew); *idem, JCS* 12 (1958), 79f • D.N. Freedman, *BA* 26 (1963), 134–39 • M. Dothan, *Yediot* 28 (1964), 176–92 (Hebrew); *idem, IEJ* 14 (1964), 79–95; 22 (1972), 166–67; 243–44 • H. Tadmor, *EI* 8 (1967), 241–45 (Hebrew) • M. Dothan, D.N. Freedman, *Ashdod I (1962), 'Atiqot* 7 (1967) • M. Dothan, *Ashdod II–III (1963–65)* (two vols. text, figures and plates), *'Atiqot* 9–10 (1971).

Ashdod, area G: bronze figurine; Hellenistic period.

ASHDOD-YAM

Identification. The site of Ashdod-Yam is circa 5 kilometers (3 miles) northwest of Ashdod, one of the five cities of the Philistine Pentapolis. Archaeological surveys carried out by the writer since the 1940's revealed a large, semicircular, rampart-like structure in the southern part of the site.

Excavations

Several excavations were conducted at the site by the writer from 1965 to 1968 on behalf of the Tel Aviv-Jaffa Museum of Antiquities. Ten cuts were made in the rampart-like structure and at its foot. In three of these cuts the city wall was revealed. It was retained on the inner and outer sides by two earthen glacis. The wall, 3.1 meters thick, was built of reddish sun-dried brick, and the outer glacis was made of varieties of earth common to the region, mainly sand and *kurkar*. The outer glacis was evidently intended to resist assaults by the siege engines and battering rams of the besiegers, whereas the inner glacis served to counter the pressure of the outer glacis.

On the basis of the pottery, two periods of occupation are distinguished at the site. The earlier, which includes the period of the construction of the

Top of brick city wall.

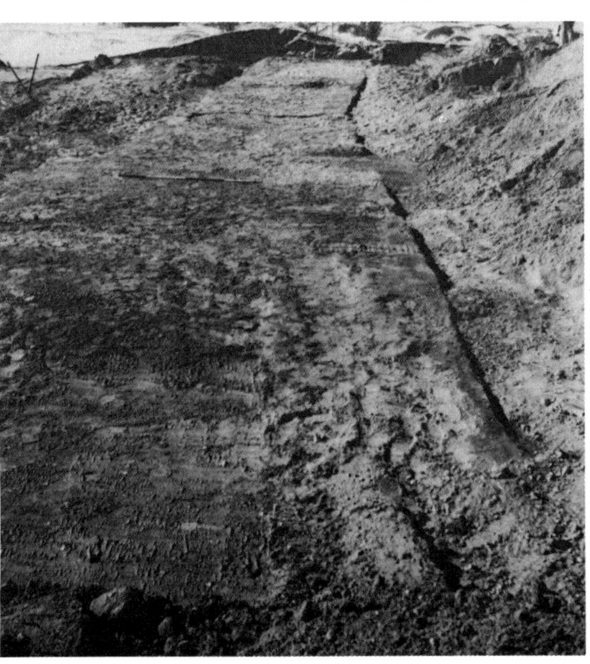

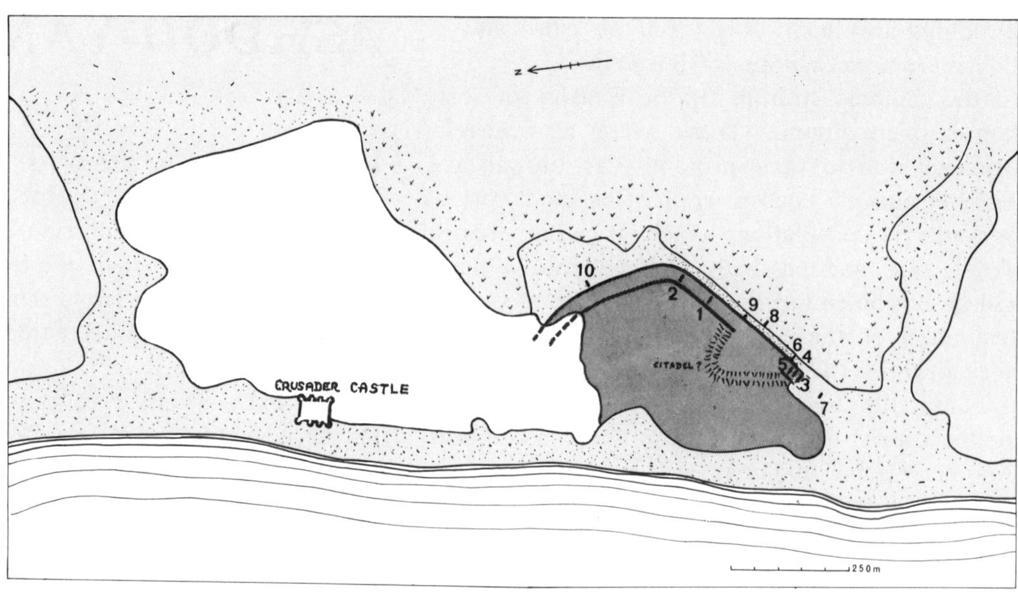

Plan of the site, showing location of trenches 1–10.

fortifications, dates to the second half of the eighth century B.C. The later dates to the seventh century B.C., when the fortifications were no longer used.

SUMMARY

Ashdod-Yam is mentioned only in documents from the time of Sargon II (742–705 B.C.), in connection with his campaign against the kingdom of Ashdod in 713 B.C. for the purpose of deposing the usurper who had seized rule in Ashdod. This usurper, called Iamani by Sargon, rebelled against him and, according to the documents, Iamani in great haste fortified three cities in the kingdom of Ashdod — Ashdod itself, Gath, and Ashdod-Yam. The last was evidently intended to serve as a rear base for the main city in times of danger. Since neither earlier nor later fortifications were discovered at the site, the uncovered wall and glacis are most certainly those erected by Iamani. J. KAPLAN

BIBLIOGRAPHY

B. Mazar, *Enc. Miqr.* 1, 750–52 (Hebrew) • J. Kaplan, *BIES* 19 (1956), 122–23 (Hebrew) • H. Tadmor, *JCS* 22 (1958), 70–80 • J. Kaplan, *IEJ* 19 (1969), 137–49.

Ruins of crusader castle.

ASHKELON

Identification. The ruins of Ashkelon cover a semicircular area of circa 12 acres, the chord of which is represented by the seacoast. Ashkelon is the only city in the southern coastal plain situated directly on the seaboard. The outline of the city is marked by a wall and towers. On the shore itself the line of the wall has been obliterated by the action of the waves.

In the middle of the semicircle's diameter, near the seaboard, stands an artificial mound (el Khadra). It is the site of Bronze and Iron Age Ashkelon. The total height of the accumulation is 13 meters. The Hellenistic level is reached at 5.5 meters, the Philistine level at 7.5 meters. South of the mound is the site of the ancient inner port, which formed a landlocked bay. Because the strata of the later periods are considerable, extensive excavation of the Philistine city is difficult. However, the finds of the later periods are among the richest in Israel

As early as 1815 Lady Hester Stanhope dug here. Her workmen found a huge statue of Zeus, which they smashed, hoping to find treasure inside it. One foot of the statue is preserved in the Rockefeller Museum, Jerusalem. In 1920–21 J. Garstang and W. J. Phythian-Adams excavated in Ashkelon. They cleared a Roman council house and dug a stratigraphic section on the shore.

Various finds were unearthed in Ashkelon during the 1930's and 1940's, among which the painted Roman grave found in 1937 deserves special mention. In 1955 J. Perrot and J. Hévesy excavated a Neolithic site on the shore of Ashkelon. In 1967 V. Tsaferis excavated a Christian basilican church with a mosaic pavement; in 1972 two marble sarcophagi with sculptured reliefs were found in the Barnea quarter.

HISTORY

Ashkelon, a coastal city in southern Palestine, was economically important in various periods, both because of its port and its location on the Philistine section of the "Via Maris."

Ashkelon is mentioned for the first time in the two groups of nineteenth-century B.C. Egyptian Execration Texts. From an Egyptian document of the fifteenth century B.C. (the hieratic papyrus, Leningrad 1119–A), and especially from the fact that Ashkelon is not mentioned in the accounts of the wars of Thutmose III and Amenhotep II in Canaan, it can be concluded that it remained loyal to Egypt throughout this period. Among the el-Amarna letters from the fourteenth century B.C. (Knudtzon Numbers 320–26 and 370) are several from Widyia, the ruler of Ashkelon, affirming his loyalty to Pharaoh. However, the ruler of Jerusalem (in Number 287) complains that Ashkelon had given supplies to the Ḥabiru, the enemies of Pharaoh. During the reign of Ramses II Ashkelon revolted but was reconquered. On Merneptah's Israel stele, Ashkelon is mentioned together with Gezer and Yanoam as cities conquered by Pharaoh's armies. It would seem then that these three cities formed the nucleus of the opposition to the declining Egyptian rule in Canaan.

Ashkelon became one of the cities of the Philistine Pentapolis following their settlement in the southern coastal plain. In the lists of city names by Amenope, probably dating from the beginning of the eleventh century B.C., Ashkelon is listed as a Philistine city (together with Ashdod and Gaza).

Stratified section of the mound; excavated in 1921.

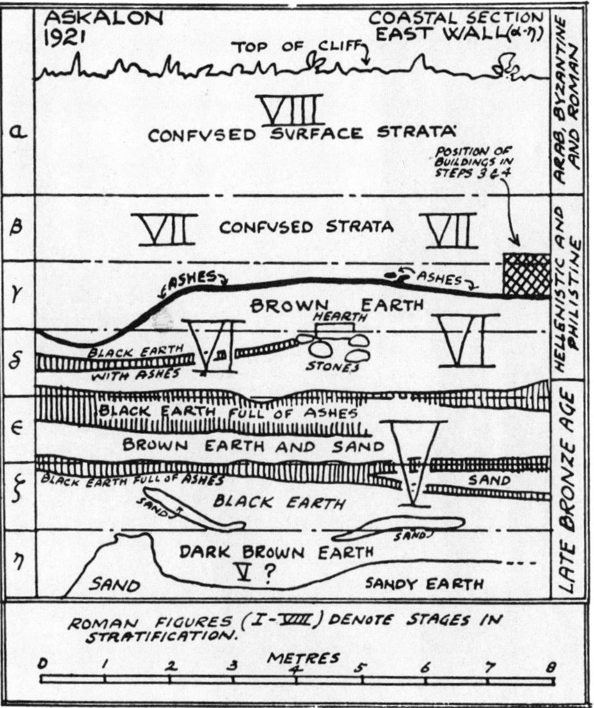

During the Period of Philistine expansion in the twelfth to eleventh centuries B.C., Ashkelon was a party in the league of the five Philistine cities, each ruled by a *seren* (Joshua 13:3, I Samuel 6:4, 17) supported by a military aristocracy. There are no written sources on the history of Ashkelon from the end of the eleventh century until the middle of the eighth century B.C.

When Tiglath-pileser III invaded Philistia for the first time in 734 B.C., the king of Ashkelon acknowledged his suzerainty but revolted shortly after. Following the defeat of Rezin, king of Damascus, by the Assyrian army, the regime in Ashkelon was overthrown (733 or 732 B.C.) in order to stave off a punitive action by the Assyrians. The leader of the upheaval, Rukibtu, was enthroned and received the approval of Tiglath-pileser III. Ashkelon refrained from taking part in the rebellious activities of the other Philistine cities during the years 732 to 705 B.C., and hence suffered no harm.

After the death of Sargon in 705 B.C., revolts broke out in the western parts of the Assyrian empire. In Palestine the leaders were Ṣidqa, king of Ashkelon, and Hezekiah, king of Judah. Judging by the prism inscription of Sennacherib and by the seal inscription *"Le 'Abdelab ben Sab'at 'ebed Metat ben Ṣidqa"* (ascribed to a king of Ashkelon at the time of Esarhaddon and Ashurbanipal — see below), it would seem that Ṣidqa was a member of the royal family of Ashkelon, and seized power by overthrowing the previous king (Rukibtu or his son Šarruludari).

In the inscriptions of Sennacherib describing his Palestinian campaign in 701 B.C., mention is made of the capture of Jaffa, Bene-Berak, Azor, and Beth-Dagon, all cities of Ṣidqa, king of Ashkelon.

When the revolt of Ashkelon was suppressed, Šarruludari, the son of Rukibtu, who had followed a pro-Assyrian policy, was proclaimed ruler of Ashkelon, but he lost the territory annexed to the Assyrian province in the north.

Mitinti, son of Ṣidqa, was among the vassals of Esarhaddon and Ashurbanipal. In 671 B.C. Ashkelon and Tyre revolted against Assyria, evidently for economic reasons. They were encouraged by Egypt. There is no information on any fighting in or near Ashkelon at this time. The city probably surrendered as the Assyrian army drew near. Since Mitinti is later mentioned among the vassals of Ashurbanipal, he was apparently not deposed for the part he played in the revolt, but he most likely had to pay a higher tribute on this account.

After the Assyrian rule had crumbled in the west, Ashkelon again came under Egyptian domination. Pharaoh Psamtik I besieged Ashdod and sent forces into Syria, probably along the inland route through Philistia. Herodotus (I, 105) relates that in the last years of Psamtik's reign Ashkelon was attacked by the invading Scythians (610 B.C.), and the temple of the Celestial Aphrodite there was plundered. According to the Babylonian Chronicle, in the reign of Nebuchadnezzar, Ashkelon was captured and laid waste by the Babylonian army, in Kislev 609 B.C.

Documents from the time of Nebuchadnezzar (published by E. Weidner) mention two sons of *A-ga-'*, king of Ashkelon, as well as artisans and singers who received oil rations from the royal household. These exiles were brought to Babylon after the capture of the city and were held in Nebuchadnezzar's palace, the same as Jehoiakin,

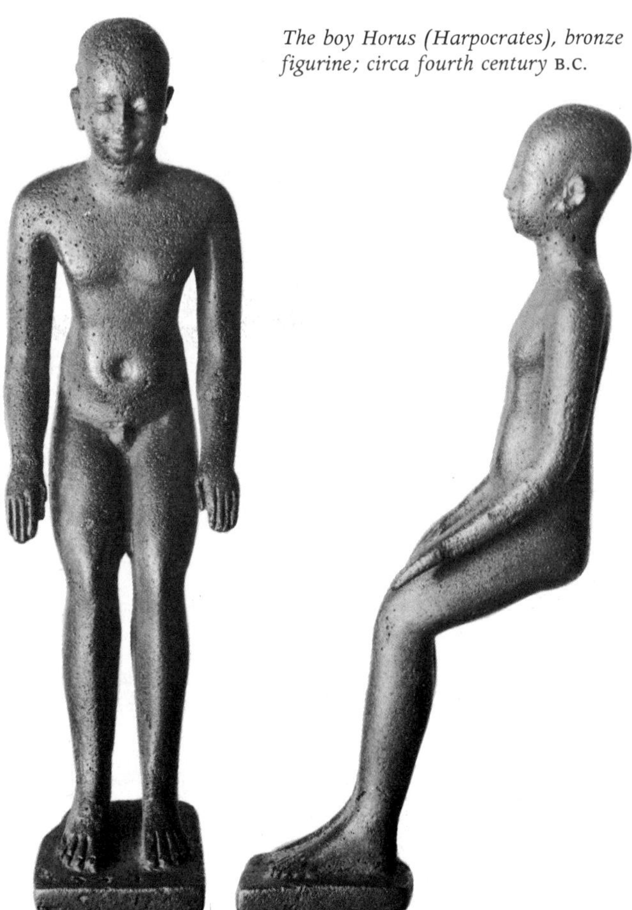

The boy Horus (Harpocrates), bronze figurine; circa fourth century B.C.

'Atlit; western wall.

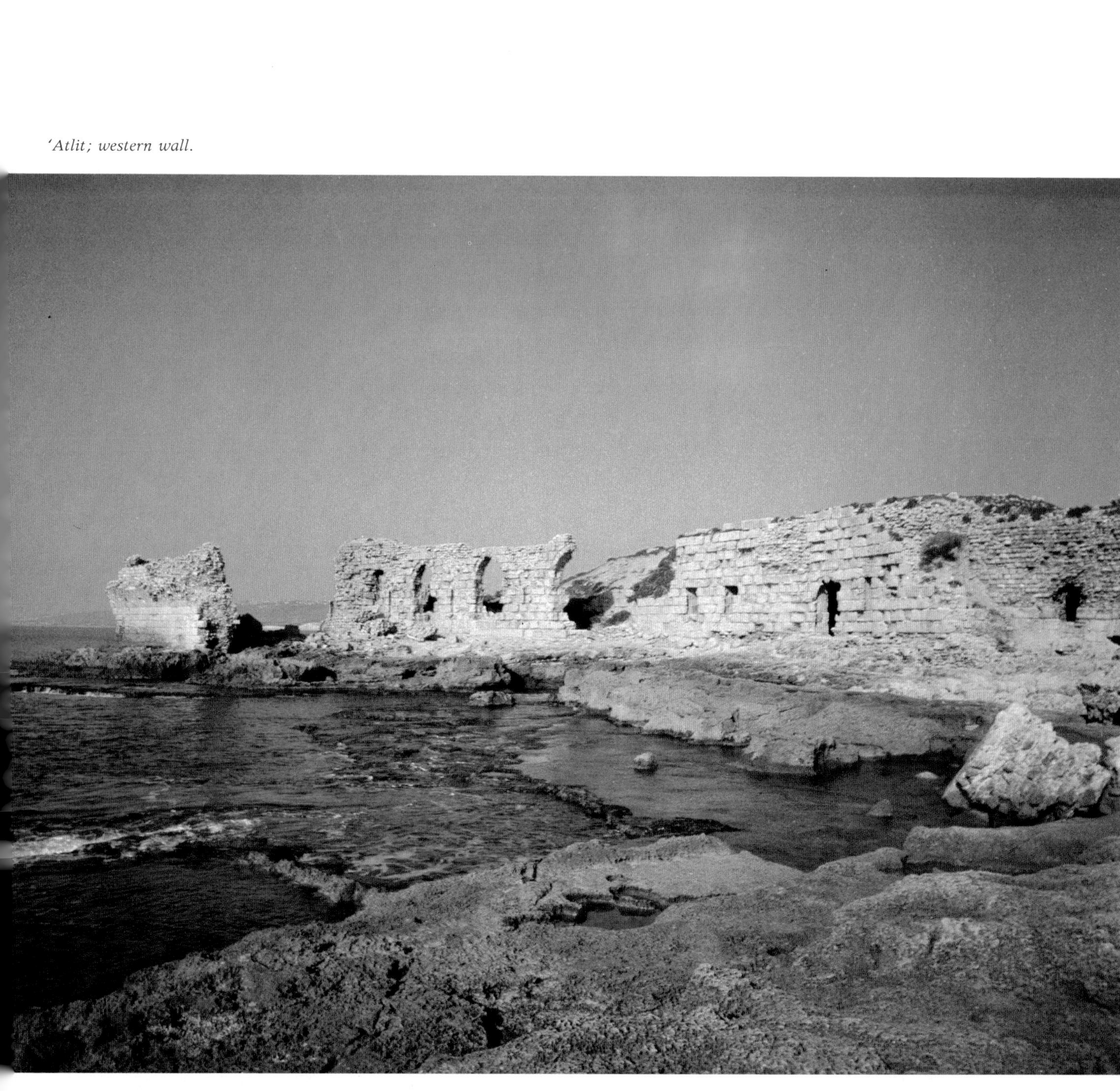

king of Judah, and his sons, who were taken into captivity in 598 B.C.

Under the Persians Ashkelon was a Tyrian possession and contained a royal palace. In the Hellenistic period its inhabitants came under the influence of the Hellenistic culture of Ptolemaic Egypt. The city retained its independence throughout the Hasmonaean period, from 104 B.C. on. In the Roman period Ashkelon flourished as "a free, allied city." Herod, who was attached to the city by bonds of friendship and family traditions, built some resplendent buildings there.

During the First Revolt the inhabitants of Ashkelon defended themselves against the attacks of the Jews. In the period of the Mishnah and Talmud, despite the fact that Ashkelon was considered to be beyond the area supposedly held by those returning from Babylonian exile — and hence outside the Land of Israel proper — many Jews resided there. Talmudic sources mention the market at Ashkelon and the gardens around the city.

At the beginning of the Byzantine period, Ashkelon was one of the strongholds of pagan Hellenism in the country, until it, too, became a Christian city. At the time of the Crusades it was a Muslim stronghold. It passed, however, into Crusader hands and was held by them from 1153 to 1187 and again from 1191 to 1247. In 1270 Ashkelon was finally destroyed by the Mameluke Sultan Beibars, never to rise again. The identification of the city with Khirbet 'Asqalan, on the coast between Gaza and Jaffa, is beyond doubt.

FINDS

Prehistoric. The Neolithic settlement on the shore yielded remains of round huts 1 to 1.5 meters in diameter and bell-shaped silos (diameter 1 to 1.5, .9 meters deep). Flint and bone tools, stone vessels, pierced shells, and mother-of-pearl ornaments were found. Animal remains include ox, sheep, goat, and pig, as well as fish bones. The stone tools bear the trace of close ties with the Paleolithic tradition. There are indications of concomitant cultural ties and relations with sites in Palestine as well as Lower Egypt.

The Bronze and Iron Ages. Apart from chance discoveries, the Bronze and Iron ages are represented by gradated sections which the excavators dug

Kneeling priest, bronze figurine; circa fourth century B.C.

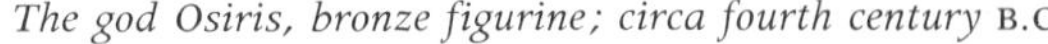

The god Osiris, bronze figurine; circa fourth century B.C.

on the seacoast in the years 1920–21. In one of these sections forty-three levels were distinguished, and in a second, eight levels. Remains of the Middle Bronze Age were found (sublevel 1, 43–41). The second level ends with a destruction layer. The third layer represents the renewal of settlement in the Middle Bronze Age. The fourth ends in new traces of destruction. The fifth level is quite thick and apparently represents the acme of a long period of growth in the Late Bronze Age. Assigned to that level are alabaster vessels from the Nineteenth Dynasty and a fragment of a basalt statue with a hieroglyphic inscription. This level ends with yet another destruction layer related to the appearance of the Philistines (circa 1190 B.C.).

The sixth and seventh levels belong to the Philistine settlement in the Iron and Persian periods, which lasted until the Hellenistic level. In the pre-Philistine levels, the Late Bronze Age Cypriot ware is prominent (a grave containing twenty-six Cypriot vessels was discovered on the seashore in 1936–37). Several Mycenaean shards were found that belong to the same period.

The excavators were generally able to distinguish

Aerial view. 1. Area of the Roman city. 2. The mound. 3. Ancient harbor.

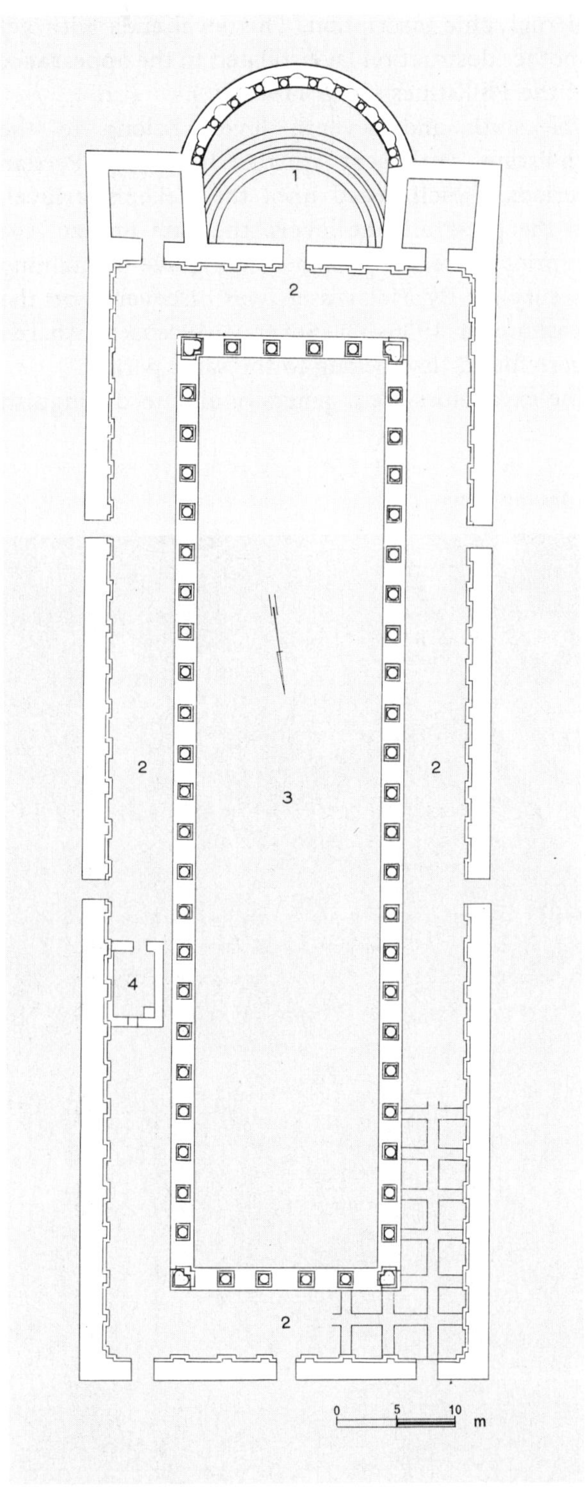

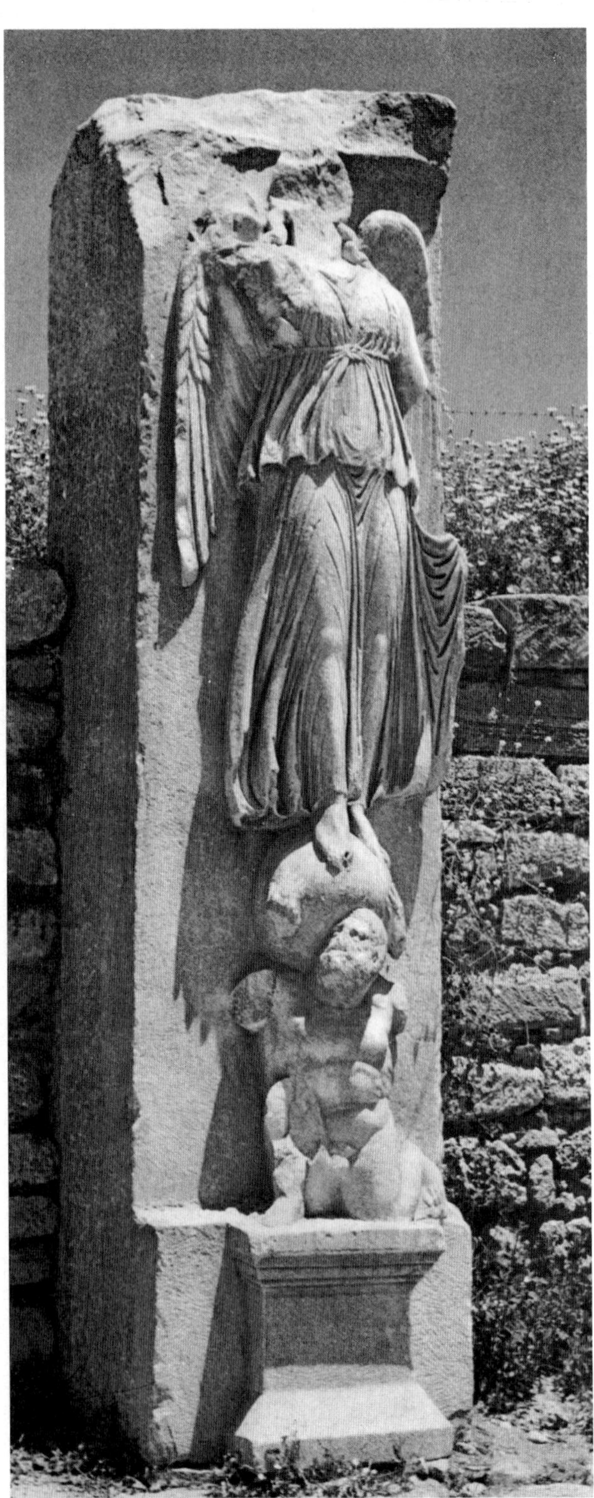

Bouleuterion, plan: 1. Senate hall. 2. Porticoes. 3. Open courtyard. 4. Temple of Apollo (?): end second/beginning third cent. A.D. *From the bouleuterion: Nike, Goddess of Victory, standing on the heavenly globe supported by Atlas (above); Isis and the infant Horus-Harpocrates (opposite page, top). Tetradrachm, city coin; second half first cent.* B.C. *(opposite page, bottom).*

between Canaanite and Philistine finds. Following the finds at Gezer, the excavation at Ashkelon formed the principal basis for establishing the pottery chronology of the Bronze and Iron ages.

The Persian and Hellenistic Periods. Finds from these periods are not extensive in Ashkelon. In addition to shards, the Persian period levels have yielded a Greek war helmet from the fifth/sixth century B.C. (fished from the sea). To the Ptolemaic period is assigned a treasure trove (circa fourth century B.C.) containing twenty-nine bronze statuettes and eleven weights (among which four are zoomorphic).

The statuettes comprise fourteen types: two are of men, in local Canaanite style; one is a weight shaped like a crouching ram, in the Mesopotamian style. The rest are statuettes of Egyptian deities in their original style. It seems that most of the statuettes had been gilded. Despite their Egyptian style they are of local manufacture. All were unearthed in a square room that had been the workshop of a smith. Hellenistic foundations were found in field 5 (the numbering of the fields follows Garstang — see bibliography), and a wall and gate were discovered in field 61.

Roman Period. Most of the finds in Ashkelon belong to the Roman period. Of the remains dating from this period, the council house (bouleuterion) is noteworthy. It was excavated by J. Garstang and W. J. Phythian-Adams in fields 61–67. The

building (110 meters long) consists of a semicircular hall in the shape of a theater (radius 13 meters), with tiers of seats. The hall was flanked on both sides by square rooms. It was entered through a forecourt (37 by 57 meters, portico included). Both sides of the hall were decorated with reliefs of winged victories (Nike) holding a wreath in the raised right hand; the left hand, close to the body, grasps a palm branch. The Victories stand poised on globes (symbolizing the heavenly sphere, universe) and were carried on the shoulders of figures of Atlas.

The courtyard adjoining the council hall was ringed by a portico (5 meters wide), with twenty-four columns on the long sides and six columns on the short sides. These columns were 8.35 meters high and bore Corinthian capitals. The inter-columnar space was 4.5 times the diameter of a column, reckoned from core to core.

In the corners stood double columns with a heart-shaped cross section. The columns, wall facing, and flooring were made of marble imported from Greece or Italy.

A relief of Isis and her son Horus (Harpocrates) was found in the south portico. In three Greek inscriptions found at this spot, two Roman citizens, Aulus Iustulius Tances, a centurion of the Tenth Legion, and Tiberius Julius Micio, a citizen of Ashkelon, are honored by the council and people of Ashkelon (*boule* and *demos*). A third-century inscription bears the legend "Prosper Ashkelon, Prosper Rome."

In the Byzantine period this building was surrounded by a thick wall, which the excavators assigned to Herod. The comparison of the style of the capitals, reliefs, and inscriptions with that of similar buildings at Sebaste (Samaria) and other places, however, proves that it is of a later date — the end of the second or the beginning of the third century A.D. Several sculptures from Ashkelon were published by J. H. Iliffe and others. They belong to the Roman period. These include the statue of Aphrodite kneeling, a complete statue of Hermes (now in the Rockefeller Museum, Jerusalem), a bust and head of Pan, a relief of Pan and a nymph, and a portrait of a Roman empress (Salonina?).

Of the graves of the period, the painted tomb excavated by J. Ory in 1937 deserves special mention. The tomb, to which one descends by three steps, consists of a single room with a round vault (4.1 meters long, 3.56 wide, 2.45 high). The surface of the rear wall and the vault are covered with painted stucco. The vault is decorated with a vine trellis forming medallions. In one of these the bust of a woman is represented, as well as a dog chasing a gazelle, a Gorgon mask, harvest scenes, doves and gazelles, Pan playing a syrinx, etc. Beneath the vine are painted, square panels separated by bands, to imitate marble. Between

them is an oval shield framed by wavy-line fillets in the corners. On the back wall are painted two seated nymphs against a background of Nilotic landscape of reeds and lotus blossoms on which birds are perched. Each nymph holds a reed in her left hand, while the right hand rests on a reversed amphora from which water pours down into a brook in which they dip their feet. To their left, an ox drinks from the stream, and on their right a crane. Fish of the tilapia species swim in the water. On the north wall are faint traces of the figures of a man and a woman, painted on each side of the door. Perhaps these figures represent the owners of the tomb. The excavator dated the tomb to the fourth century A.D., but it should probably be attributed to the third.

Lead coffins apparently made in Ashkelon are dated to the Late Roman period. Colonnettes divide the long sides of the coffins into panels, on which Hermes is represented. The panels at the short sides also show the figure of Hermes beneath an arch decorated with a Gorgon's head. The coffin lids are covered with a design of vine tendrils. Other designs include rosettes, lions, and boars. The coffins are dated to the third/fourth centuries A.D. by a coin from the reign of Constantine. A vaulted tomb of the same period, published by J.H. Iliffe, yielded gold jewelry, glass and pottery vessels, and a bronze cross.

Byzantine Period. To the Byzantine period (or perhaps the end of the Roman period) can be assigned the foundations of the semicircular city wall, which resembles the wall of Caesarea dating from the same period. The wall has round projecting towers. In field 5 a Byzantine church with one apse was excavated. In it were found Greek and Kufic inscriptions, shards dating to the Byzantine period and the Middle Ages, including glazed ware. The excavators date the church to the seventh/eighth centuries A.D. Dated to the same period are the remains of a synagogue, fragments of decorated lattice, the pedestal of a column bearing a relief of a seven-branched menorah, shofar, and ethrog. The fragments of mosaic floors uncovered in various parts of Ashkelon are also of this period. A part of the depiction of Byzantine Ashkelon has been preserved in the Madeba map.

Crusader Period. The upper section of the city wall dates from the Crusader period, but the type of construction (alternating stone and fired-brick courses) indicates a continuation of the Byzantine tradition. Ashkelon was entered by four gates during the Crusader period: the Jaffa gate to the north, the large Jerusalem gate to the east (adjoining a system of fortifications that served as the city citadel), the Gaza gate to the south, and the sea gate to the west. To the south, on the seashore, stood the Tower of the Virgins (Tour des Pucelles) and the Tower of Blood (Tour de Sang).

From the synagogue:
Chancel screen with Jewish symbols (top), chancel screen with Greek inscription (bottom).

Ashkelon-Barnea. In 1954 J. Ory excavated, on the lands of the Barnea Company, a basilical church with an inscribed apse flanked by two square chambers (prothesis and diaconicon). The nave measures 25 by 8 meters and each side aisle is 25 by 4 meters. A chapel (circa 7.5 meters wide) was attached to the south side of the church. It contains an inscribed apse and a corridor (circa 2 meters wide) running along the width of the structure and separating the apse from a cruciform baptistery (10 by 4.5 meters) with plastered walls and floor. Numerous fragments of marble flags, apparently debris of the church pavement, were discovered, as well as colored-glass tesserae, indicating that the walls had been faced with mosaics.

A second basilica was excavated by V. Tsaferis in 1966–67, 200 meters northwest of the former. Only the pavement in the north aisle and part of the narthex have been preserved. The aisle was 10.4 meters long and 6 meters wide. The pavement shows a border design of a vine trellis issuing from an amphora, with a geometric octagonal pattern in the center. A Greek mosaic inscription states that the diaconicon was completed in the month of Artemisios of the year 602 (A.D. 597) under the bishop Athanasios. A second Greek inscription contains Psalm 23:1. The fragmentary narthex pavement has geometric designs and a third Greek inscription on the east side (exactly opposite the amphora in the aisle pavement) with Psalm 93:5 and the date 597 (A.D. 493).

The marble sarcophagi with reliefs on their sides, dated to the third century A.D., were discovered in 1972 in the sands of the Barnea quarter. On one of them was a representation of the Rape of Proserpina, on the other a battle of Greeks and Gauls.

M. AVI-YONAH AND Y. EPH'AL

BIBLIOGRAPHY

B. Mazar, *Enc. Miqr.* 1, 769–77 (Hebrew) • Y. Prawer, *EI* 5 (1959), 224–37 (Hebrew) • Guérin, *Judée* 2, 135ff., 153ff. • J. Garstang, *PEQ* (1921), 12–16, 73–75, 162f.; (1922), 112–19 (with a map of the site); (1924), 24–35 • W. Phythian-Adams, *ibid.* (1921), 163–69; (1923), 60–84 • J.H. Iliffe, *QDAP* 2 (1933), 11–14, 110–12; 3 (1934), 165–66; 5 (1936), 61–68 (bronze statuettes) • J. Ory, *ibid.* 8 (1939), 38–44 (tombs) • M. Avi-Yonah, *ibid.* 4 (1935), 148–49 (lead coffins) • J. Perrot, *IEJ* 5 (1955), 270–71 • G. Radan, *ibid.* 8 (1958), 185–88 (war helmet) • M. Avi-Yonah, *Rabinowitz Bulletin* 3 (1961), 61 (remains of the synagogue) • V. Tsaferis, *IEJ* 17 (1967), 125–26.

'ATLIT

IDENTIFICATION. The promontory on which the Crusaders' castle of 'Atlit stands is situated 20 kilometers ($12\frac{1}{2}$ miles) south of Haifa. The ancient site extends over an area of nearly 200 acres (800 dunams) to the east and south. It is bounded on the west by the Mediterranean Sea, on the east by the road beyond the sandstone ridge running parallel to the coast, on the north by Wadi Dustrey (Dastri), and on the south by a line across modern 'Atlit from east to west about 400 meters south of the railway station. This area comprises the site of ancient settlement, the remains of cemeteries, agricultural areas, quarries, and fortifications from ancient and medieval times.

HISTORY

Although the name was not mentioned in the Bible, 'Atlit has been identified with Kartah of Zebulun (Joshua 21:34), since in Roman times it was part of the site called Certha — a name apparently derived from the Phoenician *qarth* ("city"). In the list of landing places between Carmel and Dor composed in the fourth century B.C. and attributed to Scylax, a famous Greek navigator, there is a Sidonian colony called Adarus, which might correspond to 'Atlit. Indeed, many Phoenician burials of this period were uncovered in 'Atlit. During the Roman period it was possibly called *Bucolôn polis* and was included within the territory of the port of Dor, which in the fourth century A.D. was transferred from Phoenicia to Palaestina Prima. The boundary between these two areas started at Mutatio Certha, a staging post first mentioned in the fourth century by the Bordeaux pilgrim (19:10), which stood on the site where the Crusaders' first fort was later built—that is, at Khirbet Dustrey.

Situated about 2 kilometers (1 mile) east of the castle where the sandstone ridge is intersected by a rock-cut defile traditionally called Bab el-'Ajal, "Gate of the Carts," Dustrey no doubt preserves the Crusaders' name, Le Destroit or Districtum (*détroit* in modern French), alternatively Petra Incisa, "Cut Rock." The actual rock cutting, however, is much older than the Crusader period: On a hewn rock are cut the Phoenician letters *'A T*. This inscription has been taken as a boundary

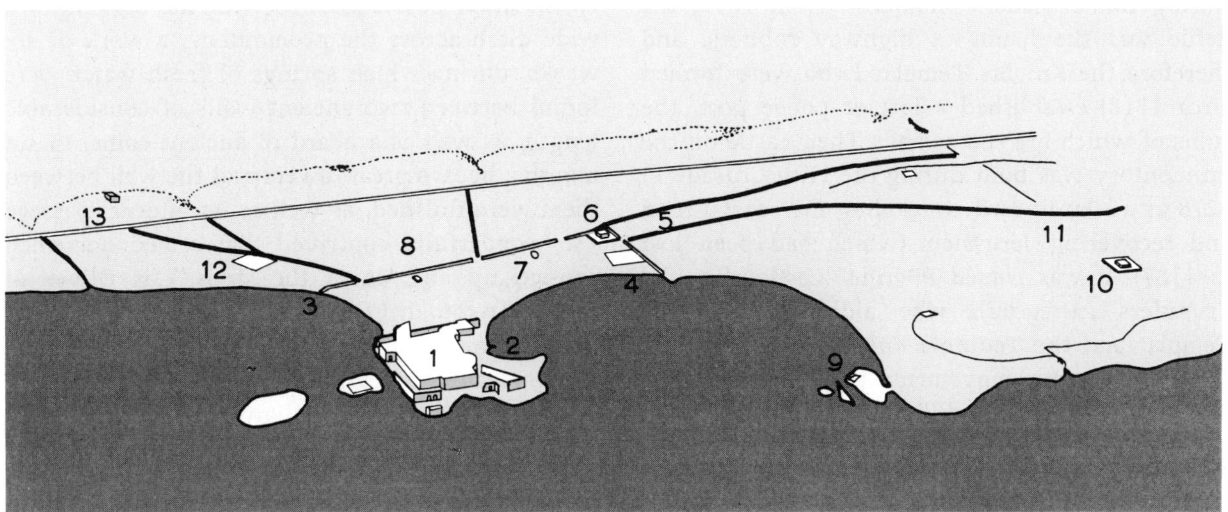

Plan of the site. 1. Castle. 2. Harbor. 3. City gate. 4. Stables. 5. Shaft graves. 6. Corner tower. 7. Church. 8. Bathhouse. 9. Outpost. 10. Tower surrounded by fosse. 11. Rampart. 12. Crusader cemetery. 13. Khirbet Dustrey. (top). View of the castle from the southwest (bottom).

mark for a Phoenician settlement also called 'Atlit, but this name is not attested before Arab times, and even if a Semitic revival, it is not found among known Phoenician names.

During the Crusaders' conquest (from 1099) the defile was the haunt of highway robbers, and therefore the Knights Templar (who were formed circa 1118) established a fort or police post, the ruins of which are still visible. Their castle on the promontory was built during the Fifth Crusade in 1218 as a step toward controlling the coastal road and recovering Jerusalem (which had been lost in 1187). It was named Pilgrims' Castle after the Crusaders *(peregrini)*, who aided the Knights Templar and the Teutonic Knights in building it. Despite menacing movements by the enemy, the castle was completed while the main army of that Crusade was engaging the Muslims at the siege of Damietta in Egypt (1218–21). The Templars, with their European revenues and permanent organization, made it one of the great fortresses of the age and manned it until the Latin Kingdom collapsed in 1291.

Fortification began in 1218 with the digging of a wide ditch across the promontory, a work of six weeks, during which springs of fresh water were found between two ancient walls of considerable length, as well as a hoard of ancient coins. In six months the two great towers and the wall between them were finished, as well as its internal passage "so wonderfully contrived that armed horsemen can go up and down the steps," as Oliver of Cologne wrote in 1218.

In its second year the castle twice defied attack, and in its third year, when besieged in force in October, 1220, its crossbowmen inflicted such loss on the enemy that they withdrew after a month's fighting.

View of the castle from the north.

In the next few years the plan took on its final form. The main east façade was doubled by the addition of a wall with three towers, then further strengthened by a low wall along the outer edge of the fosse. The original pair of great towers were raised to a height of two vaulted stages, as seen behind the east front of the north tower, itself standing a stage higher up to 33 meters. The promontory was enclosed on both sides as far as the rocks, and a chapel, hall, and other quarters erected. The hall *(palatio)* was used to feed four thousand men daily during the siege of 1220.

The lofty halls surmounting the great towers, the round church (which was just as lofty but more elegantly constructed), and the long conventual buildings beside the sea on the west — all vaulted in stone — seem to have been added by the middle of the thirteenth century, judging by their French Gothic style.

Sometimes threatened after 1220 but not again attacked seriously — even by that formidable Mameluke sultan Malik edh-Dhahir Beibars, who spared the castle when he sacked the town in 1265 — it was one of the last strongholds to be abandoned after Acre fell in 1291. For fear that it might be reoccupied, the Mamelukes dismantled the castle's defenses. Yet there was still very much to impress the traveler until the Turkish governors began stripping away the masonry to use as facing on the modern sea wall of Acre. The severe earthquake of 1837 caused still greater ruin.

MILITARY ARCHITECTURE OF THE CASTLE

The castle broadly consisted of two concentric rings, with the inner commanding the outer. In addition, three lines of defense on the east could command the front from successive tiers. Such a system of parallel supporting lines, strengthened by salient towers, was essentially Byzantine, best

Inner side of the north great tower, showing vault remains.

known from the triple land walls of Constantinople. But perhaps the Templars modeled the parallel supporting lines on the triple town walls that had confronted them at Damietta, whose system would fit the defenses of the eastern front in its final form here. The Templars elaborated on it with passages and bridges connecting the several levels, with bent or straight entrances and sliding iron doors above the gateway (herse, portcullis), by machicolation in stone (machicoulis, meurtrière) or in wood (hourd, bretèche), and by numerous very long slits (loopholes, *archières*) in recesses large enough for two or three crossbowmen (three hundred were in action during the siege in 1220).

The facing of the walls with rusticated sandstone blocks — so large that "two oxen could hardly pull each one" and the bombardment of 1220 could shift "not one from its place" — is, like the internal work, as handsome as any masonry in the proud Syrian tradition. Founded at sea level, 'Atlit was secure against undermining, such as caused the downfall of the strongest castles inland. So long as it could be supplied through its harbor, this castle was impregnable against medieval methods of siege.

EXCAVATION OF THE SITE

The British Mandatory Government undertook excavation and conservation here under the direction of the writer between 1930 and 1935. At that time the castle was still inhabited, and work was thus confined to the area of the eastern defenses and adjacent town, which produced evidence of much older occupation ranging from the end of Middle Bronze Age to the Byzantine period.

Ancient Mound. The site of the medieval town occupies a sand-covered ridge which runs from north-northwest to south-southeast and rises toward the front of the castle, the central platform of which may well cover the summit. In digging foundations for a museum about 100 meters from the castle, three distinct levels of occupation were encountered: 1) the lowest at 4 meters deep, dating to the transition from the Middle to Late Bronze ages, as dated by a deposit of intact pottery, including an amphora with a child's burial; 2) at 2.25 meters, from the Persian and Hellenistic periods, as represented by masonry and potsherds ranging from about the fifth to the second century B.C.; 3) at 75 centimeters, from the Crusader period, with ruins of a house, pottery, metal objects, and coins.

Here and at the foot of the slope verging on the north beach was some material from an occupation intermediate between 1 and 2, comparable with stratum III at Tell Abu Hawam (near Haifa). Also on the beach were coins lodged among the footings of a gateway, which showed that occupation was prolonged into the Byzantine period until the fifth century A.D. The fact that level 2 represented only part of an occupation of the Persian period (like stratum II at Tell Abu Hawam) became clear from the series of burials discovered in the south-eastern cemetery (see below).

There is evidence, then, for successive occupations whose accumulated remains have raised the ridge east and south of the castle like a mound at least as extensive outside the castle fosse as it could be inside. The ancient walls uncovered during the digging of the fosse in 1218 may well have bounded an older town or citadel that may have stood on the promontory at some remote time before the castle. This promontory sheltering a sandy beach offered just such a situation as the Phoenicians used to choose for a trading post or colony overseas.

Ancient Cemetery. So far as the cemetery on the rocky ridge beyond the southeast end of the mound has been explored, it ranges from the seventh century B.C. to Hellenistic times. The earliest burials were cremated like those at most Phoenician colonies and were accompanied by pottery unusual in Palestine but typical of Phoenician sites in Cyprus and further west, where it seems to date from the eighth or seventh century B.C. A scarab found with one of these burials dates probably from the seventh century B.C.

The next series of burials are inhumations, in rock-hewn shaft graves, like those subsequently found at Achzib. The burials at 'Atlit are later, mainly of the fifth and fourth centuries B.C., and not, in any case, before the sixth century B.C., as shown by associated Phoenician coins of silver, Attic pottery, Egyptian amulets, and scarabs of Egyptian, Mesopotamian, archaic Greek, or mixed style. One scarab has Phoenician or Aramaic letters. The hero Heracles figures not only in typical Greek attitudes but also like a Mesopotamian god or hero, raising his club in one hand to strike a lion, which he lifts with the other hand by the hind leg. The incomplete bronze figurine of an

View of northern great tower which stood to a height of 33 meters (right). Remains of the stables which could accommodate about three hundred animals with store- and workrooms (below).

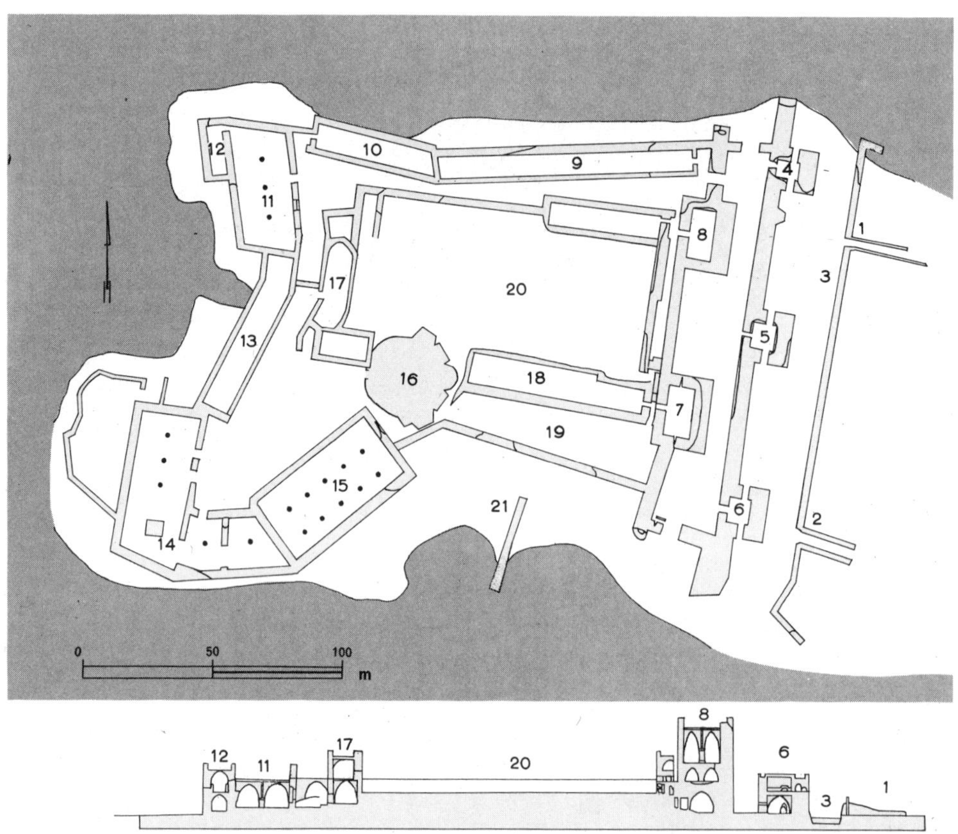

Counterclockwise: Plan of Crusader castle. 1–2. North and south outer gates. 3. Fosse. 4–6. North, middle, and south gate towers. 7–8. South and north great towers. 9. North vault. 10–11. North and northwest halls. 12. Northwest tower. 13. Western vault. 14–15. Southwest and south halls. 16. Octagonal church. 17–18. Western and southern crypts. 19. Southern outer court. 20. Inner court. 21. Pier. Corridor along eastern front of upper ward, showing descent to southern great tower (left) and doorway to upper ward (right). Hall at lower level of castle, apparently refectory. Octagonal church (plan and reconstruction).

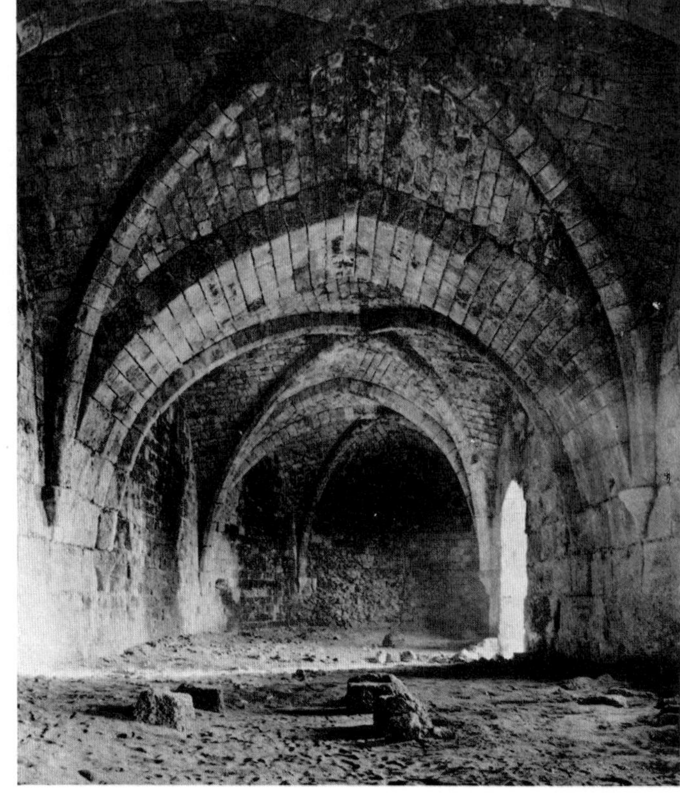

Egypto-Syrian deity was found elsewhere on the site. The attitude is as Oriental as that of the lion-slaying Persian king figuring on the reverse of the fourth-century coins of Sidon such as occurred here, yet some of the scarabs, like fifth-century coin types of Phoenician colonies in Cyprus, combine this pose with the usual attributes of Heracles as if giving their Baal a Greek disguise.

Other subjects resemble those on gems from the Phoenician cemetery at Tharros in Sardinia. Again, while other objects such as jewelry, glass, and pottery were Phoenician or local, marking the women's graves, some of the men's had bronze arrowheads that might have belonged to Greek mercenaries who served the Persians in the generation before Alexander's conquest (332 B.C.), some cultural fusion if not actual intermarriage having foreshadowed the event.

Crusaders' Fort, Twelfth Century. The first tower built by the Templars was pulled down as the siege of 1220 began, partly by the Templars themselves and finally by the enemy, leaving only its rock-cut emplacement. The sandstone rock is cut, leaving a base of only 90 centimeters for the walls of three enclosures. Likewise, the base for a rectangular tower and steps is reserved at the summit. According to the dimensions of its foundations, the tower may well have risen some 20 meters. Two cisterns are hewn near the tower and eighteen mangers in the walls of the enclosures, which would suggest that the post normally numbered from six to nine mounted men.

Crusaders' Fort and Town, Thirteenth Century. A similar outpost with square tower and adjacent stabling has been found on the cemetery ridge about 400 meters south-southeast of the castle, overlying the ancient shaft graves already noted. This became the corner tower of a wall and fosse protecting the suburb, or town as it thus became, a long rectangle roughly 600 by 200 meters. About 36 dunams (9 hectares) were habitable.

Built of large masonry like the castle, the town wall probably stood 7.5 meters above the fosse, the same height as the tower in the sea at the north end. That tower is the only part surviving at almost its full height, the rest having been pulled down to half height or less. Besides a small foot gate, the wall had three main gates, wide enough for carts, which were approached by bridges across a fosse about 2 meters deep. Two

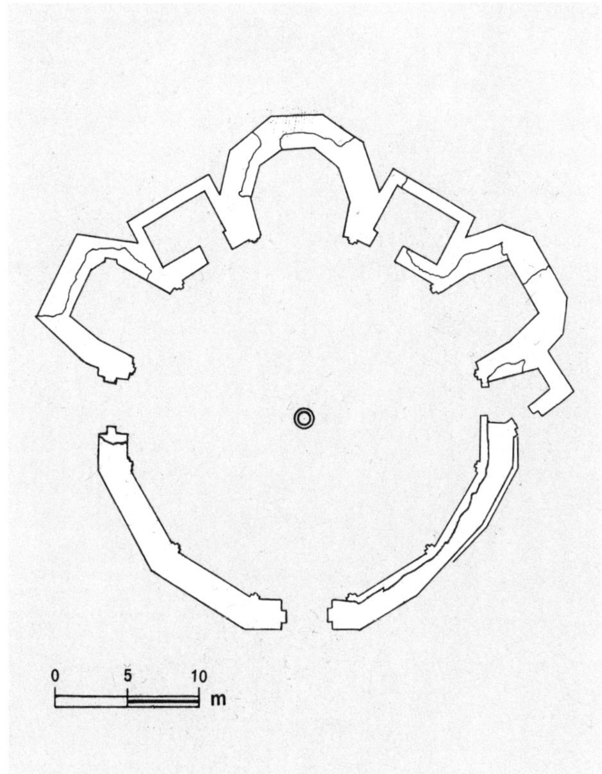

if not all three had a portcullis and therefore an upper stage. Hence they stood not less than 11 meters above the fosse. Built some time after the siege of 1220, the town was sacked in 1265.

Church, Thirteenth Century. The small church found near the east wall showed remains of stone benches for the congregation in the nave. Beyond the west wall was the start of another bay that was never completed. The stone vaulting would have risen to a height of 16 meters, by comparison with nearly contemporary churches still standing at Famagusta in Cyprus.

Stables, Thirteenth Century. Clearance of a large compound against the south wall of the town disclosed that it contained stabling for about three hundred animals, with stores, rooms for grooms, cowmen, blacksmiths, etc. The ranges have stone mangers for nearly fifty horses and continuous troughs for about two hundred and fifty cattle. All the ranges were one storied, with flat roofs carried on beams of pine and cedar. They had been destroyed by fire, and the debris

Tombstone in Crusader cemetery (below left).
Tombstone of builder (below right).

contained buried pottery, glass, iron horseshoes, and tools. Also in the debris were coins which, by comparison with those found above the debris, date the fire fairly closely to the attack of 1265.

Bathhouse in Town, Thirteenth Century or Later. The only substantial house so far uncovered is the bathhouse in the northeast part of the city. This was a plain vaulted stone structure like the traditional Arab houses inland. It contained a disrobing room, with wide benches around the walls and a basin in the middle, and next to that a sweating room over a hypocaust. This oriental arrangement may have been due to conversion in Mameluke times.

Crusaders' Cemetery, Thirteenth Century. Beside the road from Khirbet Dustrey lies an enclosed cemetery of some 1,700 Christian graves. The few carved tombstones are typically thirteenth century, nameless as was then usual in Western Europe, but marked with a cross and sometimes an emblem to show the man's status or occupation. Most of the built-up graves had their original cover made in imitation of a flat or gabled tombstone, and some are marked with a cross.

Glazed Pottery, Thirteenth Century. In the cemetery and in the town the distinctive pottery was glazed tableware, of two different classes of manufacture. More numerous is slipware in which incised *(graffiato)* designs of birds, shields, formal leaves, or purely conventional patterns were scratched on a light-buff slip and tinted with pigments that burned copper-green or yellow-brown under a transparent glaze. Varieties of this ware were widespread in the Near East, but from subsequent finds at el Mina, the Crusaders' port of St. Simeon near Antioch, and in Cyprus, it seems that much of the 'Atlit ware came from those places.

The other class has painted animal subjects, such as birds, fish, lion, deer, or human figures, outlined in purple-black, and tinted either with blue or russet-brown; or else arabesques in purple-black, some with a touch of red, or even birds painted in colors to resemble the slipware, all

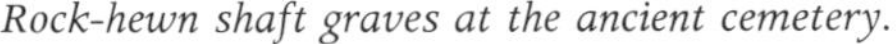

Rock-hewn shaft graves at the ancient cemetery.

under a clear tin glaze. Hardly known until found here, this ware has now been found or noted in Syria, Greece, and Sicily. Definitely thirteenth century here and at el-Mina, it is coming to be regarded as the prototype of that gay Italian ware called majolica, but its place of manufacture has still to be determined.

C. N. JOHNS

BIBLIOGRAPHY

Ancient sources: Abel, *GP* 2, 414 • K. Galling, *ZDPV* 61 (1938), 80ff.

Medieval sources: Jacobi de Vitriaco, *Historia Orientalis,* ed. Bongars, Gesta Dei per Francos, Hannover, 1611, 1131 • R. Röhricht, *Testimonia Minora de Quinto Bello Sacro, Geneva,* 1882, 99–101; *idem, Z.f. Kirchengeschichte* 15 (1895), 569–71 • Oliverus Scholasticus, *Historia Damiatina,* Tübingen, 1894, 168, 244, 254, 290 • Jacques de Vitry, *Lettres,* Leiden, 1960, a.l.

Other western sources: P. Deschamps, *Les Châteaux des Croisés en Terre Sainte* 2, Paris, 1939, 24–34.

Arabic sources: R. Hartman, *Encyclopaedia of Islam* 1, Leiden, 1960, 737.

Topography and archaeology: R. Pococke, *A Description of the East* II, 1, London, 1745, 57 • Conder-Kitchener, *SWP* 1, 293–300 • E. Graf von Mülinen, *ZDPV* 31 (1908), 167–86 • C. Enlart, *Les Monuments des Croisés* 2, Paris, 1928, 93–96 • Deschamps, *op. cit.* • C.N. Johns, *Guide to Atlit,* Jerusalem, 1947.

Excavation reports: C.N. Johns, *QDAP* 2 (1932), 41–104; 3 (1933), 145–64; 4 (1934) 122–37; 5 (1935), 31–60; 6 (1937), 121–52 • Watzinger, *DP* 2, 7–10 • B. Couroyer, *RB* 49 (1940), 243–47 • C.N. Johns, *PEQ* (1948), 88–89.

Black-figured Attic lekythos (top right). Necklace and amulet (bottom left). Blue glass vessel decorated with white wavy lines (bottom right). Glazed Crusader bowl (opposite page).

AZEKAH

SITE AND IDENTIFICATION. Tell Zakariya stands on a high hill at the northern end of a ridge, circa 9 kilometers ($5\frac{1}{2}$ miles) northeast of Beth Govrin (map reference 143123). The mound is some 400 meters above sea level and 117 meters above the Vale of Elah, which skirts the hill on the north and east. The western slope is also quite steep, but to the south it is linked to the ridge by a mountain saddle. The mound is flat topped, and only its southeastern section rises approximately 6 meters above the level of the ridge. The top of the mound is triangular in shape and attains the sizable proportions of 330 by 170 meters.

In the middle of the previous century, J. Schwartz identified Tell Zakariya as the site of Azekah on the basis of written sources. F. J. Bliss, who excavated the site, could not decide whether it should be identified as Azekah or as Socoh, since both towns, as well as the Vale of Elah, figure in the David and Goliath narrative (I Samuel 17). Bliss advanced the view that the name had been transferred at a later date from Azekah to Khirbet Shuweikeh, some 6 kilometers ($3\frac{1}{2}$ miles) farther south in the Vale of Elah, whereas biblical Socoh might conceivably be in the area of Tell Zakariya. However, after the discovery of a large Israelite site at Khirbet Abad (adjacent to Khirbet Socoh), Tell Zakariya has become generally accepted as the site of the town of Azekah.

HISTORY

Azekah is first mentioned in the story of the flight of the five Amorite kings whom Joshua defeated at Gibeon and "smote them as far as Azekah" (Joshua 10:10–11). During the encounter of David with Goliath, the Philistines camped in the Vale of Elah between Socoh and Azekah. The town lay within the confines of the northern Shephelah district of Judah (Joshua 15:35). Rehoboam (922–915 B.C.) fortified Azekah and included it within the defensive system erected after the division of the United Monarchy (II Chronicles 11:9).

An Assyrian inscription now in the British Museum (Number 131–3–23, 1–21) mentions Azekah in connection with a military campaign in Palestine. H. Tadmor maintains that the inscription refers to Sargon II's expedition in 712 B.C. against Iamani, ruler of Ashdod. The inscription reads, inter alia: "In the city of Azaqa (a-za-ka-a) his stronghold, which is situated in the mid[st of the mountains...] located on a mountain ridge like a pointed dagger [...] [it was made like an eagle's] nest and rivaled the highest mountains and was inac[cessible...] [...even for siege ra]mps and for approaching with battering rams, it was [too] strong...."

Still later Azekah and Lachish are mentioned as the last fortresses of Judah to withstand the Babylonian onslaught (Jeremiah 34:7). A similar item of information appears in one of the Lachish letters (Number 4): "He would know that for the signal stations of Lachish we are watching, according to all the signs which my lord gives because we do not see [the signals of] Azekah." The town was conquered by Nebuchadnezzar of Babylon apparently in 588 B.C., a short while before the fall of Jerusalem.

With the Return from Exile, several families of the tribe of Judah resettled in Azekah (Nehemiah 11:30). Fragmentary information from the period following the destruction of the Second Temple indicates that Azekah was still in existence. Eusebius located Azekah between Eleutheropolis (Beth Govrin) and Jerusalem (*Onomasticon* 18:10), a possible reference to Khirbet al-'Almi, east of Tell Zakariya.

The Madeba map, however, which dates from

the second half of the sixth century A.D., calls the area ***ΒΕΘΖΑΧΑΡ*** or Beth Zachariya, the present-day Kefar Zechariah, which has given its name to the mound. On the map near the indication of the village a large church is depicted with a portico and three apertures on the upper section of the façade. Behind the façade is represented a semicircular court also encompassed by a stoa. Above the drawing is the inscription "The monument of Saint Zacharias."

The elegance of the structure has led M. Avi-Yonah to conclude that it was both new and famous at the time the map was executed. In his view the court of the church was believed to contain the prophet's tomb which, in accordance with the usual practice, was separated from the adjoining church. In the Byzantine period the Christians apparently confused the prophet Zechariah with the father of John the Baptist, and hence the splendid shrine dedicated to him. The structure is first mentioned by Antonius Placentinus (A.D. 570).

Exploration of the Site

Tell Zakariya was excavated in the course of three seasons in 1898–99 (with a total working period of four months) under the auspices of the Palestine Exploration Fund. The work was carried out under the direction of F. J. Bliss, assisted by R. A. S. Macalister.

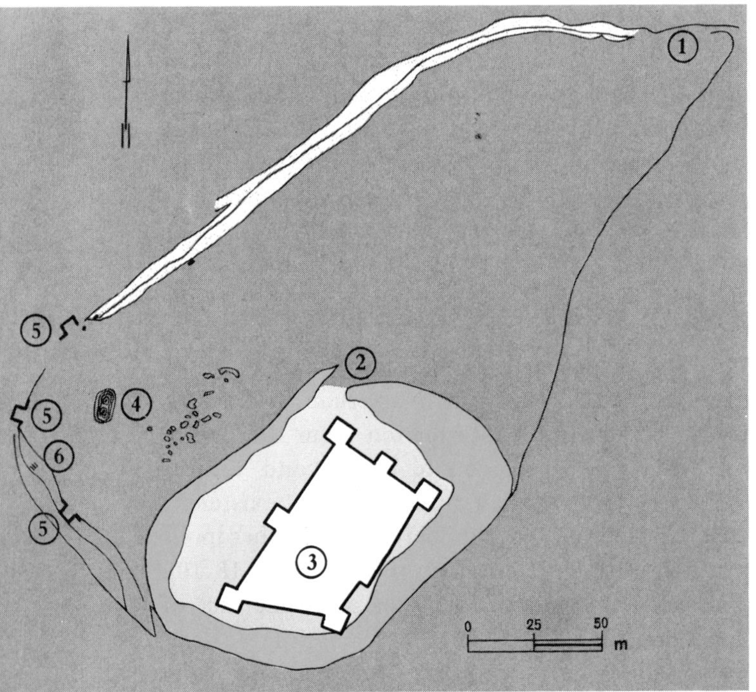

The results of the excavations of these sites were published in 1902 in a comprehensive form. Bliss described the excavation, while the summary and interpretations of the finds were the joint work of Bliss and Macalister.

EXCAVATIONS

Work was undertaken in four sections of the mound:

1. In the southwest, building foundations were examined and were found to be the foundations of three towers (6 to 6.5 meters long) built of rough stones bound with clay. There were no traces of a wall connecting the towers, which led the excavators to conclude that the towers constituted individual forts intended to protect this side of the mound, which was more susceptible to attack than the other sides. Although rubble walls were found in the vicinity of the towers, the excavators thought that these were retaining walls built to buttress the foundations of the towers, which were close to the sheer slope of the mound. Preceding the towers were a chamber and a flight of stairs leading to it. On the basis of the depth of the foundations and some ceramic finds, the towers were assigned to the Roman–Byzantine period.

2. Uncovered on the elevated southeastern section of the mound was a rectangular fortress — a shape that may have been determined by topographic conditions — with towers at each corner. Additional towers stood at the middle of the western and northern walls, and perhaps the eastern wall as well. The fortress gate was not discovered, although several doorways inside the towers were found. The entrance levels varied in height, and it thus seems that the fortress interior was not of equal height throughout.

The foundations of the fortress and tower walls were sunk in the bedrock. The parts beneath ground level were built of rubble or chipped stones bound with a mortar made of clay and gravel and set at uneven building levels. Above ground level the walls were of ashlar with marginal dressing, laid in straight courses. The rear of the towers was attached to the fortress wall without forming an integral part of it (save in one instance).

The builders intended to construct towers of equal length, yet small discrepancies are noticeable (9.15 to 10.75 meters), and this is also true for

Plan of the mound. 1. Entrance to the lower city. 2. Entrance to the acropolis. 3. Fortress. 4. Cistern. 5. Towers. 6. Stone steps.

the projections (4.75 to 5.45 meters). The walls were of rough stone, although dressed stones were used for the corners. The thickness of the wall was 1.9 to 2.5 meters.

Bliss was of the opinion that the towers were a later addition to the fortress, while Macalister assumed that the fortress and towers had been constructed at the same time by different groups of masons. Both attribute the construction of the fortress to Rehoboam (II Chronicles 11:9).

3. Half of the fortress area was excavated. Bedrock was reached at a depth of approximately 6 meters. The excavators were at a loss to attribute the buildings and other remains to their various periods, nor did they succeed in determining the exact number of periods. Although they distinguished four main occupation periods, these are not certain.

Period A is clearly defined by pottery of the type called by them Late Pre-Israelite (see below), which was discovered in rock hollows. It was impossible to attribute the pottery to any of the structures. Among the objects found was a vessel containing assorted Egyptian jewelery, including two scarabs, one with the name of Thutmose III and the other of Amenhotep II.

Period B is a plastered floor slightly above bedrock, with stamped handles containing the word *lamelekh* and the two winged scarab which, according to current opinion, belong to the later type of these seals.

In period C, which the excavators considered to be later than period B, another plastered floor was discovered, containing similarly stamped jar handles but with the four-winged scarab which, in the opinion of scholars today, is earlier than the one previously mentioned.

Period D has several rock-hewn tombs assigned to the Roman period. Here were also found Seleucid, Roman, and Byzantine shards, as well as several graves close to surface level and considered of Arab origin.

4. A trial pit approximately 30 by 20 meters was dug in the center of the mound, where bedrock was reached at no more than 4 meters. The pottery consisted mainly of shards of the Late Pre-Israelite and "Jewish" periods. Since Seleucid pottery was extremely rare and no Roman-Byzantine shards were uncovered, the excavators concluded that the mound was deserted in this period and only the fortress area was settled. Stone containers of various sizes, with stone paving between them, were found in the "Jewish" stratum and are believed to have been employed in oil production.

The finds led the excavators to conclude that the settlement had lasted, with short interruptions, from circa 1500 B.C. until the Byzantine period. Generally speaking, the finds agree with the literary sources.

Albright examined the pottery tables published in the excavation reports and suggested the following amended dates:

PERIOD	BLISS-MACALISTER	ALBRIGHT
Early Pre-Israelite	ca. ?–1500 B.C.	ca. 3000–1800 B.C.
Late Pre-Israelite	ca. 1550–800 B.C.	1800–1000 B.C.
Jewish	ca. 800–300 B.C.	1000–587 B.C.
Seleucid	ca. 300– B.C.	fourth-first cent.

Albright agrees with the excavators concerning the dating of the later periods.

Today it is possible to introduce additional revisions in the chronology of the various structures on this site. The excavators, as stated, attributed the fortress to Rehoboam (928–911 B.C.) and dated the three towers at the southwestern extremity of the mound to the Roman-Byzantine period. On the other hand, S. Yeivin assigned the construction of the fortress to the period of the Judges, and the towers, which in his opinion form part of the city wall, to Rehoboam. It was the latter who also had the fortress repaired.

Other Israelite fortresses of similar construction have since been found Kadesh-Barnea (q.v.), Khirbet Ghazzeh, Khirbet Rasm edh Dhab'a between Azekah and Tell Judeida, and at Arad, all of later date. The fortress at Kadesh-Barnea was erected in the ninth or eighth century B.C. Furthermore, since the various types of *lamelekh* seal impressions can be assigned to the end of the eighth century and the century following, it may thus be assumed that the fortress was erected at that time.

E. STERN

BIBLIOGRAPHY

Bliss-Macalister, *Excavations, passim* • Z. Kalai, *BIES* 19 (1954–55), 226 (Hebrew) • H. Tadmor, *JCS* 12 (1958), 80–84 • W.F. Albright, *The Archaeology of Palestine*, Harmondsworth, 1960, 30–31 • M. Avi-Yonah, *Madaba Map*, Jerusalem, 1954.

AZOR

IDENTIFICATION, HISTORY, AND EXPLORATION. Tel Azor is situated some 6 kilometers (3½ miles) from Jaffa, on the main road from Jaffa to Jerusalem. The name of the site is preserved in the Arab village of Yazur, and it should be identified with the Azor known from the addition in the Septuagint (Joshua 19:45), where it appears among the cities of Dan in place of Jehud of the Masoretic text. It is also mentioned in an Assyrian inscription relating Sennacherib's conquest of Azor, one of the cities of Ṣidqa, king of Ashkelon. The mound itself, at the summit of which today stand the ruins of a Crusader fortress (Château des Plains), has not yet been excavated, although a survey of the site has revealed traces of settlement from the Chalcolithic period onward. In the surrounding *kurkar* hills, especially those to the west, various remains — mainly tombs — have been found both by chance and in planned excavations. In the rich cemeteries, J. Ory, J. Kaplan, and Y. Shapira found remains from the Chalcolithic period down to medieval times.

EXCAVATIONS

In later systematic and more extensive excavations on the site, J. Perrot cleared the Chalcolithic tombs and M. Dothan those of the Bronze and Iron ages.

Chalcolithic Ossuary Tombs. The man-made burial cave in which the ossuaries were found is located in the center of the modern settlement, 100 meters south of the highway, at the edge of a *kurkar* quarry. After its accidental discovery in 1958, excavations were immediately carried out by J. Perrot. The western part of the cave was excavated in December, 1958, and the rest was cleared in May, 1959. Both before the beginning of excavations and between the two seasons, the site was damaged by illicit excavations.

The cave was dug into the *kurkar* to depth of 4 meters. The main oval-shaped chamber (7 by 11 meters) is entered from the east through a vertical shaft and a short inclined passage. At the time the cave was hewn out of the rock, a pillar was evidently left at its center to support the ceiling. In the northern and northeastern walls were three shallow niches; on a wide stone bench running in front of them, seven ossuaries were still standing at the time of discovery.

After the initial period of use, during which ossuary burial was practiced (levels 9–8), the cave was used for burials without ossuaries (level 7). In the next phase (level 6) remains of habitation were found: hearths, pottery, and other objects. After a short gap (level 5), settlement was renewed in the vicinity of the cave (level 4). Later the ceiling collapsed, carrying along rubble (level 3) containing earlier shards and shards from the

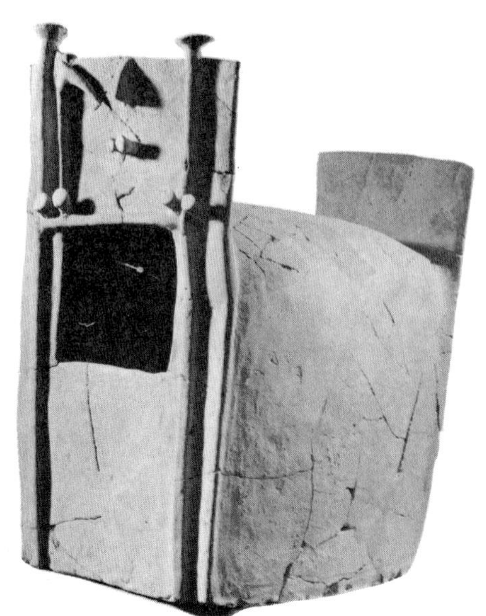

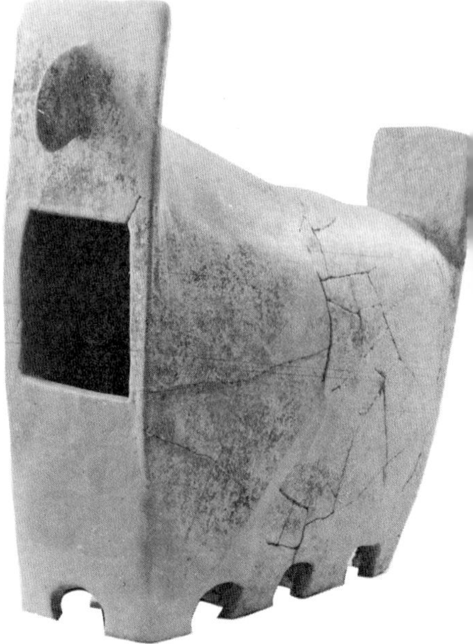

Ossuaries of the Chalcolithic period.

new settlement (locus C). This ware — typical shards of which had already appeared in level 4, which dates shortly before the collapse of the ceiling — differs from the pottery accompanying the ossuaries. The new type of pottery, well known from other sites (Wadi Zeita, Gezer, Lachish, etc.), is usually ascribed to the transitional stage between the Chalcolithic and Early Bronze ages. Its stratigraphical position at Azor is therefore noteworthy.

THE OSSUARIES. Some one hundred and twenty intact or fragmentary ossuaries were found in the burial cave. Most were house shaped and made of poorly fired clay. They average 60 centimeters long, 30 centimeters wide, and 50 centimeters high. Some are ovoid jars with an opening on the shoulder; others are zoomorphic. All the openings are sufficiently wide to allow depositing a skull within. Almost all the ossuary openings are decorated in some anthropomorphic scheme (usually a simple nose or beak), most probably of a protective nature. The ossuaries are large enough to contain even the longer bones. Each ossuary was intended to contain the bones of a single person, although they were often reused. Small ossuaries, probably models, were also found.

Several ossuaries are house shaped, with overhanging roof eaves. They have a "window" placed high in the gabled façade and a door. They are decorated with painted lattice work or a painted palm branch. These give some idea of the type of dwelling common in this period and area. The accompanying offerings indicate concern for the deceased. However, the shapes of the ossuaries do not seem evidence of any intention to provide the deceased with a dwelling after death, since some of them are shaped like common jars or even pots. Apparently they are merely containers for preserving the bones, and in their decoration some architectural elements are employed.

Wood evidently played a major part in this type of architecture. This was not necessarily the original architecture of the period, for within this culture in Palestine several basic elements of a foreign nature become evident. Hence, older traditions of local architecture may have been preserved here. In any event, the architectural style represented by the ossuaries agrees with the available archaeological data concerning building in Palestine in this period.

The funerary offerings include bowls; chalices on high fenestrated stands; several deep bowls; spherical vessels with flaring rims and, in most cases, with strainer spouts; and "churns," also with strainers. This ware, like the pottery found at Bene-Berak, is more similar in shape to the Beersheba pottery than to that of Ghassul, these being the two main phases of Ghassulian culture in the period (see Beersheba, Tuleilat Ghassul).

The discoveries at Azor have added much to the

Philistine jug, from the cemetery.

knowledge previously gleaned from the cemeteries at Bene-Berak and Ḥederah. Other such sites, as Givatayim, Yavneh, and Ben-Shemen, indicate the geographical distribution of these cemeteries, the center of which was probably in the Tel Aviv-Jaffa region. The northern limit is the base of Mount Carmel, while the southern limit lay in the Gaza area. An isolated fragment of an ossuary was found in a Ghassulian context in the small cave at Umm Qatafa in the Judean Desert.

Occupational remains from the time of the burial cave just described are known from Bene-Berak (q.v.) and Tel Aviv (q.v.). On the basis of the pottery, this site represents one phase of the Ghassulian culture in which the use of ossuaries was the characteristic feature. The custom of secondary burial links the Tuleilat Ghassul culture to the Beersheba culture, although various locations employed different types of containers: ossuaries, jars, stone cists. J. PERROT

The Bronze and Iron Age Tombs. Excavations in these tombs were conducted by M. Dothan in 1958 and 1960, on behalf of the Department of Antiquities. Three areas were excavated, two (B and C) next to Perrot's excavations and the third (D) on a *kurkar* hill next to Tel Azor and east of the Tel Aviv-Jerusalem highway. The area of the hill is circa 3/4 acre, and it stands 3.5 meters above the surrounding area.

AREA B. Above the ossuary tomb (see above) two occupational levels were uncovered. In the lower level evidence was found of ties between the settlement and the Chalcolithic tomb. In the upper level a round stone construction was uncovered, containing objects from the Late Chalcolithic period and from the transitional stage to the Early Bronze Age.

Not far to the north of this cave, another burial cave was discovered, dug in the Middle Bronze Age II. In its floor was a burial pit containing pottery of the Hyksos period. From the beginning of the Late Bronze Age down to the Early Iron Age, the cave served for human and equine burials. Several layers of human and equine skeletons were found, men and horses buried side by side. Although there was little pottery in the tombs, twenty-one scarabs were found. Besides those found at Tell el-'Ajjul (q.v.), no other such burials of human beings and horses side by side have been discovered anywhere in Palestine.

AREA D. This is the largest area excavated on the site. The earlier tombs on the cemetery hill are from the end of the Late Bronze Age, but due to their destruction during the Early Iron Age, it was impossible to ascertain their nature. The pottery found in them mostly Cypriot, including *bilbils*, knife-pared dipper-juglets, and ring-base bowls.

The majority of the tombs in the cemetery, forty-five of which were excavated, date to the Early Iron Age. From the beginning of that period down to the ninth century B.C., five methods of burial were practiced at Azor:

1. Normal burials in pits dug into the ground. The bodies were laid on their backs in an east–west position, with the head to the east, facing south. Most of these burials are from the twelfth to eleventh centuries B.C. The accompanying pottery is mainly Philistine ware, including spiral-decorated bowls with horizontal handles attached

Scarab with Negroid head; from the IA II cemetery.

to the wall and pyxidoform vessels. Found in addition to pottery in one of the Philistine burials, were a bronze mirror, a scarab from the Nineteenth or Twentieth Egyptian Dynasty depicting Hapi the god of the Nile, and an iron bracelet.

2. Burials in large pottery jars joined at their upper parts. On the basis of the jar type alone (no other finds were made in the tomb), this kind of burial may be dated to the eleventh to tenth centuries B.C.

3. Burial in brick coffins. The coffins are rectangular troughs constructed of unfired bricks laid on their side and covered with larger bricks. The few vessels found within belong to the late phase of Philistine ware (eleventh century B.C.). The skulls from the burials of types 1 and 3 are brachycephalic.

4. Cremation. Around a large store jar was found a square stone construction about 1 meter high. Inside the jar were the charred bones of one or two skeletons, and above and beneath it were offerings, including metal and pottery objects. Similar jars were found in stratum X at Tell Qasile (q.v.). On the basis of this and other finds, this type of burial may be assigned to the second half of the eleventh century B.C. It may be assumed that this method of burial was connected with the appearance of a new ethnic element.

5. Communal burials. The tombs are surrounded by a stone fence (circa 2 by 3 meters and 1 meter high). The bodies and the offerings were placed in successive layers. These tombs evidently served for the burial of several generations of the same family. The typical pottery consists of black and red juglets and Cypro-Phoenician ware of the white-painted, black-on-red, and bichrome types. Among other finds there were scarabs; conical seals; and an Egyptian amulet. This type of burial is of the tenth/ninth centuries B.C.

In addition to the above types, there were many burials of the seventh/sixth centuries B.C. on the hill, although these had been severely damaged by the Muslim cemetery at the summit. Among the Iron Age burials, a group of Israelite burial jars has survived, one bearing the Phoenician inscription *LŠLMY*.

Among the finds that could not be ascribed to a specific tomb were thick bowls with pinched rims, used in copper smelting. Another such find was a scaraboid in the shape of a Negroid head, bearing a prancing horse on its obverse, and dating to the Twenty-sixth Egyptian Dynasty.

M. DOTHAN

Burial Caves in Industrial Center. Two burial caves, dug into the *kurkar* hill about 200 meters south of the highway, were excavated by A. Ben-Tor in April, 1971.

The two caves are similar in plan. They were entered through a short, sloped stepped corridor. Opposite the entrance was a column that formed part of the rear wall of the cave. The column supported a vaulted ceiling and divided the cave into two burial chambers.

Both caves contained several layers of vessels, each layer separated from the next by a brown earth fill. That material had been brought to the caves especially for this purpose, as is attested by the presence of Mesolithic microliths, mostly lunates, in the earth fill.

Cremated burial; IA I.

Store jar with the Phoenician inscription LŠMLY. From a tomb, late seventh/mid-sixth century B.C.

Human bones were found in the two caves. There were funerary offerings only in the lowest layer. In the upper layers no bones accompanied the offerings. The burials in both caves were clearly secondary ones. There were definite indications of cremation in one cave. No signs of this practice were discovered in the second cave only 30 meters away. All the remains were found along the walls of the caves. Nothing was discovered in the center of either cave.

The caves contained hundreds of pottery vessels, the majority of them belonging to the period called Proto-Urban A by Kathleen Kenyon. There were also a few vessels with painted decoration and a number of imported Egyptian vessels. Other finds include two metal daggers and a metal javelin head, about one thousand beads of semi-precious stones, two gold beads, a number of silver rings, and a flint knife of Egyptian origin with pressure flaking.

On the basis of the contents, the two burial caves can be dated to the transition period between the Chalcolithic and the Early Bronze Age.

A. BEN-TOR

BIBLIOGRAPHY

M. Dothan, *BIES* 25 (1961), 224–30 (Hebrew); *idem, 'Atiqot* 3 (1961), 181–84; *idem, Bull. Soc. d'Anth.* 2 (11e série, 1961), 79–82 • J. Perrot, *'Atiqot* 3 (1961), 1–83 • A. Ben-Tor, *Qadmoniot* 6 (1973), 48–50 (Hebrew).

BAB EDH-DHRA'

IDENTIFICATION. Bab edh-Dhra' lies east of the Lisan peninsula in the Dead Sea, some 170 meters above the level of the sea, in the valley of the same name. The site includes a walled city and a cemetery.

EXPLORATION

The site was discovered in 1924 by A. Mallon, during a survey in the Jordan Valley carried out by the American Schools of Oriental Research and the Pittsburg-Xenia Seminary, and directed by the heads of these two institutions — W. F. Albright and M. G. Kyle. The initial reports dealt mainly with the description of the location of the site as one of the cities of the valley and only incidentally with the settlement proper, the cemetery, and the shards gathered on the surface. These were published by Albright (1924, 1926), Mallon (1924), and Abel (1929), shortly after the discovery.

Despite the considerable interest aroused, and the obvious importance of the site, it did not attract archaeologists again for nearly forty years. Interest was renewed in the mid-1960's, following the appearance of numerous pottery vessels among the antiquities dealers in the Old City of Jerusalem, which were ultimately traced to Bab edh-Dhra'. A typological-chronological analysis of a large group of vessels from the site was published by S. Saller in 1964–65.

EXCAVATIONS

Shortly afterward an expedition, on behalf of the American School of Oriental Research in Jerusalem and directed by P. W. Lapp, began excavations on the site. Between 1965 and 1967 three seasons of excavations were carried out, two in the cemetery and one in the town proper. Preliminary reports on the cemetery excavations were published by Lapp in 1966 and 1968.

The Town. No plans of this part of the site have yet been published. The town is about 40 dunams (10 acres) in area and is encircled by two fortification systems. At the beginning of Early Bronze Age II, a brick wall was built on a stone foundation, 2.5 meters wide. It had square towers (4 by 4 meters). Following the destruction of the walls and the settlement, still in Early Bronze Age II, a massive stone wall was built, 11 to 12 meters thick. This wall also had towers. It was constructed in segments so as to prevent long stretches from collapsing, if undermined. This wall stood till the destruction of the town at the end of Early Bronze Age III.

In the course of this period, the town spread beyond the walled area, and some of its structures were even built in the area of the cemetery surrounding the town. The location of the town within a sort of depression, with the fortifications built on the surrounding heights (see Arad), the construction of the wall in segments (see Jericho, Megiddo, Tell el-Far'a), and the replacement of the brick wall by a stone one (see Tell el-Far'a) are all features common to Bab edh-Dhra' and most of the known town defenses in Palestine at this period.

The Cemetery. Surrounding the town, except on the north, is the cemetery. It is the densest burial ground known in the entire ancient East. It measures 500 by 1000 meters (and possibly more). On the basis of the small section excavated, it is estimated to contain some 20,000 tombs, including some 500,000 individual burials and some 3 million pottery vessels. The tombs can be classified into three major groups:

SHAFT TOMBS. More than thirty tombs of this type have been excavated so far. The shaft, some 2 meters deep, is generally round, and at its base are entrances leading to between one and five burial chambers. Each chamber contained the bones of some five individuals, in secondary burial. The skulls were arranged along the walls, and the other bones were gathered into several heaps in the center of the chamber. The funerary offerings were mainly pottery vessels — on the average of twenty to a chamber, placed along the walls. Among the gifts were terra-cotta figurines, stone ware, sandals, wooden rods, mats, and baskets.

Battle-ax of "epsilon" type, found in tomb chamber A-44; EBA III.

A small group of special shaft tombs were noted. These consisted of a single burial chamber, containing primary burials. In each case a complete skeleton was lying in the center of the chamber. The bones belonging to earlier burials in the same chamber were pushed to one side in disorder.

CHARNEL HOUSES. Eight charnel houses have been excavated so far. These are rectangular brick structures, measuring 3 by 5 to 7 meters. All of the entrances are in one of the longer walls, and two to three steps lead down to the floor of the chamber (cf. the Early Bronze Age dwellings at Arad). On the floors, which are paved with pebbles, were heaps of bones, partly burned. One building contained the remains of some two hundred individuals. Funerary offerings included pottery vessels (more than nine hundred were found in one building), daggers, and beads. In one charnel house there was a crescent-shaped battle-ax.

TUMULI. Several such tombs have been found. The deceased was placed within a rectangular cist dug into the limestone, large enough for a single burial, which was then covered with stone slabs. These are primary burials; the funerary gifts included pottery and weapons.

CHRONOLOGY

The pottery finds within the town, and especially in the cemetery, provide the main means for determining the chronology of the site. Among the many thousands of pottery vessels found, the majority have clear parallels in the pottery known from other Early Bronze Age sites in Palestine. Only a few vessels are unique, pointing to a local tradition. The excavator applied a low chronology, and the material published so far gives the following picture:

The earliest phase on the site is represented by the shaft tombs. In this period, dated to the thirty-second to thirtieth centuries B.C., the town had not yet been founded. The shaft tombs with a single chamber are ascribed to the latter part of this phase.

In the second phase the town was founded and surrounded by a defensive wall. During the entire span of this long phase — the twenty-ninth to the twenty-third centuries B.C. — interment was in the charnel houses, although some of the shaft tombs should also be ascribed to this period.

In the third and final phase the town no longer existed. The tumuli represent the tombs of the

Burial chamber in tomb pit A-96 (EBA I). Heaped bones in center; skulls, tomb offerings at sides.

destroyers of the town and are dated to the twenty-second to twenty-first centuries B.C.

CONCLUSION

In Lapp's opinion, the excavations on this site furnish information on the character and the internal division of the Early Bronze Age in Palestine in general.

The decline of the Chalcolithic culture in Palestine would seem to have been caused by the influx of migrants from the Central Asian steppes, who came by way of Anatolia and Syria. This is indicated by the fact that instead of the brachycephalic skulls of the Chalcolithic people, the tombs of Bab edh-Dhra' contain dolichocephalic types. These migrants, lacking all urban culture, were the initiators of the shaft tombs on the site. And it is they who bore the Proto-Urban A, B, and C cultures in Palestine, according to Kathleen Kenyon's classification.

In the twenty-ninth century B.C. Palestine entered the Urban Era — under clear Egyptian influence. This Urban culture, which continued over most of the third millennium B.C., is actually an intrusive phase in the history of civilization in the country. In the twenty-third century B.C. — again under the influence of migrants from the north, who were ethnically and culturally related to the migrants who populated Palestine in the Proto-Urban period — urban settlements once again disappear from the scene.

The excavations at Bab edh-Dhra' are still in their initial stages, and many questions remain unanswered. For example, the origin of the inhabitants; the source of the burial types and the nature of the related cult; and above all the reason for the location of this huge cemetery, which obviously exceeded by far the requirements of the nearby town. The entire matter — including those points made by the excavator — still remains to be clarified.

A. BEN-TOR

BIBLIOGRAPHY

W.F. Albright, *BASOR* 14 (1924), 5–9 • A. Mallon, *Biblica* 5 (1924), 413–55; *idem, BS* 81 (1924), 271–75 • M.G. Kyle & W.F. Albright, *BS* 81 (1924), 278–85 • W.F. Albright, *AASOR* 6 (1926), 58–62 • F.M. Abel, *RB* 38 (1929), 243–46 • W.F. Albright & J.L. Kelso, *BASOR* 95 (1944), 3–13.• **New finds:** S. Saller, *Liber Annuus* 15 (1964–65), 137–219 • P.W. Lapp, *Archaeology* 19 (1966), 104–11; *idem, BASOR* 189 (1968), 12–41; *idem, Jerusalem Through the Ages,* Jerusalem, 1968, 1*–25* • Miriam Tadmor, *Qadmoniot* 2 (1969), 56–59 (Hebrew).

Tomb chamber A-21 (EBA III) after removal of bone heaps and pottery offerings.

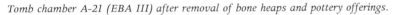

BEERSHEBA

PREHISTORIC SETTLEMENTS: IDENTIFICATION. The prehistoric settlements near Beersheba Beer Matar, Beer Safad, Horvat Batar, Bir Ibrahim, and others) are situated several kilometers from the town on both banks of the Beersheba Valley. Common to all these settlements is the fact that during at least one period they consisted of subterranean dwellings. These dwellings were cut into the sandy loam on the terrace above the valley, about 10 meters above its present-day bed. This type of habitation is found today in the Negev and was very likely used in the Bronze Age as well.

DISCOVERY AND EXCAVATION

The prehistoric sites near Beersheba were discovered in 1950 by D. Allon and Z. Ofer. They were excavated from 1951 to 1960 by the French Archaeological Mission in Israel under the direction of J. Perrot. At Beer Matar three seasons of excavations were conducted from 1951 to 1954, and at Beer Safad five seasons. A total of 2 acres was cleared. In 1952 and 1954 M. Dothan, on behalf of the Israel Department of Antiquities, excavated a part of the third settlement, Ḥorvat Batar.

Phases of Occupation. Despite the complicated stratigraphy of Beer Matar and Beer Safad, it is possible to distinguish three phases of occupation, with short breaks between them. Occupation of these sites lasted for seven centuries at the utmost. The pottery and other artifacts show almost no changes. Carbon-14 tests (M 864 a, c) yield dates for these sites that also confirm their brief occupation. The second phase has been dated to 3460 (±350) B.C. The third one has been dated to 3160 (±350) B.C. For Ḥurvat Batar, layer III, the date of 3325 (±150) B.C. was obtained. Like other similar sites in the Negev, the Beersheba settlement can therefore be dated to the second half of the fourth millennium.

The Dwellings. The earliest dwellings (phase 1) are subterranean rectangular rooms, with an average size of 7 by 3 meters, but some of them reach a length of 10 meters. Access to the dwellings was through an inclined shaft, entered generally from above the terrace and sometimes from the side. The shaft opened out into an artificial shallow depression used as a courtyard, where fireplaces and basins were found. In the floors of the subterranean rooms, bell-shaped silos were dug.

Since the soft soil was not suited for the construction of such dwellings, the rooms collapsed within a short time and were superseded in the second phase of the local cultures by dwellings consisting of a series of small oval-shaped rooms connected by galleries. Access was by one or more vertical shafts. Hand and foot holds were cut in the shaft walls to facilitate ascent and descent. Whenever the inhabitants left the place for a short time, they blocked up the entrances to the dwellings. When they finally failed to return, their houses remained nearly intact and all their equipment was undisturbed.

In the depression formed on the surface of the area, after the collapse of the first subterranean constructions, round or oval rooms of unbaked bricks were built on stone foundations. The rooms were covered by crossed beams on ground level and the ceilings were lined with pounded earth (pisé de terre). The previous entrances were blocked. The last (third) phase is represented by two layers of buildings that were constructed, after a rather long break, on the surface of the soil, above the dwellings of the second phase. These rectangular houses were built of sun-dried mud bricks on pebble foundations. The average size of these houses is 7 by 3 meters, some of them reaching a length of 15 meters.

The form of these dwellings reflects the endeavors

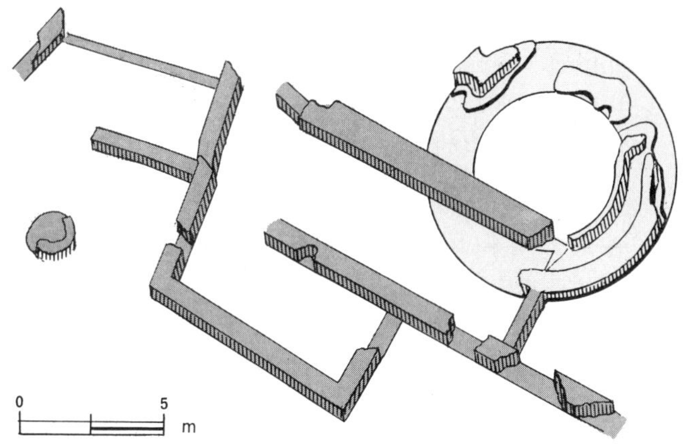

Aerial view of + Tell Beer Matar and ×× Tell Beer Safad on the banks of the Beersheba Valley (opposite page). Ḥorvat Batar; Buildings in the upper level. ▆ *Stratum I* ░ *Stratum II (right).*

of the new inhabitants to find a type of house suitable for local soil and environmental conditions, after abandoning finally the subterranean houses which several experiments had shown to be unsatisfactory.

In each of the occupation phases at Beer Matar and Beer Safad, there were at the most ten dwellings situated around one big room not used for dwelling purposes. The population of each of these settlements could not have numbered more than two hundred persons at one time.

Industry and Crafts. Metal industry in this region appears for the first time at Beersheba. Remains of the local industry in Beer Matar have been discovered: copper ore (malachite) brought from Wadi Punon that descends to the Arabah, rock anvils for breaking up the ore, fireplaces with dross, fragments of crucibles, and smelting tools. Among the products are axes, chisels, awls (points), mace heads, and various ornaments cast in the cire-perdue technique.

Flint tools were still common, although the number of types is not large. Most of the implements are scrapers, tools for cutting, and borers. Others include tranchets, sickle blades, chisels, and some axes. Arrowheads are very rare.

From the way the hard stones and ores (basalt and hematite) were worked, and from the techniques of boring and polishing, it may be concluded that the borer and also semi-mechanical processes for working basalt implements were used. Hoes and perforated mace heads were made of limestone. Small disks, plates, and cult objects were made of the local soft limestone, and the traces left on them by the flint point can still be seen.

Bone tools are relatively scarce: pickaxes, awls, needles with eyes, combs, and sickles. Saws and borers were used for working bone and ivory. From some mat imprints left on the bases of pottery, some idea may be obtained of the method of mat making. Fragments of rope made of twisted threads were also found.

Most of the pottery was handmade. Signs of the use of a potter's wheel are visible only on the most simple forms, such as bowls, which nevertheless are very abundant. In any case it is clear that the precursor of the true potter's wheel (tournette) was already in use. Clay mixed with sand is, however, not the best combination for making pottery. The color remains light, and the ware is brittle.

The dominant pottery forms are the open ones: bowls, basins, and high-footed bowls. The closed forms include hole-mouth jars, pithoi, and store jars. The characteristic vessel is the churn or bird vessel, an oblong vessel with a handle at either end of the body and a broad central neck.

The bases of the vessels are generally flat; handles are rare, which is quite remarkable for Palestinian pottery. The usual decoration is made by finger impressions on the rim or by red lines on the rim, neck, or shoulder of the vessel.

Ornaments and Figurines. The most common ornament is a rectangular or trapezoidal pendant with two holes, to be hung on a thread. These pendants are made of bone, ivory, limestone, slate, turquoise, etc. Also found were necklaces of perforated mother-of-pearl circles, of tiny beads of a glassy substance, and of grains of carnelian.

Other ornaments are small ivory plates with

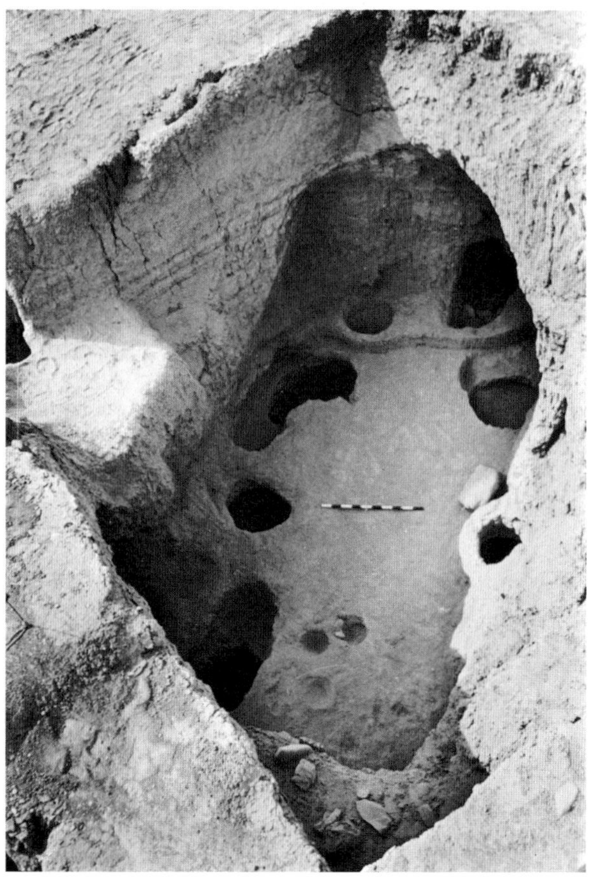

Subterranean dwellings (this page).
Aerial view of Beer Safad (opposite page).

gridlike rings, hairpins in the form of a bird or of a naked woman, small ornamented plates, a sickle, an ivory box, and other objects difficult to identify.

Especially remarkable are the ivory figurines, including several large ones, most of them of excellent workmanship. The posture of the figures is rigid, the arms held parallel to the body and the hands clasped over the belly. Some of them have holes in the cheeks, the chin, and around the head, for the insertion of a beard or hair. The eyes are inlaid.

These figurines can be compared in general with the figurines from the pre-dynastic tombs in Egypt (although all the figurines here were found in dwellings), and this applies also to their style and details of workmanship. In Beer Safad a workshop for ivory objects was discovered in a subterranean dwelling, from which it can be deduced that in Palestine there existed an independent tradition for this kind of work.

Economics. The proportion of cereals and vegetables in the food supply seems to have been considerable, as may be seen from the wheat and barely grains and the pulses found, as well as from the sickles, querns, pestles, and the numerous big silos dug in the floors of the houses or nearby. The principal source of food, however, was supplied by the raising of sheep. Cattle were less common and were perhaps used as draft animals. Horses were rare and game scarce.

The population produced enough food for their own subsistence and were thus able to maintain to a certain extent a permanent settlement in the dry region. Their level of production seems to have been superior to that of agricultural societies in Palestine during the third millennium B.C.

It is to be emphasized that a certain specialization within the whole range of industries existed in these settlements. Metal, for example, seems to have been worked at Beer Matar only. Implements of soft stone, bone, and ivory are more frequent at Beer Safad. Since these settlements are quite near each other, it may be assumed that they were largely complementary. If this was indeed so, the prehistoric settlements of Beersheba may be con-

sidered as having formed one economic and social grouping, a kind of village which, due to the scarcity of water, had to extend over a large area. In all there were only several hundred inhabitants, divided locally according to specialities. This tendency toward specialization within a community is the first step toward urban organization. The Beersheba culture disappeared, however, before having reached that stage.

Burial Customs. Infants were buried beneath the floors of the houses. Only adults were interred in secondary burials. After the flesh had decayed, the skulls and bones were collected and placed, perhaps sewn up in hides, in an unused silo or in a separate subterranean room. No funeral offerings were found in the burials, which recalls the artificial burial caves at Ḥederah, Bene-Berak, Azor, Givatayim, and other places where burial in ossuaries is not the only prevailing form. An anthropological study by Denise Ferembach shows that at least one part of the population may be connected with the Armenoid type, not known in Palestine prior to the third millennium B.C.

Painted Pebbles. On the floor of the dwellings in Beer Matar and Beer Safad, flat pebbles were found bearing various marks in red ochre (lines, points, cruciform, tectiform, and other marks). Such pebbles were found singly as well as in groups, and when in groups, always in numbers divisible by seven. The pebbles of one group always bear the same painted marks, which were applied with a finger after they had been arranged together. In one case such pebbles formed the base of a fireplace.

Chalcolithic pottery churn, basalt vessels, and copper mace heads.

Beersheba Culture in Palestine

In about 4000 B.C. Palestine entered a cultural phase in which foreign influences from the northeastern border of the Syrian Arabah can be distinguished. The settlers, who had come a short time before, brought to the region domesticated sheep and an economy that can be considered as the initial phase of an economy of production. Some elements of the first aspect of this culture are encountered in the pit-dwellings of Ḥorvat Minḥa 2 (q.v.), Gharuba (see also Central Jordan Valley), and in the mounds of Tuleilat Batashi.

Due to the stimulus this culture received from new contributions coming from the same source, it continued to develop and showed itself very adaptable to the different soil conditions in Palestine. The culture appears on both banks of the Jordan, in the Negev, and in the coastal plain, especially on sandy soils.

In the second half of the fourth millennium this culture emerges in several patterns at the same time, among which Tuleilat Ghassul and Beersheba are the outstanding and best-known examples. A third pattern may be added, in the area of Tel Aviv-Jaffa (Azor, Bene-Berak, Ḥederah, etc.) and perhaps a fourth one in the Central Jordan Valley south of the Sea of Galilee (Neve Ur, Khirbet Shune I).

The culture of the lowest levels at Beth-Shean XVII–XVI, Khirbet Shune II, Tell el-Far'a, 'Afula, and Megiddo, during the last third of the fourth millennium, is not a facet of the Tuleilat Ghassul and Beersheba culture, nor did it derive from it. These cultures differ in architecture, in their various industries and burial customs, and in their whole way of life. The later culture of Beth-Shean XVII-XVI, Tell el-Far'a, 'Afula, and Megiddo already ushers in the Bronze Age culture. That is, it is a specifically Palestinian and Mediterranean culture unlike the Jordan Valley and Negev culture, which is adapted to semi-arid regions. It flourished and extended to the whole of Palestine at the end of the fourth millennium, when the Ghassul and Beersheba culture came to an end.

The Beersheba Pattern. A pattern identical with that of Beersheba also appears 13 kilometers (8 miles) northwest of the town, at sites in the Patish Valley (Wadi Zumeili) excavated by J. Perrot in 1951. Farther to the west and south of the coastal plain are the settlements of the Patish Valley, the Gerar Valley (Wadi Shariah), the Besor Valley (Wadi Ghazzeh), the Govrin Valley (Wadi Zeita, north of Gath), and also of En-Gedi and the caves of the Judean Desert. All these represent a mixture of the patterns of Beersheba and Ghassul at various stages (violin-type figurines; high-footed basalt bowls; a great number of cornets, handles, and pottery ornaments). Dissimilar soil conditions stress the particularity of each site, as may be observed in the sites of the Besor and Govrin valleys. There is no complete homogeneity, contrary to the cultural homogeneity prevailing in Palestine during the Bronze Age.

The Beersheba pattern is known in the coastal plain as well. Finds in the burial caves containing ossuaries (see Azor, Ḥederah) and in the sites known in the Tel Aviv-Jaffa region are more similar to the Beersheba finds than those of Ghassul. On the other hand, the pottery from the sites of the Jordan Valley south of the Sea of Galilee (Tel 'Ali, Khirbet Shune, and Neve Ur) is closer to the Ghassulian ware.

Settlements in the Besor Valley. The prehistoric settlements in the Besor Valley (Wadi Ghazzeh) near Tel Sharuhen — explored in 1931 by the British Archaeological School in Egypt — were again studied in the winter of 1961–62 by the French Archaeological Mission in Israel.

The excavations uncovered semi-subterranean dwellings as well as basins, fireplaces, and silos, all of them similar to those of Beersheba. Here, too, the dwellings were grouped in small units, scattered over several kilometers along both banks of the valley. The differences between the two sites are probably to be explained, as in Beersheba, by specialization in certain industries. A very large workshop for flint implements. situated at es-Zuwewini 2 kilometers (1 mile) east of Tel Sharuhen, marketed its big-size products among all units of the settlement.

The western part of the Negev has more rainfall. Pigs were found there, which were unknown at Beersheba. In spite of better climatic conditions, however, agriculture did not develop there.

The settlements of the Besor Valley were probably poorer than those of Ghassul and Beersheba. Their culture appears to be a fringe phenomenon, and it does not seem likely that the road, by which influences from Syria and Mesopotamia penetrated into Egypt, passed through southern Palestine.

Settlement in the Govrin Valley (Wadi Zeita). The settlement of the Govrin Valley is situated about 2 kilometers (1 mile) west of Kibbutz Gath on the border between the Negev, the Shephelah ("Lowland"), and the Judean mountains. The site, cut by the trench of the Lod-Beersheba railway line, was discovered by I. Iti and excavated by the French Archaeological Mission in Israel in 1960–61. On the site are remains of a camp built on a level area several hundred meters from the valley bed. Pit dwellings with basins and several bottle-shaped silos similar to the bell-shaped silos of Beersheba were uncovered there. The difference in the shapes of the silos is probably to be attributed to the looser soil. The dwellings are scattered over an area of about 4 acres. Some of them were destroyed when other constructions were built. This was apparently a seasonal camp, occupied for short periods only.

The earliest pottery in the destroyed pit dwellings is identical with the Beersheba ware. In the general features and especially in the decoration, it is similar to the Ghassul ware. Additional Ghassulian characteristics are the high-footed basalt bowls and figurines of the violin type. Other distinctive features — such as horizontal handles, gray- and red-burnished pottery, and Bronze Age blades — are by no means accidental. They are evidence of the cultural influence of Beth-shean XVII–XVI, Megiddo, Tell el- Far'a, and others. A similar phenomenon is also seen at

Azor, in the settlement following the collapse of the cave ceiling (see Azor, levels 3–2), and, to a lesser extent, also at Mezer (q.v.).
Thus, the characteristic traits of the settlement in the Govrin Valley did not develop only because of its geographical position and soil conditions. They have a chronological significance as well.
In contrast to the Ghassul and Beersheba culture, the scarcity of flint implements at the Govrin settlement is to be emphasized. This settlement may be considered as the last phase of this culture and may even be later than the abandonment of Beersheba. This apparently is also true of site H in Wadi Ghazzeh, Azor (levels 3–2), and Mezer. In all of these, signs of contact with the culture of Beth-Shean XVII–XVI can be recognized to various extents. The settlement in the Govrin Valley is probably a little earlier than the founding of the settlement of Tell el-'Areini situated 3 kilometers (2 miles) to the east.
Disappearance of the Beersheba Culture. One of the causes for the disappearance of the Beersheba culture was probably the radical deterioration of the defense situation in the region at the end of the fourth millennium B.C. Settlements founded at about the same time in the Shephelah and in the northern Negev on the fringe of the central mountain ridge (Gezer, Lachish 4, Tell el-'Areini, Tel Arad) were all established in places suitable for defense. Their culture is closer to the tradition of Beth-Shean–Megiddo–Tell el-Far'a, which developed during the last third of the fourth millennium B.C., than to the Ghassul and Beersheba culture. J. PERROT

THE IRON AGE

Contrary to the then accepted opinion, A. Alt assumed that the remains of biblical Beersheba were to be sought at Bir es-Saba' on the site of present-day Beersheba. In recent years it has become clear that Beersheba indeed contains remains of a settlement dating from that period. In the area of the Arab town, Z. Ofer in 1953 found for the first time remains dating from Iron Age II-C lying under remains of the Roman-Byzantine period.
In connection with development work, a trial excavation of the site was carried out by R.

Chalcolithic ivory figurines of man (right) and of pregnant woman (opposite page) from Beer Safad.

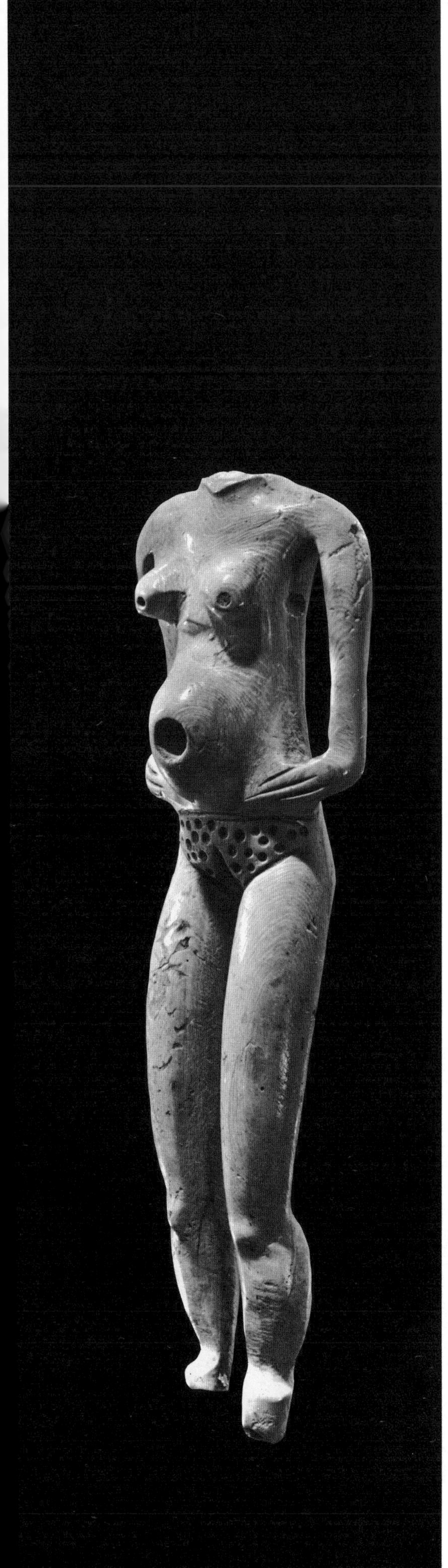

Gophna in 1962, on behalf of the Department of Antiquities. The center of the site was found to be situated approximately at map reference 130072, above the northern bank of the Beersheba Valley, where the Beersheba-Hebron road bisects the site. Excavations were carried out in two areas near the southern end of the site. In area I a house with a floor made of pounded loess was uncovered at a depth of about 2 meters under the remains of constructions of the Roman-Byzantine period. Potsherds from Iron Age II-C were found on this floor. In area II, 140 meters west of area I, an Iron Age occupation layer was cleared immediately under the surface. Fragments of loam-loess bricks were found lining the bottom of two pits dug into the earth. These pits, filled with ashes, rough stones, potsherds, and animal bones, had apparently been used as cooking pits. Under the Iron Age layer, potsherds and flint splinters dating from the Chalcolithic period were found. The finds of the Iron Age layers are assigned to the eighth/seventh century B.C.

In 1966 Yael Israeli, while excavating some Byzantine buildings north of the Beersheba-Hebron road, unearthed Iron Age II-A walls and floors dating to the tenth century B.C.

In 1968 R. Cohen continued the trial excavations on the site, to keep pace with development work. North of the road an Iron Age II-C level was uncovered beneath a Byzantine floor. South of the road the same pottery was discovered, not far from the soundings of R. Gophna.

As a result of the excavations at Beersheba, it now seems certain that a large settlement flourished there at least during Iron Age II. This settlement existed at the old traditional site, near the wells. The fortified town uncovered by the excavations at Tel Beersheba was built in the time of the Monarchy, as an administrative center.

R. Gophna

BIBLIOGRAPHY

Beersheba: J. Perrot, *IEJ* 5 (1955), 17–40; 73–84; 1967–89; *idem, Syria* 34 (1957), 1–38; 36 (1959), 6–119; *idem, EI* 7 (1964), *92–*93.

Ḥorvat el Batar: M. Dothan *et alii, 'Atiqot* 2 (1959), 1–71 • T. Josien, *IEJ* 5 (1955), 246–56 • M. Negbi, *ibid.*, 257–58 • E. Anati, *ibid.*, 259–61 • D. Ferembach, *ibid.* 9 (1959), 221–29.

Besor Valley and Govrin Valley: E. MacDonald, *Beth Pelet 2,* London, 1932, 1–21 • *Comptes rendus de la Mission archéologique française en Israël* (in course of publication) • R. Gophna, *IEJ* 13 (1963), 145–46; *idem, RB* 71 (1964), 405 • R. Cohen, *IEJ* 18 (1958), 130–31.

BEERSHEBA, TEL

IDENTIFICATION. Tel Beersheba (Tell es-Saba') is located east of the modern city of Beersheba, on the road to the Bedouin settlement known as Tel Sheva. The mound is situated between the Beersheba and Hebron valleys, which join to the west, and overlooks an extensive area. The mound is about 10 dunams ($2\frac{1}{2}$ acres) in area, and to the east of it is a much broader spur containing mainly Byzantine remains, with a few older shards from the Hellenistic and Israelite periods.

Beersheba is known in the Bible as the chief city of the Negev and as a sacred site. It is the symbol of the southern boundary of the Land of Israel — "from Dan to Beersheba" (Judges 20:1, I Kings 4:25, etc.). It occupies a prominent position in the patriarchal narratives, where it is designated as a holy place connected with the appearance of God (Genesis 21, 26, 28, 46). It heads the list of cities of Simeon (Joshua 19:2, I Chronicles 4:28) and appears among the cities of the Negev of Judah (Joshua 15:28). Samuel's sons judged the people at Beersheba (I Samuel 8:2), and Elijah passed it on his way to Mount Horeb (I Kings 19:3).

Some of the distinguished families who married into the royal family came from Beersheba: for example, Zibiah, the mother of Jehoash (II Kings 12:1). Apparently in the days of Amos a temple was still there, the existence of which was severely condemned by the prophet (Amos 5:5, 8:14). Josiah brought priests to Jerusalem "from Geba

Aerial view of the mound.

to Beersheba" (II Kings 23:8). The final mention of the city and its "daughters" in the Bible is among the cities of Judah in the period of the return from Babylon, the province then spreading "from Beersheba unto the Valley of Hinnom" (Nehemiah 11:27, 30).

The identification of the mound with biblical Beersheba is generally accepted. It is the only mound in the vicinity of Roman and modern Beersheba (Bir es-Saba'), which has kept the older name. A. Alt is the only scholar opposing this identification, and he suggested identifying the mound with Zephath = Hormah (Judges 1:17), on the grounds that, in the sources, there is no evidence of Beersheba as a fortified Canaanite city. However, since the excavations have proved that the settlement at Tell es-Saba' was founded only in the Israelite period, Alt's argument can serve merely to strengthen the accepted identification.

EXCAVATIONS

The Archaeological Institute of the Tel Aviv University, under the direction of Y. Aharoni commenced excavations on the mound in 1969. The fourth season of excavations was in the summer of 1972. Work was concentrated in two main areas: 1. A deep trench was cut through the fortifications of the city down to the lowest strata. 2. The main quarters of the last Israelite city were cleared, as well as the Roman fortress, which stood at the highest spot at the center of the mound, and the buildings beneath it from the Hellenistic and Roman periods.

Chalcolithic Period. Shards of the Chalcolithic period found in various excavation areas indicate

Plan of the Israelite city, stratum II. 1. City gate. 2. Storehouses. 3. Water system. 4. Deep trench. 5–6. Dwelling quarters. 7. Public building. 8. Governor's palace. 9. Pool in center of public building. 10. Water channel.

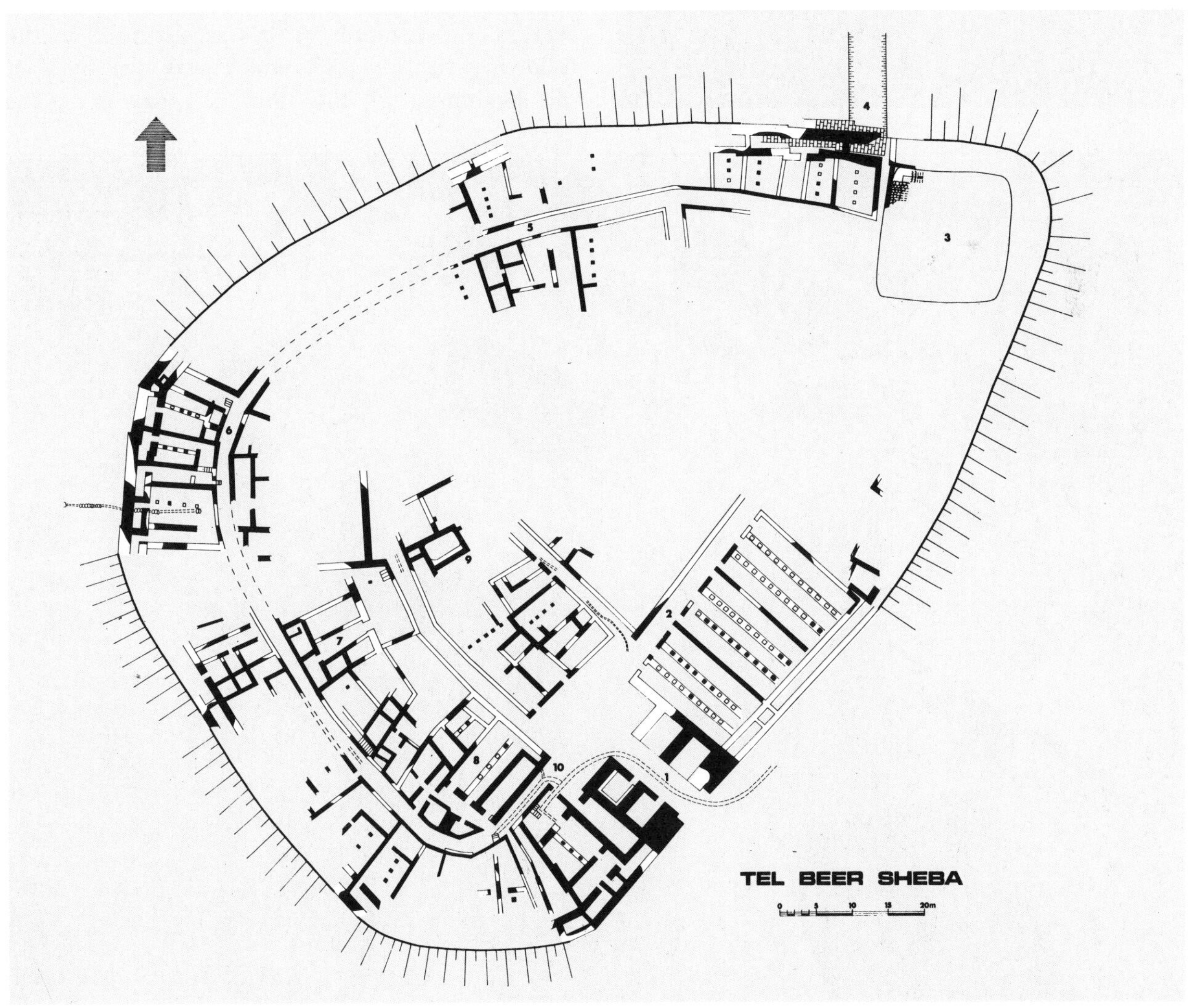

Counterclockwise: The brick wall built over the stone wall and the rampart in deep trench. The gate and water channels. A building in the western quarter.

that at least one of the corners of the mound had been occupied in this period, as at other sites investigated on the banks of the Beersheba Valley.

Israelite Period. The entire mound was settled only in the Israelite period, and its strong fortifications produced its distinctive form. Shards of the twelfth to eleventh centuries B.C., found in the deepest layer (stratum VI), indicate that the mound was settled in the period of the Judges, although it was apparently unwalled at that time.

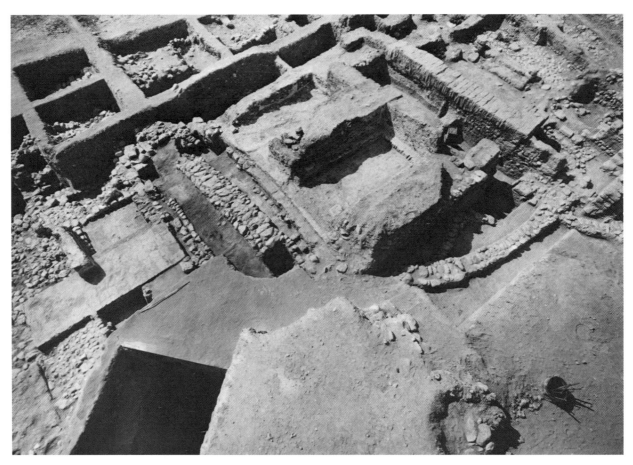

FORTIFICATIONS. Two successive city walls were revealed in the deep trench. Both were built of brick on stone foundations. The early one is a solid wall 4 meters thick with insets and offsets. It was built on top of an artificial ramp 6 to 7 meters high made of layers of pebbles, earth, and ashes, with a moat in front of it. The ramp was covered with a glacis made of layers of brick fragments and ashes, to a depth of almost 2 meters. This strong fortification was erected in the tenth century B.C. (stratum V). It was also used in the following stratum (IV), which was destroyed at the beginning of the ninth century B.C. The second wall, of the casemate type, was built in part over the foundations of the solid wall. Its dimensions are standard ones (circa 1.6 meters for the external wall and circa 1.1 meters for the internal wall), and it is reinforced by minor bends, like the solid city wall at Arad.

Over the older glacis a new one was laid down, composed of layers of earth and alluvium. This new glacis was founded on massive limestone revetments joined by tongues to the earlier layers. The upper part, which was plastered, met the city wall horizontally.

This fortification system, which recalls the fortifications of the Hyksos period, is much stronger than the other earthen works and glacis of the Iron Age also found mainly in the south of the country — for example, at Tel Malḥatah and Ashdod-Yam. It points up the great importance attributed to the fortifications of Beersheba and also indicates that, in the later part of the Israelite period, the casemate-wall system was again preferred to the others. The emphasis was apparently placed on defending the approach to the wall and on enlarging its top so as to be able to mass defenders and ammunition there.

The casemate wall was erected in the ninth century B.C. (stratum III) and continued to be used throughout stratum II, whose destruction is dated at the end of the eighth century B.C. After its ruin a final attempt was made to reconstruct the fortifications. A retaining wall consisting of layers of pebbles and earth was erected inside the casemate wall. No buildings associated with this wall have been found so far. In this period the settlement was apparently a limited one with only a fortress in the center of the mound, similar to the later fortresses.

THE GATES. The city gate was discovered at the southern edge of the mound. Two gates were uncovered, one on top of the other, corresponding to the two city walls. The early one, measuring circa 21 by 21 meters and contemporary with the solid wall (strata V–IV), is wide and massive. In plan it closely resembles the city gate at Tel Dan. It is flanked on either side by two guardrooms and a tower. Its foundations are 5 to 6 meters thick.

Between the tower and the threshold of the gate was a square in which were found remains of a platform (bamah) with a carefully constructed incense altar next to it. A similar cultic platform has also been found in the square of the gate at Tel Dan (cf. II Kings 23:8). In all likelihood these two cities were fortified according to a single plan in the early part of the United Monarchy. Hence the classical biblical phrase "from Dan to Beersheba."

The later gate, contemporary with the casemate wall (strata III–II), is narrower and lacks the front tower. It recalls the gate of Megiddo III-B in general form. In stratum III there were no partitions separating the guardrooms from the gateway. In the inner room there were benches along the walls. In stratum II the benches were no longer used and partition walls were added.

PLAN OF THE CITY. The building of the city was a carefully planned undertaking. Although Beersheba contains features that can also be seen at other cities, it is the first instance of a planned administrative city from the period of the Monarchy, a store city, in the language of the Bible. Only the last city (stratum II) has been uncovered, but it is clear from several deep soundings that most of the buildings had been repaired along the lines of the buildings of the earlier strata.

Inside the gate the square, measuring 12 by 20 meters, was surrounded by several large rooms used by passersby. From the square a peripheral road ran around the city parallel to the wall. Radial streets cut through the center of the city. Two of them started from two corners of the square. Several dwelling quarters were excavated along the peripheral road. The most complete was the western quarter. It includes three houses of the "four-room" type with a row of pillars in the courtyard. The houses are tangent to the casemate wall, and remains of stairs indicate that they had second stories. They show several phases of repairs. The entrances to the chambers of the wall were adapted to conform with the changes made in the houses. Not only were they used as part of the houses but their owners also kept them in good repair.

Several public buildings were found in the vicinity of the gate. A large building to the left of the gate, built partly of ashlars, apparently served as the residence of the local governor. Behind it was a large building of the four-room type, which contained a rich group of cult objects — mostly Egyptian. Among them was a votive cylinder seal with an Akkadian inscription, which was an offering by a man called Rimtuilani, son of Adad-idri (Hadad-ezer). In the center of the city was another public building, with a plastered pool in its center.

To the right of the gate were three adjoining storehouses, of uniform plan. Each comprised three long halls separated by two rows of pillars, similar to the pillared building at Hazor. They were founded upon a thick fill of layers of alluvim and ashes, and some of the walls were inlaid with cedar wood. The storehouses contained an abundance of pottery of various types, including cooking pots, bowls, and other vessels, besides store jars. This would seem to indicate that each of the units of the storehouses held different goods, possibly from a particular locale, and these were prepared on the spot for use, as evidenced by the grinding stones.

A Hebrew ostracon was found in one of the storerooms: 15 — *mn tld... byt 'mm....* This would appear to refer to two places in the Beersheba district, Tolad or Eltolad (Joshua 15:30, 19:4, I Chronicles 4:29) and Amam (Joshua 15:26), from which goods had been sent — a procedure similar to that referred to in the Samaria ostraca.

A broad stairway was found in the northeastern corner of the mound, possibly descending to the central water-supply system. Since there is no groundwater level here, and wells are found only in the valley beds, it would seem that this installation served to gather rainwater that had been channeled to subterranean cisterns — a project involving considerable moving of earth and stone.

Also discovered was one of the most impressive undertakings of the Israelite city — the main drainage system, which led beyond the gate. Below the pavement of the streets channels were found, covered with stone slabs to which water was conveyed from plastered gutters in the walls of the houses. The channels increase in size as they approach the gate, and in the gateway itself the channel reaches a height of 70 centimeters. This unique and excellently constructed network of drainage channels was undoubtedly intended to

Opposite page: Selection of pottery from a storeroom (top). Storerooms (bottom).

Counterclockwise: Bronze figurine of a woman. Faience falcon. Bronze double crown of Egypt. Bronze figurine of a sphinx. Bronze figurine of the bull Apis.

collect rainwater in central cisterns. Inside the gate was a 10-meter-deep cistern, but its use in the Israelite period could not be established, as in Persian times it collapsed and was cleared down to the bottom. Outside the gate the channel turned eastward, and some of the water may have flowed to the great water system in the east of the city.

The latest Israelite city (stratum II) was destroyed by a conflagration. Among the rubble was an unusual abundance of pottery and other objects. They date from about the end of the eighth century B.C., a date that also fits the script of the Hebrew ostracon. Thus, it would seem that Beersheba was sacked during Sennacherib's campaign in 701 B.C., and the settlement was not reestablished.

Among the special finds are a great number of cult objects. These include Astarte figurines, zoomorphic vessels, several small stone incense altars (one decorated, of the Persian period), and a pottery bowl on which the word *qdš* ("holy") was scratched in Hebrew.

Several vessels were found incised with the names of their owners. These appear to be examples of the early stage of the spread of writing. The letters were formed with an untrained hand and with blatant errors.

In one of the gate rooms an unusually large store jar was found bearing the royal seal *lamelekh Zif* with the four-winged scarab.

Later Periods. The settlement on the mound was renewed in the Persian period. Its importance is indicated by some forty Aramaic ostraca from about the mid-fourth century B.C. They display dates up to the twelfth or thirteenth year (of Artaxerxes III, 359–338 B.C.) as well as private names of Jews, Edomites, and Arabs, and references to quantities of wheat and barley. No building remains of this period have yet been discovered on the site. However, the settlement may have been similar to that of the Hellenistic and Roman periods, when the center of the mound was occupied by a fortress and around it were various service buildings, such as the bathhouse from the Herodian period. The latest building on the site is the Roman fortress occupying a square 30 by 30 meters, in the center of the mound. It was built in the second or third century A.D. and was used up to the beginning of the Arab period.

Bowl with the Hebrew inscription qdš *("holy") (top). Votive cylinder seal with cuneiform inscription (bottom).*

CONCLUSION

At Tel Beersheba in the period of the First Temple there was an administrative and military center well planned and with strong fortifications, although of limited area in comparison with other Israelite store cities. This royal city seems to be no earlier than the period of the United Monarchy, and it had already been destroyed by the end of the eighth century B.C. In light of these findings the identification of the biblical Beersheba, which was mentioned in the patriarchal narratives and flourished in the days of Josiah and the Return to Zion, must be reconsidered. The solution seems to lie in the remains from the Israelite period found at Bir es-Saba', within the area of modern Beersheba. Since the patriarchal narratives describe the wells as being near the valley, and since mention is later made of "Beersheba and her daughters" (Joshua 15:28, Nehemiah 11:27), it would seem that most of the inhabitants had always lived near the valley and the wells and that it was only in the period of the Monarchy, in the tenth/eighth centuries B.C., that a royal center was built on the mound. Y. AHARONI

BIBLIOGRAPHY

Y. Aharoni, The Excavations at Tel Beersheba, Report on the First Season — 1969, *Yeivin Volume* (in press, Hebrew); *idem, IEJ* 19 (1969), 245–47; *idem, The Beersheba Excavations,* I–III, Tel Aviv, 1970–72 • On the Identification of the Site: C.L. Woolley and T.E. Lawrence, *PEFA* 3 (1914), 45–47 • A. Alt, *JPOS* 15 (1935), 320–24.

Incense altar from the gate complex.

BEIDHA, WADI

IDENTIFICATION. A prehistoric site in Seil Aqlat, situated in Wadi Beidha (map reference 194977) north of Petra. It is a low mound covering an area of about .5 hectares (80 by 70 meters) on the northern bank of the wadi on a hill of aeolian sand about 15 meters high.

EXCAVATIONS

Diana Kirkbride discovered the site in 1956 and conducted excavations there during six seasons, from 1958 to 1965, on behalf of the British School of Archaeology in Jerusalem, with the assistance of the Department of Antiquities of Jordan. An area of about 750 square meters was excavated on the highest part of the mound, and two trial trenches were dug on the slope of the mound in order to examine the lowest stratum.

In the lowest part of the mound, a layer of reddish-brown sand (.5 to .75 meters thick) was discovered containing remains attributed by the excavator to a stage of the Natufian culture. Above this was a sterile layer of soft, white sand, its thickness reaching 2 meters in some places. Above it lay superimposed occupation levels, the thickness of which reaches 3 meters and more. At least six phases of building were distinguished in these levels, including remains of a material culture that the excavator attributed to the pre-pottery Neolithic.

Natufian. In the Natufian stratum, only excavated to a small extent up to now, two fireplaces were discovered in the two trial trenches. In one of the fireplaces, which is circular and bordered with slabs of sandstone, numerous animal bones and flint implements were found. One of the trenches also revealed a storage pit of irregular form, the walls and bottom of which were revetted with river pebbles.

Walls built of irregularly shaped mud bricks on stone foundations were also uncovered. Between the Natufian stratum and the Neolithic layers, an occupation gap is distinguished. However, its use was probably of short duration.

The complex of implements in the Natufian stratum consists mainly of notched blades and end scrapers, as well as obliquely truncated bladelets, microburins, geometric bladelets, lunates — most of them with ridge backs — both triangular and trapezoid. Several dentalium beads were also found. The excavator attributed this assemblage to the early stage of Natufian, on the basis of finds made in the Cave of the Valley (Mugharet el-Wad; see Carmel Caves) and excavations conducted recently in 'Eynan (q.v.).

Neolithic Strata. In level VI, the earliest Neolithic stratum discovered at Beidha, round semi-subterranean structures adjoining each other were found. The building technique indicates a combination of stones and wooden beams. Finds made in these structures include, among others, basalt axes with polished tips, numerous bone implements, a large stone bowl, the remains of a wooden bowl (40 centimeters in diameter), the remains of a pitch-coated basket, the remains of a wooden box containing one hundred and fourteen flint arrowheads, and a clay figurine representing a buck head.

In level V an improvement in the building technique is discernible and the round structures uncovered are now free-standing. In overlying level IV the building technique, both in stone and wood, is even more skilled, the structures being rectangular with rounded corners.

In levels III–II several stages of construction were uncovered, and some separate buildings could be distinguished. Two of them were wholly excavated and six only partly. The buildings are composed of a narrow rectangular corridor (8 by 1 meters). On both sides were several rooms — four rooms in one of the houses and six in the other. The size of the rooms is 1 by 1.5 meters. At least one of the houses had an entrance room (3 meters long) reached by two steps leading down from the outside, which shows that the floors were built beneath ground level. The thickness of the outer walls reached .5 to .75 meters, while that of the partition walls between the rooms in most cases was 1.5 meters and sometimes 2 meters. Since the inner walls were coated on the upper part with hard, thick, white lime-plaster, they probably did not serve as the base of a vault.

The houses are built of superimposed blocks or slabs of sandstone, the interstices being filled with small stones. The faces of the walls were straight and their corners sharply angled. The roofs were probably flat, the buildings being only one storied. The floors of the rooms were made of pounded earth (some were laid on a base of stone slabs), in some cases of lime-plaster, finished occasionally with red burnish like floors of the pre-pottery Neolithic B at Jericho (q.v.). Sometimes the plaster is hard and thick. In one of the rooms there was a fireplace (the only one discovered in all these houses) sunk into the plaster-coated floor. In some cases the ceiling was also plastered and burnished red, as is attested by lumps of plaster pound in the rubble lying on the floors.

Near some houses were rather large courtyards (one of them having an area of at least 10 by 7 meters), the floors of which were covered with hard, thick lime-plaster (in one courtyard, 7 centimeters thick). In some rooms numerous grinding and pounding implements were discovered, such as querns (both lower and upper tops) and pestles. In two opposite rooms animal bones, skulls with attached horns, bones in articulation, chopping implements of basalt, coarse flint flakes, hammerstones, and a sandstone slab used as a tabletop were found. These two rooms seem to have been some kind of butcher's shop, and the implements were apparently butcher's tools.

In another room were animal skulls with sawed-off horns, horns placed on a table made of a sandstone slab, another pair of horns nearby, a grindstone, as well as excellent bone and flint implements. These finds demonstrate that in these houses each room, or group of rooms, served as a special workshop for grinding and cutting, or for preparing the meat, or for the manufacture of tools. This complex of buildings,

Houses, levels VI-IV.

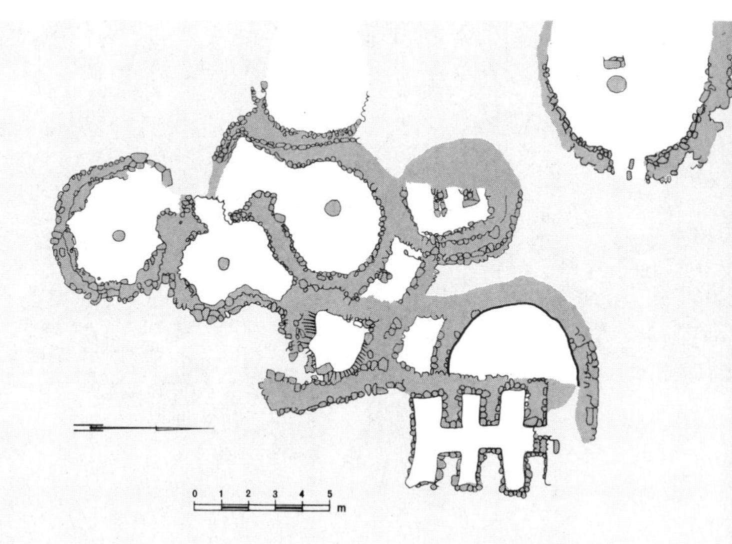

therefore, seems to have been the industrial part of the settlement.

From an earlier stage a square building with rounded corners was uncovered. Its floor certainly stood below the surrounding ground level, as evidenced by the steps leading down into it from the outside. Such structures may have been the dwelling houses.

Level I was heavily disturbed.

BURIALS. Forty-three burials were found on the site, including burials of infants. In some burials the bodies were interred intact. Others were secondary burials, and in some cases the skulls were detached and placed beneath the body. In one case the body was buried without the head.

FLINTS AND OTHER REMAINS. The flint implements, the open querns, the burials without the skull, and the plaster-coated floors finished with red burnish are among the characteristics of the pre-pottery Neolithic B phase.

Examination of the food remains discovered shows that the Neolithic inhabitants of Wadi Beidha cultivated mainly barley; cultivation of emmer occupied only a secondary place. Also found were remains of pistachio nuts and other wild plants, which used to be gathered in the surroundings. It can be assumed that the Neolithic inhabitants of Beidha had already domesticated goats, although they continued to hunt various wild animals.

Isolated obsidian implements discovered in levels III–II most probably had their source in Anatolia. Contacts between the Neolithic inhabitants of Beidha and distant regions are also attested by various marine shells, some of which were brought there from the Red Sea and some from the Mediterranean.

DATING AND CULTURAL CONNECTIONS

Reliable dates for the Natufian level are still lacking. Carbon–14 examinations place the beginning of the Neolithic settlement in level VI at about 7000 B.C. and its end at about 6500 B.C. In all, the Neolithic settlement in Beidha existed for about five hundred years.

The excavator considers that the inhabitants of levels VI–IV belonged to the first wave of Neolithic settlers that reached Beidha, their material culture being similar to that uncovered at Jericho in the pre-pottery Neolithic B levels. The finds in levels III–II represent a building tradition different from that developed in levels VI–IV, and they are ascribed by the excavator to a further wave of settlers, which probably also reached Beidha from northern regions.

The importance of the site lies in the information it provides on the wide distribution of the Natufian and pre-pottery Neolithic B industries, while its distinctive features are due to the existence of the commercial and industrial center. D. GILEAD

BIBLIOGRAPHY

D. Kirkbride, *PEQ* (1960), 136ff; (1965), 5–13; (1966), 8–72.

General view of excavation. At center, level II building; behind it workshop from levels II–III (left). Level III: part from workshop (right).

BEIT MIRSIM, TELL

THE SITE AND ITS IDENTIFICATION. The excavation of Tell Beit Mirsim was undertaken in 1926 after a visit to the site in 1924. The mound was a very impressive one, occupying about 3 hectares. Surface examination showed that it had not been inhabited after the Exile and that its occupation went back many centuries earlier. The site was the largest mound in the area. It rose about 497 meters above sea level. In 1924 it was tentatively identified with Debir or Kirjath-Sepher. The history of occupation has proved to coincide remarkably with what is known from the Bible about Debir. A short narrative has been preserved in Joshua 15 and Judges 1, partly in clear verse form with linguistic archaisms pointing to an early date for the tradition as we have it. According to biblical tradition, Debir was a royal Canaanite city in the southwestern hills or the southern Shephelah, on the edge of the Negev. It is true that the passages in Joshua 15 and Judges 1 might conceivably be taken as referring to a place in the high hill country, south of Hebron. This is impossible, however, since nothing in the hill country proper corresponds to the "basins *(gullôt)* of water" above and below Kirjath-Sepher, which are specifically mentioned by the early tradition, and since not one of the sites that have been proposed in the past can come into serious consideration. The most likely site was edh-Dhâhirîyeh, called after al-Malik edh-Dhahir Beibars (A.D. 1260–77).

The 1932 soundings to bedrock were made in thirteen places, distributed around the periphery of the site at points where the native rock is not visible today. They showed a thin occupation in the Early Bronze Age, followed by a reoccupation not later than the tenth century B.C. and ending not later than the early sixth century B.C. This was succeeded by a Roman settlement dominated by a strong fortress, followed in turn by a Byzantine occupation and finally by a late medieval Arab occupation. There is obviously no possibility here for an identification with biblical Debir, unless one discards the well-attested poetic tradition of its conquest by Caleb's son-in-law, Othniel.

The sites proposed south of Hebron, such as Khirbet Ṭarrâmah, near 'Ain ed-Dilbeh, are out of the question. The name reflects an Aramaic *Tūrā Rāmā,* "High Hill," and the pottery is almost exclusively Hellenistic-Roman and Byzantine.

In the story of the capture of Debir by Othniel, it is clear that Debir was not far from Hebron. The account of the conquest of the towns of Judah by Joshua in 10:36 relates that Joshua went up from Eglon to Hebron, from which he returned to Debir. This proves the location of the latter to be south of the direct line of march from the neighborhood of Tell el-Ḥesi to Hebron, since all the definitely located towns of the sixth district of Judah, in which Debir was situated, are much to the south of this line. Furthermore, Joshua 11:21 suggests a location for Debir between Hebron and Anab, in remarkable agreement with the actual situation of Tell Beit Mirsim. The *gullôt mayim* of Joshua 15:19 and Judges 1:15 are clearly located in the valleys above and below the town. They correspond precisely to the modern wells leading down into underground basins fed by springs that are now subterranean, deep under the accumulated alluvium. In other words, these are neither true wells *(be'erot)* nor springs *(ma'yanot),* but basins *(gullôt),* called by mistake "springs" in the English Bible.

The most important point, however, remains the location of Debir in the sixth district of Judah (Joshua 15:48–50), where it is placed with such

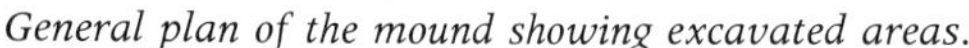

General plan of the mound showing excavated areas.

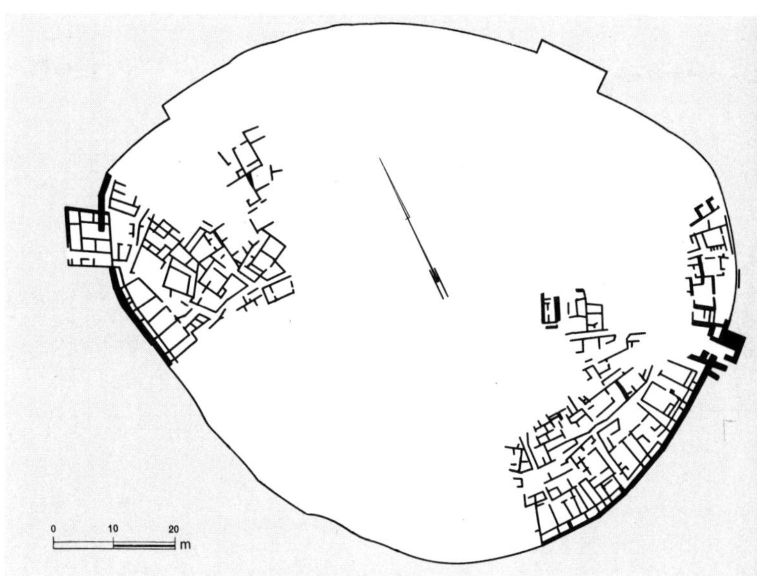

known sites as Jattir, Socoh, Anab, and Eshtemoh in the hill country south and southwest of Hebron. The identification of the rest of the eleven towns listed in this passage is still uncertain. Three names of towns at the end of the list (Joshua 15:51), which actually lie northwest of Hebron, must be transposed with the following first three names of towns in the seventh district, which lie precisely in the area already allotted to the sixth district. In other words, Goshen, Holon (Khirbet 'Alein), and Giloh (Khirbet Djâla) should be transposed to verse 52, and Arab, Dumah, and Eshean should be inserted in their place in verse 51.

The inclusion of Debir in the list of priestly towns (Joshua 21:15, I Chronicles 6:58) proves that it was an important place in the early Monarchy.

Since Tell Beit Mirsim is not in the Shephelah proper but at the edge of the high hill country, at a point where the hill country and the Shephelah merge, and since it is also definitely on the edge of the Negev where Joshua 15:19 and Judges 1:15 place it, the identification of Tell Beit Mirsim with Debir is most probable. The splendid situation and strong fortification of the site, as well as the complete agreement between the biblical data and the evidence of excavations, make the identification hard to reject, although it cannot yet be considered as certain.

As far as we can tell, the names Kirjat-Sepher and Debîr are not particularly significant, contrary to the often-expressed view that the town may have been a scribal center in the Bronze Age. A much more likely interpretation of the name would be "storehouse of the scribe," as "storehouses" was the meaning the plural still had in the Keret epic of Ugarit. The second element appears in Bêt-Sôpēr, "House of the Scribe," the name of a Canaanite town mentioned in Papyrus Anastasi I. That this word does not mean "House of the Book" or something of the kind is proved by the Egyptian spelling of the second element in syllabic orthography, which is identical with that of the Canaanite word for "scribe" in the same papyrus.

ORGANIZATION AND METHODS

After study and identification of the site in 1924, M. G. Kyle, president of Xenia Theological

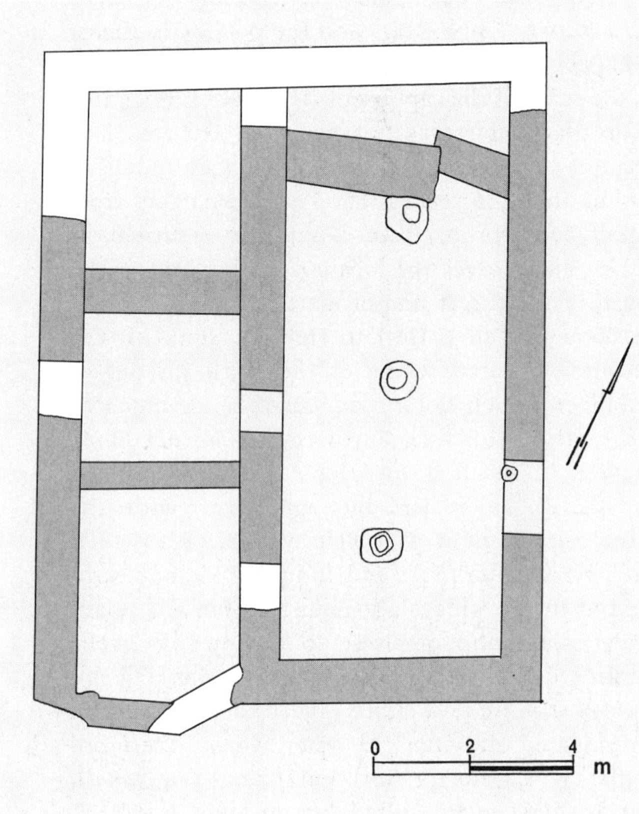

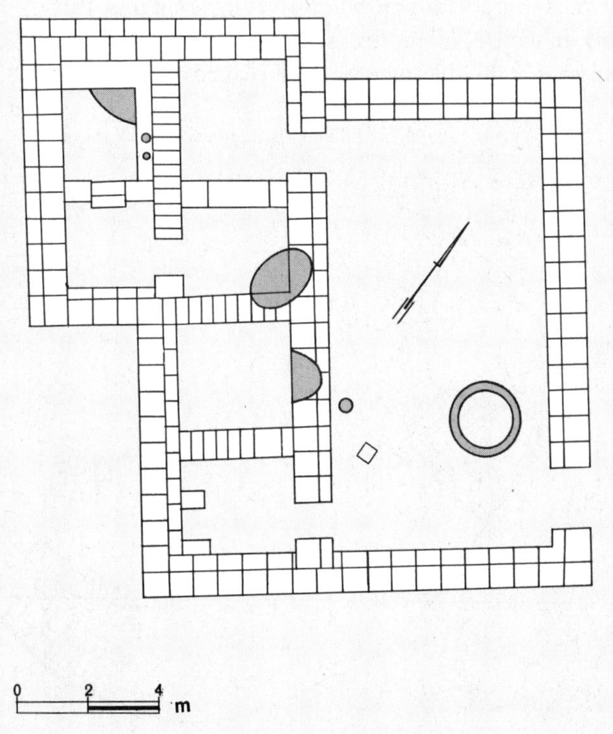

Stratum G: typical house; MBA II-A.
existing [ ] *conjectured (top).*
Stratum D: patrician house; MBA II-B (bottom).

Seminary (then in St. Louis), proposed a joint excavation by his institution and the American School of Oriental Research in Jerusalem following a successful joint undertaking of the two institutions in exploring the Dead Sea Valley two years previously. Four campaigns were carried out at Tell Beit Mirsim, the first in the spring of 1926 and the remaining three in the summers of 1928, 1930, and 1932. General coordinator and adviser was C. S. Fisher, whose plan of operation and methods of work were followed as closely as possible.

Two main areas were excavated, an extensive one in the southeast quadrant, which included the east gate, and a less extensive area in the northwest, which included the west gate and tower. No buildings were erected on the site after its destruction by the Chaldeans between 589 and 587 B.C., and not a single later shard was excavated. The surface of Tell Beit Mirsim has suffered much less from wind and water erosion than exposed sites such as Megiddo, Beth-Shean, and Jericho. The uppermost stratum (A) was well preserved, and it was possible to recover the plans and much of the elevation of a large number of houses. As work went on down to the Bronze Age, where the proportion of mud brick used in construction became much greater, a whole series of continuous burned layers or deposits was found, giving extraordinarily good clues to the stratification. The excavators followed the Reisner-Fisher method, and close attention was paid to the pottery. Thanks to well-preserved stratification and to constant checking of the pottery with pottery recovered from other sites in Palestine, it was possible to set up a provisional pottery chronology. Continuous and semi-continuous burned levels separated the strata, and care was taken to connect the phenomena indicated in vertical cuts at the sides of the excavation with material excavated at some distance from the sides.

ARCHAEOLOGICAL AND HISTORICAL RESULTS

The site was first occupied in or about the twenty-third century B.C., during Early Bronze Age III-B. This date can now be fixed by the pottery, some of which bears a striking resemblance to foreign pottery imported into Egypt in the Sixth Dynasty, as well as to native Egyptian pottery from the same period. The occupation was thin, and remains were found only in the red clay soil that was left after the hill had been burned off and the scanty soil eroded.

Strata I–H. The reoccupation of the site in stratum I probably came three or four centuries after the close of the J settlement. This new occupation took place in the twentieth or possibly even in the early nineteenth century B.C., and was characterized by pottery of the same Middle Bronze Age I, phase A, type that has been so clearly distinguished by Ruth Amiran from the earlier types of phases B and C.

The latter two phases are not represented at all

Stratum D: stele of serpent goddess; MBA II-B.

Game board and playing pieces; MBA II-B (top). Stratum C-2: stone libation tray; LBA II (bottom).

at Tell Beit Mirsim, and since they date from about the twenty-second to twentieth centuries, their absence fixes the approximate span of abandonment. Stratum I was destroyed by fire, traces of which were found in numerous places in the southeast quadrant. It was followed by the occupation of stratum H, and the end of this stratum can now be placed about 1800 B.C., since the following two strata, G and F, must be dated in the eighteenth century (see below).

There had undoubtedly been a wall or rampart around the town of H, for just inside, where the wall should have been, there were thick deposits of H debris that would otherwise have been washed away. Perhaps the H wall had been built outside the line of the G wall in this sector and its stones were used to build the G rampart. This is further indicated by the fact that H foundations were found at right angles to the G wall, under which they had continued.

It is astonishing how homogeneous is the pottery of Middle Bronze Age I (Ruth Amiran's phase Middle Bronze Age I–A) and of the last phase of Early Bronze Age (Kathleen Kenyon's Middle Bronze Age) that has been found all over Palestine as far north as the plain of Esdraelon. From Beth Yeraḥ in the north the pottery changes slightly in character — or is this more a chronological than a typological difference?

There is a striking difference between Middle Bronze Age I–A and Middle Bronze Age I–B and –C of Ruth Amiran. P. Lapp is probably correct in holding that these phases had been strongly influenced by movements from the northwest. On the other hand, Ruth Amiran has convincingly shown that the pottery of A goes back ultimately to Mesopotamia, with typological precursors in the ware of the Dynasty of Akkad. It then developed in eastern Syria and made its way down into Palestine after a substantial lag.

Strata G–F. Strata G and F, although separated by continuous burning and represented by foundations running quite differently, were characterized by identical pottery and could not have lasted more than a short time. This conclusion is not altered by the fact that there were two phases of G construction in one house complex, since the rebuilding was probably only partial and the entire stratum need not have covered more than a few decades at most.

As mentioned above, the entire span of G and F corresponds to Middle Bronze Age II–A (Kathleen Kenyon's Middle Bronze Age I), at least in southern Palestine, and is probably limited to the eighteenth century B.C., as follows from my recent demonstration that the royal tombs of Byblos I–IV were all contemporary with the Thirteenth Egyptian Dynasty. This ceramic phase ended just before the proliferation of pisé ramparts in Syria and Palestine. Of course, there are also differences between the pottery of this period in Byblos and in Palestine arising from the presence of imported Egyptian and other wares at Byblos, whereas there is apparently no such imported ware in our period in southern Palestine.

Strata E–D. The Hyksos period is represented by at least three, and probably four, phases of house construction in the E–D levels. But their exact relationship does not become clear until the final phase of D. The first phase of the external fortification of the town is marked by remains of pisé de terre walling just south of the east gate. The battered wall came later, but it is not known at exactly what stage of house construction it should be placed. In early E, after the pisé de terre phase, two large and well-built houses were preserved in the southeast.

In the eastern part of the southeast quadrant there was a well-built patrician house that yielded some of the most interesting finds of the excavation. The first construction of two large houses in the western part of the same quadrant was contemporary with a phase of E house construction to the east, which antedated two phases of the D patrician house. It is therefore possible to speak of three building phases rather than four. There was a semi-continuous level of burning between E and D, a fact that makes a four-phase hypothesis somewhat safer. None of these phases can have lasted more than a generation or so.

By far the richest phase of the town in the Middle Bronze Age was the latter part of E. This was certainly earlier than the D patrician house, since the pottery of the latter showed a marked decline in quality. The pottery of D differed from that of E chiefly in its increasingly careless manufacture, and it is not always easy to distinguish typologically between the two periods. In general the two periods together lasted from about 1700, or a little later, to about 1540–1530 B.C. This was the

Stratum A: house south of the west gate; seventh century B.C. (top). Same house looking north (bottom).

period of the two main Hyksos dynasties: the first, a Semitic group that may have ruled Egypt and Palestine for about half a century, and the second, the Fifteenth Dynasty, which ruled Egypt for about a century down to the expulsion of the Hyksos from Avaris after circa 1540 B.C. Since we made almost no attempt to hunt for tombs in the area around Tell Beit Mirsim, all the finds came from residential quarters of the town which, while giving them greater stratigraphic value, naturally reduced the quantity of pottery and other objects found.

Stratum C. Period C again shows two phases of occupation separated by burned levels. However, it is only just inside the line of Middle Bronze Age fortifications that we are able to distinguish sharply between C–1 and C–2. Building remains farther up on the site were completely destroyed, and then in many cases were eroded down to below foundation levels. When denudation had proceeded this far, the next builders often tore up the exposed foundations in order to use the stone for their own building operations.

Since the buildings of stratum D in the southeast quadrant had been thoroughly destroyed by fire and were covered by a fairly thick layer of ash-filled earth, it was possible almost everywhere to distinguish sharply between D and C constructions. During the period of abandonment, between the end of the Hyksos town and its reoccupation by the inhabitants of stratum C–1, a number of storage pits were sunk into the earth, destroying remains of D walls but also sealed by the foundations of C–1 that ran across them.

The period of abandonment may be estimated at more than a century, since there was no trace of bichrome paneled ware nor any remains of other fifteenth-century pottery types at the site. Two royal scarabs, one of Thutmose I and the other of Amenhotep III, cannot be used for precise dating purposes, since they may have served as ornaments at a later date and both were found in C debris. Neither C–1 nor C–2 was populous, as evidenced by the numerous grain pits, dated by typical Late Bronze Age pottery, scattered between the houses.

The most interesting construction in C–2 was the collapsed roof of a large building with good-size beams. A few meters from the line of collapsed roof, a crude stone lion, as well as an equally

Stratum A: shard inscribed l'z *("belonging to Uzz[iah]") (top).*
Stratum A: the northwest tower (bottom).

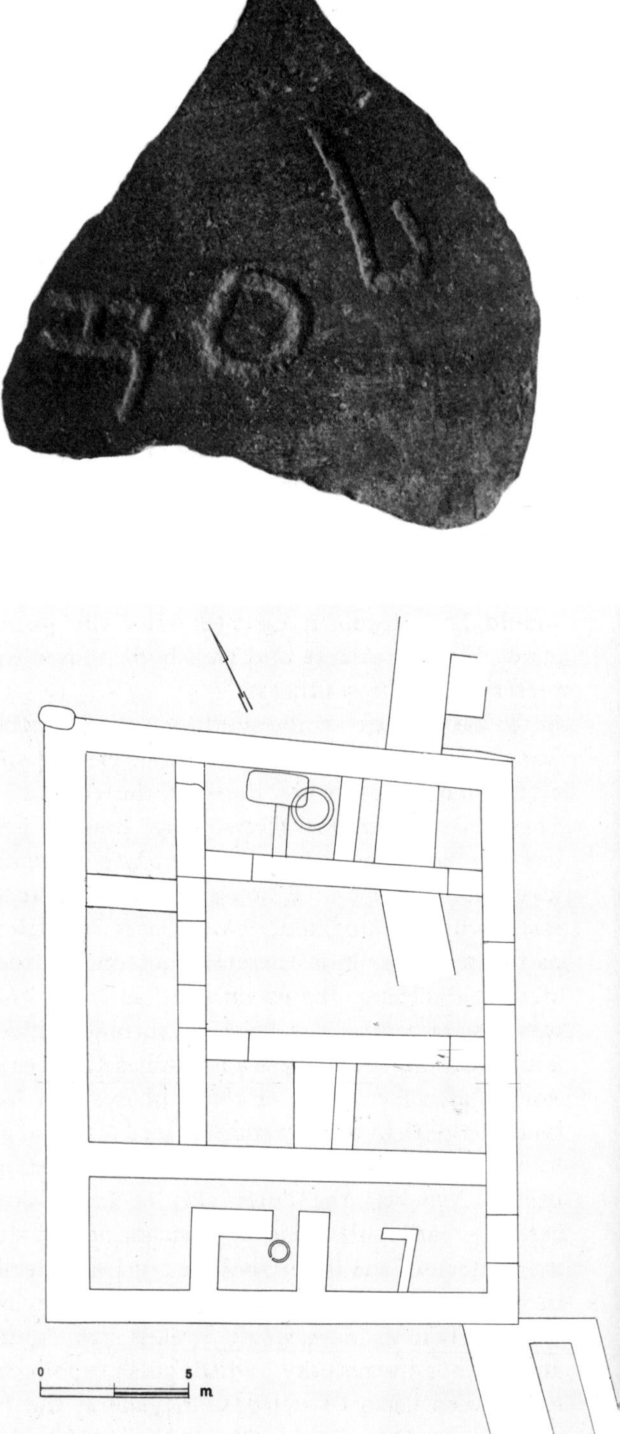

crude libation tray with a carved lioness and two lion cubs on it, was found in a refuse pit among bones of sacrificial animals.

The only fortification found at Tell Beit Mirsim that can be specifically assigned to stratum C was a short stretch of wall 2.5 meters wide, just southwest of the east gate at a particularly vulnerable point. Elsewhere it is clear that the old Middle Bronze Age battered wall was cleared and surmounted by a defense line consisting chiefly of outer walls of houses built along the edge of the summit. The same happened in Late Bronze Age at Jericho, where no trace of a wall of the period has yet been found. But the massive battered wall of Middle Bronze Age could have served as a defense wall once it had been cleared of debris and repaired.

Besides the usual imported and local Late Bronze Age pottery, some thirty Mycenaean shards belonging to as many different vases were found, nearly all in C–2 debris. It is quite possible, however, that some of them came from C–1, since there is no clear-cut evidence about the exact date at which the former was destroyed and replaced by the latter. The end of the C occupation almost certainly fell at about the same time as the end of Lachish, just after the fourth year of Merneptah, which seems to have been the critical phase of the conquest of the Shephelah by the Israelites.

All the Mycenaean shards belonged to Late Helladic III-B, which came to an end with the disruption of trade following the first major piratical raids of the Sea Peoples in the third quarter of the thirteenth century B.C. The probable date for this first movement now appears to be between circa 1235 and 1232. Evidence for this date is increasing rapidly in extent and precision.

Strata B–A. Stratum B was thinly occupied in all three phases — so thinly that in some areas where we should have expected the greatest depth of stratified debris, there was little except large grain pits. The grain pits were, in fact, almost the only structures that could be given a terminus ante quem by their pottery content. In other words, whenever the site was destroyed or the pits fell into disuse, they were filled with debris containing shards that had to be earlier in date than the filling of the grain pits in question. We were thus able to differentiate typologically among the three phases of stratum B by studying the contents of the grain pits and their relation to one another and to the extant remains of house walls.

There was a short period of occupation clearly represented only by a few grain pits, which were in use between the end of stratum C, circa 1234 B.C., and the latter part of the twelfth century B.C. This was followed by a relatively high proportion of grain pits containing pottery of the Philistine period. The latter was followed in turn by some small grain pits of the post-Philistine Iron Age I.

Some houses and other deposits could also be dated by their relationship to one another and to the grain pits, as well as by their pottery content. The first pre-Philistine phase was characterized by pottery of decadent Late Bronze Age type but without any imported pieces, as well as by the complete absence of any Philistine ware. The second phase was characterized by Philistine pottery belonging to various stages between its first importation into the hill country about 1175 B.C. and its final displacement by the purple spiral ware first isolated stratigraphically by B. Mazar at Tell Qasile. The latter pottery was in use in the Philistine plain after the establishment of the Davidic monarchy about 1000 B.C.

Although in our early work we were probably too confident that the town of stratum B was destroyed in Shishak's invasion, circa 924 B.C., that still remains the most probable date for the end of B. This was followed by phase A–1 which, strictly speaking, seems to include nearly all the walls and structures (including some which we had originally attributed to B–3), preceding the latest rebuilding of individual houses in the areas in question. Extremely little early pottery was recovered from house remains of stratum A–1, and almost all pottery from the site is late seventh or early sixth century B.C. Hence it was difficult to determine when most of the houses of stratum A were first constructed.

The house plan of A–2 appears at Tell el-Far'a in the north, as well as at various other towns in Judah, so it would seem that it was in use from the early eighth century onward. These houses were solidly built of stone often with quite massive stone pillars supporting the second floor and roof. So it is not surprising that they lasted

for two centuries, or in some cases even more.
Judging from the series of successive rebuildings at the west tower, beside the west gate of the town, it would appear that there were at least four phases of construction between the ninth century and the early sixth — although phase Delta (the fourth from the top) may go back only to the eighth century. The west tower cannot well be earlier than the ninth century, since the foundations of the west tower (to which the west gate is integrally attached) straddle the tenth-century wall. It is likely that Delta belongs to the ninth century and that Gamma dates from the early seventh, while Beta and Alpha belong to the period of Chaldean invasions.
When Volume III of the Tell Beit Mirsim publication appeared in 1943, no contemporary parallel was found anywhere for the plan of the east gate of Tell Beit Mirsim, which we had cautiously dated in the seventh century B.C. A few years later two close parallels were found by B. Alkim and H. Cambel at Karatepe in the Sheihân Valley southwest of Mara, in northern Syria. The plan of the two gates is quite similar to that of the last phase of construction at the east gate of Tell Beit Mirsim. At first most scholars were inclined to date these gates to the late eighth century B.C. From new stylistic and paleographical evidence, however, R. D. Barnett, with whom the excavators now concur, dates the sculptures in the ninth and the inscriptions probably about the beginning of the eighth. The resulting date for the east gate of Tell Beit Mirsim is therefore more than a century earlier than the date formerly accepted.
The date of the final destruction of Tell Beit Mirsim is fixed by the find of two jar-handle stamps with the impression of the seal of Eliakim, steward *(na'ar)* of Jehoiachin (*Yaukîn,* just as in the ration lists of Nebuchadnezzar from circa 592 B.C.).
An identical stamp was found by E. Grant at Beth-Shemesh, and a fourth was discovered by Y. Aharoni at Ramat Raḥel in 1962. That the original seal or identical seals belonged to the steward of Jehoiachin, who took care of his property after he had been exiled to Babylonia, is made virtually certain by the occurrence of the same situation in the case of Saul's steward *(na'ar)* Ziba. This means that all three towns were destroyed by the Chaldeans in 589–587 B.C.

SUMMARY

1. The identification of Tell Beit Mirsim with biblical Kirjath-Sepher/Debir is, in our opinion, practically certain. However, since many scholars are skeptical, we consider it advisable to use the modern and not the ancient name.
2. While the chronological results of the excavation have had to be modified in minor details (although never by more than a century or so), the early reports on Tell Beit Mirsim in 1926–33 presented the first clear picture of the ceramic chronology of Palestine.
3. From the historical point of view the most important single result was clarification of the archaeological history of Palestine during the Middle Bronze Age. This has helped essentially in providing a basic framework for the patriarchal traditions of the Bible. The period of Abraham is probably to be set in or about the nineteenth century B.C. The period of Jacob and Joseph falls in or about the seventeenth century.
4. Tell Beit Mirsim has contributed materially to our understanding of the Israelite conquest of the Shephelah by illustrating its nature and helping to fix its chronology.
5. Our site remains the best-preserved example of a town of Judah from the century immediately preceding the destruction of the First Temple. From it we can reconstruct the material culture in considerable detail.
6. Tell Beit Mirsim was the first excavated site to furnish tangible evidence that the biblical picture of the destruction of the cities of Judah by the Chaldeans in the early sixth century is correct. Our results have been decisively confirmed by subsequent work elsewhere.

W. F. ALBRIGHT

BIBLIOGRAPHY

Excavation reports: W.F. Albright, *"The Excavation of Tell Beit Mirsim* 1," "The Pottery of the First Three Campaigns," *AASOR* 12, 1932; IA, "The Bronze Age Pottery of the Fourth Campaign," *AASOR* 13, 1933, 55–127; 2, "The Bronze Age," *AASOR* 17, 1938 • W.F. Albright–J.L. Kelso, "The Excavation of Tell Beit Mirsim 3," "The Iron Age," *AASOR* 21–22, 1943.

On the excavations: W.F. Albright, *The Archaeology of Palestine and the Bible,* New York, 1932, 63–126 • M.G. Kyle, *Excavating Kirjath-Sepher's Ten Cities,* Grand Rapids, Michigan, 1934 • W.F. Albright, *apud Mélanges Dussaud* 1, Paris, 1939, 107–120 • M.W. Lightner, *BASOR* 119 (1950), 22–23 • R.B.K. Amiran–I. Dunayevsky, *BASOR* 149 (1958), 29ff. • W.F. Albright, *ibid.,* 32 • Y. Aharoni, *BASOR* 154 (1959), 35–39.

BELVOIR
(Kokhav Hayarden, Kaukab el Hawa)

IDENTIFICATION. This border fortress, named Belvoir by the Crusaders, was built by the Hospitalers at the eastern edge of the Issachar Plateau, at the top of the scarp descending to the Jordan Valley. The elevation of the ridge at this spot is 312 meters above sea level and some 550 meters above the adjacent Jordan Valley. The fortress is about 4 kilometers ($2\frac{1}{2}$ miles) from the Jordan River, as the crow flies. It commands a panoramic view reaching beyond the Sea of Galilee and the Golan Heights to snow-capped Mount Hermon to the north. Toward the east one sees the mountains of Gilead; to the south, the Gilboa and the Hills of Samaria, including the prominent peak of Sartaba; and to the west, Mount Tabor, the Nazareth mountains, and the Carmel Range.

This view gave the site its name: Belvoir, "fine view." Another name for the site in Crusader times was the French *Coquet* ("Dandy"), which is actually derived from the Arabic name for the site, Kaukab, appearing in contemporary Islamic sources. The Arabic, in turn, preserves the Hebrew name of a small town of the Second Temple period, which flourished till the fourth century A.D.

This town stood some 700 meters southeast of the site of the fortress, on a low terrace of the scarp near a small spring. Among its public buildings was a synagogue, whose stones, along with those from other buildings of the town, were used by the Crusaders in their fortress. Some of the stones from the synagogue found in secondary use bear

Aerial view from the west.

Plan of the castle. 1. Main gate. 2. Outer tower, the "Bashora." 3. East gate. 4. Court. 5. Cisterns. 6. Inner court. 7. West gate. 8. Vaults of the inner citadel. 9. Refectory. 10. Kitchen. 11. Vaults of the outer citadel. 12. Gate of the drawbridge. 13. Drawbridge. 14. Postern gates. 15. Area of industrial installations. 16. Outer towers. 17. Inner towers. 18. Moat.

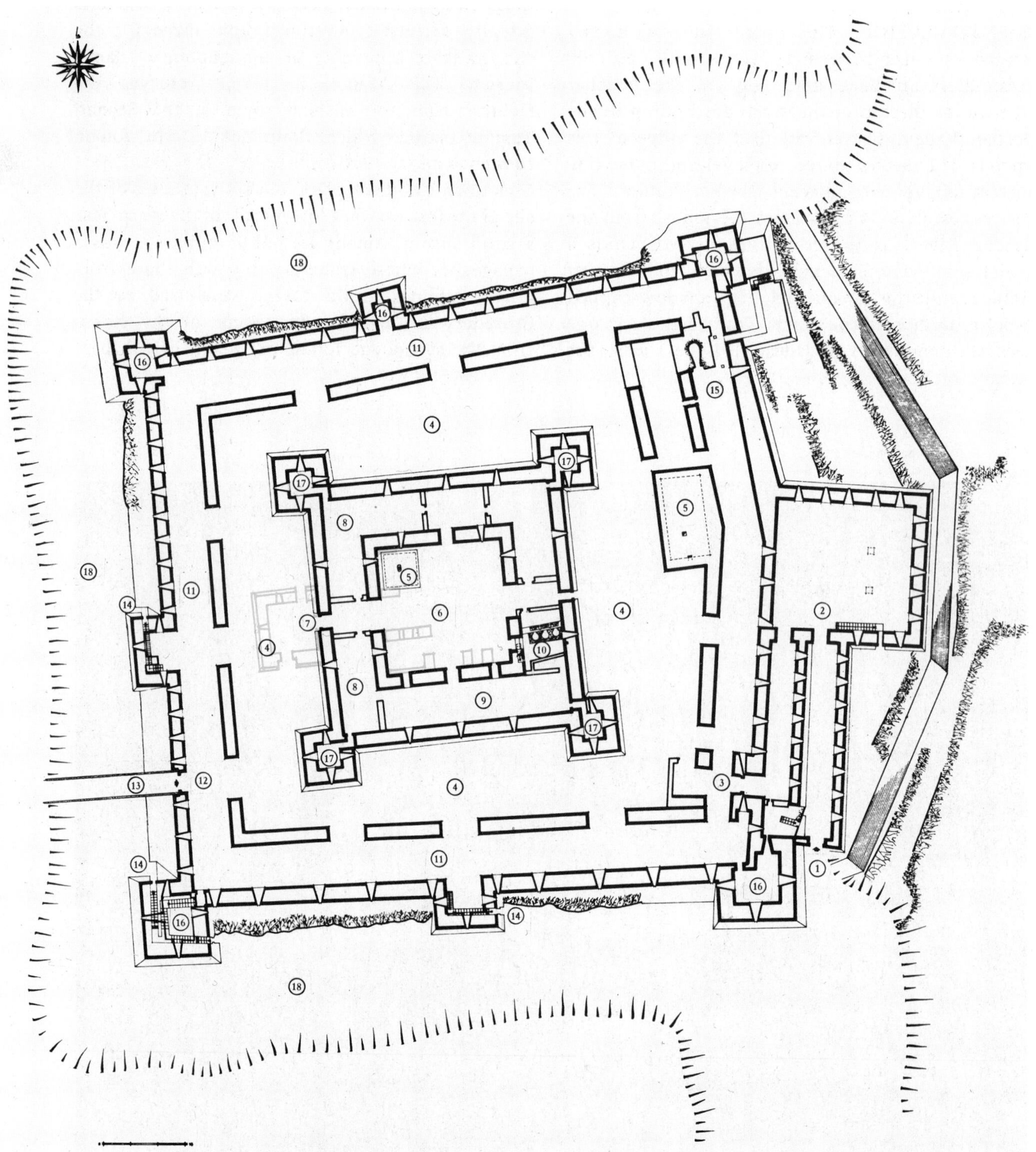

Aramaic and Greek inscriptions, as well as stone reliefs typical of ancient Jewish synagogal art in Galilee and Golan, including a basalt lintel bearing the motif of the Ark of the Law and a seven-branched menorah.

The strategic situation of the fortress is of greatest significance, for it commands a lengthy stretch of the Jordan River, once the frontier between Crusader and Muslim territories. Belvoir also controls the bridges in the vicinity of the confluence of the Yarmuk, bridges that bore the main routes to and from Damascus. Furthermore, Belvoir commands the two roads ascending from the Jordan Valley westward into the interior: the one via Beth-Shean and the Jezreel Valley, the other by way of the Tabor Valley (Wadi Bire), which joined the trade route leading to the important port city of Accho, and hence abroad.

HISTORY

It was only in the Crusader period that the upper terrace on the site was utilized for purposes of fortification. The first Latins to take advantage of the site were the Velos family, apparently in the days of Fulk of Anjou, king of Jerusalem (A.D. 1131–43). They did not succeed in taking root, however, and in 1168 the site was sold by Ivo Velos to the Order of Hospitalers. The fortress described below was built from that time on.

In 1182–83, when Saladin raided Lower Galilee and even succeeded in conquering and razing the fortress of Forbelet ('Afrabela) on the site of modern et-Taiyiba, west of Belvoir, the knights of the fortress stood up to the challenge. Despite casualties, they held the fortress and refused to surrender. The zenith in the history of the fortress came after the battle of Hattin (July, 1187).

Within a very short time Saladin gained control over all the territory of the Kingdom of Jerusalem, with only a few strong points resisting—among them, Belvoir. But these pockets of resistance also fell, and only two withstood the prolonged siege: the Templar fortress at Safed and the Hospitaler

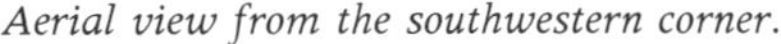

Aerial view from the southwestern corner.

Grotesque head (top). Church relief of an angel (bottom).

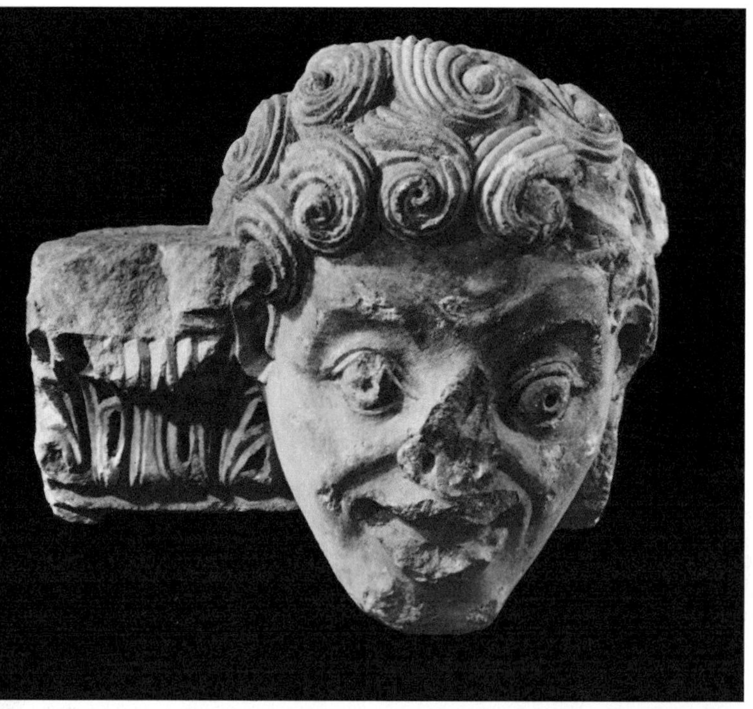

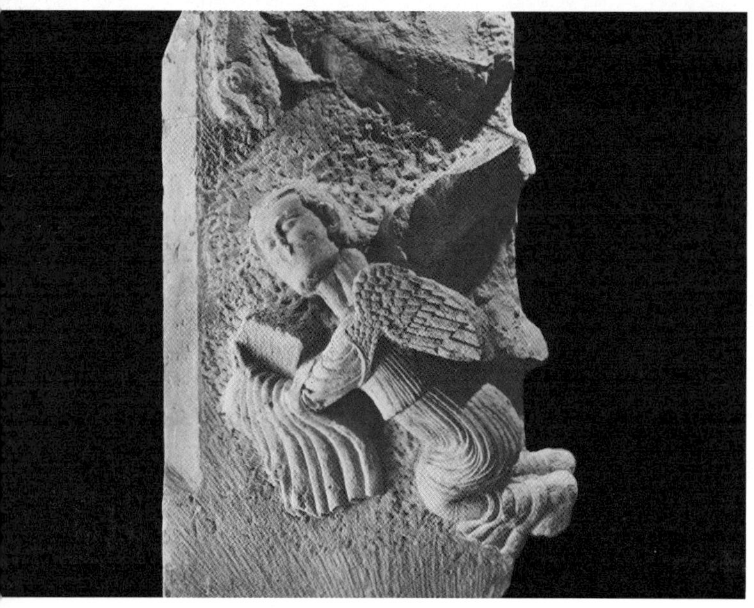

fortress at Belvoir. During the siege the knights displayed considerable military ability. Their few numbers held off great hordes and often even carried out raids outside the fortress with impunity. Saladin himself was present during part of the fighting.

When the Muslims realized the futility of their efforts, they employed expert sappers to undermine the eastern tower and bring about its collapse, in early January, 1191. Although the destruction of this outer tower left the fortress proper intact, the besieged knights saw the hopelessness of continuing the struggle and sued for peace — in return for their lives and free passage to the city of Tyre. Saladin's forces demolished the church and the gates, then abandoned the site. The desolate spot was taken over by local Bedouin, who settled in the ruins.

In the first quarter of the thirteenth century — when al-Malik al-Muazzam, ruler of Damascus, tore down abandoned fortresses to prevent their reseizure by the Crusaders — Belvoir, too, was dismantled. In 1241, by an agreement between al-Malik es-Saleḥ Ayyub, ruler of Egypt, and Richard of Cornwall, the new Crusader leader, several fortresses and towns were returned to Latin ownership, including Belvoir. The Crusaders, however, were unable to rebuild and refurbish the site. At the beginning of the nineteenth century, an Arab village named Kaukab el-Hawa rose in the ruins. It was finally abandoned in 1948.

EXCAVATIONS

In 1966–67 systematic excavations and restoration operations were carried out at the site of the fortress, on behalf of the National Parks Authority and under the direction of M. Ben-Dov.

THE FORTRESS

The plan of the fortress is unusual for Crusader fortifications, which were usually built in accordance with the topography of the site. In the present case the engineers were unlimited as to area, for the level height here provided ample room. On three sides — south, west, and north — moats were dug, up to 12 meters deep and 25 meters wide. Where the bedrock was unstable, the sides of the moat facing the fortress were lined with a stone glacis. Above the glacis stood the ramparts of the fortress. These exterior walls comprise a series of elongated, vaulted chambers.

The walls are 3 meters thick, with a width of 7 meters between them. The length of the vaults, more than 100 meters, corresponds to that of the walls.

In each corner stood a strongly built tower. In the center of each wall, midway between the corner towers, stood another tower. Almost all of the towers were built with interior staircases that had exits leading to the moat. These provided secret means for entering and leaving the fortress.

The eastern slope was heavily fortified, with walls founded directly upon the bedrock. At the foot of the terrace was an exceptionally strong external tower — the one undermined by the Muslims during the siege. There were two main gates. The one on the east was very carefully planned, with the access way turning back upon itself between the outer tower and the fortress proper. The gate on the west offered direct access to the interior by way of a bridge (partly a drawbridge) over the moat. The latter gate could be blocked during a siege and the bridge dismantled.

Inner Fortifications. Within the open space of the main fortress there was an additional fortification, which could in itself withstand a siege. This keep, or *donjon*, somewhat resembled the plan of the outer fortress. The walls consisted of four long vaults with corner towers and an additional central tower on the west. The latter tower served as the gate fortification of the keep. In the eastern wall was another small gate, only 1 meter wide. In the middle of the keep was a covered courtyard measuring 20 square meters.

The outer fortifications were built entirely of local basalt. The inner keep was made of the same stone to a height of 3 meters, above which it was built of a soft white limestone, which appears on the interior as well. The basalt had been quarried locally; the limestone came from quarries 3 kilometers to the west. Hauling the softer stone was worthwhile, for this limestone could readily be dressed or carved, and wherever the strength of basalt was not required, it was preferred.

The Church. This important building was built on the second story of the western vault and central gate tower of the keep. It measured only 7 by 21 meters and was built entirely of a harder white limestone, brought from a distance of tens of kilometers (Giv'at ha-Moreh and the Hills of Ephraim). The church was exquisitely ornamented, as is evidenced by its many remains. These

Southeastern tower of outer wall (top). Entrance tower of the inner fortress with postern gate and loophole, looking north (bottom).

include carved pillars and capitals, statues and reliefs from the cornices and the main door of the church. The statues and reliefs are significant mainly in that they can be dated precisely (1170–75); they are among the rare examples of Crusader art known from the second half of the twelfth century.

Main Hall. The main hall, with pillars and capitals made of black basalt, stood on the second story, adjacent to the church and above the northern vault of the keep.

Cisterns. Two cisterns served the entire fortress, fed solely by rainwater. One is within the outer fortress, near the baths on the east. It held some 500 cubic meters of water. The other cistern, in the courtyard of the keep, held some 120 cubic meters. No other sources of water were available in times of a siege.

Kitchen and Refectory. In the eastern vault of the keep, remains of the kitchen were found, with three ovens and their flues. In the adjacent southern vault was the refectory.

Storerooms and Stables. The extensive vaults surrounding the fortress on all four sides were utilized as stables and central storerooms. Furthermore, the northern and western vaults and part of the eastern vault on the ground floor of the keep were also used for storage and stables for the headquarters.

Workshop Area. The vaults in the northeastern corner of the fortress contained industrial and workshop installations, including a kiln built of brick, for the blacksmith, and various drainage and sewage channels.

Small Objects. Several scores of pottery vessels were found. Some were glazed and some painted, all representative of wares of the Crusader period. Iron weapons were also recovered, mainly arrowheads. Pieces of ironwork were found which belonged to the hinges and door sockets of the gates and to their metal facing. Several stone utensils were uncovered, including storage bins and grinding stones. Bronze ornaments from the church were also discovered.

M. BEN-DOV

BIBLIOGRAPHY

Guérin, *Galilée* 4, 129 ff • Conder-Kitchener, *SWP* 2, 85, 117–19 • J. Prawer, *Yediot* 31 (1967), 236–49 (Hebrew) • M. Ben-Dov, *Qadmoniot* 2 (1969), 22–27 (Hebrew).

BENE-BERAK AND VICINITY

THE SITE AND ITS IDENTIFICATION. The modern city of Bene-Berak bears the name of one of the settlements in the territory of the tribe of Dan (Joshua 19:45). It is identified at present with the Arab village Ibn-Ibraq (also known as Hiriyyeh), about 4 kilometers (2½ miles) south of the modern city. The Annals of Sennacherib indicate that Bene-Berak was located near Jaffa, Beth-Dagon, and Azor. The town was also known as the home of Rabbi Akiba. So far, no excavations have been conducted at Hiriyyeh, but surface potsherds dating from the Iron Age substantiate its identification with ancient Bene-Berak.

Five other archaeological sites have been excavated in the vicinity of Bene-Berak. These are, from north to south, Tell Abu-Zeitun, Pardess Katz, Givat ha-Radar, the hill of the Weisenitz Yeshiva, and Modi'in Street.

The ancient names of these sites are not known, but it has been suggested that Tell Abu-Zeitun (also called Tel Zeiton) should be identified with the Levitical city of Gath-Rimmon, mentioned together with Jehud and Bene-Berak in the territory of the tribe of Dan (Joshua 19:45, 21:24).

EXCAVATIONS

Tell Abu-Zeitun. In 1957 J. Kaplan excavated the site on behalf of the Israel Exploration Society. Several recent graves were uncovered in the first or uppermost level, along with a layer of ash from the Arab period and two occupation levels dating from Persian times (levels I–A and I–B). The finds from level I–A date to the fifth century B.C. and include shards of imported Attic ware and an ostracon engraved with the name "Hasshub." This appears five times in the Bible in connection with the post-Exilic period (I Chronicles 9:14, Nehemiah 11:15). The Persian stratum, with its two levels (I–A and I–B), is two meters thick. Below it was uncovered level A of stratum II, dated to Iron Age II. At the eastern edge of the site, a brick wall of the Persian I–A level was discovered. Directly beneath that was another well-preserved brick wall dating to the Iron Age II–A level. No wall from the Persian I–B level has been

Ossuary; Chalcolithic period (top). Fragment of ossuary with painting of human face with protruding nose (center). Tell Abu-Zeitun. Aramaic ostracon, inscribed Hšwb; *fifth century* B.C. *(bottom).*

revealed, which may indicate that the early Persian settlement was quite small and limited to the top of the tel.

Pardess Katz. See Tel Aviv (the Jannaeus line).

Givat ha-Radar (Bab el-Hawwah). At this site a number of Chalcolithic graves were uncovered. As in several other sites in the Sharon Plain and the Shephelah (see Azor, Sharon), burial caves were cut into the *kurkar* rock and used for secondary burials. The bones of the dead were placed in house-shaped clay ossuaries after the flesh had decomposed.

Excavations conducted in 1942 in the northwest section of the hill by J. Ory, on behalf of the Antiquities Department of the Mandatory Government, uncovered the remains of twelve burial pits and caves. In these were found fragments of fired clay ossuaries containing human bones. Pit H disclosed, among other things, human bones that had been deposited in a square hole in the rock. Pit F, where traces of an intense fire were observed, was full of potsherds. The excavator suggests that this pit was used as a pottery kiln. The ossuaries are all house shaped and identical in form and decoration with those first found at Ḥederah (q.v.). The ceramic finds included bowls, pots, hole-mouth jars, and incense burners, all typologically related to the Ghassulian-Chalcolithic ware.

J. Kaplan excavated the northeast section of the hill in 1951, on behalf of the Israel Department of Antiquities, and brought to light two Chalcolithic burial caves. One (2 meters in diameter) was completely empty. Apparently the inhabitants of the site had had no time to make use of it.

The ceiling of the other cave (7 meters in diameter) had collapsed, and most of the pottery and ossuaries in it were crushed beneath the debris. The entrance of the cave, situated at the end of a narrow corridor leading into it, was undisturbed.

The ossuaries containing human bones were placed in the corners of the cave on benches made of stone slabs. The pottery and incense burners, however, lay in the center of the cave. The ossuaries varied in size from 60 by 25 by 40 centimeters (the largest) to small ones only 15 centimeters in diameter. Most were in the form of rectangular-shaped houses with the opening placed high in one of the short ends. The side containing the opening was elevated and formed a façade decorated with a schematic representation of a human face with a protruding nose. An ossuary in the shape of a round house also belongs to this group. The opening was cut into its domed top. The lower section of the ossuary, which contained the bones, was shaped like a Chalcolithic jar. Here, too, was a curved projection above the narrow opening. On it were perhaps the reliefs of two snakes.

Of exceptional interest is a limestone tablet (48 by 12 centimeters) that was probably set upright. It represents a schematized human figure of presumably apotropaic significance.

The Hill of the Weisenitz Yeshiva. The Yeshiva stands on a high hill in east Bene-Berak. The archaeological finds were brought to light while foundations for a synagogue were being dug. In 1953 J. Kaplan excavated there on behalf of the Israel Department of Antiquities and found the remains of four building levels, all dating to the third and second centuries B.C. In their construction, dressed *kurkar* stones, rough stone, and pisé de terre were used. The finds included several bronze coins, potsherds, and fragments of lamps. It appears that this was once part of a fort or fortified domain of the Hellenistic period, erected on the hill, which was an observation point overlooking the road running from the Yarkon Basin to the Ono Valley.

Modi'in Street. Ancient remains are scattered over the hills on both sides of Modi'in Street, which marks the boundary between Bene-Berak and Ramat-Gan. Excavations conducted there by J. Kaplan and J. Ory uncovered a number of burial caves, the remains of mosaic floors, and the floor of a winepress. The dates of the caves and floors range from the second century B.C. to the eighth century A.D.

J. KAPLAN

BIBLIOGRAPHY

J. Ory, *QDAP* 12 (1946), 43–57 • J. Kaplan, *'Alon* 5–6 (1957), 21; *idem, BIES* 22 (1958), 98–99; *idem, The Chalcolithic and Neolithic Settlements in Tel Aviv and Its Environs,* Tel Aviv, 1958, 27–31 (in stencil) (all Hebrew); *idem. IEJ* 13 (1963), 300–12.

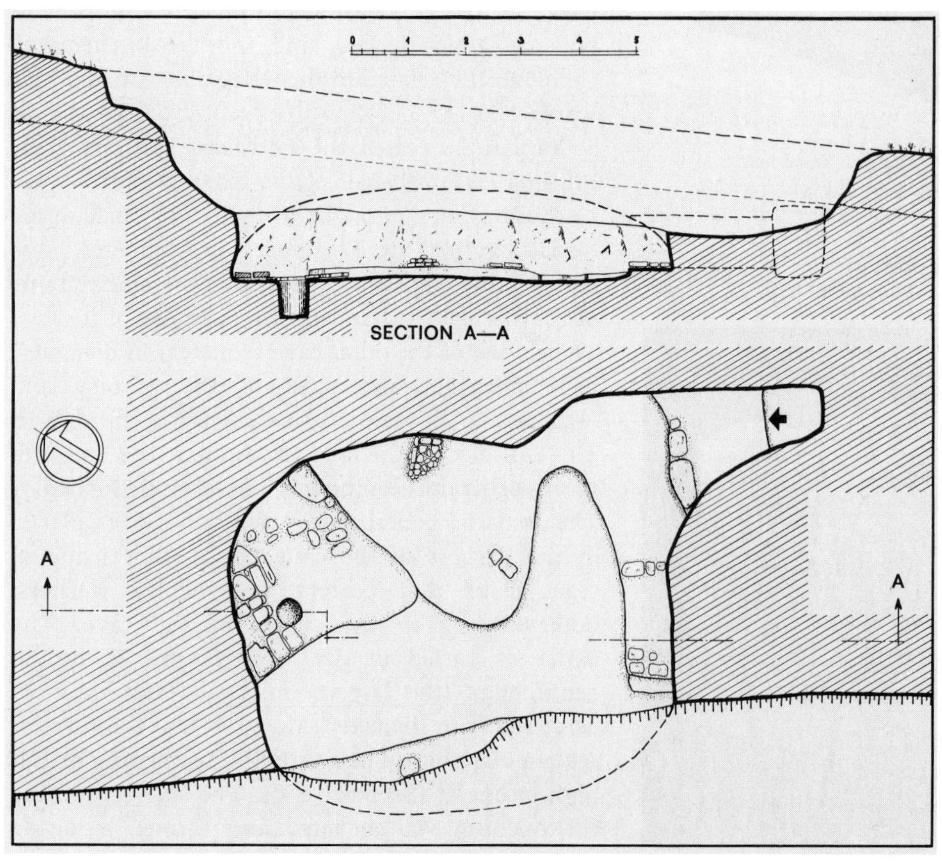

Excavations of 1951: Chalcolithic burial cave; plan and section A-A.

BETH ALPHA

IDENTIFICATION. The ancient synagogue is situated at the foot of the northern slopes of the Gilboa Mountains, on the southern side of the Harod Valley. The site was named after the adjacent ruin of Khirbet Beit Ilfa, which possibly preserves an ancient name. The place is now occupied by Kibbutz Hephzibah. In the course of digging a channel for conveying water to the fields, members of the kibbutz (then known as Beth Alpha) came upon a mosaic floor.

In 1929 E. L. Sukenik, assisted by N. Avigad, began excavations at the spot on behalf of the Hebrew University. They uncovered the remnants of a synagogue and its mosaic floor. Exploratory excavations in the vicinity of the synagogue, conducted in 1962 by the Department of Antiquities, succeeded in exposing remains of buildings and of a lower mosaic.

EXCAVATIONS

The synagogue, which measured approximately 27.7 by 14.2 meters, was situated among houses that lined the narrow streets. It consisted of a courtyard (atrium), a vestibule (narthex), and a basilical hall. The walls (.7 to .85 meters thick and standing to a height of .55 to 1.65 meters) are of undressed stone, plastered within and without. The apse of the building is oriented southward toward Jerusalem. The façade with its entrances is in the north opposite the apse.

The courtyard (9.65 by 11.9 meters) was paved with a crude mosaic decorated with geometric patterns. The form of the façade is not clear. Judging from the existing remains, it seems to have undergone several repairs. The floor of the vestibule (which is 2.57 meters wide) also has a geometric design. Three doorways lead into the hall of the synagogue. Two rows of plastered stone pillars divide the hall into a central nave (5.4 meters wide) and two aisles (2.75 meters and 3.1 meters wide respectively). It is very likely that the pillars supported an arched entablature.

Recessed in the south wall of the nave is an apse (2.4 meters deep), which served as the permanent repository of the Ark of the Law. Its floor is raised above that of the nave and three steps lead up to it. A depression (.8 meters deep) in the floor of the

Plan of the synagogue and hall and mosaic floors.

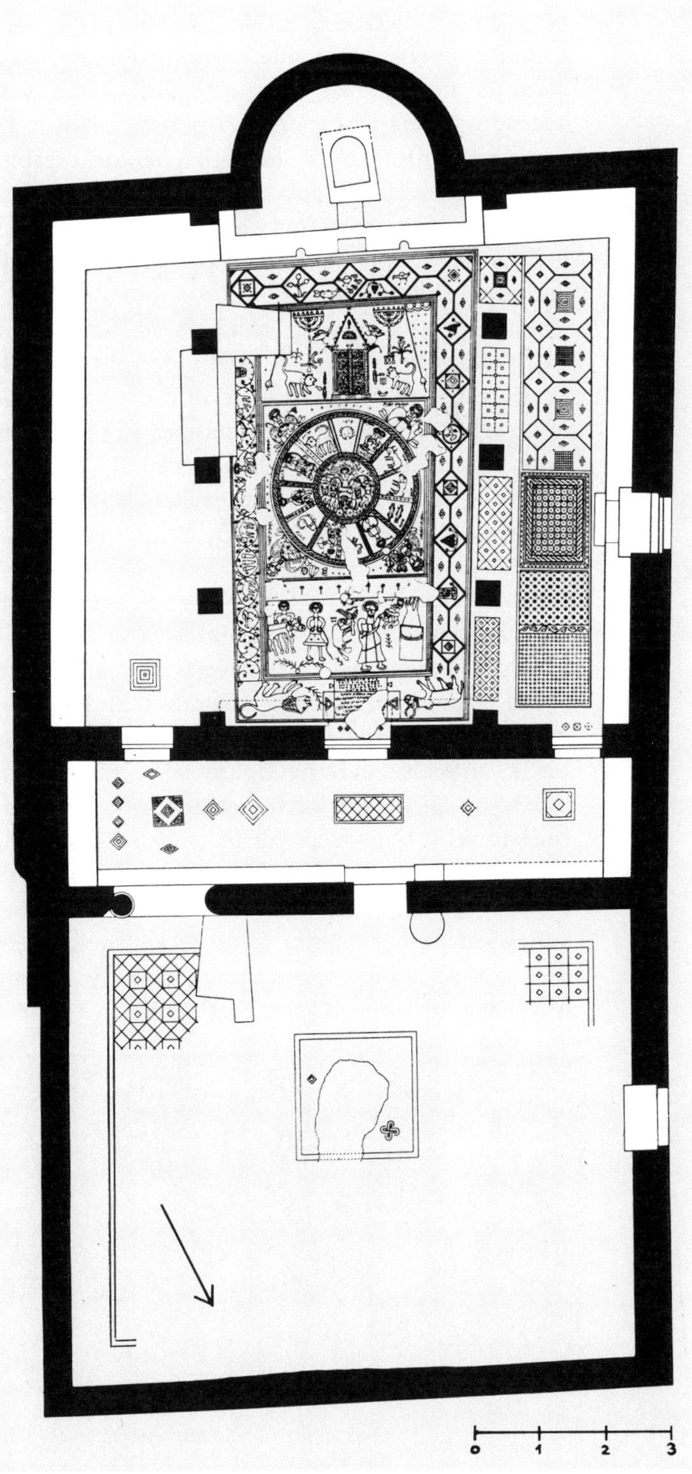

apse, covered with stone slabs, contained thirty-six Byzantine coins: hence it had served as a community chest.

Benches were built along the length of the side walls and the south wall. Near the two southern pillars in the eastern side, a platform (bema) and a bench had been erected on the mosaic floor. They were obviously later additions. A door in the western aisle opens into a side room, or annex, whose form is not known. Perhaps there were steps ascending from this room to the upper story. The remains furnish no evidence that would establish the existence of a second story, but it is reasonable to assume that there was one and that a women's gallery was built on top of the two colonnades and above the vestibule.

The whole hall is paved with colored mosaics. The floor of the western aisle is divided into squares of geometric patterns. In front of the western door is a carpet-like design. The mosaic of the eastern aisle, however, is mostly unadorned. The floor of the nave is divided into three panels, each containing a different motif: the first shows the Ark of the Law; the second, the Zodiac; and the third, the Offering of Isaac. All three panels are enclosed by a border with varied decorations: a pattern of lozenges, containing to the west fruit and to the south birds, fish, a cluster of grapes, and a pomegranate tree; to the east the tendrils of a vine with birds, animals, and the figure of a man. In the north, on either side of the entrance, a lion and a buffalo with their faces turned toward each other are placed so as to be seen from the interior of the synagogue as guardians of the entrance. The first panel was perhaps meant to duplicate the contents of the apse, which was situated directly in front of it. Behind the veil (parocheth), which is parted in the center, is a gable-roofed Ark from which is suspended an "eternal light" (ner tamid). Two birds stand beside it, facing each other in an heraldic order. On either side of the Ark is a lighted menorah, and near each are the traditional ritual objects — shofar, lulab, ethrog, and incense shovel. The Ark is guarded on either side by lions.

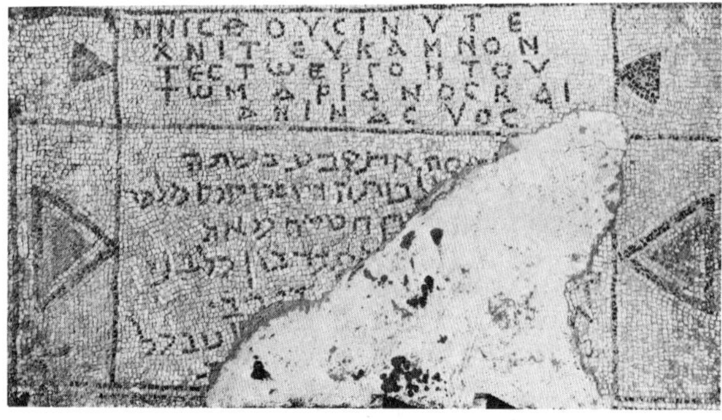

Greek and Aramaic inscriptions on the floor, at the entrance of the synagogue.

The second panel, which occupied the center of the floor, represents the Cycle of the Zodiac. The twelve signs are shown arranged in a circle. Besides each is written its Hebrew name: *Taleh* (Aries, Ram); *Shor* (Taurus, Bull); *Teomim* (Gemini, Twins); *Sartan* (Cancer, Crab); *Aryeh* (Leo, Lion); *Betulah* (Virgo, Virgin); *Meoznayim* (Libra, Scales); *Aqrab* (Scorpio, Scorpion); *Kashat* (Sagittarius, Archer); *Gedi* (Capricorn, Goat); *Deli* (Aquarius, Water Bearer); and *Dagim* (Pisces, Fishes). In the center of the circle Apollo-Helios, the sun god, is depicted driving a chariot drawn by four galloping horses (quadriga) along the dim expanse of a sky studded with stars and a moon. In the corners of the panel the Four Seasons of the year appear in the form of winged busts of women covered with jewels and surrounded by various seasonal attributes (fruit, birds, and the like). To each is attached its appropriate name: *Nisan* (Spring); *Tammuz* (Summer); *Tishri* (Autumn); *Tebeth* (Winter).

The third panel, near the entrance, depicts the Offering of Isaac. To the right is an altar from which rise the flames of a fire. To the left stands Abraham, wearing a beard and with a halo above his head. With one hand Abraham holds Isaac, who is represented as a child with securely bound hands; Abraham grasps a long knife in his other hand. The names "Isaac" and "Abraham" are inscribed above the respective figures. A hand, symbolizing the power of God, appears from above, as if emerging from a cloud, behind which rays are shining. Near it are the words of the Divine prohibition: "Thou shalt not stretch forth" ("Lay not thine hand upon the lad"). At Abraham's side a rearing ram is tied to a tree (thicket) suspended in mid-air as if there had been no place for its forelegs. Above it is the legend: "And behold...a ram." In the left corner is the ass and the two lads who accompanied Abraham.

On entering the synagogue through the main door, two inscriptions — one in Aramaic and the other in Greek — can be seen on the floor. The Aramaic inscription, which is partly destroyed, states that

Beth-Alpha; mosaic floor of the synagogue.

the mosaic was made during a certain year in the reign of Emperor Justin and that its cost was defrayed by donations of the members of the congregation who contributed in kind — wheat and the like. The floor is broken in the spot where the date was inscribed, but E.L. Sukenik was of the opinion that the floor must have been laid during the reign of Justin I (and not of Justin II, who was notorious for his severe anti-Jewish policy) — that is, in the years 518–27. The building itself, however, is older and goes back perhaps to the end of the fifth century, as may be deduced from remnants of the mosaic floor found beneath the existing floor. The Greek inscription commemorates the craftsmen who laid the mosaic: "May the craftsmen who carried out this work, Marianos and his son Hanina, be held in remembrance."

SUMMARY

The synagogue of Beth Alpha is the best preserved among the synagogues of the Byzantine type. The distinctive features of this type are the division into a courtyard, narthex, and nave; an apse facing Jerusalem as a permanent repository for the Ark; and a mosaic floor. The synagogue is not built of dressed stone, nor is it as monumental as the older synagogues found in Galilee. But the highly variegated mosaic floor is surprisingly well preserved. In its magnificent decoration three basic motifs are displayed: ritual objects, astrological symbols, and a biblical scene. The style of the mosaic is primitive, simple, and naïve, and has the charm of folk art. The two artisans, father and son, who perpetuated their names in mosaic, seem to have worked throughout the entire district, since their names are also found in the mosaic floor recently discovered at Beth-Shean (q.v.).

A highly important feature, unique to the mosaic of Beth Alpha, is the inscription indicating a date of the laying of the floor in the sixth century. This and the synagogue at Gaza are the only ones for which a date has been found epigraphically. (The Kefar Neburaya inscription gives the year of reconstruction of the synagogue.)

N. AVIGAD

BIBLIOGRAPHY

E.L. Sukenik, *The Ancient Synagogue at Beth-Alpha,* Jerusalem, 1932 • R. Vishnizer, *BIES* 18 (1954), 190–97 (Hebrew) • Y. Rinov, *ibid.,* 198–201 (Hebrew); *Biq'aat Beth-Shean* (the 17th Convention of the Israel Exploration Society), Jerusalem, 1964, 63–70 (Hebrew) • Goodenough, *Jewish Symbols* 1, 241–53; 3, 638–41.

BETHEL

IDENTIFICATION. The site of ancient Bethel is generally identified with the modern village of Beitin, circa 17 kilometers ($10\frac{1}{2}$ miles) north of Jerusalem. Its identity was first established by E. Robinson in May, 1838, on the basis of geographical references in the Bible (Genesis 12:8, Judges 21:19, etc.), in Eusebius (*Onomasticon* 40:20–21), and its similarity to the Arabic name. The houses of the modern town are concentrated at the southeast corner of the ancient city, leaving only about 16 dunams (4 acres) of the ancient site available for excavation.

In 1927 W.F. Albright, in collaboration with H.M. Wiener, investigated the site. They sank a test pit, which came down upon a massive city wall. Albright's findings demonstrated that here, indeed, was Canaanite and Israelite Bethel. Although the site had no natural defensive features, it had copious springs and stood at the intersection of major highways — the mountain road and the main road leading from Jericho to the coastal plain. Because of these assets, a flourishing town was able to develop here. The city of Bethel had been preceded in the area by Ai, situated circa $2\frac{1}{2}$ kilometers ($1\frac{1}{2}$ miles) east of it (q.v.).

Basalt conical seal. Period uncertain (above). Sewage system; LBA II (below). Pillars of IA II structure on top of a IA I wall (opposite page).

HISTORY

According to the Bible, Bethel was formerly called Luz. It was conquered by the House of Joseph (Judges 1:22–25) and resettled by the Israelites. Bethel was included in the territory of Ephraim and became a sacred site and religious center associated with the tradition of the patriarchs. Jeroboam I built a royal sanctuary at Bethel as a rival to Jerusalem, but no trace of this sanctuary has been found so far. The city was destroyed by the Assyrians at about the same time as Samaria, about 721 B.C., but the shrine was revived toward the close of the Assyrian period (II Kings 17:28–41).

Bethel escaped destruction during Jerusalem's conquest by Nebuchadnezzar, but it was razed in the transition period between Babylonian and Persian rule. The city was soon rebuilt and was a small town in Ezra's day. It prospered in the Hellenistic and Early Roman periods and was the last city captured by Vespasian before he left Judea to become emperor. It continued to prosper in the Late Roman period and reached its maximum size in the Byzantine period. Shortly after the Islamic conquest, however, the city ceased to exist.

EXCAVATIONS

The Kyle Memorial Excavations at Bethel were conducted in the summers of 1934, 1954, 1957, and 1960 by the American Schools of Oriental Research and the Pittsburgh-Xenia Theological Seminary (now Pittsburgh Theological Seminary). The first campaign was directed by W.F. Albright assisted by J.L. Kelso. The other campaigns were directed by Kelso.

In 1960 the expedition discovered a mountaintop sanctuary in the northwest corner of the site on an almost level limestone ridge. Several dark stains on the ridge were tested and found to be blood, apparently of sacrifices. Traces of numerous bonfires were also found. In the debris above and around the acropolis were many fragments of cooking pots as well as flint knives and animal bones. The earliest object uncovered was a Chalcolithic jar found in the crevice of the rocks. Most of the shards were Middle Bronze Age I, some were Early Bronze Age. Directly above this acropolis, a fine new temple was built. It was oriented to the east and had a flagstone pavement. The building appears to be Middle Bronze Age I, and it was most likely destroyed by an earthquake.

The area around the springs and the sanctuary was originally a camping ground for shepherds. It became a village in about 3200 B.C. The site was abandoned during much of Early Bronze Age, but circa 2400–2200 B.C. it was again occupied, only to be abandoned later.

Early in Middle Bronze Age I the continuous occupation of the site began. Middle Bronze Age II-A saw some rebuilding near the springs, but it was Middle Bronze Age II-B before the entire area was surrounded by a massive wall (circa 3.5 meters thick). Several sections of the north and west walls and one part of the south wall were uncovered. The location of part of the east wall was tentatively identified, but a newly paved street prevented its excavation.

Gates also were uncovered at the northeast and northwest corners of the city, and traces of gates were found in the west and south walls. Bethel's northwest gate was unique. Built directly upon the ruins of the acropolis temple, the U-shaped gateway was a rhomboid, with the north wall 14.6 meters long, east wall 9.7 meters, and west wall 9.2 meters. The gate had no south wall but abutted directly upon the city wall at its northwest corner. The minimum thickness of the walls of the gateway was 1.5 meters. The jambs of the gateway were found standing about 2 meters high. The gateway floor had originally been paved with stone slabs but was later repaired with *huwar*. There were no guardrooms, only a corridor leading from the threshold to the west wall. At that point the corridor turned south and then eastward to the inner face of the outer wall of the gateway complex, where it again turned south, apparently going through an opening in the north wall of the city. The wall is missing at this point, but just inside the walled area is what appears to be a sanctuary, since it was discovered only a few steps from the acropolis temple. The corner of this new building was uncovered. It represents one of the finest Middle Bronze Age stone buildings in Palestine. In the sanctuary was found a large quantity of animal bones and cultic ceramic ware, including store jars with serpent motifs on the bases and handles, a bull's leg, and a small stylized Hathor column.

Two distinct phases of building were found in the Middle Bronze Age II city, in several places separated by a layer of ashes. In a major reconstruction project a new section of the city's west wall had been built shortly before the city's capture (probably by the Egyptians, circa 1550 B.C.). The site appears to have lain in ruins until the fourteenth century, when it made a swift comeback.

There were two phases of Late Bronze Age occupation, of which the earlier was somewhat superior in quality to the thirteenth-century phase. Patrician houses were larger, flagstone pavements were greater in number, and a skillfully designed drainage and sewer system was installed. This represents the finest architectural phase in the city's history. An olive-oil press with its installations still in situ was found with a quantity of *zebar,* or olive refuse, nearby.

The Israelite (Iron Age I) cities are in striking contrast to those of the Canaanites (Late Bronze Age). The Israelite houses are ramshackle huts, and the pottery is poorly made and dominated by store jars and cooking pots. The Canaanite temple went out of use, and the Astarte plaques so common in the Canaanite period are very rare.

Under Joshua's conquest (1240–1235 B.C.), Bethel was assigned to Benjamin, but the excavations show that shortly thereafter Bethel was captured twice. The first conquest was probably by the Canaanites, who took over the city after the extermination of most of the tribe of Benjamin. This episode left Ephraim without any fortress for her southern border, so it was apparently at this time that Ephraim drove out the new Canaanite population of Bethel and took over that city as her own key border fortress (Judges 1:22–26). Bethel has no record of Philistine occupation. The city grew under the last of the Judges, but when David made Jerusalem the nation's capital, Bethel's growth slowed down. It was only in the time of the monarchy, after the revolt of Jeroboam I, that Bethel again became a religious center.

The excavations show that Bethel was spared in the frontier wars between the kingdoms of Judah and Israel, and the city continued to flourish. A South Arabian clay seal was found in debris outside the Middle Bronze Age city wall. An identical seal from Hadhramaut is dated to about the ninth century B.C. The seal indicates that trade relations existed between Bethel and South Arabia, which was the source of incense.

Toward the close of the Assyrian period, the shrine at Bethel was rebuilt, and the city quickly took

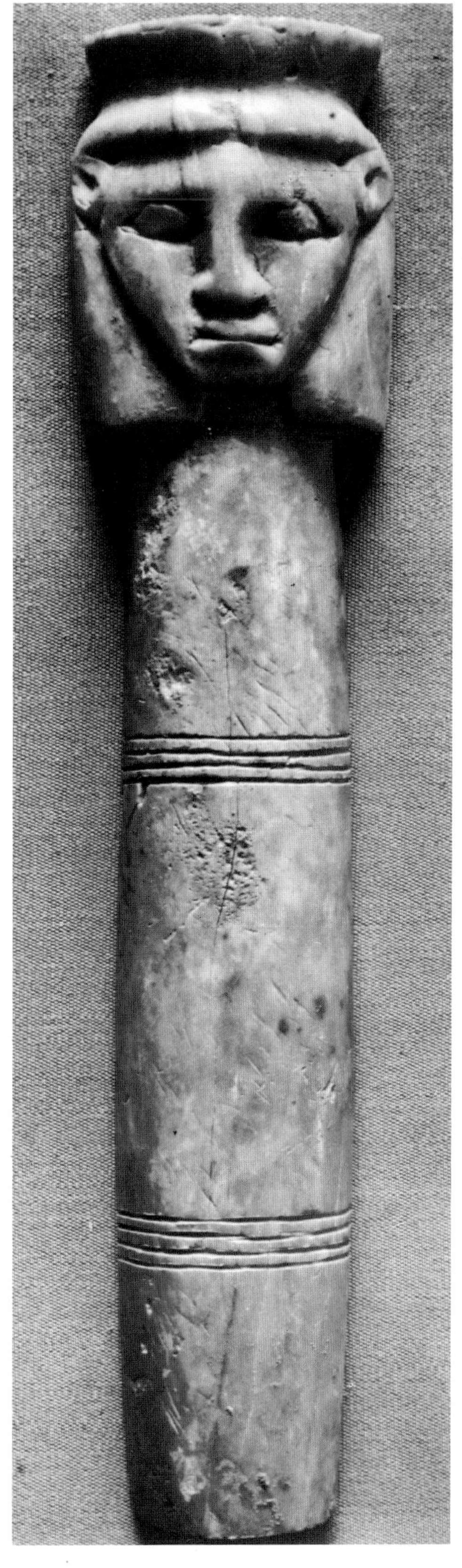

Bone handle of sistrum shaped as a Hathor column; LBA I (top). Paste scaraboid showing an animal in a boat and lotus blossoms; LBA (bottom).

on new life. Its prosperity continued until the time of Nabonidus or early in the Persian period. Since the city was not destroyed along with Jerusalem, it is a unique source for ceramic studies of the period after 587 B.C.

Ezra knew Bethel only as a small village, but by Hellenistic times it was again prominent, although not as in the Late Bronze Age. The Hellenistic period contains two phases, of which the earlier is superior. Bacchides refortified Bethel. The tumulus Rujm Abu 'Ammar on the hill east of Bethel is doubtless his work, for the surface pottery is Hellenistic of the second century B.C.

Some time during the Early Roman phase the northeast city gate was destroyed. Part of the adjacent city wall was leveled, and a house was built over it. Foundations of a new gate of this period were also found near the old south gate of the city. Within the houses of the city, however, no signs were found of burning in the Roman period.

Both Vespasian and Hadrian established garrisons here. The Roman town increased so greatly in population that, for the first time in its history, cisterns had to be used to augment its natural water supply. The Byzantine city was even larger, and a great reservoir was completed in the valley below it. Just to the east of the mound lies one of the main streets of the Byzantine city. It is the longest Byzantine street still in use in Palestine. A new northeast gate and a new east wall were erected in either A.D. 484 or 529 to protect the city against the marauding Samaritans. A large Byzantine church now used as a mosque was built, and east of it, a monastery. Churches honoring Abraham and Jacob were erected on the hill east of Bethel. Although few buildings of Byzantine times remain, pottery from nearby fields shows that the city lived on throughout the entire Byzantine era, but it seems to have disppeared shortly after the Muslim invasion of Palestine. J. L. KELSO

BIBLIOGRAPHY

History and Identification of the Site: I. Ben Dor–S. Loewenstamm–M. D. Cassuto, *Enc. Miqr.* 2, 56–67.

Excavations: W.F. Albright, *BASOR* 55 (1934), 23–25; 36 (1934), 2–15; 57 (1935), 27–30; 74 (1939), 15–17 • J. L. Kelso, *BASOR* 137 (1955), 5–10; 151 (1958), 3–8; 164 (1961), 5–14 • W.F. Albright and J.L. Kelso, "The Excavation of Bethel (1934–60)," *AASOR* 39 (1968).

The South Arabian Inscription: G.W. Van Beek–A. Jamme, *BASOR* 151 (1958), 9–16; 163 (1961), 15–18.

BETH GOVRIN

IDENTIFICATION AND HISTORY. The site was identified by the name of the Arab village Beit Jibrin, by data on the Peutinger map (32 miles from Jerusalem on the way to Ashkelon), and from milestones at various distances from the city upon which "Eleutheropolis" is written (see below).

Beth Govrin was apparently first mentioned by Josephus (*War* IV, 447) as a village in the heart of Idumea. Evidently at that time the main road running from Jerusalem to the southwest crossed the place, since it is mentioned by Ptolemy (*Geography* V, 15, 5). Several Tannaim and one of the Amoraim are known to have lived there. In A.D. 200 the emperor Septimius Severus converted Beth Govrin into a Roman colony named Eleutheropolis (*Ἐλευθερόπολις*), granting it large tracts of land stretching from En-Gedi to Gerar — the largest area ever granted to any city in Palestine.

From the Talmud we learn that Beth Govrin was fortified. The meaning of the name of the city was "City of Free Men" (חורין), but in the Midrash (*Genesis Rabbah* 41/42), it is given as "City of the Cave Dwellers" (חורים — "caves"). When nearby Marissa was destroyed, Beth Govrin took its place as capital of the district. During the Roman period the city flourished and later, in the fourth century, became a bishop's seat. In the Arab period the city was again called Beit Jibrin. The Crusaders named it Bet Giblin or Gibelin. In 1134 King Fulk built a fortress there, which was later sold to the Order of the Hospitalers.

EXCAVATIONS

In 1921 a mosaic floor was discovered on the site called el-Maqerqesh, on a hill southeast of the village. The excavation was entrusted to the Ecole Biblique et Archéologique Française. In 1921 L.H. Vincent uncovered the floor within three days. In 1927 F.M. Abel, with the assistance of N. Makhouly, enlarged the excavated area. In both excavations, remains of five periods were discovered as follows:

Period I. A room paved with a mosaic of geometric patterns in a frame of a guilloche. From the depression in the floor and the quarrying of the rock wall parallel to it, Abel considered the room to be an oil press. This is not certain, however. Another mosaic floor decorated with geometric designs found in a hall (5.8 meters wide) also belongs to this stratum.

Period II. A foundation wall was discovered .43 to .54 meters above these mosaics. The remains of this period include a hall (9.5 by 5 meters) paved with a fine mosaic (excavated in 1921) and an entrance paved with limestone flags, which led to a wide courtyard. Surrounding it was a portico paved in *opus sectile,* a mosaic of marble segments laid in the shapes of rosettes, hexagons, etc.

The mosaic floor in the hall is framed by a wide border (1 meter) representing hunting scenes. Beginning in the southeast corner of the picture, there is a house with a gabled tile roof and with a curtain folded in the doorway. In front of the house is a patch of lotus plants with birds perched on the flowers. A mounted hunter, wearing a long-sleeved tunic tied at the shoulder, gallops on his horse and holds up a wreath (?) in his right hand. In the continuation are represented an elephant and an eagle, a tree and water fowls, a farm, sheep, and a shepherd lifting his arm in greeting. Next, a wolf is depicted with its head turned backward and a hare fleeing. In the continuation a rider is shown dismounted; his horse is tied to a tree. With spear poised, he stalks an animal which was not preserved. After this, comes a break in the scene. Then a mounted hunter is shown attacking a leopard. After another break the hunter is represented with a wind-blown coat. He has dismounted and is fighting a bear. Behind the hunter, a kid is seen tied to a tree (perhaps as bait?). Here the row of pictures ends.

The figures in the margin are represented as standing on a band of hilly ground. Within the margin is a frame of lotus leaves facing inward and outward alternately. The inner field is divided by bands of geometric patterns into ten octagons arranged in two rows of five octagons each. Separating the rows is a central band of four medallions between geometric sections. Four figures are depicted in this band from south to north. First comes a figure personifying Spring (with the inscription *Ἔαρ*) — a maiden holding a bowl of flowers with a bird perched on it. The next figure symbolizes Autumn — a woman wearing a wreath of grapes and ears of corn and bearing fruits in the lap of her garment; the artist erred in his designation and called her "Earth" (*Γῆ*). Following this is a figure symbolizing

Summer — a woman (her face destroyed) holding in her right hand a sickle with a serrated blade and in her left hand a sheaf of corn. The inscription is *Θέρ[ος]*. The fourth figure in this row is missing and was replaced by a geometric decoration. The image of the fourth season, Winter, is placed in the margin. There is no inscription, but the personification is clear — the bust of a woman wrapped in a scarf and holding two ducklings. Near her is an amphora with water running out of it, symbolizing rain, and a reed.

In the octagons flanking the band of the seasons are beasts of prey and, facing them, their victims, from south to north: a hunting dog and a stag; a lioness and a ram; a bear and a boar; a lion (the figure opposite it was destroyed); a leopard and a deer.

Period III. About .47 meters above this floor level, and to the south, the mosaic floor of a small chapel was found (2.25 by 3 meters). It was decorated with vine tendrils issuing out of an amphora and forming medallions. Above the amphora, which is flanked by two rams, hovers a bird of prey. To its left a partridge is represented, and to its right, a quail. In the middle of the upper row is a pheasant; to the left, a crane; and to the right, a goose. Above the vine are two peacocks holding a wreath. Above them is a six-line inscription that mentions the laying of the mosaic by the pupils of Obodianus the priest, "the innocent and the just;" the reference is apparently to the bishop of Eleutheropolis. A coin from the year A.D. 527 is assigned to this stratum.

Period IV. Remains of an apse and foundations of a chancel screen were found at the top of this layer (70 centimeters above the level of the decorated mosaic).

Period V. A floor and a threshold of a door were found at a higher level.

THE DATE OF THE MOSAICS

In 1922 Vincent was of the opinion that the hunt mosaic belonged to a Roman villa on the outskirts of Eleutheropolis, dating from the third century A.D. However, from the mosaics discovered in Antioch, it became evident that the earliest possible date for such a mosaic was the time of Constantine (fourth century). D. Levi attributed the mosaic to the sixth century, but this date is untenable since it does not allow for a lapse of time until the later bird mosaic was laid, certainly in the sixth century.

Column drum with Aramaic synagogue inscription (top). Cave with columbarium (bottom).

This is proved by the style of the mosaic and details of decoration, which are similar to the mosaics of Shellal and Ma'on and the works of the Gaza school of mosaicists, as well as by the coin found with it. The two later periods are Late Byzantine (beginning of the seventh century) and Early Arabic.

At the beginning of World War II, a church with a mosaic floor decorated with depictions of a lion, horses, a ship, etc., was found on the site called Makhatet el-'Urj. During excavations carried out by the Department of Antiquities of the Mandatory Government, it was established that the floor had been damaged and almost all the pictures destroyed in antiquity. M. AVI-YONAH

BIBLIOGRAPHY

History of the site: G. Beyer, *ZDPV* 54 (1931), 209ff. • Hill, *BMC*, LXV.

El-Maqerqesh: L.H. Vincent, *RB* 31 (1922), 259–81 • F.M. Abel, *ibid.* 33 (1924), 583–604 • D. Levi, *Antioch Mosaic Pavements* 1, Princeton, 1947, index s.v.; *idem*, UNESCO World Art Series, *Israel Ancient Mosaics*, Paris, 1960, Pls. 15, 16.

Makhatet el-'Urj: G.E. Kirk, *PEQ*, (1946) 97–98 • C.N. Johns, *ibid.* (1948), 96, Pl. 6.

Mosaic floor of Constantinian villa (left). Mosaic floor of chapel; sixth century A.D. *(opposite page).*

ΔΙΑΜΑΘΗΤΩΝ
ΤΟΥΔΙΕΡΕΥϹΑΜΥΜΩΝ

BETHLEHEM

PREHISTORY. During the digging for a cistern in 1934, animal bones were found at a depth of 15 meters. Dorothy Bate examined the finds and defined them as fossilized elephant bones, a tusk fragment, and broken molars. An expedition on behalf of the Wellcome-Marston Fund thereupon excaved the site in 1935–37 under the direction of Dorothy Bate and Eleanor Gardner, and in 1940 under M. Stekelis. The site lies on the watershed at the highest point in the area, 790 meters above sea level.

Beneath a porous chalk layer about 3 meters thick, pockets of angular pebbles were uncovered, mixed with sticky clay. Most of the pebbles were flint nodules, chalcedony, and flinty chalk. On the southern face of the pit (18.5 by 25 by 35 meters) the excavators found a layer of pebbles that had hardened into breccia and, beneath it, gravelly clay containing fossilized animal bones.

On the eastern face of the pit were observed cracks filled by a layer of pebbles containing fossilized animal bones. It was assumed that the depression was formed by the action of water seeping into the space formed in the porous layer.

Fauna. The following are the fauna uncovered at Bethlehem, according to a list compiled by Dorothy Bate (1935–37): *Felis sp.* (size of *Panthera leo.); Hipparion sp.; Hippopotamus sp.; Rhinoceros cf. etruscus; Bos sp.; Stegodon sp.;* antelope; *Elephas sp.;* giraffoid; and small carnivore.

Dorothy Bate established that the fauna belonged to mammalia that lived in Palestine in the Lower Pleistocene. In the excavations carried out by Stekelis (1940) additional fossilized mammalian bones were uncovered, including the whole skull of a rhinoceros and the lower jaw of an elephant. Dorothy Bate was unable to complete the study of this material before her death in 1951. It was studied thereafter by D. A. Hooijer.

The following are the fauna uncovered at Bethlehem, as compiled by Hooijer:

Nictereutes megamastoïdes (Pomel); *Honotherium (?) sp.; Archidiskodon cf. planifrons* (Falconer and Cautley); *Hipparion sp.; Dicerorhinus etruscus* (Falconer); *Sus cf. strozzii* (Meneghini); *Giraffa cf. camelopardalis* (L.)*; Leptobos sp. nov.; Gazellospira torticornis* (Aymard). Hooijer omitted from Dorothy Bate's list the hippopotamus and the stegodon, which, in his opinion, were not represented among the finds from Bethlehem.

The fauna at Bethlehem belongs to the Lower Pleistocene (Villafranchian) and is of Asiatic origin. Several of the mammalia have also been discovered in East Africa. It can thus be concluded that in the period under discussion, Palestine was already a continental land bridge between Asia and Africa, and animals wandered between the two continents.

Flints. The flints discovered on the site are of special interest. After examining them, Gertrude Caton-Thompson came to the conclusion that most are eolithic, modified by nature, although it is possible to prove that several were worked by man. H. Breuil contested this, maintaining that all were naturally chipped.

After restudying the collection of flints from Bethlehem, J. Desmond-Clark reached the same conclusion as Breuil. However, since the mammalian bones were found split lengthwise in order to extract the marrow (something only man is capable of doing), it can be stated that the prehistoric finds from Bethlehem are from a period in which man was already present in Palestine. It cannot be definitely ascertained if he made flint implements or even used them. M. STEKELIS

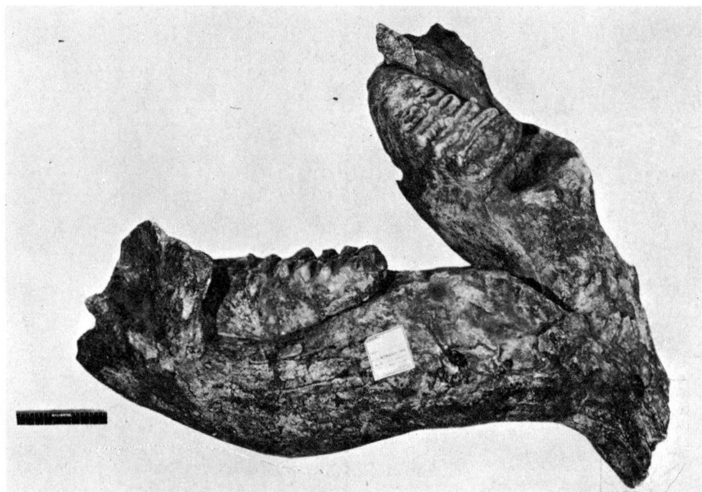

Lower jaw of prehistoric elephant (Archidiskodon). *Mosaic floor surrounding the octagon built over the Cave of the Nativity; 5th cent.* A.D. *(opposite page).*

Plan of the Constantinian Church of the Nativity.

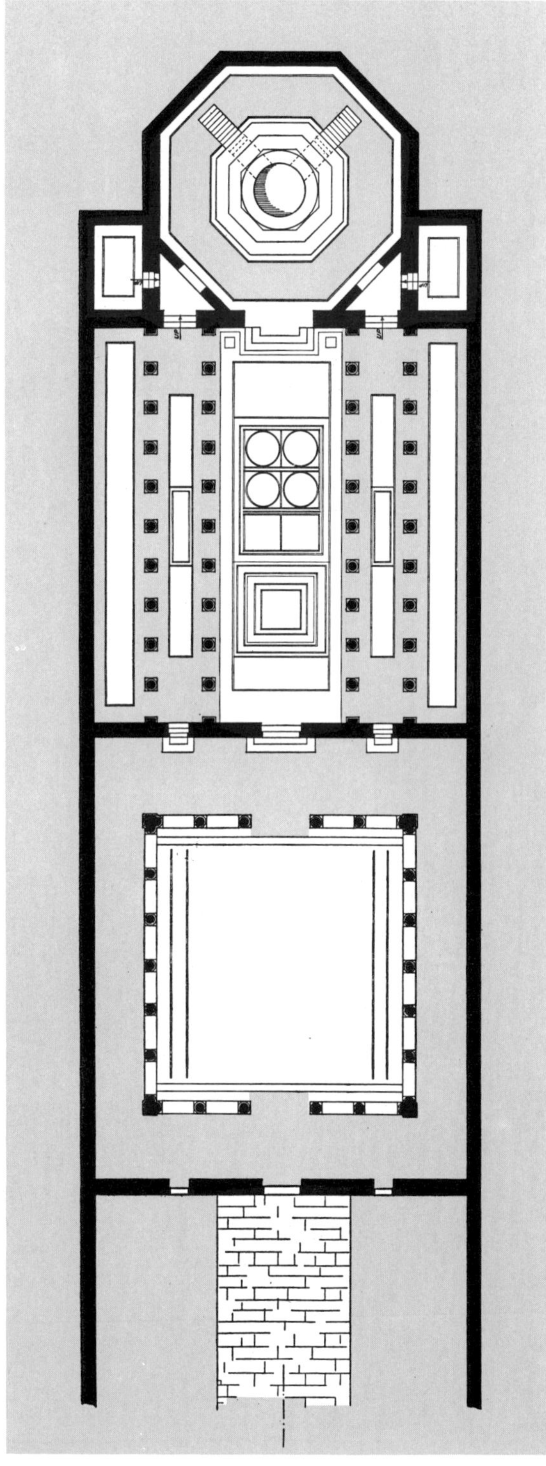

HISTORY AND IDENTIFICATION

Ancient Bethlehem is definitely identified with the modern town situated 9 kilometers ($5\frac{1}{2}$ miles) south of Jerusalem, 1.5 kilometers (1 mile) east of the Hebron road. As there is no spring in the town and all its water has to be collected in cisterns, the establishment of the town could have occurred only in the period in which cisterns were beginning to be used in the mountainous areas of the country — that is, from the Late Bronze Age. The opinion held by some that the place name *Bit ilu NIN.URTA* — in one of the el-Amarna letters — is to be read as "Bethlehem" is not sufficiently founded.

A mound with Bronze and Iron Age surface pottery exists east of the Church of the Nativity and has been tentatively identified as the site of the Canaanite town. In the Bible, Bethlehem is first mentioned in defining Ephrath, on the road to which Rachel died and was buried (Genesis 35:19, 48:7).

According to the genealogical list in I Chronicles (2:51, 54; 4:4) the inhabitants of Bethlehem were related to the family of Caleb, son of Hezron, son of Perez, son of Judah. The "father" of Bethlehem is Salma, who was among the descendants of Caleb and Ephrath. In any event, members of the family of Judah dwelt in Bethlehem, including the family of Boaz (Book of Ruth). Levites also dwelt there (Judges 17:7).

Bethlehem was evidently the northernmost settlement of the tribe of Judah, on the border of Jerusalem, since "a certain Levite" from Ephraim, on his return from Bethlehem, passed by Jerusalem on his way to Gibeah (Judges 19:11–12). Bethlehem first rose to prominence with the anointing of David, son of Jesse, as king by the prophet Samuel (I Samuel 16). The Philistines, in their wars against David, set up a garrison in Bethlehem. It appears that the city was surrounded by a wall and that there was a well or cistern at the city gate (II Samuel 23:14–16, I Chronicles 11:16).

After David was proclaimed king, and after the inclusion of Jerusalem in Israel, Bethlehem remained a small town of Judah. Because of its proximity to Jerusalem, it was included in the line of fortifications constructed by Rehoboam, to defend Judah on the southwest. According to the Septuagint, Bethlehem was included in the ninth district of Judah (Joshua 15:59ff.).

Except for one passage (Micah 5:2), Bethlehem is not mentioned again in the Bible until the days of the return from the Babylonian exile. At that time, 123 persons (Ezra 2:21) or 188 persons returned, together with the people of Netophah (Nehemiah 7:26). Micah prophesized greatness for the town (5:2), because of the relationship between Bethlehem and David's family. His prophecy had a great influence on the later history of the town.

When Herod built fortresses at Herodium and Masada, Bethlehem acquired new importance, since it overlooked the roads to those fortresses, which branched off near it from the highway following the watershed. When the aqueduct to Jerusalem was built, part of its waters were diverted to Bethlehem.

According to Christian tradition, Jesus was born in Bethlehem at the end of Herod's reign, this tradition determining the future destiny of the town. In the early centuries A.D. the birth of Jesus was located by tradition in a cave to the east of the town. A grove consecrated to Adonis (Tammuz) grew above this cave from the time of Hadrian, after the suppression of the Bar Kokhba revolt and the expulsion of the Jews from Bethlehem and its vicinity. The expulsion had created the possibility of establishing a pagan sanctuary on the spot. The Christian author Tertullian confirms that in his day (end of second century A.D.) no Jews dwelt in Bethlehem, which was then included within the territory of Aelia Capitolina which Hadrian had forbidden Jews to enter.

Under Constantine — the first Christian emperor — a momentous change took place in the history of the town. Constantine constructed three imperial churches in Palestine, one of which was the Church of the Nativity in Bethlehem, which was begun in A.D. 326. It included the traditional cave, now adapted to its new ritual role. At the end of the fourth century, Hieronymus (Saint Jerome) settled in Bethlehem, together with a group of matrons, and founded two monasteries. At that time Jews were again living close to Bethlehem.

The church of Bethlehem was destroyed during the Samaritan revolt of A.D. 529 and was rebuilt by imperial order under Justinian. Since then it has been in continuous use as a Christian place of worship. Christian legend relates that at the time of the Persian conquest, in A.D. 614, the church was saved from destruction because the three Magi

Mosaic in the northern transept.

depicted on the mosaic of the Nativity then on the gable of the building were wearing Persian attire. The conquerors recognized these figures as being of their own people and spared the church. In 634 Bethlehem surrendered to the Arabs. It was held by the Crusaders from 1099 to 1187.

EXCAVATIONS

Archaeological activity in Bethlehem, besides prehistoric research, has centered around the Church of the Nativity. The major study was undertaken in 1934 by W. Harvey on behalf of the Mandatory Department of Antiquities. His work proved that the extant church does not date to the time of Constantine I, as previously believed, but belongs to the time of Justinian. It was built in part on the Constantinian foundations. Between these two periods various repairs and alterations had been carried out, mainly the repair of the mosaic floors.

The Constantinian Church. At the center of the present churchyard a floor made of heavy stone flags was discovered at a depth of 1.3 meters beneath the surface. This evidently belonged to the outer court or to a street leading to the inner court (atrium) of the church. During the construction of the Justinian basilica, the ground level was raised, covering this floor. Beyond this pavement, in the narthex of the present building, remains of a stylobate, two steps, and a fragment of mosaic floor were found. These remains led the excavators to conclude that in front of the Constantinian church there had been a square court (27 meters each side), surrounded on all four sides by porches (3.5 meters wide).

Of the mosaic pavements in the porches, a fragment in the inner porch on the south is the best preserved. The mosaic is decorated in a sequence of geometric designs. At the corners of the rows of porch columns stood two joined half-columns with a heart-shaped cross section. On the north and south were five columns per row; on the east and

Interior of Justinian's Church, looking east.

west, only four. At the western porch a wide opening led down to the central court. The eastern porch led to the entrances of the church. The center of the court was paved at its edge in white mosaic with a guilloche band running parallel to the stairs. Since the interior of the atrium was not excavated, the whole mosaic is not known.

In the course of the examination it became evident that the western wall of the Constantinian church stood 2.8 meters east of the parallel wall of the later building, although the northern and southern walls were identical in both structures. The earlier church had three doors (central door 3 meters wide, side doors 1.5 meters wide), which were entered from the eastern porch of the courtyard by three steps (these numbers are, of course, symbolic). At the two corners of the threshold of the central door were holes for hinges. Along the doorposts were four holes for bolts. It may be assumed that the door was double winged.

The Constantinian church proper was a square basilica (26.5 meters) divided by four rows of nine columns into a nave (9 meters wide) and four aisles, two on either side (inner aisles 3 meters wide, outer aisles 3.5 meters wide). The aisles and the nave were paved in mosaics, some of them patterned. The floor of the nave has been best preserved. The entire area of the pavement was divided into two main carpets (one 5.8 meters long, the other 9.2 meters long). The level of this floor, which is some 60 centimeters lower than the floor of the present building, is higher than the level of the original bases that supported the columns of the Constantinian church. This would indicate that the mosaic was laid during the period between the building of the two churches, evidently sometime in the fifth century.

The Bethlehem mosaics have a great technical similarity to the mosaics of the Imperial Palace in Constantinople, which are contemporary, although we do not find the same richness in the design at Bethlehem. The design of the Bethlehem mosaics is even surpassed by that of the floor at Heptapegon (q.v.) of the same period.

East of the basilica stood the second section of the building complex: the octagon (7.9 meters length on each side) built over the grotto of the Nativity. Its façade corresponded to the eastern wall of the basilica. Three stairways led up to it. The central stairway, which had two steps (5 meters wide), gave access from the nave. The southern corner of the lower step, which was extremely worn and was repaired with mosaic, dates from between the time of Constantine and the fifth century. The two stairways on the sides ascended to narrower doorways that led into triangular rooms at the corners of the octagon. Openings from these rooms led to two rectangular chambers (3.5 by 6 meters), which evidently were used as the diaconicon and the prothesis for the entire basilica. These rooms architecturally connected the octagon with the basilica west of it.

In the northern room a fragment of a mosaic floor

Plan of Justinian's church. ▬ *early church* ▨ *intermediate periods* ▭ *Justinian stylobates, existing* ⬚ *inferred.*

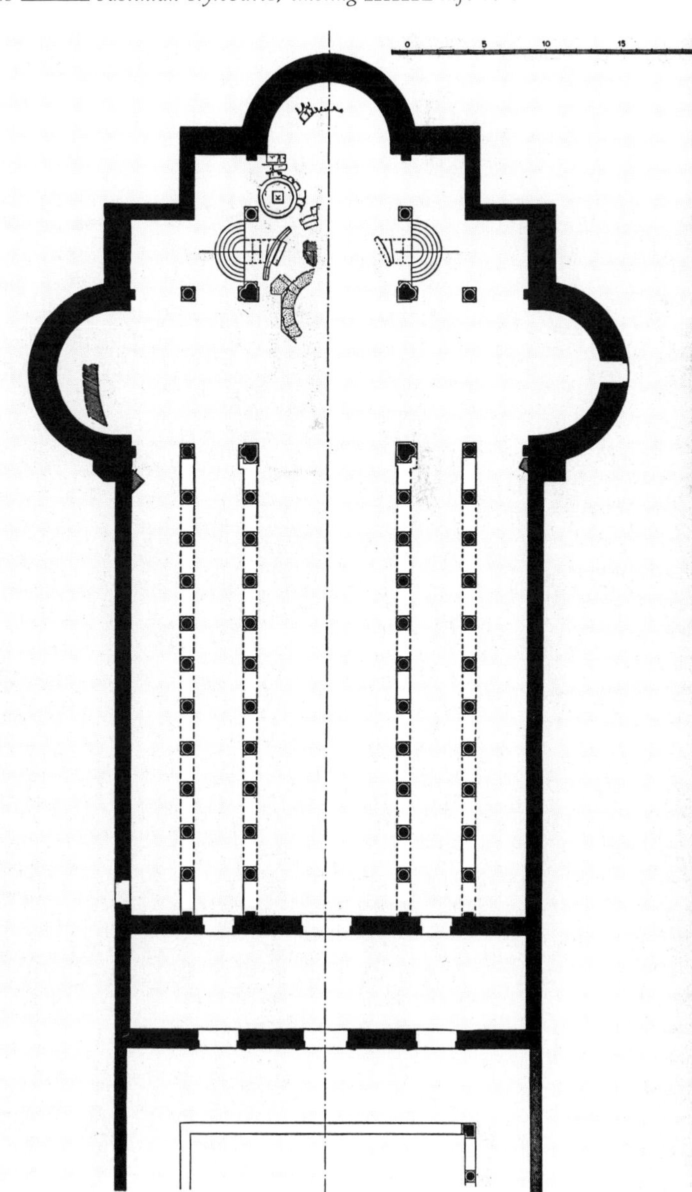

was found. It is white, and in the center is a rectangle delineated by a black band containing a pattern of crosses. This is an indication of the early date of the mosaic; after 427 it was forbidden to use the cross pattern in floors, although in this room, which was used as the prothesis, only the priests would have walked on the floor.

Within the octagon was a smaller octagonal structure (3.5 meters a side) consisting of a platform surrounded by a low step. Excavations inside it revealed a fairly large fragment of mosaic flooring (3.85 meters in diameter) surrounding the opening of the cave itself. Through this opening, which was enclosed by a railing, worshippers could gaze into the cave. Actual entrance into the cave was not allowed to every pilgrim. Scholars still disagree about the location of the entrance to the cave.

Paintings on columns: Saint (left). Madonna and child (right).

According to E.T. Richmond, there had been two entrances within the octagon, one on the northeast and the other on the southeast. J.W. Crowfoot, on the other hand, assumed that the entrance was from outside the church, through a subterranean tunnel running from the northeastern side of the octagon.

During the excavations a very narrow entrance (1 meter) containing a staircase was discovered. This entrance once led to the central opening of the octagon. According to Vincent, this was the entrance to the Nativity Grotto made in Constantine's time. However, the excavators claim that it was made by Hieronymus (according to Antoninus of Placentia, circa A.D. 570). Only in the ninth century did the two entrances on the north and south come into use; they continue to be used to this day. Their bronze doors date from the time of Justinian, while the frames are Crusader work.

The plan of the Constantinian church — a basilica intended for meetings of believers, and an octagon containing the holy shrine in the center — corresponds to the early Christian buildings of the martyrium type. These are structurally derived from the monumental mausoleums of the Roman emperors, such as the monument of Diocletian at Spalato. The Church of the Resurrection (Anastasis — now called the Church of the Holy Sepulchre) in Jerusalem is essentially the same, although in that church an enclosed court separated the basilica from the domed building erected over the tomb.

The view held by those scholars who considered that the Church of the Nativity is depicted in its original state on the right side of the apse mosaic in the Church of Santa Pudenziana in Rome seems justified. That mosaic shows an elongated building (the basilica) followed by an octagonal structure, just as it was at Bethlehem.

Justinian's Church. After the Samaritan revolt, the emperor Justinian sent an architect to rebuild the Church of the Nativity. According to the story preserved by Eutychius, patriarch of Alexandria (ninth century A.D.), the work of that architect was rejected by the emperor, who had him beheaded. The legend may reflect the fact that there was an unsuccessful attempt to restore the church and to replace the octagon by a round building 33.6 meters in diameter, inside of which a raised platform was built around the opening of the cave. The builders evidently found it difficult to raise a dome over a circular building of such dimensions, and the plan was abandoned. In its stead came the cloverleaf triple apse that still stands today.

The atrium was extended to the west, thus acquiring a rectangular rather than a square shape. A strong wall was built around it as protection against attacks like that of the Samaritans. In place of the eastern porch of the older atrium, there was now a narthex, as was common in most churches built after the middle of the fifth century. The church proper was also lengthened, becoming a rectangle instead of a square (33 meters long, instead of 26.5 meters in the Constantinian basilica). The nave was widened (10.25 meters) and the aisles were narrowed proportionally. Justinian's builders used the columns and capitals of the older building and added ten new columns and four corner columns. The imitation was so successful that most modern investigators have been misled into believing all the capitals were Constantinian. At the same time, evidently, the entrance to the Grotto at the north and south were made, for the two bronze doors are Justinian.

Since the Justinian restoration of the church, only a few minor changes have been made in it. The main door to the church was gradually narrowed to its present minuscule size, and the roof was renewed. The walls of the basilica were decorated with mosaics by Byzantine craftsmen, in Crusader times, including a representation of Jesus' entry to Jerusalem.

In 1926 the Franciscan fathers excavated next to the Church of the Nativity and discovered thirteen bells from the fourteenth century. These had been buried there in the middle of the fifteenth century, when the Ottoman rulers forbade the ringing of bells by Christians.

OTHER DISCOVERIES

The Aqueduct. In 1904, during construction work near the tomb of Rachel, masonry sections of a high-level aqueduct were discovered. Roman inscriptions on the stones mention certain centurions, most likely of the Tenth Legion.

Scholars disagree about the date of these inscriptions. J. Germer-Durand and C. Clermont-Ganneau found in one of the inscriptions mention of a consul, Julius Clemens, who was in office in A.D. 195. They thus ascribed the high-level aqueduct to the time of Septimius Severus. C. Wilson and Ruth Amiran, on the other hand, maintained that there is nothing in the inscription to indicate a date and that the aqueduct was built in the early days of Aelia Capitolina, not much later than A.D. 135.

Christian Tombs. In 1894 a rock-cut tomb was discovered in Bethlehem, in Wadi Kharrubah, opposite the Church of the Nativity to the north. It was entered through a pit shaft (5 meters long, .7 meters wide, and 3.5 meters deep) leading to a corridor continuing the line of the shaft, and then turning eastward. On either side of the corridor are vaults with two to six burial places. In all,

Capitals in Justinian's church.

sixty-one burials were found, including three that remained unexcavated. Three inscriptions were found. One, completely preserved, mentions the deacon Constantinus. The crosses and the inscriptions indicate that the burials are Byzantine.

Byzantine Crypt. In 1925 a subterranean crypt was discovered in the foundations of the Church of St. Nicholas at Beit Jalla (a large Christian village, which is a suburb of Bethlehem) The crypt had been used as a reliquary. Today the crypt is entered through a narrow passage from the west, although originally the entrance was through a corridor and four steps in the east. The main part of the crypt is a square, vaulted hall (2.3 meters a side and 2 meters high) with vaults to the sides (1.8 meters wide and 1 meter deep). A barrel vault enclosed the stairway. M. AVI-YONAH

BIBLIOGRAPHY

Prehistory: D. M. A. Bate, *Nature* 134 (1934), 219 • D. M. A. Bate–E. W. Gardner, *ibid.* 140 (1937), 431–33 • D. M. A. Bate, *ibid.* 147 (1941), 783 • D. A. Hooijer, *Bulletin of the British Museum (Natural History), Geology* 3 (Number 8), 265–92 • J. Desmond-Clark, *ibid.* 5 (Number 4), 71–90.

The Church of the Nativity: W. Harvey and W. R. Lethaby a.o., *The Church of the Nativity at Bethlehem,* London, 1910 • L. H. Vincent and F. M. Abel, *Bethlehem, le Sanctuaire de la Nativité,* Paris, 1914 • R. W. Hamilton, *QDAP* 3 (1934), 1–8 • W. Harvey, *Structural Survey of the Church of the Nativity, Bethlehem,* London, 1935 • E. T. Richmond, *QDAP* 5 (1936), 75–81; 6 (1936), 63–66 • L. H. Vincent, *RB* 45 (1936), 544–74; 46 (1937), 93–121 • R. W. Hamilton, *A Guide to Bethlehem,* Jerusalem, 1939 • J. W. Crowfoot, *Early Churches,* index s.v. • B. Bagatti, *Gli antichi edifici sacri di Bethlemme* (Stud. Bibl. Francisc. 9), Gerusalemme, 1952.

Other Remains: P. M. Sejourné, *RB* 4 (1895), 439–44 • F. M. Abel, *ibid.* 32 (1923), 264–72 • P. Cheneau, *ibid.*, 602–07 • F. M. Abel, *RB* 35 (1926), 284–88 • Ruth Kallner (Amiran), *BJPES* 13 (1947), 136–39.

Mosaic on southern wall.

BETH-SHEAN

IDENTIFICATION AND HISTORY. Beth-Shean is an important city situated between the Jezreel and Jordan valleys. It was settled almost continuously from the Chalcolithic period to modern times. The city is possibly mentioned for the first time in the nineteenth-century B.C. Egyptian Execration Texts. It definitely appears in the topographical list of Thutmose III in the Great Temple of Amon at Karnak (circa 1468 B.C.). Beth-Shean is also mentioned in the el-Amarna letters and in inscriptions of Seti I and of his son Ramses II, as well as in the Papyrus Anastasi I (thirteenth century B.C.), where it is referred to in an accurate geographical context. It figures as an Egyptian conquest in the Shishak lists at Karnak (circa 925 B.C.). The Bible deals very briefly with the site. Two essentially parallel passages (Joshua 17:11, Judges 1:27) show that the Israelite tribes did not occupy Beth-Shean and its suburbs. In I Samuel 31:12 the exposure of the bodies of Saul and his sons on the walls of Beth-Shean by the Philistines is mentioned. By implication the city and its area were conquered by David, because Beth-Shean last appears in the Bible in the list of towns comprising Solomon's fifth administrative district (I Kings 4:12).

Reference to the city in Hellenistic, Roman, and Byzantine times — when it was known as Scythopolis or Nysa Scythopolis — are too numerous to mention. With the Arab conquest, the old name

Aerial view of the mound from the west.

Bethlehem; detail of mosaic floor around the octagon in the Constantinian Church of the Nativity (top); detail of later mosaic floor of Constantine's church; fifth century (bottom).

reemerged as Beisan. In fact, the Arab victory over the Byzantines in A.D. 636 has gone down in history as the "day of Beisan."

TOPOGRAPHY

The ancient site of Beth-Shean is to be identified with Tell el Husn, north of the modern town. It had a perennial water supply (the Harod [Jalud] River flowed down north of it) and stood at the junction of important roads: the road running the length of the Jordan Valley, the roads leading from the Jezreel Valley to Gilead, and a main branch of the road to the sea passing at the foot of the mound. Thus, the site always possessed great strategic importance. The mound rises some 80 meters above the bed of the Harod and has a 30-degree slope on all sides. It can be approached only on the northwest, where a saddle of land eases access. These contours suggest that the entrance was against this saddle for many centuries, if not during the entire occupation of the site, and, indeed, the only gateway found was excavated here.

Before the excavations changed the terrain, the southeastern side of the mound was higher. This citadel-like elevation remained in use during the Hellenistic-Roman periods, chiefly as a hilltop sacred area. In Early Roman times it was occupied by a temple, possibly dedicated to Dionysus. Later, a round church replaced this pagan shrine and endured at least until the Arab conquest.

At some time during Hellenistic-Roman times, the main part of the town moved down into the valley. At its zenith, Scythopolis or Nysa had a circumvallation $2\frac{1}{2}$ miles long, enclosing one third of a square mile. For some time it was the chief city of the Decapolis, and the only one of these cities situated west of the Jordan.

EXCAVATIONS OF TELL EL HUSN. HISTORY

The central mound was excavated from 1921 to 1933 by the University of Pennsylvania Museum. In scope and in conception this was the pioneer excavation in the archaeology of Palestine. As part of the sultan's private domain up to World War I, the site was unencumbered by cemeteries or any recent constructions.

Operations were directed from 1921 to 1923 by C.S. Fisher. When he resigned, A. Rowe became director, assisted by G. FitzGerald. Excavation began again in 1925. Three years later operations were again suspended. In 1930, 1931, and 1933 small-scale excavations were carried out by FitzGerald. While the area that could be investigated became increasingly smaller as bedrock approached, FitzGerald concentrated his work in a deep sounding. Much of the early chronology of Palestine has been based on the results of this sounding.

During the first two seasons of excavation, Fisher worked on both the citadel mound and the western slope and terraces. From 1923 onward work was concentrated on the summit of the mound. Nearly the whole of the top five levels was removed before the end of operations in 1933. Because the Canaanite temples in level V were along the southern edge of the citadel, it was there that Rowe and FitzGerald concentrated their efforts after 1925,

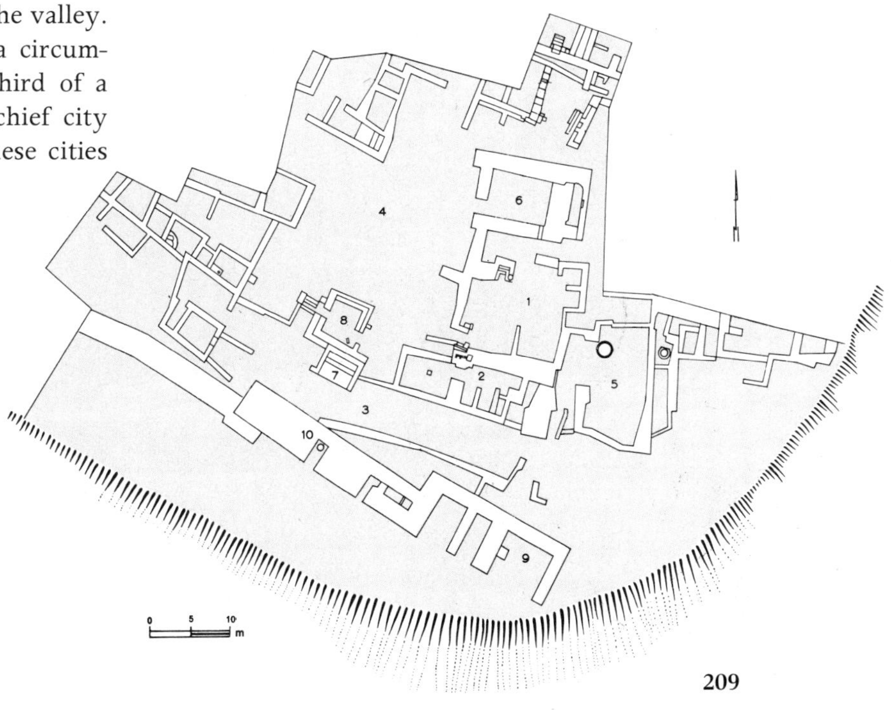

Stratum IX: plan of temple: 1. Altar court. 2. Inner altar. 3. Entrance corridor. 4. Inner court. 5. Room with oven and well. 6. Room north of the sanctuary. 7. Altar (or steps to the roof?). 8. Guard room. 9. Spot where lion and dog slab were found. 10. Water reservoir.

discovering temples from levels IX–VI lying directly beneath the southern temple of level V. Below level IX, work was confined to a very limited area, ending in the deep sounding. From time to time the cemetery cut in the cliff face along the northern bank of the Harod, just opposite the mound, was also examined. Graves were found from the Middle Bronze Age I to Late Roman times, but it was clear that the cemetery was not in continuous use during that time.

For the publication of the expedition, see bibliography. It must be emphasized that about one third of the material is still unpublished. Thus, the present article cannot be considered more than an interim report.

RESULTS OF THE EXCAVATIONS ON THE MOUND AND ITS VICINITY

Beth-Shean must have had one of the longest essentially unbroken occupations of any site in Palestine. The beginning of the settlement (stratum XVIII) is perhaps to be dated to circa 3500 B.C., and the site was in use, with gaps of a century or so, until about the time of the Crusaders.

Neolithic and Chalcolithic. In stratum XVI of

Left: Stratum VII: bronze "standard" with applied gold foil. Below: View of mound from southwest. Opposite page, counterclockwise: Stratum IX: relief found in temple representing

the deep sounding, gray-burnished Esdraelon ware was found stratified within the walls of an apsidal house. Copper implements were also found in this house. A Carbon-14 test on similar material from tomb A-94 at Jericho yielded a date — 3260 (±100) B.C. Thus, stratum XVI at Beth-Shean can be dated somewhere in the late fourth millennium. Nothing occurred below stratum XVI from which any dating might be obtained, although a general figure of 3500 B.C. for the pits in stratum XVIII has been suggested. No structures appear in the levels below XVI, so that the material from these strata cannot be used reliably in formulating a sequence of any sort. Some of the pottery from the lowest levels seems to be related to the Yarmukian, or Jericho pottery-Neolithic B culture. Some traces of the Chalcolithic period have been found in the new city of Beth-Shean (see below).

Early Bronze Age. The earliest evidence of a town, or of real buildings, occurs in strata XV and XIII (Early Bronze Age I–II). Even in the very limited area which the deep sounding reached at this stage, intersecting streets and multiroomed structures appear. In stratum XIV one house has

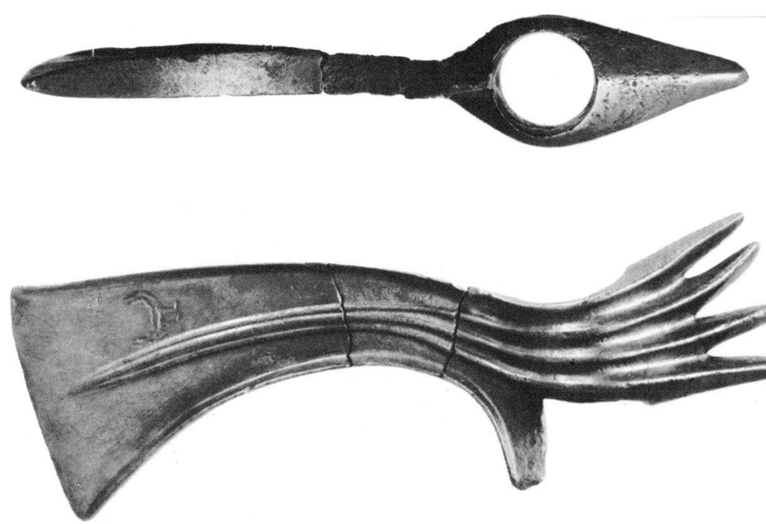

fight between lion and dog. Stele erected by Pa-Ra-em-Heb in memory of his father Amen-em-Apt, showing them worshipping Mekal, god of Beth-Shean. "Hittite" axhead; 14th cent. B.C.

rows of stones along either wall to support wooden columns. Although two more levels — XII and XI — seem to belong essentially to the Early Bronze Age, the pottery does not seem to extend as late as that found at Ai or in Jericho tomb 351, apparently indicating a break in the occupation of Beth-Shean.

Middle Bronze Age I. Relatively little material of this period was found in the deep sounding or elsewhere on the mound. Many, if not most, of the graves excavated in the Great Northern Cemetery, however, were originally cut during this period. Thus, it seems probable that the settlement had its center in some other part of the mound, or else that the occupation deposits everywhere were very slight.

Middle Bronze Age II. In burial II from the slope trench and tomb 92 in the cemetery, there is a certain amount of evidence of occupation in this period. Tomb 92 contained a fine bronze fenestrated duckbill axhead, a veined dagger, and two socketed spearheads.

On present study, the Middle Bronze Age II material from the tel seems to stop halfway through the period, as among the objects in Philadelphia, very few are later than the material in Jericho Middle Bronze Age group III, which represents roughly the middle of the period (see Kathleen Kenyon, *Excavations at Jericho,* I, London, 1960, 269). The fact that no glacis was discovered, can hardly be attributed to the fact that the deep sounding was at the very edge of the mound. The structures of stratum X-B — one of which is an example of the large, square houses built around a courtyard typical of the Middle and Late Bronze ages — seem to belong to the Middle Bronze Age phase, and it seems probable that the buildings of X-A do as well.

However, a quantity of Middle Bronze Age II material was found below the floors of stratum IX, in what FitzGerald describes as a fill. Whether this material also belonged to stratum X-A houses is unknown.

F. JAMES

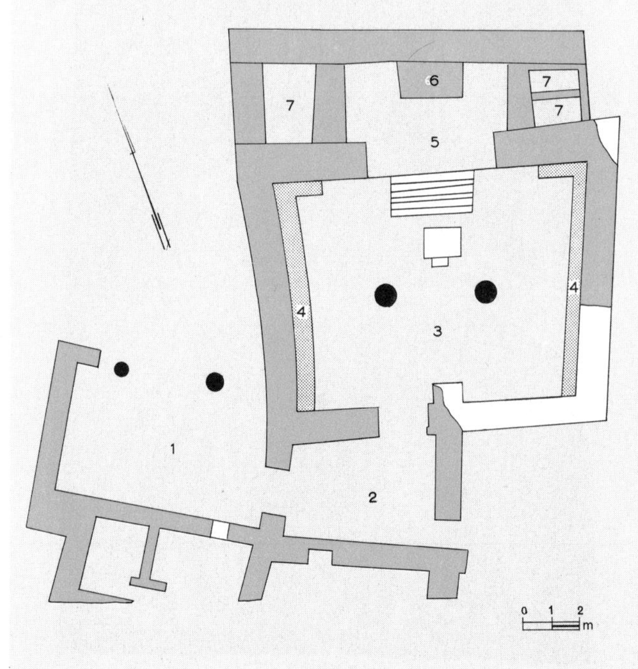

Plan of temple:
Top: Stratum VII: 1. Silo. 2. Podium. 3. Holy of Holies. 4. Steps. 5. Bench. 6. Incense altar. 7. Sanctuary. 8. Inner courts. 9. Gate. existing restored
Bottom: Stratum VI: 1. Outer court. 2. Inner court. 3. Sanctuary. 4. Bench. 5. Holy of Holies. 6. Podium. 7. Storerooms. existing benches restored

Late Bronze and Iron Age Temples
STRATUM IX. This level was attributed to the Late Bronze Age on the basis of pottery found under the floors. The plan of the acropolis was completely changed in this period. The mound no longer served for burial, and a temple was erected on it. The excavators dated the temple, which was oriented east–west, to the days of Thutmose III, while W.F. Albright proposed a date at the end of the fourteenth century B.C. The plan of the temple is extremely complex. The sacred enclosure, which was not far from the city gate, was surrounded by a wall separating it from the private dwellings outside. Steps ascended to the gate in the southern wall of the enclosure, which opened into an area of altars and cult rooms attached to the temple (building 6). The temple itself consisted of a rectangular room with a narrow cult chamber at its eastern end.

Many objects of Egyptian origin were found in the sacred area, including a stele erected by Pa-Ra-em-Heb to Mekal, the god of Beth-Shean, in memory of his father Amen-em-Apt; a scarab incised with a bull; and a cartouche bearing the name of Thutmose III. The excavators considered these finds proof of their date of the temple.

A basalt relief of a lion and dog in combat found in a room in the eastern wall suggests that a gate may have been situated at that spot and the relief set into one of its entrance rooms.

STRATUM VIII. The only remains from this level are basalt column bases that were undoubtedly part of a monumental building (temple?). The excavators assigned this stratum to the period between the end of the reign of Thutmose III and the days of Thutmose IV. Albright, on the other hand, proposed dating it at the end of the fourteenth and beginning of the thirteenth century B.C.

STRATUM VII. The temple in this level is oriented north–south, which was the usual direction of Late Bronze Age temples in Canaan. The excavators assigned it to the days of Amenhotep III and IV. W.F. Albright dated it to the time of Ramses II; and B. Mazar, to the time of Merneptah. The date proposed by the excavators, however, seems to be the most likely one. They based their conclusion on a group of objects laid as a foundation deposit

Top: Statue of Ramses III. Bottom: Lintel showing the Egyptian official Ramses-Wesr-Khapesh; reign of Ramses III.

under the altar of the temple, which included cartouches of Amenhotep III. Moreover, they found close analogies between the plan of the temple and those of a chapel and a small shrine of Akhenaton at el-Amarna, a city built at the close of the reign of Amenhotep III and the beginning of the reign of Amenhotep IV. This city was abandoned at the death of the latter pharaoh, and it is the only place where such temples have been found. It can thus be assumed that temple VII was built at the end of the days of Amenhotep III, at the beginning of the "Amarna period." The similarities between this temple and those of Akhenaton suggest that the commander of the Egyptian garrison at Beth-Shean was deeply influenced by the religious revolution in Egypt at that time.

The temple consisted of a square sanctuary in which stood columns with Egyptian lotus capitals. Steps led from the sanctuary to the Holy of Holies, which was elevated 1.5 meters above the floor of the sanctuary. In front of the sanctuary were two inner courtyards. This stratum also contained a public granary and a fortified tower *(migdol)*, which served as the residence of the Egyptian governor and the inner fortress of the city.

Among the main finds of this stratum is a stele dedicated to Ashtoret, a large group of Syro-Hittite seals, and a Syro-Hittite hand-shaped ax-head. The victory stelae of Seti I found out of context in later levels belong to the end of this level.

STRATUM VI. Temple VII continued in use in stratum VI, but with several modifications. Small rooms were added on both sides of the Holy of Holies. The period of the temple's use corresponds to the two occupation levels of the city. The excavators dated this stratum to the time of Seti I. Albright assigned it to the time of Ramses III on the basis of a lintel found in stratum V that bore the name of this pharaoh and undoubtedly came from stratum VI. The foundation deposits, however, included objects with the names of Ramses I and II. Consequently the temple may have been founded in the time of Ramses II. The two corresponding levels in the city lend support to this assumption. The stelae of Ramses II may also be dated to the first phase of this stratum.

In the vicinity of the temple were found Egyptian architectural fragments that originally belonged to the temple. Among these were painted cornices

Above: Stele of Seti I (fragmentary).
Opposite page: Stele of Seti I (completely preserved).

and numerous fragments of doorjambs with hieroglyphic inscriptions and seven T-shaped doorsills. Also characteristic of this stratum were the many incense stands decorated with painted and molded details of cultic scenes.

LEVEL V. In this level the plan of the acropolis was totally changed. Two temples were built with an east-west orientation — a characteristic feature of Iron Age temples. The southern, and larger, temple is shaped like a basilica and contains two rows of columns along the length and a "broad room" type of Holy of Holies. The northern temple is similar in plan but much smaller. In it was found a stele dedicated to the goddess Anat, which may indicate that the southern temple was the temple of Dagon (I Chronicles 10:10). The two temples were connected by a complex of rooms and storehouses.

These temples and attached structures apparently continued in use without major changes throughout the existence of the Philistine city in the later phase of this level. In the Israelite period (possibily in the time of Solomon) a monumental gate was built south of the temples. Its plan and technique are in some ways analogous to the gate of Megiddo IV-B.

A. Kempinski

Other Iron Age Remains (Stratum IV). There is probably a short break between levels V and IV, for in most places the foundations of the walls of IV appear well above the stumps of the level V walls and totally ignore the earlier layout. In some places the walls of the northern Israelite storerooms were still standing 10 to 12 feet high, so it would seem that some interval would have been necessary for the consolidation of the ground around these buildings.

Stratum IV is most unimpressive and has no evident town plan. Little, if any, imported pottery was found, and the small finds are also scanty. Probably little of the pottery is later than the end of the seventh century B.C.

The Cult Objects. The reports on virtually all the Beth-Shean cult objects were published in a single volume. In the original publication, however, it was not emphasized strongly enough how greatly the objects varied from level to level. While cylindrical cultic vessels certainly occur from IX to V, it is only in the latter level that the elaborate shrine houses and cylinders with serpents and doves appear. In fact, snakes scarcely appear in stratum IX. In stratum VII those snakes that were found were invariably cobras of the Egyptian uraeus. This level also produced a number of pig-head rhytons. Stratum VI again had few snakes, but contained a number of pottery ducks' heads. The serpent cult reached its peak in level V, with the decorated cylinders and shrine houses. The snakes on these objects are all spotted creatures with oval heads and a doughnut-shaped object on their foreheads, very different from those of stratum VII.

Hellenistic-Roman Period. Strata II and III were assigned by the excavators to this period. Because of the serious disturbances caused by construction and reconstruction of the stone buildings that came into use at this time, information about the classical

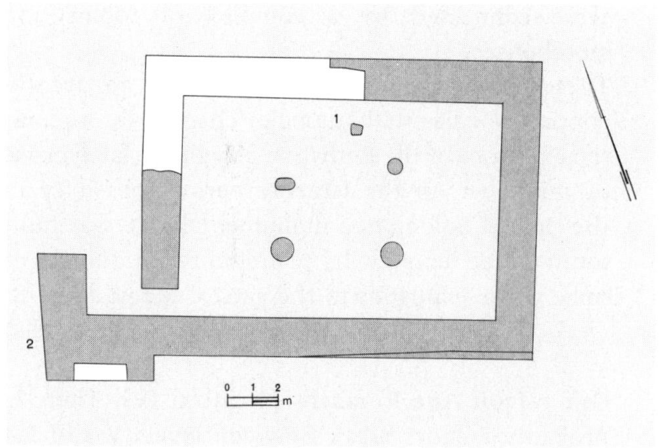

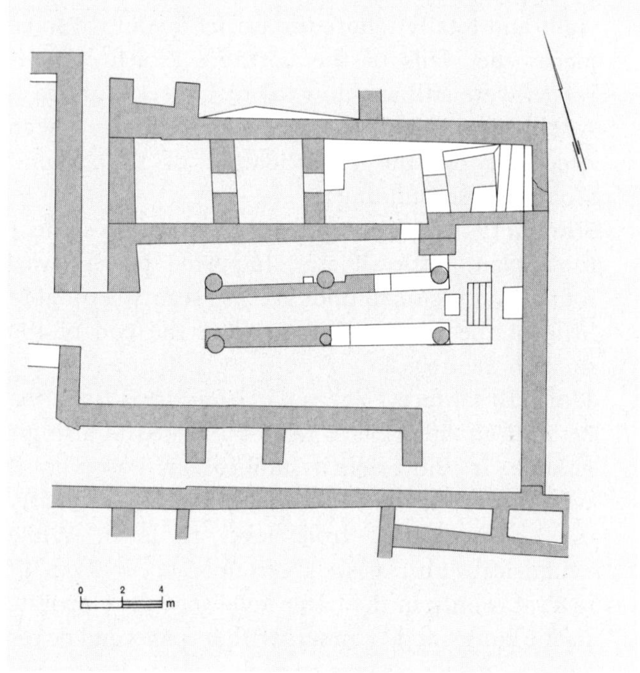

existing *restored*

Opposite page, counterclockwise: Stratum V: plan of northern temple: 1. Stele of the goddess Anat. 2. Statue of Ramses III. Stratum V: plan of southern temple (Temple of Dagon). Stratum V, southern temple: cylinder seal showing Ramses II shooting at a target with two bound prisoners beneath it. A god is standing behind the target; IA I. Jug with anthropomorphic top; LBA. Pendant showing figure of nude goddess holding a was *scepter; LBA. Below: Potsherds with paintings representing a Canaanite man and a woman; LBA II. Bottom: Fragment of a faience bowl with hieroglyphic inscription; LBA. Right: Stratum V: southern temple cult object with birds and serpents.*

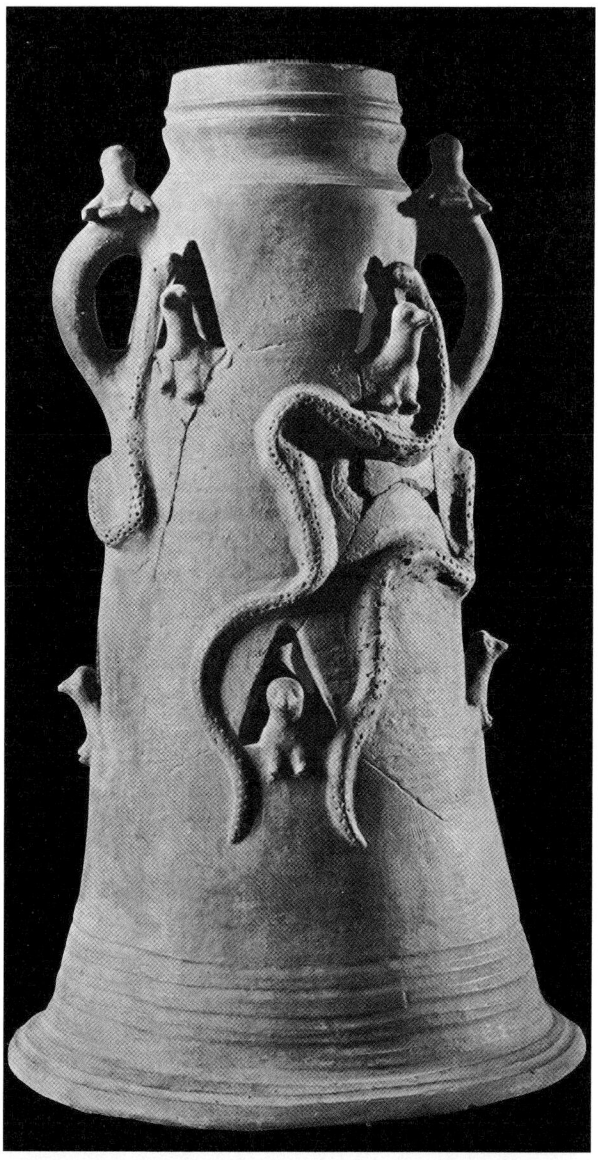

Below: Fragment of lid of anthropoid coffin.
Right: Anthropoid clay coffins (Philistine?).
Bottom: Selection of lids of anthropoid coffins.

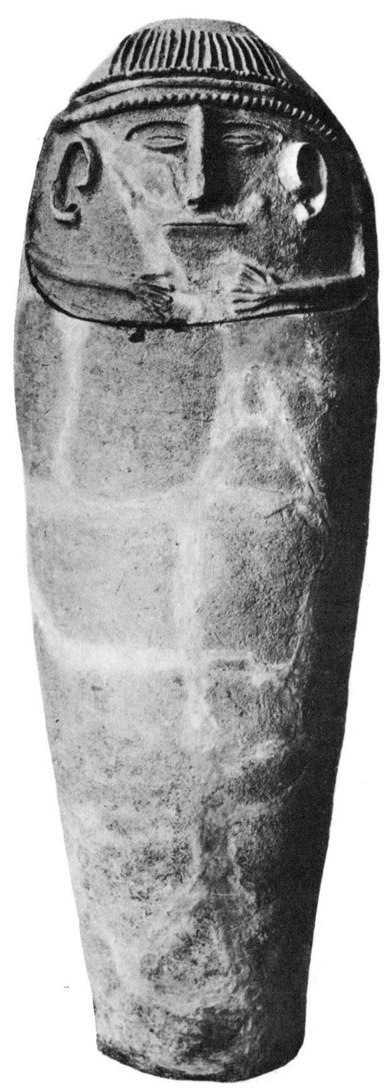

city is scanty. A quantity of Hellenistic coins and pottery occur, but it is difficult to associate them with specific buildings.

The great temple that stood at the northwest side of the summit was incorrectly attributed by the excavators to this period. A lamp found beneath the reservoir over which the temple was built provides a terminus ante quem for the construction of the sanctuary. Once thought to have been in use from the third century B.C. onward, this lamp is today considered hardly earlier than the first century A.D. The building thus seems to have been an Early Roman installation.

Except for this temple, it is difficult to assign any buildings to the same period, even though there is a good deal of pottery dating to it, including Samian, Arretine, and other first-century wares. It is possible that the hilltop shrine remained the main feature of the summit throughout the period, while a number of precinct buildings there were associated with it.

During the Byzantine period the chief architectural feature on the summit was a circular church consisting of an ambulatory around an open court. FitzGerald has dated the construction of this church to sometime in the early fifth century A.D., on the basis of similarity between the capitals of its columns with those of the Church of St. Stephen in Jerusalem. The latter was built by the empress Eudocia between A.D. 431 and 438. Furthermore, one of the mosaics from the church was of a pattern similar to one from the Church of Eleona on the Mount of Olives, of about the same period.

Dwelling houses were apparently again built on the summit of the mound during the Byzantine period. The circular church seems to have been surrounded by houses; the terraces below were also occupied. A paved roadway led from the gate in the western slope to the summit. The literary references of the time describe Beth-Shean, or Scythopolis, as a flourishing Christian city, a city of saints and scholars, churches and monasteries.

In addition to the circular church, the expedition uncovered a sixth-century A.D. monastery near the cemetery across the Harod River. Inscriptions showed that it was probably constructed sometime during the second or third quarter of the century. A hoard of coins of Heraclius I indicated that it survived the Persian invasion. There was no evidence, however, that it also survived the Arab conquest in A.D. 636. Because of this short life, finds from the monastery are most useful for dating the Byzantine period. The monastery's finest feature was a series of mosaic floors, including circular representations of the Labors of the Months grouped around the sun and moon, all personified.

Arab Period. The excavations produced little that could establish the length of time the Byzantine city survived the "day of Beisan," when it fell to the Muslims in A.D. 636. The circular church is known to have been destroyed by A.D. 806, however, for a Kufic inscription mentioning this date was found written lengthwise on one of the fallen columns. A Hebrew inscription, later than the Arab writing, occurred on the same column.

After the destruction of the circular church, a network of Arab streets was built on top of it. It is difficult to say how long this town endured. Still later buildings occur on the summit, but most of their contents had been completely looted. The latest Arab pottery seems to be the red-and-white geometric ware of the eleventh and twelfth centuries A.D. Much of it comes from the long rooms built against the outer enclosing walls, suggesting that the entire summit and terrace were in use. This pottery was used by both the Arabs and the Crusaders. Historical documents indicate that the inhabitants of Beth-Shean lived under Crusader rule. Theodoric of Wurzberg, who visited Beth-Shean in A.D. 1172, relates that Count Adam de Bethune, who took part in the First Crusade, was created first baron of Bessan and installed himself in a castle on the top of Tell el-Husn. According to William of Tyre, this castle was destroyed by Saladin in 1183.

EXCAVATIONS IN THE GREAT NORTHERN CEMETERY

Some 230 graves were excavated during the University Museum's ten seasons at Beth-Shean. All had been severely disturbed. Earthquakes, landslides, and collapses had added further confusion to the usual disturbances caused by robbing and reuse. The majority of the graves were cut in Middle Bronze Age I, and most were reused and greatly enlarged in the classical period. About a thousand individuals must have been buried here.

Middle Bronze Age I Tombs. In spite of the poor condition of the graves, a number of them were clearly similar to the shaft graves known at Megiddo. These were entered by a shaft leading

Bust of woman. Bottom: Bust of man from Roman tomb.

into a central court with rectangular chambers on three sides. The pottery from these graves is also similar to that from Megiddo and Tell el-Husn, as well as that from tombs of the same period at Jericho termed by Kathleen Kenyon Intermediate Early-Middle Bronze Age. Four-spouted lamps were numerous, while the typical weapon seems to have been a long copper javelin with diamond-shaped section and curled tang. Daggers, although much less frequent, were also found.

Middle Bronze Age II and Late Bronze Age Tombs. Few tombs dating to these periods were found in the area of the necropolis that was excavated. A small quantity of Middle Bronze Age II-A–B material occurred, as did a little from the earlier part of the Late Bronze Age I. The cemetery seems to have been completely abandoned during most of the Late Bronze Age II, however, except for a few of the earlier "Philistine" tombs.

Iron Age I Tombs. Almost none of the "Philistine" graves in this cemetery was undisturbed, but many of the "graves" were rather groups of objects associated with clay coffins that had been thrown out of their original rock-hewn chambers, presumably in Roman times. Some twenty-six such "Philistine" groups appear in the register. They may well represent a larger number of tombs, however, and certainly do indicate considerably more individual burials. Insofar as there is evidence, it would appear that the rectangular burial chambers containing the "Philistine" burials have no links with the rectangular dromos graves of the "Lords of the Philistines" at Tel Sharuhen. They were probably originally cut in Middle Bronze Age I as shaft graves. Flat-bottomed jars and ledge handles were so commonly found with the clay coffins that it was difficult to believe they did not belong together.

The lightly fired clay coffins are of two types: grotesqueries, of which no more than half a dozen are recorded; and what might be called normal faces. The latter give a definite impression of being individual portraits. It has been suggested, but that does not seem likely, that all of the latter type were women.

The pottery associated with the "Philistine" burials included quantities of lamps, pilgrim flasks, stirrup jars (some of Mycenaean ware that have not been published), and a number of white-burnished cups.

Most of the ornaments had been stolen, but poppy-bud carnelian necklaces were found, as well as heavy, crescent-shaped gold earrings typical of the Early Iron Age and bronze or iron anklets. Of weapons, only a two-pronged spear butt and a few arrowheads occurred. Several fiddle-shaped gaming boards (similar to those found in the Megiddo Treasury) were noted, as well as bronze jugs, bowls, and a lamp.

Hellenistic—Roman and Byzantine Period Tombs. By far the greatest number of tombs excavated by the University Museum expedition belong to these periods. The earliest appear in the Late Hellenistic or Early Roman period, and the latest continue well into Byzantine times. Quantities of glass were found, as well as small objects of all sorts, including a number of terra-cotta figurines, statuettes, and bronze bells. An interesting feature of many of the Roman burials is the inclusion of crude portrait busts of the dead. This custom seems to have been confined to the Beisan area. At Sebastya, rather more sophisticated examples are dated to the time of Septimius Severus.

The Roman theater.

Left: Coin of Nysa Scythopolis; second century A.D.
Opposite page and below: Monastery of Lady Mary; circa A.D. *567; mosaic pavements in main hall and in room L.*

Mosaic over Byzantine tomb chamber.

SUMMARY

Although it cannot be definitely proved whether or not the site is mentioned in the Egyptian Execration Texts of the nineteenth century B.C., there is sufficient evidence of Middle Bronze Age I and early Middle Bronze Age II material to suggest that it existed at that time. On the other hand, it is probable that none of the structures found in the excavations can be dated to the time of Thutmose III, although a certain amount of material on the tel and one or two tombs from the Great Northern Cemetery may perhaps be dated to his reign. It seems probable that there was a town here at the time of Thutmose III, but that its buildings did not reach the outer perimeter along the south where the deep sounding was excavated. (However, see above, the temple of stratum IX.)

The Nineteenth Dynasty of Egypt is well represented at Beth-Shean in both artifacts and inscriptions. These include two stelae of Seti I, one of Ramses II, and the reused fragment of a fourth royal stele that does not give a clue as to the pharaoh in whose honor it was erected. Although Beth-Shean is not mentioned in any of the topographical lists of Ramses III, a nearly life-size statue with the cartouches of this pharaoh was found. In addition, a stone-cut inscription bearing the cartouches of this Ramses was uncovered in stratum VI. Strata VIII and VII, therefore, are probably to be attributed to Seti I and Ramses II.

It is more difficult to connect confidently any of the later strata with events mentioned in the Bible. The site was occupied at least into, and probably through, the Assyrian period. But the final Iron Age occupation was almost a squatter type, and Beth-Shean certainly was not one of the great cities of Israel in that period. There is little evidence for more than sporadic occupation during the Babylonian and Persian periods, although the figurines of pregnant females and old men suggest that during that time the hilltop remained a sacred area. F. JAMES

CITY AREA AT FOOT OF THE MOUND

Since 1950 the ancient sites of Beth-Shean and vicinity have been investigated by N. Tzori, on behalf of the Department of Antiquities. Scores of sites were discovered and a few excavated. Ten of the excavated sites are discussed here.

Chalcolithic Sites. Five Chalcolithic sites were discovered within the limits of Beth-Shean itself.

Israelite Graves (Map reference 19782116). In 1951 five Iron Age II-C graves were discovered (end of the sixth century B.C.). These contained pottery, glass and bronze vessels, and silver jewelry.

Roman Villa (Map reference 19662124). In this villa of the second/third century A.D., mosaic floors with floral and geometric patterns were found, as well as a bath complete with its hypocaust. A hoard of coins was also found.

Cache of Roman Pottery, Glass, etc. (Pit 1 in Housing Project A. Map reference 19722121). In 1955 a bottle-shaped plastered pit was excavated. It contained a cache of hundreds of intact pottery vessels and lamps (of the Beth Nattif type), glass and bronze vessels, and coins of the third/fourth centuries A.D.

Synagogue I (Tel Mastaba. Map reference 19752131). The synagogue, excavated in 1962, was discovered on Tell Iṣṭaba (Mastaba), about 280 meters north of the Byzantine city wall (built in A.D. 508–09). The excavation brought to light three phases in the history of the building, from its founding at the end of the fourth or the beginning of the fifth century A.D. to its destruction between A.D. 626 and 640. The synagogue is a basilical structure with an apse to the northwest. In front of the apse, a mosaic was found with representations of the Ark of the Law (covered by a curtain), together with menorahs and the usual

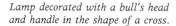

Lamp decorated with a bull's head and handle in the shape of a cross.

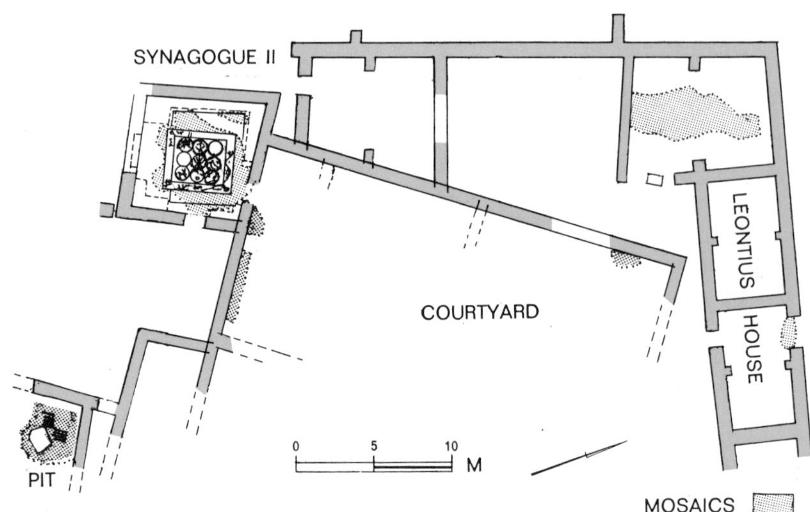

House of Leontius: Left: plan showing courtyard, chapel, mosaics, cistern. Opposite page: mosaic floor of the hall. Below: Synagogue mosaic pavement in the nave, showing the Ark of the Law; early sixth century A.D.

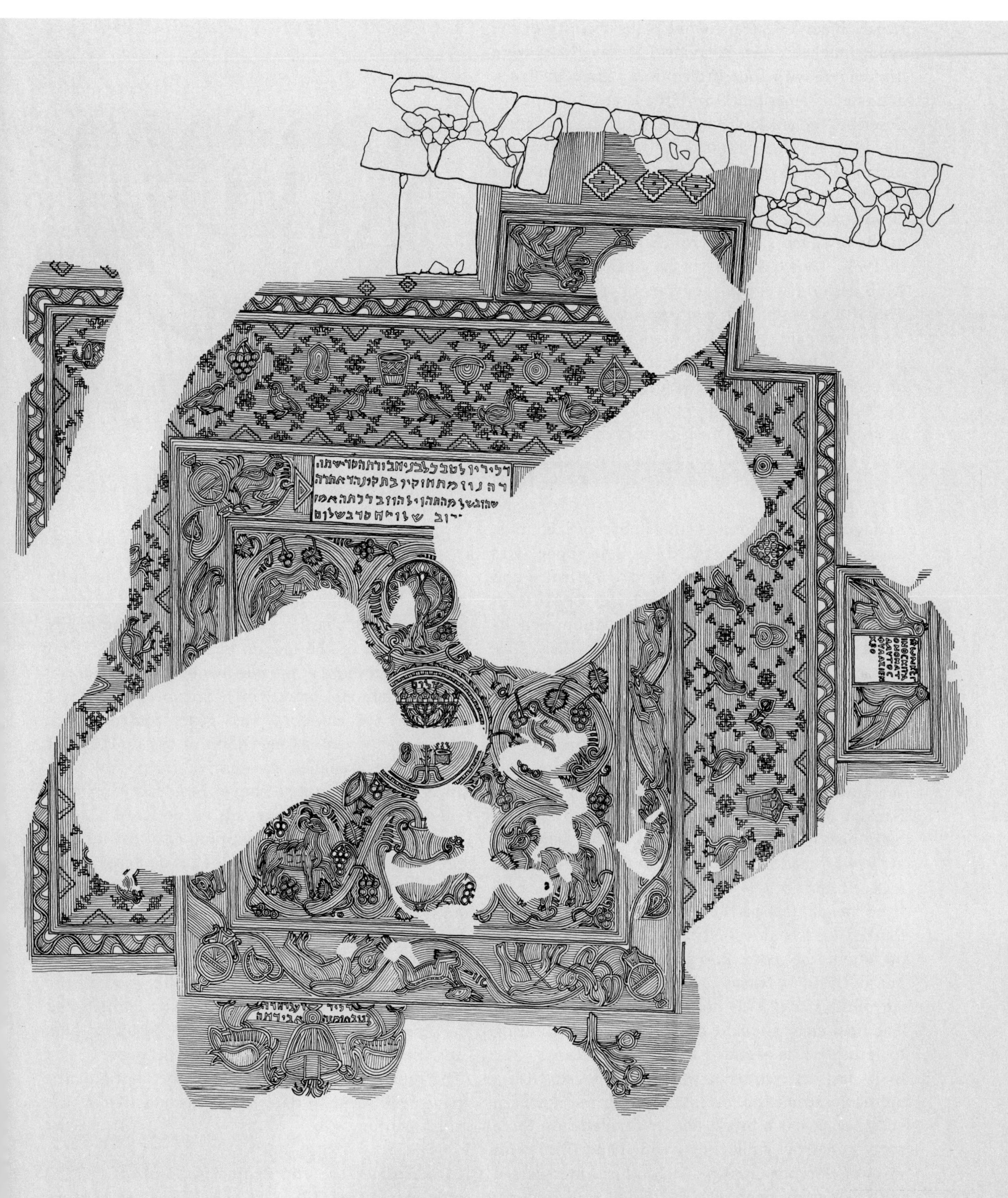

ritual objects. Several rooms in the vicinity of the synagogue were also excavated. Mosaic floors were discovered with four inscriptions, three in Greek and one in Samaritan. One of the Greek inscriptions describes the work of Hanina and his son Marianos, the same artisans who laid the mosaic floor of the Beth Alpha synagogue (q.v.). The Samaritan inscription was found in an adjacent room.

Leontius House (Map reference 1969120). Remains of seven strata were discovered at this site in 1964. They range from the Chalcolithic to the Arab period (twelfth to fourteenth centuries A.D.). The fifth stratum (fifth century A.D.), to which the excavators paid special attention, revealed a mosaic floor with two inscriptions that mention the name of Leontius, owner of the house, two scenes from the Odyssey, and Nilotic motifs.

In stratum 4, a large sixth-century building with mosaic floors in several rooms was uncovered.

N. TZORI

Synagogue; bronze handle of lamp.

Synagogue II. South of the house of Leontius, across the joint courtyard, a synagogue was excavated in 1970–72 by D. Bahat, A. Druks, and M. Edelstein, on behalf of the Israel Department of Antiquities and Museums, in association with the American Union of Jewish Communities. The synagogue consists of a single room that is roughly square (7 by 7 meters), built in the irregular shape common in Byzantine architecture.

The main entrance is on the north through the court, with a side entrance from the east. The surround in the north entrance shows an amphora flanked by two partridges. There is also an Aramaic inscription: "Remembered/be for good the artist/who made/this work." At the east entrance a Greek inscription — this time set so as to be read from inside the hall — is placed within a panel flanked by two doves. It reads: "The gift of those of whom the Lord knows the names, He shall guard them, in times...." A third panel of the surround shows two lions flanking an amphora. The existence of a niche in the south wall, pointing to Jerusalem, is assumed by the excavators.

In its last state the synagogue was paved with a multicolored mosaic, orientated from the northern entrance. It has a broad border divided into three parts: a narrow guilloche; a wide band filled with rows of fleurons crossing each other, interspersed with representations of birds, fruits, and baskets; and a narrow inner border in which a vine trellis issues from four amphorae in the four corners, with animals chasing each other along the trellis. In the field of the mosaic is another trellis rising from an amphora at the north end. The trellis forms nine medallions, six of which have been preserved. Flanking the amphora, two goats confront each other. In the central medallion of the middle row is a seven-branched candlestick (menorah) with an ethrog and incense shovel beside it (the other symbols are lost). Above this is the word *shalom,* "peace," probably the beginning of a lost inscription "Peace upon Israel." A dove is depicted in the medallion beside the menorah. Above the menorah a peacock is shown *en face,* with its tail outspread. Beside it is a buffalo. Above the peacock, in the border, an Aramaic inscription was set in a *tabula ansata.* It reads: "Remembered be for good all the members of the holy community/who contributed to repair the place/the holy: peace be upon them and blessing, Amen./... Peace, grace in peace."

The repair of the synagogue and the laying of the pavement seem to date to the second half of the sixth century A.D.

D. BAHAT

Monastery (Housing Project A "Imhoff") (Map reference 19702117). Part of a fifth/sixth century monastery was excavated in 1959. Living quarters; a public lavatory; a hall with one side opening onto a porch; colorful mosaic floors with geometric, floral, and faunal motifs; an inscription; and rare bronze vessels were found here.

Byzantine House (Map reference 19712121). On this site were discovered five strata ranging from the Chalcolithic to the Byzantine period. In the second stratum a patrician house of twenty-two rooms from the fifth/sixth century A.D. was found. A complex water-supply system, drains, and many small finds were also uncovered. The fifth stratum contained dwelling pits of the Middle Chalcolithic period, dug in clay soil.

Byzantine Potter's Workshop (Tel Magda. Map reference 19712103). In 1954–55 a potter's workshop from the Byzantine period was discovered here. It consisted of a pillared rectangular hall and a nearby kiln. Among the lamps found, one bears a Samaritan inscription. N. TZORI

BIBLIOGRAPHY

History and Topography: I. Ben Dor, *Enc. Miqr.* 2, 102–10 (with bibliography, Hebrew) • Robinson, *Biblical Researches* 3, 174–76 • Conder-Kitchener, *SWP* 2, 83, 101–14 • Abel, *GP* 1, 980–81.

Excavation Reports and Critiques: A. Rowe, *The History and Topography of Beth Shan* (Vol. I), Philadelphia, 1930; *idem, The Four Canaanite Temples of Beth Shan* (Vol. II, 1), Philadelphia, 1940 • G.M. FitzGerald, *The Four Canaanite Temples of Beth Shan: The Pottery* (Vol. II, 2), Philadelphia, 1930; *idem, Beth Shan Excavations 1921–1923, The Arab and Byzantine Levels* (Vol. III), Philadelphia, 1931; *idem, A Sixth Century Monastery at Beth Shan* (Vol. IV), Philadelphia, 1939; *idem, PEQ* (1932), 138–48; (1934), 123–34; *idem,* "The Earliest Pottery of Beth Shan," *Museum Journal* 24 (1935), 5–22 • W.F. Albright, *AASOR* 17 (1938), 76–79 • G.M. FitzGerald, *PEQ* (1940), 81 • G.E. Wright, *AJA* 44 (1941), 483–85 • F.W. James, *The Iron Age at Beth-Shan,* Philadelphia, 1966 • E.D. Oren, *The Northern Cemetery at Beth-Shan,* Leyden, 1973.

Egyptian Inscriptions: B. Mazar, *EI* 3 (1954), 23 • J. Simons, *Handbook for the Study of Egyptian Topographical Lists,* Leyden, 1937, index s.v. • Prichard, *ANET,* index s.v. • J. Černy, *EI* 5 (1958), 72*–82*.

Greek and Latin Inscriptions: G.M. FitzGerald, *PEQ* (1927), 150–54 • F.C. Burkitt, *ibid.,* 154 • M. Avi-Yonah, *QDAP* 8 (1938), 57–61; 10 (1942), 165–69 • Youtie-Bonner, *Transactions of the American Philological Society* 58, 47–78.

Coins: G.F. Hill, *Catalogue of the Greek Coins in the British Museum, Palestine,* London, 1914, XXXIVf., 75–77 • S. Ben Dor, *PEQ* (1944), 152–56 • N. Tzori, *ibid.* (1945), 47–48; (1960), 70.

Finds at City Area at Foot of Mound: N. Tzori, *Yediot* 30 (1966), 88–97 (Hebrew); *idem, Beth-Shean* (Collection), 178–79, 186–89; *idem, EI* 8 (1967), 149–67 (Hebrew); *idem, PEQ* (1958), 50–51; *idem, BIES* 18 (1954), 270–71 (Hebrew) • D. Bahat, *Qadmoniot* 5 (1972), 55–58 (Hebrew) • Y. Ben-Zvi, *ibid.* 19 (1955), 165 • Z. Ben Hayyim, *ibid.,* 106.

BETH SHE'ARIM

HISTORY. Beth She'arim is mentioned for the first time by Josephus as "Besara." It is described as a village in southern Galilee, on the border of the Ptolemais region. At that time it was the center of the estates of Queen Berenice in the Esdraelon Valley (*Life,* 119). The locality is mentioned by the same name in a Greek epitaph discovered in Beth She'arim (see below) and in a tomb inscription in Khirbet el-Qubeibah, in the vicinity of Lod. In Talmudic literature, the place is usually called Beth She'arim, although sometimes the Aramaic form is used — Beth Sh'arei or Beth Sh'arein.

In the second century Beth She'arim was a Jewish village in Galilee where several scholars lived, including Rabbi Johanan ben Nuri. There was already then a rabbinical academy in Beth She'arim (*Niddah* 27a). But the village became especially famous as the place of residence of "Rabbi," the Patriarch Judah I, and of the Sanhedrin. The Talmud contains descriptions of the life and work of the Patriarch in Beth She'arim, the city's public buildings, including the academy where the Patriarch taught, and the elaborate exedra built in his time. When he fell ill he moved to Sepphoris, and resided there until his death. After his death he was brought for burial to Beth She'arim, where he had had a tomb prepared during his lifetime. There is also a tradition that Rabbi Huna the Exilarch *(Resh Galutha)* was brought from Persia to Beth She'arim for burial. In a later period there was a Rabbi Menahem of Kefar She'arim, who was also called "a man of Beth She'arim."

The cemetery of Beth She'arim was famous from the days of the Patriarch Judah I onward, and gradually it became a central Jewish necropolis. "For people are brought here from many places like Upper Caesarea for burial in Beth She'arim" (Palestinian Talmud *Mo'ed Qatan,* 3, 5a).

The city was apparently destroyed during the repression of the Jewish rebellion in A.D. 351 against Gallus Caesar, the ruler of the Orient under the Emperor Constantius II from 351 to 354. According to Hieronymus and other sources, many Jewish cities were razed during that time, including Sepphoris and the neighboring villages.

Counterclockwise: Places of origin of the Jews buried in the catacombs. Northern slope of the hill showing catacombs 14 and 20 and their superstructures. Plan showing main catacombs; A: synagogue; B: basilica.

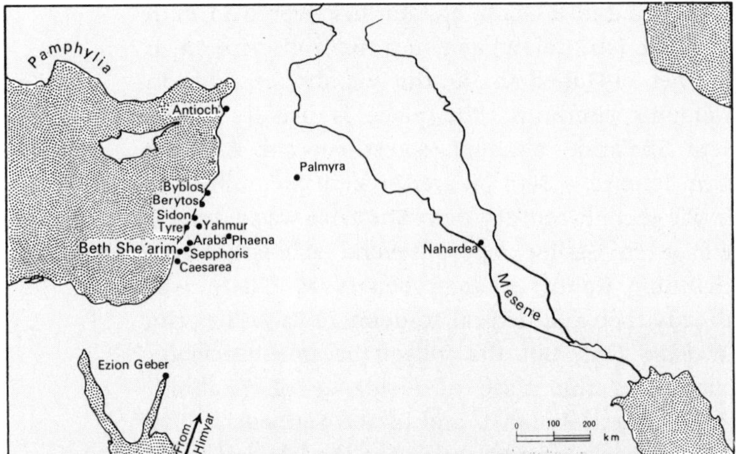

IDENTIFICATION

Ancient Beth She'arim was built on a hill once known by the Arabic name "Sheikh Abreik." It is situated in the southern foothills of Lower Galilee, facing the western limit of the Esdraelon Valley. The identification of Beth She'arim with Sheikh Abreik was based on the excavations on the site which began in 1936, on the literary sources in which Beth She'arim and Besara are mentioned, on the archaeological finds in the area of the ruins and the necropolis, and on the text of a Greek epitaph inscribed on a marble tablet, discovered in 1939 in the mausoleum near catacomb 11. The epitaph reads:

I, Justus, son of Leontios and Sappho, lie here dead,
And after I had plucked the fruit of all wisdom
I left the light, the miserable parents who mourn ceaselessly
And my brothers. Woe to me in [my] Besa[ra].
After descending to Hades, I Justus, lie here
With many of my people, for so willed stern fate.
Be comforted, Justus, no man is immortal.

The early settlement extended over the summit of the hill and its southern slopes — an area totaling more than two acres. The summit is located on the southwestern side of the hill (138 meters above sea level). From this point it slopes down to the northeast, then rises again to a height of 130 meters above sea level at the spot where the remains of a synagogue and its annexes were discovered.

The large necropolis extends around the western and northern slopes of the hill of Beth She'arim and on the nearby hills to the north and west. From surveys and excavations it became evident that this necropolis was one of the largest in the country, and almost every square foot of rock was utilized for hewing out tomb caves.

HISTORY OF THE EXCAVATIONS

As early as 1871, superficial examinations of a few catacombs were conducted by C. Conder under the auspices of the Palestine Exploration Fund, but the results were meager. Systematic excavations at Beth She'arim began in 1936, sponsored by the then Jewish Palestine Exploration Society, under the direction of B. Mazar.

In the first four excavation campaigns (1936–40) four catacombs (1–4) were unearthed on the western side, at the foot of the hill, as well as another catacomb (11) and a nearby mausoleum on the western slope. Other catacombs (5–10) on the southern foot of the hill to the west were examined and partially cleared. On the northeastern part of the hill, remains of a synagogue and adjoining buildings were discovered.

In 1953 the excavations were resumed by the Israel Exploration Society and the Hebrew University, under the direction of N. Avigad. In four subsequent excavation campaigns (1953–55, 1958), catacombs 12 to 21 were unearthed on the northern slopes of Beth She'arim, trial soundings were made in the city area, and the northern gate of the city and an oil press beside it were exposed.

In two additional campaigns (1956 and 1959) under the direction of B. Mazar, a public building in the southwestern part of the city was excavated, and remains of a mausoleum, catacombs 22 to 27, and reservoir 24 at the northern edge of Beth She'arim were discovered. M. Schwabe deciphered the

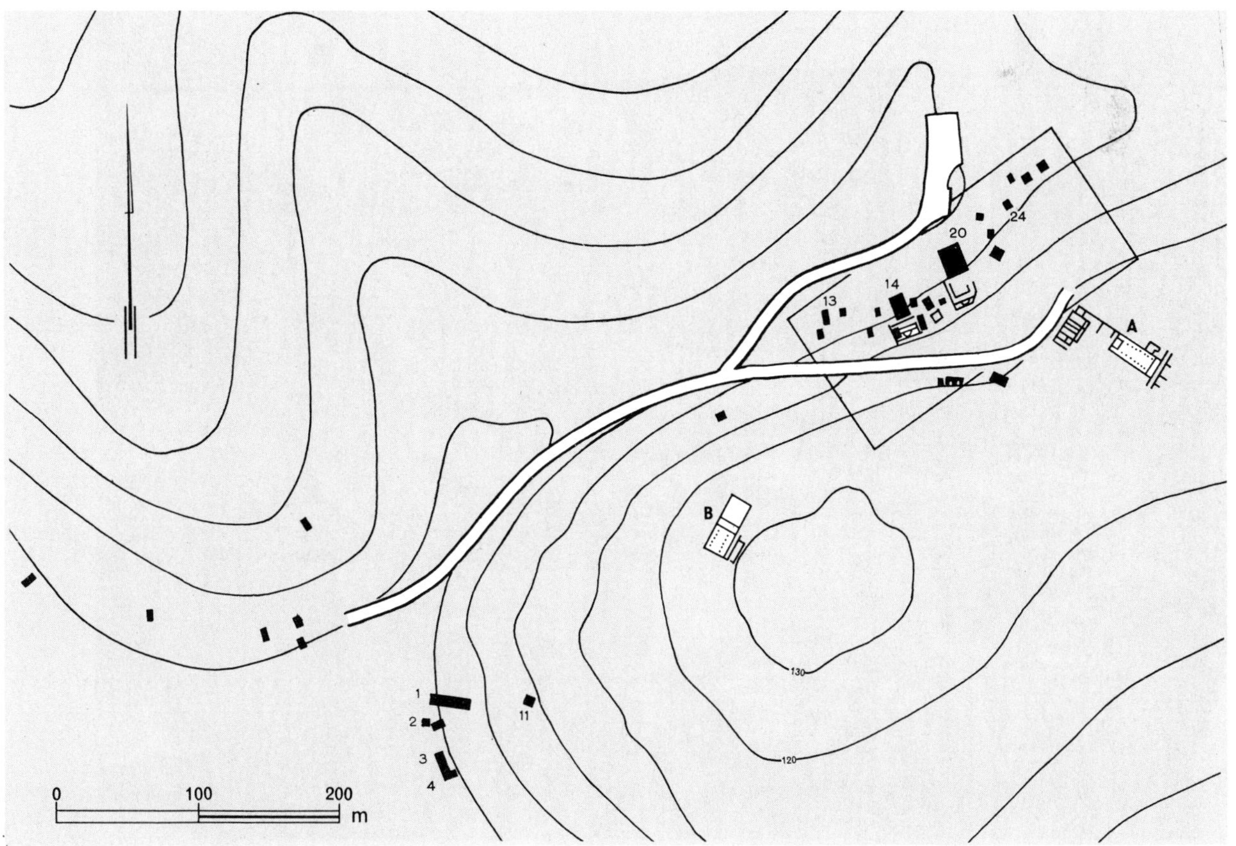

הקבר הזה
יצחק
בר

Greek inscriptions found in Beth She'arim from the beginning of the excavations (1936) until 1954. The texts were published by him and B. Lipshitz in 1967.

EXCAVATIONS OF THE CITY AREA

In the northeastern part of the summit, a complex of buildings was exposed, including a large public building (B on plan) and a synagogue (A), with buildings and courtyards between them. Several building periods could be distinguished:

Period I: A few remains of walls were preserved from the Herodian period and from the first half of the second century A.D. Typical of the constructions of this period are the small ashlar stones with protruding bosses, laid in straight courses of stretchers.

Period II: (End of the second and beginning of the third century A.D.) The buildings in this period are well planned and impressive in their fine architecture. The original plan of building B (40 by 15 meters) belongs to this period. The cellar and parts of the ground floor of the building were preserved. The walls surrounding the building are built of large ashlar stones with smooth, flat bosses, laid in courses of alternating headers and stretchers. The finds reveal that this building belongs to the most flourishing period of the town — the time of the Patriarch Judah I. It was also during that period that the large catacombs of the necropolis were begun.

Period III: (From the second quarter of the third century to the middle of the fourth century A.D.) Many changes were made in building B at that time, and various structures were added in the northeastern part of the hill. The synagogue (A) was erected — a rectangular building (35 by 15 meters) surrounded by thick walls of large ashlars without bosses.

In front of the building was an open court. Three monumental doorways in the façade of the synagogue faced toward Jerusalem. They opened onto a city street. The basilica-like synagogue was divided into a central nave and two aisles by two rows of columns. This synagogue is singular in having a raised bema in the back wall of the nave. At a later stage (III-B) the walls of the synagogue were coated with colored plaster, and marble tablets with various decorations and inscriptions were affixed to them. All the inscriptions but one are in Greek. They are dedicated to community

From catacomb 1: Opposite page: The tomb of Rabbi Isaac, son of Moqim in hall 7. Below: The corridor from the west.

officials and donors who contributed to the construction of the synagogue. In this later phase, the central opening from the court into the synagogue was blocked. Possibly a niche was built there for the Ark — i.e., a permanent Ark of the Law.

In the area between the synagogue and building B, one small structure is especially noteworthy. Two marble tablets were found in it: One contained a Greek inscription dedicated to two people who dealt with burial matters. A second inscription, also in Greek, was dedicated to "Jacob of Caesarea, the head of the Synagogue of Pamphilia," and it ended with the Hebrew greeting *Shalom* ("Peace").

All the buildings in the town were eventually destroyed and burned. This is evidenced by the traces of destruction and conflagration visible everywhere. The date of destruction was established by a hoard of 1,200 coins discovered in the conflagration level of building B. All the coins date to Constantine I and Constantius II — *i.e.,* to the first half of the fourth century A.D. No coin was found dated later than 351, the year the legions sent by Gallus Caesar suppressed the Jewish revolt. This date was confirmed by the results of an investigation of the synagogue itself.

Period IV. (From the mid-fourth century A.D. to the end of the Byzantine period) Remains of poor buildings were preserved in the city area, in the vicinity of the northern gate, and in the synagogue area. Various finds have been attributed to this period, including Byzantine coins.

Period V. Meager remains from Early Arabic and Mameluke times were assigned to this period.

Basilica. In the excavation on the southwestern part of the hill of Beth She'arim, an extensive building was discovered (40 by 15 meters). It was constructed of large ashlars with flat, smooth bosses, similar to the dressing of the masonry in building B (see above), and probably contemporary with it. The building consists of a basilica, divided by two rows of columns into a nave and two aisles. It had a wide court from which one entered the basilica through a narrow passageway (narthex). At a later stage the passageway was removed in order to lengthen the basilica proper. This structure was certainly a public building, perhaps the meeting place for business transactions. Repairs were made to it at different times. It was apparently destroyed when Gallus Caesar razed the city.

From various remains, it is evident that settlement continued in this area, both in the Byzantine and in the Mameluke periods. Beneath the floor level, earlier building remains of the Herodian and Hellenistic periods were discovered. In the debris and on the natural rock, many shards from Iron Age II-B and the Persian period were found. They are evidence that a settlement in the southwestern part of the hill was apparently founded in the ninth century B.C. and that it continued without interruption. At the edge of the summit, between two groups of public buildings, remains of a gate and an oil press were discovered, which were in use in the Byzantine period but were very likely built at an earlier date.

EXCAVATION OF THE NECROPOLIS

In the large necropolis of the second to fourth centuries A.D., many catacombs were found hewn in the rock — some belonging to one family and others of a more public character. The cemetery is huge — caves were quarried in the slopes around Beth She'arim and on the slopes of the neighboring hills. In the large catacombs there is much crowding of tombs. A great deal of epigraphic material was also discovered.

These finds prove that here was a main Jewish necropolis and that the quarrying of graves for the deceased, who were brought here from afar, was a flourishing business in the town. Since the Patriarch Judah I, his family, and his associates were buried at Beth She'arim, the place became revered by Jews in Palestine and in the entire Diaspora of the Middle East.

Hints in the Talmud were confirmed by the Hebrew, Greek, and Palmyrene inscriptions, in which the places of origin of the deceased are mentioned. Among those mentioned in the epitaphs are the head of the Council of Elders of Antioch and his family, the heads of the synagogues of Tyre, Sidon, and Beirut, men and women from Byblos, Palmyra, and Messene (in southern Babylonia). In a bilingual inscription in Greek and South Arabian, Himyarites from South Arabia are mentioned, among them the head of the community of Himyar.

From the inscriptions it became evident that those privileged to be buried in Beth She'arim were mainly people of importance in their communities, such as rabbis, holders of public offices, scribes, merchants, and craftsmen. Probably the belief was prevalent that "he who is buried in the Land of

Israel is as though he were buried under the altar" (Tosefta, *'Abodah Zarah* IV, 3).

The catacombs of Beth She'arim have courtyards or corridors from which built entrances open onto the burial halls. The portals are provided with stone doors, the majority of which still turn on their hinges. They are usually made in a style imitating wooden doors studded with nails. Occasionally a door was found still bolted, but most of them had been broken at one time or another.

Several of the courtyards were quite wide, some even paved with mosaics in colorful designs (catacombs 6 and 11). From the entrance through an elaborate façade, steps led down into a courtyard. Some of the public catacombs had several stories of burial halls placed on either side of a long corridor hewn in the rock to a sizable depth. Catacomb 11 had sixteen "halls" containing four hundred burial places.

The burial halls hewn in the rock are of various dimensions. Some consist of several rooms, with arched openings quarried in the rock between the rooms. The graves in the halls are of different types, mainly arcosolia, loculi cut into the walls (customary from the time of the Second Temple onward), and pit graves cut into the floors. Into these were placed coffins made of wood, lead, pottery, or stone — and sometimes bodies without a coffin.

There is also evidence of a continuation of the ancient practice of secondary burial: collecting the bones in an ossuary (usually of wood), or reburying them without an ossuary. In many

Counterclockwise, from catacomb 1: Palmyrene inscription: BTMLKW. Horseman relief. Hall 13; arcosolia, loculi, and shaft grave.

Above: The city; building B.
Below: Aerial view and plan of the basilica.
Opposite page: General view and plan of the synagogue.

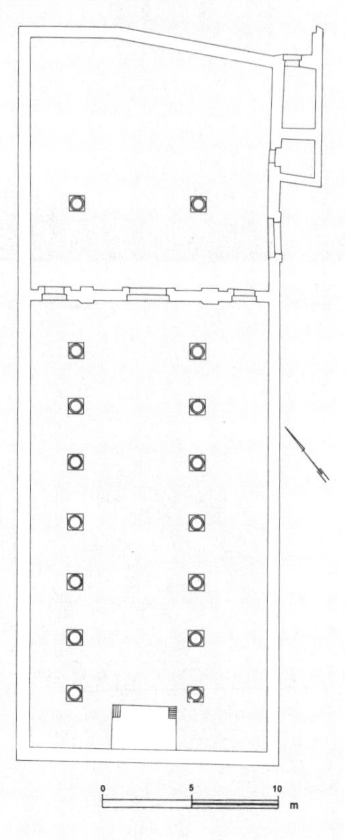

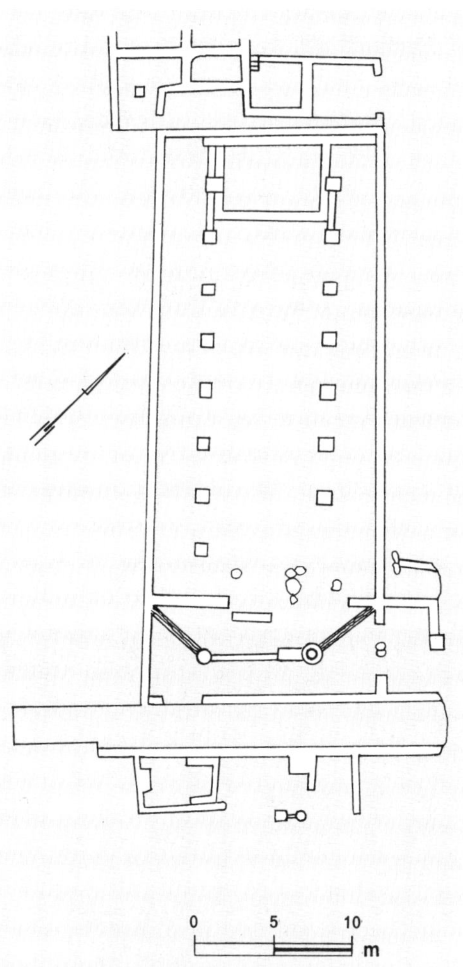

arcosolia, loculi, and troughs, angle irons and nails were found — the remains of wooden coffins. The manner of burial in Beth She'arim corresponds closely to descriptions in Talmudic literature, as, for example: "At first they used to bury them in arcosolia; when the flesh withered, they used to gather the bones and bury them in cedar-wood." (Palestinian Talmud, *Mo'ed Qatan* 81, 3–4). "An emptied coffin should not be reused. If it was made of stone or pottery, it should be broken; if it was made of wood, it should be burned." (*Masekhet Semaḥot,* 13).

The Elaborate Catacombs and Their Contents. Most of the catacombs in Beth She'arim are similar in style. However, several are different in form, and a few are outstanding in their architecture and decoration. On the walls of catacombs 1–4 are many reliefs, carvings, painted or incised pictures, and inscriptions — carved, incised, or painted in color. The decorations, which are mostly clumsy in character, reveal the Jewish style of popular art in the Roman period. The style was rooted in the artistic tradition of the Near East but was also greatly influenced by Hellenistic art. Of particular interest are the Jewish symbolic motifs, the main one being the seven-branched menorah and the ritual objects accompanying it, such as the lulab, ethrog, shofar, and incense shovel. All of these are common, conventional motifs in Jewish art.

Another common subject was the Ark of the Law, sometimes pictured within a niche and with a menorah on either side. Among the other motifs, the most frequent are geometrical designs, depictions of men, animals, and boats, and architectural designs such as an arched gate or a column with a capital.

The mausoleum adjoining catacomb 11 is of special interest from the point of view of architectural art. It is dated to the beginning of the third century. This memorial is built of ashlars, with four façades. In one of the façades is a large niche with complicated architectural ornaments, the most important of them being an animal frieze of which only fragments have been preserved. Among the ruins of the mausoleum, a large fragment of a marble sarcophagus was discovered with the relief of Leda and the Swan pictured on a short side, Achilles in Scyrus on a long side. Among the many fragments of a marble tablet, one was found on which there was carved an epitaph on one Justus (mentioned above).

On the northern slopes of Beth She'arim, catacombs 14 and 20 are the most noteworthy. Both have large courtyards, and in their façades both have three arches cut out of the rock. In catacomb 20 there are three entrances — one for each arch — and the central entrance has a double door. The large burial hall of catacomb 14 is of particular importance because of the Hebrew inscriptions

Catacomb 4. Ark of the Law in relief.

Catacomb 3. Menorah relief. Near it is the Greek inscription: "Be strong Esther, also called Amphaitha."

contained there. These mention Rabbi Simon, Rabbi Gamaliel, and Rabbi Anina (Ḥanina). It is quite possible that these are the very men whom Patriarch Judah I referred to before his death: "Simon my son shall be *ḥakham* [president of the Sanhedrin], Gamaliel my son Patriarch, Ḥanina bar Ḥama shall preside over the great court" (Babylonian Talmud, *Ketubbot* 103b). It is not improbable that this burial vault belonged to the patriarchal family. It may even be conjectured that the built tomb in the back room is the grave of Patriarch Judah I himself.

Catacomb 20 is the most important one discovered in Beth She'arim up to the present. It is certainly the largest, with over 130 limestone sarcophagi

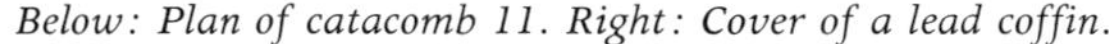

Below: Plan of catacomb 11. Right: Cover of a lead coffin.

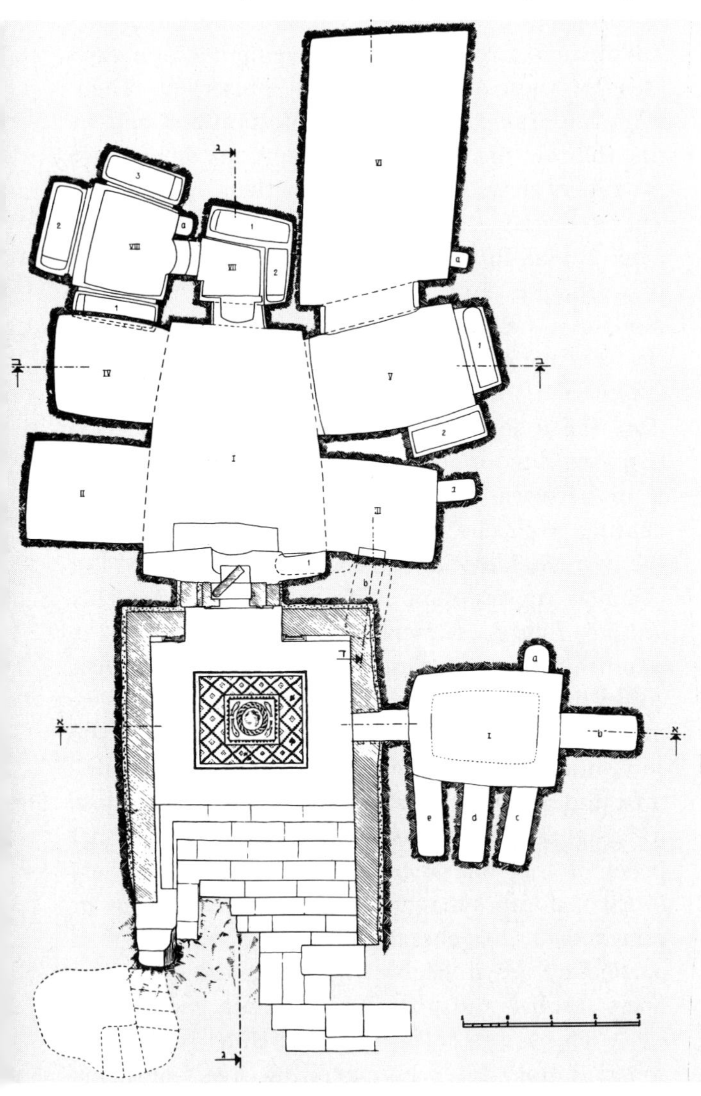

The Mausoleum above catacomb 11.
Above: Carved arch showing (left to right) fighting wolves, an eagle, lions hunting.
Below: Restored façade.
Opposite page: Plan and section of catacomb 13.

found, as well as innumerable fragments of marble sarcophagi. Three entrances lead into a hall (50 meters long); the hall was provided with extensions on either side. The hall and side rooms are full of stone sarcophagi (average length 2.5 meters). Most of these coffins are well preserved. Their main importance lies in their decorations and in the Hebrew inscriptions. There is no doubt that prominent Jews were buried in them.

The decorative motifs were generally borrowed from Roman funerary art and adapted to the style of a school of local craftsmen. The most prevalent motifs are the hanging wreaths, the heraldic eagles, the schematic heads of bulls, *tabula ansata,* and a symbolic Jewish motif — the menorah. In addition, the following motifs were noteworthy: two lions standing opposite each other, a vase or bull's head between them; a hunting scene of a lion chasing a gazelle; a bearded figure in relief on the narrow side of one of the coffins, similar to the common representation of the Greek gods. This unique figure is merely decorative, but it is astonishing that it should be found on a Jewish coffin buried alongside the tombs of rabbis.

Such coffins prove the tolerant attitude of the Jewish leaders of those days with regard to sculpture and figurative art, which by then had lost its original idolatrous connotations. Additional proof of that tolerance is revealed by the reliefs in the Galilean synagogues. All the inscriptions in catacomb 20 in general, and on the sarcophagi in particular, are in Hebrew. Among the deceased, many rabbis and their families are mentioned, *e.g.,* "This is the coffin of Rabbi Hillel [Halil], the son of Rabbi Levi, who made this cave," or "This

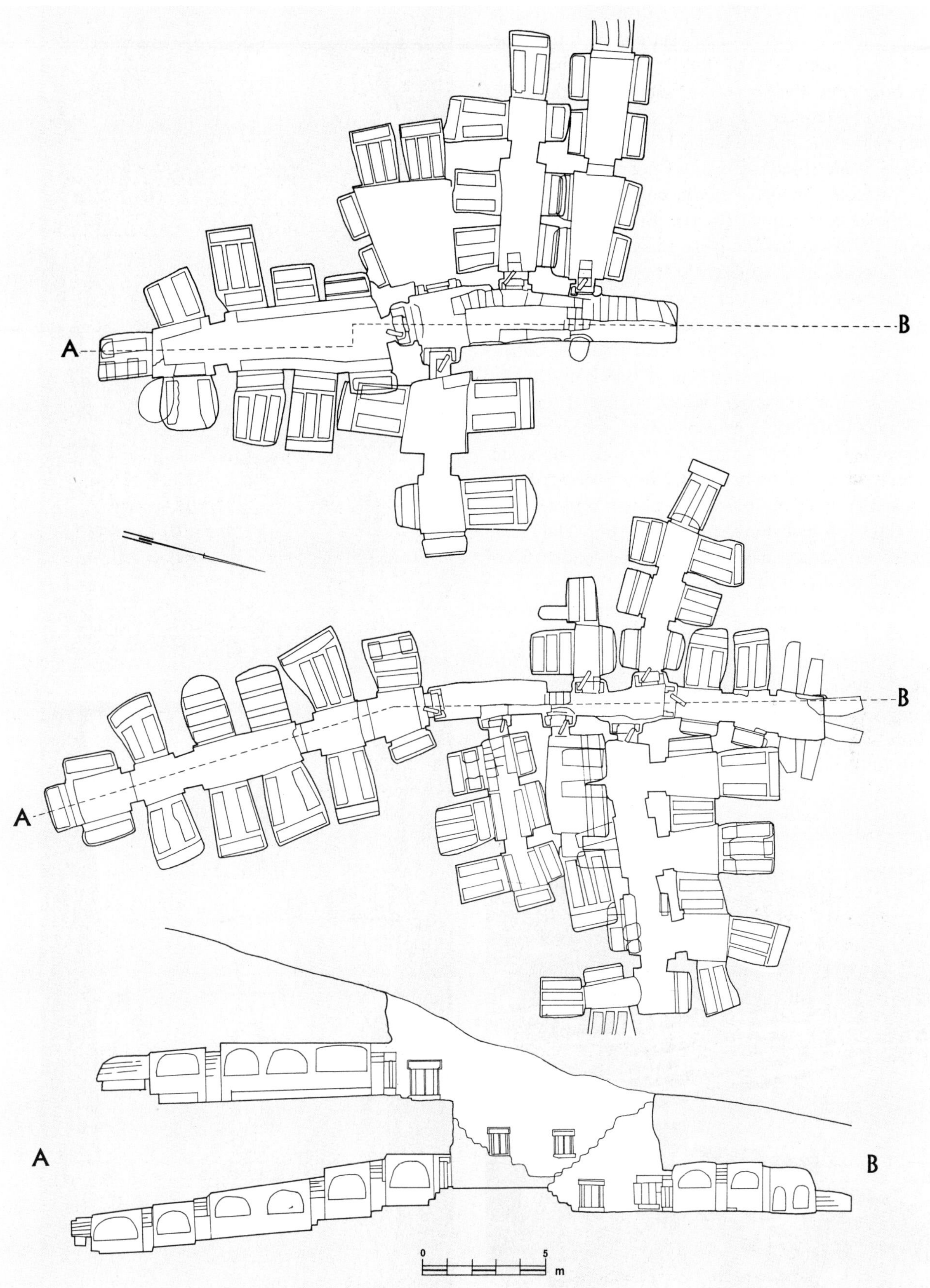
A
B
A
B
A
B
0
5
m

is the coffin of Kyra Mega, the wife of Rabbi Joshua, son of Levi, *Shalom*," "These sarcophagi, the inner and the outer, are of Rabbi Aniana and of... the holy ones, the sons of...," or "This is the coffin of...the daughter of Rabbi Joshua. [May] the memory of the just be blessed." In addition to the locally made stone coffins, the excavators found in this catacomb imported marble coffins with carvings of human and animal figures, in a purely Roman style. All those coffins were smashed in the Early Arab period, and apparently the marble was sold as raw material. Piles of fragments of figures and chips of marble are the main remnants of those sarcophagi. The fragments reveal that the coffins were decorated with scenes from Greek mythology —*e.g.*, "the Amazonomachy." (For a similar mythological motif in mausoleum 11, see above.)

Above catacombs 14 and 20 were open-air structures surrounded by benches. They were apparently used as assembly places for prayer and sermons on days of mourning and memorial. They also added architectural splendor to the landscape of the necropolis.

The structure above catacomb 20 is approximately square (22 by 18 meters). On its northern, narrow side, toward the courtyard, it has a balustrade. On the other three sides it is surrounded by walls, alongside which are rows of stone benches. A niche was located in the middle of the southern wall (directed toward Jerusalem).

Below: Benches in the structure above catacomb 20.
Right: The mask and eagle sarcophagi; catacomb 20.

Catacomb 20. Stone sarcophagi in hall 8. Bottom: The shell sarcophagus.

A group of separate graves, unique at this site, was discovered on the northern slope of Beth She'arim, west of the upper structure of catacomb 20, and near the surface. Some were quarried in the rock as rectangular shafts; others were built of stone slabs in the shape of a box. These graves were covered with layers of stones placed one above the other or arranged in the form of a gable. Lead coffins were discovered in these graves, decorated with reliefs common on such coffins in the Roman period. It is likely that they were brought here from one of the Phoenician cities, where such coffins were mass-produced. On two of them, traditional Jewish symbols were added: the menorah, lulab, ethrog, shofar, and incense shovel.

Funerary Inscriptions. The Greek inscriptions in the Beth She'arim cemetery are more numerous than the Hebrew ones. Those in Palmyrene and Aramaic are scarce. The short inscriptions mention the name and burial place of the deceased, and some add a sentiment, such as "Peace" or "Alas" in Hebrew. The considerable number of longer inscriptions were written mainly on the walls of the burial chambers and on marble tablets. In them are given the lineage, description, and occupation of the deceased, and conventional formulas like the Hebrew inscription on a marble tablet: "This grave is of Rabbi Isaac son of Moqim. *Shalom.*" The following are examples of a few of the Hebrew inscriptions on the walls of the burial chambers: "This is the resting place of Yudan, son of Levi, forever in peace. May his resting place be [set?] in peace. Of Yudan, son of Levi." "This place belongs to priests. Alas."

Examples of the Greek inscriptions are thus: "This is the grave of Leontios, the goldsmith, father of Rabbi Paregorios and Julianos, the *palatinus*" (on a marble slab), or "Benjamin, the son of Julios, the textile merchant, son of the most excellent Makrobios," or "We [are the sons] of Leontios from Palmyra, the banker," or "The tomb of Aidesios, head of the council of elders, from Antiochia" (on the wall of a burial chamber). A Palmyrene inscription reads: "The burial hall of Thyme, of the family of Amase." An Aramaic

From top to bottom: Catacomb 20; the gate, the lion, and the eagle sarcophagi. Opposite page, top: Fragment from sarcophagus showing Leda and the Swan. Bottom: Sculptured fragments of marble sarcophagi; part of an Amazonomachy.

Top to bottom: Catacomb 20: "These sarcophagi, the inner and the outer, are of Rabbi Aniana and of...the holy ones, the sons of..." Aramaic epitaph from catacomb 12 about Shim'on son of Yohanan. Mugharet el Jehannum; graffito of a boat.

inscription: "He who is buried here is Shim'on the son of Yoḥanan, and on oath, whoever shall open upon him shall die of an evil end."

A marble tablet with Jewish symbols and a Greek epitaph runs as follows:

This tomb contains the mortal remains of noble Karteria
but it preserves forever her immortal memory.
Zenobia brought her here for burial,
fulfilling thus her mother's behest.
For you, most blessed of women, your offspring,
whom you bore from your gentle womb, your pious daughter,
for she always does actions praiseworthy in the eyes of mortals,
erected this monument so that even after the end of life's term
you may both enjoy again new indestructible riches.

Such inscriptions are evidence of a belief in the resurrection of the dead.

Other finds. All the catacombs in Beth She'arim were broken into and looted by grave robbers in later periods. Of all the graves and coffins, a few only escaped destruction and were found intact. From these the excavators derived much information about the burial customs of the period. The objects left in graves include jewelry, pottery, glass vessels, and coins. Such objects were not always placed in the tombs and on many occasions only bones of the deceased were found.

SUMMARY

The reconstruction of the history of the cemetery at Beth She'arim, especially the catacombs, is fraught with difficulty. Nevertheless, a general picture is revealed by the architectural, epigraphic, and other types of finds. Accordingly, it is possible to trace the various phases of the evolution of public and private catacombs, their enlargement, and the changes that took place in them in the course of generations.

Only a few graves are from the Herodian period and the second century. The quarrying of the graves and the building of the magnificent catacombs and mausoleums began, without doubt, in the period of Patriarch Judah I. From his time onward, prominent Jewish families from the Land of Israel and from the Diaspora would bring their dead to Beth She'arim for burial. This custom continued without interruption until the Jewish revolt suppressed by Gallus Caesar in 351. After this date, the burials in Beth She'arim decreased greatly, then ceased altogether in the Byzantine period.

The excavations at Beth She'arim have vastly increased our knowledge of Jewish architecture and art in the period of the Mishnah and the Talmud, known heretofore mainly from the synagogues in Palestine and neighboring countries, and from the catacombs in Rome. Much new knowledge of burial practices was obtained, as well as of Judeo-Greek, Hebrew, and Aramaic epigraphy. The new finds in all these fields are a considerable contribution to Talmudic research and to that of the social, religious, and economic aspects of the period of the Mishnah and the Talmud.

N. AVIGAD AND B. MAZAR

BIBLIOGRAPHY

The Excavations: B. Mazar, *BJPES* 4 (1937), 79–82, 117–18; 5 (1938), 49–71; 6 (1939), 101–03; 9 (1942), 5–20; *idem, Kedem* 1 (1940), 66–76 (all Hebrew) • N. Avigad, *IEJ* 4 (1954), 88–107; 5 (1955), 205–39; 7 (1957), 73–92, 239–55; 9 (1959), 205–20; *idem, EI* 4 (1957), 85–103; 5 (1959), 171–88; 6 (1961), 61–67 (Hebrew) • B. Mazar, *BIES* 21 (1957), 153–64; *idem, Beth She'arim, Report on the Excavations During 1936–40,* (Vol. I), New Brunswick, 1973 • N. Avigad, *Beth She'arim* III, Jerusalem, 1971 (Hebrew).

The Inscriptions: M. Schwabe, *IEJ* 4 (1954), 249–61 • M. Schwabe and B. Lipshitz, *Beth She'arim. Greek Inscriptions* (Vol. II), New Brunswick (in press).

Below: Catacomb 18; epitaph of Karteria, set up by her daughter. Bottom: Mausoleum above catacomb 11; epitaph of Justus in which Besara is mentioned.

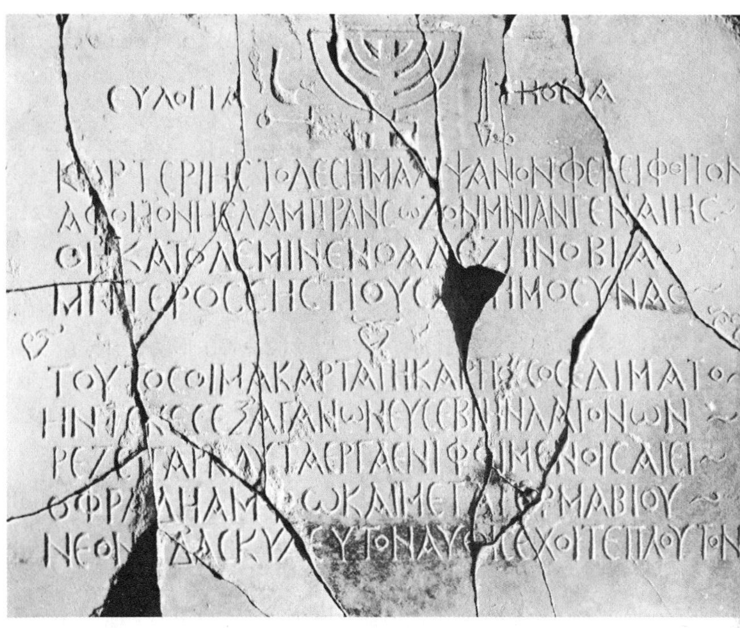

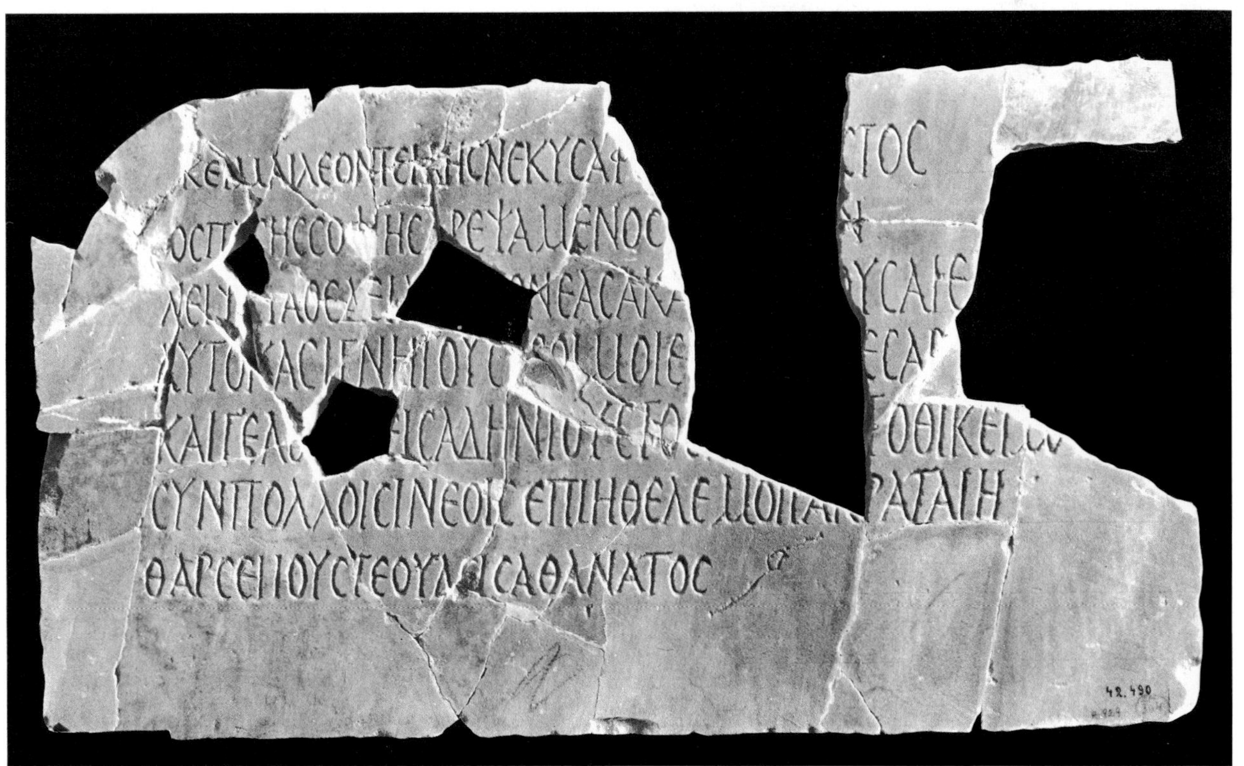

BETH-SHEMESH

IDENTIFICATION AND HISTORY. A city in the northeastern Shephelah (Lowland), Tel Beth-Shemesh is near the modern city of Beth-Shemesh, 20 kilometers (12½ miles) west of Jerusalem. The city was founded in the Middle Bronze Age and existed, with interruptions, until the Byzantine period. Except for the Bible, it is not mentioned in ancient documents. Its name is apparently of Canaanite origin and is meant to designate a city where there was once a temple to the sun god. It is called *'Ir-shemesh,* "City of Sun" in Joshua 19:41.

Other biblical references indicate that it was located near Zorah, Eshtaol, and Ekron (I Samuel 6:9, etc.). Eusebius identifies it (Bethsamis) with a site 10 miles from Eleutheropolis (Beth Govrin) in the direction of Nicopolis to "the east" (*Onomasticon* 54:11–13). Its name was preserved in the Arab village 'Ain Shems. E. Robinson identified the ancient site with Tell er-Rumeilah immediately west of 'Ain Shems, basing his theory on the above-mentioned evidence.

The mound stands on a long, flat ridge in the midst of the Valley of Sorek, 250 meters above sea level. The ridge is between two valleys: Sorek to the north and Illin to the south. These meet a short distance west of the site. The area of the ancient city on the summit was approximately 7 acres. Since the mound is not steep, rising only some 30 meters above the valleys, its eastern side was connected to the mountain range. Because it lacked an adequate water supply, it was not an easily defensible site.

Although between circa 1700 and 900 B.C. a fortified town was built there, it could never have been the center of a city-state in the Bronze Age. It was probably always a dependency of a larger city to the north, west, or south. During the tenth century it was a defensive outpost and provincial center in the Kingdom of Judah.

In Israel's tribal lists (Joshua 19:41), Beth-Shemesh is allotted to Dan, but is also appears on the northern boundary of Judah and as a Levitical city in Judah (Joshua 21:16). Whether the Danite list is a secondary compilation, as is frequently maintained, or an earlier list of towns from the twelfth century before the northward migration of the tribe of Dan (Judges 18), or an administrative list from the time of the United Monarchy, is a difficult and much debated issue. Strangely enouth, however, the Judean list of towns by provinces (Joshua 15:20 ff.) does not mention Beth-Shemesh, Zorah appearing in its place (verse 33).

The city was clearly Israelite in the tenth century B.C., when it appears in Solomon's second district (I Kings 4:9), and presumably also as early as the time of Samuel when the Ark was returned there from Philistia (I Samuel 6:9ff.). It is not mentioned as a site of importance in Israel's history after the tenth century. Rehoboam fortified Zorah instead of Beth-Shemesh (II Chronicles 11:10), although the town is mentioned as the scene of the battle between Joash of Israel and Amaziah of Judah (II Kings 14:11, II Chronicles 25:21).

During the reign of Ahaz, the Philistines seized the city from Judah (II Chronicles 28:18). This is the last biblical reference to the city. The Talmud describes it as the smallest village between Gabatha and Antipatris (Palestinian Talmud, *Megillah* 1, 70a, and parallels). Eusebius lists it as a small village.

Opposite page: Clay model of an axhead inscribed in Ugaritic. Below: Philistine jug and bowl. Bottom left: Potsherds with proto-Canaanite inscription; LBA. Bottom right: Libation bowl with zoomorphic decoration; LBA.

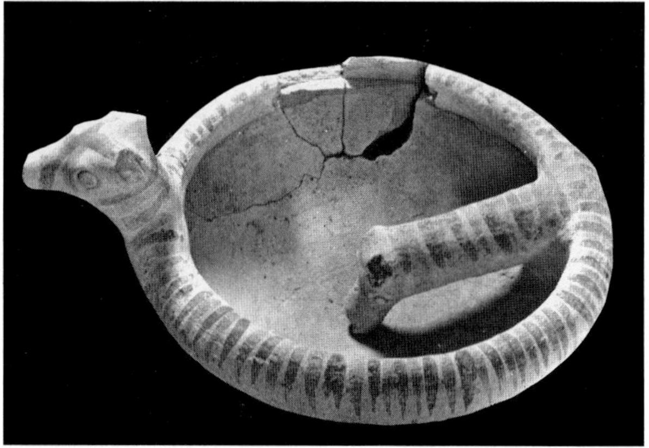

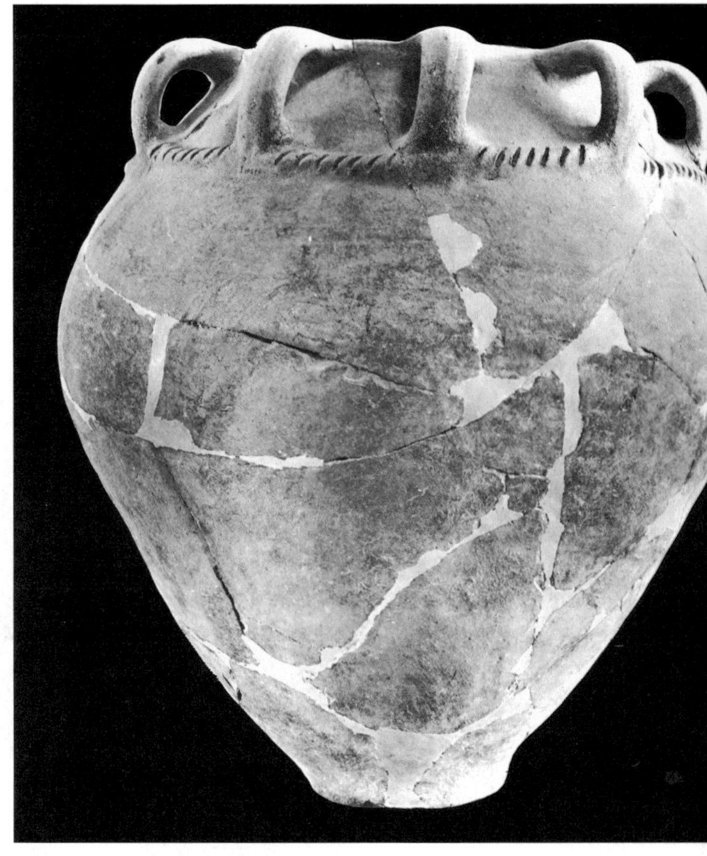

EXCAVATIONS

Beth-Shemesh was first excavated by D. Mackenzie for the Palestine Exploration Fund in 1911–12. A Bronze Age city wall was followed throughout its course around the city, and a city gate belonging to it, with three entries, was excavated on the south side of the mound. Four strata were distinguished. The earliest, from the Bronze Age, ended with the cessation of Mycenaean and Cypriote importations. The second stratum was characterized by Philistine ware, which Mackenzie was then able to identify as such and describe adequately for the first time. The city of this stratum was destroyed by a conflagration, which was the most conspicuous feature of every section through the mound. The third stratum was believed to contain two phases, the first interpreted as ending with the invasion of Sennacherib in 701 B.C., and the second as a reoccupation in the Late Israelite Period. The upper level of occupation consisted of a Byzantine monastery at the southeastern edge of the mound.

Five seasons of excavation by the Haverford College Expedition were conducted in 1928–31 and 1933, under the direction of E. Grant, assisted by C. S. Fisher and A. Rowe. The writer prepared a report of the work, *'Ain Shems Excavations,* Parts IV and V (Haverford, Pennsylvania, 1938–39), from such material and records as existed in Haverford College (now in the University Museum, Philadelphia).

Except for occasional Neolithic and Chalcolithic flint implements, which turned up in later contexts, the material found indicated that the earliest occupation of the site was during the Middle Bronze Age I. This material, together with shards of Middle Age II-A, was found on the rock surface or virgin soil, which were accorded the designation "stratum VI."

Stratum V was dated to the Hyksos period of Middle Bronze Age II-B and C (late eighteenth through the mid-sixteenth century). At this time a well-built city wall (circa 2.2 to 2.4 meters wide) was erected on bedrock around the summit of the city, the lowest course consisting of large boulders, some almost a meter in thickness. The upper part of the wall was built of brick, masses of which were encountered in excavation. The city gate of

From left to right: Tomb; Philistine horn-shaped vessel (with mirror reflection). Jar with nine handles. Burnished store jar; IA I.

three entries is a good, though comparatively small, example of the typical Bronze Age type.

Three towers were uncovered, one at the northeast, one at the west, and one at the southwest. They protected critical points in the fortifications, although at least one of them — that at the southwest — is a later addition, while the western one was rebuilt at least once after destruction.

Three tombs (numbers 9, 17, and 13), dating from the late eighteenth through the mid-seventeenth century, appear to antedate the city wall. Another tomb (number 12), from the seventeenth to sixteenth centuries, is perhaps contemporary with it. If so, then the wall was erected not before the middle or second half of the seventeenth century. It is very likely that the fortifications of Beth-Shemesh, as in other fortified cities of this period, included a glacis and a lower battered wall. However, insufficient work was done along the slopes to recover them. One fine house, erected against an offset in the western wall, was excavated.

In 1933 Rowe included in stratum V a few loci that contained bichrome ware of the early fifteenth century. This would mean that the destruction of the Middle Bronze Age city could not date much before circa 1500 B.C. at the very earliest. These loci, however, may well contain mixed material from strata V and IV-A. Indeed, it would now appear more likely that the end of stratum V occurred during the Egyptian reconquest of Palestine in the mid-sixteenth century, such a date being more in accord with the other pottery found in the stratum.

A most prosperous period in the city's history was that of stratum IV in the Late Bronze Age. Its debris reached nearly two meters in depth. Two phases were distinguished: one from the fifteenth and early fourteenth centuries, the other from the fourteenth to the thirteenth century. A large building was recovered in the second phase. One room contained two brick smelting furnaces with holes in the sides through which air could be forced into the fire by a blowpipe. Nearby was a furnace of a different type — long, narrow, and probably open. It was filled with ashes, and drops of crystallized slag adhered to the side walls.

In this period for the first time numerous cisterns were dug into the rock, with narrow necks built up through the debris to the occupation level. Each had a small depression in the center as a sump hole. The number of the cisterns is such that one must assume the invention of a hydraulic cement efficient enough to keep the water from seeping away through the rock.

The most interesting objects found in this stratum were a tablet written in Ugaritic cuneiform script, the signs being impressed on it backward, and an ostracon bearing letters in early Canaanite alphabetic script. Tombs 10 and 11 preserve a fine series of thirteenth-century pottery, which belongs to the end of stratum IV.

The city of stratum IV was destroyed at the end of the thirteenth or the beginning of the twelfth century, but the data are not sufficient to identify the destroyers. Two silos (numbers 515 and 530), contain transitional pottery of the period circa 1200 B.C. They are later than IV-B but earlier than stratum III, which was built over them. They suggest the same pre-Philistine phase of Iron Age I as Albright's Tell Beit Mirsim B-1. Hence, it may follow that stratum IV was destroyed in the late thirteenth century, presumably by the Israelites whose presence is represented by these silos.

Stratum III, with debris approximately 1 meter in depth, contains a fine collection of Philistine ware. The era of this stratum was a flourishing one for the town. The city wall on the west side had been breached but was repaired at this time. Although houses were built simply, one large residence with a courtyard was recovered. The furnaces for copper smelting found in stratum IV seem to have continued in use, and pieces of several ceramic blowpipes were recovered. As in the preceding stratum, cisterns were again found under private houses.

This evidence of prosperity, together with the city's geographical location and its quantity of Philistine pottery, suggest that it was under the political and economic domination of the Philistines, despite its Israelite population. Since we now know that during the second half of the eleventh century fine Philistine pottery ceased to be made, we must infer that the destruction that laid waste to the city occurred not later than the early part of the third quarter of the eleventh century. If so, then Beth-Shemesh may be assumed to have been destroyed with great violence by the Philistines shortly after their destruction of Shiloh and the subsequent removal of the Ark from Beth-Shemesh to Kirjath-Jearim (I Samuel 6:1–7:2). Large quantities of Philistine pottery were found because they were preserved within the thick layers of the debris of destruction.

The city of **Stratum II-A** dates from the early tenth century B.C., when the site was retaken by David. A casemate repair of the old city wall was found. The dimensions of walls and casemates were so close to those of Tell Beit Mirsim that one must presume the erection of both under common direction. A large residence for the district governor was built, and it was reused in subsequent periods. It has never been completely excavated. Southeast of the governor's residence was an even larger public granary, consisting of three long parallel rooms surrounded by well-built walls (1.5 to 1.75 meters thick). The residence is elevated and may have been built on a filling (millô?), as was the building of similar age and type at Lachish and the *millô* in Jerusalem.

Beth-Shemesh was without doubt a center for the provincial administration of Israel's United Monarchy, and the above-mentioned structures are evidence of that fact. A large stone-lined silo (diameter circa 7.5 meters on the north–south axis and 6.5 meters on the east–west) for grain storage was found east of the residence but within its precincts. It was plastered to a depth of circa 4 meters, but its base may have been deeper. Its size suggests public rather than private use, but whether this great silo was erected in II-A or II-B is unknown. At any rate, this construction, as well as the above-mentioned ones, is not common.

The excavated sections of stratum II-A indicate that it had been burned. The pottery of the stratum is similar to much of the pottery common in the destruction layers of stratum III, and it seems to precede that part of the tenth century when chordal and spiral burnishing of red-slipped bowls had become the usual decoration. Consequently, the writer dated the brief interruption in the city's life at the end of II-A to either late in the reign of David or early in that of Solomon (circa 975–940 B.C.); that is, before the end of Tell Beit Mirsim B-3 and the invasion of Shishak (circa 924 B.C.). Only further excavation with new methods of digging can determine whether this conclusion is correct.

Strata II-B and II-C are identified by the writer's artificial separation of the pottery without clear architectural correlation. After the tenth century the site was an unfortified village. The building remains of the seventh century are so incoherent and eroded that little can be made of them. Quantities of pottery from the end of the Iron Age II suggest, however, that the site was destroyed in the Babylonian conquest of Judah. Houses of the period between the tenth and eighth centuries were published as belonging to one level.

On the western side, the town's outline, established in the time of stratum II-A and continued subsequently, shows houses built around the edge of the mound and facing inward upon a street that turned in a large semicircle within the occupied area. Evidences of reconstruction were plentiful in the houses, but the buildings cannot now be dated. From the 1933 expedition, large numbers of shards from the late tenth or early ninth century were recovered, but almost nothing was found that can be dated to the ninth century. This may indicate that the city was destroyed in Shishak's invasion (circa 924 B.C.).

In any event, it is clear that Rehoboam did not consider the site sufficiently defensible to include among the Judean cities he fortified to protect the country. Instead he fortified Zorah (II Chronicles 11:10). However, the history of the city between circa 950 and 587 B.C. cannot be reconstructed from the remains found in the excavation. Copper working continued, vats for the olive oil and dyeing industries, and large numbers of grape presses were discovered. The most important activity was apparently the making of wine.

Stratum I was the designation of a variety of late materials including second-century B.C. coins as well as Roman, Byzantine, and medieval pottery.

A fine series of tombs from the period of stratum II were excavated by Mackenzie. Tomb 1 is the earliest, from the tenth century B.C. The others belong to the eighth/seventh centuries and are excellent examples of late Judean tombs. They consist of a room in the slope of the rock, entered by a square-cut door with steps leading down into it. On three sides are benches for the burials. At the rear a pit or repository was dug, perhaps to store older bones when new burials were made. The entrance was sealed by a stone plug, its edges carefully rabbeted to fit snugly. The uncommon feature of the main series of these tombs is that they form a coherent family group opening around a central area. The usual number of eighth/seventh century seals and royal stamped jar handles was found in the town. Of special interest was the stamped handle with the inscription *l'lyqm (n)'r ywkn,* "Belonging to Eliakim, Steward *(na'ar)* of Jehoiachin *(Yawkin).*" It was stamped with the same seal as two stamped handles found by Albright at Tell Beit Mirsim.

G. ERNEST WRIGHT

BIBLIOGRAPHY

Identification and history of the site: N. Avigad, *Enc. Miqr.* 2, 100–18 (includes bibliography) • Robinson, *Biblical Researches* 2, 224 • F.M. Cross Jr.–G.E. Wright, *JBL* 75 (1956), 202–26 • Y. Aharoni, *BASOR* 154 (1959), 35–39 • W.F. Albright, *ibid.* 173 (1964), 51–53.

Excavation reports: D. Mackenzie, *APEF* 1 (1911), 41–94; 2 (1912–13), *passim* • E. Grant, *Beth Shemesh, A Report of the Excavations Made in 1928,* Haverford, 1929; *idem, Ain Shems Excavations* 1–2, Haverford, 1931–32; *idem, Rumeileh,* Haverford, 1934 • E. Grant–G.E. Wright, *Ain Shems Excavations* 4–5, Haverford, 1938–39.

BETH YERAḤ

IDENTIFICATION. Tel Beth Yeraḥ (known also by its Arabic name, Khirbet el-Kerak) covers an area of approximately 50 acres along the southwestern shore of the Sea of Galilee. The western boundary of the mound is the old bed of the Jordan River. The southern boundary is the issue of Jordan from the Sea of Galilee. The suggestion that Khirbet el-Kerak be identified with Beth Yeraḥ or Talmudic Ariaḥ was made in the nineteenth century. Some authorities have identified the site with the Philoteria built by Ptolemy II Philadelphus. Others have suggested identifying it with Sinnabri, mentioned by Josephus as the northernmost border point of the Jordan Valley and the camping ground of Vespasian's army (*War* III, 447, IV, 455). In Talmudic literature, Beth Yeraḥ is frequently mentioned as a mixed settlement of foreigners and Jews near Sinnabri.

EXCAVATIONS (HISTORY)

In surveys prior to the excavations, it had become clear that the site was settled in the Early Bronze Age, and from the Hellenistic to the Arab periods. A special kind of Early Bronze Age pottery first discovered here was named by W.F. Albright Khirbet Kerak ware. The typical features of this ware are red and black burnish, and incised or ribbed decoration. Since the discovery of this ware at Beth Yeraḥ, similar pottery has been found at many other sites in Palestine and northern Syria. Its style attests that this ware apparently originated in Anatolia.

The first excavations at Beth Yeraḥ were carried out by the Jewish Palestine Exploration Society in 1944–45 under the direction of B. Mazar (Maisler), M. Stekelis, and I. Dunayevsky. The expedition excavated an area in the south of the mound. In 1945–46 M. Stekelis, M. Avi-Yonah, and I. Dunayevsky continued work in the south and began excavating in the north of the mound.

Excavations since 1949 have been carried out in the northern part of the site by the Department of Antiquities, at first under the direction of P.L.O. Guy and later under P. Bar-Adon. More extensive excavations in the south of the mound and soundings in various places in the center and western part were directed by P. Bar-Adon (1949–55). In

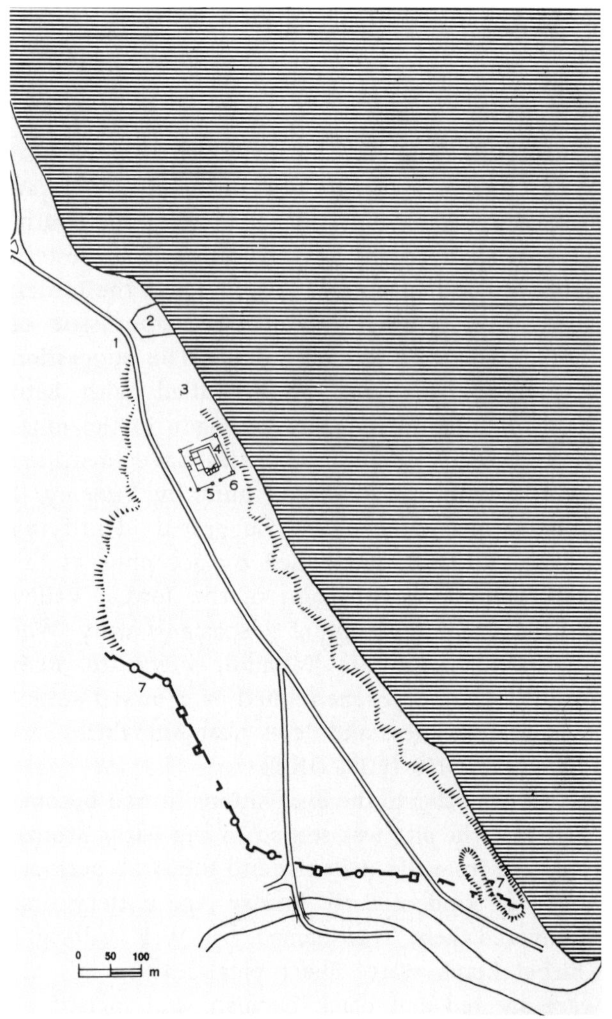

General plan. 1. Remains of the Roman-Byzantine bridge. 2. Modern cemetery. 3. Byzantine church. 4. Synagogue and fortress. 5. EBA building. 6. Late Roman therms. 7. Hellenistic city wall.

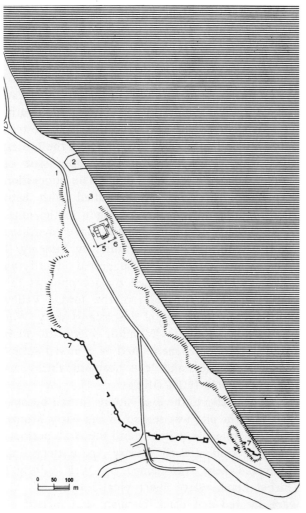

the course of the latter excavations, residential districts were exposed, and the lines of the different city walls were examined. In 1952–53, 1963–64, additional excavations and soundings were undertaken by the Oriental Institute of the University of Chicago under the direction of P. Delougaz, in the later seasons assisted by Helene Cantor. The work was concentrated mainly in the northern part of the mound and, to some extent, in the center.

Fortifications of the City. The city walls in the different periods were built in the southwestern and southern sides of the mound. On the east, the Sea of Galilee offered a natural defense. The Jordan, which flowed in its old bed until much later (at least till the Middle Ages), formed a natural protecting border on the north and west of the mound.

The first fortifications are attributed to the beginning of the Early Bronze Age. Six phases were distinguished by P. Bar-Adon. In the south of the mound was discovered part of a wall running east–west. The wall (up to 8 meters wide) was built of mud brick in three adjoining sections. Two superimposed gates were exposed. The door jambs of these gates were made of basalt, and the stepped paths that descended into the city from the west were also paved with basalt. Outside the gate, but close to it, were a group of upright basalt stones (perhaps tombstones), which are assigned to the early phase of the wall. Within the gate were two

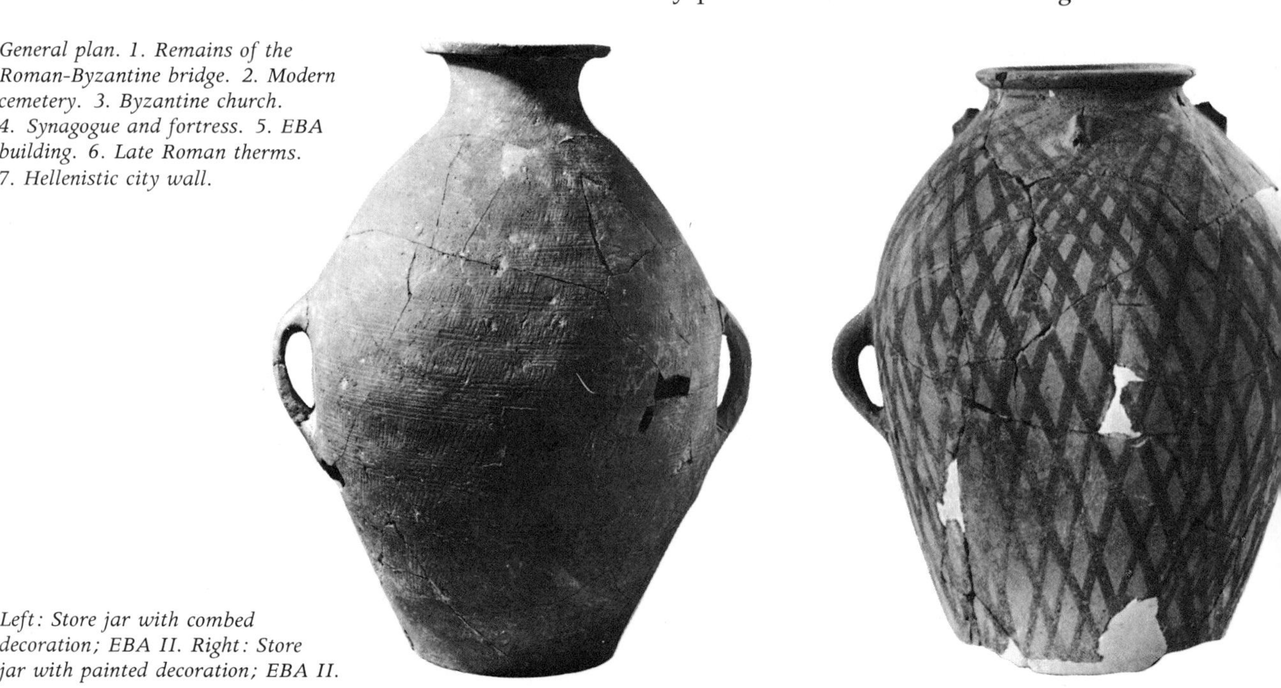

Left: Store jar with combed decoration; EBA II. Right: Store jar with painted decoration; EBA II.

guardrooms dated to a later phase. Remains of early fortifications have been preserved from all phases of the Early Bronze Age to the Middle Bronze Age I. From the Hellenistic period, 1,300 meters of city wall were discovered. Adding the other parts found so far, the total length was likely to have been 1,600 meters. The wall follows the western and southern borders of the mound and is constructed on a huge basalt foundation, topped by a brick wall of which only a few courses remain. The wall was built in sections contiguous to each other. It was fortified with outward-jutting, alternating square and round towers.

Southern Section of the Mound. Early Bronze Age. In the south of the mound, remains of the Early Bronze Age were exposed under the Hellenistic stratum, with only a thin layer of earth separating them. Along the fortification wall the excavators reached virgin soil at a depth of 7.3 meters. The four phases of the Early Bronze Age could be distinguished. They were named Beth Yeraḥ I–IV.

BETH YERAḤ I. The inhabitants of the earliest settlement did not live in houses but in roofed-over pits (circa .5 to 3.5 meters in depth, 3 to 4 meters in diameter). Remains of ashes, shards, and animal bones were found in them. The shards are of the gray-burnished type.

BETH YERAḤ II. For the first time, rectangular houses with mud-brick walls were found in this

Selection of Khirbet-Kerak ware; EBA III.

stratum. Remains of a courtyard paved with basalt slabs were discovered, as well as corners of rooms. The pottery is characterized by red burnishing and band slips. It includes hole-mouth vessels and ledge handles. A tournette for making pottery was also found.

BETH YERAḤ III. In this stratum the walls of the houses are built on basalt foundations of one or two courses. No Khirbet Kerak ware was found, and on the basis of the pottery Beth Yeraḥ III has been assigned to Early Bronze Age II. The city wall built of mud brick has been attributed to the same period. On the floor of one of the houses with mud brick walls several jars stood undisturbed; they were similar in style to the jars in a grave at Kinneret (q.v. Volume III). A cylinder-seal impression was also discovered.

BETH YERAḤ IV. The settlement of this period had a longer life than its predecessors. Four phases are distinguished in the approximately two-meter-thick stratum. Most of the houses are built of basalt, with only a few of mud brick on a basalt foundation. A building measuring 7 by 8 meters and oriented north–south was uncovered. Aside from the large amount of pottery, five figurines of animals were discovered, two pottery models of houses, and the fragment of a pottery figure of a roaring lion. Among the flint tools, the knife blades are noteworthy. The pottery of Beth Yeraḥ IV is dated to Early Bronze Age III, and Khirbet Kerak ware is abundant.

Ivory bull head; EBA III.

Southeastern Part. In the southeastern part of the mound, P. Bar-Adon made a ten-square-meter sounding down to virgin soil. The large occupational gap is of shorther duration than that previously found in the excavation in the south of the mound. Here, twenty-three phases were distinguished: four phases of Early Bronze Age I (including an apsidal house); five of Early Bronze Age II (brick walls, a paved street, and traces of drainage); six from Early Bronze Age III, including a conflagration layer; three phases of Middle Bronze Age I, including a potter's workshop; and a grave from Middle Bronze Age II. A stratum from the Persian period, not uncovered on the mound until then, was also found.

HELLENISTIC REMAINS. Part of one of the Hellenistic quarters of the city was uncovered in the southern section of the mound. Several building complexes were discovered on either side of a street running southeast–northwest. The largest of these buildings is a spacious residence with a courtyard paved with river pebbles. The court is enclosed on three sides by eleven rooms. According to the pottery (Rhodian jars) and the coins, it dates to the Ptolemaic period.

Bar-Adon found additional Hellenistic houses. A few were preserved up to the level of the windows, which looked out east to the Sea of Galilee. The walls of one of the houses was ornamented with colored plaster, imitating black, red, and green marble veneering.

The Roman period is represented in the southern part of the mound by sections of a large building, of which a corner of the outer walls remains.

The Northern Section of the Mound

THE BUILDING WITH THE CIRCLES. On the northern side of the mound was discovered a large rectangular building (30 by 40 meters), dating from Early Bronze Age III. The building was constructed

Beth Yeraḥ; Khirbet Kerak bowl; EBA II.

of basalt rubble, and its entrance on the east overlooked the Sea of Galilee. The northeastern section was damaged by a Roman-Byzantine bath constructed above it. The building consisted of a broad wall on top of which were stone circles, which had been sunk 10 centimeters below the level of the pavement. There were four circles along the southern wall, three along the western wall, and two along the northern wall. The edge of another circle is visible near the entrance on the eastern wall, and there were probably another two circles along the northern wall: twelve circles altogether.

The interior of each circle was divided by four stone partitions. These started from the perimeter and were built toward the center of the circle, but stopped short of it. From the entrance of the building on the east, a corridor led to an inner court paved with stone slabs. In the southern wall of the courtyard, a threshold was found and steps leading to the area between two circles. Near the threshold, a clay oven was discovered. In the northwestern corner of the court was another oven. A third oven, cleared in the middle of the court, contained small bowls and Khirbet Kerak ware. An apparently roofed-over area ran along the length of the west side of the court.

A paved street extended around the building on the south, west, and north sides (and perhaps also on the east). From the north side it descended stepwise eastward to the sea.

This building was probably a public granary, its plan being similar to a stone model discovered on the island of Melos.

ROMAN PERIOD. The Fort and the Synagogue. North of the building with the circles was discovered a large, square Roman fort (60 by 60 meters), with square towers at its corners. The main gate was in the middle of the southern wall. It was flanked by towers similar to the corner towers. The foundation of the fort consisted of a rubble fill faced with large, smoothly dressed stones on the outside and smaller stones on the inside.

Within the area of the Roman fort, Guy and Bar-Adon uncovered the remains of the foundations of a synagogue (22 by 37 meters). The building was divided by two rows of columns into a nave and two aisles. There was an apse in the middle of the southern wall, oriented to Jerusalem. The nave was paved with a colored mosaic, partially preserved, depicting plants, birds, lions, etc. On the base of a column were carved a menorah, lulab, ethrog, and incense shovel. Several rooms, unearthed south and west of the synagogue, were undoubtedly for public use. In the same area, a branching water and drainage system was brought to light.

THE ROMAN BATH HOUSE. In the north of the mound a Roman bath was discovered. The main

"Building with the circles"; EBA. Detail (left) and plan (right).

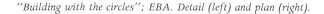

Opposite page: Drainage pipe of the Roman therms.

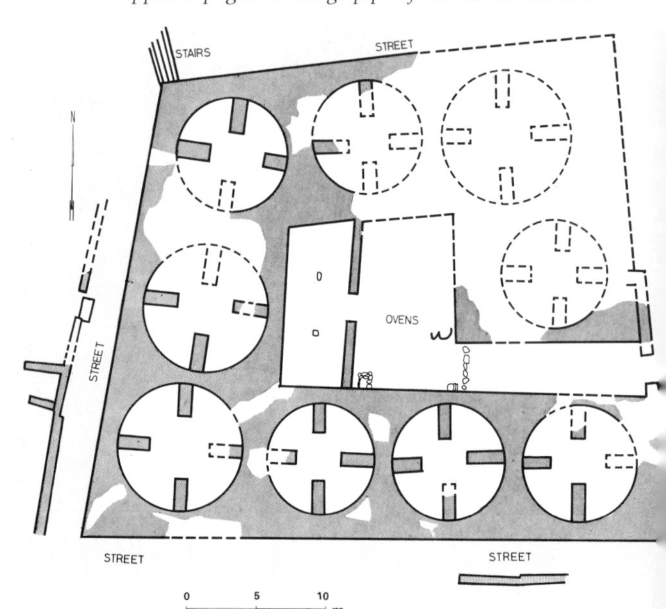

Late Roman therms; plan. Bottom: Pool in the center of the frigidarium.

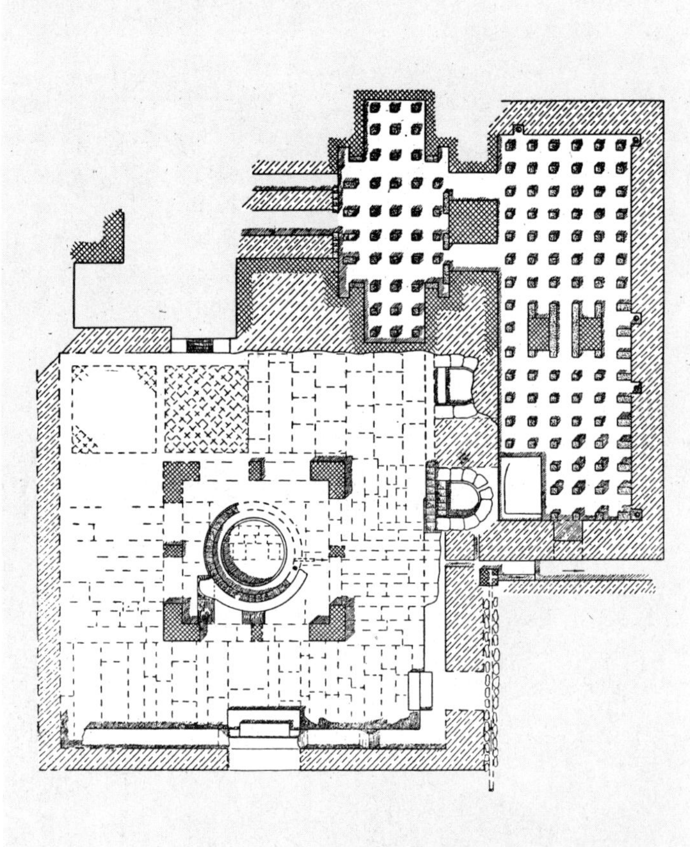

parts were a frigidarium, a tepidarium, a caldarium, the two latter built over a hypocaust. The frigidarium is almost square, the main entrance being from the west with another entrance from the east. It was once paved with marble flags and had a pool in the center with a roof supported by columns (some bases were discovered). The walls of the frigidarium were decorated with a colored and gilt mosaic. Benches were built along the western wall and at the western end of the southern wall. The southern wall and the southern part of the eastern wall were twice as thick as the other walls, for they separated the frigidarium from the caldarium and the tepidarium. Their function was to carry the weight of the arches and to insulate the heated rooms. Two bathtubs were found by the southern wall.

The cellar of the hypocaust was L-shaped. Its ceiling was supported by a series of posts and arches made of baked brick. Additional support was provided by several stone pillars. Clay pipes and apertures for hot air were found in the walls. One section of the floor of the hall above the hypocaust cellar was preserved. This floor was also paved with marble flags.

The caldarium was built above the short arm of the hypocaust cellar, and the tepidarium was built on the south side. The water for the bath was conveyed by clay pipes from the large aqueduct to the southwest, which ran from the Yavneel Valley (Wadi Fajjas) to Tiberias and branched off to Beth Yeraḥ.

THE BYZANTINE AND ARAB PERIODS. P. Delougaz and R. C. Haines of the Oriental Institute, University of Chicago, uncovered remains of a church in the north of the mound. During its existence the church was rebuilt, restored, and modified several times, and therefore had not been originally planned in the form in which it was found. The walls (.6 to 1.2 meters wide) were built of large, rough stones, with a fill of small stones. The church is a basilica, with a hall (domus — 11.5 by 12.5 meters) divided by two rows of columns into a nave and two aisles, terminating in three projecting apses. The floors were of varied material — pisé de terre, crude slabs of stone, and soft limestone. The atrium, the narthex, the halls, and the diaconicon were paved with mosaics decorated in floral and geometric designs. Only a few fragments have survived. Since the church buildings spread over the whole width of the mound, the entrance was placed in the south, not in the west as was customary. The entrance led to a kind of elongated porch south of the large courtyard. A large opening divided by two columns led from the porch to the rectangular courtyard (10.5 by 21 meters).

In the center of the apse, in the place of the altar, a recess for the reliquary was found.

The rectangular diaconicon (6.8 by 5.2 meters) is a later addition to the original building. Its floor and the apse in the eastern wall adjoining it were paved with a colored, geometric mosaic that contained a three-line Greek inscription laid in black tesserae. The inscription mentions the names of the donors and the date of its construction.

On the basis of the architectural evidence, C.H. Kraeling dated the construction of the original church to the first half of the fifth century A.D. According to the inscription in the diaconicon, the third (last) phase was built in A.D. 528–29, during the reign of Emperor Justinian I. The history of the church came to a close at the end of the sixth century or the beginning of the seventh.

An Arab building was discovered above the remains of the church. The building is entered from the west through an opening that leads through an elongated vestibule to a large inner courtyard. On the west and south side of the courtyard, a single row of rooms was built. An opening on the north of the courtyard leads to a row of rooms running northward the length of the

Late Roman therms; view from the east.

courtyard. Only a few of these rooms were excavated. To the east, three rows of long rooms were built, two rooms to each row. The walls were faced on both sides with large stones, with a fill of rubble and earth between. The corners and door jambs were built of well-dressed, squared stones. Five soundings were made around the church to examine the stratigraphy, but no important remains were discovered.

SUMMARY

Tel Beth Yeraḥ was settled from the beginning of the Early Bronze Age I to the Middle Bronze Age II, but the whole mound was apparently not occupied during this period. Remains of the Early Bronze Age III settlement were found in the north and south, but not in the center. The most important structure of this period is the "building with the circles." So far, remains of Middle Bronze Age I have been found only in the south of the mound. From Middle Bronze Age II only a grave was found in the south of the site. During the Bronze Age the site was fortified and surrounded by a wall. Settlement was renewed in the Persian period. The city expanded in the Hellenistic period. Among the remains from the Roman period, the fort is of special interest; and from the Byzantine period, the synagogue and the church. Beth Yeraḥ was also occupied in the Arab period.

RUTH HESTRIN

BIBLIOGRAPHY

History and identification of the site: L. Mayer, *IEJ* 2 (1952), 183–87 (includes bibliography) • P. Bar-Adon, *EI* 4 (1956), 50–55 (includes bibliography) (Hebrew).

Excavation reports: B. Maisler, M. Stekelis, M. Avi-Yonah, *IEJ* 2 (1952), 165–73, 218–29 • P. Bar-Adon, *ibid.* 3 (1953), 132; 4 (1954), 128–29; 5 (1955), 273 • P. Delougaz–R.C. Haines, *A Byzantine Church of Khirbat al-Karak*, Chicago, 1960.

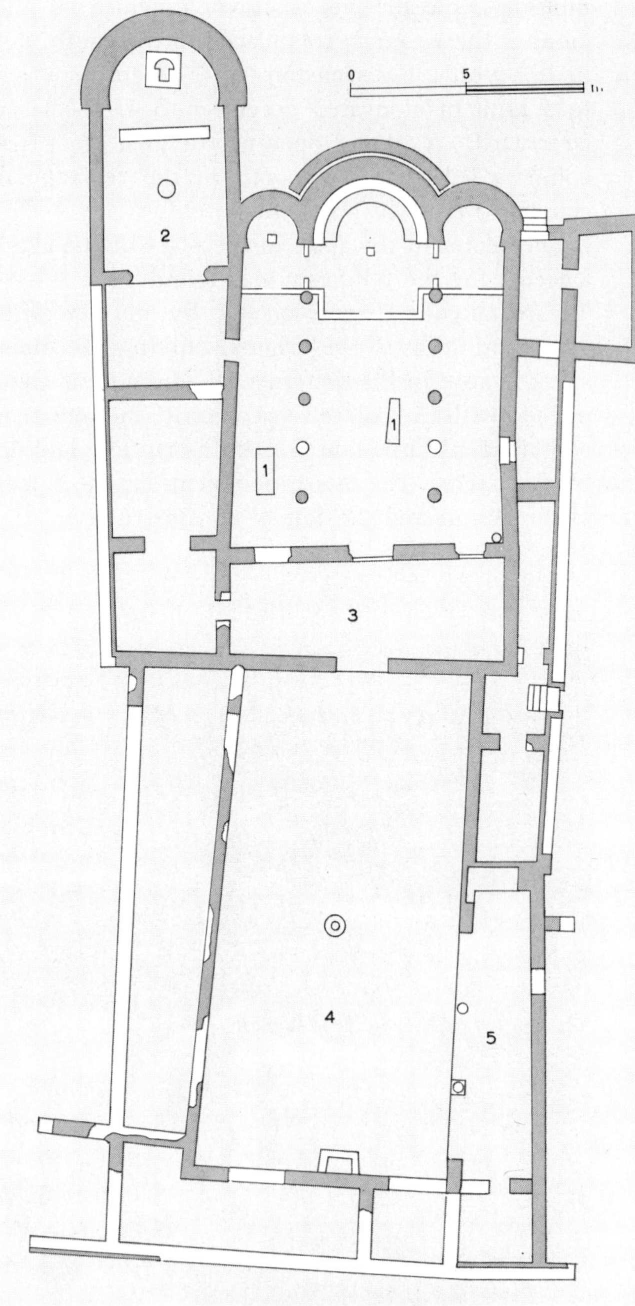

Plan of Byzantine church: 1. Tombs. 2. Diaconicon. 3. Narthex. 4. Atrium. 5. Portico. Below: Inscription in the mosaic floor of diaconicon mentioning donors and year of foundation (528/29).

BETH-ZUR

IDENTIFICATION. Beth-Zur was a city in Judah situated on the old Jerusalem–Hebron road, about 30 kilometers (20 miles) south of Jerusalem (II Maccabees 11:5, Eusebius, *Onomasticon* 52:2) and about 6 kilometers ($3\frac{1}{2}$ miles) north of Hebron, on the boundary between Judaea and Idumaea. It commanded not only the southern approach to Jerusalem but important routes to the Shephelah (Lowland). The name has been preserved at Khirbet Burj eṣ-Ṣur, but since this site exhibits only Byzantine and Arabic remains, W.F. Albright and O.R. Sellers proposed to identify it with adjacent Khirbet eṭ-Ṭubeiqah.

Khirbet eṭ-Ṭubeiqah is a natural conical hill (1,007 meters above sea level, one of the highest ancient sites in Palestine). It rises some 100 meters above the valley to the north, but only 22 meters above the valley to the south. To the east it slopes down gently to 'Ain edh-Dhirweh, where its nearest water supply lay. The hill was doubtless terraced in ancient times, as in the modern era, with the terraces providing differing street levels for the village. Its physical features lent themselves to the establishment of a citadel, which, when endowed with cisterns, reservoirs, and defensive walls, could serve as a bulwark for Jerusalem against incursions from the south.

HISTORY

Beth-Zur was occupied sporadically during the Early Bronze Age, but it did not become a stronghold until the Hyksos period (Middle Bronze Age II-B). Hyksos Beth-Zur was apparently destroyed in the Egyptian reconquest of Palestine, in the late sixteenth century, and it remained unoccupied for some three centuries.

Beth-Zur was rebuilt in the beginning of the Israelite period. According to II Chronicles 11:7, it was one of the cities in Judah fortified by Rehoboam. Beth-Zur also appears in a town list of the territory of Judah (Joshua 15:58 and I Chronicles 2:45), which some archaeologists date to the time of Josiah (Alt) and others, earlier, to the reign of Jehoshaphat (Wright and Cross). The archaeological evidence indicates that Beth-Zur was occupied during the eleventh century by the Israelites, who repaired the Hyksos fortifications. For some unknown reason the Iron Age I settlement came to an end circa 1000 B.C. Thereafter the hill was slowly resettled, but it was not until the second half of the seventh and beginning of the sixth century that an extensive and prosperous community had come into existence. This city came to an abrupt end with the invasion and conquest of the country by Nebuchadnezzar.

On the basis of the archaeological evidence it is difficult to account for the Chronicler's attribution of the rebuilding of Beth-Zur to Rehoboam, or for the town list in Joshua 15, if that indeed originated in the time of Jehoshaphat.

Beth-Zur was a district capital during the Persian period (Nehemiah 3:16) and is mentioned during the conflict between the Ptolemies and Seleucids (third century). It achieved its greatest importance as a citadel during the wars between the Maccabees and the Seleucids (second century), and is often mentioned in the first book of the Maccabees and by Josephus (I Maccabees 4:29, 6:7, 26, etc.). In 165 B.C. the Syrian regent Lysias was defeated by Judas Maccabaeus at Beth-Zur in an open field encounter. Beth-Zur, as yet unwalled (see below), played no direct part in the battle. Judas Maccabaeus rebuilt the old citadel in 165–163 and erected a wall around the town to provide a first line of defense. When Lysias returned in 163 for his second campaign, the city was already fortified, and it was conquered only after a long siege. Beth-Zur remained garrisoned by the Syrians until Simon recaptured it in 145–143. This put an end to the struggle over the city. With the disappearance of the Idumaean threat under John Hyrcanus, Beth-Zur lost its importance as a frontier citadel. Although a thriving town in the period 140–100 B.C., it was subsequently abandoned and never again occupied.

EXCAVATIONS (HISTORY AND RESULTS)

The first campaign at Beth-Zur took place in June–July, 1931, under the joint sponsorship of the Presbyterian (McCormick) Theological Seminary (Chicago) and the American Schools of Oriental Research. The excavations were directed by O.R. Sellers, with W.F. Albright as archaeological adviser.

It was not until 1957 that Sellers was able to organize a second campaign under the same sponsorship. H.N. Richardson served as archaeological adviser. The results of the 1957 excavations were published by the writer and by P. and N. Lapp, members of the expedition.

In the 1931 excavations nearly 8,000 square meters of the summit were cleared to bedrock (average depth of debris — 1 meter). A sizable portion of the city was thus exposed, although the shallowness of the debris, caused by the repeated abandonment of the site and quarrying on the part of Byzantine and Arab builders, prevented a precise stratification. The Hellenistic builders, moreover, had sunk their foundations at many points to bedrock, resulting in an almost incredible mixture of debris.

Three areas on the east side of the city were selected for excavation in 1957. Fields I and III on the northeast were intended to explore the city-wall system and, if possible, to locate stratified debris. (Field II on the southeast proved to lie outside the city wall altogether.) Although the 1957 campaign was modest in comparison with that of 1931, it had the good fortune of selecting areas for excavation that supplemented each other as well as the results of the earlier expedition.

Early Bronze Age. Pockets of Early Bronze Age shards, found scattered over bedrock, indicate that the hill was occupied sporadically in the third millennium B.C.

Middle Bronze Age. Beth-Zur appears to have been settled in the seventeenth century B.C., but its fortifications were not erected until the sixteenth

Aerial view of the site.

century B.C. They were repaired once, and were apparently enlarged at a later date. A massive city wall 2.5 meters thick surrounded the city. On the southwest side the wall was strengthened by a tower (5 by 10 meters). On the northeast side a series of inner guard or storage rooms was added, perhaps also to buttress the wall.

The wall is of typical Hyksos construction: huge stones, often polygonal, not laid in regular courses, and filled with smaller stones (cf. the nearly contemporary walls at Bethel, Tell Beit Mirsim, and Shechem). Other than the storage rooms, no buildings could be attributed to the Middle Bronze Age.

There is some evidence that the Middle Bronze Age city, from 8 to 15 dunams in size (the wall has not been traced on the north), suffered a violent destruction by fire at the close of the Hyksos period (circa 1550 B.C.).

Iron Age I. Remains of the Iron Age I settlement are concentrated for the most part on the north side of the hill. Numerous walls and piers of houses were attributed to this period in 1931. In 1957 it was discovered that during Iron Age I the city area had been reduced in size on the north and a new city wall built. The early Israelite city exhibits poor masonry, the reuse of earlier structures (for example, sections of the Middle Bronze Age city wall were repaired and restored to use), and a shrinking of the city limits. There was also evidence that this Israelite city was destroyed in a conflagration, probably toward the close of the eleventh century.

The pottery finds also date to about this time. Two interesting pieces of inlay came from Iron Age I contexts: the broken handle of a bone cosmetic spoon that represents Egyptianizing Canaanite art and may belong to the Middle Bronze Age period, and an ivory sphinx inlay that so far is without parallel.

Iron Age II. As indicated by the pottery, the last phase of the Israelite city belongs to the second half of the seventh century B.C. Occupation in the intervening period — *i.e.*, circa 1000–650 B.C. — is attested by only relatively few shards. The settlers in the time of Josiah apparently made no use of the earlier fortifications, nor did they build any of their own. Part of the Iron Age II city was found outside the old wall. As in the earlier periods, little architecture from the seventh century was

Hellenistic bathtub or dyeing installation. Bottom: Hellenistic fortress.

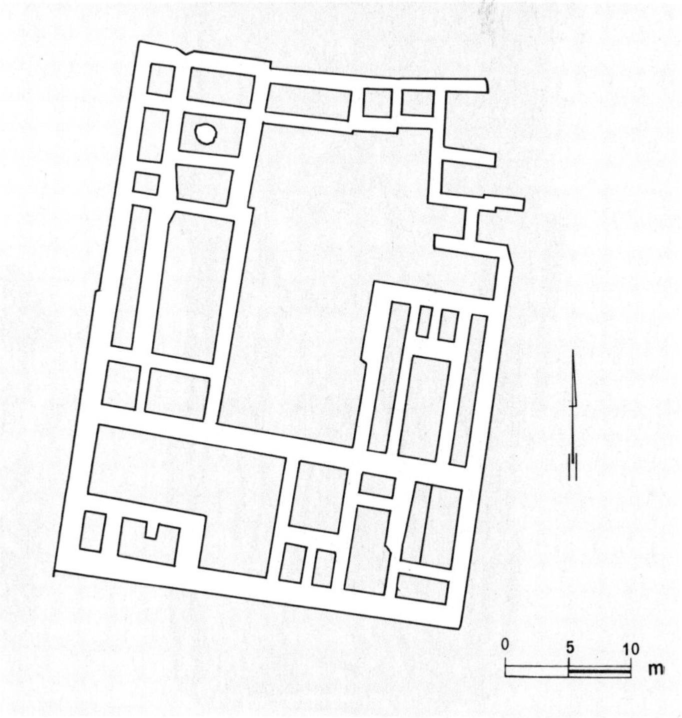

found, but eleven *lamelekh* jar handles stamped with the two-winged symbol and five handles stamped with the rosette appeared in the stratum.

The scattered evidence of a violent destruction circa 587 B.C., found in 1931, could not be confirmed in 1957.

The Post-Exilic City. The archaeological evidence indicates that occupation during the Persian period was sparse and was not resumed until perhaps the fifth century. A coin with the legend "*Hzqyh Pḥh*" ("the governor [*peḥa*] Hezekiah") was found in this stratum. It is probable that the first phase of the citadel was erected during the third century, as Beth-Zur assumed new importance in the conflict between the Ptolemies and Seleucids.

Beth-Zur reached its zenith in the second century during the Maccabean wars. Two distinct strata belonging to this period were identified: stratum II, 175–165 B.C., from the time of Antiochus IV Epiphanes; and stratum I, 140–100 B.C., from the time of John Hyrcanus. These strata lay outside the city wall and therefore belong to the periods which preceded and followed the struggle over Beth-Zur.

With the aid of datable loci, coins, and a careful analysis of the literary evidence, the following picture of the city can be reconstructed: Under Antiochus IV, Beth-Zur was a peaceful, prosperous town. Notable features included numerous bathrooms (a bathroom was found complete with bathtubs, a basin, and a foot bath, and twelve single tubs were found scattered over the city); a marketplace (inn, butcher shop, tavern, and other shops); and a large number of cisterns and reservoirs.

Following his victory in 165 B.C. Judas Maccabaeus reconstructed the old Middle Bronze Age wall around the city and probably built phase II of the citadel (the first two phases are Oriental in character, the third typically Greek). It can be assumed that when Lysias regained control of the city in 163–162 he strengthened its defenses. He was followed by the Syrian general Bacchides, who in 161 built the third citadel.

Toward the close of the reign of Jonathan, Simon besieged Beth-Zur and conquered it. He probably repaired the defenses, but the city quickly resumed a peaceful existence, as the renewal of occupation

Left: Fragment of a decorated bone object with incised designs. Right: Coin with the legend Hezekiah peḥa; *fourth century* B.C.

outside the walls demonstrates. Typical of this occupation is a house complete with bathing and laundry facilities, built against the outside face of the city wall on the northwest side. The population gradually declined in the following years and ended circa 100 B.C.

Since the evidence of the coins remarkably supports the other archaeological and literary evidence, their distribution is worth noting (dates represent the reigns of the rulers issuing the coins): nine Greek and imitation Greek (fifth/fourth centuries B.C.); fifty-six Ptolemaic (312–181 B.C.); 180 Seleucid (225–96 B.C.); twenty Maccabean (125–78 B.C.). None of these coins came from hoards. Thirty-five of the Ptolemaic coins were attributed to Ptolemy II (285–247 B.C.) and 131 of the Seleucid, to Antiochus IV. A total of twenty-nine stamped Rhodian jar handles and others with seal impressions were attributable to the Hellenistic period.

SUMMARY

The history of Beth-Zur may be summarized in tabular form:

V. EBA (third millennium): sporadic occupation.

IV. MBA II-B (Hyksos, 17th–16th centuries): founding of the city, fortifications.

III. IA I (Israelite, 11th century): reuse of MBA structures, reduction of city limits.

II. IA II (Israelite, ca. 650–587 B.C.): peaceful community.

I. Post-exilic city.

- F. Outpost (fifth/fourth centuries B.C.).
- E. Citadel, phase I (third century B.C.).
- D. Antiochus IV Epiphanes (175–165 B.C.): peaceful, prosperous community.
- C. Judas Maccabaeus (165–163 B.C.): rebuilding of city wall, citadel, phase II.
- B. Bacchides (ca. 161 B.C.): citadel, phase III.
- A. Jonathan, Simon, John Hyrcanus (142–100 B.C.): peaceful community.

R. W. FUNK

BIBLIOGRAPHY

O.R. Sellers, *The Citadel of Beth-Zur*, Philadelphia, 1933; *BASOR* 43 (1931), 2–13; *QDAP* 1 (1932), 158f.; *BA* 21 (1958), 71–76 • W.F. Albright, *The Archaeology of Palestine*, Harmondsworth, 1960 • Watzinger, *DP* 2, 24f.; *RB* 65 (1958), 266f. • R.W. Funk, *BASOR* 150 (1958), 8–20 • P. & N. Lapp, *BASOR* 151 (1958), 16–27 • P. Lapp, *Palestinian Ceramic Chronology 200 B.C.–A.D. 70*, New Haven, 1961 • O.R. Sellers *et al.*, *The 1957 Excavations at Beth-Zur*, *AASOR* 38 (1968).

EL-BUQEI'A

DESCRIPTION AND IDENTIFICATION. The Judean Buqei'a is a small isolated plain lying immediately east of Khirbet el-Mird (ancient Hyrcania) and west of the escarpment that falls away abruptly to Khirbet Qumran and the Dead Sea. The barrier of Wadi Mukellik and the Dabr system bound it on the north. Wadi en-Nar on the south forms a basin roughly 8 kilometers by 3 or at most 4 kilometers, oriented north–northeast by south–southwest. M. Noth is undoubtedly correct in identifying it with the biblical Valley of Achor, "Valley of Trouble."

EXPLORATION

The first systematic exploration and excavations in the Buqei'a took place in 1900. The little valley, now desolate and visited only by seminomadic shepherds, proved to have supported a rather intensive occupation in antiquity, between the ninth (or eighth) century B.C. and the late seventh or early sixth century B.C. (Iron Age II-B–C). The occupation of the Buqei'a was based on a complex irrigation system, the first that can be attributed with certainty to the Judean kingdom, since,

Map of the Buqei'a Valley.

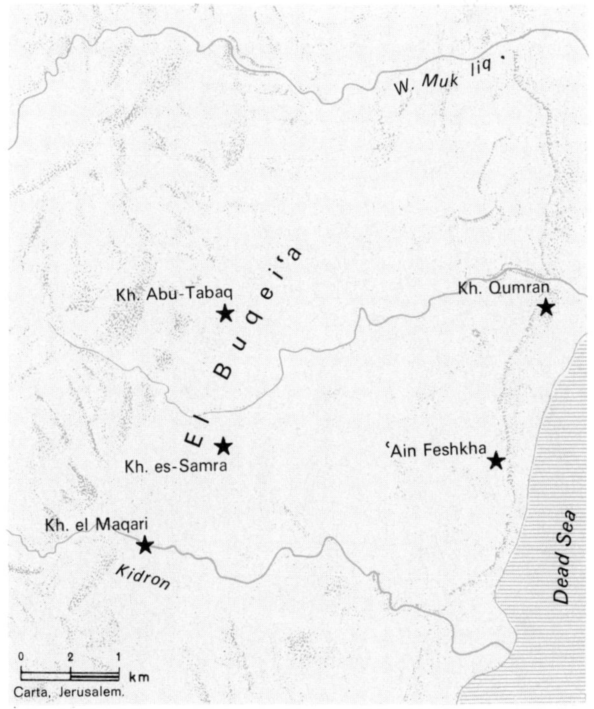

Right: Khirbet Abu Ṭabaq: wall line of Dam 1 in foreground; looking north. Bottom: General view of the U-shaped farm (Dam 1) circa 150 m south of Khirbet Abu Ṭabaq; looking west.

contrary to the usual situation, no remains of earlier or later date were associated here with the Iron Age installations.

EXCAVATIONS

Soundings were made in three small fortresses in the Buqei'a: at Khirbet Abu Ṭabaq in the north (map reference 18861276); at Khirbet es-Samrah, the central and largest of the settlements (18731251); and at Khirbet el-Maqari in the south (18621231).

Khirbet Abu Ṭabaq. Also called Khirbet Karm 'Aṭrad after its adjacent dam, Khirbet Abu Ṭabaq is situated atop a hill that controls an intersection of ancient roads: the north–south track connecting Jericho and Bethlehem, and the road leading west from Qumran and 'Ain Feshkhah. The village fortress is a small, rectangular enclosure measuring 59 by 30 meters. Its walls, averaging about 1.25 meters thick, are of roughly dressed ashlar masonry. Occupation debris had eroded from the crown of the hill, forming silted layers above the ashy levels and floor levels of undisturbed debris on the lower slopes, retained by the enclosure walls. On the surface and in the silted levels, soundings produced mostly Iron Age II-B–C shards, with a sprinkling of Roman and Byzantine pieces. Lower levels produced unmixed, homogeneous Iron Age II-B–C pottery, an assemblage of poor forms characteristic mostly of the eighth/seventh centuries. The only notable peculiarity of this and other Buqei'a sites was the absence of deep, rilled-rim cooking pots usually dominant in Judean sites of this period.

At the foot of the northern slope of the hill is a rock-cut cistern (called Mugharet Abu Ṭabaq by the Bedouins). It was tunneled into the hill to a depth of 34.7 meters beneath the northern wall of the fortress.

Immediately south of the ruins is a large dam system constructed of low, fairly substantial walls, controlling the shallow bed of a southern tributary of Wadi Qumran. Two low dams run across the wadi bed. Long, low walls (the longest 740 meters) run parallel to the wadi bed, presumably to deflect and spread winter torrents, creating a broad, flat bottom land that would retain its moisture long after the rains were over.

Nearby on the west is a cemetery, compared by E. W. G. Masterman in 1903 with the cemetery of Qumran. On closer examination, however, it proved to be a recent cemetery of a Bedouin clan, different in type and orientation from that of Qumran (q.v.).

Khirbet es-Samrah. This fortress lies on a dominating hill in the central Buqei'a. Its defensive walls form a rectangle about 68 by 40 meters, with the longer walls on the north and south. On the north, south, and east, the main defensive walls (about 1 meter thick) are paralleled by inner walls (.6 meters thick). On the eastern side of the fortress, the *intervallum* is cut by some twelve transverse walls, forming narrow rooms. The fortress is thus constructed on a model of the casemate system characteristic of this period.

Soundings here established that the site, like Khirbet Abu Ṭabaq, had a single level of occupation of Iron Age II-B–C date. A royal jar handle from the second half of the seventh century B.C. came from one phase of the single stratum. In the southwest quarter of the fort was a large pool-cistern. No fewer than three separate dam and terrace complexes were found in the valley beds adjacent to the ruin, on the north- and southwest.

Khirbet el-Maqari. The southernmost of the three sites, Khirbet el-Maqari is situated on a flat ridge bordering Wadi Maqari. The outer walls of the enclosure are poorly preserved but appear to be 32 meters long a side. The details of its plan were not fully established by soundings. Apparently the site suffered two violent destructions, marked by distinct phases in occupation debris. However, all pottery was of Iron Age II-B–C date, and the span of occupation exactly that of the two sites to the north. The settlement was sustained by twin rock-cut cisterns tunneled into the ridge supporting the *khirbeh.* An enormous dam system on a northern tributary of the valley no doubt is to be associated with the ruin, although it is located a kilometer and a half west of it.

SUMMARY

The excavations in the Buqei'a show that settled occupation there belongs to a single period. The foundation of the three sites can be dated no earlier than the ninth century B.C. They were abandoned at the beginning of the sixth century B.C., coeval with the fall of Judah. The pattern of construction of the fortresses, their plans, masonry, cisterns, and the extensive set of similar irrigation systems, together with their identical pottery repertoire, suggest that the settlement of the Buqei'a was organized at one time by a central authority. Jehoshaphat or Uzziah (at the latest) may have been responsible for settling and developing the Buqei'a. Both kings are credited with building operations, and it was specifically stated that Uzziah was active in the wilderness (II Chronicles 17:12, 26:10). The sites in the Buqei'a cannot be separated from similar Iron Age forts at En-Gedi and at Qumran. The latter is remarkably similar in size and plan to that of Khirbet es-Samrah. These five sites all belong to the "desert district" of Judah (Joshua 15:61–62). In the list of cities in this district between Beth-Arabah and En-Gedi are the "City of Salt" ('Ir ha-Melaḥ), to be identified with Khirbet Qumran; and Middin (better Madon), Secacah, and Nibshan, to be identified respectively with Khirbet Abu Ṭabaq, Khirbet es-Samrah, and Khirbet el-Maqari. F. M. CROSS JR.

BIBLIOGRAPHY

F. M. Cross, Jr. and J. T. Milik, *BASOR* 142 (1956), 5–17 • F. M. Cross, Jr. and G. E. Wright, *JBL* 75 (1956), 223–26.

CAESAREA

NAME AND IDENTIFICATION. The name of the site has been preserved in its Arabic form, Qaisariye. Herod, the founder of the town, gave it the name Caesarea in honor of Caesar Augustus. To distinguish it from other towns bearing the same name, it was given several surnames such as Caesarea on the Seashore or Caesarea-on-Sea (Caesarea Maritima). Some authors call it Caesarea Sebaste, Caesarea of Palestine, or Caesarea of Judea.

Vespasian made Caesarea a Roman colony. Henceforth it bore the title *Colonia primo Flavia Augusta Caesariensis*. Under Alexander Severus it received the title of *Metropolis Provinciae Syriae Palestinae*. In Jewish sources the town appears under the

Left: Khirbet es-Samrah: one of the fourteen store rooms on the east side of the fort; looking west.

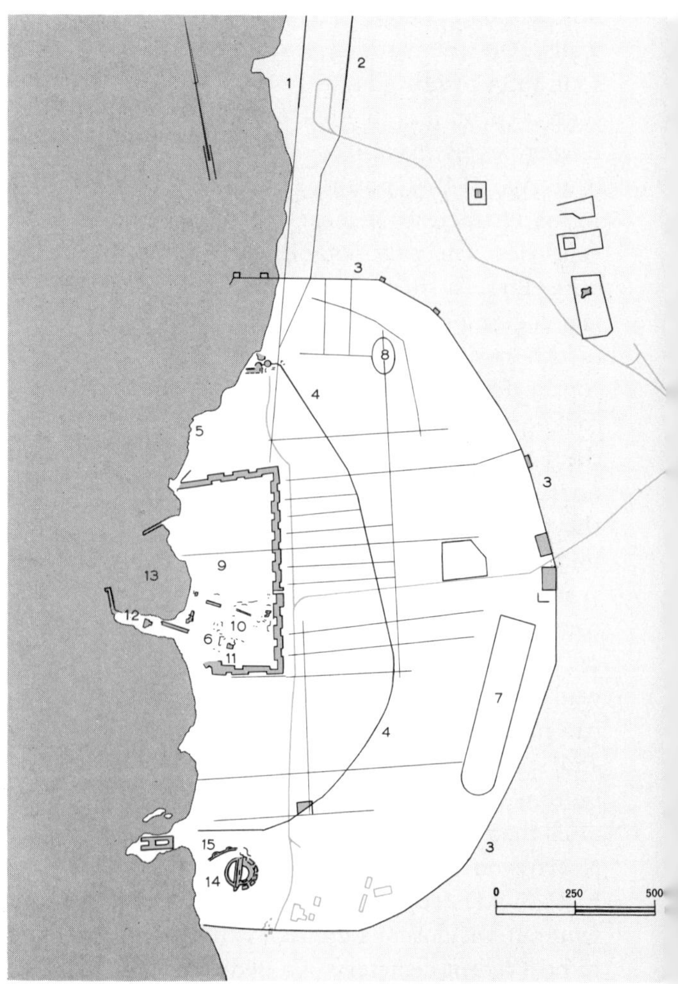

Plan of site. 1, 2. High- and low-level aqueducts. 3, 4. Byzantine and Herodian city walls with north gate. 5. Site of Straton's Tower, later Jewish quarter and synagogue. 6. Byzantine church. 7. Hippodrome. 8. Amphitheater (?) 9, 11. Crusader city and church. 10. Temple of Augustus. 12. Crusader harbor watchtower. 13. Later harbor. 14. Theater. 15. Byzantine-Crusader castle.

names of Qesari, Qisari, Qisarin. Herod named its important harbor the Port of Sebastos in honor of Augustus (*Sebastos* in Greek). Accordingly, the town is often mentioned as Caesarea near the Port of Sebastos.

The settlement that preceded Caesarea was called Straton's Tower, a name also preserved in one of the numerous names given the new town, Straton's Caesarea. In Jewish sources the name of this town appears as Migdal Sharshon.

HISTORY

Herodian Caesarea was built near a naval station of the Sidonians founded at the end of the Persian or the beginning of the Hellenistic period and bearing the name of Straton's Tower. Abdashtart (corresponding to the Greek Straton) was the name of two Sidonian kings, and the town was probably built under the second of them, who reigned in the time of Alexander the Great. The name of the site appears for the first time in a document from the archive of Zenon, in 259 B.C., when a harbor already existed at this site. At the end of the second century B.C., Zoilus, the ruler of Dor, took possession of Straton's Tower. Not long afterward the town fell into the hands of Alexander Jannaeus and was incorporated into the Hasmonaean kingdom for about one generation. It is to be assumed that Jewish settlement in the town began at that time. In any case the "border of the people which returned from Babylon" as defined by Talmudic law was extended by the rabbis up to the walls of the town, making all its territory (except the city itself) part of the Holy Land.

In 63 B.C. Pompey returned the town to its Gentile citizens and added it, together with the other towns on the seashore, to the Roman province of Syria. Pompey's legate Gabinius rebuilt the town shortly afterward. Mark Anthony gave it to Cleopatra VII, queen of Egypt, but when Augustus won at Actium, the half-ruined town was given by him to King Herod (30 B.C.).

In 22 B.C. Herod began building the new town, which was inaugurated in 10–9 B.C. The magnificent new city and its spacious port are described in detail by Josephus Flavius (*Antiquities* XV, 331ff., XVI, 136ff.; *War* I, 408ff.). After Archelaus, Herod's son, was deposed in A.D. 6, Caesarea became the residence of the Roman procurators and hence the official capital of the province of Judea. Agrippa I was the last Jewish king to reign over the city. Although the majority of its citizens were Gentiles, there also existed in Caesarea a very numerous Jewish community, which occupied a powerful position in the economy of the town. A state of permanent tension prevailed between the Jews and Gentiles. This led to disturbances and bloodshed in the term of office of the Roman procurator Felix, and once again under Gessius Florus. It then sparked off the general revolt of Judea, A.D. 66.

Vespasian, who had been proclaimed emperor by his legions during his stay at Caesarea, raised the town to the rank of a Roman colony but with limited rights. Alexander Severus granted it the title of Metropolis.

During the Middle and Late Roman periods an important Jewish community existed in Caesarea. Christianity was preached there in the apostolic age (Acts of the Apostles 10:23–26). At the end of the second century A.D. it was already the see of a bishop.

During the Byzantine period Caesarea remained the capital of the Province of Palaestina. From the third century onward there existed in the town an important Christian school and a famous library collected by Origen, one of the early Church fathers. From 315 to 330 the historian Eusebius was archbishop of Caesarea and head of the churches in the province. In 451, however, Jerusalem was raised to the rank of a patriarchate, and its bishop obtained precedence over that of Caesarea.

In the sixth century the town also had a numerous Samaritan community, which together with the local Jews revolted in 548 against the Byzantine governor. In 639 Abu Obeida, the general of Caliph Omar, captured Caesarea. The Muslims ruled at Caesarea for the next 460 years. At the beginning of the First Crusade, Caesarea paid tribute to Godfrey of Bouillon and was not attacked. But in 1101 Baldwin I occupied it, slaughtering most of the Muslim inhabitants and sacking the city. Under the Crusaders Caesarea began to decline rapidly. Even the fortifications erected by Louis IX of France in 1251 did not render it safe. The Crusaders held Caesarea intermittently until 1265, when Sultan Beibars conquered it. In 1291 Sultan Malik al-Ashraf turned it into a heap of ruins. In 1878 a small settlement of Muslims from Bosnia was founded there which lasted until 1948.

EXPLORATIONS AND EXCAVATIONS (HISTORY)

In April, 1873, the Palestine Exploration Fund carried out the first survey of the remains of the Crusader city, the town walls, and the aqueducts, under the direction of C. Conder and H. Kitchener. They drew up a map of the remains of the city. This became a document of considerable importance, since it recorded the surface aspect of the area as it was before the foundation of the Bosnian village. Later, L. Haefeli conducted a general exploration on the site, without excavating. His work was continued by A. Reifenberg, who made use of aerial photographs of Caesarea and its surroundings.

Most of the archaeological discoveries made in Caesarea up to 1958 were made accidentally. Fragments of hundreds of inscriptions, statues, and architectural details were discovered during field work or road building. In 1945 J. Ory conducted excavations on the site of the synagogue on behalf of the Department of Antiquities of the Mandatory Government. In 1951, as the result of the discovery of a porphyry statue, the area east of the Crusader city was cleared. The excavations carried out in the area by S. Yeivin on behalf of the Department of Antiquities led to the finding of another statue and a street section of the Byzantine period. Yeivin also excavated a church which had been accidentally discovered east of the wall of the Byzantine city.

In 1959 the Archaeological Mission, acting on behalf of the Istituto Lombardo in Milan, initiated systematic excavations in Caesarea under the direction of A. Frova. During the excavation campaigns of 1959–63, the Roman theater was cleared, and trial soundings were carried out at the city walls and at the aqueduct. From 1960 to 1962 A. Negev, on behalf of the National Parks Authority, carried out extensive excavations in the area of the Crusader city and south of it. The fortifications of the Crusader city and other remains of the Roman, the Byzantine, and the Early Arab periods were uncovered.

In 1956 and 1962, excavations in the Jewish quarter of Caesarea, under the direction of M. Avi-Yonah on behalf of the Hebrew University, linked up with another excavation in the area of Straton's Tower under the direction of A. Negev. In the summer of 1963, during excavations on behalf of the Parks Authority, a further section of the high-level aqueduct was uncovered and inscrip-

Aerial view of the theater from the north.

tions of Roman legions dating from the period of the Bar-Kokhba revolt were found. In 1971–72 R. Bull, working on behalf of the American Schools of Oriental Research, conducted soundings at the northern extension of the Byzantine street, in the course of which a marble statue of Roma was discovered.

EXCAVATIONS (RESULTS)

The Hellenistic Period. In the summer of 1962 the area north of the Crusader city and east of the synagogue was cut by a sounding trench. It appeared that this area actually formed an inconspicuous, flat mound. The trench (5 by 50 meters) exposed the corner of a large house. The two extant courses are built of local sandstone laid in headers and stretchers. The corner of the house was covered by a considerable accumulation of Hellenistic pottery characteristic of the third and second centuries B.C., such as Megarian bowls, stamped wine-jar handles from Rhodes and other islands of the Aegean Sea, lamps, etc. The latest pottery in this context was eastern terra sigillata A (and of this only the early types dating to the second half of the second century B.C.). Pottery from the first century B.C. has not been found in the area. This suggests that the area was abandoned after its conquest by Alexander Jannaeus.

Remains of walls and early Hellenistic pottery were found in the lowest stratum in the synagogue area near the seashore. It therefore seems probable that the Jewish quarter of Caesarea was built on and near the site of ancient Straton's Tower. The remains of a massive wall can be seen in the sea close to the synagogue. Perhaps these are the remains of the mole of the harbor of Straton's Tower. Ancient texts also suggest that the Jewish quarter of Caesarea was close to the harbor.

Remains of the Hellenistic period were found in several excavated areas. At a small distance from the mound of Straton's Tower, the Italian mission uncovered a section of a wall that incorporated two big, circular towers similar to those discovered at Samaria. This wall was repaired several times (some of the added parts were not even essential for the fortifications). It continued in use at least until the Late Roman period. The excavators dated the wall and towers to the reign of King Herod. In light of the parallel at Samaria, however, it seems that they should be assigned to the Hellenistic period.

One of the main sewers of the town, which was certainly built during the reign of Herod or later, was found at a distance of about 150 meters north of the wall — that is, outside the walled area. The high-level aqueduct was also probably built during the reign of Herod, a considerable time after the old wall and the towers had fallen into disuse. When the builders of the aqueduct had to continue it into the town area, they were compelled to pass it over the wall. In order to accomplish that, they built a massive basement to a height equal to that of the remnant of the wall but not incorporated in it. We may therefore quite safely conclude that in Herod's time the town was not surrounded by a wall.

The Roman Period

THE PODIUM NEAR THE HARBOR. The excavation of the Crusader city showed that the elevation east of the harbor was not a natural hill but a wholly artificial podium. In its northern section this podium consists of a complex of big cell-like compartments continuing eastward from the wall, a fact that had already been noted by the explorers of the Palestine Exploration Fund. The builders had filled these compartments with rubble of cut sandstone. Only a small quantity of pottery was found in the filling of the podium. The finds are mostly of Early Roman ware — *e.g.,* Arretine terra sigillata — and a few are Late Hellenistic pottery, perhaps also dating from the building period itself.

The southern part of the podium has a row of vaulted constructions. One of them (measuring 21 by 7 by 13 meters — the last dimension being the height up to the top of the vault) was excavated in its entirety. The walls on the south and on the east are built of big stones, dressed in a manner characteristic of the Herodian period. They are laid in courses, one stretcher alternating with two headers. Above the vaults is a filling similar to that found inside the cell-like compartments. At present the whole of the podium reaches a height of 15 meters above the level of the area situated westward, but at the time of its construction it must have been considerably higher. It may be assumed that Herod intended to erect a podium for the acropolis of the city. The vaults probably served as storehouses of the port (see below).

Close to the eastern gateway of the Crusader city a part of the sewer was uncovered. It ran north–

south, parallel to the seashore. West of the sewer and above it was part of a street, paved with big slabs of hard limestone. Several small openings were provided for drainage from the street into the sewer. The sewer, 1.8 meters high and 1 meter wide, probably belongs to the Herodian town. However, the buildings of that period were partly demolished during the Early Arab period. They were completely destroyed during the period of Crusader rule, when the city wall was built.

THE HERODIAN HARBOR. The descriptions given by Josephus indicate that the harbor was one of Herod's most remarkable building works in Caesarea. From investigations carried out by the Link Mission for Underwater Exploration (1960), it appears that the southern breakwater, shaped like a large arc running from southeast to northwest, was 600 meters long. The northern breakwater was 250 meters long. The harbor was entered from the northwest, as is related by Josephus, and its water area was circa 3½ acres.

During the excavations west of the podium, a section of a wall (about 10 meters wide) was uncovered, which is connected by a vault to the western wall of the podium. The excavators distinguished two phases of construction here, and they have assumed that the wall was probably part of one of the inner moles of the harbor. Excavations north, south, and west of this wall showed that the numerous buildings set up in this area were not earlier than the sixth and seventh centuries A.D. Only from this time up to the Crusader period was the zone densely built up and inhabited. It may therefore be assumed that part of the Herodian harbor had been dug into the land and that mooring berths for ships as well as storehouses (the vaulted buildings) had been erected there.

In the earthquake of A.D. 130, the moles and other port installations were heavily damaged. At that time the wall to the west of the podium and the vaulted buildings were probably repaired. By the end of the Roman period, and certainly in Byzantine times, it had become impossible to use the eastern part of the harbor because of the sanding up of the mooring berths. Various installations were gradually built in the sanded-up area. The Byzantine harbor, which had to be cleared of sand by the emperor Anastasius in the sixth century, and the other, later ports — which were much smaller than the Herodian port — were situated outside the present-day seashore. A. NEGEV

Counterclockwise: Coin of the city from the time of Nero (A.D. 54–68). Crystal head, probably of a Roman emperor; .35 m high. Statue of Diana of Ephesus; third century A.D.

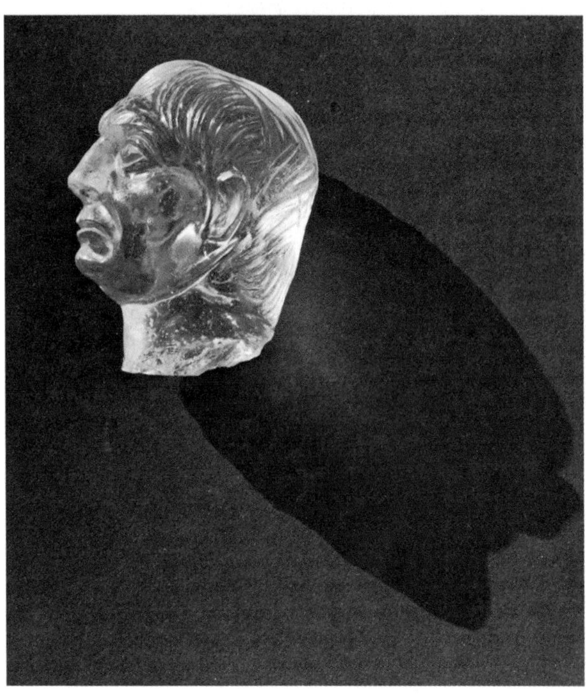

THE THEATER. From 1959 to 1964 the Italian Archaeological Mission uncovered the theater situated in the southern part of the town. The theater of Caesarea proved to be a kind of palimpsest for the history of the antique theater from the first century A.D. until the Byzantine period. Then a fortress reinforced with semicircular towers was built over its remains.

From its foundation period — *i.e.,* the age of Herod — remains have survived of the cavea with its stairways, the *euripus* (the channel for the evacuation of water running round the orchestra), and the concentric gangway (built after the model of the theater of Eretria). The floor of the orchestra was coated with a layer of painted plaster, which was remade in fourteen successive seasons. It was decorated with various ornamental patterns—floral, geometrical, and fish-scale. The orchestra wall was decorated in an imitation of marble paneling. The theater of Ceasarea has the earliest instance of such decoration; one of later date was found in the theater of Leptis Magna in Roman Africa.

The *scenae frons* is built in the Hellenistic style and has a central square exedra, on the two sides of which were smaller concave niches. Their front parts facing the podium were covered with very fine plaster work; the painted *pulpitum* (front part of the stage facing the public) was ornamented corresponding to the plaster work of the niches.

In the second century A.D., when the theater was reconstructed, the central exedra of the *scenae frons* was made semicircular; it was flanked on both sides by deep square niches. The exedra and the walls facing the public were ornamented with superimposed rows of columns. The front of the *pulpitum* was rebuilt and provided with alternating square and semicircular niches, which were coated with marble. The orchestra (diameter 30 meters) was provided with a marble paving and the seats in the auditorium were also made of stone (in the previous, Herodian theater they had been made of conglomerate).

Various periods of construction can be distinguished in the seating area. In the lower part of the auditorium there were six (possibly seven) *cunei* ("wedges") each with thirteen tiers; in the central *cuneus* there was a rectangular compartment (the seat of the provincial governor). There was a passage below the seats of the lower part and another above it. From the latter six entrance vaults *(vomitoria)* lead into the auditorium. These vaults were entered from the outside from a concentric ring-shaped gangway. The exit from the gangway was by six vaulted gates alternately decorated with groups of attached columns and pilasters.

In the third century A.D. a semicircular platform was added behind the stage, resembling that in the theater of Dougga in North Africa. During the

late Imperial period (third to fourth century A.D.), the orchestra area was turned into a large basin *(columbetra)* for nautical games, similar to such installations discovered in the theaters of Athens and Corinth. At that time water cisterns were added to the theater complex, which were also used later by the Byzantines and the Arabs. An earlier stone with an inscription mentioning "Pontius Pilatus, Praefectus Judaeae," and the "Tiberieum" (a building dedicated by him in honor of the Emperor Tiberius) was reused in the late Imperial period as a step in the theater.

Decorations in the theater dating from the Herodian period include several delicate architectural details made of stucco-coated stone. In the Roman period (second and third centuries A.D.), architectural details were made of marble. Among the finds from the theater are many big pottery lamps from the Herodian period, offering bowls with Greek potters' marks, and later lamps found under the *hyposcenium*. The roofing of the *hyposcenium* was supported by a system of arches resting on pillars. In the theater area were found a statue of Diana of Ephesus; several statues of clothed women; a female, mask-like head; and fragments of statues, reliefs, and inscriptions.

BYZANTINE FORTRESS AND WALL. In the Byzantine fortress (probably from the reign of Justinian, with Arab additions) a small hoard of gold objects was found, including jewelry and crosses as well as a silver box for cult objects.

The Italian mission found evidence that the external wall of Caesarea, which follows a semioval line outside the city, is to be dated to the Byzantine period. They uncovered a wall section with semicircular towers that they dated to the Herodian period (but which A. Negev regards as Hellenistic; see above).

The Italian mission also began to clear the line of the aqueduct and identified the plan of the ancient city on Israeli aerial photographs. A Christian building outside the city wall was also excavated by them.

A. Frova

THE SYNAGOGUE. North of the Crusader city, a capital carved with a seven-branched menorah was found in the 1920's on the seashore. In 1947 J. Ory excavated on this site on behalf of the Department of Antiquities of the Mandatory Government and discovered two superimposed mosaic floors. The upper mosaic was white. On the lower an inscription was found mentioning a donor, a certain Julius, and the area of the mosaic floor donated by him. Another mosaic fragment was decorated with a colored guilloche.

In 1956 and 1962 excavations were carried out on the site on behalf of the Archaeological Department of the Hebrew University, under the direction of M. Avi-Yonah, assisted by A. Negev. The excavators reached virgin soil, at a depth of 7 meters and identified five superimposed strata.

STRATUM I. On virgin soil, 2.8 meters above sea level, were found the foundations of Hellenistic houses (see above), which were perhaps connected with the anchorage site of Straton's Tower nearby. In this stratum, vessels typical of the Hellenistic period were discovered, such as Megarian bowls, and West Slope ware (referring to the western slope of the Athenian Acropolis).

STRATUM II. This stratum includes the remains of a square building (length of one side 9 meters). The thick walls of this building (up to 1.2 meters) go down to 1.4 meters above sea level. Above the foundations (3.9 meters high) are five courses (each .27 meters) of hewn stones laid in alternating headers and stretchers.

The pottery found in this stratum includes Herodian lamps, spindle-shaped bottles, and some fragments of Herodian (pseudo-Nabatean) ware.

The eastern wall of the building and a considerable part of the southern wall up to the southwestern corner were fairly well preserved. Part of the walls of this building were incorporated into the walls of the synagogue of the fourth century A.D. (see stratum IV, below). It may therefore be assumed that the house served as a synagogue in the reign of Herod and afterward. It may even have been the synagogue *Knestha d'Meredtha* (*i.e.*, the "Synagogue of the Revolt") mentioned in Talmudic sources. Around that synagogue centered a conflict that kindled the revolt of A.D. 66 (Josephus, *War* II, 285–91).

STRATUM III. From Augustus until the third century a part of the Herodian building served as a plaster-coated cistern. In the fourth century this cistern was filled up with rubble, and among it were found fragments of terra-sigillata ware, coins of the procurators, and Roman pottery.

Tel Dan; Mycenaean charioteer vase.

STRATUM IV. Over the rubble fill a synagogue was built in the third century. For its walls, part of the walls of the Herodian building from stratum II were reused. This might be the synagogue in Caesarea which according to Talmudic sources was situated near the seashore. The floor of this building stands at a height of 4.9 meters above sea level. The synagogue (18 by 9 meters) was directed southward, but its entrance was in the short eastern wall, in the direction of the town. On the southern side a number of small constructions (perhaps shops, as in the synagogue of Sardis) had been added. Alongside these ran a paved street.

In the synagogue, mosaic floors were discovered, as were fragments of a Hebrew inscription giving the order of the "priestly courses" and their places, as detailed in late liturgical hymns. Several lamps, impressed in the mold with the seven-branched menorah, were also discovered.

Near one of the walls of the synagogue a hoard of 3,700 bronze coins was found, almost all from the time of Constantius II. As some of these coins bear the effigy of Julian Caesar, we may assume that the hoard was hidden about A.D. 355 and that the building was therefore destroyed in the middle of the fourth century A.D. When its was reconstructed, the hoard was forgotten.

STRATUM V. In the middle of the fifth century a new synagogue was erected on the ruins of the fourth-century building. Oriented on a north–south axis, the later building had a long, narrow entrance hall (11 by 2.6 meters) paved with a white mosaic floor. Set in the floor was the inscription: "Beryllus, archisynagogus and administrator, son of Ju[s]tus, made the pavement work of the hall from his own money." This vestibule formed the entrance to another hall, in the center of which was a circular area paved with stone (.5 meters in diameter), surrounded by a mosaic floor.

To this building belonged marble columns, one of which bears the inscription: "The gift of Theodorus son of Olympus for the salvation of his daughter Matrona." There are also several Corinthian capitals. The columns and the capitals are of two different sizes, some of them having a diameter of .5 meters and some of .25 meters; they perhaps belonged to the hall and to the gallery respectively. Carved on two of the capitals is the seven-branched menorah. Distinguishable on the third capital is a group of letters forming a monogram, which can be read "Patricius" on one side and "Con[sul]" on the other. The building was therefore reconstructed in A.D. 459, in the consulate of Patricius.

Between periods IV and V, a covered sewer running from east to west (toward the sea) was constructed

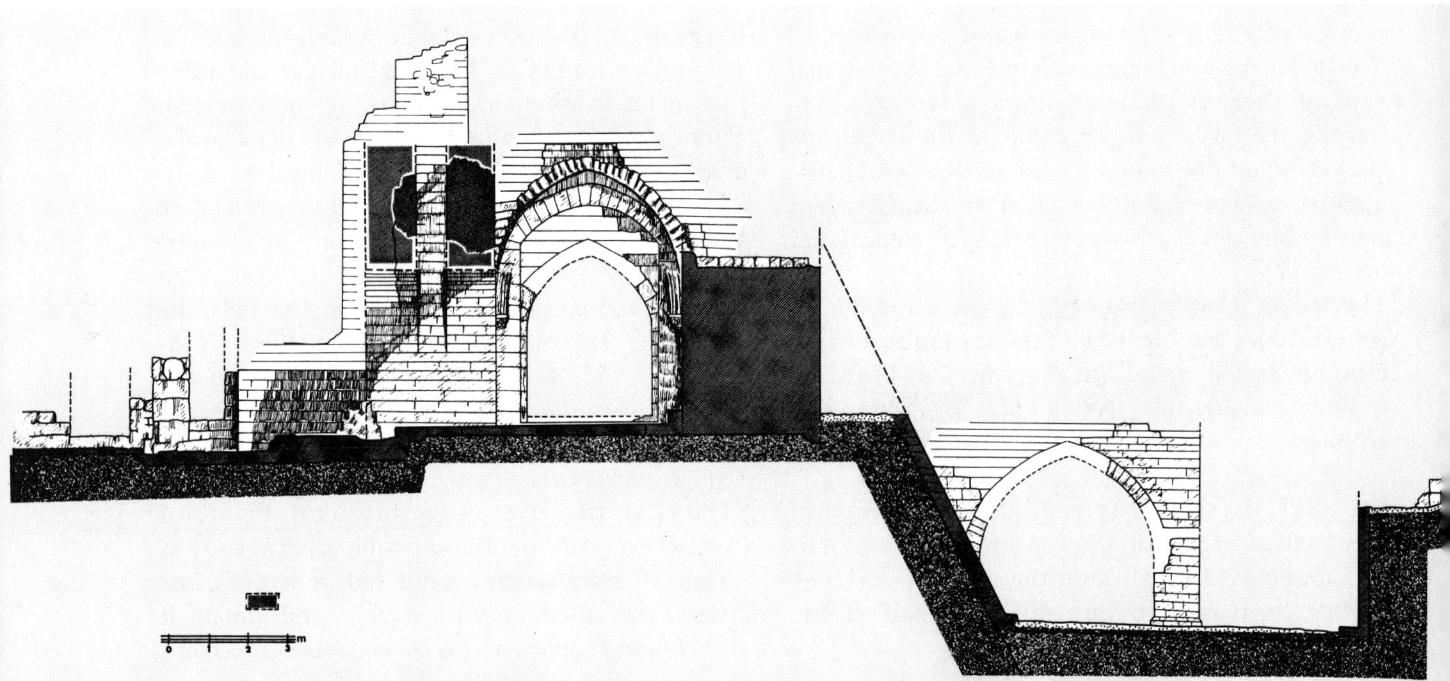

above the level of the earlier building, the hall of the later building being superimposed on it.

East and west of the building, water channels with pottery pipes were found. Among the smaller finds are small columns (of the Ark?), a marble slab carved with a menorah, fragments of marble inlays, fragments of marble mosaics with an inscription reading: "God help us! Gift of the people in the time of Marutha," and another inscription with the same name "Marutha." The synagogue was destroyed by fire, and the heat caused the mosaics to change color. Brimstone was found on the floor.

At the beginning of the Arab period the floors were repaired with a mixture of marble and stone fragments embedded in a layer of plaster. No signs of occupation after the fifth century A.D. are found on the site. M. AVI-YONAH

THE WATER SUPPLY. The water supply system of Roman Caesarea was one of the most perfected in the country. Water was brought to the town from two sources: from springs on the southern slopes of Mount Carmel by an aqueduct carried on arches (the so-called high-level aqueduct), and from a dam across the Zerqa River (Naḥal ha-Tanninim) by the low-level aqueduct. The high-level aqueduct, which is more than 9 kilometers long, is formed at its beginning by a rock-cut channel continuing up to Shani (Maiumas, map reference 146216). At Shani it also collected water from the abundant springs near the Roman theater. Thereafter the water was carried by a system of pottery pipes placed on a base constructed of stone and mortar. The aqueduct crosses the Zerqa River on a low bridge, and from there it is carried on arches across the Kabara swamps.

The aqueduct carried on arches actually consists of two conduits joined together. On top of each system of arches is a built channel, each with three pottery pipes (diameter of each pipe 17 centimeters) in which the water flowed. In the Kabara swamps the two conduits are separated. The second branch was possibly built on higher, dryer ground after the destruction of one branch because of excessive pressure on the miry soil. In the sandstone ridge running parallel to the seashore, the aqueduct continues as a cut tunnel about 400 meters long. After emerging from the ridge, the aqueduct is once more carried on arches, running west–southwest up to a point near the seashore, and from there along the shore to the north end of the city itself.

In this section of the high-level aqueduct it could be ascertained that the eastern of the two conduits (see above) was built first. Near Caesarea the

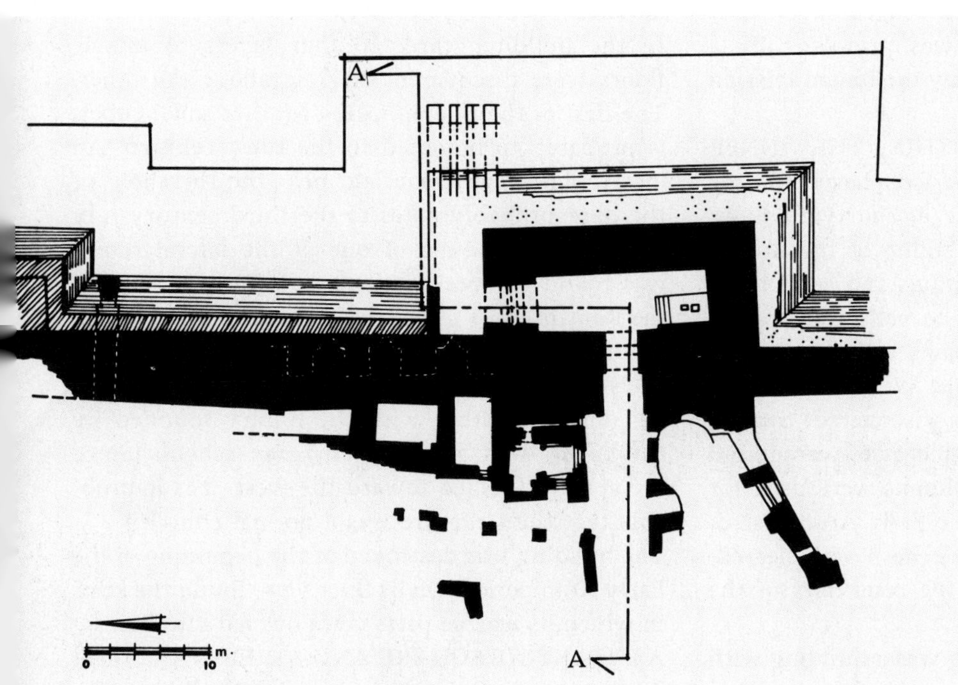

Plan and section of the eastern gate of the Crusader city.

aqueduct has been completely eroded by the action of the waves.

The construction of the high-level aqueduct dates from the reign of Herod. It was repaired by units of the Second Legion (Traiana Fortis) and the Tenth Legion (Fretensis) at the beginning of the Bar-Kokhba revolt, when the town became the headquarters of the Roman army that was rushed into the province to quell the Jewish revolt.

As previously mentioned, the low-level aqueduct, which is about 5 kilometers long, draws its water from a dam built on the Zerqa River. At its beginning it is an open, rock-cut channel running at the foot of the sandstone ridge, parallel to the seashore. In its continuation the aqueduct is built of sandstone and is roofed by a vault (circa 2 meters high). A small section of the low-level aqueduct was cleared north of Caesarea. Its lower part is made watertight by a plaster coating.

The date of the low-level aqueduct is unknown, but it seems that both aqueducts were in use at the same time. The high-level aqueduct probably supplied drinking water, whereas the low-level aqueduct conveyed water to irrigate the gardens near the town.

The Byzantine Period. Excavations conducted in the Byzantine levels have not yet established a clear-cut conception of the town. However, it may be concluded that during this period the town attained its maximum size, the length of its walls reaching 2.5 kilometers. It was protected by a semioval wall, partly cleared by the Italian mission (see above).

BYZANTINE REMAINS WITHIN THE INNER CITY. During the Byzantine period a large building (30 meters long) consisting of a big courtyard, halls, and rooms was built on the filling of the Roman period. Only its deep foundations and sections of the floor are extant today. The halls were paved with grayish-white marble slabs and the smaller rooms had floors of opus sectile. West of the building a big polygonal apse was discovered. Several Corinthian capitals carved with crosses were found in the rubble. The marble columns were used for the repair of houses during the Early Arab period.

East of this building a water cistern was cleared, which was probably one of the reservoirs of the aqueduct.

Also west of the Roman filling was a building with two apses on its eastern side and a floor covered by a mosaic of rough stones. At the western extremity of this structure were the remains of a square building surrounded by a screen. Storage jars (for water?) were found placed below the level of the floor. No corroboratory evidence of the nature of the structure was found, however.

Throughout the area of the Crusader city are scattered numerous cellars or underground stores. In some of them the roof vaults are still preserved. The massive walls of these structures are built of small stones embedded in clay mortar and revetted with well-dressed stones. Evidently goods brought in by sea were stored in these structures.

REMAINS SOUTH OF THE INNER CITY. South of the fosse dating from the Crusader period, the excavations on behalf of the National Parks Authority brought to light the foundations of a large public building, more than half of which was destroyed when the Crusaders dug out the moat. From the few remains left it can be surmised that in the east side of the building there was an exedra leading to two small entrance rooms, paved with opus sectile and with mosaics of rough cubes. West of the entrance rooms was a long hall, paved with small mosaic cubes. At its western extremity was a small apse (it is not clear, however, whether the building was a basilica). In the rubble of the apse tiny stone and gilded glass tesserae were found, belonging probably to the wall or ceiling mosaics.

In the building, three to four layers of mosaic floors were discovered laid one above the other. The first of the floors, made of rather small cubes, is probably to be dated to the third century. An inscription of welcome laid near the threshold of the door probably dates to the third century A.D. In the white mosaic of one of the lateral rooms was found in Greek a passage from the Epistle to the Romans 3:13. Among the remains of the buildings a statue of the Good Shepherd was found.

A. Negev has suggested that this building should be identified either with the library founded by Origen or with an early Christian school. (Since the apse is directed toward the west, it is improbable that the structure was a normal church.)

The building was destroyed at the beginning of the Early Arab period. On its floor were found the kilns in which its marble parts were burned into lime.

A BYZANTINE SQUARE AND STREET. At a small distance east of the Crusader city, S. Yeivin, on behalf of the Department of Antiquities, cleared a section of a street. The excavators uncovered three main strata, the uppermost dating from the eleventh to the thirteenth century A.D., the middle one from the eighth to the ninth century A.D., and the lowest stratum to the Byzantine period. In the two upper strata few building remains were found. In trial soundings carried out beneath stratum III, signs of occupation from the Late Roman period (Stratum IV) were found. They were not explored further, however. The excavator ascribes this lowest layer to the fifth and sixth centuries A.D.

In the south part of the excavated area a large public square, paved with big reused marble slabs, was discovered and cleared to a length of 30 meters. In the northern part of this square there was a tripartite gate having two marble columns in its center. East of the gate stood a porphyry statue representing a man sitting on a throne of green granite. West of the gate was a statue of white marble also representing a man sitting on a throne; the upper and lower parts of the figure do not correspond to each other. The porphyry statue probably represents the Emperor Hadrian and originated from the Hadrianeum known to have existed in Caesarea. Both statues were apparently transferred to a public square here in the Byzantine period.

North of the tripartite gate is a rectangular room (10 by 5.1 meters) paved with rough, white mosaics. It leads to a flight of ten steps that ascend to another street 1.5 meters higher than the area to the south. On the floor of the platform an inscription was found mentioning a Byzantine governor, so far unknown, as well as the city mayor during whose term of office "the wall, the apse, and the stairway" were repaired.

The street north of the stairway is paved with rough white mosaic cubes and was cleared over a length of 15 meters. A trial sounding carried out at a distance of 80 meters north of the limits of the excavated area proved that the street continued in that direction. On the sides of the big square and along the street, building remains, probably of shops and workshops, were discovered. The

From top to bottom: Synagogue fragment of capital. Synagogue inscription: "God help us! Gift of the people in the time of Marutha." Synagogue fragment of mosaic floor and inscription.

excavator assumed that the whole complex was the central marketplace of Caesarea, and that the open place north of it was the cattle market.

THE BUILDING OUTSIDE THE WALLS. East of the city wall, on the top of a hill rising about 26 meters above sea level, S. Yeivin has also uncovered a Byzantine building, probably a church. It is near the cemetery whose remains were found between the wall and the hill. The structure (13.5 by 11.5 meters) is oriented to the east. No traces of roofing columns have been found on the floor and it seems that this floor area was a court open to the sky, perhaps intended for ceremonies before burial. The floor is paved with mosaics. On its margins are drawings of wild and domesticated animals among stylized fruit trees. In the main field there are medallions in which various birds are represented.

In the narthex and in the extraordinarily narrow aisles, which were only partly cleared, the mosaics were decorated with geometric patterns. The remains of another building paved with mosaics were found 14 meters east of the building, and nearly at the same level. Its eastern wall (28 meters long) and its central apse (diameter 4.5 meters) are still extant. The axis of the apse of this building does not, however, correspond to the axis of the court to the west. Judging by the style, the latter building should be dated to the second quarter of the fourth century. It was destroyed during the Arab conquest in A.D. 640.

The Early Arab Period. Remains of this period have been found all over Caesarea wherever excavations or soundings were made. It follows that during the Arab period the size of the town did not decrease from that of the Byzantine period. The big Byzantine building erected upon the Roman filling was repaired in the Early Arab period with stones removed from the building itself. For the most part only the floors of the structures had been preserved. The sewage channels and the water-supply system from the Roman and Byzantine periods ceased to function in the Early Arab period, and therefore cisterns, fountains, and sewage pits were dug over the whole area.

West of the filling, remains of various workshops were found. The southern vaulting, which is completely preserved, was used in the Early Arab period as a workshop for casting iron, as may be seen from the thick layer of iron slag and cinders covering the floor. Under this layer was hidden a big jar in which silver bracelets were concealed and a small jar containing jewelry of gold, bronze, and precious stones. All these objects date from the tenth century A.D.

West of the filling, in a stratum above and west of the Byzantine building, there were found remains of crucibles for copper smelting, as well as remains of buildings, of storerooms, and of numerous early Arab sewage pits.

The Crusader Period. The Crusader city is the smallest of the several towns built at Caesarea, its area being about 22 acres (either one sixth or one tenth the area of the Roman and the Byzantine towns, depending upon the various evaluations).

THE CITY WALL AND GATES. The Crusader city was walled on all sides. The seashore wall has been almost completely destroyed; remains are only left close to the shore. The eastern wall measured about 650 meters and the northern and southern ones about 275 meters each. The fortifications consisted of a counterscarp (still extant to a height of 4 to 6 meters), a fosse (bottom width 7 meters), and a glacis (its gradient being 60 degrees and its length up to the base of the wall 8 meters). The wall rising above the glacis was about 10 meters high, but only a small section of its is preserved near the southern gate. Loopholes were cut into the wall at regular intervals. Two have been preserved in situ near the southern gate. The inner and outer face of the fortifications are built of rather small stones bedded in strong white mortar. The filling of the wall was made of clay, mortar, and any available material. Nine towers are incorporated into the eastern wall, four in the southern one, and three in the northern. The towers (10 to 17 meters long) project 7 to 8 meters beyond the wall. Opposite every tower on the wall is a recess in the counterscarp of the fosse. There are three gates in the city wall.

The Northern Gate. The northern gatehouse is built in the middle of the north wall. A bridge was supported across half the fosse by an isolated pillar (1.75 by 4.25 meters). In the distance from the glacis up to the pillar the bridge was built of arches.

Opposite page, left: High-level aqueduct. Right: Latin inscription from aqueduct mentioning repair in Hadrian's time. Bottom: Crusader fosse (eastern section); built in 1251.

IMP TRAIANO
HADRIANO AVG
VEXILLATIO
LEG X FRE

It leads to the road in front of the gateway. The doorway of the gate (3.2 meters wide and 4 meters deep) looks westward and is thus protected against arrows shot from the north.

The hall of the gatehouse is square (length of each side 8.25 meters), with a ceiling formed by four cross vaults resting on four pillars set in the corners of the hall. The pillars and their capitals, which are decorated with plant motifs, are preserved in situ. In the southwestern corner of the hall is a stairway leading up to the tower above the gate. An opening in the southern wall opened into the town itself.

This, gate, like the other two, is built according to the principle of indirect access. This fact is of chronological importance, for such gates were not built in the Crusader period prior to the middle of the thirteenth century. The excavator therefore attributed the Caesarea fortifications to the latest phase of the Crusader period, the time of Louis IX, King of France.

Another staircase, east of the gate, led to its top floor, of which only the lowest courses and the foundations of the loopholes (opening toward the road and the glacis) are still extant. Near the northern and eastern corner tower, at some distance from the gateway, there is a secret passage in the wall, leading from the town into the fosse. It consists of a sloping gallery (7 by 1.1 by 3 meters), which opened on the outside into the glacis, but was probably blocked during the siege by Beibars in 1265. The other secret passages were also blocked by strong constructions.

The Eastern Gate. This was the main entranceway to the city; it is situated in the middle of the eastern wall and entered by a bridge. The remains of four pillars and four arches, supporting the bridge across the fosse and the glacis, are preserved in situ. The outer doorway of the gatehouse looks northward. In the continuation of the parapet of the bridge the doorway is protected by a system of loopholes. Inside the doorway (3 meters wide, 4 meters deep) are the installations for pouring out burning materials; a slot for an iron grille; a threshold made of a marble block; and the upper holes for the hinges of the gate, made of marble columns cleft lengthwise.

The hall of the gatehouse (15 by 4.5 meters) is paved with small, rectangular stone slabs. In its southwestern corner is a well and a basin. Along its eastern wall is a bench built of stone, attached to the wall. In the middle of the western wall of the gatehouse is a doorway leading into the town. The ceiling of the gatehouse rests upon three cross vaults, built upon pillars. The capitals of the latter are decorated with plant motifs, which have been preserved. This gatehouse also had an upper story, reached by a staircase attached to the western wall. There were loopholes in the north, east and south walls of the passage leading to the upper floor.

The excavators could clearly distinguish two phases of construction in the eastern gatehouse. All remains just described belong to the last phase, *i.e.*, to the time of Louis IX. To the first phase the excavators assign two sections of the wall, north and south of the western doorway of the gate chamber. These are built of big hewn stones, in contrast to the other parts of the gatehouse, which are built of small stones, only slightly chipped.

A sounding made inside the wall revealed remains of the doorposts of an earlier gate, to which the above-mentioned two sections of wall had belonged. It therefore is clear that initially a much wider gateway had been built on this side. It had no hall in front of it and was built with a direct access. When the fortifications were built by Louis IX, the gateway was narrowed by adding doorposts built of small stones. It is also possible that this change in plan occurred during the year in which these fortifications were under construction. Thirty meters north of the eastern gate there was another secret passage (7 meters long) of outstanding workmanship, built with gradually descending cross vaults.

The Southern Gate. Because this gate was known prior to the excavations, only soundings were carried out here. It seems that the construction of this gate was never completed. The Crusaders had succeeded in building only its outer gateway, the plan of which was similar to that of the northern one. Near the southeastern corner tower was a third secret passage (14 meters long). Although similar to the northern one it was less sloped than the others and of inferior workmanship.

CRUSADER STREETS. Inside the town several sections of the Crusader city's network of streets were discovered. One of the streets led from the eastern gateway westward and was paved with big slabs of hard limestone, identical to the pavings of the Roman period. It is evident that these stone slabs were reused, although the street itself probably dates from the Roman period. Further Roman remains have been discovered close to it, and on the same level.

An additional section of a street, roofed by a cross vault, was found alongside the eastern wall. In its pillars there were holes for tying up houses. A third section of the street was uncovered above the podium. It runs from north to south, passing above the western part of the large Byzantine building in the direction of the big Crusader church. This street is paved with small stones, characteristic of the last phase of Crusader building. In its foundations were embedded Roman capitals of the Ionic order.

THE CRUSADER CHURCH. Within the city itself the southern Crusader church was uncovered, the construction of which had not been completed. The church was built on the southern part of the podium. According to its plan, the western half of the nave and the northern aisle were to have been built above the three southern vaults of the podium. In order to adapt the podium for this purpose, its western area was reinforced by four strong buttresses. Afterward three apses of exceptionally well-dressed sandstone were built on the top of the elevation, at the eastern end of the podium. Only then was the construction of the northern wall of the church begun. But before half of it could be completed, two of the vaults collapsed, and the remains of the wall were buried under the debris. The builders were thus compelled to abandon their initial plan. In front of the original central apse they built another apse of very poor workmanship. Reused columns, discovered in situ in the nave of the church, correspond to the lines of this second apse. The columns were sunk deeply into the floor and had no bases.

The church is paved with small stone slabs like those of the road to the eastern gate. In soundings carried out under the southern aisle, the foundations of mosaic-paved rooms, perhaps of a mosque or of a church, were found. In addition, cell-like compartments of the podium were discovered, filled with pounded sandstone.

THE HARBOR FORTRESS. At this spot only limited trial soundings were conducted. It appears that this fortress was built on a narrow land tongue, probably once part of the southern breakwater of the Herodian port. This fortress was evidently built by the Crusaders in the twelfth century or at the beginning of the thirteenth. It is separated from the town by a channel 20 meters wide. Its western access was protected by two strong towers. One of the entrances from the harbor to the fortress was discovered in its northeastern corner. A narrow passage, probably roofed, leads from the main hall of the fortress to a big gateway, almost completely preserved. Both the hall and the gateway are covered at present by rubble. Under the fortress a subterranean hall was discovered.

A CRUSADER HOUSE. Southwest of the eastern gate, near the roofed street, a large residential house was discovered. The beginning of its construction is dated to the Early Arab period. Debris of columns were covered with stones and earth, and the floor laid upon the filling. Under this floor a hoard of gold and silver coins from the tenth century was found.

This house had two courtyards with wells in each of them. The rooms of the house were built around the courtyards, and in one courtyard was a stairway leading up to the roof. There were also subterranean storerooms. The house was apparently occupied for a considerable time, for it had undergone many repairs and modifications in the course of its existence.

A. NEGEV

BIBLIOGRAPHY

Conder-Kitchener, *SWP* 2, 13–29 • L. Haefeli, *Caesarea am Meer,* Munster i.w., 1923 • A. Reifenberg, *IEJ* 1 (1950–51), 20–32 • S. Yeivin, *Archaeology* 8 (1955), 122–29 • M. Avi-Yonah, *BIES* 20 (1956), 194–95 (Hebrew) • A. Frova et alii, *Caesarea Maritime (Israele), Rapporto preliminare della 1-a campagna di scavo della Missione Archeologica Italiana,* Milano, 1959 • C.T. Fritsch and I. Ben-Dor, *BA* 24 (1960), 50–59 • E.A. and M.C. Link, *An Underwater Expedition to Israel,* New York, 1961 • A. Negev, *Bible et Terre Sainte* 41 (1961), 6–15 • A. Frova et alii, *Scavi di Caesarea Maritima,* Milano, 1965.

The theater: A. Frova, *Caesarea Maritima,* Milano, 1959; *idem, Quattro campagne di scavo della Missione Milanese a C.M., La Lombardia a l'Oriente, Milano Ist. Lombardo,* 1963; *idem, Ann. d. Sc. Arch. di Atene,* 39–40 (1961–62), 649–57 • *idem,* in *Ill. London News,* April 4, 1964; *idem, Note alla Va Campagna di scavo, Rend. Ist. Lomb.,* 1963 • A. Albricci, *L'orchestra dipinta di C., in Boll. d'Arte,* 1962 • A. Frova et alii, *Scavi di Caesarea Maritima, Milano,* 1965, 55–244.

The synagogue: M. Schwabe, *Jubilee Volume for Alexander Marx,* New York, 1950, 433ff. • M. Avi-Yonah, *EI* 7 (1956), 24–28 (Hebrew) • E.L. Sukenik, *Rabinowitz Bulletin* 1 (1949), 17; 2 (1951), 28–30 • M. Avi-Yonah, *ibid.,* 3 (1960), 44–48; *idem, IEJ* 6 (1956), 260–61; 13 (1963), 146–47; *idem, The Teacher's Yoke, Trantham Memoriam Volume,* Waco, 1964, 46–57.

The aqueducts: A. Negev, *Yediot* 30 (1966), 136–41 (Hebrew); *idem, IEJ* 14 (1964), 237–49; *idem, IEJ* 22 (1972), 52–53.

CAPERNAUM

IDENTIFICATION. The site consists of a town (as yet almost unexplored) from the Roman period and a synagogue of the third century A.D. It is located on the northwestern shore of the Sea of Galilee and is identified with the Capernaum mentioned in the New Testament, Josephus, the Kefar Naḥum of Talmudic literature, and later sources. A Roman centurion built a synagogue there (Luke 7:2–5). Jesus preached and performed miracles in Capernaum (see Matthew 8:5ff.; Mark 1:21ff., 2:1ff., etc.) and cursed the place (*e.g.*, Matthew 11:23ff.). Josephus relates that he was brought there after being wounded in battle near the Jordan (*Life*, 72). Talmudic sources relate that in the beginning of the second century A.D., and perhaps even later, a Judeo-Christian community existed in Capernaum *(Minim)*.

In the fourth century the Comes Joseph built a church in Capernaum, as he did in other centers of Judeo-Christian heresy. But in the sixth century A.D. wealthy Jews still lived there, as is shown by an Aramaic inscription in the mosaic floor of the synagogue at Ḥammath Gader, which mentions a donor from Capernaum. In medieval Jewish tradition the site is called Kefar Tanḥum, or simply Tanḥum, and hence the Arabic Tell Ḥum. Various pilgrims mention that local inhabitants robbed stones from the ruins.

EXPLORATION

Among the black basalt stones of the ruined village, the remains of the synagogue, which are of white limestone and had obviously been brought from afar, stand out in sharp contrast. E. Robinson, in 1838, was the first to identify the site and the synagogue. In 1856 C. Wilson and R.E. Anderson uncovered a portion of the building, and in 1881 H.H. Kitchener excavated an additional section. These activities prompted further looting of stones. In 1894 the Franciscan Order purchased the site and at present holds it in custody. H. Kohl and C. Watzinger excavated the ruins of the synagogue (1905) and published the results of their research in their monumental book. The Franciscans, under G. Orfali, continued to unearth the synagogue and to reconstruct parts of it. Excavations were resumed by V. Corbo and S. Loffreda from 1968 onward. The village proper, to the east of the synagogue, has been only partly excavated. Various objects of basalt found among its ruins have been gathered together near the synagogue.

SYNAGOGUE

The synagogue consisted of a main building (20.4 by 18.65 meters) and a court to the east (11.25 meters wide at the front). Along the façade of the building, which faces south — toward Jerusalem — ran a raised, paved platform. Access to the platform was by stairs on either side. At the northwestern corner of the building, a room was appended having an external staircase leading to the upper story (now missing).

The three entrances of the façade opened into the interior, which was divided by two parallel rows of columns forming a nave and two aisles. A third aisle was formed on the north by a lateral row of columns. A bench ran along each of the longer walls. The floor was paved with flagstones. On the east an opening led to the court, which was surrounded on three sides by a portico. This trapezoidal court was also paved with flagstones

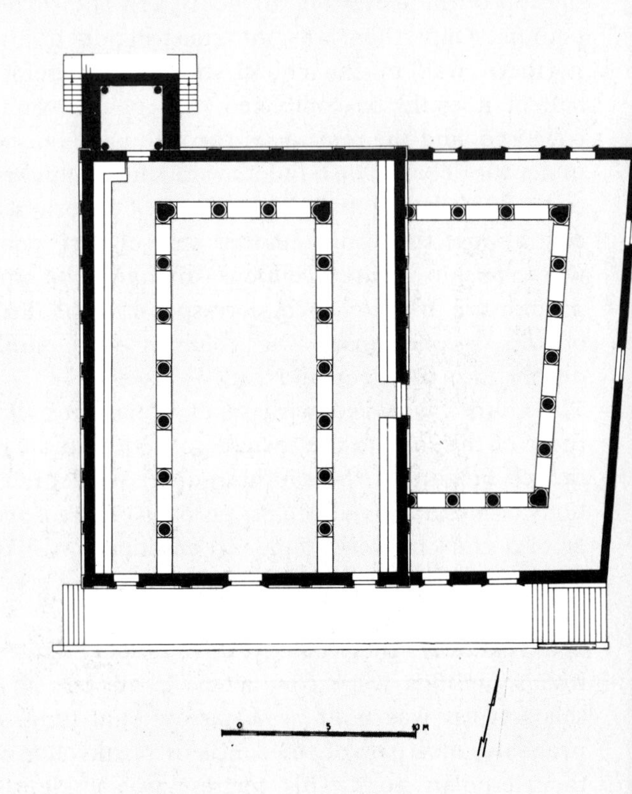

and had several entrances on its three sides.

Of the synagogue walls — which were about 60 centimeters thick — there remain only one to four courses of ashlars, each 40 to 60 centimeters in height. On the outer face, pilasters appear at regular intervals. Most of the column pedestals were found in situ.

The architectural members of the building found strewn about were so numerous as to enable a plausible reconstruction of the original appearance of the synagogue in all its details. The Franciscans have accordingly reconstructed a part of the north and east walls, as well as the row of columns on the north.

The façade was divided into three horizontal fields marked by architectural elements: the lower story, the upper story, and the tympanum of the gable. The lower façade was divided by pilasters into three fields, each pierced by a doorway. The middle one led into the nave and the outer two into their respective aisles. These doors were topped with lintels adorned with varying motifs: vine tendrils, date palms, figures that seem to be eagles, and lions and cupids supporting festooned garlands. A cornice separated the two stories. In the center, above this cornice, a large arch framed a window. This window was flanked on either side by smaller windows, each resembling a temple façade consisting of two pairs of colonnettes with oblique fluting, supporting a Syrian gable with a shell in its center. Above the large arch was a double window of the same type as the flanking ones.

The cornice of the Syrian gable crowning the building was richly adorned with architectural and floral patterns as well as a horizontal frieze that arched in the middle. This frieze bore a continuous acanthus pattern from which emerge poorly preserved animal figures, apparently lions. The gabled roof was covered with tiles.

The interior was composed of two stories of colonnades, forming aisles below and galleries above. These surround a high, central nave on three sides. The columns stood on pedestals resting on stylobates. The bases, carved of one stone together with the pedestals, were of the Attic type. The capitals were of the Corinthian order. The

Left: Plan of the synagogue.
Right: Reconstruction of the façade.

entablature above was composed of architrave, plain convex frieze, and cornice, reaching to the floor of the upper gallery at a level of 7.3 meters above the ground floor. This upper story served as the women's gallery. Little has survived of the upper columns. They apparently had molded capitals and no bases. Between the columns ran a stone screen.

The walls of the gallery were adorned with pilasters bearing a convex frieze and a cornice, both richly ornamented. The decoration of the frieze consisted of medallions of leaves encircling various floral and geometric patterns: rosettes, bunches of grapes, pomegranates, pentagrams, hexagrams, etc. One remaining portion of the frieze shows a carriage, which may be interpreted as an Ark of the Law similar to the Ark of the Covenant appearing in the frescoes of the synagogue at Dura-Europus. On a remaining portion of the cornice are a hybrid sea horse and two eagles holding a garland in their beaks. These are the only animal figures in the synagogue that have not been damaged by iconoclasts. The restored location of these friezes — in the upper gallery, far away from the view of the worshippers — is strange. However, there seems to be no other suitable place for them.

The position of the Ark of the Law had been a matter of dispute. Kohl and Watzinger interpreted certain fragments of minor architecture as portions of the ark and proposed to locate it along the width of the nave, before the entrance. Sukenik, however, observed that these fragments were part of the double window belonging to the façade and that the Ark of the Law — as a rule portable in early synagogues — did not have a fixed position within the prayer hall.

Two inscriptions, one in Greek and the other in Aramaic, were found incised on columns. They read, respectively: "Herod, son of Mo[ki]mos, and Justus his son, together with the children, erected this column," and "Ḥalfu, the son of Zebidah, the son of Yoḥanan, made this column. May he be blessed."

SUMMARY

The synagogue at Capernaum belongs to the earlier type of Galilean synagogue. It is attributed to the third century A.D. on the basis of contemporary

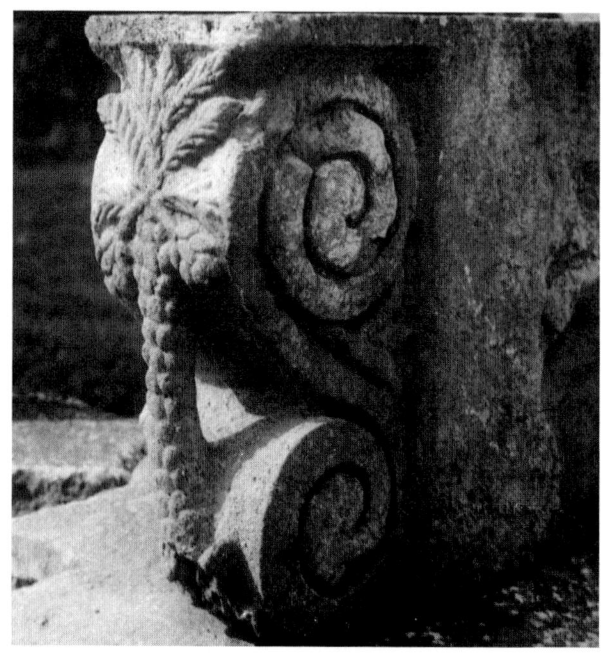

From top to bottom: Capital with relief of menorah, shofar, and incense shovel. Fragment of gable. Console with relief of a palm tree.

Above: Frieze with relief of medallions encircling floral and geometric patterns.
Below: Cornice with relief of hybrid sea-horse and two eagles holding a garland with their beak.

Below: The benches along the western wall, synagogue interior.

architectural parallels in Syria, as well as local historical considerations. The finest example of this type, its remains are also the best preserved. The plan of the building is that of a basilica. The construction is of ashlar masonry with ornamentation carved in the stone. The repertory of decorations is quite diversified, including floral, faunal, and geometric motifs. Human figures are rare.

While most of the decorations are merely ornamental, some of them have symbolic meaning. The menorah, the shofar, and the incense shovel depicted on a Corinthian capital, and the Ark of the Law, are religious symbols common to ancient synagogal art. The vine, the pomegranate, and the date palm evidently appear as symbols of three of the Seven Species (Deuteronomy 8:8). The pentagram and hexagram may have had magical meaning. All but one figures of living beings were purposely obliterated by iconoclasts.

The Franciscan fathers V. Corbo and S. Loffreda who renewed the excavations at Capernaum in 1968 made also soundings in the area of the synagogue. On the basis of the numismatic evidence, the excavators now claim for the existing structure a date in the middle of the fourth century A.D.

This astonishingly late date has been challenged by G. Foerster. He argues that the coins on which it is based were not found underneath the intact flagstones but below spaces from which the pavement had been removed. They should therefore be ascribed to later restorations. Historical and architectural reasons make it very difficult to assume that the Galilean synagogues are contemporary with the totally different type of synagogues of the Byzantine period.

The Franciscans also continued the excavation of the octagonal building south of the synagogue, which was previously unearthed by G. Orfali. This building is now defined as a church built above the remains of St. Peter's house in the first half of the fifth century A.D. N. AVIGAD

BIBLIOGRAPHY

Kohl-Watzinger, *Synagogues*, 4–40 • G. Orfali, *Capernaüm*, Paris, 1922 • Sukenik, *Ancient Synagogues*, 7–21; *idem, Rabinowitz Bulletin* 1 (1949), 19f.; *idem, Kedem* 2 (1945), 121–22 (Hebrew) • Goodenough, *Jewish Symbols* 1, 181–92; 3, Figs. 451f. • V. Corbo, S. Loffreda, and A. Spijkerman, *La Sinagoga di Cafarnao dopo gli seasi del 1969*, Jerusalem, 1970 • V. Corbo, *The House of St. Peter at Capernaum*, Jerusalem, 1969 • G. Foerster, *Qadmoniot* 4 (1971), 126ff. (Hebrew); *idem, IEJ* 21 (1971), 207–11 • M. Avi-Yonah, *ibid.* 23 (1973), 43–45 • S. Loffreda, *ibid.*, 184.

CARMEL CAVES

THE SITE. The Cave of the Valley (Ma'arat ha-Naḥal, Mugharet el-Wad), the Cave of the Oven (Ma'arat ha-Tannur, Mugharet eṭ-Ṭabun), and the Cave of the Kid (Ma'arat ha-Gedi, Mugharet es-Sukhul) lie on the southern escarpment of the Valley of the Caves (Naḥal ha-Ma'arot, Wadi el-Mughara) where it opens into the Coastal Plain, about 2 kilometers (1 mile) from the Haifa–Tel Aviv highway and several kilometers north of 'Atlit.

These caves, opening to the northwest, are of a karstic nature. The remains of the "chimney" in the Cave of the Oven and the marks visible in the Cave of the Valley are evidence that water once flowed inside them.

EXCAVATIONS (HISTORY)

In 1929–32 excavations were carried out in these caves, under the direction of Dorothy Garrod, on behalf of the British School of Archaeology in Jerusalem and the American School of Prehistoric Research. In 1932 T. D. McCown directed the excavations on behalf of the American School of Prehistoric Research. In 1967–68 A. Jellinek continued to work in the Cave of the Oven on behalf of the Museum of the University of Michigan and the University of Arizona. The abundant archaeological finds discovered in the three caves can be dated to over 150,000 years ago, *i.e.*, to the period when groups of hunters and food gatherers settled there at the end of Lower Paleolithic Age. They continued to use the caves until the emergence of an agricultural society at the beginning of the Natufian period.

The finds give a most detailed conception of the world of prehistoric man, enabling us to draw numerous conclusions regarding the development of man — his material, religious, and artistic culture — as well as the flora and fauna of the period and the modifications of them through climatic changes.

EXCAVATIONS (RESULTS)

The Cave of the Oven. The southernmost of this group of caves, the Cave of the Oven is situated on the spur of the escarpment at the beginning of the bar of rocks that blocks the valley 63 meters above sea level and about 31 meters above the level of the valley. During the excavation campaigns, the central chamber, the area of a funnel, and a small terrace in front of the cave were excavated. Ten layers, labeled A to G, have been uncovered. Their total depth reaches 15.5 meters.

LAYER G. The excavator (Dorothy Garrod) termed this layer Tayacian, whereas C. F. Howell called it Tabunian (European and Near Eastern prehistoric cultures are not always coeval, and this requires the use of a different nomenclature). Layer G was found directly on the bedrock slanting toward the basin in the center of the cave. The color of the earth is light, the thickness of the layer 3.8 meters. Within the limited excavation area a small number of animal bones and about 424 flint implements were found, including scrapers (11.2 percent of the total number), carinated scrapers (1.65 percent), burins (.7 percent), and chipped retouched flakes (the remainder).

LAYER F. This layer, 3.6 meters thick, belongs to the Upper Acheulian culture. This layer, too, is slanted, following the floor of the cave. The earth is dark at the bottom and light at the level of contact with layer E. The animal remains found are of great variety, with primitive types predominating. Dorothy Bate even considered that a tropical climate may have prevailed at this time. In this layer 3,887 flint implements were found, including hand axes (31.76 percent of the total), side scrapers (42.01 percent), carinated scrapers (4.26 percent), and burin (.92 percent).

LAYER E. This layer, 7 meters thick, is divided into four sublayers (horizons), E-a to E-d. At first defined as Upper Acheulian-Micoquian, it was later designated Acheulian-Yabrudian (by Dorothy Garrod in 1956). The color of the earth is light in the center and dark near the walls of the cave, where it becomes harder. At a depth of 6.3 meters, marks of flowing water can be distinguished. Two fragments of human bones as well as animal bones were found there, including bones of a hippopotamus, fallow-deer, ox, gazelle, and horse.

The distinction between the four sublayers (horizons) is based only on the typology of the flint implements, not on any geological modifications. Even during the first season the excavator noted an assemblage of Upper Paleolithic implements. They are frequent in all of the four horizons, but especially in three of them (Dorothy Garrod, 1956). This is the case also in the rock shelter in Yabrud (Syria). It was labeled by A. Rust pre-Aurignacian and by Dorothy Garrod (1961) Amudian. This Amudian assemblage is part of the so-called Acheulo-Yabrudian complex (Dorothy Garrod, 1962). The following table lists the type of implements, discovered in the various horizons of layer E:

Layer	E-a	E-b	E-c	E-d
Hand axes	1,003	1,866	616	3,618
Sidescrapers, type A	3,746	6,327	2,763	8,803
Sidescrapers, type B	514	1,594	784	2,938
Carinated scrapers	448	815	215	803
End scrapers	21	67	8	79
Points	78	127	20	54
Burins	59	97	34	115
Cutting tools	320	1,057	379	1,643
Retouched blades and flakes	81	223	19	37
Audi points	10	21	—	—
Châtelperron points	51	76	—	—

Sidescrapers are made of broad flakes with flat chipping (retouch) and can be divided into two groups: those with the bulb of percussion at the center of the base; and those with the bulb of percussion on the side.

LAYER D. This layer, 2.7 meters thick, belongs to the Mousterian culture, characterized by the

Map showing the Carmel Caves.

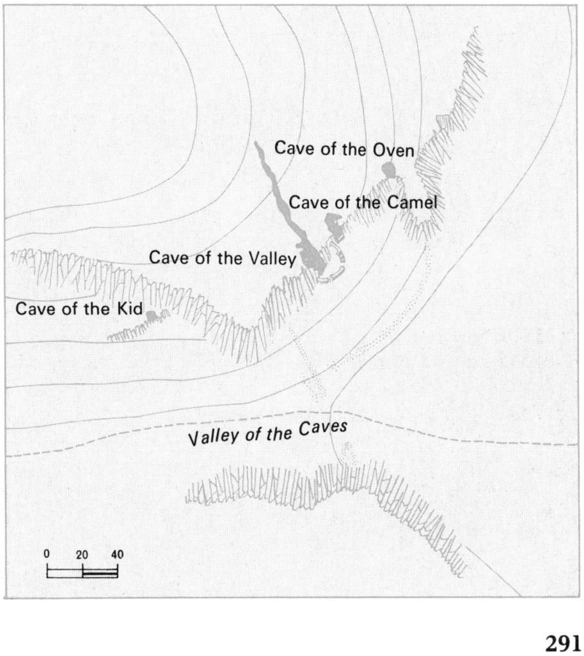

Cave of the Oven
Cave of the Camel
Cave of the Valley
Cave of the Kid
Valley of the Caves
0 20 40

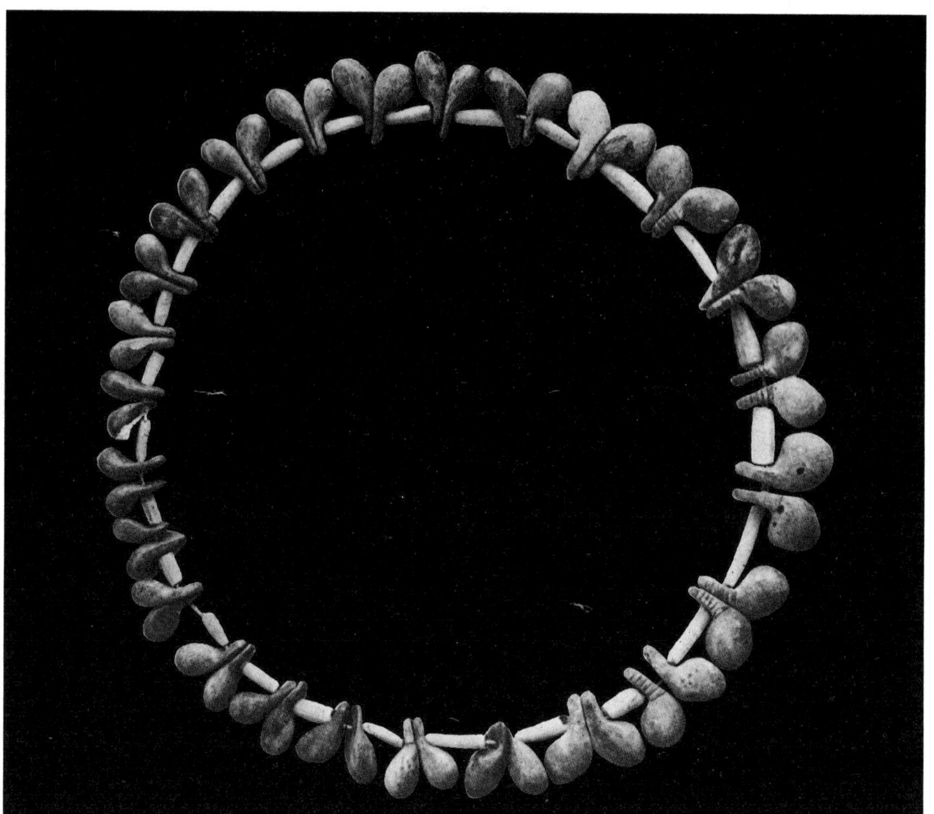

Right: Cave of the Valley; necklace of dentalia and bone from a grave; Natufian period. Below: From right to left: Cave of the Oven, Cave of the Kid, Cave of the Valley.

early Levallois technique (Levallois-Mousterian). It was excavated in the major part of the cave and the terrace. Rock debris has been found in this layer, and some scholars link this fact with a period of rainfall. Animal remains are numerous and varied.

The flint industry is mainly represented by flakes and points — 1,188 implements of which side-scrapers constitute 45.94 percent and points 27.6 percent. In addition, other types of scrapers, hand axes, burins, retouched flakes and points, cutting and other implements have been found.

LAYER C. Like the preceding one, this layer belongs to the Mousterian culture, characterized by the Levallois technique. Its thickness is about 2.2 meters. The earth, hard and dark, was excavated over an extensive area. The most important finds are a human skeleton and a separate lower jawbone. The skeleton, known as the Woman of Tabun, of the Neanderthal type, was found in the opening of the cave, lying on its back with its legs flexed.

The flint industry comprises 767 implements. The major part are made of broad flakes, the Levallois technique that can be easily identified. Side-scrapers represent 50.83 percent of the total, points 10.79 percent, and implements showing notches 12.09 percent.

LAYER B. This layer belongs to Upper Mousterian characterized by the Levallois technique (Upper Levallois-Mousterian). It was uncovered over the whole area of the cave, including the area of the chimney. The earth shows a reddish tint and contains stone debris and some fragments of human bones. A considerable change takes place in the fauna at this period. The large, primitive animals are disappearing, replaced by animals showing present-day characteristics. Dorothy Bate called this phenomenon the "crisis of the fauna," but some scholars believe that the disappearance of some types of animals was gradual.

The flint industry is represented by 568 implements, the retouching technique differing from that of the preceding layer. Among the implements found are sidescrapers (57.35 percent), points (13.19 percent), burins (2.3 percent), and others.

LAYER A. Remains from historic times up to the Byzantine period were found in this layer.

In the years 1968–71 A. Jellinek and W. Farrond made a section of the back part of the cave. Each item found there was listed in its place. There is another pit close to the chimney area.

It seems that the lower layers F and E became stratified when the sea was closer to the cave. Possibly this happened in the Inter-Glacial Riss-Würm period. Fractions in the various layers indicate various local geological events. Over eighty stratigraphical elements have been found. The findings have not yet been studied in detail, but in general, the following may be stated:

In layer E hand axes were found belonging to Late Acheulian. In the upper part of this layer, concentrations of pre-Aurignac tools were found. Jellinek assumes that there is no specific culture but that there is tool making for specific work.

In layer D 25 percent of the flint industry belong to the Levallois technique. Blades and points of the Levallois type were also found.

In layer C large fire areas are common. Large Levallois flakes are extant. In the lower part of this layer about 25 percent of the flint implements are characterized by the Levallois technique, while in the upper part the Levallois type is even more prevalent. During this period the chimney area started to collapse. This becomes more evident in layer B.

The main periods of occupation of the cave were E-a and C-d.

The Cave of the Kid. This cave lies about 100 meters east of the Cave of the Valley on an isolated escarpment, about 11 meters above the level of the valley. It opens to the north, and there is a small terrace in front of it.

In trial soundings carried out in 1929 and during two seasons in 1931–32 (the latter under the direction of McCown), the entire cave and its terrace were cleared and two layers, B and C, were discovered.

This cave is outstanding in its rich finds of human skeletons, all dating from the Mousterian period. It apparently served as a burial place in prehistoric times. The skeletons were mostly discovered in layer B within the cave itself and on the terrace in front of it. Ten skeletons were found, among them three complete ones, two of which were adults. Some of the skeletons were found embedded in a hard breccia, so it took the excavators a considerable time to extract and prepare them.

Dorothy Garrod and McCown equated the above layers with layers D–C in the Cave of the Oven, but objections have been raised against this hypothesis. E. S. Higgs, for example, considers that the layers of the Cave of the Kid should be placed between layers B and C of the Cave of the Oven. Layer B is divided into two sublayers. In horizon B-1, 1,032 flint implements were found, and in B-2, 653. In layer C this industry is scanty and the finds mostly broken.

The Cave of the Valley. This cave is situated about 70 meters east of the Cave of the Oven, approximately 45.5 meters above sea level and 12 meters above the level of the valley. It is 71 meters long, its form being similar to that of a winding brook. The cave consists of two chambers, a large opening, and two recesses. In front of the cave is a large terrace (radius 55 meters). Excavations were carried out in the cave from 1929 to 1932. Nine layers were uncovered. The finds provided evidence for the chronological continuity from the end of the Mousterian to the beginning of the Natufian periods between this cave and the Cave of the Oven and the Cave of the Kid.

LAYERS G–F. Uncovered in both chambers and in the long narrow part (gallery) of the cave, these layers form a 2.2-meter thick deposit over the grit accumulated in the basin on the floor of the cave. Initially Dorothy Garrod considered that layer G belonged to the Upper Mousterian, but she later ascribed it to the Upper Paleolithic I. This layer may even have been preceded by an earlier occupation layer eroded by the action of the water flowing through the cave. Besides sidescrapers, points, and burins, the finds also included Emireh points, Châtelperron points, and blunted-back blades.

LAYER E. This layer, .4 to .6 meters thick, dates from the Upper Paleolithic III. The earth is black. Between layers E and F, marks left by flowing water can be distinguished. Numerous animal bones and fragments of two human skulls of the Cro-Magnon type have been found there. The industry includes 2,181 flint implements and seven bone points. Among the flint implements are scrapers (64.03 percent, of which 40.03 percent are carinated scrapers), burins (23.35 percent), and Font Yves points.

LAYER D. Comprising two horizons, layer D belongs to the Upper Paleolithic III–IV. It is found expecially in chamber II and in part of the gallery. The earth is dry and its color light brown, except in the corners of the cave where it is black and moist. Gravel and stone debris is scattered throughout the whole layer.

The division into two horizons is based mainly on the typology of the implements. In D-2 the percentage of retouched implements is considerable, and their retouching shows workmanship of outstanding quality. In D-1 their number is 1,888, and in D-2 1,862. Most of the implements are scrapers (84.06 percent in D-2, 73.73 percent in D-1). In D-2, 22 percent of the scrapers are carinated ones, whereas in D-1, end scrapers form the most important group, representing about 27 percent. Font Yves points are scarce in comparison with their number in the preceding layer. The Levallois technique still prevails in the chipping of the implements. The other implements are convex-faced flakes, cutting tools, blades, and points.

LAYER C. This layer belongs to the Upper Paleolithic V and has been named Atlitian. It was uncovered in chamber II and in the gallery. The earth is dry, hard, and black and includes some fragments of human and animal bones. This complex has been given the name "Atlitian" since it was discovered for the first time in the Cave of the Valley. Some 4,280 implements were found, most of them Peonean burins (25.59 percent) and carinated scrapers (35.93 percent), while blades or points are rare (3.17 percent). The flint came from various sources, tabular flint being used there for the first time.

LAYER B. This layer is Natufian and extends over the whole terrace and both chambers. Its thickness is 3 meters. Only in 1931, when the terrace was completely excavated, was the distinction made between Upper and Lower Natufian.

ARCHITECTURAL REMAINS. The wide terrace before the cave was probably the main dwelling place of Natufian man, which accounts for the numerous finds made there. In the center of the terrace several cup marks and a 41-centimeter-deep pit were hollowed out of the rock. The rim of the pit was accentuated by a border cut into the stone. To the east is a semicircular wall, built of big and small unhewn stones directly on bedrock, except for its eastern part, which stood on earth containing remains from the preceding stage. Between the wall and the cup marks were parts of a pavement made of large, flat stones. It is impossible however, to determine with certainty whether

Cave of the Valley.
Above: Haft of a sickle; the end is carved in the form of an animal head; Natufian period.
Below: Natufian burial; the skulls are decorated with dentalia.

these architectural remains are remains of dwellings, of a burial place, or of both.

BURIALS. On the terrace and in both chambers about eighty skeletons were found. Two main groups can be distinguished, probably belonging to two phases of the Natufian. (A) Group burials: The bodies are laid in a tightly flexed position. They wear necklaces of dentalia and bone ornaments, characteristic of Early Natufian. The heads rest on a layer of stones. (B) Individual burials: The position of the bodies is only slightly flexed. The skulls bear no ornaments. Most of the heads rest on a layer of stones, and in some cases the skeleton was covered with stones. These burials belong to the Late Natufian.

FLINT IMPLEMENTS. About 8,000 flint implements dating from Lower Natufian were found, most of which were small blades and 7.7 percent sickle blades. The tool that appears for the first time in the Natufian is the sickle blade of flint, clearly showing on the cutting edge the luster resulting from its use in harvesting. A few fragments of bone hafts were also found, into which the sickle blades had been set. In this layer a new technique of retouching can be distinguished in implements to be fitted into the hafts. Retouching was done on both faces of the same side, diminishing the thickness of the tool (Helwan retouch). It is found in 44.5 percent of the implements.

In the layer belonging to Upper Natufian, 4,400 implements were found, of which most are small blades and 8.8 percent sickle blades. The method of retouch, so frequent in the preceding stage, becomes less common and is found in only 19.2 percent of the implements. Other implements found are burins, scrapers, blades, and cutting tools.

STONE IMPLEMENTS. A varied complex of such objects is part of the Natufian culture. It includes mortars, stone bowls, and grinding stones made of basalt and limestone.

BONE TOOLS. About sixty complete bone tools and about 170 fragments were found. The most common are points made of animal long bones, harpoon points, fish hooks, flat bone implements, and sickle hafts. Most of the last are broken, yet their remarkable workmanship is noticeable. Two sickle blades fitted into one of them are still preserved.

ART. The Natufian is the first prehistoric culture

in Palestine in which art objects were found, carved in bone or stone. Animals are represented in a realistic style. Most of the art objects are tool hafts, decorated at their ends with an animal head. In the Cave of the Valley a human head carved in limestone was found. Other finds include stone pendants and beads made of animal bones and also of cardium and dentalium shells.

SUMMARY

The Human Type. In layer C of the Cave of the Oven, the skeleton of a woman (Tabun I) and a jawbone (Tabun II) were found. Examination of the skeletons showed that they were clearly of the Neanderthal type, although the jawbone was slightly more developed. The cranial capacity of the Tabun I skeleton is 1,271 cubic centimeters. The brow arcade is prominent and the skull base oblong. The skeleton of Tabun I is similar to skeletons found in the parallel cultural complex of the Shanidar Cave.

In the Cave of the Kid about ten skeletons were found, including two complete skeletons of adults (Skhul IV, V), one skeleton of a child, clear fragments of a female and a male skeleton, and fragments of five others. The cranial capacity of IV is 1,554 cubic centimeters and that of V, 1,450 cubic centimeters. The age of the adults did not exceed forty years. The skeletons of the Cave of the Kid show a strong affinity to *Homo sapiens* — the bones of the arcades are smaller, the chin is developed, and the skull base is shorter.

There is a longstanding controversy regarding the skeletons of the Cave of the Oven and the Cave of the Kid. McCown and A. Keith are of the opinion that the skeletons of these two caves belong to the same period and represent a type of man in the course of development from the Neanderthal type to *Homo sapiens*. They illustrate their viewpoint by two tables.

The first table shows the differences and similarities among the Neanderthal, the Cro-Magnon, and the Carmel Man and points to the fact that, of the twenty-five items basically belonging to the structure of the skull, only three items are similar to those of the Neanderthal Man, eight to those of the Cro-Magnon, eleven to the Intermediate, while three are undetermined. This means that the Carmel Man is closest to the Cro-Magnon Man.

In the second table which enumerates eighty-six items belonging to the structure of the skeleton, thirteen are similar to those of the Neanderthal Man, twenty-four to these of the Cro-Magnon, thirty-five to the Intermediate, while ten are undetermined, and four are specific to the Carmel Man only. Therefore, McCown and Keith suggested that the Carmel population and especially that of the Cave of the Kid represents the Intermediate stage which fills the gap between the Neanderthal and the Cro-Magnon. The Carmel Man reached this stage not by hybridization but by "natural and separate evolutionary history." It should be kept in mind, however, that the woman of the Cave of the Oven is closer to the Neanderthal and also that there is a close resemblance between the bones of that woman and those found in layer E of the Cave of the Oven.

After the publication of the report several scholars attempted to explain the phenomenon of the different types of man in the same period. Three kinds of approach can be distinguished:

1. The Intermediate type is not the outcome of hybridization but a stage in a "natural and separate evolutionary history."
2. There were two taxonomic groups, clearly associated with crossbreeding between them. This is the trend of Hutton, Thomas, and others.
3. There exists a chronological difference between the Neanderthal and other types. Specifically this difference is evident between the findings in the caves of the Kid and of the Oven. This is the view of D.R. Brothwell, T.D. Stewart, and E.S. Higgs. The latter thinks that there is a difference of 10,000 years between the population of the two caves. F. Bordes (1951) suggested that the Neanderthal man was not the only one to belong to the Mousterian period.

The numerous skeletons from the Natufian belong to the Mediterranean type.

Chronology and Paleoclimatology. Few chronological data were available to the excavators for dating the cultures of the Valley of the Caves. No ancient sea terraces were found; the northern shore had sunk; and there had been strong erosive activity (considerable quantities of erosion material were accumulated). During the excavations the sediments and the palynological finds from the different layers in the caves were not investigated sufficiently. These could have helped in the study of the climate and consequently have provided a description of the environment around the cave

It was thus necessary to rely on geological data found inside the caves, on comparative stratigraphy,on faunal remains, and on absolute chronology. Dorothy Bate and F.E. Zeuner tried to draw conclusions regarding climatic fluctuations from changes in the frequency of two animals—the fallow-deer *(Dama),* which lives in a moist climate and wooded areas, and the gazelle *(Gazella),* which is found in a dry climate. In Bate's and Zeuner's opinion, the three peaks in the proportion of deer bones mark three pluvial periods: the first in layer E-c in the Cave of the Oven, the second in layer B in the same cave, and the third in layer D in the Cave of the Valley. The first one is contemporary with the last Riss glacial period, the other two with the two Würm sub-glacial periods (Würm interglacial). Higgs established the existence of a dry climate according to the quantity of bones of bovines. He claims that layers B and C in the Cave of the Kid do not correspond to layers C and D in the Cave of the Oven, whereas layers C and D in the Cave of the Kid do indeed correspond to layer B in the Cave of the Oven. Higgs also based his opinion on analogies on the shores of the Mediterranean.

E. Tchernov reached a conclusion opposite to that of Dorothy Bate and Zeuner. He used in his research a sample of small rodent fauna. His conclusion was that in the Coastal Area, from the Middle Pleistocene, the climate had practically become dry. The swamps vanished in the Upper Mousterian.

J. Bouchud (1969) in his faunal research in the Qadzeh Cave shows that the faunal finds in the Mousterian layer indicate a wet climate, while in the Upper Paleolithic layer the climate was dry.

This method of trying to determine chronology on the basis of the fauna met with strong criticism. Numerous scholars argued that due to the interference in natural conditions made by man as a hunter, this is by no means an objective criterion. Another method of dating is mainly based on geological phenomena inside the caves. R. Neuville and F.C. Howell, for example, contend that the first evidence for the pluvial period is to be found only in layer D of the Cave of the Oven, where big quantities of gravel were discovered. This layer is accordingly to be ascribed to the first Würm sub-glacial period, whereas the preceding layers date from the Riss-Würm interglacial. Howell considers that all layers of the Cave of the Valley demonstrate that a dry climate prevailed there. He bases this on the fact that there are no remains from the pluvial period in the Valley of the Caves and, furthermore, in the Cave of the Valley there is a cultural rift between layers E–F and layers B–C which dates from the pluvial period. In the palynological studies carried out by M. Rossignol (1963) in the Carmel Area, wet climatic conditions appear in the Upper Pleistocene.

The geologists who dealt with sediments and with geological factors in the Coastal Plain found it difficult to define the findings because of the very narrow coast and because of tectonic effects. The studies of Slatkin and Rohrlich (1964), H. Michelson (1968), A. Issar, and L. Picard (1969) point, however, toward terrasses rising to 78 meters, 55 meters, 12 meters, and 4 meters above sea level. According to Slatkin and Rohrlich the terrasse of 78 meters and that of 55 meters both precede the formation of the caves, the 12-meter one belongs to the Middle Tyrrhenian and the 4-meter one to the Late Tyrrhenian. Farrand while summing up the climate of the Upper Pleistocene points out that it was 5 to 6 grades lower than today.

In his 1950 paper Howell summarizes the various concepts and presents a table wherein the climatic and cultural events are listed, as well as the data related to them. Garrod in her 1962 paper agrees with most of Howell's conclusions. In his 1968 paper J. Perrot also presents a summary table, but he puts the beginning of the historic layers in the Cave of the Oven at a slightly later period.

If we consider the early stratigraphy, layers G to E in the Cave of the Oven belong to the Riss-Würm interglacial, their date being 80,000 to 55,000 B.C. The Levallois-Mousterian layers belong to the beginning of Würm, their date being 55,000 to 35,000 B.C. With regard to the layers of the Upper Paleolithic, the early layers in the Cave of the Valley (G, F) belong to the Gottweig interpluvial, the Aurignacian, and later layers, until 15,000 B.C. The Natufian layers belong to the period 10,000 to 7,500 B.C.

Absolute Chronology. The Mousterian culture characterized by the Levallois technique is found on the shores of the Mediterranean and on the shoreline of the Tyrrhenian transgression III (Tyrrhenian III) corresponding to the Würm glacial period I–II. At Ras e-Kelb in Lebanon is a Mousterian culture somewhat earlier than layers C and D of the Cave of the Oven. It is dated by

Carbon-14 to about 52,000 years ago. Layer D at Shanidar is also early Mousterian, dated by radioactivity to 50,000 years ago. It follows that the beginning of the early stage of Mousterian is to be dated to the Würm interglacial II–I. The developed phase of Mousterian at Kabara and in the Geulah Cave (see below) is to be dated to 42,000 years ago, and at Qetzer 'Aquil to 44,000 years ago, *i.e.*, from Würm interglacial III to Würm II.

TAMAR NOY

GEULAH CAVE (MA'ARAT HA-GEULAH, MAP REFERENCE 15042446)

This cave is situated on the eastern slope of Mount Carmel, 205 meters above sea level. It is 2,500 meters south of the point where the outlet of Naḥal Gibborim — *Wadi Rushmiya* in Arabic — flows into the Mediterranean. The site lies now in the built-up area of the Geulah quarter of Haifa. The cave, as well as a narrow, undisturbed ledge along the face of the rocky cliff, are remnants of a former larger cave destroyed by recent quarry operations. Excavations in the two chambers of the cave and on the ledge — called a terrace by the excavator — were carried out by E. Wreschner in four seasons, 1958, 1960, 1963, and 1964.

Three layers were discovered, identical in archaeological content throughout the excavated area, their thickness varying in the cave and on the terrace. In layer B two stages could be distinguished and were designated accordingly.

Layer A. This layer, 10 to 30 centimeters thick, with gray dusty soil, contained Levallois-Mousterian flint implements, 2,176 animal bones, and horn and teeth fragments.

Layer B-1. This layer, 25 to 40 centimeters thick, with brown powdery soil, contained Levallois flint implements, bone tools, animal bones, ochre, and coproliths of *Hyaena*.

Layer B-2. This layer, 40 to 90 centimeters thick, with blackish-brown soil in which were charcoal fragments, contained Levallois flint implements of uniform size (all larger than those found in layer B-1), bone tools, and animal bones.

The two B layers yielded 9,412 bones, including horns and teeth; 318 bone tools; and three small bone fragments of humans.

Layer C. This layer, 5 to 20 centimeters thick, with light-brown powdery soil, rested on bedrock, filling cavities and crevices. It was found to be sterile.

DISTRIBUTION OF FLINT IMPLEMENTS

	LAYER A	LAYER B-1	LAYER B-2
Points	15.1 %	20.0 %	20.9 %
Levallois flakes	21.2 %	23.4 %	25.7 %
Racloirs	12.1 %	—	2.3 %
Scrapers	9.1 %	1.1 %	—
Knives	9.1 %	6.6 %	9.4 %
Denticulated pieces	—	—	4.6 %
Notched tools	—	3.3 %	—
Various flakes	33.4 %	39.0 %	27.9 %
Cores	—	3.3 %	4.6 %
Hammerstones	—	3.3 %	4.6 %

A sediment analysis of layers C to A (from bottom to top) by Elisabeth Schmid of Basel showed a change from a warm, humid climate (layer C) to a warm, dry one (layers B-2–B-1), followed by a change to colder, wet conditions (layer A).

A Carbon-14 examination of charred bones from layer B-1 gave a date of 42,000 ± 1,700 (Groningen Nr. 4121).

G. Haas of Jerusalem, in comparing the Geulah fauna with those from the Cave of the Oven C and the Cave of the Valley G, tends to believe that the Geulah fauna B-2–A represents a gradual change and not a faunal break.

E. WRESCHNER

BIBLIOGRAPHY

D. A. E. Garrod and D. M. A. Bate, *The Stone Age of Mount Carmel* 1, Oxford, 1937 • T. D. McCown and A. Keith, *The Stone Age of Mount Carmel* 2, Oxford, 1939 • E. Wreschner, M. Avnimelech, and S. Angress, *IEJ* 10 (1960), 78–89 • R. Vaufrey, *Revue Scientifique* 1939, 390–406 • A. Rust, *Die Höhlenfunde von Jabrud (Syria)*, Neumünster, 1950, *passim* • R. Neuville, *Le Paléolitique et le Mésolitique du Désert de Judée*, Paris, 1951, *passim* • D. A. E. Garrod and D. M. A. Bate, *JRAI* 81 (1951), 121–32 • D. A. E. Garrod, *Journal of World History* 1 (1953), 13–38 • F. Bordes, *L'Anthropologie* 59 (1955), 486–507; *idem, Neanderthal Centenary, 1856–1956*, Koeln-Graz, 1958, 175ff. • D. A. E. Garrod, *Quaternaria* 3 (1956), 39–59 • M. Stekelis, *EI* 4 (1956), 24–33 (Hebrew) • R. S. Binford, *New Perspectives in Archaeology*, Chicago, 1968, 49–60 • J. Bouchud, *International Quaternary Association, 8th Congress*, Paris, 1969, 118 • W. R. Farrond, *The Cenozoic Glacial Ages*, ed. K. Turekian, Yale University, 1968 • A. Issar and L. Picard, *Bull. Assoc. France, Etudes Quaternaires* 6 (1969), no. 18, 35 • M. Rossignol, *Israel Journal of Earth Sciences*, 12 (1963), 207 • H. Michelson, *ibid.*, 19 (1968), 71 • A. Slatkin and Rohrlich, *ibid.*, 13 (1964), 125–32.

Geulah Cave: E. Wreschner, M. Avnimelech, E. Schmid, G. Haas, and R. A. Dart, *Quaternaria* 9 (1967), 69–105 • E. Wreschner, *Actes VII Congr. Preh. and Protoh. Sciences*, Prague, 1970, 280–83 • E. Petter and E. Heintz, *Bull. Mus. Nat. d'Hist. Naturelle*, 2e série, Vol. 41, Nr. 5 (1969–70), 1292–98 • J. Heller, *Israel Journal of Zoology* 19 (1970), 1–49 • H. Frenkel, *ibid.*, 51–82.

CHOROZAIN

IDENTIFICATION. Chorozain (Chorazim, Khorizin in Talmudic sources), a Jewish city of the Roman period, is mentioned in the New Testament (Matthew 11:20–24, Luke 10:12–16), together with Bethsaida and Capernaum, as one of the three cities that Jesus upbraided for failing to accept his teachings. The Talmud (*Menahoth* 85-a) refers to it in connection with the laws of the *'Omer* offering. Eusebius (*Onomasticon* 174:23) states that Chorozain was two Roman miles from Capernaum and was in ruins in his day.

Until the middle of the last century, there were differing opinions as to the exact location of the city. Ancient Chorozain is now identified with a site 4 kilometers (2½ miles) north of Capernaum, called by the Arabs *Khirbet Karazeh.* At the western edge of the site flows the brook of Chorazain, which carries a large quantity of water during the winter. To the north an ancient road crosses the Jordan River near its entry into the Sea of Galilee and joins the main road running from the Bridge of the Daughters of Jacob to Damascus.

Plan of the synagogue. ▒ *existing* ☐ *conjectured.*

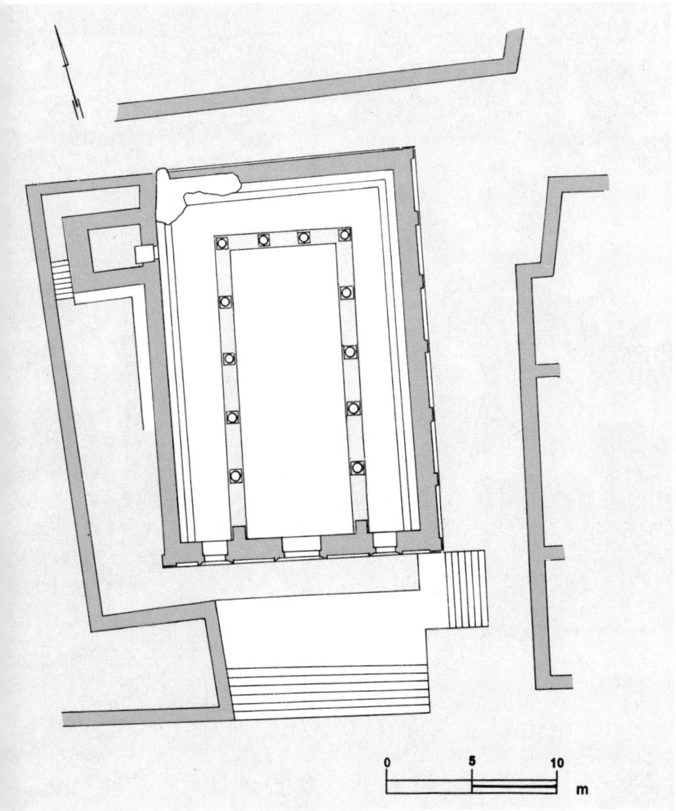

TOPOGRAPHY

The city lies in a mountainous area strewn with basalt stone. It covers the northern, southern, and eastern slopes of a low-lying hill (45 to 61 meters above sea level, 267 to 273 meters above the Sea of Galilee). About 300 meters east of the city is the spring Bir Karazeh, which carries the rainwater to the eastern section of the city. In the whole area around the city many dolmens are still standing. Near the spring are some scanty remains of a settlement dating from the Chalcolithic period.

The town of Chorazain itself covered an area of approximately 12 acres and was built on a number of terraces that divided it into several distinct quarters. a) A central quarter was situated on the highest elevation (61 meters above sea level). This included the most important public buildings, such as the synagogue, which, like the rest of the city, was built of basalt stone (see below). b) Another quarter, situated on the lowest terrace to the south (50 meters above sea level), contained, among other structures, two oil presses and a roofed-over water cistern. c) The third quarter, the most densely built, was situated on the western side of the hill. It was probably a residential area, which covered several broad terraces descending from an elevation of 55 meters above sea level down to the middle of the slope of the hill.

HISTORY

The city was evidently built after Bar Kokhba's revolt, probably on the ruins of a former settlement whose remains have not yet been excavated. With the growth of Jewish settlement in Galilee in the second century A.D., the city expanded. The synagogue, erected at the end of the second or the beginning of the third century, was demolished, apparently together with part of the city. This occurred in the second half of the fourth century —*i.e.,* after the death of the emperor Julian— when attacks by Christians against the synagogues and the Jewish community in Galilee were intensified. It seems that the normal life of the community, which had been resumed in the fifth century, was again interrupted at the end of the seventh or at the beginning of the eighth century. The site was deserted until the thirteenth century, when it was again settled. That settlement lasted until the fifteenth century. The Arab village of Karazeh arose only in the nineteenth century.

EXPLORATION

The City. Three excavation campaigns have thus far been carried out in the area. The first two were in the synagogue (see below). The third, undertaken by Z. Yeivin in 1962–63 on behalf of the Department of Antiquities, was chiefly concerned with excavating the structures of the central quarter surrounding the synagogue. This excavation uncovered a series of rooms in a large building bordering on the northern wall of the square in which the synagogue stood. This building complex also included three subterranean chambers, one of which was a cistern for storing water (with a capacity of circa 250 cubic meters), and another possibly a *miqve,* or ritual bath (3.5 by 2 by 4 meters). Adjoining them was a third, smaller room that probably served as a storeroom. A large building was uncovered to the east of the synagogue with a series of rooms that connected it to the eastern wing of the synagogue. In the west the periphery of the residential area, which also adjoined the synagogue, was cleared. All the buildings were erected without mortar (in dry masonry), using local basalt stone.

The architectural finds have made it possible to distinguish three stages in the construction of the synagogue area. The first stage is that of the original structure. The second is the period following the destruction of the synagogue, during which the surrounding buildings continued to function as

View of the synagogue from the northwest.

they formerly had. The third stage is assigned to a much later date.
The pottery and coins found in the area belong to the three main periods: second to fourth centuries, fifth to eighth centuries, and thirteenth to fifteenth centuries. Z. YEIVIN

The Synagogue

EXPLORATION. The synagogue was first identified by C. Wilson in 1869. Its remains were subsequently described by V. Guérin and H.H. Kitchener. In 1905–07 H. Kohl and C. Watzinger excavated part of its ruins on behalf of the Deutsche Orient-Gesellschaft. The presence on the site of a hut belonging to some Bedouins prevented the Germans from completing the excavations. It was only in 1926 that the synagogue was completely cleared, by N. Makhouly and J. Ory on behalf of the Department of Antiquities of the Mandatory Government. In the course of further excavations conducted by Z. Yeivin in 1962–63 in the city and in the vicinity of the synagogue, additional details connected with the building were unearthed.
PLAN. The synagogue (22.8 by 16.7 meters) was built of local basalt stone. It was situated in the interior of the city and surrounded by a block of large buildings. Several courses of ashlar are preserved from the walls. Of the southern wall, however, nothing remains above floor level. The façade of the building, which faces south toward Jerusalem, has three entrances. A courtyard, 5 meters wide, extends along the western wall. At the northern end of this courtyard was a small room adjoining the wall of the synagogue. It was entered from the hall. Several steps are preserved between this room and the walls of the courtyard. Apparently, these were part of a staircase leading to the upper story. On the northern and eastern sides, the synagogue is bordered by streets. At the southern side of the building (its façade) is a wide square (up to 9.5 meters from the façade) that was reached by steps ascending from the south and probably also from the east (see plan on page 299 for the proposed reconstruction of the steps).
The many architectural fragments found here, as in Capernaum, enable the interior and exterior features of the synagogue to be reconstructed with a fair degree of certainty.
THE FAÇADE OF THE SYNAGOGUE. The synagogue was divided by cornices into three horizontal sections—a lower story, an upper story, and the tympanum of the pediment. The height of the building to the highest point of the roof was about 16.5 meters. The façade of the lower story evidently had only two pilasters at the corners. It had three entrances: a large entrance in the center and a smaller one on each side. All were surrounded by molded frames. Above the lintel of the main entrance (3.2 meters wide) was a cornice supported by two decorated consoles, and above the cornice there was probably an arched window.

Three different stages of construction (Roman I, III, and IV) from the city area near the synagogue.

The façade of the second story seems to have been provided with three windows decorated with conches, which were found among the ruins. Two of the conches terminated in an arch, and the third was surmounted by a pediment. The decorated cornices of the roof pediment terminated at their bottom in horizontal platforms. According to one opinion, these platforms were occupied by sculptured lions, parts of which were found in the course of the excavations. Other scholars, however, believe that the lions were placed at the sides of the Ark of the Law. Below the cornice of the pediment and parallel to it there was probably a frieze decorated with the stylized form of lions protruding from acanthus leaves. This pedimental frieze was crowned with an eagle, of which the head and feet are now missing.
Pilasters with Attic bases and Ionic capitals divided the eastern wall of the building into five sections. Above the pilasters was a cornice, and it is certain that the second story had windows on the south, east, and west sides.
INTERIOR. The interior is divided by two longitudinal and one transverse row of columns into a

nave (6.6 meters wide) and aisles (3.2 meters wide) that surrounded the nave on three sides. Two rows of benches, parts of which are missing, run along the length of all the walls except the wall at the entrance. A large boulder, which for some reason had not been removed during the construction of the building, is conspicuous in the northwest corner. Ten of the twelve square pedestals and two semi-pedestals, on which the columns rested, were found standing on stylobates. Each column pedestal and Attic base is made of one stone block. A number of fragments of the monolithic columns were uncovered. Several capitals displaying two different styles were also found. Some are in a quasi-Ionic style, with four smooth volutes. Some are in a quasi-Doric style, with two consoles protruding at the sides. The general height of a column with all its parts was approximately 5 meters. The fact that not a single fragment of an architrave came to light led to the conjecture that there must have been arched colonnades. Fragments of smaller columns apparently belonged to the upper story, which served as the women's gallery, as was common in most of the synagogues.

The fragments that are presumably parts of the upper story mainly include the decorated friezes, which were found in great numbers. As in Capernaum, they had been placed (according to Kohl–Watzinger) along the upper part of the walls of the gallery. The walls were divided by pilasters with Attic bases and Corinthian capitals.

DECORATION. Above the pilasters were the friezes, crowned by a separately constructed cornice. The convex friezes were decorated with reliefs. They are distinguished from the decorations found at Capernaum by their schematic style and by the fact that human and animal figures frequently appear alongside the floral patterns. The recurrent basic motif of the decorations is a medallion of acanthus leaves with patterns of rosettes, shells, wreaths, or other objects carved in the center. The figures of men and animals have been better preserved here than in the other synagogues of Galilee, but the hand of the iconoclasts is much in evidence, especially in the mutilation of the human faces. Only one face, that of a Medusa, has been preserved undamaged.

Among the decorations worth noting is a vintage scene set amid vine tendrils, depicting two men either bearing clusters of grapes or treading grapes; a galloping centaur; a lion attacking a centaur; a beast suckling its whelp; and a lion devouring its prey. The protruding sections of the friezes above the capitals are decorated with various patterns — a recumbent figure holding a cluster of grapes with the wings of an eagle in the background; an architectural motif resembling the form of a window commonly found in the synagogues, that is, a gabled conch carried by two colonnettes. Fragments of the branches of a menorah carved in relief were also found.

One of the noteworthy finds of the synagogue is an armchair made of basalt stone in the form of a square block, its back decorated with a rosette pattern. On the chair is an engraved memorial

A seat (cathedra) of Moses; basalt, with an Aramaic inscription. Bottom: Arch with conch.

inscription in Aramaic which reads: "Remembered be for good Judan b. Ishmael who made this portico [stoa] and its staircase. As his reward may he have a share with the righteous." This chair seems to be of the type referred to in the New Testament (Matthew 23:2) as the Seat (Cathedra) of Moses. It was designed to serve as a seat for the sages, and is also alluded to in Talmudic literature. A more simple seat of this kind was discovered by N. Slousch in 1921 in the synagogue at Hammath-Tiberias (q.v. Tiberias).

The Chorozain synagogue, like the other early synagogues in Galilee, had no fixed place for the Ark of the Law. The portable ark was apparently kept in the adjoining annex on the west and brought into the main hall only when needed.

Summary. The synagogue of Chorozain is one of the earliest synagogues of Galilee built of dressed stone in the form of a basilica with carved decorations. According to literary sources, it was in ruins at the beginning of the fourth century. It follows then that it had been built as early as the third century. Although smaller in size, it closely resembles the synagogue in Capernaum in the form of its façade and its profusion of interior decorations. The rigid, primitive carving of the decorations is usually explained as being the result of the use of a hard basalt stone. In any case, there is no doubt that the decorations were made by several artisans employing different styles. It also bears a marked resemblance to the highly formalized and rigid Byzantine carving, despite the centuries that separate them. There are numerous representations of human figures, of other living creatures, and of mythological animals. Since the reliefs of images in Chorozain were not mutilated by religious fanatics as were those in Capernaum and Kefar Bar'am, their style and subject matter are better known.

N. Avigad

BIBLIOGRAPHY

C. W. M. van de Velde, *Memoirs to Accompany the Maps of the Holy Land,* Gotha, 1858, 304 • Robinson, *Biblical Researches* 2, 346–60 • Guérin, *Galilée* 1, 241–42 • Conder-Kitchener, *SWP* 1, 400–02; *idem, Palestine Pilgrim Texts* 3, London, 1891, 16f. • Abel, *GP* 2, 299–300 • E. L. Sukenik, *Tarbiz* 1 (1930), 145–51, 135–36 (Hebrew) • N. Epstein, *ibid.,* 152 • Z. Yeivin, in *All the Land of Naphtali,* Jerusalem, 1967, 135ff. (Hebrew) • *idem., EI* 11 (1973), 144–57 (Hebrew) • J. Meshorer, *ibid.,* 158–62 • H. Kohl–C. Watzinger, *Synagogen,* 4–58 • E. L. Sukenik, *Ancient Synagogues,* 21–24 • E. R. Goodenough, *Jewish Symbols* 1, 193–99.

CHURCHES

The earliest church thus far discovered is at Dura-Europus, dating from the first half of the third century. In Christian sources references are made to churches built at that time in Caesarea, Gaza, and other places. Numerous churches were erected in Palestine from the beginning of the fourth century (after Christianity had attained the status of a recognized religion) to the eighth century. The Emperor Constantine built large basilicas at Bethlehem (q.v.) and Jerusalem (q.v.). He also contributed to the construction of churches in Jewish cities of Galilee in an effort to spread Christianity. However, the majority of the churches whose ruins have survived in Palestine were built from the middle of the fifth to the beginning of the seventh century.

Most of the excavated churches have been dealt with under the various headings in this encyclopedia. Only those that did not warrant a separate entry are grouped here.

'AGUR (Khirbet al-'Anab)

Northwest of the village of 'Agur (map reference 142122). In 1957 the remains of a basilica situated on a hill and dating from the end of the fourth or the beginning of the fifth century were cleared by R. Gofna, on behalf of the Department of Antiquities. The church has a semicircular, external apse (2.7 meters in radius). The east section of the nave (13 by 10 meters) with a mosaic floor laid in geometric patterns was uncovered. The nave had been separated from the northern aisle by two columns whose bases were found in situ. A section of the atrium's northern wall and a small chamber attached to the southern wall of the hall were also cleared. The fragment of a baptismal font was found on the plastered floor of the chamber.

Among the finds were fourteen bronze coins, attributed to the fourth century, discovered in the area of the bema. Also found were the fragments of a marble chancel screen, a small marble reliquary with no lid, and a marble column 1.75 meters high.

'AIN HANNIYA

Circa 7 kilometers ($4\frac{1}{2}$ miles) southwest of Jerusalem (map reference 165128). In 1932 a basilica dating from the fifth/sixth century was excavated

Map showing sites where churches have been excavated
The sites shown by ▲ appear as separate entries.

here by D.C. Baramki, on behalf of the Department of Antiquities of the Mandatory Government.

The atrium (circa 10 meters long) had been paved with white tesserae and surrounded by porticoes. The east portico, resting on a stylobate, had given access to the narthex. The latter (10 by 3 meters) is paved with mosaics laid in a scale pattern enclosed by a border of small flowers. Of the three doorways in the eastern wall, the central one had opened into the nave and the side ones into the aisles. The hall (15 by 10 meters) had been divided into a nave and aisles by two rows of five columns. The mosaic floor of the nave (circa 5 meters wide) is decorated with a vine trellis, which forms round medallions and apparently issues from an amphora located on the west side. The schola cantorum had been set one step higher than the nave. Two other steps lead into the semicircular inscribed apse (2.5 meters in radius), which is paved with flagstones. Traces of an altar, beneath which a marble reliquary had been set, were found in the chord of the apse.

The mosaic floor of the southern aisle (circa 2.5 meters wide) is also laid in a scale pattern. The diaconicon, which had been paved with white tesserae, contains traces of an altar and of a niche in its southwest corner.

The northern aisle is paved with mosaics in intersecting bands forming squares, with a floral design in the center of each square. One step leads from the aisle to the prothesis, which had been paved in mosaics and ornamented with crosses around the site of the altar.

D.C. Baramki, *QDAP* 3 (1933), 113–17.

ʿAIN KAREM

Circa 4½ kilometers (3 miles) west of Jerusalem (map reference 165130). The present church dedicated to Saint John is built on the ruins of a Byzantine church, of which a fragment of a mosaic pavement was discovered as early as 1674. The remains of the latter building were excavated by S.J. Saller in 1941–42.

West of St. John's Church were cleared the remains of a Chapel of the Martyrs, parts of which had already been discovered in 1885. Another section of the structure came to light in 1939, but only in 1941 was the chapel completely cleared by Saller.

Of the chapel (17 by 12.5 meters), the east, west, and north walls (the last-mentioned forming the

Plans. *Top: 1. Khirbet Kufin. 2. Khirbet Asida. Bottom: 1. Suḥmata. 2. 'Ain Hanniya.*

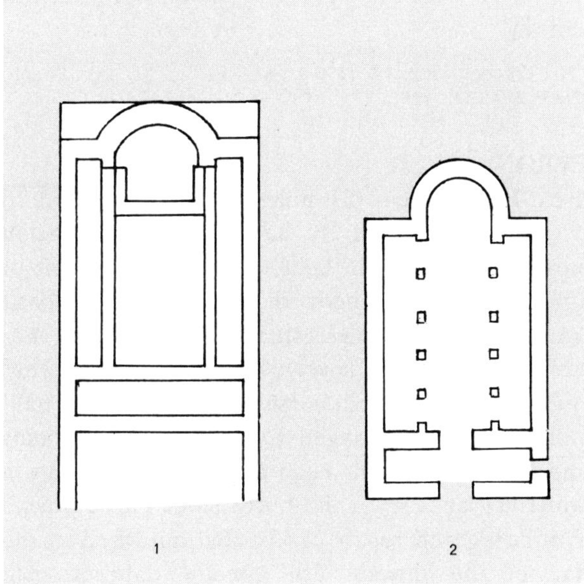

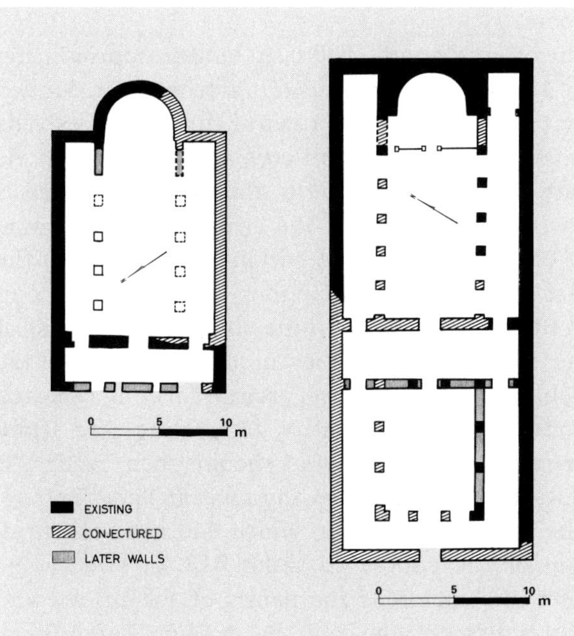

west wall of the church) have survived. Two rock-hewn tombs were discovered in the apse.

The schola cantorum of the chapel is raised about one meter above the hall. Its mosaic floor is decorated with a large rhombus motif surrounded by a border of acanthus leaves. A pair of doves and a plant are represented in each of the upper corners. Two peacocks face each other in the lower ones. Each of the large rhombi contains nine small ones arranged in three rows and filled with various guilloche patterns. A four-line Greek inscription is set in a square in the center of one rhombus. The schola cantorum is flanked by rooms on either side. In 1941 Saller discovered near the southern wall of the Chapel of the Martyrs another chapel (13.1 by 8.3 meters), with an external apse (2.7 meters deep). This he called the Southern Chapel. Its inner walls are plastered, and the schola (8.5 by 2.5 meters), which had run along the whole eastern wall of the chapel, is raised .5 meters above the hall level. A fragment of a mosaic pavement laid in geometric patterns is preserved on the northern side. A chancel screen had separated the schola from the hall, as attested by the discovery of four screen-post bases and fragments of others.

Both chapels are attributed to the sixth century.

S.J. Saller, *Discoveries at St. John's, Ein Karim 1941–42*, Jerusalem, 1946.

'ASIDA, KHIRBET

Circa 10 kilometers (6 miles) north of Hebron (map reference 160113). In 1932 a basilica of the fifth/sixth century was excavated by D.C. Baramki and M. Avi-Yonah, on behalf of the Mandatory Department of Antiquities. The narthex, containing two doorways in the south and west sides, had been paved with a mosaic floor ornamented in a scale pattern. The western doorway leads into the hall (12 by 9 meters), which had been divided into a nave and two aisles by two rows of four columns. The mosaic floor of the nave has a vine trellis emerging from an amphora and forming round medallions in which bunches of grapes, pomegranates, a caged bird, and a flamingo are depicted. The church bears visible evidence of the activity of the iconoclasts in the eighth century who transformed the shapes of the birds and beasts (a lion) into plants. The floors of the aisles are paved in mosaics laid in a simple design.

D.C. Baramki and M. Avi-Yonah, *QDAP* 3 (1933), 17–19.

BAḤAN

North of Tulkarm (map reference 152195). In 1955 J. Ory excavated this site on behalf of the Department of Antiquities. A sixth-century basilica was unearthed, with two superimposed mosaic pavements in the nave. The upper mosaic (a section circa 5 to 6 meters was explored) is divided into two equal fields. The eastern part is ornamented with various geometric patterns, while the western has a uniform pattern. The lower, of which the western edge has been uncovered, is decorated with a vine trellis issuing from two amphorae and forming round medallions containing representations of animals and birds. A Greek inscription in one long line mentions the names of the donors.

In the center of the south side of the nave, a seven-line Greek inscription in a round medallion mentions the "brothers Porphyrius and Marcus." East of it is another inscription of six lines set in a *tabula ansata,* which also mentions names of donors. A third inscription of ten lines enclosed in a frame includes the verse: "...Holiness becometh thine house, O Lord, for ever" (Psalms 93:5).

Fragments of mosaics in geometric patterns are preserved in the northern aisle. In the southern aisle two superimposed mosaic floors were cleared. The upper one is bisected by a border. The western section is filled with a scale pattern, while the eastern section is decorated with a design of interlaced circles that form four-petaled flowers. The mosaic floor of the lower level is laid in a geometric pattern and contains a six-line dedicatory inscription in Greek that mentions the priest Julianus and the first Christian martyr, Saint Stephen. The narthex, the floor of which is paved with mosaics in patterns similar to those in the church, is provided with three doorways. One leads into the nave, the others to the aisles.

BEIT JIMAL

Circa 25 kilometers ($15\frac{1}{2}$ miles) west of Jerusalem (map reference 147125). In 1916 the ruins of a basilica were discovered here. It measures 15 by 10 meters and has a rectangular external apse. A section of the mosaic floor of the nave was uncovered. It is decorated with geometric designs. In its center is a Greek inscription, of which only the ends of five lines are preserved.

F.M. Abel, *RB* 28 (1919), 244f. • M. Avi-Yonah, *QDAP* 2 (1932), 148.

DEIR SHA'AR (Beit Sha'ar)

Circa .5 kilometers west of Kefar Ezion (map reference 182117). In 1902 the remains of a church with an inscribed apse were discovered here. A fragmentary four-line inscription in Greek in the mosaic pavement mentions the names of several donors. The church has been dated to the end of the sixth century.

L.H. Vincent, *RB* 12 (1903), 612–14 • M. Avi-Yonah, *QDAP* 2 (1932), 149.

'EVRON

Circa 9 kilometers ($5\frac{1}{2}$ miles) north of Accho. In 1951 M. Avi-Yonah, P. Kahana, and Y. Landau excavated the site on behalf of the Department of Antiquities. They uncovered a fifth-century basilica (14.5 by 10.6 meters), which is divided into three halls by two rows of five pillars. Another row of pillars found outside, south of the hall, apparently had belonged to a loggia. Two rooms (one of which had been a diaconicon) and a baptistery appear on the north side. Three phases of building and repair can be distinguished in the plan of the church. The specific date of each alteration is stated in several inscriptions (fourteen in Greek and one in Syriac) discovered in the floors.

The original church had been built in approximately 415. It had consisted of an atrium surrounded by porticoes with two rows of three columns. The mosaic floors of the porticoes are laid in geometric patterns. On either side of the entrance, which is at the western end of the atrium, the monogram of Christ (☧) is placed within a guilloche. To the east, two Greek inscriptions are set directly in front of the entrance to the church. In the first of the five remaining lines of one inscription, the Hebrew letter *yod,* in its archaic form, is repeated three times, apparently designating the Holy Trinity. The inscription should then read: "O Holy Trinity, remember thy servant Timothy."

The second inscription, which dates the construction of the church to about 415, is twenty-one lines and mentions the names of the priests and the craftsmen who laid the mosaics. Later floors covered the remains of the first structure in the whole of the building except for a single room on the north side. In that room the original pavement is preserved, though it, too, has undergone repairs. The church had been thoroughly renovated in

Shavei Zion; mosaic pavements.

442–43. A nine-line inscription dating from that year was discovered in the nave. It is the longest inscription found on the site and relates that the church had not only been provided with new beams and mosaics, but totally reconstructed. The mosaics from the second phase of building are all decorated with geometric patterns. A square, unpaved area in the nave marks the site of the altar. The upper floors of two other side rooms also belong to this period. One of these rooms had originally served as a diaconicon; the other had been a baptistery. In the diaconicon a depression in the floor was found, which apparently had served as a basin for washing the agricultural tithes presented to the church. Dedicatory inscriptions were found in these rooms; one mentions a *φωτιστήριον* ("place of light"), *i.e.,* it had served as a baptistery.

In 490 the building had been further modified by the addition of a narthex. The foundations of the narthex walls were laid over the original floor of 415, as stated in the fragmentary eleven-line inscription set in a round frame at the center of the mosaic floor of the narthex.

The chancel screen posts, which had been set into the pavement at a later date (442–43), may also belong to this period of construction. According to the traces remaining on the floor, the chancel screen had run along the whole width of the nave and had been provided with a narrow passageway giving access to the enclosed area.

M. Avi-Yonah, *Christian News from Israel* 5 (1955), 21–22; *idem, 'Alon* 5–6 (1957), 34–35 (Hebrew) • Y. Buk in *Western Galilee and Its Coast,* Jerusalem, 1961, 78–80 (Hebrew).

ḤADAT, ḤORVAT (Khirbet el-Hadatha)

Near Kibbutz Sha'albim (map reference 151143). In 1962 a basilica of the fifth century was excavated here by R. Cohen, on behalf of the Department of Antiquities. The church, which had been constructed in two phases, is built of well-dressed limestone (thickness of walls, 1.1 meters). The apse is external and its mosaic pavement has a floral design.

Two entrances leading into the nave (8.3 meters long) were uncovered. The nave had been separated from the aisles by rows of three columns. The intercolumnar spaces are paved in geometric designs placed within a border. Another mosaic pavement decorated with varied geometric motifs was uncovered in the south aisle. A post of the chancel screen was found. A mosaic with a guilloche ornamentation was found beside it. The nave is paved with mosaics, and at the east end, near the steps leading to the bema, the mosaic contains a three-line inscription in Greek enclosed in a rectangular frame: "As the hart panteth after the water brooks, so panteth my soul after Thee, O God" (Psalms 42:1).

ḤANITA

Excavations on the site were begun in 1940 by M. Avi-Yonah, on behalf of the Mandatory Government Department of Antiquities. The remains of a basilica of the sixth century were uncovered. The excavations were resumed in 1956 by M. Prausnitz for the Israel Department of Antiquities.

The basilica (17 by 14 meters) has an external apse and is divided by two rows of four columns into a nave (13 by 7 meters) and two aisles. The mosaic floor of the nave is decorated with geometric patterns. A hunting scene is depicted in mosaic in the narthex, together with two inscriptions in Greek. One mentions the names of the priests who served at the time the church was built. The other inscription apparently contains the names of the donors.

M. Prausnitz in *Western Galilee and Its Coast,* Jerusalem, 1961, 68–69 (Hebrew).

ḤAZOR-ASHDOD

Circa 17 kilometers ($10\frac{1}{2}$ miles) northeast of Ashkelon (map reference 123130). In 1956 J. Ory, on behalf of the Department of Antiquities, excavated the ruins of a basilica (12.5 by 10.5 meters) here. The apse had probably been external. The two aisles (each 2.5 meters wide) had been separated from the nave (5 meters wide) by two rows of three columns. In the western wall of the church, three doorways had led into the narthex (3 meters wide). Also found were the remains of a hall that had run along the entire north side of the church. The mosaic pavement of the nave is composed of a single field within a wavy border. Its center is divided into seven rows of three medallions each. Fifteen of the twenty-one medallions are preserved. A vine trellis rising out of an amphora located in the center of the bottom row frames the other medallions. The amphora is flanked by lions on both sides. In the other medallions are representations of various beasts (a deer and a wolf, etc.) and birds. The aisles are paved with mosaics laid in geometric patterns.

At the foot of the steps leading to the schola cantorum in the east side of the nave, a six-line inscription in Greek is set in a round frame. It states that the laying of the mosaic was completed on the tenth day of the month of Daesius in the year 615 of the fifth indiction (A.D. 512).

EL-ḤUBEILA, KHIRBET

Circa 10 kilometers (6 miles) southwest of Bethlehem (map reference 160119). In 1925 the French Biblical and Archaeological School in Jerusalem uncovered a basilica here. It had been 16 by 12.5 meters with an external apse and dates from the fifth/sixth century. Two rows of four columns had separated the nave from the two side aisles.

The mosaic pavement of the nave consists of a field set in a guilloche border. The field is ornamented with a pattern of flowers with twenty-four petals. Each flower is divided into four zones by diagonal bands of black leaves. Part of a rectangular panel decorated with two fishes and plants is preserved in front of the apse. In the west side of the nave, in front of the doorway, is another panel filled with interlocking geometric designs.

The southern aisle is paved with a geometric pattern of squares with tiny crosses in their centers.

F.M. Abel, *RB* 34 (1925), 279–82 • L.H. Vincent, *RB* 48 (1939), 87–90.

EL JADUDA

Twelve kilometers ($7\frac{1}{2}$ miles) south of 'Amman. Only the apse and part of the entrance remain of the church. The length of the church had been 16 meters. On the mosaic floor of the nave, in front of the doorway, was found an eight-line Greek dedicatory inscription that states that the church was erected in the days of the bishop Theodosius, in the year 653.

R. Savignac, *RB* 12 (1903), 436; 36 (1927), 589 • A. Alt, *ZDPV* 55 (1932), 132–34 • S. Saller, *JPOS* 21 (1948), 143.

KAFR KAMA

Twelve kilometers ($7\frac{1}{2}$ miles) southwest of Tiberias. In 1961 and 1963 the Finnish Oriental Society, under the direction of A. Saarisalo, uncovered a baptistery and a chapel, dating from the sixth century, which had been part of a complex of buildings belonging to either a church or a monastery.

In the baptistery, which had had an apse and a baptismal font, were found two superimposed mosaic pavements ornamented with floral and faunal designs and geometric patterns. Three Greek inscriptions in the floor mention the names of the bishop and church officials. An invocation to Saint Thecla is included in two of the inscriptions.

North of the apse of the baptistery is a chapel containing an inscribed apse (3.5 meters in radius) with a mosaic floor in geometric design. Of special interest among the finds is a small marble chest set in the mosaic pavement. It had served apparently as a reliquary.

A. Saarisalo, *IEJ* 11 (1961), 197; 13 (1963), 149.

KEFAR TRUMAN

North of Lod (map reference 143154). In 1958 remains of a sixth-century basilica were excavated here by Warda Sussman on behalf of the Department of Antiquities. No trace of the apse was discovered. The mosaic floor of the nave (.5 by 5.4 meters) is laid in a pattern of scales and small squares and contains a five-line inscription in Greek, which mentions Eusebius, a priest, who is also called "abbot." It is thus likely that the church was part of a monastery. The mosaic floor of the two aisles (.5 by 1.7 meters) is laid in colored squares. The diaconicon (1.4 by 1.7 meters) and the prothesis (2.1 by 1.7 meters) were also uncovered.

KUFIN, KHIRBET

Circa 11 kilometers (7 miles) north of Hebron (map reference 160114). In 1931 D.C. Baramki, on behalf of the Mandatory Government Department of Antiquities, excavated a basilica (20 by 12 meters) with an inscribed apse, narthex, and forecourt. The walls of the church had been destroyed below floor level. The site had apparently served as a dwelling place after the destruction of the church.

D.C. Baramki, *QDAP* 4 (1934), 118–19.

MA'IN (biblical Ba'al Ma'on)

Eight kilometers (5 miles) southwest of Madeba. In 1937 the remains of church were excavated here by R. de Vaux, on behalf of the French School of Biblical Archaeology in Jerusalem.

Only the western part of the nave (16.5 by 9.5 meters) and a chapel on its northern side are preserved. The remaining sections of the mosaic floor indicate that it had consisted of a field of geometric patterns enclosing a fruit basket, bunches of grapes, hunting scenes, etc. The field had been surrounded by a border (.7 meters wide) containing representations of churches. The name of a Palestinian city is written in Greek above each church, as in the Madeba map (q.v.) The churches are separated from each other by branching trees. The border seems to have originally contained twenty-four churches, but only eleven have survived: Nicopolis (Emmaus), Ashkelon, Maiumas, Gaza, Odroh, Kerak-Moab, Areopolis, Gadora, Heshbon, Ba'al-Ma'on, and another that may be either Lod or Beth Govrin.

The artist had attempted, with little success, to depict the churches according to their types of structure, *e.g.*, as basilicas, cruciform churches, rotundas, and churches with transepts. At the east end, near the bema, was found the fragment of a mosaic containing the verse "Then shall they offer bullocks upon thine altar" (Psalms 51:19) in Greek. The mosaic pavement at the west end of the nave, near the doorway, contains another Greek inscription with verses from Psalms and the date 614. The excavators calculated it according to the era of Provincia Arabia — *i.e.*, A.D. 720 — but the true date seems to be that of the era of Heshbon (Esbus) (circa A.D. 394).

Little has survived of the mosaic floor of the chapel. It had been decorated with a vine trellis issuing out of a goblet and, left of it, was found the fragmentary image of a beast described in the Messianic prophecies. Above it is the Greek inscription: "And the lion shall eat straw like the ox" (Isaiah 11:7).

R. de Vaux, *RB* 47 (1938), 227–58.

MICHMASH (Muḥmas)

Ten kilometers (6 miles) north of Jerusalem (map reference 176142). In 1931 the remains of a sixth-century basilica were excavated here under the direction of R.W. Hamilton, on behalf of the Department of Antiquities.

The church had been almost totally destroyed by later Arab building, and only fragments of the floor of the nave were uncovered. The two rows of columns separating the nave from the aisles seem to have contained at least three columns. The mosaic floor is decorated with geometric patterns and contains a six-line inscription in Greek, mentioning the name of a donor who had provided funds for the construction of the church and the laying of the mosaics.

R. W. Hamilton, *QDAP* 1 (1932), 103–04 • M. Avi-Yonah, *QDAP* 3 (1933), 35–36.

MISHMAR-HA'EMEQ

The remains of a church were excavated in 1936 by R. Giveon, on behalf of the Department of Antiquities, uncovering the nave and the southern aisle. The eastern and southern walls of the wall (10 by 4.5 meters) are built of large ashlars, whereas the northern wall is built of rubble. A column base was found in situ in the southern wall.

Several phases of construction can be distinguished. An external apse, of which only the foundations remain, had been added to the eastern side of the building at a later date. A marble cross (16 centimeters high) discovered in the area of the apse apparently had been part of the chancel screen.

The mosaic floor of the nave is ornamented with colored geometric patterns that form two octagons. Guilloche and various other patterns fill the octagons and the spaces around them. To the west of them, in the center of the western part of the pavement, a seven-line Greek inscription set in a circular frame states that the floor had been donated by a deacon named John, in memory of his relatives. The inscription is surrounded by geometric and floral designs and rows of conches.

Coarse white tesserae had been used to repair the mosaic floor. The southern aisle is paved in the same manner. According to the ceramic evidence, all the various phases of building had been done within a brief period of time, apparently in the fifth century.

Archaeological News 9 (1964), 19–20 (Hebrew).

OZEM

A village built in part over the site of Khirbet Beth-M'amim (map reference 121116). In 1945 R. Gofna, on behalf of the Department of Antiquities, cleared the remains of a basilica that had been partially destroyed during the building of a medieval structure.

The mosaic floor of the nave appears to have been set in a border framing a field decorated with geometric patterns. The latter consists of hexagons and squares, as well as medallions and lozenges. Figures of animals are represented on the field. In the western section of the border, which is preserved, appear two lions on either side of a cross. At the upper part of the cross are the Greek letters ☧ , and at its foot are the initials I(- *'Ιησοῦς*) and X(-*Χριστός*). The still-existing northern side of the floor is decorated with figures of birds. Of the three Greek inscriptions laid in the mosaic floor, one, of five lines set inside a circle, mentions the year in which the construction of the church was completed. Another inscription, inside a semicircle, refers to a monk, one Zomnus.

The mosaic floor of the northern aisle is laid in geometric patterns made up of intertwining large and small circles. It contains a seven-line Greek inscription that mentions the Virgin Mary and a woman called Marcella. Intertwined hexagons similar to those of the northern aisle make up the mosaic pavement of the narthex.

EL-QUWEISMA

Three kilometers (2 miles) south of 'Amman (map reference 238148). The mosaic pavement of a basilica discovered here is the best preserved part of the building. In the nave, the mosaic is ornamented with intersecting circles filled with representations of plants and animals — a ram and a lion — and birds. A one-line Greek inscription was found: "Lord, protect this building." It appears in front of the schola. The southern aisle is paved with intersecting circles and squares in which three churches and a pitcher are depicted. West of it another Greek inscription relates that the church had been renovated during the first indiction of the year 780. S. Saller believes that the date is to be reckoned according to the era of Pompey and corresponds to A.D. 717/718.

In the eastern intercolumnary space of the southern aisle, a fragment of a mosaic pavement with a fourteen-line inscription in Syriac has survived.

S. Saller and B. Bagatti, *Town of Nebo,* Jerusalem, 1949, 251–68.

RESHEF (APOLLONIA)

In the vicinity of Herzlia (map reference 132177). Following the discovery of a mosaic pavement here, excavations were carried out on behalf of the Department of Antiquities in 1962. A church dating from the sixth century was partially cleared. The section of the nave explored is bisected by

two pillars. It is paved with a delicately colored mosaic ornamented with medallions that contain geometric designs and a cross. There are also rows of small birds. A spacious court paved with multi-colored marble flags was also found.
A Greek inscription in three lines, 2.5 meters long, was found in the west side of the pavement of the nave. It contains a poem written in hexameters, which describes the church and its construction by a certain Marinos.

RIḤAB

Twenty kilometers (12½ miles) northwest of Gerasa (map reference 225205). Of the numerous remains from the Byzantine period discovered here, the most outstanding are the ruins of four churches and a monastery. According to the existing mosaic pavements and the Greek inscriptions, the church of the Prophet Isaiah was the earliest built on the site. The second church, that of Saint Basil the Martyr, is a basilica with an inscribed apse, prothesis, and diaconicon. The base of an altar and a reliquary were found in the apse. This church was completed in A.D. 594. The third church, that of Holy Wisdom (Hagia Sophia), seems to have once been part of a monastery. Two Greek inscriptions, laid in the mosaic pavement of its nave, mention the names of its builders and the date of its inauguration — A.D. 604. The fourth church, that of Saint Stephen, the protomartyr, was built in A.D. 620.

M. Avi-Yonah, *QDAP* 13 (1948), 68–72.

ROGLIT

Circa 22 kilometers (13½ miles) southwest of Jerusalem (map reference 150120). Excavations near this village, in which a basilica (14 by 10.7 meters) dating from the fifth century was cleared, were begun by R. Gofna in 1959 and continued by Warda Sussman, both on behalf of the Department of Antiquities.
The apse of the church was not uncovered. The parts of the building cleared include a trapezoid-shaped narthex, the central doorway in the western wall of the church, and another doorway in the southern wall. Near the last a recess paved with mosaic was found. From the narthex — which is paved with tiny white tesserae — three doorways open into the interior of the church. Near the middle doorway — the widest of the three — were found two sockets into which the hinges of double-wing doors apparently had been set.
Spaces left for columns in the mosaic pavement indicate that the nave had been separated from the aisles by two rows of three columns. The north-western column was found in situ. A pillar base, a Corinthian capital, and fragments of other capitals were also found. The mosaic floor of the hall is divided by intersecting geometric bands into medallions ornamented with green leaves. The southern aisle is paved with geometric patterns — interlacing polygons (octagons, hexagons, squares) filled with stylized floral ornaments. The center of the pavement is decorated with an octagon containing a pomegranate tree, a bowl of figs, an ethrog, a lemon, and the Greek letter *A*. A marble panel of a chancel screen decorated with a Maltese cross set in two intersecting squares was also found. In the middle of the screen is an opening with a step leading up to the schola cantorum. The latter is paved with a red-and-black pattern of circles set in a white field.
The mosaic pavement of the northern aisle is decorated with guilloche work laid in geometric patterns. It is preserved in its entirety. A circular medallion fills the center of each field thus formed. In one of them are two bunches of grapes rising out of an amphora.

SHAVEI ZION

Seven kilometers (4½ miles) north of Accho. The church, discovered in 1955, was excavated by M. Prausnitz on behalf of the Department of Antiquities in 1955, 1957, and 1963.
Two main phases of building were distinguished in the church. The first phase had measured 27 by 16 meters and consisted of an apse (it is now impossible to ascertain whether it had been an inscribed one, since the eastern part of the church is destroyed), a nave, and two narrow aisles. Several rooms had been attached to the north side of the church. The façade, which faces the sea, had overlooked an atrium (circa 400 square meters) paved with flagstones and containing a cistern. The church, which had stood 1.3 meters above the atrium, had been reached from the south and north sides of the atrium by flights of stairs, the remains of which were cleared. Another flight of steps had led from the atrium down to the seashore. The mosaic floor of the nave is of a simple design.

On the east side, in front of the apse, are two large crosses with four depressions around them. These seem to indicate that a table (mensa) had been placed here. Of particular interest is the central medallion in the pavement of the northern aisle, which is decorated with a cross, pomegranates, and fish. The mosaic floor of one of the rooms on the northeastern side of the church is decorated with five crosses.

In the second phase the original nave continued in use, but the mensae were enclosed by a chancel screen. The rooms on the north side were enlarged, and in one of them a new mosaic floor was laid over the floor decorated with crosses. The outer narthex, whose length exceeds the total width of the nave and aisles, also appears to have been added in this phase. In the narthex is a ten-line dedicatory inscription in Greek, set in a circle, and mentioning the name of the donor and the date, A.D. 485/86. In the same year a new mosaic floor, decorated with a great variety of geometric designs, was laid in the original (inner) narthex.

Archaeological News 7 (1963), 16, 17 (Hebrew) • M. Prausnitz, *Excavations at Shavei Zion,* Rome, 1967 (with a chapter on the mosaic pavements and inscriptions by M. Avi-Yonah and on the glass finds by D. Barag).

SHELLAL

Twenty-one kilometers (13 miles) south of Gaza. In 1917 Australian troops stationed here discovered the mosaic pavement of a church. Its edges had been damaged but the center has survived. The pavement seems to have originally measured 15 by 8 meters. The mosaic pavement of the nave consists of a single field within a border of squares, some of which are filled with a guilloche pattern and others with animal figures. One of the squares contains the head of a man.

The central field is divided into round medallions arranged in rows of five medallions each. These are formed by a vine trellis that emerges from a broad amphora situated in the center of the bottom row. The medallions in the central, vertical row, above the amphora, are filled with a double basket, a pair of doves, a basket filled with fruit, an amphora, a bird in a cage, and another basket. In the side rows there is a symmetrical arrangement of animals on one side (leopard, lion, hare, lamb, deer, goat) and birds on the other side. The animals and birds face each other. The amphora in the bottom row is flanked by two peacocks.

In the east of the floor, a four-line inscription in Greek, set in a *tabula ansata,* relates that the church was decorated with mosaics in the year 622, according to the era of Gaza, in the tenth year of the indiction, *i.e.,* 561/62. Another Greek inscription, in nine lines, in the west section of the pavement, is almost completely obliterated.

There is a strong similarity between this pavement and that of the synagogue at Ma'on (q.v.), which is located not far from Shellal. The Shellal mosaic pavement is now in the Australian War Memorial at Canberra.

A.D. Trendall, *The Shellal Mosaic,* Canberra, 1957.

SUḤMATA (present-day Hosan)

Circa 18 kilometers (11 miles) east of Nahariya. N. Makhouly and M. Avi-Yonah excavated the site on behalf of the Mandatory Government Department of Antiquities in 1932. They cleared a basilica of the sixth century.

The church has a round external apse (3.5 meters in radius). The narthex (2.5 by 10 meters) has a mosaic floor decorated with geometric patterns, including a central circle, lozenges, and semicircles. Three doorways in the eastern wall of the narthex had led into the hall, which had been divided into a nave and two aisles by two rows of four columns. A fragment of mosaic floor was discovered in the north side of the nave. It is decorated with garlands in diagonal bands and squares formed by sprigs were scattered among them.

A Greek inscription, divided in three columns, was found in front of the bema. The middle column, of five lines set in a *tabula ansata,* is well preserved. It mentions "John the archbishop and Cyriacus, the chorepiscopus," together with other persons in whose time the floor was laid (possible date: August, 555).

The mosaic floor of the northern aisle (2.35 meters wide), whose outer wall was completely cleared, is preserved in its entirety. It is laid in a continuous pattern of circles and elipses with an amphora near the entrance, flanked by two peacocks. Out of the amphora rises a vine trellis.

The intercolumnar spaces are paved in geometric designs, with the exception of the second space which is decorated at the four corners with branches of pomegranates and birds.

N. Makhouly and M. Avi-Yonah, *QDAP* 3 (1933), 92–105.

UMM JARAR, KHIRBET (Ḥorvat Gerarit)

Ten kilometers (6½ miles) south of Gaza. In 1917 the remains of a basilica dating from the sixth century were discovered here. The church apparently had had an internal apse. Large sections of the mosaic floor of the nave, aisles, and diaconicon have survived. The mosaic field adjacent to the apse is composed of three interlocking circles. A square is inscribed within each circle. A basket with grapes fills the central circle, and peacocks are represented in the flanking ones. Two other panels containing fowls appear on either side. To the left of the section adjacent to the apse, a fragment of a mosaic floor, decorated with geometric designs, was uncovered. The mosaic floor of the nave consists of a floral field surrounded by a border of alternating circles and squares. The circles contain birds. The squares contain geometric motifs. The aisles are paved with an identical geometric pattern of squares. A border of lotus flowers surrounds the colored mosaic floor of the diaconicon.

F.M. Drake, *PEFQSt* (1918), 112–24 • M. Avi-Yonah, *QDAP* 3 (1933), 33–34.

UMM ER-RUS

Twenty kilometers (12½ miles) southwest of Jerusalem, near the village of 'Aviezer (map reference 152121). In 1898 a basilica dating from the fifth/sixth centuries was excavated here. The apse had been an external one. The mosaic floor is decorated with geometric patterns in colored cubes. In the center of the floor is a large cross, with small crosses set in squares at the end of each arm. Another cross appears in the pavement in front of the altar and, west of it, intertwining vine tendrils emerge from a goblet. It is flanked on the right by an inscription in Greek "Saint John's," and on the left by an Aramaic inscription, *mara Yoḥana, Yona Kohen* ("Saint John, Jonas Priest"). A word that appears to be written in Hebrew can be distinguished to the left of the cross.

Among the rubble many ashlar stones and a fragment of a tombstone bearing a Greek inscription were found. A stone on which a human figure is carved, and bearing traces of a Greek inscription, was also found.

L.H. Vincent, *RB* 6 (1898), 611–15; 7 (1899), 454–55 • R.A.S. Macalister, *PEFQSt* (1899), 200–04.

DAN, TEL

HISTORY AND IDENTIFICATION. Biblical Dan, repeatedly mentioned in the scriptural phrase "from Dan to Beersheba," is generally identified with Tel Dan (Tell el-Qadi) in northern Israel at the foot of Mount Hermon. It is a fairly large mound, of about 50 acres, in the center of a rich and fertile valley. The abundant springs in and around the mound form one of the tributaries of the Jordan River. The name "Dan" first appears in Genesis 14, but the original name of the city was Laish (Judges 18:29, Joshua 19:47). That name appears in the Egyptian Execration Texts and in the Mari documents of the eighteenth century B.C. Thutmose III lists Laish among the cities captured by him. The tribe of Dan, after conquering Laish, changed its name to Dan, by which it was henceforth known.

Jeroboam I established one of his royal sanctuaries at Dan to mark the northern boundary of his kingdom, just as that at Bethel (q.v.) marked the southern limit. The city was destroyed early in the ninth century by the Aramaeans but was soon rebuilt by Ahab. It must have served Jeroboam II as an important outpost, but the prophets condemned the worship of the Golden Calf there and held it responsible for the calamities that befell Israel. Nevertheless, the city survived until the days of Jeremiah and continued to exist during Hellenistic and Roman times.

The identification of Tell el-Qadi with Dan was first suggested by E. Robinson in 1838. However, as early as the fourth century A.D. Eusebius speaks of a large Jewish village called Dan, four Roman miles from Caesarea Philippi (Banias). That is the exact distance between Tel Dan and Banias. Pottery collected on the site supports this identification. In 1935 W.F. Albright suggested that Tell el-Qadi (Tel Dan) be considered one of the Hyksos cities, which are distinguished by sloping

Bronze bowl from the Mycenaean tomb.

ramparts. But Tel Dan, with its ramparts, differs somewhat from other mounds of this type in that its surface is not flat but quite concave. From the high circumference of the mound there is a gentle slope inward, toward the center. An explanation of this phenomenon was provided by the excavations.

EXCAVATIONS (HISTORY)

The excavations on the site began in 1966 by the Department of Antiquities and Museums. Originally started as an emergency, or salvage, operation, it has continued every year since, under the direction of A. Biran and members of the department. During the first season a trench was cut into the southern slopes of the mound from top to bottom. At the same time a number of squares were opened on the mound itself to examine the stratigraphic sequence. In subsequent years additional areas were excavated, and in 1971 another trench was cut into the eastern slopes of the mound.

EXCAVATIONS (RESULTS)

The Ramparts. Excavations on the southern side of the mound revealed a sloping rampart with a stone construction 6.3 meters thick serving as its core. The material used for the exterior had been amassed from the debris of the previous settlements on the site, mainly of the Early Bronze Age. This loose material was covered with a layer of smoothed clay. For the construction of the inward-sloping rampart, natural soil was taken from the surrounding valleys, in which almost no pottery was found. The same type of rampart construction was also found on the eastern side of the mound. However, the material used for the earthen fill on both sides of the stone core was the natural red soil of the area in which virtually no pottery was found. The stone core revealed by the trench made on the east side seems to indicate that the builders of the ramparts had found this stone construction (perhaps a city wall from some previous settlement, possibly Early Bronze Age or Middle Bronze Age II-A) and used it as the core to hold the rampart together. A brick wall was then added on top.

In the excavations on the southern side of the mound, a number of burials in jars were found in the inner slopes of the rampart. They are to be

dated to the end of the Middle Bronze Age II-B or Middle Bronze Age II-C. Hence it can be assumed that the rampart was built before the end of the Middle Bronze Age II-B. In the undisturbed layers of the settlement, under the outer rampart, two strata of Middle Bronze Age II (one Middle Bronze Age II-A and one Middle Bronze Age II-B) and three of Early Bronze Age could be distinguished. This proves that the rampart was built after the beginning of the Middle Bronze Age II-B. Complete vessels found in the stone construction under the earthen rampart of the eastern trench also date to Middle Bronze Age II-A or Middle Bronze Age II-B. The ramparts at Tel Dan could be dated, accordingly, to sometime in the second half of the eighteenth century B.C.

The Middle Bronze Age Levels. At least one Middle Bronze Age II-B level could be definitely established: the floor of a house with a large number of vessels found in the debris of the destruction, including cooking pots, jugs, and juglets, which can be dated to the end of Middle Bronze Age II-B period. Other evidence for the

Opposite page: Aerial view of the site. Top right: Clay head; eighth century B.C.
Right and bottom: Mycenaean crater; tomb 387.

opulent settlement of this period comes from the burials found in various parts of the excavation area, all of which date from the latter part of Middle Bronze Age II-B and Middle Bronze Age II-C. An unusual feature of the early Middle Bronze Age II-B and possibly the Middle Bronze Age II-A are vessels found in the levels that preceded the construction of the ramparts, which resemble pottery found at Ṫell Kalil and Alalakh.

The Mycenaean Tomb (Tomb 387). A tomb built of rough basalt stones was found dug into the earthen work of the inner rampart. The floor, built of flat stones, measures 2.4 by 2.2 meters. The walls, which were built at an incline of 32 degrees, are 2.4 meters high. The entrance was from above. In the tomb the remains of forty-five skeletons of men, women, and children were found in a state of utter disorder. It seems that the skeletons and funerary offerings had been periodically pushed aside to make room for additional offerings and interments. The tomb contained imported Mycenaean ware, pyxides, amphorae, juglets, flasks, and a charioteer vase (the only one found so far in Canaan) as bronze objects (bowls, an oil lamp, swords, and arrowhead), ivory cosmetic boxes, gold and silver jewelry. A large number of locally made vessels, stone implements, and Cypriote imports complete the repertoire in the tomb. On the basis of the ceramic evidence, it appears that the tomb was used for a generation or two from the middle of the fourteenth century to the beginning of the thirteenth century B.C.

The Iron Age Levels. Stratum V of the Iron Age was especially rich. A large quantity of vessels was found in it. The destruction of this stratum can be safely assigned to the middle of the eleventh century B.C. The distinctive collar-rim vessels were found in the final phase of this stratum as well as in its earlier stages. This level of occupation is ascribed to the Danite conquest that probably took place in the middle of the twelfth century B.C. Some Philistine pottery from this time was also found in the eastern section of the excavation during the 1971 season.

The Settlement at Tel Dan persisted throughout the Iron Age. A Phoenician inscription (*lb'l plṭ*, "Belonging to Ba'al Pelet") is evidence of the latest stratum of occupation at the beginning of the sixth century B.C. When Jeremiah (4:15, 8:16) refers to Dan, he speaks of it as an existing city.

Opposite page, top: Inscribed shard: l'mṣ *("belonging to Amoz" or "Amaziah"); eighth century* B.C. *Opposite page, bottom: Mycenaean tomb 387, looking east. Below: Area A; stratified section. Bottom left: Some of the 300 juglets found in situ; eighth century* B.C. *Bottom right: Burial in a jar; MBA II-B–C.*

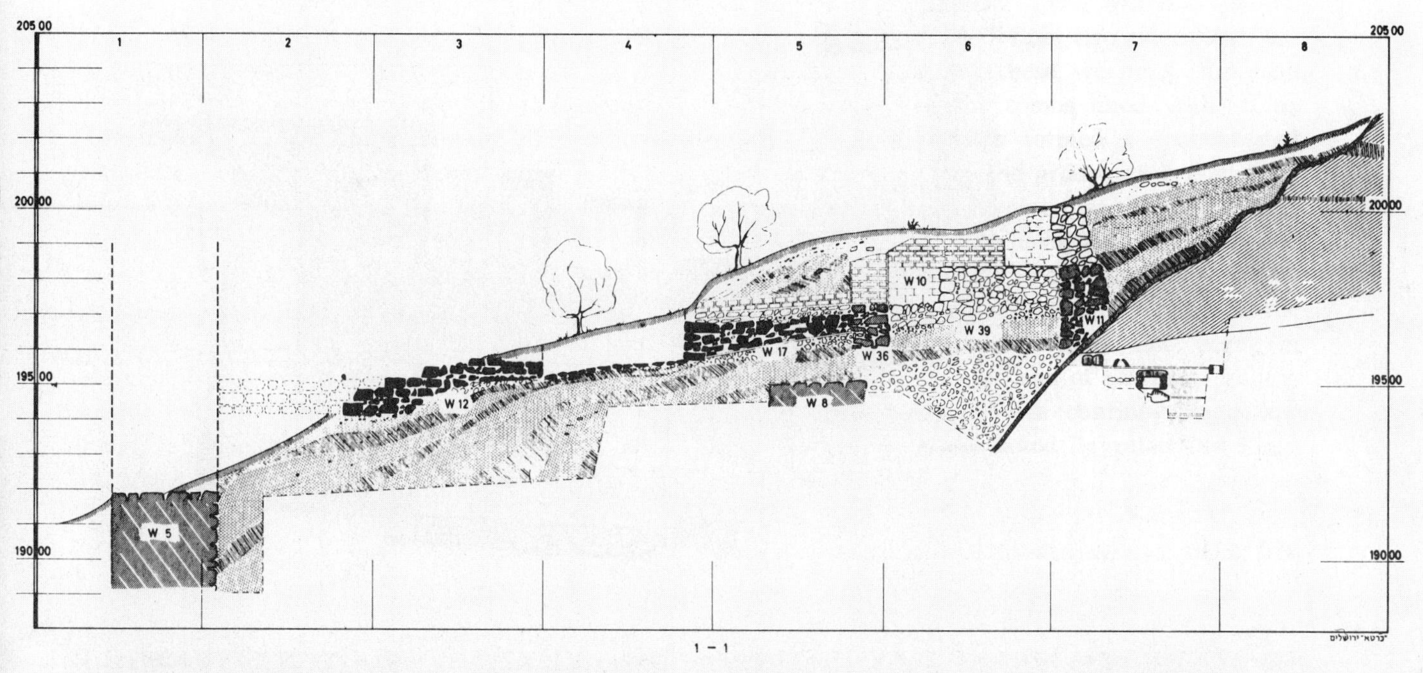

The IA city gate complex, area A. Upper: Plan. Lower Paved entrance, looking west.

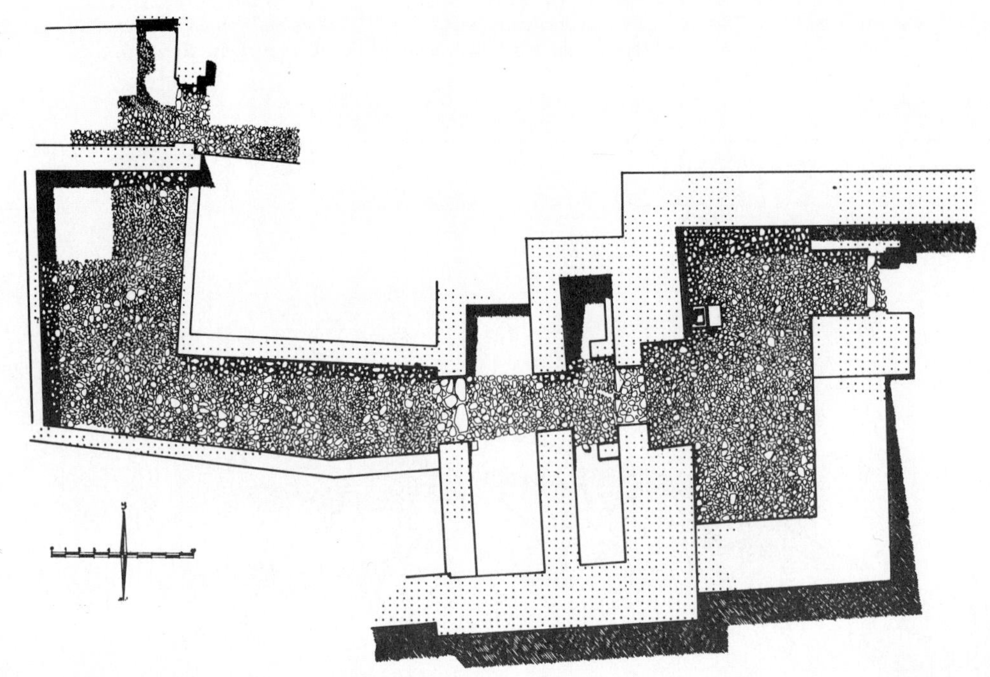

Upper: Isometric reconstruction of the bamah. Lower: Steps leading to the bamah.

From top to bottom: Stone column base, apparently of canopy. Structure supporting canopy in the city gate. Eastern wall of the bamah in typical Israelite masonry: hewn stones with margins laid in headers and stretchers.

THE CITY GATE AND WALL

A complex of the Israelite period with an outer and an inner gate, a stone-paved square, a stone-paved road, and massive city walls was discovered. The main, inner gate, built of large basalt stones, measures 29.5 by 17.8 meters. It is composed of two towers and four guardrooms. A paved street, the royal processional route, led westward from the four-meter threshold, then turned northward on a 28 degree incline up the slope of the mound. Of the outer gate, the threshold (3.7 meters wide) with its doorstop, sockets, and right- and left-hand piers were found. Between the two gates a paved rectangle 19.5 by 9.4 meters served as a gathering place. It may provide an illustration for the expression *reḥov* often found in the Bible (*e.g.*, Judges 19:15, II Chronicles 32:6).

Next to the eastern wall of the southern guardroom an unusual structure and bench were found. This structure, built of hewn limestone, may have supported a king's throne or a cult statue. Four decorated bases or capitals (one of which is missing) were probably of columns that supported a canopy (see left). The bench, which runs some 5 meters to the city wall, may have been used by the elders of the community.

The entire city-gate complex was built on top of an earthen fill. The city wall, 3.6 meters thick, must have risen to a height of some 12 meters above the plain. The city gate and wall were probably built by King Jeroboam I and destroyed during the attack of Ben-Hadad of Damascus. Pottery found under the stone pavement and in the level of destruction on the floor dates the gate and wall to the end of the tenth and their destruction to the beginning of the ninth centuries B.C., respectively. Remains of a later building were found above the destroyed city gate. In one of the rooms some three hundred juglets belonging to the middle of the eighth century were found. Among the finds is a Hebrew inscription *l'mṣ* ("belonging to Amotz" or "Amatziah").

THE ACROPOLIS

At the northern side of the mound an almost square platform (18.7 by 18.2 meters) was excavated. It is built of fine masonry laid in headers and stretchers, characteristic of the classical masonry of the Israelite monarchy. This platform was probably erected by Jeroboam I and enlarged during the reigns of Ahab and Jeroboam II. The space enclosed by the four outer walls was filled with basalt stones laid closely one on top of the other in such a way that a wide platform was created. A flight of steps, 8 meters wide, was built against the southern wall of the platform, providing access to it. The platform may thus have been an open-air acropolis, or bamah.

Potsherds collected from the stone steps point to a date in the middle of the ninth century B.C. This open-air cult place was probably built on the site of an earlier one, which ceramic evidence suggests may have been in use during the Middle Bronze Age II. The bamah was continuously enlarged by the addition of rows of large stones. It must have continued in use during the Hellenistic and Roman periods. To the Roman period belong the nymphaeum excavated to the north of the acropolis, as well as the Aphrodite statue accidentally found in the fields some 200 meters from the mound.

SUMMARY

The earliest remains discovered so far at Tel Dan belong to the Early Bronze Age II. The abundance of pottery and its excellence indicate that during the Early Bronze Age a large city existed here by the rich springs. Evidence for a Middle Bronze Age II-A occupation also was found. During the Middle Bronze Age II-B the city was strongly fortified with huge ramparts. This is the city mentioned in the Execration Texts and the Mari documents.

Tel Dan continued to enjoy prosperity during the Middle Bronze Age II-C and Late Bronze Age. The people of that time, as well as those of the Iron Age I, lived within the enclosure and safety of the earthen ramparts. Neither did the tribe of Dan venture outside these ramparts. Jeroboam I extended the city beyond the limits of the ramparts and built a massive wall and city gate. In the Assyrian conquest the city suffered the fate of other cities in northern Israel, but it continued to be inhabited, and the acropolis was used as a place of worship.

A. Biran

BIBLIOGRAPHY

Robinson, *Biblical Researches* 3, 358 • W.F. Albright, *JPOS* 15 (1935), 224 • B. Mazar, EI 3 (1954), 28 (Hebrew) • Y. Yadin in *Western Galilee and Its Coast,* Jerusalem, 1965, 42ff. (Hebrew) • A. Biran in *All the Land of Naphtali,* Jerusalem, 1967, 21ff. (Hebrew); *Qadmoniot* 13 (1971), 2ff. (Hebrew); *IEJ* 20 (1970), 92ff. • A. Malamat in *Essays in Honor of Nelson Glueck, Near Eastern Archaeology in the Twentieth Century,* New York, 1970, 164ff.; *idem, Biblica* 51 (1971), 1ff.; *idem, IEJ* 21 (1971), 35ff.

DEIR 'ALLA, TELL

IDENTIFICATION. This mound, one of the prominent ancient sites in the Jordan Valley, is situated 12 kilometers (7½ miles) north–northeast of the junction of the Jabbok and the Jordan rivers. It was settled in the Chalcolithic, Late Bronze, and Iron ages I–II. The site is generally identified with biblical Succoth (Genesis 33:17, Joshua 13:27, Judges 8:5, I Kings 7:46), for which the valley of Succoth was named (Psalms 60:6, 108:7). Among the evidence for this identification is the mention in the Talmud of a locality called Ter'ela or Der'ela (Palestinian Talmud *Shevuot* 8:2, 38–d), identified with Succoth. In the writer's opinion, however, the excavations at the site have not furnished proof for this identification. Following F. M. Abel, we prefer to identify Succoth with Tell el-Ahṣaṣ, 2½ kilometers (1½ miles) west of Tell Deir 'Alla, which is a translation of the word *succoth* ("booths"). Since Tell el-Ahṣaṣ is smaller than Tell Deir 'Alla, the latter was most likely the main city of the valley of Succoth. Ter'ela, mentioned in the Palestinian Talmud, may have been the name of the extensive Roman-Byzantine village immediately to the east of Tell Deir 'Alla.

HISTORY

Deir 'Alla is situated in an ancient delta formed near the junction of the Jabbok and the Jordan rivers. In Chalcolithic times a village was built on an outlying hill on the southern bank of the Jabbok. The present course of this river is relatively recent and probably dates from medieval times. At the end of the Chalcolithic period the site was deserted, and only at the beginning of the Late Bronze Age was the top of the hill leveled and the area enlarged for building operations. A large sanctuary was built with adjoining rooms. They were destroyed about 1200 B.C. A fairly continuous occupation, however, was maintained until the Persian period, when the site was finally abandoned. It was used as a cemetery in medieval times.

EXCAVATIONS

Five seasons of excavations have been carried out since 1960 by a Dutch expedition headed by H. J. Franken of the University of Leyden. The aim of the expedition has been to obtain an accurate chronology of the transition from the Late Bronze to the Iron Age cultures, based on a stratigraphical rather than a typological study of the remains. The methods used follow those introduced by Kathleen Kenyon in her excavations at Samaria and Jericho.

Chalcolithic Village. The buildings on the mound are mainly of mud brick without stone foundations. Hence there is an extremely fine stratification consisting of levels varying from the width of a brick to only a very few centimeters. A trench dug through the northern slope of the mound revealed that the Chalcolithic village was completely destroyed by the Late Bronze Age settlers. Its artifacts are found only along the edge of the slope.

Late Bronze Age Sanctuary, House, and Chapel. The Late Bronze Age consisted of a sanctuary complex with various stages of rebuilding. The oldest stage was constructed on an artificial mound so that the cella of the temple rose about one meter above the surrounding buildings. The absence of a defensive wall indicates that Late Bronze Age Deir 'Alla was probably an open sanctuary whose sanctity was its only defense in a period so politically unsettled. This is in sharp contrast to the strong fortifications usually encountered in this period. The sanctuary appears to have been the shrine of wandering Bedouins. On the north–south axis of the cella two piles of stone slabs were found, most probably the successive bases of pillars.

The last sanctuary was destroyed by an earthquake followed by a fierce conflagration. A badly burned collection of ritual pottery vessels, pottery "shrines," cylinder seals, beads, a gold ring, and fragments of bronze armor plating were recovered in the sanctuary. Also found were the remains of an Egyptian faience vase bearing a royal cartouche, which has been identified as belonging to the wife of Seti II, Taousert (1214–1194 B.C.). Thus, the sanctuary was destroyed early in the twelfth century B.C.

An important collection of local and imported pottery, cylinder seals, and worked bone objects came from a Late Bronze Age house on the northeast slope of the mound. Excavations in this building have thus far uncovered a kitchen, a pantry, and an adjoining room that apparently served as a chapel, since a pottery shrine was also found there. This house was also destroyed by an earthquake followed by fire. The floor of the chapel was split open by the earthquake, and a victim of the disaster was found buried under the debris in the kitchen. In two of the rooms to the east of the sanctuary, three inscribed and eight uninscribed clay tablets were found. The script of these tablets apparently is related to Phoenician.

Iron Age I Metal Workers' Settlement. The phase following this destruction level seems to date to the Iron Age I (twelfth to tenth centuries B.C.), but there is no evidence of a permanent occupation of the mound during this period. None of the town walls or houses can be associated with the period. It can be assumed that at the time the place was used by seminomadic metal workers, who worked bronze in the winter months. Traces of furnaces for smelting bronze were found, along with a number of pits dug into the slopes of the tel. In addition to the furnaces and a few insignificant walls, the accumulation of this phase consists entirely of open areas, often covered with layers of straw, perhaps to facilitate walking up the slippery mud slopes during the winter. The many flint sickle blades indicate that crops were grown. Post holes, 5 centimeters in diameter, found in the ground, were probably from tents that had been set up.

Aramaic Settlement (Iron Age). A new group of settlers followed, with a different tradition of pottery techniques. They built a walled town with rectangular houses, which were found to have gone through several building phases. An unpaved street runs across the excavation area. The pottery is not characteristic of Western Palestinian traditions, and there is an accumulation of about 6 meters of debris before the typical wheel-burnished ware of the eighth and seventh centuries appears. The material culture of this town undoubtedly developed under Syrian-Aramaean influence, as can be seen in the terra-cotta male, female, and animal figurines.

One of the town walls was built on a layer of reeds, and some buildings were erected on wooden beams laid under the walls. An unusual feature of this period is a round tower attached to the outside of one of the town walls. Sometime during this period a circular pit, 8 meters in diameter, was dug to a depth of approximately 3 meters. Houses were pulled down to make room for it, but the purpose of the pit is uncertain.

In one of the rooms adjoining the temple of this

Top: Temple; clay model of a sanctuary; circa 1200 B.C. *Bottom: Clay tablet with alphabetic inscription (perhaps a late stage of the Mycenaean II script brought by the Philistines); circa 1200* B.C. *Right: Faience vase with the name of the Egyptian queen Taousert (1214–1194* B.C.*).*

period, fragments of an Aramaic inscription written on wall plaster were discovered in 1967. Stratigraphical study showed that the inscription does not come from that room. It fell into the room, together with the wall to which it was attached, during or sometime after the earthquake and fire that destroyed the next phase of occupation. That phase appears to have been quite long, perhaps several centuries judging from the rather thick (1 meter) deposit of regularly built-up courtyard levels running east–west through the center of the excavated area.

This Aramaic inscription is the longest in that language found so far. It should enable scholars to broaden the knowledge of the development of the language. The text of the inscription mentions a non-Israelite biblical prophet, Balaam.

Arab Remains. The upper levels of the mound were extensively disturbed by Arab graves that had been dug into them. In order to reach the Iron Age layers, the Arab cemetery had to be excavated. It consisted of single graves containing glass bangles and bronze trinkets and some glassware. No coins were found. This created the problem of dating the cemetery. Thus Tell Abu-Gurdan, located several hundred meters from Tell Deir 'Alla, was excavated. Tell Abu-Gurdan was an Arab settlement that lasted from the period of the Islamic conquest to approximately A.D. 1500, with two breaks in occupation of unknown duration.

The numerous fragments of pottery found in twenty layers of the courtyard levels did not make possible an accurate dating, since this pottery is relatively unfamiliar. However, on the basis of the pottery-making techniques, the importance of this region in the sugar industry in the Arab period was seen. An industry that produced sugar molds began in the second period of occupation and continued to the end of the third. That industry is unrelated to the techniques of the local potters. Fragments of these molds are found by the thousands in connection with the sugar-mill stones in the vicinity of Tell Abu-Gurdan.

SUMMARY

The development of various types of pottery, several of which were hitherto unknown, are being studied in relation to their stratigraphical position on the tel.

Tell Deir 'Alla, the first Late Bronze Age site in Transjordan to be excavated, reveals trade relations reaching as far as Mycenae. Evidence has been found of an Early Iron Age seminomadic tribe whose pottery bears no connection with that of the Late Bronze Age. The later fully developed Iron Age I culture of this region shows different characteristics from that of Western Palestine.

H. J. FRANKEN

BIBLIOGRAPHY

Annual reports: H. J. Franken, *VT* 10 (1960), 386f.; 11 (1961), 361f.; 12 (1962), 378f.; 14 (1964), 377f.; 417f.; 17 (1967), 480f.; *idem, PEQ* (1964), 73f.; *idem, Excavations at Tell Deir 'Alla. A Stratigraphical and Analytical Study of the Early Iron Age Pottery* (with contributions by J. Kalsbeek) 1, Leyden, 1969; *idem, Excavations of the Tell Deir 'Alla Medieval Arabic Cemetery and the Medieval Arabic Tell* (Tell Abu Gurdan) (in press).

The Aramaic text will be published shortly.

DEIR EL-BALAḤ

THE SITE. The Late Bronze Age cemetery near Deir el-Balaḥ is buried deep (5 to 12 meters) beneath the sand dunes some 13 kilometers (8 miles) south of Gaza. There is no evidence as yet of any settlement in the immediate neighborhood with corresponding levels of occupation.

EXCAVATIONS

In 1971–72 illicit digging led to the discovery of about fifty large and striking anthropoid clay coffins of the "slipper" type with movable face lids. Also found were quantities of bronze, alabaster, and faience vessels; ushabti figurines; scarabs; gold jewelry; semi-precious gold beads; and a large collection of pottery (Mycenaean, Cypriote, Egyptian, and local Palestinian). All belonged to the Late Bronze Age, fourteenth to thirteenth century B.C. Four inscribed Egyptian burial stelae also came to light in the cemetery. Consequently, a rescue dig and survey of the area was undertaken in March, 1972, by Trude Dothan and Y. Beth-Arieh. The work was continued on a larger scale in June of the same year.

The area of the cemetery so far examined measures 150 meters from north to south and 200 meters from east to west. The coffins were found in roughly rectangular tombs cut into the natural marl. All were oriented generally toward the west (*i.e.*, to the Mediterranean) and were found in groups of three or four, about 3 to 4 meters apart, with unoccupied space or plain interments between the groups.

Tomb 114. In the first season, in a hitherto untouched area buried deep beneath the dunes, a pottery anthropoid coffin was found with burial offerings still in situ. The coffin was shaped with a well-defined head and shoulders, and naturalistically rendered features (tomb 114). Around the coffin were arranged large offering vessels — a combination of local Canaanite, Egyptian, and Mycenaean pottery. At the head of the coffin stood a large four-handled storage jar closed with a bowl. Slightly to the side was a small tall-necked Egyptian juglet. At the foot and to one side of the coffin were three vessels set in a row: a Canaanite jar (the upper part smashed in), a complete

Deir el-Balaḥ; lid of anthropoid sarcophagus.

Below: Tomb 118; coffin before opening. Opposite page, from top to bottom: Tomb 118; coffin after opening; two skeletons with funerary offering arranged alongside. Tomb 114; burial offerings around and on the coffin. Tomb 116; upper part of coffin.

Mycenaean III-B three-handled pyriform jar, and a complete tall-necked Egyptian jar.

Inside the coffin lay two complete skeletons, male and female, with traces of two others. The burial gifts in the coffin included a number of bronze objects: a wine set consisting of bowl, strainer with ring handle, and small dipper-juglet inside the strainer (such sets are well known in Egyptian and Canaanite contexts of the Late Bronze and Early Iron ages); a mirror; and three bronze knives — one cast in one piece with the handle in the form of the foreleg and hoof of a deer (a similar knife is known from Megiddo, and others from New Kingdom contexts in Egypt).

There were also five bone pellets (gaming pieces?) with a different sign incised on each, small carnelian and gold beads, and a small Bes amulet of gold. Also found were two carnelian scarabs still in their gilded settings — one with its silver ring. On it was engraved a cartouche of Ramses II.

On the basis of the pottery (primarily the Mycenaean III-B pyriform jug) and the cartouche of Ramses II on the silver ring, the burial is to be dated to the thirteenth century B.C.

Tombs 116 and 118

In the second season (June, 1972), which was undertaken on behalf of the Hebrew University and directed by Trude Dothan, the dunes were removed (8 meters deep) along a strip 50 meters long and 20 meters wide north–northwest of tomb 114 and adjacent to it. Two anthropoid coffins were uncovered here (Numbers 116, 118). In the area were scattered traces of plain burials with only a few funerary offerings of pottery, a recurring type being a standing storage jar with a bowl as a lid. Such jars also mark the more elaborate graves where the dead were interred in anthropoid pottery coffins. A dipper-juglet inside the storage jar was another common feature.

The coffins, about 1.8 to 1.9 meters in length, were laid in rectangular graves about 3.25 meters long, 1.7 meters wide, and 1.7 meters deep (from the original surface). The graves, cut roughly in the marl, sloped inward at the bottom and were slightly rounded at the head, following the outline of the coffin. After the coffin had been laid in the grave and the burial offerings arranged, the grave was filled in with sand and marl, and the storage jar was placed at the head of the grave as a marker.

Tomb 116. The coffin in tomb 116 looked intact

at first but apparently had been robbed or disturbed in ancient times. Only a few burial gifts remained inside. Others were piled on the coffin in "throw-out" groups or scattered nearby. The throw-out contained pottery (a Mycenaean three-handled pyriform jar and a local flask and bowls), carnelian beads in the shape of a lotus bud, and a well-cut carnelian seal bearing the name of Ramses II and engraved with a chariot scene.

The coffin in tomb 116 was of the type in which the head and shoulders are not delineated. The face mask was rendered in high relief. The lid seemed to have been fired at a far higher temperature than the body of the coffin. It was thus possible to remove it almost intact, whereas the body was friable and broke easily. A small intact jug was found inside the coffin near the skull. In the area of the chest was a broken and scattered Mycenaean stirrup jar. There were also five lentoid disks, most probably gaming pieces. On the bottom of the coffin, under the skeleton in the area of the hands, was a steatite scarab bearing the two first signs of the fourth name of Ramses II.

Tomb 118. The third tomb in this group, tomb 118 is located about 4 meters south of tomb 116. The coffin found inside contained two skeletons, male and female, with their burial offerings intact.

The vessels were arranged alongside the right-hand skeleton, the female, from below the skull to the knees. They included three pottery flasks with concentric circles—a type known in Canaan in the thirteenth century. Next to them was a lotus-shaped alabaster goblet decorated with petals. Resting diagonally in the hip area was an alabaster cosmetic spoon in the form of a swimming girl. Her head, made separately, is pegged into a depression in her back, and she holds the spoon in her outstretched arms. This type of cosmetic vessel is well known from Egypt (New Kingdom) in ivory, wood, and alabaster, and occurs in ivory in the Megiddo treasury.

The bronze objects included a tanged bronze mirror with traces of cloth adhering to it, a set of two bronze vessels, a flat bowl (also with traces of cloth adhering to it), and a jug with matching handles incised with lotus flowers. The vessels are Egyptian in shape and decoration, and have parallels in the New Kingdom.

On the finger bones of the right-hand skeleton were two seal rings, one of gold alloy and the other of dark red carnelian. Most of the other jewelry (gold earrings, gold and carnelian beads) and scarabs, on the other hand, were grouped around the skull and on the chest of the left-hand skeleton (the male).

Fourteen scarabs of carnelian, steatite, and faience were found in the coffin, some with their silver and gold mounting still intact. The scarabs include private, royal, and religious types. Three bear the name of Thutmose III, one the name of Amenophis III. The name of Ramses II does not appear, but there are enough datable objects that cannot be earlier than the period of Ramses II. This tomb thus fits chronologically into the same framework as tombs 114 and 116, *i.e.,* the thirteenth century B.C.

SUMMARY

The coffins from Deir el-Balah display a striking spectrum of types and levels of execution. They differ greatly in style, technique, shape, and workmanship. The excavation of tombs 114, 116, and 118 has shown that lids of diverse types can be more or less contemporaneous.

The cemetery seems to have been in use from the fourteenth century B.C. to the last phase of the Late Bronze Age. Although the finds reflect the cosmopolitan flavor of that period, the Egyptian element predominates, as is attested by the very custom of burying the dead in anthropoid coffins and by the stelae and associated objects, which reflect Egyptian culture.

As yet no trace has been found of the settlement to which this cemetery belonged. It may have been a central burying ground for a wide area, serving people of the same cultural background. The dead buried here may have been high-ranking Egyptian officers and officials serving in Canaan, or members of the Egyptian garrisons stationed in Egyptian strongholds in Syria-Palestine, or possibly Canaanite rulers and dignitaries steeped in Egyptian culture.

Later coffin-burials (twelfth to eleventh centuries) from Beth-Shean and the Philistine tombs at Tel Sharuhen show that the custom of burying the dead in anthropoid pottery coffins was adopted by the Sea Peoples, including the Philistines.

TRUDE DOTHAN

BIBLIOGRAPHY

Trude Dothan, *Qadmoniot* 5 (1972), 21–25 • Trude Dothan and Y. Beth-Arieh, *ibid.,* 26 (both Hebrew) • Trude Dothan, *IEJ* 22 (1972), 65–72; 23 (1973), 129–51.

DHOBAI, WADI

EXCAVATIONS. In Wadi Dhobai, situated about 60 kilometers (37 miles) east of Rabbat Ammon, A. Kirkbride discovered two prehistoric sites, and following him L. Harding found another two. An expedition subsequently organized on behalf of the British School of Archaeology in Jerusalem, under the direction of J. Waechter and V.M. Seton-Williams, worked there for about four months in 1937–38, discovering six further sites and excavated two of them.

The culture of five of these sites (A–D and E–1) was called Dhobainian and that of other three sites (E–2, I, and K), Aurignacian. (On the validity of these terms, however, see below.) The finds at the remaining two sites (G and L) were too few for a clear definition.

Of the two sites excavated, one (B) was defined as Dhobainian and the other (K) as Aurignacian. At the first site, signs of a round stone structure were discerned on the surface, and the excavation was carried out by cutting a short, narrow trench (3 by 1 meters) across the structure at its southern end. Three layers were uncovered, the lowest of which is of white earth of varying thickness, not exceeding .15 meters, which directly overlay bedrock. The middle layer is of fine gray sand .3 meters thick, and the uppermost layer of light sand .1 meters thick.

The stones of the building stand upon the lowest layer or — where that is missing — directly on bedrock. Three holes cut into the rock — certainly the sockets of the posts supporting the ceiling — are filled with the gray sand of the middle layer. Two fireplaces full of ashes were also found cut into the surface of the middle layer down to bedrock. Thus the building was erected during the occupation of the second layer.

Implements were discovered in all three layers, forming a homogeneous assemblage. Most are burins and scrapers, and a smaller part are arrowheads, points, pestles, and blades. Quantitative proportions vary between layers, but the composition remains essentially the same, except for the lowest layer.

This assemblage is very similar to the proto-Neolithic one at Jericho (q.v.). The excavators have indeed stressed the link with the finds discovered by J. Garstang in his excavations. Therefore, the term "Dhobainian," suggesting a separate culture, seems unnecessary.

Site K consists of three hillocks covered with flints. A short, narrow trench (3 by 1 meters) was dug by the excavator between the two eastern hillocks where five layers were uncovered without reaching virgin soil. In all layers — the lowest, nearly sterile, always excepted — flint tools and animal bones were discovered. In the second layer from the top, remains of fireplaces and a human tooth were found. In the third layer a floor of pounded earth 5 centimeters thick was cleared. The material is homogeneous throughout the layers. The tools are of small size and sometimes even miniature. All of them are scrapers and bladelets, with retouch, and obliquely truncated. The number of scrapers always exceeds that of the bladelets.

This complex is similar to those found at many open-air stations as well as in some caves in Western Palestine, which have been defined as belonging to the Kebaran culture, the sixth phase of Late Paleolithic in Palestine and Syria. For that reason the definition of the culture of site K as Aurignacian can be discarded.

The importance of this site lies in the evidence it provides for the wide dispersal of the Kebaran culture.

EFRAT YEIVIN

BIBLIOGRAPHY

J. Waechter and V.M. Seton-Williams, *JPOS* 18 (1938), 172–85 • L. Picard, *ibid.*, 186 • D.M.A. Bate, *ibid.*, 292–96.

LAYER	NUMBER OF IMPLEMENTS	BURINS	SCRAPERS	ARROWHEAD POINTS	BLADES
Upper	155	61%	32.0%	6.5%	0.5%
Middle	60	43%	18.0%	35.0%	4.0%
Lowest	69	35%	8.5%	10.5%	46.0%

DIBON

IDENTIFICATION. A city in Moab first settled in the Early Bronze Age, Dibon was the capital of the Moabite Kingdom in the Iron Age and an important center in the Nabatean and later periods.

The site of biblical Dibon is adjacent to the modern village of Dhiban (map reference 224101), 64 kilometers ($39\frac{1}{2}$ miles) south of 'Amman on the road of Kerak and 4 kilometers ($2\frac{1}{2}$ miles) north of the Arnon River. Of the two natural hills lying to the west of the highway, the southern is occupied by the modern village and the northern is the site of the ancient city. The northern hill (200 by 150 meters), which is by far the more defensible of the two, is protected on the west, north, and northeast by deep ravines. On the south and southeast today, however, there is a broad saddle joining the mound proper with the hill of modern Dhiban. Excavation has indicated that this is largely artificial, a result of wash, and does not reflect the original contours. There is every indication that the original city site (Early Bronze Age, probably, and almost certainly Iron Age I) and the enlarged later Moabite site (Iron Age II) were well protected on their southern flanks by natural ravines or depressions.

The site of ancient Dibon was first established by its similarity to the name of the Arab village. Its identity was subsequently confirmed in 1868 by the discovery on the site of the Mesha stele.

HISTORY

The chief sources for the history of Dibon are the Bible and the Mesha (Moabite) stele. In general, the city's fortunes were directly linked with those of Moab, especially with that part of the kingdom lying north of the Arnon River. It was an important Moabite city as early as the thirteenth century B.C. It is referred to in Numbers 21:30 as one of the cities seized from Moab by Sihon, king of the Amorites. When the invading Israelites defeated Sihon, they took Dibon. Tradition assigned the territory to the tribes of Gad (Numbers 32:34) and Reuben (Joshua 13:15ff.), but it probably had stronger ties with Gad, since it is also called Dibon-Gad (Numbers 33:45ff.).

Dibon was Mesha's birthplace (stele, lines 1–2) and apparently also the capital of his father. It is thus not surprising that Mesha made it his capital and erected monumental buildings there. The details of his building activities in Qarḥoh (probably the city's royal citadel) are described in line 21 of the stele. Biblical references to Dibon (Isaiah 15:2,

Opposite page: View of south-east corner of the mound and gate area, fortifications of city, and foundations of Nabatean-Roman temple (1953 excavations). This page: Stele of Mesha, king of Moab; circa 850 B.C.

Jeremiah 48:18) indicate that it was the chief Moabite city in the time when Moab had achieved some limited independence from Assyria and Babylonia. Dibon is again mentioned in the fourth century A.D. in the *Onomasticon* of Eusebius, where it is described as "a large town near the Arnon" (16:18). The latest reference to Dibon is to be found in the writings of the Arab geographer Yaqut (A.D. 1179–1229), who speaks of the village Dhiban.

EXPLORATION

Excavations were carried out in Dibon by the American School of Oriental Research in Jerusalem, beginning in the autumn of 1950. There were four campaigns: 1950–51 under the direction of F. V. Winnett; 1952 under W. L. Reed; 1952–53 under A. D. Tushingham; and in the spring of 1955 under W. M. Morton. The first three campaigns were limited to the southeast corner of the mound. The fourth campaign was confined to the northwest, the northeast, and the summit and center of the mound.

EXCAVATIONS

Early Bronze to Iron Ages. There is evidence for an Early Bronze Age occupation of the mound. At the southeast corner, a few shards of this period (apparently mostly from Early Bronze Age III) have been found. These are mixed with later Iron Age shards and apparently are not associated with any structures. Farther to the north, however, pure Early Bronze Age levels resting on bedrock have been reported and, in the northeast, a section of a curved and sloping wall that has been dated to this period.

After an apparent gap in occupation, there is evidence for an early Moabite occupation (Iron Age I) on the summit of the mound. A major structure there seems to have been a sanctuary, and with it was associated a terra-cotta incense stand of the Iron Age I Beth-Shean type. Other large buildings in the northeast may represent public buildings of the same period.

It is from the southeast corner, however, that most of the evidence for the Moabite period comes. It is all Iron Age II, from about the middle of the ninth century B.C. down to the destruction of the city by Nebuchadnezzar in 582 B.C. We must assume from the architectural and stratigraphic evidence (interpreted in the light of literary sources) that this area was a royal quarter, presumably built by King Mesha, on a small hillock outside the earlier south wall of the city. It had been separated from the older town site by a branch valley (or valleys) running up from the deep ravine to the east. It was delimited on the west by a broad bay running up from the ravine on the south.

If the architectural remains and associated deposits in this area have been correctly interpreted, three structural periods of this citadel can be distinguished. The first period, presumably that of Mesha, consists of a wall running around the east, southeast, and southern parts of the hillock, connecting up with the earlier defenses to the north and west (?). Within this loop are the remains of a building, but its plan is not clear. The construction of the Nabatean temple over eight centuries later on the same site removed too much of the evidence. A second structural period is to be dated to the last quarter of the eighth century B.C. on the basis of the pottery in the fill behind new retaining defensive walls and a square tower.

Finally, to counteract the thrust of the fill, and possibly also to strengthen the defenses themselves, great battered walls of large blocks were leaned against the period 2 walls on the east and south. The construction date of this period 3 is probably the end of the seventh or early sixth century B.C., *i.e.*, only a few years before the destruction of the city in 582 B.C. Unfortunately, following the destruction, serious erosion during the more than five centuries while the mound was deserted removed the occupation levels of periods 2 and 3 and, with them, any evidence of structures of these periods within the defense walls.

Nabatean to Byzantine. In the Nabatean period, a temple was constructed at the southeast corner overlying the remains of the Moabite period just described. Approached from the north by a monumental stairway, the temple itself consisted of a broad *pronaos* and an equally broad *naos*, behind which was a tripartite adytum. In plan, and in many details, it resembles the larger and better-preserved temple at Petra, called Qasr Bint Far'un. The temple was surrounded by a paved elevated platform that was retained at the east and south by strong walls. These were not defensive walls, however, for a broad, open staircase ascended from the south to give access to the platform.

No evidence of other structures of the period,

either public or domestic, have been found in this area. It therefore appears that the temple was a shrine to which pilgrimages were made and was not part of a larger urban complex. On the basis of the distinction of two periods in the staircase and of a rebuilding of the retaining walls, the following chronology has been proposed for the temple: construction about A.D. 10; damage (from earthquake?) in perhaps the third quarter of the first century followed by a reconstruction; and then final abandonment, probably, in A.D. 106 when the Nabatean kingdom was absorbed into the Roman Empire.

That there was a Roman occupation of the site appears clear from the discovery of two inscriptions (one probably of A.D. 201 and the other of A.D. 245/46) and coins. But in the southeast corner of the mound, where most of the excavation has taken place, there is very little (if any) structural or stratigraphic evidence. Exceptions may be a bath complex, a small portion of which was excavated in 1950–51, and a stretch of a defense wall. It seems probable that, at best, the Roman presence was merely a small fort with a garrison to protect the north–south road at this point north of the Arnon River.

In the time of Eusebius, Dhiban was a small, unwalled town, but its fortunes improved in the fifth century with the general prosperity of the whole country. Two churches (probably of the sixth century) and other structures have been excavated, but later robbing has destroyed much of the evidence. They were not elaborate, however. The Byzantine period at Dhiban seems to have come to an end at about the time of the Muslim conquest.

Arab to Mameluke. The site appears to have remained derelict for about a century. The next evidence is of an Umayyad occupation. The churches and other earlier structures were robbed to obtain stone for new buildings. The major structure, west of the old Nabatean temple, has been interpreted as a fortified manor house. By the early ninth century, the site was again abandoned. Finally, in the medieval (Ayyubid-Mameluke) period, there was a reoccupation of the manor house and some other minor building, but the Arab village had moved to the southern mound where the modern town now stands.

Cemetery. Tombs of the later Moabite and the Byzantine periods were found at Dhiban. Of the former, only one was intact, the remainder having been more or less seriously looted. The best-preserved Byzantine tombs were those inserted into the podium of the Nabatean temple, but many of those had also been robbed. Despite active exploration, no Nabatean cemetery has been found. This may corroborate the assumption that in the Byzantine period the temple at Dhiban was a shrine for pilgrimage, and there was no permanent population at the site, except, of course, for the priests and other religious personnel who must have lived near the temple.

SUMMARY

The meager literary evidence for the history of Dibon has been supplemented by archaeological evidence. Dibon's beginnings go back to the Early Bronze Age. With some apparent gaps — the most obvious being the Middle Bronze and Late Bronze ages — it has continued to exist in some form to the present day. The evidence of walls, tombs, and pottery of the later Moabite period — ninth century B.C. to destruction by the Babylonians — indicates a highly developed civilization, which, although in many respects parallel to that of Israel and the other kingdoms east of the Jordan River, retained its own native character. If we may judge from the pottery on the mound and in the tombs, Assyrian influence in Dibon was much weaker than in the Ammonite kingdom to the north and east.

The Nabatean shrine throws some additional light on the culture and history of what in many ways is still a very mysterious kingdom. The Byzantine churches are a footnote to what is already known of the comparatively prosperous times of the sixth and seventh centuries A.D.

A. D. TUSHINGHAM

BIBLIOGRAPHY

N. Glueck, *Exploration in Eastern Palestine* 3 (*AASOR* 18–19 [1937–38]), 115, 242ff. • S.J. Saller, *Rivista di Archeologia Cristiana* 15 (1938), 160–62 • F.V. Winnett, *BASOR* 125 (1952), 7–20 • R.E. Murphy, *ibid.*, 20–23 • W.L. Reed, *BASOR* 128 (1952), 7 • A.D. Tushingham, *BASOR* 133 (1954), 6–26 • A. Alt, *ZDPV* 70 (1954), 16f. • A.D. Tushingham, *BASOR* 138 (1955), 29–34 • W.H. Morton, *BASOR* 140 (1955), 5f. • W.L. Reed, *BASOR* 146 (1957), 6–10 • A.H. Van Zyl, *The Moabites*, Leyden, 1960, 77–80 and *passim* • G.R.H. Wright, *BASOR* 163 (1961), 26–30 • F.V. Winnett and W.L. Reed, *The Excavations at Dibon (Dhibân) in Moab* (*AASOR* 36–37 [1961]) • A.D. Tushingham, *The Excavations at Dibon (Dhibân) in Moab, 1952–53* (*AASOR* 40 [1972]).

DOR

THE SITE AND ITS IDENTIFICATION. Biblical Dor, known as *Δῶρα* in most Hellenistic sources, is identified with a mound known as Khirbet el-Burj (map reference 142224), on the seacoast south of Kibbutz Naḥsholim and north of Ṭanṭūra. Northwest of the mound are the remains of a port, and to the south are ruins of a Crusader fortress whose existence is preserved in the Arabic name of the mound. According to the Greek and Latin sources, Dor was located between the Carmel Range and Straton's Tower (later: Caesarea). The *Tabula Peutingeriana* map places Dor 8 miles north of Caesarea, and Eusebius states that the distance is 9 miles (*Onomasticon* 78:9, 136:16). On the basis of these sources it is possible to locate Dor at Khirbet el-Burj.

HISTORY

Dor is first mentioned in an inscription of Ramses II (thirteenth century B.C.) from West Amarah, Nubia. The inscription contains a list of the settlements along the *Via Maris*, including its western branch from the Sharon to the Accho Plain (q.v.). It is most likely that Dor, like other cities on the seacoast such as Tell Abu Hawam was founded during the Late Bronze Age II shortly before the reign of Ramses II. At that time commercial relations between the Mediterranean East Coast and the Aegean islands were thriving.

In the Bible, Dor appears for the first time in connection with the Israelite Conquest. It was one of the cities that joined the coalition headed by Jabin, King of Hazor, in the war against Joshua (Joshua 11:1–2). Its king, too, suffered defeat at the hands of the Israelites (Joshua 12:23). The Canaanite city of Dor, located in the territory of the tribe of Manasseh, was not conquered until the time of David.

In the account of Wen-Amon's journey to Byblos (circa 1100 B.C.), the port of Dor is mentioned, as is its ruler, Beder, king of the Tjeker (one of the Sea Peoples who invaded the eastern Mediterranean area at that time). In the reign of Solomon, Dor became the center of his fourth administrative district; it was governed by Abinadab, the king's son-in-law (I Kings 4:11). In 732 B.C. Tiglath-Pileser III conquered the city along with that section of the Coastal Plain which belonged to the kingdom of Israel. He turned it into the capital of the Assyrian province of Duru, extending from the Carmel to Jaffa.

The Eshmunezer inscription suggests that during the Persian period Dor was ruled by the Sidonians. This probably accounts for the error of the Greek writers, who attributed the founding of the city to the Sidonians. There was apparently a Greek colony at Dor in Persian times, and it might even have been a member of the Attic Sea League, in its Carian division.

During the Hellenistic period the city became an important fortress. In 219 B.C. it was able to withstand the attack of Antiochus III and the Seleucid army. Eighty years later, the pretender Tryphon entrenched himself there during his war against Antiochus VII Sidetes. At the end of the second century B.C. the tyrant Zoilus ruled both Dor and Straton's Tower, until Alexander Jannaeus took both cities from him. Pompey put an end to Hasmonean rule in Dor and awarded the city autonomy and the right to mint coins. Its coins indicate that Zeus as well as Dorus (a son of Hercules, Dor's mythical founder), and Astarte-Aphrodite were worshipped at Dor.

A Jewish community and synagogue are known to have existed in Dor at the time of Agrippa I (A.D. 41–44). Hieronymus relates that the city was entirely in ruins in his time (end of the fourth century A.D.). On the other hand, it is known that bishops resided there until the seventh century A.D. After that time the site was abandoned until the construction of the Crusader fortress of Merle.

EXPLORATION

In 1923–24 two seasons of excavations were carried out at Dor under the sponsorship of the British School of Archaeology in Jerusalem. The excavations were begun under J. Garstang and were expanded a year later. In 1950 and 1952 J. Leibowitz conducted some excavations north of the mound, on behalf of the Israel Department of Antiquities.

EXCAVATIONS

The first excavations at Dor by the British School of Archaeology in Jerusalem were carried out in the early 1920's, when archaeological methods

Opposite page, top: Plan of the 1924 excavations. Bottom: General plan of the site, showing excavated areas. 1. 1923 excavations. 2. 1924 excavations.

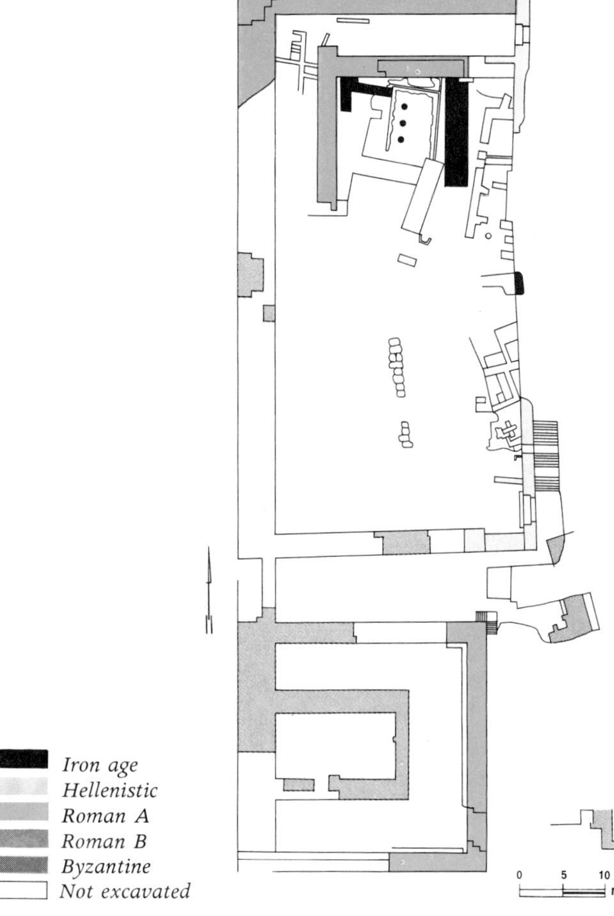

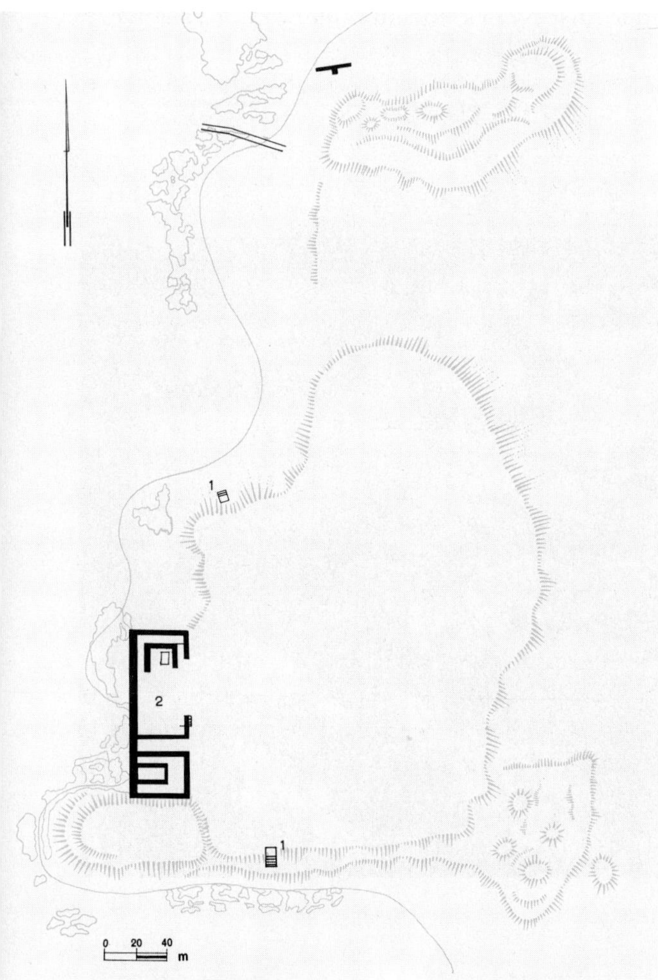

were still rather primitive. As a result, the short and rather incomplete reports published by the excavators do not supply much information. Nonetheless, it is possible to reconstruct a more or less complete picture of the general history of the mound.

Trenches cut in 1923 (some of which were enlarged in 1924) revealed that the first settlement was established at the beginning of the Late Bronze Age. It was destroyed in the thirteenth century B.C., as is proved by the traces of conflagration found between the remains of the earliest settlement and the next occupation stratum, dating from Iron Age I.

Because of the limited excavations in the lower strata of the mound, very meager architectural remains from these two periods came to light. The ceramic finds include Late Bronze Age Cypriote imported ware, along with local ware, and Philistine and other Iron Age I pottery. More extensive architectural remains were excavated in the Hellenistic and Roman levels. In the north trench a wall was uncovered, constructed of well-dressed stones set in a plaster that apparently dates to the Hellenistic period. On top of that wall was a Roman wall. These may have been walls of the city fortifications mentioned by Stephanus Byzantinus.

The remains of a large building were uncovered in the southwestern corner of the mound during the 1924 season. However, in their reports the excavators discuss only the northern part of the structure, which was apparently a self-contained unit separated from the rest of the building. The southern part is only shown on their ground plan, and it is not mentioned in the reports. The structure consists of a *temenos* (sacred precinct) measuring 70.4 by 41.6 meters, with a raised podium 24 meters wide in its center. The length of the building is not recorded, although its entire southern side is shown on the plan and its foundations were excavated. Two openings giving access to the podium were made in the eastern wall of the *temenos,* which faced the city. The entire structure is made of well-dressed stones set in plaster. The western side of the structure was severely damaged by the sea.

On top of the podium was a floor with pillar bases dating from the Late Roman period. The plan and nature of the structure to which this floor belonged are not known. During the Early Roman period the space between the *temenos* walls and the podium was filled in first by natural debris and later by intentional dumping. In this rubble were found Attic bases and plain Ionic capitals, without floral decoration, similar to those uncovered in the pre-Herodian level at Samaria and in the Hellenistic level at Miletus. The excavators suggest that pillars were erected on top of the podium — at least in the northern section. They interpret these remains as a temple built on top of the podium (with a *temenos* around it), similar to the Roman temples dedicated to Poseidon in Syria. However, they date the building to Hellenistic times, which makes it rather difficult to understand why they compare it to Roman temples in Syria, the earliest of which dates to the first century A.D. C. Watzinger felt that these bases indicated the presence of colonnades only.

The ceramic finds are mixed and indicate that during the fifth and fourth centuries B.C. many vessels were imported from Greece. Among these were Attic red-figured ware, black glazed ware, West slope ware, and others. From the third to the first century B.C., Hellenistic pottery predominates. Late terra sigillata ware shows that occupation of the site continued into the Early Roman period.

In 1950 J. Leibowitz uncovered several sections of a Roman theater (60 meters in diameter) north of the mound. He cleared the eastern end of the *diazoma,* the eastern *vomitorium* at *scena* level, a small portion of the *scena* itself, and the orchestra (which had a plastered floor on limestone foundations). The limited area excavated and the meager finds make it difficult to determine the exact date of the theater, but it was most likely built sometime in the second or third century A.D. As yet, only a preliminary report on the finds has been published.

In 1952 the remains of a basilica were excavated southeast of the mound of ancient Dor by J. Leibowitz on behalf of the Department of Antiquities. A semicircular apse and sections of the nave and northern aisle were uncovered. The mosaic floor of the northern aisle is decorated with a geometric pattern of square medallions. It contains a Greek inscription in a *tabula ansata* that mentions the name of the bishop Acacius. Other discoveries include the top of an ivory

View of the mound from the sea.

scepter shaped like a hand, and a marble column. The latter has a small hole into which a chip of a rock had once been set and held by bronze nails. Four crosses are incised around the hole. A Greek inscription states that the hole contained "a stone of Holy Golgotha." A similar relic has been discovered on Mount Gerizim.

SUMMARY

In spite of the limited and incomplete publications of the British School of Archaeology, a reasonably clear conception of the mound's history can be pieced together from the excavations, primarily on the basis of the ceramic finds. This history corresponds well with what is known about Dor from literary sources.

The first settlement on the site was established in the Late Bronze Age; its destruction may be ascribed to the Tjeker. Dor was apparently a flourishing city during the Iron Age, but the excavators did not record any traces of occupation down to the fifth century B.C. From that time onward appears an abundance of imported Attic ware demonstrating close mercantile connections between Dor and Athens. The ceramic and numismatic evidence further indicates that a rich and flourishing settlement occupied the mound until the third or fourth century A.D.

The structures excavated by the British expeditions are not adequately described. Many dimensions are lacking, and the height of the walls is indicated only by the number of courses remaining. The southern section of the building shown on the ground plan is not described, nor are the earlier building remains beneath the Hellenistic structure. Other architectural remains, such as the theater and the basilica (both apparently belonging to the fourth century A.D.), are located beyond the limits of the mound proper, indicating that the city grew and expanded considerably during the Roman and Byzantine periods. G. FOERSTER

BIBLIOGRAPHY

Schuerer, *GJV* 2, 3–4, 35, 138ff. • J. Garstang, *BBSAJ* 4 (1924), 34–35; 6 (1924), 65–75 • G.M. FitzGerald, *BBSAJ* 7 (1925), 80–98 • W.F. Albright, *JPOS* 5 (1925), 31ff. • Watzinger, *DP* 2, 27ff. • J. Leibowitz, *'Alon* 3 (1951), 38–39; 5–6 (1957), 35 (Hebrew); *idem, Christian News from Israel* 5 (1954), 22–23 • M. Avi-Yonah, *Enc. Miqr.* 2, 579–81 (bibliography) (Hebrew) • B. Mazar, *Yediot* 27 (1963), 139–44 (Hebrew) • F. Lucaini, *Biblica Oriente* 6 (1964), 207–18 • Y. Aharoni, *The Land of the Bible*, London, 1966, Index.

DOTHAN

THE SITE AND ITS IDENTIFICATION. The biblical city of Dothan is identified with Tel Dothan, situated in a broad valley 22 kilometers ($13\frac{1}{2}$ miles) north of Shechem (map reference 173202). Eusebius locates it in the territory of Sebaste, 12 miles north of Samaria (*Onomasticon* 76:13). Eshtori ha-Parḥi, in the fourteenth century, described it with great accuracy as situated a four-hour's walk north from Samaria. In 1851 it was identified anew by C.W.H. Van de Velde.

The mound rises some 60 meters above the valley. The area at the top of the mound is about 10 acres, and that of the slopes is 15 acres. The settled area thus consisted of some 25 acres. One of the most important highways leading from the hills to the Jezreel Valley passed along the foot of the mound.

HISTORY

In the Bible, Dothan is first mentioned in the story of Joseph and his brothers. Joseph, following his brothers who had wandered from Shechem in the direction of Dothan, "found them in Dothan" (Genesis 37:17). According to the narrative, there were extensive pasture lands in Dothan, and caravans passed through it on their way to Egypt. Other than the Bible, Dothan is not mentioned in any written sources. G. Maspero attempted to identify it with the city of *t-t-y-n* listed ninth among the cities conquered by Thutmose III. This identification however, is not plausible, for *t-t-y-n* appears in one context with cities of Syria.

In the period of the Israelite Monarchy, Dothan is described in the Bible as a walled city. The king of Aram dispatched an army there to bring out the prophet Elisha (II Kings 6:13–14). Dothan is mentioned three times in the Book of Judith (3:9, 4:6, 7:3) in connection with the campaign of Holofernes.

EXCAVATIONS

Excavations were carried out at Dothan almost every year from 1953 to 1960. These were under the direction of J.P. Free of Wheaton College, Illinois. To date, preliminary reports of seven seasons of excavations have been published (1953–55, 1957–60). These reports, however, are incomplete and lack a general summary, so information on the site is still fragmentary.

Work was carried out in five areas. Areas D and K on the slope of the mound contain strata from the early periods of settlement down to virgin soil. In these areas, situated at the edge of the occupied area of the mound, are remains of the city's fortifications. On the summit of the mound the three other areas, A, T, and L, were excavated, and buildings from later periods were uncovered.

Chalcolithic Period. Settlement at Dothan began at the end of the Chalcolithic period. No building remains were found, but Chalcolithic shards (bases of cornets, handles, etc.) appeared in the lowest levels of area D.

Early Bronze Age. In the Early Bronze Age, Dothan was a large settlement surrounded by a wall, like other cities in Canaan in this period. Early Bronze Age remains were found on the slopes of the mound in areas D and K. Seven levels of occupation and at least one system of fortifications were uncovered in area D from Early Bronze Age I–III. A wall built of undressed stones was found preserved to a height of about 5 meters. Its outer face was vertical and the inner face sloped. The width at the base of the wall reached 3.25 meters. A flight of steps was excavated on the slope leading up to the wall. The beginning and end of the steps were not traced, but the excavators assume they led to the city gate.

In area K two Bronze Age city walls of undressed stone were cleared. One wall, 4 meters thick, is preserved to a height of 2 meters. According to the excavators, there was a gate in the second wall. From the meager information in the published reports, however, it is difficult to ascertain the plan of the gate and the second wall or their relationship to the first wall. It is also impossible to determine whether a connection existed between the fortifications of areas K and D, both of which are assigned to the Early Bronze Age.

Middle Bronze Age II-B. This is the next period represented on the site. Remains were found on the slope of the mound in areas D and K. Two levels of settlement were uncovered in area D. In one there was a burial of an infant. The city wall was discovered in area K with occupation remains of the period adjoining it.

Late Bronze Age-Iron Age I. Few remains were found from these periods. According to the excavators, the settlers continued to use the Middle Bronze Age wall. There were remains of occupation on the summit and on the slopes of the mound. A small pottery vessel was found containing fifteen metal pieces, mostly silver, including a ring and pieces of jewelry that might have served as currency. The prosperity of the city can be seen in a large tomb dug into the slope of the mound, which was in use in the second half of the second millennium B.C. The tomb held about one hundred bodies and one thousand complete vessels.

Iron Age II. The main finds of Dothan come from the Iron Age. Occupation levels of this period are reported to have been found on the slopes of the mound (areas D and K.), but only the finds in areas L and A on the summit are described. In area A there were several levels with remains of buildings. Streets were cleared between the buildings; one street was more than 30 meters long. Inside the houses were storage rooms as well as ovens, pottery, and other common household articles. One of these settlements was destroyed by fire, apparently in the ninth century B.C. A Carbon-14 test of a piece of charred wood from this level dated its destruction to 804 (±80) B.C.

Four Iron Age II levels were excavated in area L. In the lowest level (4) a large public building was

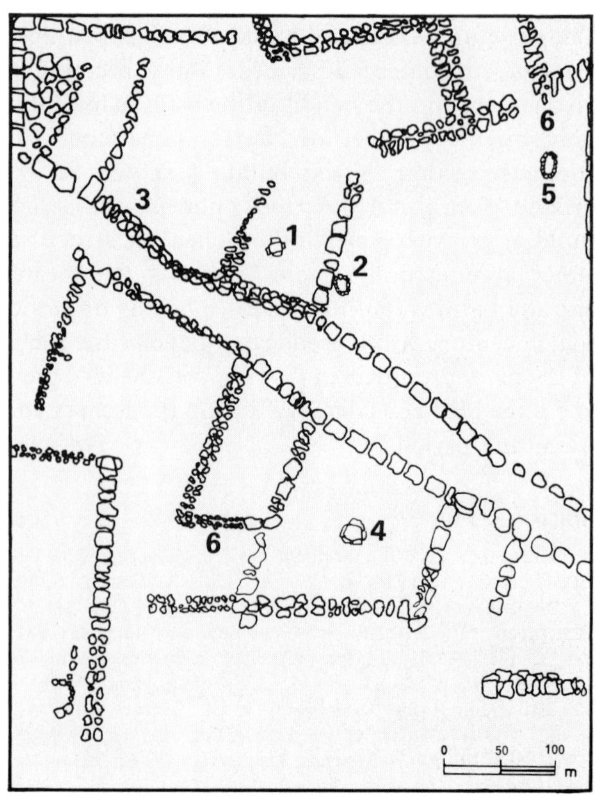

found with thick, solid main walls, indicating it may have had several stories. Finds among its ruins and on the plaster and stone floors indicated that it was a public building, perhaps of administrative character. Some rooms contained ovens, complete vessels, and charred grains of wheat. In one room there were about one hundred storage bins identical in shape and volume. Scores of similar bins were discovered in other rooms. The building was apparently in use in the tenth/ninth centuries B.C. It was destroyed by fire, possibly during the Aramaean invasion. The excavators do not state whether there was a connection between this destruction and that noted in area A. The building was restored (level 3) and more storerooms were added at the end of the ninth century B.C. It was in use until the beginning of the eighth century B.C.

The following settlement (level 2) contained remains from the eighth century B.C. It was destroyed either during the Assyrian conquest of Tiglath-Pileser III in 732 or with the fall of the Israelite Kingdom in 721 B.C.

Under Assyrian rule the settlement was rebuilt (level 1) and existed only a short time, from the end of the eighth to the beginning of the seventh century B.C. The ceramic finds included carinated bowls of Assyrian origin from the eighth century. Similar bowls have been found at Calah in Assyria, at Tell el-Far'a (q.v.), and at Samaria (q.v.). An eighth-century ostracon was found with cursive Aramaic script reading *RŚB* (Albright).

Hellenistic, Roman, and Mameluke Periods. Dothan was not resettled until Hellenistic times, when a small settlement was built on the summit of the mound. Several levels of Hellenistic occupation were found in area A. Among the finds were stamped Rhodian jar handles and coins.

From the Roman period only a few shards were found. In area T, on the summit of the mound, a large Mameluke building was partly excavated. From what can be seen on the surface, it consists of about six courts and 150 rooms. One court and twenty-five rooms around it were cleared.

D. USSISHKIN

BIBLIOGRAPHY

History and Identification: Eshtori ha-Parḥi, *Kaftor va-Feraḥ*, Jerusalem, 1899, 294 (Hebrew) • Abel, *GP* 2, 308 • M. Noth, *ZDPV* 61 (1938), 56 • B. Mazar, *Enc. Miqr.* 2, 772–73 (Hebrew).

Excavation Reports: J.P. Free, *BASOR* 131 (1953), 16–20; 135 (1954), 14–20; 139 (1955), 3–9; 143 (1956), 11–17; 147 (1957), 36–37; 152 (1958), 10–18; 156 (1959), 22–29; 160 (1960), 6–15.

Opposite page: Plan of area A (IA) showing diagonal street and houses. 1. Working stone. 2, 5. Storage pits. 3. Leaning wall. 4. Large working stone. 6. Doors. Left: Multiple-handled crater; IA I.

CHRONOLOGICAL TABLES

The Archaeological Periods in Palestine

Palaeolithic (Old Stone Age)	25,000–10,000 BC
Mesolithic (Middle Stone Age)	10,000–7500
Neolithic (New Stone Age)	7500–4000
Chalcolithic	4000–3150
Bronze Age	
Early Bronze Age I A–C	3150–2850
Early Bronze Age II	2850–2650
Early Bronze Age III	2650–2350
Early Bronze Age IV (IIIA)	2350–2200
Middle Bronze Age I	2200–2000
Middle Bronze Age IIA	2000–1750
Middle Bronze Age IIIB	1750–1550
Late Bronze Age I	1550–1400
Late Bronze Age IIA	1400–1300
Late Bronze Age IIB	1300–1200
Iron Age	
Iron Age IA	1200–1150
Iron Age IB	1150–1000
Iron Age IIA	1000–900
Iron Age IIB	900–800
Iron Age IIC	800–586
Babylonian and Persian Periods	586–332
Hellenistic Period	
Hellenistic I	332–152
Hellenistic II (Hasmonean)	152–37
Roman Period	
Roman I (Herodian)	37 BC–AD 70
Roman II	AD 70–180
Roman III	180–324
Byzantine Period	
Byzantine I	324–451
Byzantine II	451–640
Early Arab Period	640–1099
Crusader Period	1099–1291

Selected List of Kings

Egypt

Pre-Dynastic Period		
4th and 3rd millennium		
Proto-Dynastic Period		
Ist Dynasty	c. 3100–2890 BC	Narmer
IInd Dynasty	c. 2890–2686	
IIIrd Dynasty	c. 2686–2613	
Old Kingdom		
IVth Dynasty	c. 2613–2494	
	Snefru	
	Khufu	
	Khafre	
Vth Dynasty	c. 2494–2345	
VIth Dynasty	c. 2345–2181	
	Pepi I	
First Intermediate Period		
VIIth Dynasty-Xth Dynasty		
Middle Kingdom		
XIth Dynasty	c. 2133–1991	
XIIth Dynasty	c. 1991–1786	
Amenemhet I	1991–1962	
Senusert I	1971–1928	
Amenemhet II	1929–1895	
Senusert II	1897–1878	
Senusert III	1878–1843	
Amenemhet III	1842–1797	
Amenemhet IV	1798–1970	
Sebeknefrure	1789–1786	
Second Intermediate Period — the Hyksos Period		
XIII–XVIIth Dynasties		
New Kingdom		
XVIIIth Dynasty	1567–1320	
Ahmose	1570–1546	
Amenhotep I	1546–1526	
Thutmose I	1525–1512	
Thutmose II	c. 1512–1504	
Hatshepsut	1503–1482	
Thutmose III	1504–1450	
Amenhotep II	1450–1425	
Thutmose IV	1425–1417	
Amenhotep III	1417–1379	
Amenhotep IV (Akhenaton)	1379–1362 BC	
Smenkhkere	1364–1361	
Tutankhamon	1361–1352	
Eye	1352–1348	
Haremhab	1348–1320	
XIXth Dynasty	1320–1200	
Ramses I	1320–1318	
Seti I	1318–1304	
Ramses II	1304–1237	
Merneptah	1236–1223	
Seti II	1216–1210	
XXth Dynasty	1200–1085	
Ramses III	1198–1166	
Ramses IV–XI	1166–1085	
End of New Kingdom		
XXIst Dynasty	1085–935	
XXIInd Dynasty	935–730	
Shishak I	935–914	
Osorkon II	914–874	
XXIIIrd Dynasty	817–740	
XXIVth Dynasty	730–709	
XXVth Dynasty (Nubian or Ethiopian)	750–656	
Shabaka	716–695	
Taharka	689–664	
XXVIth Dynasty	664–525	
Psamtik I	664–610	
Necho II	610–595	
Psamtik II	595–589	
Psamtik III	526–525	
XXVIIth Dynasty (Persian)	505–404	
Cambyses	525–522	
Darius I	521–486	
Xerxes	486–466	
Artaxerxes	465–424	
Darius II	424–404	
XXVIIIth–XXXth Dynasties	404–343	

Assyria

Shalmaneser I	1274–1245 BC
Tiglath-Pileser I	1115–1077
Ashurnasirpal I	1049–1031
Shalmaneser II	1030–1019
Tiglath-Pileser II	966–935
Adadnirari II	911–891
Ashurnasirpal II	883–859
Shalmaneser III	858–824
Adadnirari III	810–783
Shalmaneser IV	782–772
Tiglath-Pileser III	745–727
Shalmaneser V	726–722
Sargon II	721–705
Sennacherib	704–681
Esarhaddon	680–669
Ashurbanipal	668–631

Neo-Babylonian Kingdom

Nabopolassar	626–605 BC
Nebuchadnezzar II	605–562
Amel-Marduk	562–560
Nabunaid	556–539
Nergal Sarussur	560–556

Persia

Cyrus	559–530 BC
Cambyses	530–522
Darius I	522–486
Xerxes	486–464
Artaxerxes I	464–423
Darius II	423–404
Artaxerxes II	404–359
Artaxerxes III	359–338
Arses (Xerxes II)	338–336
Darius III	336–331

The Kings of Judah and Israel

THE UNITED KINGDOM

Saul	ca. 1020–1004 BC
David	1004–965
Solomon	965–928

JUDAH		ISRAEL	
Rehoboam	928–911	Jeroboam	928–907
Abijam	911–908	Nadab	907–906
Asa	908–867	Baasha	906–883
Jehoshaphat	867–846	Elah	883–882
Jehoram	846–843	Zimri	882
Ahaziah	843–842	Omri	882–871
Athaliah	842–836	Ahab	871–852
Joash	836–798	Ahaziah	852–851
Amaziah	798–769	Jehoram	851–842
Uzziah	769–733	Jehu	842–814
Jotham	758–743	Jehoahaz	814–800
Ahaz	733–727	Jehoash	800–784
Hezekiah	727–698	Jeroboam	784–748
Manasseh	698–642	Zechariah	748
Amon	641–640	Shallum	748
Josiah	640–609	Menahem	747–737
Jehoahaz	609	Pekahiah	737–735
Jehoiakim	609–598	Pekah	735–733
Jehoiachin	597	Hoshea	733–724
Zedekiah	596–586		

The Hasmoneans

Jonathan	152–142 BC
Simeon	142–134
John Hyrcanus	134–104
Aristobulus	104–103
Alexander Janneus	103–76
Salome Alexandra	76–67
Aristobulus II	67–63
Hyrcanus II	63–40
Matthias Antigonus	40–37

The Herodians

Herod (the Elder)	37–4 BC
Archelaus	4 BC–AD 6
Herod Antipas	4 BC–AD 39
Philip	4 BC–AD 34
Herod Agrippa I	AD 37–44
Agrippa II	53–100(?)

The Procurators

Coponius	c. AD 6–9
M. Ambibulus	9–12
Annius Rufus	12–15
Valerius Gratus	15–26
Pontius Pilatus	26–36
Marcellus	36–37
Cuspius Fadus	41–46
Tiberius Alexander	46–48
Ventidius Cumanus	48–52
Antonius Felix	52–60
Porcius Festus	60–62
Albinus	62–64
Gessius Florus	64–66

Seleucid Kings

Seleucus I Nicator	311–281 BC
Antiochus I Soter	281–261
Antiochus II Theos	261–246
Seleucus II Callinicus	246–225
Seleucus III Soter	225–223
Antiochus III the Great	223–187
Seleucus IV Philopator	187–175
Antiochus IV Epiphanes	175–164
Antiochus V Eupator	163–162
Demetrius I Soter	162–150
Alexander Balas	150–145
Demetrius II Nicator	145–140
Antiochus VI Epiphanes	145–138
Antiochus VII Sidetes	138–129
Demetrius II Nicator	129–125
Cleopatra Thea	126
Cleopatra Thea and Antiochus VIII Grypus	125–121
Seleucus V	125
Antiochus VII Grypus	121–96
Antiochus IX Cyzicenus	115–95
Seleucus VI Epiphanes Nicator	96–95
Demetrius III Philopator	95–88
Antiochus X Eusebes	95–83
Antiochus XI Philadelphus	94
Philip I Philadelphus	94–83
Antiochus XII Dionysus	87–84
Antiochus XIII	69–64
Philip II	67–65

The Ptolemies

Ptolemy I Soter	304–282 BC
Ptolemy II Philadelphus	285–246
Ptolemy III Euergetes	246–221
Ptolemy IV Philopator	221–204
Ptolemy V Epiphanes	204–180
Ptolemy VI Philometor	180–145
Ptolemy VII Neos Philopator	145–144
Ptolemy VIII Euergetes II	145–116
Ptolemy IX Soter II	116–107
Ptolemy X Alexander I	107–88
Ptolemy IX Soter II (restored)	88–81
Ptolemy XI Alexander II	80 BC
Ptolemy XII Neos Dionysos	80–51
Cleopatra VII Philopator	51–30
Ptolemy XIII	51–47
Ptolemy XIV	47–44
Ptolemy XV	44–30

Overlapping dates usually indicate co-regencies.

Roman and Byzantine Emperors

Augustus	27 BC–AD 14
Tiberius	AD 14–37
Caligula	37–41
Claudius	41–54
Nero	54–68
Galba	68–69
Vespasian	69–79
Titus	79–81
Domitian	81–96
Nerva	96–98
Trajan	98–117
Hadrian	117–138
Antoninus Pius	138–161
Lucius Verus	161–169
Commodus	176–192
Septimius Severus	193–211
Clodius Albinus	193–197
Pescennius Niger	193–194
Caracalla	198–217
Geta	209–212
Macrinus	217–218
Diadumenianus	218
Elagabalus	218–222
Severus Alexander	222–235
Maximinus	235–238
Philip the Arab	244–249
Decius	249–251
Trebonianus Gallus	251–253
Valerian	253–260
Gallienus	253–268
Aurelian	270–275
Probus	276–282
Diocletian	284–305
Maximianus	286–305
Constantinus I	293–306
Galerius	293–311
Constantine I	306–337
Magnentius	337–353
Constans I	337–350
Constantius II	353–362
Julian	361–363
Valens	364–378
Valentinian	364–375
Theodosius	379–383
Honorius	393–423
Arcadius	383–408
Theodosius II	408–450
Marcian	450–457
Leon I	457–474
Zenon	474–491
Anastasius I	491–518
Justin I	518–527
Justinian I	527–565
Justin II	565–578
Tiberius II	578–582
Focas	602–610
Heraclius	610–641
Constans II	641–668